Life of an

INDUSTANI

Six Degrees of Separation

Life of an

INDUSTANI

Six Degrees of Separation

Shiv Kunal Verma

Title: Life of an INDUSTANI: Six Degrees of Separation
Author: Shiv Kunal Verma

ISBN: 978-93-92209-15-4

Edition: 1

Published by:
BluOne Ink LLP

Publisher's Address:
306, Tower-I, Assotech Business Cresterra,
Plot No. 22, Sector 135,
Noida 201305.

Website: www.bluone.ink
Email: publisher@bluone.ink

Printed in India by Thomson Press India Ltd.

For my parents,
Usha and Ashok Kalyan Verma...

Table of Contents

Prologue

There was something about Delhi that so naturally made it 'home', even though until then I had hardly lived in the city. I especially loved the mornings, when twittering sparrows and screaming parakeets would welcome the grey light of dawn, and if one was lucky, you could hear the occasional meowing call of a peacock. Regardless of how late one had gone to bed, it used to be impossible to sleep once the cacophony of bird song started. One thing was for sure, thirty-seven years previously, at the end of October the temperatures were a lot cooler than what they are today. On the fateful morning in 1984, I switched on the radio in the kitchen that was perennially tuned into the main All India Radio frequency and made myself a mug of tea. My living room, tiny as it was, looked a real mess. In one corner was a blue-coloured movie projector on a table that had been 'borrowed' from the World Wildlife Fund (WWF), and next to it were four huge cans with the yellow-and-black label of Eastman Kodak containing prints of a film on the Canada goose.

An overflowing ashtray, empty beer mugs and the furniture all askew meant the flat needed serious cleaning. Tired by the effort, I decided to stretch out on the solitary sofa in the living room and must have been fast asleep for four, maybe five, hours. The incessant banging on the door woke me up. Madhusudan Srinivas, who was to work in television with distinction in later years, was breathing heavily, and he brushed past me as I opened the door. 'You were sleeping?' His tone was incredulous. 'There's a rumour the Iron Lady has been assassinated!' Just in case it hadn't registered with me, he added, 'She's probably dead!'

I stared at Madhusudan, not quite believing what I had just heard. He always referred to Prime Minister Indira Gandhi as the Iron Lady, but I still asked the obvious question. He nodded in the affirmative. The radio was playing a monotonous tune, but despite its funereal quality, it meant nothing. Generally, unless All India Radio was broadcasting film songs, rarely did one notice what they were churning out on the airwaves.

The bush system through which news used to spread like wildfire was more often than not deadly accurate. I quickly got ready, grabbed a black jacket and my small bag that housed my Pentax K1000 camera with its accompanying 200 mm lens, and came down the two flights of stairs three steps at a time, leaving Madhu to lock up behind me. 'In case David comes here, give him the keys,' I yelled. Kick-starting my white Vijay scooter that had 'Press' stencilled on its front panel in maroon, I set course at top speed for Parliament Street. Though it was a Wednesday, the roads by then had already started to thin out. It was almost as if the city was holding its collective breath.

At Associated Press (AP), the tension was palpable. Samuel, who managed the office was watching the teleprinter as it hammered out short bursts of information, while in the inner office, Vicki Graham, the chief of bureau, was standing next to her desk. I cannot recall if the two other correspondents, Seema Sirohi and Brahma Chellaney, were present or not. Kuldeep Nayyar, who at 61 was the senior journalist at AP and looked to me like he had been carbon-dated, was continuously shaking his head and making clucking noises, which indicated he was deeply distraught. Vicki waved me into her room. 'Still no official confirmation,' she said, 'but it seems Mrs G was shot by her own guards; you have your camera?' She handed me a pack of Ilford black and white 100 ASA rolls. 'Don't wait Kunal, see what reactions you can get on the streets. Come back as soon as you have something for me.'

There was nothing happening 'on the streets' and so I headed off to Lodhi Estate where Leslie George and Manju were also huddled by the radio. 'I'm hungry,' I announced. While Manju made me something to eat, All India Radio finally stopped the mewing sounds it was emitting since the morning, and in the gravest of tones, the death of Mrs Gandhi was formally announced to the world at large. I don't recall if the newsreaders said anything about who had assassinated the prime minister, but by then the 'bush system' was raging like a wildfire and soon the news was out that she had been killed by two Sikh personnel who were part of her security.

I wandered around in the area between Lodhi Gardens, Khan Market and Parliament Street, literally watching the riot develop. The khaki-clad cops, who were usually visible in street corners, had either been whisked off or simply got into civilian clothes. The identity of the assassins now being known, just where and against whom a backlash would develop, was hard to say. As the afternoon gave way to the evening, there were isolated fires, and on Prithviraj Road I found a Sikh, probably around my age, scurrying along the road, half running, half walking. His turban was dishevelled, and he was constantly looking behind him, the whites of his eyes reflecting the sheer terror of his situation. I pulled up beside him and told him to get on the scooter. He obeyed without a moment's hesitation, and I opened the throttle and sped down the road towards Lodhi Estate. Manju heard the scooter coming and with no questions asked or words spoken, he was quickly hidden under a settee. I asked for some water, gulped it down and headed off again. There was still daylight left, and I had not as yet taken any photographs. Instinctively I set course for the Ring Road, reaching the intersection at the All India Institute of Medical Sciences (AIIMS), from where I turned right.

Barely half a kilometre away I could see black smoke, and at the Sarojini Nagar–Kamal Theatre intersection (there were no flyovers then) two trucks were burning furiously. Pulling up on the side, my legs still straddling the scooter which had its engine running, I snapped off a few shots. Realizing I was much too close in case the fuel tank exploded, I moved back to a side and parked. Running around towards the front of the burning wrecks, I got the shock of my life. Somehow, I had presumed the trucks were on fire but the inhabitants in the cabin must have escaped.

Surrounding the cabin, armed with spears, were three or four men on either side. They were jabbing at the side of the cabin and to my horror,

I realized they were not letting the two men inside get out of the inferno. 'You bastards,' I yelled and ran towards the men, who seeing me coming, turned to face me with the spears now pointing in my direction. The man closest to me had a chequered shawl and I got a good look at his face—just an ordinary, run-of-the-mill person on the streets of Delhi, now a murderer. The burning men inside the cabin made no move to escape, and I realized they were not only dead, but their skulls were showing, the hair and the skin having peeled off. It was gruesome and I felt the bile surge upwards and I doubled over and threw up. One of the men laughed scornfully, turned his back on me and again started to prod the dead man on his side of the truck.

I turned to the second truck and there too the situation was the same, with another half-a-dozen men blocking the exits. My having thrown up somehow seemed to make me no longer a threat to the group who contemptuously ignored my presence. I staggered back towards the scooter, shooting as I backed but soon, I was out of my thirty-six frames. I quickly rewound the film and with shaking hands, loaded another reel. The men were standing a little further away now, watching their handiwork with a sort of detached look. It was almost fully dark by then, but the bright glow of the flames had lit up the entire area.

I was so intent on changing the film, I hadn't looked over my shoulder. An army convoy had moved up to the burning vehicles and stopped about 40 metres short. The lead vehicle was an RCL jeep minus the gun, and with the driver, on the front seat was a Sikh officer, who from his rank badges was a lieutenant colonel. The formation sign was the head of the urial, which I guessed was the insignia of the Bhopal-based 22 Infantry Division. In the flickering light from the burning trucks, I thought the officer was from the Mahar Regiment. The men who had set fire to the trucks also seemed unaware of the army's presence, for they stood in a gaggle looking at their horrific handiwork.

Impulsively I ran up to the jeep and told the Sikh officer to 'do something' but he just sat there and stared back at me, his eyes seemingly not registering a thing. Ignoring me completely, the driver then put the jeep in gear and cautiously began to thread his way past the two burning wrecks, the rest of the convoy following. The second half of the convoy consisted of Gorkha troops, who just sat in their trucks, their face stoic and stony, and went past almost as if on parade. I counted seventy vehicles, mostly the usual three-tonne trucks, interspaced with jeeps and the odd one-tonne vehicle.

It was fully dark now and I made my way back to Parliament Street intending to deposit the roll of exposed film and perhaps file a story on the carnage I had been a witness to. Some more vehicles were also burning en route but thankfully there were no corpses. With the police having completely disappeared, the entire city seemed deserted. I parked outside Narendra Place and entered the AP office but strangely, there was no one there even though all the lights were on. In all my comings and goings, there had never been an occasion when I had not found Samuel at his desk and so this was indeed strange. My gaze then fell on Vicki Graham's desk, where a thick sheaf of papers had been folded lengthwise and were neatly lying there.

I looked around for Samuel again, but there was no sign of him. Once again, my gaze went to the papers. What can best be described as a brain fade, on an impulse, I darted into Vicki's cabin, picked up the papers and tucked them into my jacket like a common thief. Turning around, I quickly exited the building, started the scooter and went around 70 metres, after which I stopped under a streetlight. Still straddling the scooter, I looked at the papers in the yellowish mercury light, hoping it would be something routine that I could then place back on Vicki's table.

The sheets were cyclostyled and though in places the print was faint, it was readable. It seemed to be some sort of a voter's list of Ward No. 32 in Trilokpuri. I cannot recall the number of pages, or if I even counted them, but the list had at least 700 names on it. Some serial numbers were circled in pencil, with the message 'do not kill', but these could not have been more than four or five in totality. It didn't require rocket science to understand what was happening—the organized killings were about to start in real earnest. For me it was the moment of truth—I could go back to the office, get assigned to cover Trilokpuri and secure my journalistic future, or I could try and do something about it. Just what, I had no clue. I put the papers back in my jacket, engaged the gear of the scooter and took off in a daze, hardly aware of where I was going!

BOOK I

1

The DNA: Six Degrees of Separation

I remember the Dehradun of the 1960s in flashes. The first recollection is of the Indian Military Academy (IMA), House No. 7 that was opposite the club. Then there was the manicured triangular patch near the Plunge Bath, where the commandant's horse-drawn buggy would appear every morning, with Brigadier Prem Bhagat, Victoria Cross, returning my salute, which I am told was almost a daily ritual. I remember the multitude of gentleman cadets (GCs) in their maroon and grey striped blazers who all had bicycles with reflectors at my eye level. I remember the passing-out parades at the IMA, the band playing Colonel Bogey March, the adjutant on his white charger, the crunch of boots on Drill Square and the staccato gunfire—as I kept up desperately with my father and his buddies as they flushed out grey partridges and jungle fowl in the mustard fields beyond Mohand Pass, the gateway to Dehradun. Then there was the maddeningly exotic smell of cordite from spent 12-bore cartridges, and finally, there is this distinct memory of three dead elephants at Barkot which is near where the Jolly Grant airfield is located today.

Even when he was a GC at the IMA, my father was passionate about hunting and fishing, and not surprisingly he was the president of the shikar club. As a platoon commander posted back to IMA in early 1962 after a tenure at Walong, North-East Frontier Agency (NEFA), with his battalion, 2 Rajput, he simply carried on from where he had left in June 1956. It seems around that time the number of elephants on the western side of the Ganga had grown disproportionately and the Uttar Pradesh government was looking for people who could help cull some of the herds that were straying into human habitation. The IMA was an obvious choice to look for volunteers, and my father, then a captain along with his younger brother, Lieutenant Vijay Dhruv, promptly signed up along with Captain Sushil Pillai who was a forest officer's son from Kerala but commissioned into the Assam Regiment.

News soon filtered through that their 'quota' of a tusker and two females had been met. I distinctly remember the *sal* forest and my father holding some jungle fowl chicks in his hand while someone hoisted me onto the tusk of the dead elephant, which had collapsed into a kneeling position and died. Then, with me sitting there, my uncle started hacking at the flesh of the tusker and I remember the *khukri* exposing the pink insides. I was not yet two, but somehow that visual never, ever, left me.

Then the Chinese attacked on 20 October 1962 and 2 Rajput was deployed along the Namka Chu, and just about everyone who were 'family' was either killed or taken prisoner. Even the arrival of my younger sister Teesta a few days previously failed to lift the gloom. No one knew what had happened in NEFA and according to my mother, news of what had happened trickled in only in bits and pieces. My father was begging the commandant to let him go and search for remnants of his battalion, and eventually, Prem Bhagat sent him off. What he went through in the following days is a story that only he could tell, but it was a living hell for everyone—without doubt. Just when and how the news arrived that Lieutenant Colonel Brahmanand Avasthy, who had been the adjutant at the IMA and my father's mentor in 2 Rajput, had also been killed, I do not recall but it was to further impact our lives in many ways. The battalion had ceased to exist, and my father carried the guilt on his shoulders that when the crux came, he was not there with his men. Somehow, in a strange sort of way, we all collectively lived with that guilt.

Besides the IMA, the city of Dehradun too was home. My paternal grandparents lived in a house called 'Patur' on Turner Road in Clement Town while my mother's parents lived in an equally huge bungalow, though on the first floor, on Inder Road in Dalanwala. Large families being the norm then—my mother had six brothers and two sisters while my father had two elder sisters and a younger brother—the family tree was much too complicated for a little child to come to terms with or comprehend. But as we grew older, one began to understand the extent of one's roots. At one level, the two families were poles apart, and yet both sides had known each other for years, and I suppose my parents were destined to get married.

My grandfather's—Narendra Singh Verma—biological father was a Kashmiri Pandit, Vishnu Dutt Okhal who was a barrister by profession. A tall and imposing figure, he had looks that could almost pass off as Caucasian. Under the influence of the Arya Samaj movement[1], he had sallied forth from the valley and set up his practice in Moga in Punjab, where he met and married Yashodha out of caste. She, in turn, was the daughter of Subhadra and Shiv Rattan Verma, who was a Rajput originally from Kannauj, whose ancestors had migrated to the Deccan. They carried considerable clout, for a cluster of villages in Patur (in what is now Akola District in Maharashtra) were bestowed to the family as a jagir by the rulers of Berar.

Yashodha would die at childbirth and my grandfather was all but orphaned as his father decided to hand over the baby to his grandmother, Subhadra, who was fondly known as Ammaji, after which he returned to Kashmir. I am not sure at which point Shiv Rattan Verma died, but after his demise, Ammaji with the little boy in tow moved to Jalandhar where she became the hostel warden at the Kanya Maha Vidyalaya (KMV). The first-ever women's educational institution to be set up in North India, it was founded in 1886 as a result of the renaissance that the Punjab witnessed at the time by the crusader of women's education, Lala Dev Raj. When Ammaji arrived, one of the prominent educationists associated with KMV was Dr Dilbagh Rai Varma, a close associate of Swami

[1] Arya Samaj was a Hindu reform movement that was based on the infallible authority of the Vedas. Advocating that there was but one supreme being universally referred to as God, the movement also played a major role in bringing about changes in matters pertaining to civil rights and social issues since the early 1800s.

Shraddhanand, a doyen of the Arya Samaj movement at that time. Dilbagh Rai had lost his wife, who was from the well-established Sikand family, at a fairly young age and he was bringing up his two daughters, Satyavati and Saraswati, and a son on his own. As luck would have it, the young Narendra Singh and Saraswati became inseparable, and the little boy (called Dev by Saraswati) was soon bestowed the status of a brother by the tying of a *rakhi*. It was also laughingly suggested that when they grew up and had families of their own, maybe one day their children could get married.

The KMV, then more than two decades old, was a hub of the Indian nationalist movement. Lala Dev Raj had steered the college in an era in Indian society when sending the girls out to study was considered nothing short of blasphemy. Focused on keeping the Indian methodology of teaching at the core of the institution, Lala Dev Raj had also repeatedly shunned any grants from the British government, surviving to a great extent thanks to the Maharaja of Kapurthala.

However, a girl's college was not quite the place for the young man, and in keeping with the prevailing ethos and the Arya Samaj mindset, Narendra Singh Verma was sent off to Haridwar.

Like most youngsters of my generation, in my early twenties I too had little or no idea about my family's history other than the broad facts of who was whom. The first real glimpse in the rear window of time would present itself from the most unexpected quarter.

In 1983, after I joined *India Today*, the first assignment I was sent on was to Haridwar where Pramod Pushkarna, one of the established photographers on the magazine's payroll, was to do a photo feature on Gurukul Kangri. I was the 'feature' part of the assignment but nevertheless, shoved my trusted Pentax K1000 and 200 mm lens into my bag. As I was leaving for Haridwar, my father said, 'Gurukul Kangri? That's where your Dadaji studied!' In the taxi, Pramod never spoke to me—perhaps smarting from the fact that a junior chap had been assigned to accompany him. After looking out of our respective windows, we reached the gurukul and it was quite an education watching Pramod at work. I had three rolls of Ilford black and white film, so I was quite circumspect in taking a few shots, after which I got busy talking to people.

Back in Delhi, the editor, Suman Dubey looked at the rolls and rolls Pramod had shot through his eyepiece, and he kept shaking his head. Then being a typical editor, he told Pramod the shots were too contrived, and we needed to go back. Turning to me, Suman brusquely said, 'You too ...' Just then he saw the three rolls of negatives drying on the side and he looked at them. Turning to Pramod he said, 'Why didn't you show me these before? This is the kind of stuff I want!' Pramod hadn't a clue what Suman was talking about, but he must have guessed. Anyway, he was smart enough to keep quiet and off we went again, this time Pramod being a lot more friendly. I then said that maybe, after we finished shooting, we could go and interview my grandfather who then lived in Dehradun as well, which we did. The subsequent photo feature got quite a few pages, and though none of my shots was used, it sure gave me a lot of confidence. Until then, all my photography had been restricted to shooting in Zanskar and Ladakh.

Life at the gurukul was tough but fun. Every morning, be it summer or winter, low or high water, the boys would swim both ways across the Ganga. 'We would battle the current and often land up way downstream,' my grandfather would say (in the story I had to go with the *India Today* style and say 'said Verma' which felt very odd), 'and it shaped our bodies and minds like nothing else could.' A bright student, he would graduate from the gurukul and appear for the Indian Civil Service exam. Having made the cut, he was then required to proceed to London where he was to do his initial training at Cambridge. However, around that time Ammaji became unwell. Not willing to leave his grandmother behind in India, Narendra Singh opted to join the Provisional Civil Service instead, and being heavily influenced by his mother's roots, he asked for and was assigned to the Central Provinces and Berar cadre.

Meanwhile, still at the KMV, Ammaji was on the lookout for a suitable girl for him. Sheila Sharma's family was originally from Batala, and she had eight or nine brothers and an elder sister who was twenty years her senior. Her father was with the railways and had moved to East Africa to help build the railway lines there, and her eldest brother, Vidya Ratan Sharma, had joined the Colonial Service in Uganda. The rest of the brothers were spread across the world. Shiela's sister was married to Badrinath Sharma, better known as Pandit Sudarshan, who went on to become a well-known writer considered to be at par with Munshi Premchand. Apart from his many books and stories that included *Haar ki Jeet* where a man protects his horse from a famous dacoit, Pandit Sudarshan was perhaps the most sought-after scriptwriter in Bombay in the 1930s, penning among others the films *Ramayan* (1933, starring Prithviraj Kapoor, Dadabhai Sarkari and Indubala), *Kunwari Ya Vidhwa* and *Dhoop Chhaon* (1935). Sheila had been sent back to India to study in Jalandhar and she was, by all accounts, quite a head-turner whose main pass-time was to look gorgeous. I am not sure of the exact timeline here, but she probably married Narendra Singh Verma in 1929 or 1930.

With his wife Sheila and Ammaji accompanying him, my grandfather now went through a string of postings that saw him serve in Akola, Chandrapur, Jabalpur, Bilaspur, Raipur and Mandla. By all accounts an extremely kind and involved person, he used to tour the countryside extensively and was soon a well-known figure in the remotest of areas. Meera was his first born in 1931, followed by Kamla in 1933 when the family was posted in Akola. Two years later, my father, Ashok Kalyan arrived at Chandrapur, and he was then followed by Vijay Dhruv who was born in Jabalpur. Far removed from the nationalistic hustle and bustle of the Arya Samaj movement in the Punjab, the fast-expanding family was in a world of its own. During the British period, the administrative service, the Indian Civil Service was often referred to as the 'Heaven Born'. Being a part of the Provincial Civil Service meant you would not quite be a part of the Delhi circuit, but life in many ways was perhaps even better.

Sometime in the late 1930s, Jhilpa was terrorised by a man-eating leopard which had by then killed over sixty people. The remote areas of the Central Provinces were sparsely populated and even the administration was hard-pressed to get to some of the villages. This leopard had got bolder with each attack and was by then literally walking into the town and carrying off children and other victims at will. Armed with his trusted hammer 12-bore gun loaded with LGs[2], my grandfather sat in vigil and fortunately for him, it was not long before the rogue cat sauntered into his field of fire. Hardly had the blast of the shot felled the leopard, virtually every door in the area flew open and men and women armed with axes, knives, sticks and sickles rushed towards the hated enemy and within minutes the carcass had been dismembered completely.

With cholera outbreaks common, cases of man-eating tigers and leopards were frequent in the Central Provinces, and Narendra Singh was invariably the 'go-to' person. From the perspective of the four children, life assumed a high-octane pace. With their Morris Bentley, perhaps the only car within miles, it was but natural for the two boys to get sucked into the spirit of things, and my father would shoot his first leopard when he was barely 12 years old. While my elder aunt, Meera was packed off at a very young age to a boarding school, Kamla was home schooled. The two brothers would swim across the Narbada to go to school when the family was in Mandla, after which they were packed off to Nainital to join the newly opened Birla Vidya Mandir (BVM).

From the few photographs that one remembers seeing, the family retained its roots with Kashmir, though my grandfather never forgave his father for abandoning him. Vishnu Dutt Okhal, in the meantime, had remarried and sired another four children, two sons and two daughters. The family dropped 'Okhal' and adopted 'Nath' as the surname; the eldest was Jitender, the second was again named Narendra, while the daughters were Vimla and Shama, both of whom went on to teach in Srinagar University before eventually settling down in Jammu. The physical resemblance between Shama and my aunt Kamla was incredible.

While either moving up to Kashmir or while returning, my grandfather also decided to visit his childhood friend Saraswati Varma. Having completed her masters in Hindi from KMV, she had married Harcharan

[2] 'Large Goose' cartridges had nine large lead balls fired from sporting guns. It was good enough at close range to kill deer and sometimes even a tiger.

Singh Hoon, a widower who had three children from his earlier marriage with Niranjan Ratra—Sanyukta, Ranjit and Nirmal. The son of Jwala Singh Hoon—whose ancestors were the Huns of Central Asia and had subsequently served in Maharaja Ranjit Singh's army—Harcharan had spent his early life in Amritsar where he had served in the police. The kind and gentle Saraswati not only filled the void of a mother in the lives of the three children, but also had four boys and two girls of her own. In order of appearance, there was Ravi, Shashi, Jati, Sudhir, Usha and Sudha.

Saraswati's elder sister, Vidyawati, was also highly educated and she had married Swami Das Dhawal, a civil engineer who had graduated from the Thomason College of Civil Engineering (later Indian Institute of Technology Roorkee) which was then the oldest and most respected technical institution in India. Involved in the construction of Model Town in Lahore in the early 1920s, Swami Das was later honoured by the Government of India with the title of 'Rai Saheb' for building either the India Gate or the Durbar Hall. Model Town, as the name implied, was being built to provide housing to eminent Indians that included retired judges, civil and provisional service officers, engineers, doctors and businessmen. The spacious bungalows were to be built following British standards, and Model Town was to be a garden city with Muslims, Hindus, Sikhs and Christians all living together. Encouraged by Vidyawati and Swami Das who had settled in Model Town, Harcharan and Saraswati also decided to relocate, and they shifted into No. 11C which was three houses away from the Das residence.

All Saraswati's six children were born in Lahore, with Usha, my mother, arriving in 1938. The two elder boys, Ranjit and Nirmal, were beginning to find their feet as businessmen with their father, and while the younger siblings were all having a blast, there was high drama unfolding in the case of Sanyukta, the eldest daughter.

Wooed extensively by Tikka Sahib, the crown prince of Guler, she eventually married him in 1941 much to the chagrin of her father. Much to Sanyukta's horror, her husband turned out to be an alcoholic and he died shortly thereafter, leaving her a penniless widow with two children, Praveen and Brijesh, the eldest of my 30-odd first cousins from my mother's side.

Having moved back to her father's house in Lahore, Sanyukta adored my mother Usha, who was quite the star. Hers was an amazing fun-filled childhood—a huge mansion, fruit-laden gardens, a tennis court, a fountain, servants, uncles, aunts. She had a plethora of hilarious stories about growing up in Lahore and the antics of her brothers, especially Shashi, who was always up to some scheme or the other. When the Verma entourage came visiting in the mid-1940s, my mother remembered them but had little or no interaction with the elder boy, Ashok Kalyan.

In the build-up to Independence, my mother vividly remembers the visit by Dhillon, Sehgal and Shahnawaz, the three stalwarts who had been Subhas Chandra Bose's key men in the Indian National Army (INA). All children around her age were used to shouting '*Inqilab zindabad*' and proudly carrying the Tricolour—my mother was chosen to render the INA song, *Kadam kadam badai ja* in their honour. Though there was talk of Partition, and rumblings of trouble brewing in Sialkot, Rawalpindi and other areas, no one had an inkling of what was coming. Aged 9, my mother for the first time heard the word 'rape' being used, albeit in hushed voices. Harcharan, by then one of the well-to-do citizens of Model Town, believed that whatever happened, nothing would impact the family.

One of the brothers had earlier gone down with typhoid and he then had a relapse. To get him away from the heat of the summer, the Hoon family had travelled to the Doon School in Dehradun towards the end of July 1947 at the invitation of Vishwa Nath Kapur. The first Indian to break the monopoly of British masters by being given charge of Jaipur House by the headmaster, Arthur Edward Foot, Kapur was my grandmother's first cousin and his elder daughter, Savita, would subsequently become one of my mother's closest friends. At the time, the Hoon family had no idea that they had left their beloved Lahore for good, for by then, hell had broken loose as the British abruptly left behind a partitioned subcontinent. The Radcliffe Line suddenly had a meaning, and an exodus began from either side of the new border. One of the brothers had stayed behind, and while he was escaping from Lahore with a cousin, the latter was pulled off the train, murdered and mutilated in full view of the others.

They were the lucky few who got away with their lives as 1,100 of the 1,300 families living in Model Town had to hurriedly leave everything behind and literally, flee with just the shirts on their backs. Even as it dawned on them that they were now refugees, with nowhere to go, they were acutely aware of the fact that the family had escaped the actual carnage. What the Partition would do to the collective psyche of families and the subcontinent is well documented—and I don't think any of my mother's family ever forgot those horrifying days. Yet, in all our growing up years, never once did anyone, ever have anything negative to say about Muslims. I remember my mother watching the film *Garam Hawa* starring Balraj Sahni years later and crying silently. There was so much potency in those tears. As a result, I don't think it ever mattered to either me or my sister in later years as to who followed what religion.

With the term starting, they could no longer stay on at the Doon School and they shifted to an evacuated property in Ajmeri Gate that was allotted to them in Delhi. To the grandparent's horror, the other side of the street was occupied by sex workers, and the children were instructed not to look in that direction, let alone venture that side. On 30 January 1948, Harcharan's eldest son, Ranjit Hoon, was married to Visharda, who was my mother's first cousin being Vidyawati's daughter. The wedding ceremony was soon abandoned as news of Mahatma Gandhi's assassination swept through the city like wildfire. My mother would talk of running in the streets and the distinct memory of seeing Bapu's face as he lay in state before the funeral.

The Delhi sojourn would end soon, but perhaps not soon enough as far as Saraswati was concerned. She was mortified to hear one of her sons singing a song sung by the sex workers. The family would then move again to Dehradun where they shifted into 1 Balbir Avenue, which would become the family's base in Dehradun and where the young Usha Hoon would start coming into her own!

Back in the Central Provinces, around the same time, the Verma family was quite removed from the traumatic scenarios unfolding in the Punjab and parts of North India. In the lead up to India's Independence, along with Mahatma Gandhi, Jawaharlal Nehru and Sardar Patel, Govind Ballabh Pant who had been the chief minister of the United Provinces between 1937 and 1939, was a key figure. Arrested and imprisoned by the British in 1940 for helping organize the Satyagraha movement, he was again arrested in 1942 for signing the Quit India resolution, after which he had spent three years cooling his heels at the Ahmednagar Fort with Nehru and other top leaders. Fortunately, for India and Indians in general, in July 1945, the hardliner government of Winston Churchill faced a landslide defeat at the hands of Clement Attlee's Labour Party and was sent packing. One of the first things Attlee's government did was to order fresh elections to the provisional legislature in the United Provinces. This resulted in the return of Govind Ballabh Pant as the chief minister in 1946.

Perhaps it was his Gurukul Kangri background, or maybe it was just a quirk of fate, Govind Ballabh Pant chose Narendra Singh Verma to draft the bill that would abolish the zamindari system that had been introduced in India by the British to economically take control of the vast countryside. As the chief minister who presided over India's most populated state through the next few years, the abolishment of the zamindari bill is considered to be among Pant's finest achievements.

Call it serendipity but the link with educational institutions was to continue. Govind Ballabh Pant was determined to establish a public school in the Kumaon region before the country became independent. By the beginning of 1947, Ghanshyam Das Birla had purchased one of the most spectacular estates which at the time was the Hallet War School. The property was situated just below the summit of Sher-ka-danda, 'the most easterly of the peaks surrounding Nainital ... it commanded a stunning panoramic view of the town, the *tal* and the drop to the plains of India' in the words of Martin Booth in his book *Carpet Sahib: The Life of Jim Corbett*. The history of the place warrants telling for it would have a profound impact on my father's personality subsequently. The estate had originally been owned by J. W. Waugh, and in the 1870s the Oak Openings High School was established there. One of the boys educated there was Jim Corbett, whose subsequent exploits and writings would capture the imagination of millions across the globe. In 1905, the Philander Smith Institute of Mussoorie was amalgamated with Oak

Openings and it became the Philander Smith College. This then became home to Orde Wingate, who also studied there and went on to become one of the most famous generals during World War II. The exploits of his 'Chindits' in Burma had also captured the imagination of the world. In a strange quirk of fate, despite their birthplaces and schools being the same, Corbett never met Wingate, even though during the war as a lieutenant colonel and senior instructor in jungle craft, he was responsible for the training of many of Wingate's Chindits at Chhindwara, which was situated in the Central Provinces.

By July 1947 BVM had been established and the two boys, Ashok Kalyan and Vijay Dhruv, had been bundled off to Nainital from Nagpur where the family had been posted. Inside the premises of the school, they were physically protected from the events that were beginning to unfold across the country. Fredrick Gordon Pearce, who had a Maharashtrian wife and two sons, both of whom joined the Indian Navy subsequently, had moved from the Scindia School as the first principal of BVM and one can only guess what the prevailing atmosphere inside the school was by drawing inferences from what my father would tell me in later years. There were daily updates on the developments in the country as the countdown to Independence reached a feverish pace, and these were regularly shared with the students. The entire school posed for a photograph on that historic day, but the euphoria was tempered by the horrors of Partition. Then, even before the embers of the exodus on either side of the new border had begun to cool down, the fighting over Jammu and Kashmir had erupted on 27 October 1947 when DC-3 Dakotas of the Royal Indian Air Force (RIAF) and other civil airlines began to airlift Indian troops into the valley to combat the tribal *lashkars* that were making a beeline for Srinagar. Sometime in 1948 Pearce was replaced by T. B. Kankan, who had come directly from the UK to take over the school, and the tradition of daily updates on the country continued, especially special bulletins on the fighting and then, as my father would tell me, 'one day in 1948, Mr Kankan, solemnly announced that Dakotas belonging to the IAF had successfully landed on an improvised airstrip at Poonch and the much-needed 25-pounder artillery guns were even then, as he spoke, engaging the Pakistani artillery that had laid siege to the surrounded garrison.' That was the day when Ashok Kalyan Verma told himself, come what may, he was going to join the Indian Army. With him, many others, including his brother, would then choose the same path.

What Ashok Kalyan or the others in BVM did not know at the time was that his father, Narendra Singh, was playing a major role in the Police Action, code-named Op Polo that was unfolding in the Deccan almost simultaneously. Mir Osman Ali Khan, the Nizam of Hyderabad, had initially refused to accede to either India or Pakistan and opted for Independence. With the Razakars threatening to take on the princely state's irregular army and set up a communist regime in the heart of the subcontinent's hinterland, the Indian Army moved into the state in September 1948. Though Hyderabad then signed an instrument of accession and joined the Indian Union, the countryside continued to remain extremely volatile on communal lines. Prime Minister Nehru, then looking for an able and competent officer to take charge as the civil administrator of the erstwhile princely state, gave the responsibility to Narendra Singh.

Hyderabad! This was perhaps the crowning glory of my grandfather's life, and by all accounts, he handled an extremely difficult job successfully. The Nizam was one of the richest men on the planet at the time and making sure none of the assets was misappropriated was a major challenge. While the inventory of the Nizam's personal weapons was being done, a pistol inscribed with the name 'Shiv Rattan Verma' was discovered which further confirmed the fact that my grandfather's grandfather had close links with the Nizam and was not just restricted to the princely state of Berar. When I was born, my mother wanted to name me Kunal after Emperor Ashok's son, but since my grandfather wanted me to carry his grandfather's name, I eventually would be named Shiv Kunal.

In 1992 while shooting the J. R. D. Tata-funded film *Salt of the Earth* on the history of the IAF, bad weather forced me to land at Begumpet airfield which was a diversionary stop that day. The pilot with me had a girlfriend in Hyderabad, and he disappeared leaving me high and dry. In flying overalls and with nowhere to go, I managed to call Wing Commander Sadatullah Mohamed who was a close friend of my father. He picked me up after a while, and after making me buy some presentable clothes, took me to the Secunderabad Club in the evening. As word got around as to whose grandson I was, quite a few old-timers started coming to the club just to say hello. That to me was the biggest tribute anyone could pay the man after all those years.

By then my elder aunt Meera had been married to Madhu Sudan Seth, an artillery officer who was from the second batch of the Doon School. My father remembered meeting Flying Officers Nirmal 'Nimmi' Suri and Dalbir 'Dolly' Yadav, both of whom were from the 1st JSW (Joint Services Wing, Clement Town, later the National Defence Academy or NDA) course and were doing their advanced fighter training at Hakimpet during this period. Dolly Yadav would marry my younger aunt, Kamla, a few years later.

Still very much on Nehru's radar, Narendra Singh finished his tenure in Hyderabad and moved to Bombay where he was Custodian Evacuee Property in the Ministry of Rehabilitation. Living in a spacious apartment on Marine Drive, those were heady days. A photograph of the family's prized golden retriever, Toby, even featured on the cover of the *Illustrated Weekly of India*, at the time perhaps the most prestigious magazine in the country. My aunt Kamla recalled decades later, 'Nehru would often call and talk endlessly to daddy, as he was very invested with most of the business families, including that of Mohammad Ali Jinnah. We used to wonder; doesn't the prime minister have anything better to do?' I am not sure now, but my grandfather either presented the prime minister with golden retriever puppies or they both got them from the same litter—there was a 'doggy' connection as well!

During this period, my father had developed quite a reputation as a 'naturalist-shikari', having moulded himself on his hero, Jim Corbett. In 1950, in his final year at BVM, he became the first head boy of the school and then graduated after having completed the Uttar Pradesh Board's High School and Intermediate Education as a 15-year-old. From there it was a small step to Dehradun, where he was part of 8 JSW. The first ten batches were housed in Clement Town in the old prisoner of war (POW) barracks that housed mainly Italian and a few German and Austrian POWs during World War II. It was from here that Heinrich Harrer, an Austrian climber, escaped and made his way to Lhasa, where he was subsequently employed as a teacher for the young 14th Dalai Lama. The book and the film, *Seven Years in Tibet*, were both classics. The spartan POW-like conditions would soon be history when JSW became the NDA and moved to the sprawling environs at Khadakwasla, near Pune. Vijay Dhruv and my mother's brother, Sudhir Hoon, were both part of the batch that would make the transition.

At the IMA, life carried on in much the same vein. More interested in running the shikar club than in the humdrum of training, Ashok Kalyan was part of 17 Regular IMA. In 1955, all the state colours were laid to rest at the IMA, and my father participated in the impressive parade that was held then. As a result, years later when I made the IMA film, *Making of a Warrior*, everyone was amazed at the fact that I knew where what had been stored in Chetwode Hall. On 3 June 1956, with Mohammad Reza Pahlavi, the Shah of Iran taking the salute, my father like so many before and after him, went up the steps from Drill Square into Chetwode as the band played *Auld Lang Syne*. Later, on that fateful day, he was pipped by his father and was commissioned into 2 Rajput as a 2nd lieutenant. His journey in the army had begun!

Usha Hoon, in the meantime, had migrated to Calcutta where the two elder brothers, Ranjit and Nirmal, were trying to rebuild the family fortunes. After doing her Matric from the Modern High School in Calcutta, she did her Intermediate at the Gokhale Memorial Girl's College, before coming back to Dehradun and enrolling in Dayanand Anglo-Vedic College, where Sheel Vohra and R. D. Singh, both subsequently masters at the Doon School, were her contemporaries. Her natural flamboyance severely curtailed by her father's uncompromising strictures and curfews, she was only too glad to join her elder brother Ranjit's family in Madras, where they had moved recently. The ringleader, with her nephew Vinoo and two nieces, Varuna and Vineeta in tow, Usha did her Bachelor of Education along with her much older sister-in-law, Visharda. Those were two carefree years in Madras (now Chennai), for she would often talk about the fun she had and would rarely miss an opportunity in later years to head off to the South.

Back in Dehradun in 1957, the *Illustrated Weekly* again came into play. Very fond of dressing up and getting her photograph taken, she was the 1st runner-up in the Miss Photogenic Contest and her photograph, with her head covered by her sari *pallu,* made it to the magazine. In December, both Vijay Dhruv Verma and Sudhir Hoon passed out of the IMA and the two families got together after their passing-out parade. This was the start of a whirlwind romance, for at the time 2 Rajput had just moved into Sabatoo near the Simla Hills as a part of 4 Infantry Division. With 1 Balbir Avenue now the centre of Ashok Kalyan's universe, stories abound as to how after riding down on a motorcycle from Sabatoo, getting into the barricaded house of the former policeman, Harcharan Hoon, was nigh impossible.

Before moving on from the year 1957, one must also mention that my mother's youngest sister, Sudha and her niece, Praveen Guleria (both coincidentally born on the same day) joined Welham Girls' School as the first batch of ten girls that also included Subhasini Sehgal, the daughter of Colonel Prem and Lakshmi Sehgal, who were part of the INA. Having set up the Welham Boys' Preparatory School a decade and a half earlier, Miss H. S. Oliphant had set her heart on opening a girl's school as well. The task had been entrusted to Miss Grace Mary Linnell, and much to my aunt Sudha's chagrin, she was robbed of being the first school captain of Welham Girls' because she had to be shifted to the neighbouring St Thomas School in her final year to do her final exam as Welham did not have the requisite number of girl students in her class.

Anyway, the die had been cast and my parents were to be married on 11 June 1959. The association with educational institutions was far from over, as my uncle Jati Hoon, by then was an integral part of the Doon School landscape. A popular and likeable individual, he was a close friend of John Martyn, the second headmaster and had also been adopted by Mrs Dhawal, the dame of Hyderabad House, who had earlier tragically lost her only son. Jati Hoon, according to family lore, was responsible for Sheel Vohra getting a job in the school for he had introduced him to John Martyn and told the latter to 'just close your eyes and hire him!' Sheel Vohra, known to generations of DOSCOs as 'Bond', would go on to become one of the iconic masters.

More pertinent to my immediate story, when my uncle, Jati told John Martyn that my mother was getting married to Ashok Kalyan Verma, the headmaster graciously offered and insisted the wedding must take place in the Doon School itself, since the school was closed for the summer vacations. Since from my father's side most of the officers from 2 Rajput attending the wedding would be coming from Sabatoo, Jaipur House was allotted to house the *baraat*. On D-Day, the only officer in Sabatoo was Captain Tarun Kumar Ghosh, who had been left behind to man the fort by the commanding officer (CO), Lieutenant Colonel Maha Singh Rikh. Loath to miss out on the wedding, Ghosh too decided to follow and in blatant disregard to orders, was present at the appointed hour.

Photographs of who were present make for interesting viewing, for many of those present were later killed in the opening hours of the Chinese onslaught twenty-five months later when 2 Rajput was holding the thin red line on the Namka Chu in NEFA. There were others present too including the then second-in-command, Major Brahmanand Avasthy, who was my father's mentor and would be killed by the Chinese after the ceasefire at La Gyala Gompa while commanding 4 Rajput. But the person that dominates the dinner photographs is the large figure of John Martyn, who was sitting at the head of one of the tables. Much to my mother's embarrassment, who at that point had been married for less than half an hour, the headmaster bellowed across the tables ... 'Usha ... Ashok ... remember to register your son the day he is born for the Doon School.' I guess that sort of sealed my yet-to-be-born fate—I was *doomed* for *Doon*!

2

Tic Tac Toe: The Early Years

I suppose being the first child in the family has its advantages. Among other things, you get your own personal 'baby book' and I had this off-white, slightly padded book which when opened had telegrams stuck across double spreads saying things like, 'Joy! Joy! It's a baby boy!' My first photograph as a newborn was with my father's classmate, N.P. 'Nirpoo' Singh. Then, my poetic introduction to the world at large having been made (and dutifully recorded for posterity), I was, according to my aunt Sudha, brought home to 1 Balbir Avenue from the Doon Hospital and cooed at by one and all.

2 Rajput, along with the rest of 4 Mountain Division, had by the end of 1959 moved from Sabatoo and was deployed at Walong. The NEFA, until then, had no army units, the area being administered by the Ministry of External Affairs (MEA) with two Assam Rifles battalions looking after the entire region.

Getting in and out of Walong depended on a flight in a Twin Otter, which ferried men and material between Tezu, which was the battalion's rear. Maybe one of the telegrams in the baby book was to my father, though I doubt if NEFA had a telegraph service then. Nevertheless, as is the case with so many soldiers, they are not always able to be at home even on such occasions. Finally, he did get some leave and strapped himself into the co-pilot's seat in the Otter next to a Flight Lieutenant Sandhu. The aircraft taxied to the top of the grass-strip that served as a runway and then throttled down, gathering speed to take off. Just then, the back wheel gave way or something odd happened, for the aircraft turned 90 degrees towards the makeshift air-traffic control (ATC) hut. Pulling on the stick and muttering 'Come on baby! Come on baby', Sandhu not only got the aircraft off the ground, missing the ATC shack by the skin of his teeth, he managed to bank sharply to avoid going into the hillside. During the rest of the flight, other than mop his brow a few times, Sandhu said nothing to my father. He did ask the ATC at Tezu to confirm if his wheels were alright, and after making a couple of passes for visual confirmation, put the plane down without any further ado.

Three months later, in the winter cold of January 1961, my parents landed at Jorhat from Calcutta in a Kalinga Airways DC-3 Dakota with me in a basket. The vast Brahmaputra, covered in mist was crossed by ferry, while Gangetic dolphins seemed to escort the boat, much to my mother's delight. Finally, to get to Tezu, the Digaru had to be crossed, for which 2 Assam Rifles had an elephant that would swim across the river. The trip had a deep lasting impression on my mother's psyche, for according to her, while my father sat behind the mahout on the elephant's neck with me in his lap, she was left to fend for herself at the back, somehow surviving the crossing by hanging on to the animal's tail!

At Tezu, waiting for us to arrive, was a sparkling new *basha* built out of bamboo by the Tai Khamti chief, Chow Khamoon Gohain, who would later become a Member of Parliament. Just east of Tezu, the Lohit debouches out of the hills and the river then braids, creating multiple islands which in those days had herds of wild buffalo. True to form, my father had linked up with Chow Khamoon who was equally obsessed with shikar, and the Khamti Raja had helped him shoot two spectacular heads. There were at the time no families at Tezu, and during the buffalo-hunt, plans were made to make the basha, into which we, mother and child, plus a black cocker spaniel, were deposited. My father then got into a Twin Otter and headed off to rejoin his battalion at Walong, which was busy constructing the defences on both sides of the Lohit should the Chinese attack and get past Kibithu.

It was a wild and desolate country in those days. Again, according to my mother, the cocker spaniel was a delicacy that was being eyed by every tiger in the area. After sunset, the dog would go mad as the big cats would circle the basha, sometimes testing the framework with their paws. Having no previous experience of dealing with ferocious felines, my mother would sit with me inside the mosquito net and pray the tiger would leave, or sometimes, the men living in their quarters nearby would bang utensils to scare off predators. Sambar alarm calls, were frequent, as was the barking of *kakar* (barking deer) which was indicative that a tiger was around. It was then, it seems, that my eyes would light up and I would gurgle with delight. Trying to hush me up, my mother for the first time began to suspect she had produced an idiot son!

The stay at Tezu also impacted my life in many other small ways. Major Ranjit Singh Dyal, subsequently the hero of Haji Pir, once decided to visit my mother. Ferrying his jeep across the Brahmaputra, he arrived with the back of the vehicle stuffed with *lauki* (calabash or bottle gourd). I suspect around the time I got quite an overdose of the blasted plant, because even today I run a mile from certain vegetables. It was during this period, that Lieutenant General S. P. P. Thorat had visited Walong and accurately predicted the date when the Chinese would attack along the Lohit. Years later, when the general's autobiography, *From Reveille to Retreat* was republished in Marathi, it would be my singular honour to have the family invite me to write the foreword for the book.

We were in Tezu till my father got posted to the IMA. 1 Balbir Avenue was still my mother's family home in Dehradun, but we proceeded to Ujjain for a short break where Narendra Singh Verma was the commissioner. According to my aunt Kamla, Nehru had offered my grandfather a governor's job, but with retirement looming, he had refused. In June 1956, when the family had come to Dehradun for my father's passing-out parade, they had zeroed in on a house on Turner Road in Clement Town that was then occupied by a missionary family. This sprawling bungalow, with some 3 or 4 acres of land, was finally bought around 1961 and was renamed 'Patur'. In Ujjain, Kamla and Squadron Leader Dolly Yadav were expecting their first child, Vir Vikram, while my aunt Meera was already the mother of two—Rajeev and Suniti. A black and white photograph of me sitting on my father's shoulders with my mother and my grandfather's golden retrievers Toby and Sheeba recaptures those early days. When we moved from Ujjain to Dehradun, there was another vital addition to the family. Tipu was a magnificent retriever, with a tail that looked like a Tibetan prayer flag. Wherever I would go, he would too, and he was my first real all-weather companion.

My mother was expecting my sister Teesta by the time we moved into IMA, and she duly arrived on 28 September 1962. She would never forgive my parents for not having bought a baby book for her as well, but then those were extremely dark days with the threat of a border clash with China by then a real possibility. In many ways, even though we had been mauled and conquered by the British and so many invaders before that, India as an entity had never lost a war. The attack on the Namka Chu and the subsequent disasters all over left deep scars on the country's psyche. In many ways, even today, almost six decades after the event, I don't think we have quite recovered our equilibrium vis-à-vis our northern neighbour.

However, it wasn't just the Chinese who were rocking the boat! By then I was old enough to understand that all was not too well on the home front. By the late 1950s, my mother's second-oldest brother, Nirmaljit Singh Hoon, had created quite a business empire for himself. He had married Roma Rani Mitter, a wonderful Bengali lady, and shifted his base to London where they lived with their three children, Indrajit 'Indu', Prithvijit 'Notu' and Gouri. Gregarious by nature, and with plenty of money to boot, he had hosted not only my father's parents but the two sisters also when they had visited Europe, the two girls staying on for a while even after my grandparents returned to India. Whatever the dynamics of the situation, after my parents got married, Nirmaljit perhaps failed to deliver on certain promises made or implied, and my aunt Meera became openly hostile towards my mother. Some of the verbal attacks were vicious and I remember clinging to my mother's sari and wondering what the hell was going on. My father, being completely devoted to his side of the family, would refuse to believe his wife.

Meera had always been my grandfather's favourite, and not only was she not checked, but my grandmother too got into the act, resulting in a typical *saas–bahu* scenario that plagues so many families, especially in India. To make matters even worse, Vijay Dhruv was at the time in love with a girl who was a Catholic and wanted to marry her. The girl's family laid down the precondition that he converts, which resulted in not just a collapse of the relationship but also plunged my uncle into a clinical depression leading to a major breakdown. Mortified that a son of his could have 'mental problems', my grandfather refused to have anything to do with Vijay Dhruv, which then left my father with no choice but to bring him to the IMA where he was then treated.

Upset by the constant taunts, even though Teesta was then still a babe in arms, my mother decided she needed to start working. The family had been fortunate that in 1961, a young Nepali widow, Sharda, had come looking for a job and soon she was an integral part of the family, a virtual surrogate mother to both me and my sister. Having borrowed a cycle from my aunt Sudha, the first port of call for my mother was the Welham Boys' School where she was interviewed by Miss Oliphant, who told her she would receive the appointment letter in a day or two via the dak. Despite having landed the job, mother impulsively decided to cycle down to St Joseph's Academy as well, where she was interviewed by the head Patrician, Reverend Brother Dooley. Without much ado, he walked the then 25-year-old to an adjacent barrack and told her, 'That's your class, Mrs Verma. Start teaching!' The sign on the door read: *Class 2-A*.

Determined to silence her sister-in-law Meera's taunts, my mother also sold off some of her jewellery and after a few months, presented my father with a black-coloured Ambassador car. Just what a momentous achievement that was can be gauged by the fact that no one else in the IMA at my father's level of seniority had a car!

I distinctly remember the day Prime Minister Nehru died, though I was just 4 at the time. The news had come on the radio, and everyone was talking in hushed whispers. That night, alone in my room, I could hear the tap dripping and was convinced it was the sound of wolves coming to get me as with Nehru's passing, the world was about to come to an end. When finally, the grey light of dawn dimmed the darkness, I heaved a sigh of relief. The world had not ended after all, and I had soon forgotten about Nehru. Not that I knew him before either.

My father was then nominated to attend the Staff College course at the Defence Services Staff College that was situated in the Nilgiris in Tamil Nadu. Mostly officers who were already holding the rank of major attended the course, so my father as a captain was relatively junior. After the debacle with the Chinese in 1962, the Indian Army was going through a massive transition, with new battalions and formations being raised all over the country. As a result, the year-long Staff Course was shortened by a few months.

The main casualty of the move to the South was the Ambassador, which was sold in Dehradun. We made our way to Madras where we briefly stayed with my uncle Ranjit and his family. Vinoo, the eldest of the cousins, had also passed out from the Doon School around the same time and everyone was hoping that he would get into the Indian Institute of Technology. The 1964 batch included both Sanjay Gandhi and Kamal Nath, both of whom were close friends of my cousin. The Ambassador was replaced by the more modest Standard Herald, a five-seater sports car that was then being manufactured in Madras.

We arrived in Wellington and perhaps because my father was a junior captain, we were given accommodation in Conoor, the house overlooking the Wellington Gymkhana Club and Golf Course. The house had a massive eucalyptus tree on which Nilgiri langurs would sit and tease poor Tipu, who otherwise would roam around Wellington in solitary splendour. Once while one of the syndicate classes was on, and the commandant was also present, the golden retriever strolled in to see if all was well with the world. My father pretended he had nothing to do with the dog. However, he needn't have worried, for Tipu looked right through him and then wandered out, after which the interrupted class resumed.

Wellington was heaven—there is no other word for the place. The carefully trimmed hedges, shaped in the form of an owl (the institution's formation sign) lined the college, and just as you entered the main gate, on the left there was a small yellow two-room barrack that was the kindergarten school. To get there, I had to come down to the golf course, then climb up to the college, and then say goodbye to Tipu. After the three hours of play or whatever they made us do in those days, I would step out, meet the faithful waiting Tipu and head back the same way.

The highlight of the Wellington stay was the arrival of my uncle Sudhir, then a lieutenant or a captain who had been commissioned into 62 Cavalry. He had gotten married to Asha 'Molly' Ahluwalia, whose family was well established in Hong Kong, and their stay with us was a part of their 'honeymoon'. The bridal chamber in the house allotted, everyone went to bed. As the night progressed, there was a severe rainstorm, and like all good army houses, this roof too started to leak like a sieve. After Molly Aunty's shrieks had subsided, the couple spent the rest of the night with a bucket between them catching the water!

The Staff College course didn't only test the officers, it tested their wives as well who tried to share the workload and sat with their husbands working late hours. My father did well enough not to let the family down and got graded 'D' (Distinction). However, just then, he would get the shock of his life, for he received his posting orders for Fatehgarh, which was the Rajput Regimental Centre. This effectively meant he was being taken off the roll of 2 Rajput and was being transferred to a new raising, 18 Rajput. This led to collective howls of protest, but the army is the army, and it is not for you to question why.

This time around my parents had no intention of selling the car. So, our baggage and Tipu along with an escort having been loaded onto a railway freight wagon and placed at the mercy of the Indian Railways, the entire family bundled into the Standard Herald and started the long journey that would take us to Fatehgarh on the banks of the Ganga in Uttar Pradesh. We promptly ran into trouble, for Tamil Nadu at the time was in the midst of the anti-Hindi riots. It was quite a frightening experience to see a mob at work, and we were lucky to get away with just a crack running across the windscreen.

It must have been May or June, for I remember the heat and my mother buying green grapes as we entered Hyderabad. This was familiar ground for my father, and he was reliving his own past with his little family in tow. We then reached Kanha, and by then he was almost beside himself with excitement, for when my grandfather had been in Mandla, Kanha Kisli had been a virtual playground for the two brothers. Even now, fifty-six years later, I can picture the inside of the car—my father driving, his elbow out of the window, my mother in the passenger seat and in the gap between them, the .357 Magnum Winchester Rifle laid out next to the hand brake. Teesta was sitting behind our mother, Sharda in the middle, and me on the right. Having built up Kanha, my father was trying to keep our spirits up, for ever since we had entered the sanctuary from the Mukki side, we hadn't seen a thing! For some strange reason, he was repeatedly muttering, 'Not a *sauset* ... not a *sauset*!'

Just as I was about to ask what a 'sauset' was, the track took a slight bend and stretched across the red dirt track, was a magnificent male tiger! He was enormous, and for a while he just lay there, ignoring the Standard Herald while all of us just gaped at him, mesmerised. After a few minutes, the tiger got up and very casually stepped off the road onto the raised embankment on the right. He was now looking down on us, his massive face just about seven or eight metres from my father and me. Again, time froze as he stood there, peering into the Herald in a detached sort of a way. Then he raised his tail, and my father's hand instinctively moved towards the rifle ... but the tiger was spraying, after which he turned around and melted away into the undergrowth.

Further down the road, a bullock cart was coming, and it was carrying a white man. I had never seen such a strange-looking, semi-reddish creature before, and we watched in awe as my father told him we had just seen a tiger a few kilometres back. The man was George Beals Schaller, who even today is one of the biggest names in conservation, and who at the time was doing a feature for *Time-Life* on Kanha and writing his book, *The Deer and the Tiger*.

By then the 'Kanha bug' had got deeply implanted in us, and after getting to the rest house, we were off on an elephant, perhaps Teesta's first ride on a pachyderm. This time fortunately my mother had nothing to complain about, as all of us were seated in a civilized manner. We saw another tiger, which was a little far off, and though we tried to close the gap, we only got fleeting glimpses of it. In the evening, we met up with Schaller and he and my father talked of other areas in the Central Provinces. In the morning we walked through what seemed like tall grass to me, where Schaller had put up some sound recording equipment in a tent. Standing there in the open, in the middle of a meadow, the place suddenly erupted with the alarm calls of chital, and I watched in fascination as the tape recorder's spools began to rotate. Thanks to the calls we could pinpoint the location of the tiger, which was again quite far off from us. But it felt exciting to be then walking in tiger country as we headed back the way we had come on foot.

As we got into the car, Schaller, who was probably around the same age as my father, was looking at the rifle. He turned to ruffle my hair, and said, 'Remember son, when you grow up, shoot tigers with a camera, not with a gun!' I don't particularly remember this myself, but my mother would describe the moment to me a few times in later years, though I don't think she ever realized who George Schaller really was. His other book, *Stones of Silence: Journeys in the Himalayas* was also a classic read that was part of my growing years. He was perhaps the first man to introduce the world to the majestic snow leopards, photos of which appeared in the *National Geographic* for the first time in the 1970s.

We were in Fatehgarh briefly, but life in the Rajput Regimental Centre gave one a glimpse of what life in the British garrisons must have been like. The Mess dominated the Ganga and on the sandy beaches, every evening, the Mess staff would make ice cream by churning the ingredients in wooden buckets that were also loaded with rock salt and ice to cool the containers within. There was also a huge stuffed marsh mugger that was placed in the corridor. It had been shot by Major D. P. Singh, and maybe it's a relative thing, but I never saw a bigger crocodile in my life.

Two events happened in Fatehgarh that I clearly remember. The first was that my father got promoted from a captain to a major, and he came home on a cycle carrying a four-foot long *lauki* to mark the occasion. We also used to get lots of watermelons that grew along the Ganga, and in the evenings would sleep outside on cots protected by mosquito nets. The second was the arrival of Sushila Avasthy, with her two daughters—Niharika (Bulbul) and Aradhana (Bela). They had earlier stayed with us at the IMA for a month, and this was their second visit. Bulbul was a great favourite of mine for she would fuss and carry me around, while I remember fighting all the time with Bela. I also discovered around that time that I could sketch, for in my baby book, I had drawn a railway engine and some bogeys. The engine was with a blue pencil, while red was the colour for the coaches. And the wheels were black. So much for my fast-developing sense of colour!

Pakistan, or to be more specific, Field Marshal Ayub Khan and Zulfikar Ali Bhutto, were beginning to flex muscle by then and various things were happening on India's Western front. 18 Rajput, then being commanded by Lieutenant Colonel Zail Singh were to be a part of 23 Infantry Division. With the battalion due to move, we were again bundled into the Herald and deposited in Dehradun, this time at 38 Inder Road, the Hoons having given up 1 Balbir Avenue for this much bigger place, even though we occupied only half of the first floor. The house was huge, and the area in front had a massive *kathal* (jackfruit) tree. With talk of war in the air, my grandmother was most perplexed as all the pillows in the house had disappeared. Finally, the elders zeroed in on me as the culprit. Having decided all pillows represented Pakistani soldiers, I had arrested the lot and locked them up as prisoners of war. I got my ear pulled and was told to go dig a trench for myself under the jackfruit tree, which I then proceeded to do.

In September the war came, and all the windows had black paper pasted on them. My slit-trench was deep and wide enough to accommodate me, but what of the rest of the family? Ah well, I guess I then figured it was each man for himself! Then as the fighting intensified, my father arrived in the dead of the night in a jeep with a driver and one more soldier. 23 Infantry Division was on the move and was heading for the Sialkot Sector. He had peeled off from the battalion at Ambala where he had driven past St Paul's Church, which had just been hit by the Pakistan Air Force's Canberra bombers and was burning furiously. He stayed for three to four hours, and I still remember the feel of his trousers as he hugged me goodbye. My mother was smiling as he left, but I knew inwardly she was crying like hell. Fortunately, in the next two or three days, the ceasefire was declared and 18 Rajput, except for some shelling, never saw any action.

My uncle Vijay was at Jassoran and had been a part of the Battle for Chawinda. As a part of 20 Rajput, he was occupying the Alhar railway station (in Sialkot District, Pakistan) and even after the ceasefire was holding the line. My father joined him there and together the two brothers went over the entire ground. 18 Rajput was then sent off to Sikkim and deployed at Nathu La while my father received his posting orders to proceed to 77 Mountain Brigade as the brigade major. Deployed just below Se La at Nuranang, he was back in the sector where 2 Rajput had been decimated just three years earlier.

In 1966, we shifted to 19-A Inder Road, just a stone's throw away from my grandparent's house. One morning, much to everyone's horror, Tipu was found lying in the basement and he was dead. It was heartbreaking. He was then loaded onto a bicycle, and we went to the Rispana river and buried him there. As we started back, while crossing the stream, I lost my slippers and had to walk back barefoot. Tipu's passing was the first time someone or something close to me had died. I remember my mother, tears streaming down all our faces, sitting on the steps later in the evening, telling both Teesta and me about life and death. I think she was also wondering how on earth would she break the news to my father. She was a pretty good artist, who could do wonders if she had something to copy. She had this letter pad and had painted little birds on each page, using Salim Ali's plates as a reference. Each day a different bird would go to my father, who would also write back diligently. One such page with a bird was smudged badly, for it carried from Dehradun to NEFA the news of a golden retrievers passing.

So badly were Teesta and I affected by Tipu's death, my mother decided to do something about it. Living nearby in Dalanwala, was an Afghan falconer, Sirdar Mohamed, who used to have hawks that he had trained for hunting. We went to his house and there was this litter of cocker spaniels, and after we picked a female puppy, little Amber came into our lives. She would not only wag her little stump tail, but her entire hindquarters also used to shake almost as if she was dancing.

With my mother teaching in St Joseph's Academy, it was but natural for me to be enrolled there as well. There were quite a few Anglo-Indian teachers, and if I recall correctly, my class teacher in class 1-A was Mrs Huntley. In my class, there was an Assamese boy, Parthasarthy Roy Choudhary, and the two of us were earmarked as being 'naughty' right from the start. We were taught from the English Reader, which had a story about Kate who goes swimming and is rescued by her dog. The story made me cry every time for it reminded me of Tipu and it infuriated Mrs Huntley, who thought I was playing the fool, trying to disrupt her class. A couple of times she threw a piece of chalk at me, then when I would 'not behave' she let fly with a duster. I wonder what she was thinking, for the duster was a solid block of wood with felt attached on one side. Self-preservation made me duck and poor Parthasarthy got hit just above the eye. There was a lot of blood, a bit of self-berating on Mrs Huntley's part, and angry-looking Irish brothers shaking their heads in disbelief! My contribution towards the abolition of classroom violence was further reinforced by the huge bandage that Parthasarthy went around with for the next week or so.

Besides that, the bun samosas we got near the gate were the top draw and I got to act in the junior school play because my mother was directing it. I had to play this fat prince (a cushion was tied around my waist) and one had to shuffle in, only to be rejected by the princess who was to choose a husband on the grounds that I was overweight. It's a different matter that when I shed my robes and the cushion, what came out was a scraggly looking character that could give any stick some serious competition. I also hated the smell of the glue that was used to stick on the artificial moustache and beard, but what the heck, it was a small price to pay for stardom!

Parthasarthy and I were separated the next year as he went to 2-A, which was my mother's class, while I was sent to 2-B which was being taught by Mrs Dixit. Parthasarthy's mother was the sister of Bipin Pal Das, one of Assam's leading politicians, who subsequently would become India's minister of external affairs. His younger brother, Satyen Pal Das, was at the time a young fresh-faced captain who after his schooling in the Rashtriya Indian Military College (RIMC), had gone the usual route through NDA, Khadakwasla and IMA, Dehradun before being commissioned into 14 Dogra. An excellent football player, he was perhaps one of the most likable human beings who got along with just about everybody, regardless of who they were or what their age was. I don't think my aunt Sudha had a choice in the matter—for the family had literally adopted him. They were married in the September of 1967.

All this while, my father was sitting in Nuranang, from where they could see the lights of Tawang across the Mago Chu that flowed down below, joining the Namgyang Chu a little to his west after which the river entered the Kingdom of Bhutan. During his tenure with 77 Mountain Brigade (Chindits), he would serve under two outstanding brigade commanders—Brigadiers Ajit Kumar Mitra, who was from the Dogra Regiment and then Harry Singhal. In his case, fate had willed that every time his battalion got sucked into a clash with the Chinese, he would be away from his unit.

In 1967, 18 Rajput was deployed at Nathu La facing the Chinese who were in the Chumbi Valley on the eastern side of Bhutan. The Rajputs were asked to escort a detachment of sappers who were to lay barbed wire between Indian and Chinese positions that stretched from Yakla to Nathu La on the North Shoulder and then across the South Shoulder to Camel's Back. The pass itself was situated at a height of 14,140 feet (4310 m) and connected China's Yadong County with Sikkim, at the time a small kingdom ruled by the Chogyal, but whose defence was the responsibility of India's 33 Corps. Ever since the People's Liberation Army (PLA) adopted a belligerent stance during the India–Pakistan War in 1965, the Indians had initially back-pedalled and abandoned Jalep La that was then under 27 Mountain Division. The line at Nathu La, however, had held as Major General Sagat Singh commanding 17 Mountain Division had refused to pull back. This had irritated the PLA which for the last few months had become even more boisterous at Nathu La, but apart from the odd shove and push, no major incident had developed.

In 2016, my book on the Sino-Indian conflict, *1962: The War That Wasn't* had been out for a while and it was getting some great reviews. I received a phone call from Colonel Anil Bhat, an armoured corps officer, who post-retirement had emerged as a prolific writer and had very good connections with both the media and the film world. He told me he was helping J. P. Dutta, a well-known Bollywood film director, make a movie called *Paltan*, which was to be based on the Nathu La incident. '18 Rajput is your battalion,' he said, 'this is the time to tell the story.'

I knew the broad details of what had happened but needed to find out more, so officers and junior commissioned officers who were present at Nathu La were traced down in the next few days. The fencing ordered by Sagat Singh had started early in the morning of 11 September, the sappers laying the wire down the North Shoulder, which was held by a company of 18 Rajput commanded by Major Harbhajan Singh. 2 Grenadiers were holding the South Shoulder to the right of Nathu La and the men were standing outside their bunkers listening to the Chinese broadcasts as the PLA was vociferously opposing the laying of the barbed wire. Then suddenly there was the sound of a whistle, and the few visible Chinese soldiers also disappeared. A PLA officer (some said he was a major) then appeared with a red handkerchief in his hand.

The Chinese officer threw the handkerchief into the air and then all hell broke loose. The initial volley of gunfire caught the sappers and the Rajputs, including Major Harbhajan Singh, out in the open. At the same time, Chinese mortars also started to pound the Indian posts on both Shoulders. Unfortunately, so unexpected was the coordinated Chinese onslaught that 2 Grenadiers on the South Shoulder literally froze, and they too took casualties, including Captain Prithvi Singh Dagar. For a while, it looked like it was going to be a repeat of 1962 as 2 Grenadiers began to abandon their positions on the South Shoulder. By 0645 hours, most of the exposed Indian troops were either dead or were dying.

Lieutenant Colonel Zail Singh, unable to communicate with Harbhajan Singh, ordered Major S. Chandrashekar commanding 18 Rajput's Bravo Company to move from their location below the pass at Teghuk to Nathu La on the double. The company assembled and was on the move by 0700 hours, reached Sheratang in two hours and began the final climb towards the pass. At 0930 hours, the 120 mm mortars of the supporting light regiment got its orders to finally engage the Chinese at Nathu La. At 1040 hours Chandrashekhar reached what is now known as the Ghol Ghar (then Centre Pump) where the brigade commander,

Brigadier M. M. S. Bakshi (who was awarded the MVC two years earlier while commanding Hodson's Horse) was present with his detachment and protection party. Leaving the company behind, Chandrashekhar climbed up to the North Shoulder just around the time the Indian medium artillery guns finally opened fire.

An artillery observation officer was present at Yakla and had a commanding view from there. He was directing the fire extremely well and Chinese positions started taking a plastering. 'It had taken us more than four hours to get our act together, but when we did, it was quite a sight.' The Chinese had not moved to occupy either North or South Shoulder and by 1400 hours, 18 Rajput's Bravo Company had reinforced the depleted company of Major Harbhajan Singh. Later that evening, Sagat Singh would order Chandrashekar to launch a frontal attack on Chinese positions at Nathu La, telling him that another company of 2 Grenadier was on its way to add to his attacking strength shortly.

The attack never materialized, for as Chandrashekar put it, 'Only ten men of the promised company materialized, resulting in the question being asked again. What was I to attack with?' This response was to earn him Sagat's wrath and a severe reprimand that effectively finished his career. Next four days nothing happened. On 16 September the Chinese political officer appeared with a white flag and said, '*Hum ladai bund kar rahen hai ... hum aapki laashe waapis karna chahate hai*' (We are stopping the fighting. We want to hand over your dead bodies). Sixteen dead, including the bodies of Harbhajan and Dagar were handed back to the Indian side.

'Wait a minute,' said Anil Bhat, as I passed on the details to him subsequently. 'We killed 300 Chinese at Nathu La and then Cho La ... according to this ...' Anil Bhat had let it hang as he realized the implications of what I was telling him. India had lost 88 lives and another 163 wounded, with a higher degree of casualties at Cho La when the Chinese once again attacked on 1 October. It was obvious that when it comes to India's military history, Bollywood would always make it nigh impossible for our people to really know what happened as their own formulae aimed at the box office remained the driving force. The Indian line at Nathu La and then Cho La had held, and to a great extent the myth of the nine-foot Chinaman had been demolished, but we then have our own brand of storytelling. To me, it always seemed disrespectful towards the men who had died, that their real stories were never told.

Back in Dehradun, in 1968 we had been allotted a 'separated family accommodation' in the cantonment area. We were on the first floor, while Lieutenant Colonel M. L. Chibber (later Lieutenant General and one of the key figures in the Siachen saga) was our downstairs neighbour. The area was secluded but one day a beggar, probably with mental health issues, accidentally drifted into the residential area. All of us children, probably frightened of the strange-looking and unkempt man, ganged up on him and started driving him away. My mother was in the meantime, coming in the car and she saw what was happening. She immediately put a stop to it and I was told to get into the car. Reaching home, she then proceeded to give me the thrashing of my life. Apart from everything else, what struck me was that while she was belting the daylights out of me, she herself was crying, repeatedly saying, how could you do something like this. The lesson was not lost on me, for though I got into plenty of brawls later in life with bigger and senior kids, I don't think I ever raised a hand on anyone smaller or junior to me.

All this time, ever since the IMA and Staff College days, we hardly saw my father who was still the brigade major with 77 Mountain Brigade, coming home for his annual leave of two months, and then another 14-day casual leave that the army granted to soldiers. Then came the news that he had been nominated to attend the year-long Allied Infantry Officers' Course run by the US Army in Fort Benning, something which sent a ripple of excitement through all of us.

India in the 1960s was economically still finding its feet after a few centuries of colonialism. One of the biggest problems for officers going on foreign courses abroad was that they were reduced to penury by the finance ministry bureaucrats who would allow them a daily allowance that for their contemporaries from other countries would amount to 'loose change'. The existing system was such that the United States government would double what the home country was giving, which in my father's case was a paltry $4 per day. The amount was so low that the Americans objected, saying there was no way anyone could hope to survive on that allowance. This behind-the-scenes wrangling was going on, while my father was running around getting all his other things in order. The family had said goodbye to him, reconciled to a years' separation, and he even boarded the Pan Am flight, when matters came to a head, and he was taken off the flight. Equally surprised was his brigade commander when my father was back in 77 Brigade, to spend another year of wistfully looking at the Tawang lights across the valley.

Amazingly, he was nominated for the same course yet again and was to leave in the beginning of 1969 for the United States. By now, my mother was fed up with being alone, and she was determined to accompany him for a year. Everything went into a frenzy ... the car, the fridge, just about everything that could be monetized, was sold off and little Amber, Teesta and I were shifted to Patur in Clement Town to live with my grandparents. St Joseph's Academy from Clement Town was too far for us to commute, so we were shifted to St Mary's School which was about a kilometre from our house. My two cousin brothers, Vir Vikram and Vijit, my aunt Kamla's two sons, were also in Clement Town. Vijit, in a freak accident, had sat down in a steaming hot pot of dal, as a result of which had to walk around starkers.

Then the day came when my parents had to leave Dehradun for their last-minute paperwork in New Delhi. We were to drive down three to four days later to see them off. The family was gathered at the Dehradun railway station and until then, everything was quiet, almost akin to a calm before the storm. Then a whistle went off and the guard at the back of the train began to wave a green lantern, and the train gave a little jerk and began to move forward. That was when Teesta came into her own—she let out such heart-rendering and anguished screams, I am sure the entire population of the city must have heard her. As the train and my mother's receding figure got smaller, the screams got louder. I am not sure if I put in a supporting act, but even if I did, in the retelling of the incident, my role was always ignored by those who were present at the station.

Amber quickly settled down with the two golden retrievers. Leaving her with Sharda, my grandmother and two cousins, Teesta and I then drove to Delhi with my grandfather to see my parents off. It was to be a short trip, just two or three days and we were accordingly carrying virtual overnighters. However, the news of my sister's theatrical performance had reached my uncle Nirmal, who then told my mother to 'take the two kids along' as well, offering to pay for our tickets. To make matters even more interesting, after a year's haggling with the US government, the babus had increased my father's daily allowance from $4 to $6, which now would amount to $1.5 per person and when doubled (thanks to Uncle Sam) to $3. We would later learn the Pakistani officer on the same course got $32 (doubled to $64) per day. So much for accountancy and financial studies! You don't have to have the IQ of an Einstein to know when you are well and truly below the poverty line.

The Pan American Boeing 707 lifted off from Palam with the four of us on board, delighted at the thought of being together. If my parents were worried about how we were going to manage, they sure did not communicate it to us. We first landed at Tehran, refuelled, then did the hop to Beirut, refuelled, got to Istanbul, again refuelled, then made it to Frankfurt. I had the window seat and I remember it was raining. My father got off the plane with me and we went and bought a Voigtlander camera from the duty-free shop in the transit lounge. To get the focus right, you had to get two yellow squares aligned in the viewfinder. Then we took off again, and then we landed at Heathrow. To receive us, there was my uncle Shashi who along with his brother Ravi was living in London. Apart from them, there was my aunt Roma and cousins Indu, Notu and Gouri. Our year-long overseas adventure had begun!

3

Guns and Roses: The Fall of a Barbet

London in the early part of 1969 was a scary place. It was grey and gloomy, and we were mostly confined to the apartment in Richmond that my two uncles shared. If Teesta or me so much as jumped out of bed onto the reddish wooden floor with a thud, within one minute the doorbell would ring and an angry-looking landlord who must have been a librarian all his life would sternly put his finger on his lips and say 'ssshhh ...' The apartment had a black and white television, something we had never seen before. Though I had seen plenty of White air hostesses, I also had my first close encounter with a White woman during this period and it left me shaken. Ravi, the eldest of my grandmother Saraswati's brood, had a long-time steady Spanish girlfriend, Inez de la Morena, and though she even visited us in India, they never did get married. Shashi, my mother's favourite brother, had married a German lady, Annette Zumloh, whose father had been one of Adolf Hitler's Panzer commanders. From this liaison he had a son, Amrit, who was around my age, but Shashi being Shashi, he had moved on to other relationships and while we were there, he had this blonde lady friend called Beryl, who smelled of perfume and had large teeth along with other eye-catching attributes, who would leave a lasting impression on me. Just as she couldn't understand our 'Queen's English', we couldn't make head or tail of what she said, so there would be a lot of teeth baring on her part to make us feel comfortable.

Just my luck, I opened the bathroom door and crept in, afraid I might otherwise upset the overzealous landlord who probably had a stethoscope attached to his roof, and lo and behold ran into a stark-naked exhibit of the female Anglo-Saxon race. Beryl let out a gurgle, then tried to reach for a towel but it was out of arm's length. By then, she had probably zeroed onto my two saucer-like eyes (I had myopia, but no one was aware of it then) and probably realized my level of panic was far greater than hers. So, she bared her teeth in an embarrassed sort of way and tried to pat me on the head. Having seen enough of the female anatomy for a start, I fled from there and then sat and shook for quite a few minutes. Subsequently, the fully dressed avatar of the said White woman, smelling of a double dose of perfume sashayed past a few times, but neither Beryl nor I ever spoke of the said encounter again.

My father had left us behind while he had carried on across the Atlantic to the US. We were to follow him after a two-week hiatus in London and another week-long stop in New York with my uncle Jati. Shashi had a pista-green two-seater sports car which sort of suited his personality, so Teesta and I were put in the open boot, and he drove us around London. We went to London Zoo where we met Leo, the lion who had become very famous after he had become Metro-Goldwyn-Mayer's mascot. Like good tourists we were then shown Piccadilly and Madame Tussaud's museum where my mother asked a bobby in full uniform directions before realizing he was made of wax. These White folk sure knew how to complicate life.

The Pan Am flight to New York was fascinating as we flew across the Atlantic. I was glued to the window and could see merchant ships below leaving white wakes behind them, and then there was the Statue of Liberty after which we landed at John F. Kennedy International Airport. The two brothers in London had given a huge box of Indian sweets for Jati Uncle's family, and I was carrying the golden coloured box that was rather conspicuous. Ahead of us, at the customs counter was an American girl carrying a sweet apple, which we would shortly learn was for her dying mother from her UK-based son. The US customs officer just refused to let her take the apple through and eventually it was thrown in the trash. Then it was our turn. The officer ticked two of the three bags with chalk and asked my mother to open the third. Notoriously bad at packing unlike my father who was fastidious, she cheekily told the officer she would happily open it, but he would then have to help her close it again. It became a bit of a joke as the poor chap, after insisting the bag be opened, had to eventually sit on the suitcase for it to be closed. We were then waved through, with me still holding the humongous box of sweets. Jati Hoon, who was watching from the visitor's gallery, just couldn't get over the miracle of the sweets.

It was snowing in New York, and I remember looking at the traffic lights suspended overhead while snowploughs worked to keep the roads clear. There were lots of yellow taxis and there was the Empire State Building, at the time the tallest skyscraper in the world. Jati Hoon had married Barbara and they lived on Long Island, a suburb of New York City. They had three children—Seema, Johti and Sanam—and they were our 'American' cousins. Sanam was barely one and was mostly confined to a playpen which made her look like a caged stuffed toy.

Either on the first night or perhaps it was the next day, Jati laid into my mother, telling her she had no idea what life in the United States was like and just what was she thinking when she decided to bring Teesta and me along. The bottom line was he had his own family to feed and there was nothing much he could do to support us. Though the tirade upset my mother, she became more determined to manage entirely on her own.

We were at Long Island for a month and learnt how to use sledges in the snow. On one occasion, we had gone to downtown New York with my aunt Barbara and as we were coming out of a shopping mall, there was a man handing each exiting child candy bars. Seema, Teesta and Johti took their share and went through the door, but I politely said a 'thank you'. Immediately, a klaxon sounded, and some people came rushing forward. It seemed the management was waiting to see which kid had good manners. When we got home, my mother was so proud of me. That was another lesson ingrained into me at a fairly young age, and by and large, I've always been excessively polite.

Finally, we got the green signal from my father to proceed on to Fort Benning. It must have been March by the time we landed in a Southern Airlines Boeing 737 at Columbus, Georgia where my father was waiting for us along with Major Bill Curtis, his wife Sue and their year-old baby daughter. Bill Curtis was a US Army officer (later rose to the rank of a lieutenant general) and he and his wife were our military sponsors. As per the existing system, there was also a civilian sponsor, which in our case was Dr Mac Molnar and his wife Jean, who was of Red Indian (later referred to as Native American) descent. They had three children, Susan, Mac Junior and Kathy, all of whom were older than us, with Kathy perhaps being around my age. Call it the luck of the draw or whatever, we could not have asked for better people.

The house allotted to us was still not ready and we were shifted into a huge double-storied square-shaped complex. The next morning, we had accompanied my mother to the laundry machines that were placed at a common juncture, when lo and behold we heard someone whistling in the courtyard below *'Main kya karu Ram, mujhe bhooda mil gaya'* which at the time was quite a popular Hindi song. Not quite believing our ears, we rushed to see who it was. A dandy looking person with a jaunty walk was coming along, and after he saw us gaping at him, he came up to where we were. He was from the Pakistan Army, and his name was Major Sarfraz Hussain, and he lost no time in making my mother *bhabhiji* and extracting a promise from her that she would make him *aaloo ka paranthas*. A Special Forces officer, he subsequently would often drop by and both he and my father would discuss military matters endlessly. In the 1965 War he had been captured by the Indian Army and had once escaped from a POW camp, only to be captured again. On one occasion I remember him telling my father, 'Ashok, next war when you are captured by the Pakistan Army, tell them you are my friend. They will then treat you nicely.' These words were to come and bite the honourable Major Sarfraz Hussain firmly in the butt when he was captured by 2 Rajput at Chittagong two years later. He, of course, wasted no time in dropping my father's name, but whether he got any preferential treatment or not is debatable.

Fort Benning is one of the largest military bases anywhere in the world. Mainly situated in the state of Georgia, part of it is also in Alabama, the two states separated by the Chattahoochee River. Where we were allotted a house, one could see the three large parachute towers that dominated the base. The US Army was extremely well organized, and even before we knew what was happening, Teesta and I had been enrolled in the Wilbur Elementary School. The American system meant that the academic year would end in May, so I was admitted into grade IV where I barely did two months. My class teacher was a pretty and petite Jewish lady, who was known to us as Miss Spavvy. Maybe to impress her, I told the class that if you waded out into the sea off Marina Beach in Madras and stood on your father's shoulders, from India you could see Australia. This created havoc in the school. First Miss Spavvy was running around with a globe, then the principal got involved, and finally, my mother was sent for. For the Yanks it was a big thing because none of them had a clue about anything outside of the United States. I got a few solid whacks on my bottom for my creative fable.

The Americans took everything, especially their sporting activities extremely seriously. A US Army squad car pulled up outside our house a day or so later, and an African American soldier with a measuring tape caught hold of me as I was loitering outside. He took my measurements and was gone, without saying a thing to anyone else. The next day the squad car was back, and in the presence of my mother, I was ceremoniously handed over my baseball uniform, cap and kit. I was assigned to Team Orange and had this shirt which had the Infantry School motto emblazoned on it—'Follow Me'. The Benning Little League was serious business with regular coaches and cheer leaders. First time I went out to bat, I swung and connected with the ball, and even though I had no idea about the rules, the ball cleared the fence. After that the coach would holler, 'Send that Indian kid up ...' What I remember most vividly was the post-match picnics where we would roast our own hot dogs and eat large slices of watermelon. It really amounted to living life king size.

The Wilbur School was walking distance from our house, and the route was through some beautiful pine forest. If you were lucky, you could see deer, while rabbits were extremely common. My father had walked us down the trail to the school one day and we were walking back when a huge Alsatian dog came charging around the corner. Hard on Rommel's heels was Karen McKay, who was then a US Army captain. It wasn't long before she and her sister became almost a part of the family. Karen was a paratrooper then, and subsequently her rise through the hierarchy of the CIA would make her a key player in the rise of the Mujahideen in Afghanistan. Now in her mid-eighties, she continues to be in touch with both Teesta and me.

By then my mother had become quite a star at Fort Benning. She was busy making paintings and those were being bought by an increasing number of people, plus was holding television shows on diverse subjects like how to tie an Indian saree, using the likes of Jean Molnar and Sue Curtis as models. One day an American officer came and bought a painting she had made on jute, and paid her a hundred dollars for it. My father arrived just as the Yank officer left, and he felt the officer had paid too much money for the painting. I was told to cycle after the American officer and after a few minutes I caught up with him and told him my father had sent the money back as he felt too much had been paid for the scroll. The American laughed and told me to go back and tell my father to take lessons in art and wife appreciation. It sure tickled my mother pink.

Her innovativeness meant the moment we reached Fort Benning, we even had a car, a white Volkswagen Beetle and though we were not flush with funds, we were never short of cash either. Columbus was fairly close to Fort Benning and we would often visit the city. There were trips to Callaway Gardens and Six Flags, but the real big trip was to Panama Beach in Florida with the Molnars. Situated some 330 kilometres south of Benning, the Molnars had their house amidst some of the whitest sand I had ever seen. We had ambitious plans to do some deep-sea fishing, but the weather began to pack up as a hurricane started to develop off Florida. Much to our collective disappointment, we had to truncate the trip as weather warnings were being flashed by the local authorities.

The transition to grade V was painless, at least for me. Dr Molnar, around that time presented me with a Daisy BB gun, which was an extremely accurate weapon, especially in the hands of a soon to be 9-year-old. Bill Curtis too had bought the same gun for me, and much to my greedy self's regret, he then had to return it. My parents were not at home, when a neighbour's son, a boy called David, came along and at a range of 25 metres, challenged me to shoot him in the stomach, which like an idiot I promptly did. To my horror, David doubled up in pain, and was soon howling like a wolf. As people came out of their homes to help him, I bolted home and prayed to God he wouldn't die. By the time my parents returned, I was waiting for them, and as they entered the house, I told them to beat me up. David's mother registered a formal protest, and two large US Army Military Police sergeants came in a car with a blue light flashing on top. I got a severe lecture about being careless with weapons, but luckily for me, after about a month, I got my beloved Daisy gun back.

Letters from my grandfather in Dehradun were sporadic but kept my parents abreast with what was happening at home. I came home one day to find my mother most distraught, and she blurted out that Amber was dead. Just like that my little world imploded, and I started to sob uncontrollably. There had been an altercation with a servant in Clement Town, and he, in turn, had poisoned the dogs, killing my grandfather's beloved Toby and Sheeba and Amber. My mother quickly tried to rectify the situation by saying it wasn't true and that she was only testing me, but I wasn't fooled by her backtracking statements.

Our time in Fort Benning coincided with two major events. First, the Vietnam War was at its peak and the activity at the base was almost frenetic. Every day, hundreds of Bell helicopters, better known as the Huey, would fly past, and from home, we could see the three towers constantly winching up and releasing parachutes. There were also frequent para jumps as the 101 Airborne Division was training there at the time. Every night, we would watch the flickering black and white images of what was happening in Vietnam and Cambodia. Sometimes my father would sit me down and explain to me what was going on, and I remember thinking the Vietnamese were an Asian country just like us. However, quite a few officers doing the course with my father were South Vietnamese and they were so integrated with the US forces that even their uniforms and mannerisms seemed similar.

Then came the biggest event of them all. Apollo 11 blasted off for the moon from Cape Kennedy in Florida and the entire American continent was glued to the television sets. As the lunar module Eagle with astronauts Neil Armstrong and Buzz Aldrin approached the moon's surface on 20 July, we moved to the next-door house to watch the final moments on a colour television set. It was heady stuff, and for the Americans, it was even more special. Even after the landing, we watched spellbound as to how the astronauts were recovered, and I still remember the visuals as President Nixon and all the bigwigs crowded the bridge of an American warship to be present at the site of the splash down.

I went into grade V with a renewed sense of respect for the United States. Neil Armstrong's famous words, 'a small step for man and a giant step for mankind' had fired up my imagination. My classmates may not have known the distance between Madras and Australia, but they could identify every spaceship and rocket that was displayed in the school along with an abundance of the Stars and Stripes. One of the most noticeable things about the United States was that every house had the flag, which was something one did not associate with India.

The course wound up in October and it was a proud moment to watch my father receive the best foreign student award while Bill Curtis took the trophy among the US officers. It was time to go home, and the Beetle was sold for the same price that my parents had paid for it when it was bought. Overloaded with bags and baggage that included a 26-volume *New Book of Knowledge* and a Remington typewriter, we flew from Atlanta to Washington, D.C. where we stayed for a few days with the Indian military attaché. Driven around the American capitol, we did all the usual stuff tourists do, but what stuck in my mind was the US Marine Corps Memorial, also known as the Iwo Jima Memorial, that was located near the equally stunning Arlington Cemetery. It was late in the evening but so struck was I by the statue of the six Marines raising the US flag, I begged the military attaché to drive around it once again. I didn't know it then, but the original photograph on which the sculpture was based was taken by Joe Rosenthal, an AP combat photographer. Four years later, as a C Former at the Doon School, I would make a painting depicting the same scene, and the painting would that year be given pride of place during Founder's Day. I had painted the scene from memory, and the only change was that the Tricolour had replaced the Stars and Stripes.

After a brief halt of four to five days in New York, we were back in London, where we stayed with my aunt Roma and our cousins in Regent Square. Indu and Gauri took us to see swans in the park opposite, after which we were not given a breather by our parents as they took us all over, from the Tower of London to just about every landmark in the city. It was honestly a huge relief to catch the BOAC flight from Heathrow to Paris a few days later, but there too we were driven around the bend as we got an overdose of the Louvre, assorted cathedrals and museums. The arrival of my uncle Shashi was a welcome relief, especially since he took us to a restaurant where the main course was presented with a couple of sparklers throwing sparks in every direction.

By the time we landed in Italy, I was ready to rebel, but my mother would have none of it. 'You are an ungrateful wretch. This is such a wonderful opportunity.' In Rome we stayed in a quaint little hotel near the Colosseum and the 'sightseeing' continued in real earnestness. One day we were to go on a tourist bus to see some palace or ruin or something. The owner of the inn had by then become quite friendly with my parents. 'Be careful,' he warned, 'the bus is mobbed by these chaps who will try and sell you two folders containing slides of Italian monuments. They will ask for $16 per folder ... do not pay more than ten dollars ...'

My father was looking hurt at the thought of having to buy transparencies, for his Voigtlander had been extremely busy on the trip. Sure enough, as we reached our destination, a swaggering Italian with curly hair who thought he had looks to kill zeroed in on my mother, who in her attire was looking every bit the Indian tourist. 'Pretty Indian lady,' he started off, 'For you ...' he offered the two folders, one yellow and one light blue, '$32 ... special price!'

My mother had her schoolteacher expression on her face, and she told the Italian to take a hike. But he was a persistent chap. By now everyone in the bus was watching this engaging duel. Finally, more to get rid of the fellow, she then made her offer ... 'one dollar ...' she said.

The expression on the Italian's face had to be seen to be believed as it went into various contortions that suggested a severe and sudden lack of oxygen in the atmosphere. He then put his forefinger against his temple and made the universal gesture that her screw was loose. He departed.

In 30 seconds, he was back ... perhaps he was a masochist who revelled in self-inflicted injuries. 'Sixteen dollars ... for you! Pretty Indian lady ...' The last three words were said I suspect, for self-protection, for the tone had lost the earlier swagger. My mother held up one finger. Again, he gestured she was nuts and stomped off ... only to be back again, each time the price going down by half. Finally, much to my mother's horror, he said, 'Ok ... one dollar ... for pretty Indian lady!' My mother, who did not even want to pay the dollar, was momentarily stumped but paid 'Curly' the amount and I was handed over the two folders which had slides of all the monuments in Roma.

Back at the inn, the owner saw me carrying the folders and he shot off to my mother and said I hope you didn't pay more than ten dollars. When he learnt what had happened, he took off his golf cap, threw it on the ground, and began jumping on it. 'I don't teach you ...' he said, 'You please teach me!' The Italians were indeed emotional people!

From France to Italy, we had flown Air France, but for the final leg of the return journey we were back with Pan Am. As the aircraft lifted off from Rome, I could see the city sprawled out below. After a brief halt at Karachi, we landed at Palam in November. We had been out of the country for almost eleven months in all, and in many ways, the Fort Benning tenure completely changed our lives. Teesta, of course, having celebrated her seventh birthday in September, was by then talking like a Yank, her dietary preferences being 'potato wedges, French fries and mashed potatoes!' All three were said in a rush with the sound partly coming through the nasal passage!

18 Rajput had since moved from Nathu La to Nasirabad, a small town near Ajmer in the Rajasthan desert. Coming back from the lush environs

of Fort Benning to an environment where everything was khaki, including the uniforms and the colour of the vehicles, it was a completely different world. Never having seen, let alone lived, in such arid conditions, I was quite fascinated by the countryside. Lieutenant Colonel Balwant Singh was commanding the battalion, and for the first time, one got to feel what it was like to be living among troops. As a senior company commander, my father was allotted a huge independent bungalow that neighboured the house of Colonel Bhavani Singh, the Maharaja of Jaipur.

My Daisy gun, with almost unlimited ammunition, came into its own in that environment. The first bird I shot was a shrike, and after having knocked it down, I spent time studying its feathers and colours. Guns do terrible things to people, and even though every time I shot a bird, or a palm-stripped squirrel, I always felt a twinge of remorse, but would just carry on mindlessly. The first time I shot a pigeon, it was sitting far away on the roof. After the bird came tumbling down, I realized I was being watched by Captain Jimmy Abraham who was passing by on his bicycle. After he had said a couple of nice things about my marksmanship, he slyly asked if I was interested in learning a new sport. 'Good,' he said, 'I'll pick you up at 3 p.m.' Sharp on the appointed hour, he arrived with a strange-looking contraption, which was attached to a longish rope.

That part of Rajasthan had a plethora of large wells, each one with water that was eight or nine metres from the top. It was quite dark, but the craggy rocky sides had plenty of place for blue rock pigeons to make their homes. For the Abraham family, pigeons were a delicacy, and though the bulk of the birds took to wing the moment my head would appear, there was always the one-odd bird that was still there. Shooting downwards is never easy, and to make matters worse, it was fairly dark inside. After making a few adjustments, I had sent half-a-dozen birds crashing into the water. Jimmy then took the contraption and one by one lifted the six birds out. I don't know how, but my mother got wind of the fact that I was slaughtering pigeons. I again got a thrashing, after which the Daisy was confiscated for a month.

There were no schools worth the name in Nasirabad, so I was enrolled into St Anselm's School in Ajmer. This involved getting into a 3-tonner every day and doing the commute from Nasirabad. Having just come back from Benning, the rest of the kids started calling me USA, something that I hated. Luckily, before any serious brawls could break out, my father was told to report to Mhow, where he was posted to the PC Wing in the Infantry School.

My father had been introduced to three things in Fort Benning, and like all late converts in life, he was quite fanatical about all three. While Doctor Molnar had got him hooked onto golf and skeet shooting (he picked up an over and under 12-bore Falcor from Italy with the last of the remaining dollars), Bill Curtis had introduced him to the world of the labrador retriever. Originally from Newfoundland in Canada where it would retrieve fish from trawlers in the icy waters, the labrador as a breed was fast gaining in popularity in UK and the US. In India, at the time, other than a few royal families that had imported the dogs, no one was familiar with them in 1970. Shortly after we had returned to India, Bill Curtis had enquired if my father wanted a pair of labrador puppies as the new US military attaché who had been posted to New Delhi was arriving soon with his pregnant dog. Having had a comfortable flight across the various seas in a C-130 transport aircraft, the said female duly whelped and after the mandatory period of 49 days of being with their mama, two beautiful little girls arrived in a wire mesh cage at Mhow.

It was love at first sight for there is nothing as endearing as a labrador puppy. The more golden of the two who had yellow piercing eyes was named Sona, while the other puppy, lighter in colour, was to be called Sandy. However, a few days after the puppies arrived, my parents felt my education was becoming a matter of serious concern and decided that I would be sent back to Dehradun to live with my mother's parents at 38 Inder Road. Though the term had begun, I was admitted into Marshall School in Class V. There I was to meet Anoop Seth and Pushpindar Singh Maini, and Miss Rafo Kichlu taught us in a classroom resembling a garage. My mother had taught Pushy in St Joseph's Academy, so it was comforting to know I wasn't the only one leading a nomadic existence.

My year at Marshall was ordinary, as was evident when on Sports Day my grandmother, Saraswati, who was invited to be the chief guest, wryly said to me, 'Out of shame you could have won at least one of those cups!' Considering there were but a handful of us, it indeed was a rather poor show. Also in academics, try as I might, Miss Kichlu always ranked Anoop Seth one notch above me.

Meanwhile, after yet another short stint at Mhow, my father was instructed to move back to 18 Rajput in Nasirabad. Though he was not the second-in-command, he was told he would be taking over the battalion, which was then due to move to Agartala, in Tripura. Since Agartala was then a non-family station, it meant my mother too would have to move back to Dehradun, which automatically meant that both Teesta and I would be back on the rolls of St Joseph's Academy. The second move to Nasirabad coincided with my winter break, so I was back too. Sandy had already been despatched to my father's brother, while Sona was beginning to come into her own. My father had been training her well, for even at that young stage of her life, she was shaping up extremely well as a gun dog. Thanks to Sona's training schedule, I got to do a solo crawl with a single barrel shotgun, get within range, and shoot my first common teal. Though I had handled 20-bore weapons at skeet ranges in Fort Benning, the blast and recoil of the 12-bore weapon almost dislocated my shoulder.

Promoted to the rank of lieutenant colonel, my father took over 18 Rajput. The Indian Railways had already positioned a special train for the battalion's move, and the CO had a special saloon car which was labelled 'Tiger'. Sona's wire mesh cage in which she and Sandy had arrived was loaded into the compartment and she would undertake the 21-day journey in royal style. My mother, Teesta and I were to travel with the battalion up to Lucknow, after which we were to catch a connecting train back to Dehradun. Just before we embarked ourselves from Nasirabad, the old subedar major (SM) retired after more than forty years of service. I remember watching as the 'SM Saab' stood in his uniform and each man of the battalion put a marigold garland around his neck. After a while, you could no longer see the man, who along with his handlebar moustache simply disappeared among the heap of flowers. It was a moving experience and underlined the bond that exists in infantry units. The number of men who had tears streaming down their cheeks was incredible.

Only those who have travelled in an army 'special train' will know the pleasures that were associated with it. Even mail trains, notorious for being slow, looked like they were super-fast jumbo jets as they went past our long line of bogeys that were pulled by various steam engines which all seemed well past their 'use by' date! In 2009 I would do the book for the Dimapur 3 Corps and would half in jest refer to the 21-day haul from Nasirabad to Agartala. Since the book was about an army formation, it had to go for the mandatory look through by the military intelligence branch. The only thing they objected to was my putting on paper the number of days it took thirty-nine years previously, to get from point Nasirabad to Agartala.

The train first stopped at Fatehgarh where the battalion had to leave behind its colours. The band played on the platform and there was a lot of presenting of arms, drums rolling and cymbals clashing. While all this was going on, no one noticed an incoming train and Teesta ran onto the track, turned around and just escaped being run over by the skin of her teeth. It was a terrifying moment, and I think I was the only one who saw it. The next morning, my mother with the two of us said a tearful goodbye to my father and Sona at Lucknow. Since the train to Dehradun was only at night, we hopped onto a cycle rickshaw and spent the day looking at the various sights in the city of nawabs.

Back in Dehradun, after a brief stay again in a rented house in Dalanwala, we were allotted separated family accommodation in the cantonment. My mother rejoined St Joseph's Academy and so did Teesta and I. Somehow, after having done a truncated grade IV, I seemed to have been in a perpetual grade V state of mind—starting with the Wilbur School in Benning, then St Anselm's in Ajmer, and finally Marshall School in Dehradun. Mrs Shamshi was my class teacher in grade VI, and she was a wonderful person, apart from being a close friend of my mother. Home now was a separated family flat opposite the sprawling estate that was the circuit house (now the residence of the governor of Uttarakhand) and for all practical purposes, I had the run of the place. Armed with my faithful Daisy, I was back to my evil ways, shooting everything that even remotely looked like a target.

Right across our house was a Gorkha Regiment School which had a peepul tree growing along its wall. I was standing in its shade, and as was my wont I was scouting the foliage for victims when I saw a greenish blur. The Daisy barked once, and almost in slow motion, a green barbet (also known as a coppersmith) tumbled down. I stared at the little bundle of green feathers and then the dazed head looked up at me, the beak opening slowly as the bird prepared to die with some dignity. But it wasn't the coppersmith that was dying, it was me. Filled with the usual remorse at what I had done, it became a mission with me to save the bird somehow. I tossed the Daisy aside, scooped up the bird and for the next four hours sat next to a dripping tap keeping the little fellow alive. Finally, it had recovered and was ready to fly again. I think that was the day when the wanton killing stopped. I would use the Daisy only to shoot at paper targets after that.

There was now yet another dimension to going to school, for my mother, me and my sister all had cycles and we would roll downhill from Haathi Barkala and Rajpur Road to St Joseph's Academy. Sometimes other kids used to ride with us, and I remember Kirti Pandey would join us sometimes. She later went on to marry Deepak Kapoor who would be India's 22nd COAS.

By April 1971, we knew a big war was coming as refugees started pouring into India from Bangladesh. Suddenly, the mood in the cantonment became sombre, for, in our locality, almost all officers were posted in frontline areas, either in the Western or the Eastern Theatre. News of what was happening in East Pakistan was limited to All India Radio bulletins, so we all started listening to the BBC as well. With the Mukti Bahini coming into play and the killings intensifying, we all knew it was a matter of time before India intervened. Sometime in August my mother told me I had to appear for the Doon School entrance exam, and though the family were unlikely to have the requisite funds to send me to the school even if I passed, she expected me to do well. There would be four papers, English, general knowledge, Hindi and maths. Other than this one early warning conversation, I don't think I had any clue of what to do, or what I should prepare for. I think the exam took place in September, but by then there was such a build-up for the coming war, I think the papers were done almost as an aside.

With the war looming, my father had in the meantime driven down from Agartala in a grey-coloured Fiat car that had been allotted the rather fancy registration number TRA 1111 with Sona for company. She was by then almost a year-and-a-half and was quite an outstanding specimen and had been mated, and, in about a month was expected to litter. Because of her large head and imposing personality, almost everyone always mistook her for a male. At the same time, another lady, though belonging to our own species, was also standing up to Pakistan's two *langotiya yaars*, President Richard Nixon and Secretary of State Henry Kissinger, our very well-known Prime Minister Indira Gandhi. Even to us children, the horror of what was being unleashed by the West Pakistanis on their own Bengali population was so obvious, it was baffling why the Americans continued to support the Pakistani generals.

'All this talk of freedom and liberty, good versus evil, goes out of the window when it comes to themselves,' my mother would say of the United States. 'It's a genocide, that's what it is,' she then explained to me and my sister what the word meant. Her generation, victims of Partition just a quarter of a century earlier, knew exactly what it meant to be displaced and the people butchered all around them. With war now a distinct possibility, every evening, my mother would join the other wives as they covered their heads and said whatever prayers they could think of to keep their husbands alive in the days to come.

Everyone was frantically collecting money for the Bangladeshi refugees by then, and we also had our hands full with the arrival of the puppies. Labrador retrievers in those days being almost unheard of, there was a long line of people wanting Sona's pups and two were sent all the way to Agartala since they had been promised by my father to the famous music composer, S. D. Burman. One female, named Missy by Teesta in honour of her best friend in Benning, was given to my aunt Sudha, who at the time was residing with her husband Satyen Pal Das, then a major, in a house just across the road from the Doon School.

Then the Battle of Boyra happened on 22 November and India collectively felt a shiver down its spine as Indian Gnats from 22 Squadron shot down two F-86 Sabre jets in full view of thousands who watched the thrilling dogfight. On 3 December, Pakistan, believing in the dictum that the fight for the east would be fought in the west, launched a pre-emptive strike against Indian airfields and as the lights went off across the country due to the enforced blackout, we all clustered around the radio and heard the announcement that India was at war with Pakistan. All of us had waited for the inevitable for days, and it was a relief that at last things were happening. In what was becoming a habit I guess, according to my sister, I promptly dug a trench inside the Gorkha Regiment School premises.

18 Rajput, still a relatively young battalion, was a part of 311 Mountain Brigade that made up 57 Mountain Division. The general officer commanding (GOC) was Major General Benjamin Gonsalves, and his immediate boss was Lieutenant General Sagat Singh, who was commanding 4 Corps. We of course knew nothing about what was happening, but in the Agartala Sector, 18 Rajput was to play the pivotal role in the capture of Akhaura, with 10 Bihar in support and 4 Guards (1 Rajput) in reserve. On the face of it, Akhaura seemed to be beyond the capability of a single brigade group to capture and secure, for it was a heavily built-up area defended by an adequate number of Pakistani troops. Ben Gonsalves felt the best that could be done was to keep the Pakistanis on the defensive, so that they, in turn, could not threaten Agartala. By all accounts, it was to be a formidable task and to make matters worse for my father, 311 Mountain Brigade was being commanded by Brigadier R. N. Misra, who was my father's direct boss.

To understand the dynamics of the situation one must go back to 20 October 1962 when at dawn, the Chinese attacked 2 Rajput positions on the Namka Chu. Pathetically deployed at the bottom of the valley, the battalion stood no chance whatsoever and 282 men were killed while the CO, badly wounded, was taken prisoner with the rest of the surviving men. Only one officer along with some men from Alpha Company managed to disengage and pull out. Deployed to the right of 2 Rajput, was 9 Punjab, a proud battalion with an outstanding record. Commanding this unit was the then Lieutenant Colonel Misra, who unfortunately had the previous evening tapped into the brigade commander, John Dalvi's conversation with the GOC, 4 Mountain Division, Major General Niranjan Prasad. Realizing the hopelessness of the situation and that the higher commanders had no plan 'B', Misra had colluded with the CO of the battalion on his right, 4 Grenadiers, and the two had actually run away the next morning, abandoning the men from their own battalions.

In the aftermath of the debacle, no one was held accountable, thanks mainly to Y. B. Chavan, the then defence minister's whose brief was to ensure that the prime minister was protected at all costs. Even the Henderson-Brooks-Bhagat report that dealt mainly with 4 Corps operations at the time, was classified and even today remains so. Misra then subsequently found himself still commanding 9 Punjab in 1965 and even got a Vir Chakra (VrC) as part of the dole-outs for the fighting in Chhamb–Jaurian, thereby clearing his way to a higher rank. *Trouble was, my father knew what Misra had done at Namka Chu, and even worse, Misra knew he knew!*

Before the actual war was declared, there had been a sharp action fought at Dhalai by the Indian Army against set Pakistani troops. There had been heavy casualties, including the brigade commander, Brigadier Shiv Dayal Singh Yadava, who was then replaced by Kailash Prasad 'Tom' Pandey, Kriti's father. My father had been present when they evacuated Yadava from the Agartala airfield, and the lessons of the engagement were not lost on him, just as they were not lost on General Sagat either, who was perhaps one of the most adaptable commanders the Indian Army has ever had. Evolving different tactics and bringing into play all that he had learnt at Benning, my father led the assault on Akhaura on 5 December and 18 Rajput took the objective with five men killed. In the build-up to the attack, three others had been killed on 2/3 December, but the lack of serious casualties in capturing Akhaura had everyone sit up and take notice. Both 18 Rajput and 10 Bihar were subsequently awarded the Battle Honour 'Akhaura'.

However, for my father and 18 Rajput, the real test was yet to come. From the initial orders issued by Eastern Command, it is obvious that Dacca initially was not the objective. The army chief then, General (later Field Marshal) Sam Manekshaw was fairly conservative in his approach and the initial plans catered for a war of attrition. This mainly aimed at pushing the one Pakistani division and two brigade groups holding the eastern flank of East Pakistan west of the Meghna River. Straddling the expanse of the river was the bridge that linked Ashuganj on the east bank with Brahmanbaria on the west. Should the Indians succeed in their objective of boxing up the Pakistanis, then Sagat Singh knew he had a chance at taking Dacca.

There is enough evidence to suggest that Misra was aware of the exact number of Pakistani troops at Ashuganj when he called my father and told him to move along the railway embankment that ran from north to south before swinging across to the right across the Meghna Bridge and take Ashuganj. The narrow approach meant only one company could approach Ashuganj at a time. 10 Bihar were again in support, and 4 Guards yet again the reserve battalion. A troop of PT-76 (three tanks) under then 2nd Lieutenant (later Major) Rajinder Mohan Shrivastava from 63 Cavalry were allotted for the assault. Captain 'Shammi' Mehta, the squadron commander was also present for the attack.

Misra would tell a journalist years later he saw a shadow of fear across my father's face, which was not surprising for the orders were all but suicidal in nature. Nevertheless, despite suspecting what Misra was trying to do, my father got on with the job in hand. I have had officers from the East Bengal Rifles (EBR) who witnessed the Rajput advance tell me what happened subsequently and by all accounts, it was a desperate but determined affair. Pakistani pill boxes, situated to cover exactly the approach taken, opened up with devastating effect, and 18 Rajput would lose 27 men killed and another 80 wounded. The only reason the death rate was not any higher was because the battalion literally hugged the embankment and the Pakistani MMGs could not depress their line of fire beyond a point. Mohan's tank took a direct hit and he was badly burnt, but he was pulled out alive by my pigeon shooting companion, Jimmy Abraham and my father. Mohan never forgot the incident and despite being extremely ill in 2015, would be by my father's side every day when it was his turn to cross over the Rainbow Bridge.

Somehow, the Rajputs hung on, and then amazingly the Pakistani troops—almost a brigade if not more—began to withdraw across the Meghna on the road cum rail bridge. When the defenders occupying the pill boxes started to disengage, Major T. L. Sharma, commanding Alpha Company chased after them on the bridge, covering a fair distance before he was felled by an MMG burst to his head. Then, in what is etched in every man's head who was there, two spans of the bridge were blown by the Pakistani sappers. A confused and disoriented Pakistani commander then decided to move with his withdrawing troops north towards Sylhet. Watching all this from a helicopter was Sagat Singh, who then promptly landed and asked his kin, Air Commodore Chandan Singh, to put together a fleet of Mi 4 helicopters and airlift 311 Brigade's reserve battalion, 4 Guards (1 Rajput) across the Meghna to Narsingdi. The gates to Dacca had been prised open.

After the surrender, my father got some leave and arrived in Dehradun to be with my mother on her 33rd birthday. However, the day was marred by tragedy, for Sona had caught a chill and she died in our arms that day. As a family, we were devastated, but even before we could come to terms with her passing, my father was recalled, for Misra had been caught by the military police stealing gold bars that had been in possession of the Pakistani troops. He decided to take me along with him, and my mother and Teesta were to follow by air after a few days. We got to Calcutta from where we boarded an Indian Airlines Fokker Friendship and landed at Agartala. Misra was among three brigadiers who were court-martialled for misappropriation, one of the others being Shabegh Singh, who later appealed, got reinstated and retired as a major general, only to be killed in the Golden Temple as Bhindranwale's right-hand man in June 1984. Owing to the disgrace brought upon the army and himself, 311 Brigade never got its due and even T. L. Sharma, who was recommended for a Param Vir Chakra (PVC), was downgraded to a VrC. My father was Mentioned-in-Despatches and for the rest of his life, he would carry the cross that he had failed to get his men the recognition they deserved, and even after 18 Rajput became 13 Mechanised, he tried in vain to get them the Ashuganj Battle Honour.

Our stay in Agartala was brief, during which time two incidents of note took place. I stole the Jonga keys from my father's driver, Havildar Punj Raj and promptly hit a tree, earning a well-deserved thrashing. Second, my mother and Teesta, following in our wake, met an intelligence havildar from 18 Rajput at the Dum Dum airport. When Indian Airlines announced boarding, my mother had taken Teesta to the washroom. The intelligence havildar, overawed by the fact that the CO's wife was travelling on the same plane, insisted there had been no announcement. By the time they thought of enquiring what had happened, they were told the plane had already landed in Agartala. At our end we got a shock when only the suitcases appeared but no mother or sister. The next day they arrived unheralded on another unscheduled flight, mainly because the airline couldn't argue with my mother anymore. She even fought with the airline staff and brought the shamefaced intelligence havildar along!

4

The Doon School: North to South

Back in Dehradun, after hectic last-minute preparations, I arrived at the Doon School wearing a pair of green trousers. Since my cousin Vinoo Hoon had been in Hyderabad House, the 'Sorting Hat'[3] or its equivalent did not have to tax itself and I was assigned to Hyderabad B. Dr S. D. Singh, who had been my father's tutor in Birla Vidya Niketan, Nainital was my housemaster and Amitav Ghosh my house captain. My grandfather, Narendra Singh, also knew a forest officer who lived in the Forest Research Institute, and his son, Ramchandra Guha was told to 'look after me'. Coincidentally, as I reached school, he was perhaps the first person I met and he said to me, in no uncertain terms, that he didn't want to 'see me my *f*#%ing face* for the rest of the year!' The second person I met was a Sikh who had hair sprouting from his face and I would learn later he was known as 'Uppal Surd'. I tried to get past him, but he caught me and asked why was I wearing olive green pants. I honestly told him my mother had cut up my father's old pants and made mine.

Uppal Surd's collective wisdom and deduction powers (he had been in Doon at that point for four years at least) came to the fore. 'Your pop is in the army?'

---

[3] In the Harry Potter series, the Sorting Hat was a sentient magical hat at Hogwarts that determined which of the four school Houses each new student belonged most to. These four Houses were Gryffindor, Hufflepuff, Ravenclaw and Slytherin.

'Yes,' I said, drawing myself up to my full height, which was four feet something at the time.

'Oh, I see ...' Then he decreed, 'Your name from today is going to be "Rifleman Fauji".' Luckily for me, the 'Rifleman' bit got dropped, but I was 'Fauji' from that day onwards.

Quite a few of my batchmates were sons of old boys and had then been groomed for the Doon School by spending four years at Welham Boys', which was then a preparatory school. This lot were miles ahead of us D Formers (grade VII) for they knew the ins and outs of what was expected of us, plus they had been in Doon for a year as well, having joined in E Form (grade VI). Nevertheless, one settled down quickly, and I was just beginning to get used to the daily routine when things started to go drastically wrong.

On a weekday I was surprised to see my mother struggling across the Main Field. From a distance, she resembled an orangutan, as both arms were holding two bags that were clearly extremely heavy. I sprinted across and asked her what on earth was she doing in school. She shooed me off and disappeared into my housemaster's bungalow, where I dared not follow. So, I waited, and three minutes later she was back minus her load. Again, I asked her what was she up to. I was obviously irritating her with my persistence, so she sat me down in the car, and told me that I had actually failed the Doon School entrance examination and it was Dr Singh's extreme kindness and the fact that he had been my father's tutor, that he had inflated my marks so I could get in. Since he had done this huge favour, he had politely enquired after that if my father's liquor card could be used, of course scrupulously on payment, for he as a housemaster had a huge social requirement for whisky and rum. Hence the orangutan act!

I was blown sky-high by this revelation and suddenly hated being in Doon School. I wanted to run away but had no clue where to go. I was 11 years old, and quite honestly, my world had fallen apart.

There were twelve of us D Formers in Hyderabad B. Both Hari Krishan Dar (408) and Abhiram Singh (147) were from Welham and were in their second year in school. I was loitering around somewhere when they told me my batches' entrance exam papers were being burnt by the *maalis* near Chestnut House. What made me take off like a jackrabbit and get there I have no idea, but I found all four of my papers still intact and the overall mark sheet which was only partly singed before I pulled it out of the fire. I folded the papers and put them inside my shirt, after which I went towards the Central Dining Hall, where I then looked at the final mark sheet. I could hardly believe what I was looking at; in English, I had topped the exam, was second in general knowledge, had flunked Hindi and was not too hot in maths, but then nor were the others. It didn't take my partly developed brain to figure out what had happened.

I burst out crying and was sitting near the Main Field sobbing in solitary splendour, for it was around 3 p.m., which was Rest Hour and actually, as per the rules, I should have been in my room. Just my luck, Amitav saw me and presuming I was having the new boy blues even after a couple of months, he came and sat next to me and started to give me the usual stuff about loneliness and homesickness, how it was but natural and I could always come to him when I felt blue. After a while, I just took out the answer papers and the mark sheet and gave it to him, in the process blurting out what had happened.

Amitav looked shocked, and then he abruptly stood up and said, 'Come with me,' and started to walk towards Dr Singh's residence. By then, I knew my housemaster, like everyone else in the school, had a nickname, and he was known as 'Saand' which was slang for a bull! I was in no mood to go to him, but Amitav said there had to be some misunderstanding, and before I could scream out 'Noooo' we had entered his bungalow and rung the bell.

Mrs Singh, who was an extremely good-natured and kind lady, answered the doorbell, saying Dr Singh was asleep. Amitav said it was a matter of some urgency, so after a while, a very angry-looking Saand appeared at the doorway. My knees were banging together, and I was trying to hide behind Amitav, but my great house captain shoved me forward, handed over the sheaf of papers to the Saand and said, 'Fauji has something to say to you sir,' and he fled the scene. If this had been a Shakespeare play it would have had a footnote ... Exit Brutus! I had no choice but to blabber some nonsense about my mother and whisky and actual results. By then, with his years of experience in handling a crisis, the

Saand asked me, 'Where did you get these papers? Don't you know it's a yellow card (YC) offence to steal school property?' I was of course by then jelly! I duly got a YC the next day from my headmaster, Colonel Eric Simeon, who never asked me if I had anything to say in my defence.

That same morning, earlier at breakfast, Saand had announced at the Hyderabad House dining table that I was a 'cad' and a 'bounder' and he had my father's permission to whip me if required. This then of course made me fair game for all the bullies in the house and the next few years I had to fight almost daily physical battles to survive. Complaining to my father was out of the question, for he was then in Mizoram, 18 Rajput having moved there from Agartala after the war. In any case, no one could say anything about his family, his 'Guruji' or anyone who had his unquestioning loyalty.

Years later, I think it was 2016, Amitav, by then one of India's most celebrated authors and I were both at the Times Literature Festival and had been put up at the Taj Mahal Hotel in Mumbai. Though he remembered his last day in school when I had been sitting with him listening to Bengali poetry, he did not remember the incident where he had left me high and dry with the Saand. Anyhow, after school, even the greatest catastrophes then seem funny. It always reminded me of Kipling's famous lines that are also emblazoned at Wimbledon's Centre Court ...' If you can meet with triumph and disaster ... And treat those two imposters just the same.'

The Doon School taught us many wonderful things and the five years spent there shaped and moulded us. Injustice was a way of public school life, and you learnt to live without moaning and groaning about it, for there was no one to listen to you. On our second day in school, I remember trooping into the art school. Sitting in a corner was Rathin Mitra, the most eccentric of all our teachers. I am not sure if Pablo Picasso had died just then or a few months earlier, but by way of an introduction, he asked who was the greatest artist of all. Since we all incoherently mumbled something or the other, he went down the line, giving each one a stinging slap. Corporal punishment was not allowed, but who amongst us was going to tell our lunatic art master that and risk a second *jhaap*? Nevertheless, just to cover his hand warming exercise, the good man then gave us all a postcard that had his line drawings on it and we were supposed to be the privileged ones.

Three days later as we entered the class again, Rathin Mitra from his corner fired the same question at us but he slyly added the word 'alive' under his breath. Even before the chorus saying 'Pablo Picasso' had finished, he was at it again, saying to us, *when Rathin Mitra is alive, how can it be Picasso?* Yet, he was a brilliant master and could teach you techniques that made an otherwise half dead painting come alive. As time passed, I made a series of war paintings that adorned the walls of the art school. Even today, a lot of my classmates and contemporaries insist I got my nickname Fauji because of that, but then they are taking away from Uppal Surd's creative genius.

Despite being at war with Dr Singh for my entire five years (so much for pastoral care), I started to enjoy myself. A lot had to do with the younger crop of masters who were in a different league by themselves. The Saand was also HOD of the English Department and even if I topped my class in trials (exams), I would constantly get demoted. We had a system where the bright boys were in 1 and the duffers were in 4. Masters had classrooms and we were graded as per our performance in English, maths and Hindi. In grade IX if you were good in English but usually flubbed maths and Hindi, you would be B1B4B4 or whatever. I think I was in C Form when two masters, Rajendra Pal Devgan (RP) and Krishna Kumar Candeth (KK), both of whom taught English, stood up in the weekly meeting of masters (Chambers) and told Dr Singh he was being extremely unfair to me. It didn't change anything, but I realized I was indeed getting the rough end of the stick and wasn't just being paranoid.

This boosted my confidence considerably. KK was from Kerala, and he had a great sense of humour. He had started a publication called *Hell'uva Fag* and it was the closest thing you could have in school to *Mad* magazine, as it lampooned both masters and students alike. Screwing up my courage, I walked up to him and asked him if I could join the editorial board of *Fag*. Though KK knew who I was, he had not taught me, and he looked at me with the tilt of the head that I would later get very familiar with. 'Really?' he said, 'And what might be your interests?'

'Deep-sea fishing and big-game hunting,' I replied.

KK didn't know quite how to react to that, so keeping a straight face he meekly said, 'Ok, you're on!' He then went to his room and had a belly full of laughs.

When a door closes, another one opens elsewhere. The school by and large had some outstanding masters who made classes fun. I had by then developed a fairly simple philosophy in life, which in the long run was actually not such a good idea. By the time I reached B Form, I told myself I would pay full attention in class, absorb as much as I could, but as a matter of principle, would not study either at 'Toye Time' (prep) or particularly prepare for exams by mugging up things. I am not sure how this line of thinking came into my head, but I was to stick to it quite doggedly even through my college years. Sometimes you need a good counsellor, or perhaps just a tight whack on the bottom to see the light! At first, my grades seemed to improve, but then gradually began to fall away. Academically it was pure hara-kiri.

The classes I enjoyed the most were those of 'Guru', or Gurdial Singh. His mountaineering days were behind him, but he still used to stride across the Main Field with a rainbow-coloured golf umbrella as if he was marking his run-up for a hop, step and jump event. We called him 'Gaida', and at times he was the 'Mountain Goat'. No issue of Fag was ever complete without some reference to Guru or the other and he in turn used to love it. We were studying grid maps one day and suddenly Guru stopped and asked the class ... map reference so-and-so, what will you find there? The area under consideration had scrub vegetation, so after a suitable pause I replied, 'Sir, grey partridge!'

'Well, why not the black francolin?' Guru was delighted someone had responded. His voice was quivering with excitement.

'Because sir the black prefers a bit of water.'

That month I got the highest possible grades from him on my report card. Guru had been my uncle Ranjit Hoon's classmate at Government College Lahore. My subtly reminding him about that on other report card days had cut no ice, but the partridge sure hit the jackpot!

In 2017, Vikram Seth, the author of *A Suitable Boy* and I set off together from Gurgaon/Noida to Chandigarh to visit Guru who was then 93. Guru was more or less confined to bed, but he was delighted to see us, especially since he shared a particularly close relationship with Vikram whose housemaster he had been. Guru said he had had a wonderful time till he was 'ninety-two and a half' after which he was confined to quarters. His biggest fear, as he went on to say, was 'losing my memory'. Guru then recalled his first impressions of a young Vikram, with whom he had an involved discussion about Mozart and classical music. Considering he was talking of their first meeting that was half a century ago, the recall was amazing. Then the two of them started talking of Thomas Hardy and the various nuances in *Far from the Madding Crowd*. The two of them could not only remember each character, they even knew the blasted page numbers where certain events had been alluded to. I too had done the same book for my Indian School Certificate in 1976, and I couldn't even recall what the cover of the book looked like! And Guru was worried about his memory!

While in school, our friendships more or less were confined to our own batch. We had quite a diverse bunch, and the most 'driven' characters were invariably the second-generation DOSCOs. Dhruv Khanna, better known as 'Dodo', was the second son of Tishi Khanna who had groomed his boys to be school captains or perish in the attempt to get there. The elder Dodo, Vinit Khanna, who was my house captain in 1974, had been pipped to the school captaincy by Rajiv Sarin, who till this day remains a close friend of mine. Dhruv would get the coveted appointment alright, and even though he wasn't particularly talented, he made up for it with his sheer hard work. We were good friends until as the Hyderabad House tennis captain, he released a list of six names with himself at the top and his younger brother, Nalin, bringing up the rear.

Most teams were hard to break into if you were not there already, but in tennis I had initially spent a lot of time hitting balls at a wall and then, in the Vohra Cup, narrowly lost to Niraj Sardana in the semi-finals. I should have been a natural choice for the house team, but found myself excluded, the Dodo well aware of the fact that I had no forum for appeal given my frosty relationship with Dr Singh. In front of the entire house, I then challenged Dhruv to play a set the next day, and 'if he so much as got a game off me' I would not press my claim any further. With nowhere to hide, the Dodo was soon 4-0 down when he feigned a twisted ankle and ran off. On the grounds that the game hadn't finished, I was still excluded from the side. This was too much for me to take, so the next day I led the Tata House cheering squad as they played against Hyderabad House.

R. D. Singh (RD), who taught history, was also the housemaster of Hyderabad A. Related to the royal family of Poonch, he too like Sheel Vohra, had been introduced to John Martyn by Jati Hoon. RD was also a good friend of my father and he had with him Nawab, one of Sona's puppies who had grown into a handsome young retriever. Even though I was a S Former then, RD caught me by the ear and marched me away from the tennis courts. 'You bloody *ullu*, do you know what happens to traitors on the battlefield? They are shot!'

'I'm trying to make a point sir ...' I held my ground.

'You can always convince yourself you've been wronged and justify your actions. I am sure there are other ways to protest,' said RD, 'But no matter what the provocation, you never let your side down.' It was another of those lessons that get stored away in one's brain.

Hashim Tyabji, batch of 1974, was the chief editor of *Fag*, and since he wanted to 'concentrate on his final exams' he resigned from the job. KK looked at me pensively ... 'You ready for some big-game hunting Fauji?' he asked. 'You're the Top Cat now!' *Great,* I was thinking ... *I can attend this year's Socials with Welham Girls' now*! Being chief editor in B Form was unheard of, and though we were nowhere close to what the *Doon School Weekly* editorial board did week after week, I was at least theoretically, at par. We continued to have great fun, and around then I was joined by Arun Kumar aka 'Spy' who was a brilliant cartoonist as well with a wry sense of humour. The next year I got the two Rahuls on board—Rahul Bhagat and Rahul Roy. However, not all our protagonists liked to be featured on our pages which was perhaps once a term or maybe, if we were in a creative mood, twice. In one issue we had analysed Bull Surd's (batch of 1975) brain and come to some drastic conclusions. He was waiting for me two nights later and hit me with a hockey stick on my face, leaving me spitting out teeth. With a swollen, blue face, I was quizzed by the 'authorities' but had to steadfastly maintain I ran into a lamp post!

Ah, Doon School was fun, though we didn't always think so while we were there. More than anything else, I think it was the mid-term break that shaped our personalities. Dehradun's geographical location was almost perfect, with the Ganga flanking the Doon Valley to the east and the Jamuna to its west. We just had to roll out of bed and head north and we were in the hills of Mussoorie, while to the south were the oldest mountains of the subcontinent, the Shivaliks. It was here that I perhaps had my narrowest shave with death, and even today exactly what happened forty-six years ago remains a mystery.

We had an extended weekend and our deputy housemaster, A. N. Dhar (later the principal of Scindia School) who was known as AD or Bheeku (because he was always bumming cigarettes from other masters) decided to take all twelve of us A Formers on an overnight cycling trip. The plan was to get to Lachiwala, and from there follow the forest road to Kansrao, before cycling back from the Clement Town side. AD was the only master who insisted on calling me Shiv, and at Lachiwala, he asked me to take the lead while he brought up the rear. Our torches had all but flamed out, but it did not matter because the moon was out in all its glory, and the newly laid tarred road was like a grey ribbon stretching ahead of us. The tall *sal* trees were throwing numerous shadows across the road, and since it was downhill, I was clipping along at quite a pace. I can still recall Sanjeev Sethi (205) egging me on ... 'Faster ... Faster ...' and then I know that I looked at this shadow about a hundred metres ahead of me. It was just another shadow, but as I got to it, I was literally braking for my life. The entire lot of cycles telescoped into each other, and we finished in one big heap on the road.

'What happened Shiv?' AD's voice was more of a groan from among the heap of bodies.

'I don't know sir ...' I said shakily.

Meanwhile, Nakul Bhubna (416) had managed to get a faint glow out of his torch, and it was passed up to me. In that dim light, my blood froze. The entire road had disappeared, creating a yawning gap some 10 metres wide. The road had sunk down and below us were just jagged rocks. AD was to write about the incident in the *Doon School Weekly* and I still remember his opening lines ... 'Shiv was born under a lucky star ...'

Till today I have never figured out what happened, yet something did. Later that night, we also ran into a police ambush. This time we were trudging along on foot, not wanting to mount our bikes after what had happened, and AD was in the lead. It was a wonder he didn't have a heart attack when suddenly in the middle of the jungle, lights came on all around us along with the sound of multiple rifle bolts.

Around then, while I was still an A Former, there was an unexpected visitor. Bela, or Aradhana, was then in her third year in Medical College in Gwalior. I remember she wore a gent's watch with the dial turned inwards, and whether that had anything to do with it or not, I was smitten so bad I couldn't think of anything else for days. For the next four years, including most of my time in college, I would remain in correspondence with Bela and sometimes even jump off moving trains to visit her and Mrs Avasthy in Gwalior. It was only when she was engaged to a doctor based in the UK, that I finally came out of a perennial state of puppy love!

S Form came and went, and in a final act of defiance, I refused to attend Dr Singh's farewell dinner at his residence. We were to be the last of the Indian Senior Cambridge batch, which meant the lot after us would pass out after doing an extra year. There was a lot of confusion, for we too were switched to the new system, which was then referred to as the 10+2, but then told we were reverting to ISC. This meant we had lost an entire term, and subjects that had been earlier covered by masters in three weeks, were summarized within a day. My policy of not studying anything outside of class was in tatters, especially since I was the only one in my batch who had opted for the arts with additional maths. To make matters even worse, when we walked in for our Indian history paper, we were dumbfounded, as the characters we were being quizzed about had not even remotely figured on our radars. 'Chaps,' I remember R. D. Singh going on to the stage and announcing, 'There has been a botch-up. Just do your best.' In the final analysis, I was lucky to have got away with a second division, despite having topped the English language paper.

The Doon School forged friendships that have lasted decades. Two of my best buddies in school were Mohit Whig (501) and Sanjeev Singhal (528), both of whom were coincidentally from Jaipur House and both of whom joined the NDA and then the army and IAF respectively. Mohit was to meet a tragic end in 1997 when he was killed in the Kupwara Sector in Jammu and Kashmir when his vehicle ran over an IED. Receiving his body and his subsequent funeral was perhaps one of the most difficult things some of us had to do. Anoop Seth (523) and Pushy Surd aka Pushpindar Singh Maini who were with me in Marshall School resurfaced in Doon School and we continue to be thick as thieves, as is the case with Jagatbir Singh (272) and Atul Bahadur Singh (68) plus some others who are among my 'go-to' guys whenever I need anything. Most Hyderabad House guys—Hari Krishan Dhar, Abhiram Singh, Sanjai Bannerji (387), Hemant Jain (59), Nakul Bubna, the late Vipin Malhotra (157), Janardhan 'Jerdi' Kapoor (170) are more like family, and that list includes quite a few from Hyderabad A as well. The bond of a shared childhood is something very special—M. Ct. P. Chidambaram (135), Anupam Swaroop (22), Ashok Khosla (139), Sunil Wadwani aka Toady (20) among them. The last-named had twin sons and he named them Shiv and Kunal. He swears to this day that it has nothing to do with me! I told him so long as he doesn't secretly call his wife 'Fauji', it's OK!

The books we read also had a lasting impression—I remember reading Paul Carell's *Hitler's War on Russia* in C Form, when I was 12 years old. Hemingway was but a natural favourite, and I particularly liked his collection of writings in *Byline*. James Herriot and his animal stories, Jim Corbett, Kenneth Anderson and P. D. Stacey's *Elephant Gold* were my virtual bibles, and I used to leaf through them often, re-reading chapters at random. However, the book that moved me the most was a part of our curriculum, Alan Paton's *Cry the Beloved Country*. Someday, I would often muse, I want to be able to write like that!

On the home front, after Sona's most unexpected demise, shortly after I joined the Doon School, Missy reverted to us, my aunt Sudha giving her up despite the fact that she had been with her for more than a month by then. 18 Rajput by then had left Agartala and deployed in penny packets all over Mizoram, and in the summer holidays we got to visit Silchar and Warangte, which was where the Jungle Warfare School was situated. Back in school, I felt most upset that none of my batchmates or friends had any idea where Mizoram was, and worse, no one was particularly interested in rectifying that.

Having finished his command tenure, my father then got posted to Mhow in 1974 where he was nominated to attend the prestigious Higher Command Course. After a fairly long stay in Dehradun, my mother, along with Teesta, Sharda and Missy joined him there. To everyone's delight, my father then got posted to the Defence Services Staff College as a directing staff (DS) and by the end of 1974, the family was back in Wellington. For me, this was to be a logistical nightmare, but just being in the Nilgiris compensated for all the travel related hardships one had to endure.

At the end of the term in June 1975, I was still 14 when I had to make the journey from Dehradun to Wellington. The Doon School on its part had a Delhi Party that sent us by bus and offloaded us at Sundar Nagar. While in school, we were not allowed to keep any money, so my father had sent ₹150 to my grandfather, who in turn drove down from Clement Town, searched for me for a while, then went back home. With a residual princely sum of ₹15 that was given to me by Dr Singh as my balance pocket money, I then took an auto-rickshaw to my aunt Sudha's place in Sardar Patel Marg, where she and her family had shifted from Dehradun. Army families in those days were so short of cash, my uncle Satyen Pal Das took me to the New Delhi railway station, bought me a ticket in an unreserved compartment of a 'Holiday Special', and with some serious shoving and pushing, I got into a compartment through the window. The train was cram-full of sweaty bodies, but I at least had a window seat. Looking around for my uncle in growing panic, I finally spotted him as the train began to move. Running alongside, he gave me half-a-dozen oranges that he had bought, but in all the confusion, he forgot to give me any money.

The train chugged through the night, the open window throwing bits of coal into my eyes. I had my bag, which I held tight, and felt sorry for the others who were fast asleep in a standing position. By the morning, some of the standing bodies had got off, so we now had some breathing space. I was rationing my oranges but had nothing to eat or drink. At Jhansi, one of my co-passengers who had his wife and relatives with him got out from the window and bought some *puri–aaloo* for his lot. Thank God for the milk of human kindness, he bought some for me as well. Feeling (and looking) like a beggar by then, this was to be my last meal on this railway journey as the kind family got off in the afternoon at Bhopal. The next day, we were somewhere near Vijaywada when the train was further held up for five to six hours. 'Rice smugglers,' someone whispered darkly, and since others all nodded, it must have been the case. Another day was to pass, and finally, after nearly 72 hours, the Holiday Special steamed into Madras Central.

By then the entire train was empty, and I staggered out, with the intention of getting to the nearest pillar and going to sleep. Hardly had I plonked down, when a voice incredulously asked, 'Kunal?' It was my cousin Vineeta, who for the last twenty-four hours had been checking every train arriving from Delhi. I hardly remember being driven home to the house in Kodambakkam, but the water was like black sewage after I was put into a tub. After that I just slept, every now and then being fed something to keep me alive.

After a forty-eight-hour break, I boarded the Nilgiri Express with a ticket Vineeta had bought and reached Coimbatore early in the morning. The train then terminated at Mettupalayam an hour or so later, from where I had to switch to narrow gauge and take the toy train to Coonoor. I had been in such a daze that I had forgotten to ask for money again, and to my horror realized I needed a fresh ticket for the last leg of the journey. Seeing a soldier from the Madras Regiment, I begged him for a ₹10 loan, and after signing all sorts of papers and giving him my watch as collateral, he advanced me the money. Finally, a few hours later after the train pulled into the station, I heaved a sigh of relief to see my father standing there. After paying the good soldier his money and recovering my watch, I finally was home where everyone including Missy was waiting. It had taken me six days.

Returning to Dehradun was no big deal, but the journey from the north to south was a virtual nightmare that was to repeat itself three more times. However, the day I would reach (we lived in a house called Mansarovar that overlooked the road to Kotagiri) my father would have all the fishing reels out and the first weekend after my arrival, we would hit the upper lakes running. Upper Bhawani, Avalanche, Mukurti ... they were teeming with rainbow trout. On other weekends we would head down from the Nilgiris and go fish the Lower Bhawani, and though the fish there were monsters (my father caught a 49 lb *mullee*) I personally preferred spending entire weekends stalking trout, even though they were hard to catch in the crystal-clear waters. The Nilgiri weather, with the drizzle sweeping along with the mist, made each trip surreal. Getting back home, we would cook the trout in butter and then pick each fish clean.

On 7 December 1975, Missy gave birth to seven puppies in my father's study. Armed with a sterilized scissor, I watched as each little creature popped out in what looked like a cellophane bag. There were three males and four females, each with their eyes screwed tightly shut. Helping Missy with the water bags, I had never seen anything so wonderful. In the next few days, as the litter started to find their feet, one little chap caught everyone's attention, for even then he stood, his tail wagging furiously and his eyes always dancing with delight. One evening he jumped out of the enclosure and somehow managed to get to a bottle of calcium tablets, which he proceeded to demolish. Though he was violently sick the next day, this act probably saved his life for the other puppies subsequently got affected by pneumonia, and the other two males died. The little guy was then named Sher Khan, after a tree pie that my father had when he was a growing boy in Mandla. For the next decade-plus, Missy and Sher Khan were to completely take over our lives.

Sher Khan was a year-old by the time I passed out from the Doon School and arrived in Wellington for my six-month hiatus in December 1976. I was perhaps one of the first to leave from my batch, and the last few days had been an emotional roller coaster. Until it was time to leave, I hadn't quite realized just how deeply ingrained into my system the school had become. 18 Rajput by then had moved from Mizoram to Dehradun and being the former CO's son, they extended me the courtesy of dropping me off at the railway station, for this time around I had too much baggage to proceed with the Delhi Party. As the train pulled out, my father's driver, Punj Raj and the others with him all saluted. At that point in time, I was determined to join the army and get commissioned into 18 Rajput. Quite honestly, until then, it had not even occurred to me that I might have an option.

In Wellington, apart from the weekend frenzy of chasing grey jungle fowl and rainbow trout, I started playing tennis regularly at the Wellington Gymkhana Club. The club with its immaculately polished wooden floors and heads of bison and tiger on the walls also served some excellent lemonade bottled by Spencers. The tennis marker, who taught all the ladies and called them 'Missies' because of his own colonial hangover, was ambidextrous and on the red-clay surface, almost impossible to beat. Wing Commander Mohan Vasudeo Kashikar, the DS in charge of tennis, also suffered from the same fate, and the two of us would watch the marker in action and plot how to get past the 'man with no back hand'. I'm not sure if I ever managed to win two sets in a row, but the near-obsessive attempt was to pay its own dividends subsequently.

A few days before leaving school, while working on my last edition of *Fag*, KK had looked at me quizzically and said, 'You know Fauji, I know you are planning to join the army. However, when you go through Madras, go to this place called Tambaram. There is no harm in widening your horizons a bit.' He had left it at that, and I too had forgotten all about it. Ironically, despite Wellington being a major defence hub, there was actually no information available on the entrance examination for the NDA, and even though I filled the requisite form, I had no clue even what subjects one needed to prepare for.

I was having breakfast with my father when I decided to raise the subject. 'I'm seriously thinking,' I let that sink in, noticing the slightly one raised eyebrow, 'of not joining the army. I might want to be a writer ... or join the merchant navy.' I even then had no idea where the navy came in, for it certainly wasn't on my agenda. My father's raised eyebrow had come abreast of the other and he was by then scowling. 'To be a writer,' he said, 'you need to be an intellectual.' Given my ISC grades, I was in no position to even look remotely hurt. 'You cannot just start writing. You have to specialize in a field, understand it, and then express yourself. Who put the idea of the merchant navy in your head?'

'The guys were saying it's good money ...'

The look I got cannot be described. Contempt, a feeling of sadness, disgust, complete lack of OLQ (officer like qualities), all combined with a tinge of pity, more so for himself than me, for he was solely responsible for having created the creature who put money above country and duty. 'Join the army,' he said, pushing back his chair and standing up, 'or go to hell!' Exit father. It was also the end of the one and only attempted career counselling session in my life.

I decided to rebel at that point. Years later, when I made the film on the NDA, *The Standard Bearers*, I would repeatedly kick myself in the pants for having done so. Sent off to do the exam in Madras two weeks later, I just reported at the centre, wrote my name and roll number, and exited after the mandatory half an hour. Having ensured I would get a sum total of zero in all four papers, I then began to worry about the repercussions when the results would be declared and even thought of running away for good. Back in the Nilgiris, all that was forgotten as I got on with the serious business of defeating the blasted tennis marker. But K. A. 'Toots' Chengappa, who was the chief instructor's nephew, the then Brigadier (later Lieutenant General) B. C. Nanda, and who was madly in love with his cousin, got the story out of me. Scratching his chin while sipping a lemonade, he said philosophically, 'I thought I had problems. But man, you're *fucked*!'

Fate intervened. While playing golf at the Ootacamund Golf Club, the up and down nature of the terrain resulted in an officer not realizing the group ahead of him was still in range, and he hit my father on the head with a ball hit from 180 yards away. This meant two things; in the long term, it ensured my father, having been knocked on the head, would certainly become a general; and in the short term, it fast-tracked him to the military hospital in Wellington where he was laid up when my NDA exam results arrived and he could not tear me apart as had been predicted by Toots and others who were in on the impending disaster.

Two months later, in February 1977, having sunk my NDA boat, I was again on the train to Madras, this time to seek admission in college. The previous day a letter had arrived from Colonel Eric Simeon, the Doon School headmaster, which said that owing to my 'exceptional performance'

in the English language paper, Delhi University colleges would be inclined to view my application favourably should I plan to apply. However, I was in no mood to even contemplate going up and down between Wellington and Delhi by train, so the idea was rejected out of hand. As I left home, my mother, who was an old Madras veteran having done her teacher's training there, said to me sternly, 'Any college, but Madras Christian College (MCC).' And, she added, 'They are heavy into drugs,' as if it was information supplied by the Intelligence Bureau under an oath of secrecy.

'Where is it?' I asked, since most of the talk had until now centred around Loyola College.

'Tambaram, it's a bit far from Madras, but it's connected by a suburban train.'

One look at Loyola and the other city colleges, I started to regret having not joined the army. The word Tambaram kept niggling at me, and then I remembered what KK had said. The next day, I was on the train, heading south past Meenambakam Airport to take a look at this college of junkies! Sitting opposite me was an extremely attractive girl, and since I was wearing a new pair of dark glasses, I screwed up the courage to say hello. She was from Mauritius, her name was Ruby, and she was going to MCC to see if she could get admission there. *Aha,* said I to myself, but then we were at the Tambaram station and after crossing the overbridge, entered the lush environs of the institution. Ruby soon disappeared down the corridor and I went looking for the English department.

There were two lines there. One had a motley line of three candidates who all looked bored, while the other seemed to stretch around the block, and each hopeful had properly combed hair and looked like eager beavers. I asked someone what the longer line was for, and he reverently said, 'B. Com *Maccha*!' I had no idea what 'Maccha' meant, but one thing struck me with absolute clarity, this commerce must be worth doing if I was to get a job after college! Why I stood there, I still don't know, but had obviously held my place long enough to hear the words 'next' when I reached the top of the line. Dr Swaminathan, his right arm but a shrivelled stub from polio, looked at my papers and asked me why I wanted to do B. Com since I had not done accountancy in school. Before I could truthfully say I had no idea why I was sitting there, his eyes widened and he said, 'You've done additional mathematics? I've never seen an arts student ever opt for that before.' Before I could say anything, he stamped my application with the word 'Admitted' and that was that!

I thought I'd go find Ruby now that I had the admission part out of the way, but no sooner had I stepped out of Swaminathan's room, I was accosted by a bunch of characters who looked like goons from outer space. Their eyes were uniformly red-shot, and their hair looked like bee-hives that had gone wrong. 'Junkies,' I thought in panic, but they had me properly surrounded and there was no place for me to run and hide. One of them had taken my file and was leafing through it, 'Admitted, huh?' he said, a cigarette dangling from the corner of his mouth. Then he let out a short triumphant yelp, 'Hey *Maccha* ... he's from Doon School!'

Assigned to Bishop Heber Hall, the next two weeks were pure hell! My moustache was half shaved off, I had to sweep, clean, and wash endless rooms, run around the women's hostel with a lungi raised over my head yelling 'I am a eunuch! I am a eunuch!' And if that wasn't enough, was subjected endlessly to the 'Commando Course' where one had to crawl in the gymnasium while a heavy knotted rope swung just over me. If the head came up even by a centimetre, the knot would hit you like a tonne of bricks. My diet during that period was mainly 'Tambaram Grapes' which were the sick smelling and bitter fruit of neem trees. Being a DOSCO was such a rarity, I was told later how even '*Macchas* from other colleges came all the way to have fun!'

The only respite I got before I was 'initiated' in a pond with all the other freshers, was when this rather large looking character took pity on me. His name I was to learn later was David Davidar, and after telling me to clean his room, he said he would lock it from outside and I could sleep '*under his bed*'. As he closed the door, he said the magic words, 'If you need to pee, do it outside the window!'

I was soon wishing he hadn't said that, for the brain latches on to these things and I was desperate soon enough. The room was on the first floor, and I had no idea what was outside the window. Stepping onto a slanting surface in the pitch dark, I promptly fell on my butt and was lucky I didn't get seriously hurt. David got a shock when he came around after a while, for I was hiding under the stairs. He was kind enough to let me sleep there for a couple of nights, a kindness I never forgot! After the ragging period was over, I ran into Ruby, who was sitting on one side of a gutter and staring into her eyes was no one else but David Davidar. Life! Who said it's fair. I would meet Ruby in Mauritius in 2018 when she was the director of the Maritime Oceanographic Institute or something equally impressive sounding. When I told her how she had broken my heart, she said, 'That bloody David!' Davidar was by then my publisher, and I was only too happy to echo her sentiments!

5

See See See! It's MCC! Onto Ladakh

I believe people who have spent their school years in a particular region, should go to another end of the subcontinent for their undergraduate studies! Being in Wellington, the insular nature of the army did not expose any of us to South India as such, but the three years in Bishop Heber Hall would completely change the way I looked at the southern peninsula. Had I stayed at my uncle Ranjit Hoon's house and been a day scholar, one may not have been exposed to the diverse mix of people. It took a bit of time, but I soon learnt to distinguish a Malayali from a Tamil, a Kannadiga from a Telugu, or a Coorg from another Coorg (given the fact that they all had long noses and each one thought he looked like Alexander the Great). We also had a few people from Mizoram, a Tibetan, one Nicobari, some Nigerians and even an Iranian. As one learnt to differentiate one from another, one wondered how on earth could everyone south of the Vindhyas be classified as a 'Madrassi' or, for that matter, everyone to the north of the same geographical feature be clubbed as a 'Sardar-ji'!

After the ragging got over, I settled down quickly to my new life. The freedom one suddenly enjoyed, where, unlike school, life was not regulated by various bells going off, led to a complete collapse. The first morning I didn't feel like attending classes, I just rolled over in bed and went back to sleep, missing the first two sessions. No one asked me why I hadn't turned up in the morning, so the next day again I skipped a couple of classes. Those became days, and days became weeks at a time and by the end of the first semester, the degeneration was complete. I had become a real foul-mouth where I couldn't speak two sentences without bringing in the choicest swear words, my room was filthy and out of the four or five subjects that we had done, I had failed in all, including English.

What saved me from complete and absolute ruin was tennis. The day I was initiated and did not have to live any more like a squirming rat hiding from junkies, I made my way to the college courts where the physical director, K. C. David was selecting the college team as quite a few entrants had got in on a tennis scholarship, whatever that meant! My five months with the tennis marker in Wellington paid immediate dividends and with a fairly lethal forehand, I virtually walked into the side along with my batchmate, Murali 'Sweetie' Padmanabhan. My captain in the first year was K. A. Aiyana, who was Toots' cousin, and who was more obsessed with his nose and sex appeal than focussing on his backhand which was his weakness. I would take over as the captain in my second year itself, and with Murali as my vice-captain, we powered MCC up the inter-collegiate ladder.

Despite the tailspin I had gotten into, tennis kept me well clear of any drugs, and other than once smoking 'pot', I stayed more or less restricted to cigarettes. My first-semester mark sheet brought me back to my senses. I still believed in the mantra that I would concentrate only in class and will not study outside, but then I realized if I was not in class, I was going to bleed to death—and the worst part is, no one would give a damn! The first thing I did was clean my room, make the bed, get myself a haircut, get back into shorts and hit the tennis courts, this time with the intention of clearing my thought process. Swearing and general abuse were out, and though it took a few weeks, I was back on track. Classes were fun, and there were quite a lot of us who would engage the professors in lively discussions. P. H. Mani, Ranjit Kuruvilla and Thomas Mathews, the last two being from Lovedale in the Nilgiris while the tall lanky Mani was from Bokaro in Bihar (now in Jharkhand), would also ask questions but the others in the class never opened their mouths. The four girls in our class sat together in the front row, and they were extremely quiet, generally sticking to the traditional half sarees and flowers in the hair. One of them, Sudha, wore large hoops and had a beautiful neck, which sitting behind her, was admired often, especially if the class got boring.

I had just been appointed captain of the MCC team when I noticed I was being stalked by David Davidar. It was unnerving, so I accosted him near the cafeteria and asked him why he was behaving strangely. David looked like Vijay Amritraj, and though he couldn't hit a tennis ball to save his life, he was fanatical about the game. He was going to pass out of MCC that year, he said, and his one unfulfilled wish would be that he never got to play on the college courts. As a rule, unless you qualified to wear the MCC colours, no one was allowed to play on the main surface. There were courts in all the three Halls—Bishop Heber, Selaiyur and St Thomas's—that were meant for lesser mortals but since David had let me sleep in his room when I was dying, I said go ahead. However, the next day again he was back. What now? I have no one to play with, said the Davidar who wore size 12 shoes and carried a racquet like it was a fly swatter. If I was seen playing with him, I wondered what worse a calamity could there be, so I went and changed up and we played a 'set'. David, to his credit, to this day has never forgotten to be immensely grateful, though the last time we met, in his telling of the story, he claimed he got a game off me! Age does strange things to people!

As luck would have it, his tenure at the Staff College over, my father was posted to the Cabinet Secretariat in New Delhi. On a fishing trip just before he left, he had slipped and fallen, hurting his hand. To keep the pain down, someone gave him an aspirin which he took on an empty stomach. This nearly killed him, for it created serious internal haemorrhaging, but it was handled well by the army doctors in Wellington. It had come as a shock to me, for until then, my parents to me had been immortal. Teesta and I had been lucky, with almost all family members on both sides living healthy long lives. The shift to Delhi meant I would once again have to do the Madras–Delhi train journeys, and though it gave me the heebie-jeebies, I told myself I was no longer a kid, and those days were history.

Little did I know! I was heading to Delhi in 1978, after a gap of two years. Dressed in a white kurta and pyjama and Kolhapuri slippers, I wanted to get some water at the Bhopal railway junction. The ticket collector (TC), a nasty sort of chap, told me not to get down, as commuters would try and get in if I opened the door. There was no one on the platform, so I dashed across and started filling my bottle, during which time the train started to move forward. Used to alighting and climbing from moving trains, I got on easily enough but found the door locked. By now the train was gathering speed, and the TC asked me sadistically what the matter was. I asked him, politely enough, to open the door but I spoke in English, for I was completely out of touch with Hindi. The next thirty minutes, the man lectured me about rashtra bhasha and how he detested us 'Tamils'. I couldn't believe the levels of racism while I hung on for dear life. Finally, someone came along and let me in. Though I searched the train for the TC with the intention of throwing him out of the moving train, luckily for both of us I couldn't find him.

By my third year, I was completely at home in MCC and enjoying every minute of my time there. The campus, neighbouring the IAF Tambaram Station, was pure heaven with a rich and diverse bird life and even some deer. Sometimes some of us would crawl through the tall grass, get to the IAF perimeter and watch Kiran Mk-I and HPT-32 aircraft take off, skimming just over us. Just what were we trying to do, I have no idea, for had any DSC[4] guard seen us, he would have been justified to shoot to kill. MCC was also brimming with talent, especially Bishop Heber, which in my third year, boasted of literally all the game captains. All four members of my tennis team were from Heber which meant the other two halls were not interested in holding the annual inter-hall tennis tournament. Monopoly sometimes has its disadvantages!

It was 5 October 1979, and I had turned 19 that morning. I was to play Ramesh Krishnan later in the evening in the Bertram Tennis Tournament at Egmore Stadium. He had just come back to India after winning the Wimbledon and French Junior titles and I was informed just before the match that it was going to be televised, which was scaring the daylights out of me. Getting thrashed is one thing, but getting thrashed live on television, is quite another thing. Just when I thought life couldn't

---

[4] The Defence Service Corps, comprising mostly retired soldiers, are entrusted tasks such as the security of airfields.

get worse, I got a message that there were some visitors waiting for me near the entrance to the hall. Wondering who on earth it could be, I walked across and was amazed to see Mrs Avasthy and Bela, the latter all decked up in a blue sari, sitting there. They were on their way to Pondicherry to see Bela's prospective match, the doctor from England, who she had dismissed earlier in her letters as having a Punjabi accent! When the heart shatters, it shatters! And boy, did it break into a million pieces. The two ladies carried on to Pondicherry, I got whacked 6-0, 6-0 and after refusing to see the match clippings on Doordarshan News, I cried myself to sleep.

But the next day was another day in paradise, and I said to myself, what the heck, let me go check out this guy. So, I thumbed down a truck on the Tambaram–Pondicherry Highway, climbed onto the canvas at the back, and made the four-hour journey with enough wind on my face to blow all my woes away. To the credit of the Sud family, into which Bela shortly got married, they didn't shoo me off from JIPMER, where they were doctors! To make matters worse, I kind of liked the guy with the Punjabi accent, so I caught a ride back the next day. But obviously, I was all screwed up inside, and so I sat down and instead of the ritual of writing to Bela in the evening, I hammered out an article for the MCC magazine. I titled it 'The Pseudo Society', and it was all about drug abuse and peer pressure that created havoc in young minds. The next morning, I walked across to Mr Rajani, who was the professor who handled the MCC journal, and after handing him my article, I forgot all about it.

Our music and cultural groups invariably swept every festival and in 1980, we conceived MCC's very own festival. I remember sitting with K. P. Achuthan, who was also the college hockey captain, and he said our campus was so wild it reminded him of the jungles of Africa. Those days one of the most popular comic strips featured the Phantom, and K. Prasad, who was Erapally Prasanna's nephew, promptly said, '*Machha*, I got it! Let's call it "Deep Woods"!' And Deep Woods it was, which even now forty years later is a much looked-forward-to calendar-event for colleges across the country.

I graduated from MCC in May 1980, and with my trunk, holdall and tennis racquets boarded the Grand Trunk Express for the last time.

The train crossed Gwalior and I looked wistfully out of the window, fully aware I would soon be twenty and for all my platonic relationships, had not even come close to kissing a girl yet! Wistfulness was giving way to panic by the time the train pulled into New Delhi, for the walls for the last few kilometres were all carrying this ridiculous message '*Dulhan wahi jo Pathakji dilwayein*'.[5]

Hardly had I reached Delhi, my father had the fishing gear out, and we set off for Dehradun. I suspected he had a hidden agenda, for whomsoever I would meet, they would look at me gravely and tell me how concerned they were about my future. Being a regular soldier, my father did everything by the Army Act, so he had these 1-inch maps of the Uttarkashi region, and I dutifully followed his finger across the alarmingly sharp-looking grids to a small lake called Dodital. I was familiar with the place even though I had never been there, for it was a popular destination for Doon School groups during mid-term breaks. However, our preparations were not just limited to the study of maps. We got these fancy rucksacks from the IMA's trekking club, and then with an arm-long shopping list went to the CSD canteen. Top of the list was a plastic jerrycan with 5 litres of XXX Sikkim Rum, followed by 5 kilograms of rice, 5 kilograms of flour, 1 kilogram each of assorted dals and God alone knows what else. Added to the list were pressure cookers, frying pans and if I remember correctly, *proper* plates, forks, knives and spoons.

We took a local bus to Uttarkashi, a 10-hour haul with people either side of us hanging out of their windows puking their guts out intermittently. When we offloaded our rucksacks and the holdall with provisions at the bus stop, it finally dawned on my father that we could not move even an inch with the load we were carrying. Somehow, we got to the local National Cadet Corps (NCC) unit, and it was decided to junk at least 80 per cent of the stuff we were carrying. Restricted to just the

[5] A matrimonial for brides, 'Pathakji' was obviously quite a hot shot as a marriage broker!

rucksacks that were over 25 kilograms each, I asked him what were we to do with the dead weight that was the rum! It was like the deer, the grass and tiger—if we left it behind, the NCC staff would almost certainly drink it. 'We'll take it with us,' decreed the father. I rolled my eyes!

The NCC jeep dropped us at the roadhead the next morning, and from there we began the arduous climb towards Aghora. By the time we reached the small guest house three to four hours later with our heavy loads, I was all set to go home. We offloaded some more provisions, and the grateful chowkidar's eyes were bulging at this unexpected booty from two strangers in transit, so he offered to carry the rum halfway plus a bit of our other baggage as well. With shaky knees that were by then wobbling like bicycles about to fall, we trudged along till we ran into a *gujjar* camp. The head gujjar, who had a flowing red beard, took pity on us and gave us a white horse, a blob of white butter and a *degchi* of milk. His son, who would lead the horse, would return in the evening after dropping us. With the rucksacks now on the horse, suddenly life was different, and one started to enjoy the trek. After a while, the track opened into a valley that had this heavenly lake, the size of perhaps four football fields.

While Lakhi Ram, the chowkidar who looked after the small forest rest house at Dodital, offloaded our stuff, both my father and me had already hit the lake and our fishing lines were singing out over the clear waters. We arrived just when the fish were biting, and in the next hour we had caught almost a dozen trout. Since it was then time for our gujjar friend and the white horse to take leave, we magnanimously gave him six trout. This became a daily ritual, for the gujjar would arrive with a blob of butter and milk and take back fish for his family. The barter system was well and truly alive in the hills.

We were there for a week, and we fished and fished, and had trout for breakfast, lunch and dinner, cooking them in the fireplace with dollops of white butter. Some of it would land in the pan, but some also fell in the fire and the flames would burn a bright yellow. If I remember correctly, we did not touch the other provisions, and could barely finish the daily quota of milk and butter.

On the third night, stuffed with trout cooked in butter, I was fast asleep, when I was rudely woken up by my father who told me I was snoring 'like an old man'. Under the Army Act, section something or the other, he then gave me an order, 'Stop snoring!' I was most put out, but there was no point saying anything because my father had already gone back to sleep. I turned around, tucked up and followed suit, but was again woken up. 'I told you to stop making an infernal racket!' The pattern repeated itself a couple of times, and then thankfully the grey light of dawn began to creep in through the window which was just above our heads. At daybreak, usually, Lakhi Ram would come in cheerfully, stoke up the fire and make tea which was nine-tenths milk. However, that morning there was no sign of him, though we could hear him moving around in his neighbouring hut.

Finally, he arrived and breathlessly enquired how had we coped with the leopard sitting on our window ledge most of the night. Not more than three feet from us, perhaps even less, the feline had been sawing every now and then. When my father would wake up and start telling me to shut up, the leopard would stop and watch us squabble, if you can call a one-sided conversation that.

As the day progressed, people from neighbouring villages started arriving at the lake in their hundreds, each group accompanied by a drummer, for it was the day of the 'Ganga Mela'. With the trout spooked by the noise, there was no point fishing, so we retreated to our room and decided to get some shuteye. An hour later, Lakhi was frantically waking us up. A woman was thrashing around on the lawn, obviously in the throes of an epileptic fit, while someone was trying to make her smell his shoe. Every time the smelly thing was pressed against her face like a mask, she would start off again. My father had rushed across by then and he pushed the man with the shoe away and turning to me, ordered me to get the XXX Sikkim Rum. Pulling the inner lid off with his teeth, he then poured a capful down the gasping and frothing woman's throat.

It was magic! The rum obviously made her splutter and choke, but suddenly her eyes were wide open and she seemed to have been shocked out of her state. Gathering herself with the help of her group, she was taken away while others collected around to look at the white jerry can with a reverence that is usually reserved for the *devtas* in their temple abodes. Half an hour later, we were woken up again, and this time there was a line a kilometre long outside our door, all of whom wanted darshan of *doktar saab*. If someone had a bum knee, he got a capful; if his elbow was scratched, he or she got a capful; stomach and headaches, blisters and ulcers, they all got the same treatment. Even then, at the end of the medical session, we still had about 2 litres of rum left.

The day we were to leave, while the white horse was being loaded with our rucksacks, I saw something out in the lake that seemed to be thrashing around. I ran across and realized it was a green tit. Big trout, the size of my arm, were circling the little bird, which I somehow managed to retrieve by creating ripples by casting near it so that got it close to the shore. Like the woman, the little guy's eyes were also rolling, the white membrane clouding over. By now I think everyone knew what to do. The rum was brought, but instead of a capful, a dropper was used to plop a single drop into the open beak. It does not matter which gods one prays to, for once again there was a miracle. After hopping around from my hand to my shoulders, the tit flew away after a while, and we started our walk back, the jerry can swishing along on the horse's back.

The hidden agenda of the trip was to convince me to apply to IMA as a direct entry. On returning to Delhi, I did that and was then told to report to Dehradun to the Services Selection Board (SSB) where I would have to clear the medical and physical tests. I was to leave at night by the Mussoorie Express when the *dakiya* (postman) came along in his khaki uniform, and after asking me my name, handed me a registered letter from Bennett Coleman & Company. There was a letter inside with a demand draft in my name for a few thousand rupees, which at that point of time was a lot of money. The letter congratulated me and said my entry in the All India Essay Competition had won, and as per the terms and conditions, I was to report to the *Times of India* office the next day either in Delhi or Bombay. It was all extremely intriguing because, for the life of me, I could not remember having entered any competition of the sort at any level.

Much to my father's annoyance, I decided to skip the SSB, and made my way to the Times of India Building, where there was a desk near the reception that had a banner saying 'All India Essay Winners – Report Here'. Since I was the main winner, someone took my photo and then I was taken up to the third floor where I was warmly congratulated by Inder Malhotra, who had a sign on his door saying 'Resident Editor'. By then I was feeling extremely foolish, so I took out the letter and the draft and placed it on his table. 'There has been some mistake, sir,' I said regretfully, 'I never took part in any competition.'

The look on Inder Malhotra's face was of sheer disbelief. 'How on earth ...' he muttered and left the room, only to return three minutes later with Girilal Jain, who I presumed was even senior to him. 'What are you saying?' He barked at me, and I started to explain how I had not entered any competition.

'Ask Bombay to send me his entry,' said Girilal Jain. I was then asked to wait outside, and I watched in awe as the entire floor buzzed with editorial activity. After half an hour I was called in by Inder Malhotra and was shown the essay I was supposed to have written. It was the article I had given Mr Rajani titled 'The Pseudo Society' though the heading had been changed to something else. Taking the initiative, he had filled the forms, and I vaguely recalled that one day he had asked me my address in Delhi. Since Rajani often visited Manali, I had presumed he wanted it in that context. A visibly relieved Inder Malhotra then shook my hand and said I could report from tomorrow as I would be in his department as a trainee correspondent as per the terms of the competition. An hour later, I was given an appointment letter and was on a DTC bus heading home.

Just then, we also shifted house from near the IIT crossing to the flats on Sardar Patel Marg. Our building overlooked the site where the Taj Man Singh Hotel would come up subsequently, while across the road was the ridge area where I used to take Sher Khan and Missy and flush partridge to my heart's content. The new location also was a stone's throw from the Defence Services Officers' Institute in Dhaula Kuan, so I could happily get back to playing tennis as well. Sweetie Padmanabhan, my erstwhile vice-captain, also came visiting from Madras, and since neither of us had ever played on grass courts, we decided to go knock a few balls.

Used to skidding a bit on clay, I promptly twisted my left foot. At the time, I didn't quite realize that I had had a hairline fracture.

Unable to get through on the telephone, I finally turned up at the *Times of India* with my foot in plaster up to the knee after an enforced break of a week. I was straight away called into his cabin by Inder Malhotra who told me that the correspondent's vacancy had been filled since he presumed, I was not interested in the job. Seeing my crestfallen expression, he then said he was transferring me to the Advertising Department where I would work under Lakshman Tandon, until he could get me back into the editorial side. With no choice in the matter, I then reported to my new boss, who was quite a television personality since he conducted a weekly quiz show on Doordarshan.

Honestly, I hated the job. I was assigned *Sandhya Times* and all I had to do was make sure all the advertisements that brought in the money came in on time. There were quite a few people in the Advertising Department, but my two immediate colleagues who became good friends were SanJeet, who was Durga Das's[6] grandson, and Priti Thapar, whose father was from the Madras Sappers. Though I was by and large bored stiff, there were a few lighter moments. Lakshman Tandon wanted me to get a feel of various departments and so I found myself downstairs in the Classified's Section. Being the junior-most, everyone had gone for lunch leaving me to hold the fort.

After a while, a middle-aged Muslim man came and said he wanted to put a marriage advertisement for his daughter. I fished out a form and gave it to him, but he very politely asked me to fill it for him while he dictated the content. '35-year-old very beautiful divorcee with two children. Belongs to XYZ sect. Highly educated, virgin ...'

'Whoa ...' I said, and pointed out, equally politely, his daughter could not be a virgin with two children from her previous husband.

The man was equally adamant on keeping the word 'virgin', and things were beginning to get a bit heated under the collar. Finally, I picked up the phone and called up Laxman Tandon ... 'Sir, I have a problem ...'

[6] Durga Das (1900–1974), a veteran Indian journalist, author and social worker, was founding president of the Press Club of India. A longtime parliamentary correspondent and editor, he served as the editor-in-chief of *Hindustan Times* from 1957 till 1959.

and I went on to explain the developing crisis. After I finished saying what I needed to say, Tandon asked me a simple question, 'Kunal, who is paying for the advertisement?' and hung up. Game, set, match!

I had been with the *Times of India* for almost three or four months by then and was up to my ears with *Sandhya Times*. I used to check with Inder Malhotra if a vacancy had come up every third day, so more out of exasperation, he spoke to Lakshman Tandon and sent me off to the floor above to edit copy for the *Economic Times*, which was even duller. I was howling about the slow death I was dying to my mother when she said, 'Why don't you and Teesta go to Nepal.' She suggested we spend a couple of days with Visharda Aunty who was then the principal of the Kendriya Vidyalaya School in the Indian Embassy in Kathmandu. And so, it was we boarded the Royal Nepal Airlines Corporation (RNAC) Boeing 727 on a cold, foggy morning. The last time I had sat in a plane was a Fokker Friendship from Silchar to Calcutta ten years previously and quite honestly, I was a bit apprehensive when we lifted off from Palam.

In the seat pocket was the RNAC inflight magazine. There was an advertisement on the first page asking for naturalists for Tiger Tops Mountain Travel's expanding footprint in India. It was the organization's logo—a tiger's head—that had caught my eye initially, and I could hardly wait to get back to India and apply for the position being offered. I was back in Delhi after a week, while Teesta stayed on in Nepal a bit longer. I then promptly called the number.

Lute Jerstad looked like Robert Redford, and behind his boyish demeanour, was the heart of an accomplished mountaineer. Along with Barry Bishop who then was an important cog in the management of *National Geographic*, the two of them were the first Americans to summit both K2 and Mount Everest. Subsequently, Lute, along with Jim Edwards, Chuck McDougal and Colonel Jimmy Roberts had come together and transformed the face of tourism in Nepal. The organization's focus in the last year or so had shifted to India, and the group had set up

Ladakh Sarai at a place called Stok, which was across the Indus River from Leh. My job, Lute explained, would be to explore and open new trekking routes between Srinagar in Kashmir and Leh in Ladakh. It would be a virtual expense paid holiday if one liked that kind of life, but the salary on offer was about a quarter of what I was getting in the *Times of India*.

Around then my father picked up his rank and was posted to a place called Kiari, also in Ladakh, where he was to command 70 Infantry Brigade. Maps were laid out on the dining table and we stared at purple-coloured patches that indicated extreme high altitudes. Kiari was about 126 kilometres upstream along the Indus from Leh, which itself was situated at 10,700 feet (3262 m). As was the norm in the army, we were allotted a first-floor separated family house in Pratap Chowk, Delhi Cantt and shortly after we shifted there, my father left for Ladakh to take up his new assignment.

I think it was around this time the Army Welfare Housing Organisation (AWHO) came into being and my parents applied for a flat, which would take three or four years to complete. There were to be two complexes constructed, one in New Delhi's R. K. Puram and another, larger complex in a place called Noida, which no one had heard about. Given my father's seniority, we were quite sure he would make the cut for what was later called Som Vihar, but either way, the princely sum of ₹3.4 lakh had to be paid over the next three or four years. My father's take-home salary at the time was in three figures, and though my mother and I were supplementing the family income, the word 'panic' was never too far whenever economics were discussed.

In 1973 when my father had done the Higher Command Course, his air force colleague and close friend, Wing Commander Sadatullah had literally put a gun on his head and forced him to apply for a 1,000 square yards plot on Jubilee Hills in Hyderabad. When it was allotted to him, Sadatullah paid part of the money which was then paid back to him in instalments. The price of the land had since escalated beyond belief, especially since N. T. Rama Rao (NTR), had built a film studio somewhere there, or so we were told. In a complete knee-jerk reaction, my father decided to sell it. Since Sadatullah could not talk him out of it, he said, alright, NTR's daughter was keen to buy the plot and she would arrive on such and such date *by air* from Hyderabad to negotiate the deal.

Only those who have grown up in the army will relate to what happened next, for it bordered on pure insanity. The fact that the lady was coming by air created an aura around her, and when she arrived, before she could make an offer, my father had given her a lecture about black money, politicians, corrupt bureaucrats, unethical businessmen and a few other pet subjects which army officers always kept under their pillow. He then launched off into the second phase about dying for your country, hard-earned money, AWHO, the flat and its total cost and how he wanted just that much and not a penny more. When Sadatullah got to know what had happened, he being a Canberra pilot, had to be restrained from flying to Delhi and dropping a 1,000 lb bomb on my dear father. We, the family, who were witness to our future financial security go down the drain, were curtly told to shut up when we tried to clear our throats. Even my mother, who was the financial brain of the family, seemed to have frozen at this very critical moment.

Not too surprisingly, my father was diddled out of getting a flat in Som Vihar and was allotted one in Noida, but by then we were resigned to things falling jam side down when it came to property and money. But what the heck! We lived in great style and continued to do so. Sher Khan and Missy flew in the pressurized cabin of the An-12, and together the new commander and the dogs arrived and took over the Kiari Brigade. My father's office was on the right bank of the Indus, and it was connected to his residence across the river by a suspension bridge. The initial descriptions that were coming from Ladakh along with some photographs, were painting the picture of a virtual moonscape with a river running through. By early May, while I was preparing to move up by road with a consignment of canvas and bamboo to construct more yurts (Mongolian-styled tents) in Ladakh Sarai, my mother and Teesta flew up to Leh and joined my father.

In New Delhi, I was beginning to get a taste of what life in Tiger Tops might be like. Inderjit Singh was an immaculately turned-out character whose father was a general from the Corps of Signals. Giving him company was Ronesh Mehra, who was the son of Romesh Mehra, a tea garden veteran from Assam who had moved to Bangalore and was looking at expanding Tiger Tops operations into South India. While we ran around Naraina and other parts of Delhi getting parts fabricated for the yurts, Ronesh in particular painted a picture that made it sound like naturalists and trek managers in the field were like trapeze artists swinging from one sexual encounter to another. I don't think I ever had the guts to tell them I was nowhere near any cherry on any cake, but they were so full of their exploits, they never asked me either.

Finally, on 1 May 1981, I set off from New Delhi in a loaded truck for Kashmir, where I would have to change the vehicle and proceed to Ladakh. The driver was a 40-year-old Sikh, Satnam Singh, whose only expression was a constant smile. Above the cabin was a 'tool box' and I spread my bedding there, alternating between sitting with Satnam or taking a nap on top. In the morning, we were just short of Ludhiana when he pulled up near a tube well. Taking out a Lifebuoy soap from the glove box, Satnam cut it in half and the two of us then had our baths. With the sheer volume of the gushing water, the mustard fields in the background with partridge calling, it was the closest one could get to nirvana.

The next day, late in the afternoon, we went through the Banihal Tunnel and I got my first view of the Kashmir Valley, and it was beautiful. Perched up on top in the tool box, we crossed Anantnag and drove along the placid looking Jhelum until we entered the city of Srinagar, where we pulled into Nedou's Hotel. There a standalone smaller building had a white board with the by now familiar-looking tiger-head logo. There was such a different feel about the place, it was like stepping into a completely different world. Coming out to meet the new arrival and the truck, there was Colonel John Wakefield, better known as 'Papa John', Jeff Campbell, who would be my immediate boss, and Captain Alok Chandola, who was an ex-Guards officer who had been aide-de-camp (ADC) to the President of India. Alok was from the 1962 batch of the Doon School, and he had got hold of a Unimog, a German vehicle that resembled a half-track, which he was driving up to Leh once Zoji La opened.

I then followed Jeff Campbell past Dal Lake where the sun was setting and the lights of the hundreds of houseboats were beginning to twinkle, along the boulevard and then finally we came to the bungalow that had a common wall with Shalimar Gardens. There the 'sherpas' were waiting, and I was introduced to the lot of them. About ten of them were from the Lahaul/Manali region, while there were also a couple of Tibetans. Because of our Nepalese operations, they were collectively called sherpas which seemed to suit everyone. While the rest of the staff lived downstairs, Jeff and I had rooms on the first floor, plus there were another two guest rooms for transit staff. We unloaded the truck in the morning, and I was sorry to see Satnam drive away. Three days on the road together and baths under tube wells is enough to forge extremely strong bonds.

While we waited for the official opening of Zoji La, I got to explore Srinagar, starting with our own office complex. Nedou's Hotel was owned by Omar Nedou and his wife Daisy, and they lived in a house to the right of the main building. Behind that, within our complex, was the chief minister's residence, since Sheikh Abdullah's wife was from the Nedou family. What struck me then was the absolute lack of security, for there was just the odd guard around. In our office, we had an English girl whose name shall be kept under the wraps for obvious reasons. The chief minister's son, whose privacy also shall be honoured, but who was a doctor by profession who alternated between London, Delhi and Srinagar, used to pick her up on his motorcycle and she would return with pine needles sticking to the back of her dress.

Finally, after five days, we received news that Zoji La would open the next day. Another truck was hired, once again with another Sikh driver, but joining me in the tool box on top of the cabin was a tall, lanky Englishman, John Sanday, who was the 'architect' of Ladakh Sarai. Since he carried a bottle of Black & White Scotch, I was quite happy to share my space with him. I also received a message from my parents, who were then visiting Kargil, that they would meet us on the other side of the pass forty-eight hours from then. Jeff Campbell gave me a last-minute briefing, instructing me to spend a fortnight in Ladakh, after which I was scheduled to fly back by the Indian Airlines flight. 'This'll be your first big job. I want you to do a reconnaissance of the Umasi La that links the

Chenab Valley to Zanskar. While you're up in Leh, see what information you can get on this route.'

After the 'Down Convoy' had reached Sonamarg, the 'Up Convoy' was given clearance after lunch. Dozens of engines came to life, and vehicles began to lurch forward. John Sanday and I had climbed down from the tool box on top and were buying some Cadbury chocolates when we saw our truck also flash past. Luckily for us, there was an Ambassador car, into which we jumped and James Bond-style told the driver, 'Catch that truck!' On the slushy slopes that had just been cleared of ice by the Border Roads Organisation, it was easier said than done. However, just short of the notorious 'Captain's *mor*' where so many people had earlier come to grief as was evident by the plethora of memorials marking the spot, a vehicle had broken down and the entire convoy including our truck had stopped. We clambered on board after giving our driver a mouthful, and then wrapped ourselves into the sleeping bags, waiting for the forward movement to begin again.

We survived the bitterly cold night swigging Scotch and breaking off chunks of rock-hard chocolate, but even at daybreak, we were yet to get across the pass. My parents waited in vain for the convoy to show up at Gumri, then they went back to Drass. I had no idea where they were, so when we finally did get through, after spending the night parked at Kargil, we set course for Leh in the morning. With daylight illuminating the landscape around us, I just drank it all in—Batalik, Fatou La, then the loops as we dropped down past Lamayuru and saw the Indus River in the distance for the first time, then the long black ribbon of a road as it ran for another couple of hundred kilometres before we reached Leh. Bypassing the town itself, we turned east and then crossed the Indus at Choglamsar and finally reached the Ladakh Sarai camp at Stok where we were met by two black and white pied magpies who looked quizzically at us. Smiling broadly, his hand extended in welcome, was the camp manager, Tsering Angdu and for the first time, I heard the Ladakhi greeting, *Juley*!

After a brief sojourn, I flew back to Srinagar as instructed and began to prepare for the Umasi La reconnaissance. I was issued my North Face equipment, which consisted of a golden coloured pup tent, a blue down jacket, a foam mat that was to be used as a mattress, a pair of cream-coloured boots and was assigned two sherpas, Muccho and Tashi. Jeff Campbell himself worked out the daily rations, and calculated everything down to the basic minimum, so different from my father's earlier planning for Dodital where even if we had taken shopping carts along, we couldn't have carried half the stuff. 'Ok,' said Jeff to me when we were about to leave, 'Remember you're the boss, but these two guys with you have years of experience. Learn from them, don't get into trouble, and off you go!'

We exited the Kashmir Valley at Banihal, then after crossing the Chenab, left the National Highway and followed the river eastwards, past Kishtwar to the road head at Garah. There were a team of mules waiting for us there, and all the pre-packed rations were loaded onto the animals. The main muleteer was from Hoshiarpur, and his vocabulary was enough to make even the most foul-mouth character blush. What he had to say to the mules, sounded even more colourful and graphic in Punjabi, and for the next few days, as I walked behind him, I couldn't stop laughing.

After we set up camp on the first day, high above the raging Chenab, the muleteer stuck his head into my tent and asked for a cigarette. As we sat and looked at the river below, he asked me if I knew of the 'Umasi La legend'. '*Woh kya hai?* (What is that?)' I asked.

The man from Hoshiarpur cleared his throat and lowered his voice and said anyone who crosses Umasi La will die!

'Heh,' I gulped. I hadn't heard that one before. Hoshiarpur reached for my cigarettes and helped himself to another one, which he lit by using the earlier stub. Ah! He's fibbing to bum another cigarette. '*Phir aap kyon ja rahe ho?* (Then why are you doing the trip?)' I asked, cleverly having figured out a way of trapping him.

He looked at me sadly. Then he asked me if I had heard of Maharaja Gulab Singh's[7] *senapati* (general), Zorawar Singh. He had crossed the pass more than a hundred years ago when he first went and captured Ladakh, but in the process, many men had died at the Rewa and their bodies were still there, buried in the ice. People from Zanskar, if they had to trade, came to a point and returned, while people from Machail, the last

[7] Gulab Singh (1792–1857) was the founder of the Dogra dynasty and the first Maharaja of the princely state of Jammu and Kashmir, the second largest princely state under the British Raj, which was created after the defeat of the Sikh Empire in the First Anglo-Sikh War (1845–46).

village above the tree line, went from this side. No one crossed over. I'm only hired to go till Machail, he informed me, you have to get porters from there. I thought you had people meeting you from Zanskar on the other side of the pass, but your Tashi says no such arrangement has been made.

I called out to Tashi and Muccho who said they were aware that people from Zanskar did not cross the pass, but they were not aware of the fact that it also applied to the Muslim population on this side, for Kashmiri traders were a common sight in Padam on the Zanskar side. Hoshiarpur looked at the two dimwits and said, *those Kashmiris come by bus from Kargil, they don't walk across Umasi La with carpets*!

The muleteer was right, for after we had crossed the Chenab at Atholi and then climbed almost vertically up along the Bhuma River to the tree line, the villagers simply refused to porter for us. We camped there for the night, and I spent hours haggling with the local population the next day. Finally, after agreeing to a rate that was six times what Jeff had told me, I went to sleep with my boots on. My last thought was that if we were going to die in any case, obviously there would be no audit, so why should I haggle at all?

We set off in the morning through the Valley of the Pregnant Horses! In all my years since I have never seen anything as beautiful. We were surrounded by hanging glaciers and were walking along an endless meadow, a carpet of edelweiss fringed with blue buttercups and an assortment of other tiny alpine flowers. My friend from Hoshiarpur was walking along with me, giving me a detailed account of the sex lives of donkeys, which was the dramatic opposite of mine. Every now and then there would be a herd of wild-looking horses, usually, about a dozen animals and in between each there would be a donkey. All the horses were females, and at the end of their 12-month gestation period, they would give birth to mules. Soon we found 'his' herd, and when he whistled, the horses trotted across to him. There were a couple of three- or four-month-old foals, which he would take back with him. His last words to me were, '*Khote khote honde hai ... aap toh kuch nahi kar sakde*! (Mules are mules and they themselves cannot do anything!)' then having convinced us all that we were going to be history soon, he cheerfully said, *see you in Hoshiarpur whenever you pass that way—just ask for me*!

We climbed up to the Rewa, which was effectively a rocky cliff, and set up camp there at 17,550 feet (5350 m). Our plan was to break camp in the early hours of the morning and cross the massive snow field. In all probability, there would be dangerous crevasses, so it was imperative the entire party be roped, and with a bit of luck get to the Zanskar side of the pass by daybreak. Since there was the possibility of high winds in the latter half of the afternoon, I told everyone to buckle down and crawled into my pup tent. If I had trouble with the porters at the other end of the snow field, I planned on leaving the loads there, get to Padam and come back with porters from Zanskar. It would delay us by two or three days, but that was the best I could hope for under the circumstances.

At around 3 p.m., my tent was unzipped from the outside and a frowning Muccho stuck his head in, saying somewhat incredulously, '*Woh toh gaya! Woh toh gaya*! (They have left! They have left!)' Neither he nor Tashi had seen them depart, but the six porters had hightailed it shortly after we had reached the Rewa, without taking the money that would have been due to them until then. There was nothing else that we could do, so we quickly separated the essential items into three loads and hid the remaining two-thirds in a corner and covered it with a canvas sheet weighed down with rocks. At the stroke of midnight, roped and heavily loaded ourselves, we started to move cautiously across the ice. Muccho was in the lead, and with me in the middle, Tashi was bringing up the rear.

It took us close to five hours to traverse the distance, and at daybreak, we were at the Zanskar end, which was marked by a heap of stones and a few heads of bharal and ibex. The two sherpas offered prayers and green apples, and then Tashi began to unrope himself. There was a clearly visible track going down along the ridge, but 2,000 feet (610 m) below us there was another glacier. Though the rope made the going cumbersome, I insisted we retain it, and said I would now take the lead from Muccho, who in turn would bring up the rear. As soon as we changed positions and made sure the knots would hold, I suddenly lost my footing and plunged down a small patch of snow, coming to a stop just inches from where it was a free fall to the glacier below.

I had partly dragged Tashi off the track, but luckily Muccho had held his position, but only just. I saw a look of absolute terror on Tashi's face and watched in horror as he produced a Swiss army knife and started to lash at the rope. Muccho, seeing what was happening, yelled at Tashi in Tibetan who then sheepishly put the knife away. Badly shaken, I crawled back onto the track, leaving a trail of blood on the snow for I had cut myself on the abrasive ice as I fell. The Umasi La legend had almost claimed us, but after crossing the Malung Togpo over a perennial ice bridge, we made it to Padam without any further incident.

We set up camp near a small stream and I had sent Muccho to see if he could get some porters from Padam to help recover the baggage we had left behind. The idea of going back up onto Umasi La was not very appealing, but we had to try, nevertheless. Besides, I still had a long way to go to get to the pick-up point near Lamayuru and in Padam we could not get anything to replace our partly abandoned rations. I was contemplating all our options when a foreigner appeared. He was carrying a rucksack out of which were protruding two aerial like objects. The man was French, and he was a tour operator who had heard that we had not only got across the pass but had also survived. After enquiring about my health, he offered to pay me twenty rupees if I'd make him a map of the route followed by us. Highly offended, I told him to take a hike, when my gaze fell on the two tubes and I asked him what they were.

The Frenchman unfolded the two US Air Force (USAF) maps; the first one was of the Northeastern states of India and the other was the entire state of Jammu and Kashmir which included the areas that were also under the occupation of Pakistan. There were some strange-looking grid-like things on the northern side of the map, but I was looking at the sheer printing quality which was a top draw. I told the Frenchman I would make the map if he gave me these two maps. Our barter in place, I then sketched out the route for him, marking out potential camping sites. The two maps, now my prized possessions, were like two fragile babies and I was extremely careful with them. Once we reached Ladakh Sarai, I took a fountain pen and neatly wrote my name on the right-hand bottom corner. Three days later, my father sent a vehicle for me and with my maps in tow, I arrived at Kiari where Missy and Sher Khan greeted with great glee.

My idea of rest and recuperation at Kiari was to take the dogs and flush chukar partridge in the nearby valleys, but they were rather difficult to shoot on the wing, especially since they would run uphill and then hurtle towards you like white missiles after they got airborne. Afternoons would then be spent sitting near the suspension bridge catching snow trout in the Indus. My mother and Teesta had already gone back to Delhi, and it was only on the third evening, I remembered the maps and in the light of a petromax, showed them to my father. Early in the morning, I thought I heard the high-pitched whine and the chop-chop of a Cheetah helicopter but turned around and went back to sleep.

My father returned two days later and nothing more was said about his abrupt absence. Years later, after he had retired and I was writing my book, *The Long Road to Siachen*, he told me that the printed notations on the map had been USAF markings and the Americans had drawn a straight line from a place called Chalunka (later it became quite famous as NJ 9842) to the Karakoram (KK) Pass that effectively placed the entire Siachen Glacier in Pakistan's control. My father, along with the GOC 3 Division had then flown to Army HQ in Delhi along with the corps and army commander, and Mrs Indira Gandhi had been shown this brazen cartographic aggression indulged in by the Americans. Colonel Narendra 'Bull' Kumar, who had already done a skiing expedition to the Siachen region, had previously also got a tourist map from a German rafting expedition that showed the same area as belonging to Pakistan. After the USAF map surfaced, Bull Kumar was sent again to immediately scout around for any evidence of Pakistani activity. The race to occupy Siachen, which climaxed two years later, had begun.

On my return to Ladakh Sarai, I was delighted to find Inderjit Singh at the camp, having recently moved up from Delhi. Until now, the promised land had not thrown up anything from the opposite sex that remotely matched the stories that I had been fed in Delhi by Ronesh and Inderjit and I was beginning to think they had also been seeing the Yeti. Now I would have a chance to watch the master at work and would learn a few invaluable tips on the art of seduction. Sure enough, within 24 hours, his scarf and turban neatly in place, Inderjit had invited two Ladakhi girls to the Sarai for lunch the next day (one for him, one for me, I thought deliriously). As lunch hour approached, he had me sitting on the gate with field glasses looking for any approaching jeep while he played 'cool' in his yurt '*because you don't want to appear to be too eager*'. Fair enough!

The two young ladies arrived shortly, and while I sat with 'mine' on a hammock facing Inderjit's yurt into which he had taken 'his', things soon began to happen. There were grunts and strange sounds and at times the left side of the yurt would bulge, sometimes the right. So fascinated by this display were we, that I and mine even forgot to hold hands! After twenty minutes or so, the two emerged. 'His' was smiling sweetly in a satisfied manner while Inderjit Singh looked positively dishevelled. As we sat down for lunch under the weeping willow trees, a hushed whisper informed me that 'his' was in fact from the anti-hijacking squad deployed at the airport and she had just given 'him' a real-life demonstration of how to handle 'suspects'. The speed with which the two surprised ladies were packed off post-lunch was then but a foregone conclusion.

At Ladakh Sarai, two more people had moved up at the same time. My cousin Vineeta Hoon had arrived to take over and run the camp (having followed me into Tiger Tops) and the other was the retired Brigadier Mark Valladares, who was overseeing the construction of the new dining hall. Mark Valladares was from the Bengal Sappers, and he had been an active member of various mountaineering expeditions and was also an avid angler. He more or less kept to himself, and generally had a pretty poor opinion of the management, most of whom he referred to in the most derogatory terms. He also was least bothered about his appearance and spent most of the time in a shabby vest.

Major General K. K. Sudan was commanding 3 Infantry Division and he was my father's direct boss. His ADC was an artillery officer, Captain Rakesh Chugh, and one evening after knocking off an entire bottle of rum in his room in Alpha Mess, Inderjit and I decided to walk back to Ladakh Sarai in the 'moonlight', partly because Mark Valladares had appropriated the only Jonga in the camp. It was nearly a 20-kilometre walk and somewhere along the way I had such a reaction to XXX Old Monk, I have never been able to drink rum again. The next morning, nursing hangovers, we were surprised to see the brigadier wearing a fresh shirt and driving off in 'our' Jonga. A couple of hours later, he was back with his wife and daughter, who had flown in from Delhi.

Sitting on a hammock stretched between two willow trees, with water gurgling past my feet in a small channel, I watched Kavita Valladares walk across to a yurt that had been allotted to her. My head was spinning, and daylight was hurting the eyes, so I shut them both and took a nap. An hour later I ran into the lady near the showers, while I was soulfully whistling *Nights in White Satin* and she smiled and said hello. 'You look terrible! Late night out?' I'm not sure if I said anything at all, I was just mesmerized by her. In the evening I still had a headache and had turned to her for help. She had short, cropped hair and was wearing a black polo neck. Until that moment, I had never kissed a girl. Four days later, by the time her plane lifted off the runway, I knew I had had it!

That night, by the light of a petromax, I wrote two letters. One was to Bela, with whom I had no communication whatsoever post Pondicherry, and I told her I was smitten. Then I wrote to Kavita, hoping and praying she hadn't forgotten about me the moment she had taken off from Leh. I lived in terrible suspense until her first letter arrived a week later. One of the reasons I remember a lot of detail from the treks is because I would subsequently write to her almost daily, describing everything—the birds, the flowers, the wildlife, the people.

That year I crossed Umasi La yet again (and survived), recovering our rations stashed on the pass, and then did some other fabulous treks, including the reconnaissance of the Old Mughal Road that ran from South Kashmir across the Pir Panjal to Poonch. We also fished the Bringhi, which had some very good-sized trout. Captain Surendra Vikram Gurung, a former British Gurkha officer and one of our senior managers visiting from Nepal, stunned everyone by landing a 9-pounder brown trout. Until then, one had no idea trout that big even existed, though I had seen some pretty big specimens in Dodital. Since our office was in the Nedou's Hotel complex, I would also have breakfast with Sheikh Abdullah on a few occasions, the chief minister curious to know from me the condition of some of the remoter villages. While in Ladakh, I got to travel extensively, visiting Tso Morari and then driving up the Yankee-1 axis to Chushul and Pangong Tso. By then, Brigadier R. K.

'Ramu' Gaur had taken over as the deputy GOC of 3 Infantry Brigade. He was a wonderful photographer, and I would learn a lot from him.

After five action-packed months, I was looking forward to the end of the season. I had hatched a plan to visit Kavita who was then studying at the National Institute of Design in Ahmedabad, and just when I was all set to fly out of Srinagar, Papa John sent for me and said the Delhi office was sending a small batch of clients who were to be taken to Ladakh over Kanji La. I looked at him incredulously, for I had never been sent with a group till now. Besides, by the beginning of October, all the passes would freeze over and no one in his right mind would risk running those routes at this time of year. But Papa John was adamant, 'Houseboat owners take groups across till mid-October. Take a good team of sherpas. You'll be fine. You then fly out of Leh to Delhi.'

Jeff Campbell and his wife Christina had already left Kashmir, and so had most of the staff. Luckily, one of the most experienced sherpas, Norbu, was still around and with him as my right hand, we set off from Kashmir. The group consisted of some eight clients, all of whom were what New Delhi called 'walk-in clients', so there was no cohesion as such between them. As expected, the going was extremely difficult, for icing had begun and even the streams were beginning to freeze over. The route ran past the Rangdum Monastery to Lamayuru and the pass itself was at an altitude of approximately 17,000 feet (5000 m).

It was 4 October when we reached the top of the pass. Earlier, we had been picking up signs that there was a group ahead of us, but we had dismissed it as being sheer madness and not paid much attention. However, at the very top, there was a dead mule, and from the amount of snow on the corpse, it was not more than two days old. There were some tracks heading off into a snow field, but they abruptly ended where there was a semi-buried saddle. It was all very perplexing, but there was nothing we could do, so we dropped down from the pass and camped a kilometre short of Kanji village which was itself situated at 12,713 feet (3875 m). That night I tossed and turned, trying to figure out if we had missed something, for the mystery of the dead mule and the tracks was baffling.

The next morning, having turned 21, we broke camp and started for Kanji. There was a fast-flowing stream to our right, across which some stone shelters had been constructed almost like bunkers. For some reason, Norbu had waded across and gone and looked inside the shelters. I saw him stagger out and throw up. By then I was running, jettisoning my rucksack and plunging into the ice-cold water myself, for instinctively I knew something was seriously wrong. Seeing me, another sherpa also followed and we entered the stone shelter, literally having to crawl into it. The stench was unbearable and to my horror, in the dim light, I could see what looked like a body. We pulled the man out and realized his feet and hands were completely frostbitten and the rotting flesh was responsible for the terrible smell.

Since rigor mortis had not set in, I presumed he must be alive and the three of us then took turns to try and resituate the man, alternately giving him mouth-to-mouth and then breaking away to vomit. By then two other sherpas had arrived and everyone was rubbing his limbs or pumping his chest. Amazingly, after about fifteen minutes, one of the man's eyelashes fluttered. Somehow, we got him to Kanji village and the local womenfolk then took over, keeping night long vigils for the next three days. I had sent the group on, asking them to send an ambulance to the road head seventy-two hours later. In Leh, the man would lose all his fingers and feet, but he would survive. All of us, the sherpas and me, had pooled in the money for the authorities to fly him out of Leh to Srinagar once he recovered, which I learnt subsequently was only in January 1982.

After a brief halt in Delhi, I told my mother I was going to photograph flamingos and on the eve of Diwali landed at Ahmedabad. The flamingo was waiting at the airport, and then I was smuggled into the Women's Hostel at the National Institute of Design. Kavita's roommate was Sujata Keshavan whose boyfriend was Ramchandra Guha who had unceremoniously told me to make myself scarce in Doon School exactly a decade earlier. Anyhow, after watching flocks of starlings fly over the Sabarmati River for a few days and getting acquainted with all of Kavita's friends, which included Alpana, Bharat Upadhaya and his girlfriend, Shefali, I flew back to Delhi to face the music for by then just who the flamingo was, was no longer a secret.

6

Nepal and Ladakh: India Today and AP

Once again, on 25 December, I boarded a RNAC flight to Kathmandu for my winter training and was initially assigned to spend time with Himalayan River Exploration (HRE). Promptly I received an invitation to join John Edwards and my friend from Zoji La, John Sanday, for a Christmas bonfire dinner. Jim's younger brother, the amiable and easy-going John, ran the Nepal operations and within minutes, he had put me at ease. After a while he started talking about a rafting expedition that was to run the virgin Marsyangdi River that originated northwest of the Annapurna massif and after running its course over 150 kilometres, joined the Trishuli at Mugling. An Austrian expedition consisting of world-class white-water specialists had come a cropper a fortnight previously. According to John, the water levels were slightly higher now, so there was a good chance the HRE expedition that was being planned would succeed.

It suddenly dawned on me that the entire conversation was for my benefit. 'We need four guys for each raft,' said John, plonking a nice fat slice of roasted turkey on my plate, 'Unfortunately we only have seven. So, you're going to be the eighth. All you have to do is hang on and stay in the raft. If you get pitched out, just get back on. It's a piece of cake!'

It was anything but that! The first hour itself, after we had put in on the river, I got pitched half-a-dozen times. The first few times it was terrifying, for in the fast-flowing current one got tossed around like a twig. Soon I figured the trick was not to fight the water, but 'sit on it' with one's feet stretched downriver. This way, even if you came on a rock, it just slid under your bum, and you could then get to the side where the others would pick you up again. Having been initiated into the world of white water, I spent the next ten days with the HRE boys, all of whom were Nepali. There were some wonderful chaps—Mahesh, Yogi and some others, and their 'success rate' with the opposite sex was amazing. Before me, Ronesh Mehra was the only other 'Indian' to have been trained in white water. I also began to realize where Ronesh had picked up some of the stories, passing them off as his own!

My initial training with HRE over, I was put on a flight to Pokhara and told to report to the legendary Colonel Jimmy Roberts at his pheasant farm near the airfield. Had life been fair, Roberts should have been the leader of the Mount Everest expedition in May 1953 that put Tensing Norgay and Edmund Hillary on the summit for the first time, but he was replaced by Eric Shipton who himself was replaced by John Hunt at the last moment. Roberts then decided he would work as a porter on that expedition. He would subsequently go on to play a major role in making Nepal a major trekking destination and would partner with Tiger Tops and HRE and create a brand that would become dominant in adventure tourism. After introducing me to his incredible collection of birds, he then pulled out a map of Ladakh and we spent some time looking at the Shyok River Valley as a potential area for our India operations. I was amazed at his depth of knowledge, and perhaps said so. He smiled and said that was the area where they did the entire training for Everest.

The next day I was given a sherpa and along with a grumpy Englishman, we set off for the Tatopani trek that took us into the heart of Gorkha country from Pokhara. Walking along the base of the Annapurna Massif, we came to an area where even the waterfalls had frozen, forming gigantic chandelier-like vistas and the trees were covered with lichen and moss. This had been the inspiration for J. R. R. Tolkien's description of the 'enchanted forest' in his incredible book, *The Hobbit*. At some point, since India were playing England in a test match, I pulled out my small

Grundig transistor radio and caught up with the commentary. My English companion was most invested in the scores, but when I got back to Kathmandu, John Edwards told me he had formally complained about my radio. I told John the English have always been rotten losers and had the Brits won, there would have been no complaint. In any case, I couldn't have given a damn!

The next day we set off in rafts on the Trishuli for the Tiger Tops Jungle Lodge in Chitwan National Park. I think it took us two days, for I remember camping along the way. Once the river entered the Terai, it became the Rapti and it was hard work rowing the laden rafts. Finally, exhausted, we reached the famous lodge, and I was allotted tented accommodation situated on one side, while the elephant camp was on the other flank. The chief naturalist was K. K. Gurung, who was also a great artist, but he had a deep-rooted dislike for us Indians. I was delighted to find Hashim Tyabji there, for not only had I taken over Fag magazine from him in Doon School in 1974, he was also in Loyola College trying to get educated when I was in MCC and we had met every now and then.

Charles 'Chuck' McDougal, who had authored *The Face of the Tiger*, used to run the show at the lodge that was serviced by an airstrip at Meghauli. Tiger Tops had a large stable of elephants that were used to ferry guests from the airfield to the lodge. Apart from the lodge itself, we had a tented camp, and there was also Tharu Village. Apart from a healthy population of both tiger and leopard, there were quite a few one-horned Indian rhinoceros, including one called 'Old George' who more or less lived in our camp. Unfortunately for me, during most of my stay, Chuck was away in England and only got back just as I was due to leave.

At the lodge, every evening buffalo calves used to be staked inside a couple of ravines inviting a tiger to take the bait. The moment a 'kill' would occur, and the tiger would settle down to eat the calf, watching members of the staff would radio back to the lodge. There, usually, a slide show would be running, or guests would be having their dinner. A bell would go off and everyone would drop everything and dash across to the waiting Land Rovers. The ravines had hideouts overlooking them and once a batch of people were inside, battery operated lights would illuminate the tiger sitting on his or her kill. There would be a lot of 'ooohs' and 'aaahs' and then the exercise would repeat itself all over again the next day. Along with the buffalo calves, in another ravine, a goat would also be tied to attract leopards. I went with the Gorkhas one day to tie the goat and was amused to see the leopard already sitting there in anticipation.

I was back in Delhi by March and was promptly sent off to the Corbett Tiger Reserve where we had a fishing camp on the Ramganga River. Catching mahseer and the occasional goonch, a freshwater catfish, we also had the run of the park in those days. While I was catching 8 to 10 lb mahseer on conventional plugs and 12 lb line, one of the guests at the camp was a Frenchman who used a light-weight fly line with, amazingly, a tiny snick of Amul cheese. Standing on a rock near a deep frothing pool, he hooked onto a 35 lb golden mahseer. The sun was setting and in the orange light, he played the fish almost as if he was conducting an orchestra. The hook was so tiny in the mouth of the fish, I couldn't even see it in the fading light. Then, after weighing the pulsating and exhausted fish, he cradled it like a baby and let the water rush through its gills. With a powerful thrust of the tail, the fish then swam away to liberty and freedom. 'Catch and release,' said the Frenchman. All of us who had been bludgeoning our victims to death stood around shamefaced. I for one never killed a mahseer after that day.

After another quick trip to flamingo country, I flew back to Srinagar, quite looking forward to my second season in paradise. Breathing in the fresh mountain air, I stepped into the airport building where one had to register one's name at a desk near the entrance door. The moment I did so, there were many excited voices in Kashmiri and a policeman scanned a list of names, after which he politely asked me to follow him. In a room, I was asked to sit while the list was double-checked, and then I was told there was an FIR against my company. I was not being placed under arrest, but later in the afternoon, I was to report with Colonel John Weikfield at the Lal Chowk police station. 'What are the charges?' I asked for the tenth time, before someone whispered in my ear, 'Attempted homicide!'

Papa John was wearing a grey-coloured safari suit, and he was getting rather exasperated. I had been told to keep my mouth shut, so I just sat there with a blank expression. For the tenth time, he repeated, 'The horseman was not part of our group. My boys not only saved his life, they even had him flown out of Leh to Srinagar at their own expense.' It seemed when the poor unfortunate soul had reached his village, a virtual cripple, everyone thought he was a *mušrān* (evil spirit). His fellow horsemen had not only left him for dead, but they had also told everyone they had personally buried him at Kanji La and both his mules had died with him. Since the houseboat owner who they worked for and half-a-dozen people from the village were involved, it was decided to file a case against Tiger Tops Mountain Travel instead.

The next day the police took us to the village, and on seeing me, the boy (he was barely 16) started to cry and beat his chest violently. Nothing more was said about the case to me after that, but the police managed to ask Bhardwaj, our accountant in Srinagar, for a few sleeping bags and tents to formally bury the case. The management in Tiger Tops was spooked enough to subsequently issue a written note advising all employees that if we did get involved in any humanitarian work in the future, the company could not be expected to hold our hands.

In 1982 we had shifted our office from Nedou's Hotel to a houseboat called the Star of Zanzibar, which was anchored 100 metres upstream of Zero Bridge in downtown Srinagar. It was said that the original owners were slave traders, and the boat was haunted. Papa John used to sit at a desk and snore through most of the day, waking up to enjoy the lunch that was served, before going right back to sleep. When in Srinagar, I would occupy the other desk and put a fishing line out in the Jhelum, catching carp the size of my hand, and then watch them swim lazily away when released. It wasn't long before I was asked to prepare for another run into Ladakh, but this time around I would be accompanying a small group of Americans, led by Lila Bishop who was Barry Bishop's[8] wife. Once again, we took the Kanji La route and the entire experience was so very different, which underlined the fact that the right time of year was so critical. Alpine flowers were blooming everywhere, and yellow wagtails danced around our feet as we traversed through boggy marshes.

American groups were generally good fun, but their over-reliance on technology even in those days was sometimes killing. They had

[8] Barry Bishop (1932–1994) was an American mountaineer, scientist, photographer and scholar. With teammates Lute Jerstad, Jim Whittaker, Willi Unsoeld and Tom Hornbein, he was a member of the first American team to summit Mount Everest on 22 May 1963.

pedometers (to count the number of steps) and altimeters to keep track of their altitude, and with each step, they needed to refer to the book. If one of the pamphlets they carried said your face would go green at 15,000 feet (4500 m), a group of grumpy Martians would trudge past you, but if it said oxygen was plentiful, they would start behaving like Julie Andrews in the *Sound of Music*. 'It's all in the head,' said Leela to me, the evening before we were to start climbing up to Kanji La. Since I was familiar with the route, I took off an hour earlier and had made it to the top of the pass from where I then got the most spectacular view of the ranges—with K2 towering over the rest about 180 kilometres to the northwest. After a while, the first of the group were visible making their way towards the top, so I settled down on a clearly visible rock and lit an unfiltered Camel cigarette, blowing rings so no one could miss the fact I was smoking. 'Wow, gee man, he's smoking!' I heard some voices say in awe, and sure enough, they promptly forgot about being sick. I do feel a tinge of guilt though, for I also think in the process of watching me smoke and expecting me to drop dead, they missed out on seeing K2.

When we reached Ladakh Sarai, Leela gave me two books, both of which were my constant companions for years. Apart from the second edition of *Medicine for Mountaineering*, a beautifully illustrated guide to alpine flowers made it possible for me to identify various species subsequently. Even if one couldn't quite zero in on the exact species, one at least knew the botanical family they belonged to.

One continued to explore the remoter parts of Ladakh in between the trans-Himalayan treks. With Vineeta running Ladakh Sarai, Ranjit and Visharda Hoon along with Varuna and her husband, Raman Mahajan also visited Stok and Kiari. One evening I took Raman on a chukar shoot along the Upshi–Manali road and by the time we got back, it was late. The entire Hoon clan was waiting at the gate, worried that something had happened to Raman. The son-in-law syndrome meant I was of least concern to anybody. To add to my woes, I got it in the neck for having 'exposed' Raman, who incidentally, had had a complete blast until then.

Another friendship that developed then was with Karan Bilimoria, who was also visiting Ladakh. We seem to have got along well for we continued to correspond even after he left. Karan's father, then a major general, Faridoon Bilimoria was Adi Sethna's first cousin. Both were from the Doon School but very senior to me. Sethna had been the commandant at Defence Services Staff College, Wellington, and our house, Mansarovar, was one of the three facing the big man's residence.

With the season winding down, I asked Papa John if I could get Kavita up to stay with me and take her on a trek. He looked at me from behind his desk, suddenly wide awake, for Papa John was an old woman at heart who loved a scandal. 'That Valladares girl?' he asked, trying not to beam benevolently. He gave me the go-ahead and plans started being made for 'Project Marmot'.

Two days later, on 8 September, I was driving back from Kokernag with Puneeta who alternated between the Srinagar and Delhi office. I was driving the Tiger Tops Jonga when I was stopped by some policemen just short of Anantnag. They told me Sheikh Abdullah had passed away and I better fly a black flag on my vehicle. As we drove past villages, one could see people standing around in clusters on either side of the road. Women were wailing, some of them lifting their phirans to beat at their exposed breasts. Amidst all this, all shutters were down and there was no way I was going to get a black cloth.

I pulled up by the side of the road near some isolated fields and turned to Puneeta who was looking positively scared. 'What colour bra are you wearing?' It was a rhetorical question for I could see through the fabric and knew it was black. 'Quickly, take it off ...' She started to say something, but I had already turned my back. 'Just do it!' There was some rustling, then she handed it over my shoulder. I quickly wrapped it around the rear-view mirror. It wasn't a flag, but something was better than nothing. Then, without any further drama, I sped ahead and got her and myself back to the Star of Zanzibar.

Kavita arrived in Srinagar and the sunsets on Dal Lake took on a new meaning. We were all set to leave for our trek in a couple of days when Papa John sent for me. 'There is a slight problem,' he said. 'There's a new group who Puneeta has signed on (déjà vu) and they arrive tomorrow.' The route I had planned for ourselves centred around the Overa Aru Wildlife Sanctuary, the Lidder Valley and Pahalgam.

Coincidentally, or maybe it was sheer spite, New Delhi wanted to follow the same plan but in a reverse manner, with the 'walk-in clients'! After we had left for the trek, Papa John had a bad fall and fractured his foot, which resulted in his being admitted in hospital.

The trek had gone well enough but because of heavy snowfall, I had to call off the first part, which was to get to the Kolahoi Glacier further up the Lidder Valley. The extra days in Overa Aru were well spent, but when we got back, the Delhi office was up in arms about the 'Valladares girl' and my 'deliberate cancelling' of the Kolahoi part of the trip. Kavita and I, along with Hashim Tyabji who had come up to Srinagar, went and met Papa John in the hospital where he was propped up in bed with his leg strung up.

Mark Valladares had parted with Tiger Tops in 1981 itself, and his parting verbal salvos had left the top management in Delhi, which mainly meant Sammy Malik, reeling. Puneeta was Sammy's niece and now they had a knife which they wanted to turn. Papa John said he would stand by me, but I told him not to make an issue of it for I was planning to quit anyway. All the sherpas shed a tear along with me as we left the next day, and then the aircraft lifted off from Srinagar, shutting the door behind me on my Tiger Tops days.

Just as my entry into Ladakh coincided with my father's move to Kiari, he too got posted out around the same time, going as the deputy GOC of the Amritsar-based 15 Infantry Division. I don't think he spent any real time there, for he was asked to help make a short documentary film with a Bombay-based producer. Shortly after that, he was selected to attend the extremely prestigious year-long course at the National Defence College (NDC). Accordingly, the family then left Pratap Chowk and moved to Raksha Bhawan, our first floor looking out at the India Gate which was about 500 metres away. Below us was Air Commodore Denzil Keelor, VrC, one of the two brothers who had become the face of the IAF in the 1965 India–Pakistan War, while a lot of families that had been with us in Wellington, were also living in the same complex.

In the first few months of 1983, Kavita and I set up a company called 'Format' and one of the first jobs we were commissioned to do was to produce a poster, 'Cats of India'. Kavita would do the illustrations and it then adorned many an office for decades. More important than the poster, it brought me in touch with H. S. Panwar, then the director of Project Tiger and S. K. Mukherjee, who was looking after the newly formed CITES (Convention on International Trade in Endangered Species of Wild Fauna and Flora) cell that monitored wildlife trade in India. In those days, even though Project Tiger was a decade-old, no one talked of wildlife conservation, even though the alarm bells had begun to ring across the globe about the dwindling tiger population.

Recognizing my need to be mobile, my parents finally said I could buy a scooter, being adamant not to let me buy a motorcycle. With much fanfare, I then bought my Vijay scooter, on which I would drive Kavita around. Our new company, however, was not going anywhere and after a few months, I wandered into *India Today's* office in F-Block in Connaught Place. I had become friendly with Ajit Ninan, who was also from MCC and the cartoonist for the magazine, and he had suggested I go see Aroon Purie, who seemed quite bemused by the fact that I could want a job with his organization. The only blazer I had in those days was a Doon School Old Boys' one, and I was wearing that. 'Which batch are you?' said a voice from behind me, and I turned to look at Suman Dubey, then the managing editor. 'We haven't done any environment-based stuff, but your background seems interesting. Give us five minutes.' I was officially put on the desk as a sub-editor, but when I said that was not what I was looking for, Suman dismissively said, 'Don't worry about that!' Two days later, much to the disbelief of the other subs (as they were called) I was off to Gurukul Kangri with Pramod Pushkarna.

Shortly after the photo feature was published, in a story datelined 15 November 1983[9], I got my first independent story on how Srinagar had become the biggest chink in the fight against poaching of animals in the subcontinent. The Indian Wildlife (Preservation) Act of 1972 had, thanks to Jammu and Kashmir's then special status, bypassed the state

[9] Kunal Verma, 'Srinagar becomes major outlet for poachers throughout India,' *India Today*, 16 July 2013, https://www.indiatoday.in/magazine/environment/story/19831115-srinagar-becomes-major-outlet-for-poachers-throughout-india-771211-2013-07-16

altogether. Mir Inayat Ullah was then the chief wildlife warden of Jammu and Kashmir and he, along with the political lobby, had put pressure on the Government of India to exempt the state from treaties like CITES as well on the grounds that there were 60,000 artisans in the Kashmir Valley who made their living from the wildlife trade. A special committee that included the likes of Nalini Jayal and S. L. Singla, both at the time holding the rank of joint secretaries, had not only ratified the state government's position but (in all probability without physically checking) certified that there were a massive number of animal skins already in stock.

The scale of the killings was mind-boggling, and the methods adopted were barbaric. For example, meat as bait would be placed in a hollow of a tree in Rajasthan. Two or three nails would then be positioned pointing inwards to ensure the head could not be withdrawn. Trucks with as many as 3,000 to 4,000 skins would be caught, but for each that got apprehended, a dozen or more got away. To top it off, an elaborate system was put in place where the Jammu and Kashmir wildlife department would issue Legal Procurement Certificates stating even coats made from snow leopard pelts belonged to a mythical creature called *moolen* (*Pardus domesticus*). The story created an uproar in Parliament, and I was extremely chuffed about it when the doorbell in Raksha Bhawan rang.

I had come home for lunch and was whisked away to South Block. After the briefest of waits, I was ushered into Prime Minister Indira Gandhi's presence. She asked me to sit down and brief her about the story. I took my time and gave her as much detail as I could, for Mukherjee and Panwar had given me reams of supporting material which obviously could not all be used in the report. Throughout she had her elbows on the table and her fingers interlocked in front of her face, but I could see the flicker of emotion. When I finished, she got up and walked me to the door. 'I'll do what I can,' she said, 'you've done a great service to the country.' When I told my mother I had met the prime minister a short while ago, she said, '*Satte na maar*' (Don't pull fast ones).

Panwar Saab, as he was called, had by then become an extremely close friend and we would constantly look at how to help sort out issues for the various tiger reserves across the country. One day he called me to his office. Rajesh Gopal, who was later the field director at both

Bandhavgarh and Kanha tiger reserves and then also the director of Project Tiger, was also present. 'See this,' Panwar Saab pushed an anonymous letter written to Indira Gandhi with a copy to the finance minister, Pranab Mukherjee that accused a member on the Board for Indian Wildlife, and his sons, of inappropriate financial behaviour. The letter claimed that at the member's request, the honourable prime minister had directed the Government of India to most kindly give an exemption of duty to bring in film cameras worth a certain amount per person. Since all three had availed of the option being given to 'Indian wildlife filmmakers', the letter claimed they had brought in the requisite amount of equipment, of which half had then been 'sold in black' which was deplorable and so forth. The immediate knee-jerk reaction to the charge had led to the withdrawal of the exemption, but a subsequent enquiry proved that the charge was pure rubbish.

Then Panwar Saab put another sheaf of letters, which were letters written by the same member of the Board to an assortment of people. In the anonymous letter, one of the keys was slightly out of alignment. The same key was also out of sync in exactly the same manner in all the other letters. 'Masterstroke,' said Panwar Saab, 'Close the door for everyone else! How do you a function in a country where there are no ethics?' You didn't need forensics to tell you what the obvious conclusion was.

My footprint began to expand, as I got a few more stories on some other subjects as well. Punjab was beginning to play up and I asked Suman Dubey if I could be assigned a story, any story. However, Punjab and the entire Khalistan movement was the turf of Shekhar Gupta, so Suman just nodded and said, 'All in good time!' Shekhar would sometimes be at my house, talking to my father, with whom he was quite friendly. Being a senior correspondent, he along with the others, would be polite but not friendly with the younger lot. At the desk, I remember there were quite a few of us—Anita Kaul Basu, Simrin Bhargava, Paran Balakrishna and David Devadas among others. Most stories filed by correspondents, especially the outstation ones, were quite pathetic and needed a major rewrite.

The worst copy used to come from Prabhu Chawla, who it was uniformly acknowledged could not 'write to save his skin'. The grapevine had it that he was not too ethical in his dealings and from day one, he did not like me. He would constantly needle me by whispering 'Doon School, Doon School!' whenever no one else could hear him, and even though he irritated me no end, I could only ignore such juvenile behaviour.

When I wasn't in the *India Today* office, I used to go to the library at the NDC and go through anything I could find, especially concerning Ladakh and Tibet. There was a lot of material on the Great Game and as I was getting more and more invested in reading up about geopolitics, I would also discuss every little detail with my father. One day I ran into Brigadier (later Lieutenant General) Amar Kalkat in the library, and we started discussing Tamil Eelam and the developing situation in Sri Lanka. After a while we were joined by an Indian Police Service officer whose name I cannot now remember, and he said the Mossad were key players in the developing situation within the island nation.

My father came home one day with a book he had drawn from the library and gave it to me, saying there was a section on Nasirabad that had caught his eye. The book, published in 1960 was titled *Army Diary 1899 – 1926* and had been authored by Colonel R. Meinertzhagen, who was serving in the War Office in the immediate aftermath of World War I. The initial part of the book, covering the period when Meinertzhagen was a young officer serving in India, Kenya and Egypt was mainly anecdotal, but the book got really interesting when policy matters were being handled by him as a mid-level officer. On 24 March 1919, he lunched with the British prime minister, Lloyd George and they discussed Zionism and the Middle East, especially the sovereignty of the Sinai. This was followed up by a long letter to the prime minister which was stunning for its amazing clarity of long-term strategic thought, for it virtually predicted the 1966 Yom Kippur War. The British having laid two eggs of Arab and Jewish nationalism, then discuss what they have to do to protect their interests in the Sinai Peninsula.

After a few days, when I went to return the book to the NDC library, I had time to spare and started browsing around. Meinertzhagen's name had come up in another conversation in relation to the Australian attack on Gallipoli during World War 1. Almost by chance, I found a file in the refence section that also had his name on the first page, and I settled down to browse through it. At first, I failed to realize the real importance of what I was looking at, but then I started making notes, for in front of me was a document that stood history on its head. Illustrated with maps, the document was a virtual blueprint for the partition of India. The first part was a brief report about the Indian troops that had fought in Europe, the second section dealt with their expectations and the third talked of British interests that necessitated the requirement for a Hindustan that was minus Pakistan and Princesstan!

I had my tail up and after I thought I had enough material to do a definitive story on the lack of strategic thought on the part of Indian leaders which allowed for India's Partition in 1947, and I asked Suman Dubey to let me do an article on those lines. At that point, even I had not connected the dots and would only subsequently realize that the Meinertzhagen proposal pre-dated the first mention of Pakistan in Indian history by almost a dozen years! Suman was listening to me quietly, when I also started talking of Israel's interest in Sri Lanka. Seeing me talking, Dilip Bobb, who was a senior correspondent, had wandered across and unknown to me, had heard the last bit. He let out a short guffaw and started to ridicule me in the calculated way senior journalists have to make youngsters look stupid! There was a map of the world on Suman's wall, and Dilip actually held his belly, climbed on to a chair to point out, 'Here's Israel ... and here is Sri Lanka. What the fuck do they have in common?' In all this, the partition of India story got forgotten.

New Year's came and went. George Orwell had warned of totalitarianism in his book, titled *1984* which had been published in 1949. In reality, at the rate at which things were unfolding in the Punjab, it looked as if the Indian government was completely losing the plot. I had had a bad scooter accident near Khan Market and was laid up with a bum leg, passing the time playing scrabble with Kavita, while my parents moved to Jalandhar where my father was posted as brig adam, 11 Corps after the completion of the NDC course. Teesta had got a job at the Taj Man Singh Hotel and the two of us shifted to a one-bedroom apartment in Pragati Vihar.

The year started badly. I limped into Suman Dubey's office making sure Dilip Bobb was preening somewhere else, with the intention of getting him to give the green signal for the Partition story. Before I could say anything, he looked up at me and stroking his bearded chin thoughtfully, asked me, 'You involved with Mark Valladares's daughter?' Besides having been on mountaineering expeditions together, Suman's father was also from the Bengal Sappers. 'I met him recently. He wants me to fire you!' I could only shrug my shoulders and backtracked from his cabin. I knew he wouldn't do it, but if I put a foot wrong, he would not hold my hand either. I called up Kavita, and then sitting on the grassy patch over Palika Bazaar with her, I told her what had happened. She had lit a cigarette and with a slightly detached air, said, 'You know, you'll never be able to afford the kind of lifestyle I want.'

In March, I managed to get Suman's nod to do a special report on rhino poaching in Kaziranga[10], especially since reports were coming in that ninety-one animals had been butchered the previous year. I landed at Guwahati and caught the train to Barpeta Road where I met Sanjay Deb Roy, who was perhaps one of the country's most dedicated forest officers. He was then the field director of the Manas Tiger Reserve, but he had earlier been in Kaziranga and turned things around when the population of rhinos was down to just fifteen animals. He briefed me about the modus operandi of the poachers and the powers who were behind the massacre. After spending two nights in Manas, I returned to Guwahati and then drove down to Kaziranga, where I hunkered down waiting to see if the poachers would strike while I was there.

Early morning, one of the forest posts reported that there had been screams of an animal a few hours ago, suggesting that a rhino had been trapped in the grasslands. Moving while it was still dark, I got to the post where four guards armed with .315 rifles were waiting for me. Moving through the grass in the grey light of dawn, we soon found the distraught animal. Rhinos have a strange habit of defecating at a particular point, and the animal every time backs the last seven or eight metres, before he does his job on an ever-increasing pile of rhino dung. This makes it easier for poachers, who dig a pit, then put *punjis* (sharpened bamboo stakes) inside and then wait for an animal to tumble into their trap.

---

[10] Kunal Verma, 'Indian rhinoceros perilously close to extinction at Kaziranga National Park in Assam,' *India Today*, 31 March 1984, https://www.indiatoday.in/magazine/environment/story/19840331-indian-rhinoceros-perilously-close-to-extinction-at-kaziranga-national-park-in-assam-802913-1984-03-31

The look on the helpless animal's face, with blood oozing from the corner of its mouth and a stake sticking through his body, was heartbreaking. I was standing less than a metre from those eyes, and I had never seen anything as horrific as this. I turned to the forest guard and told him to shoot the animal. Though they had undoubtedly seen this before, the guard had tears streaming down his face, and he just handed me his rifle. Placing the muzzle where I thought the brain was, I started to squeeze the trigger when suddenly the grass parted on the other side and three men literally stumbled into us. Two were carrying weapons while one man had a saw. Seeing us, they turned on their heels and bolted.

I don't know what I was thinking, for I took off after them, the rifle helping to keep the sharp blades of elephant grass off my face. Then suddenly, abruptly the grassland finished, and I was flying through thin air, landing on the muddy slope which angled down to the Brahmaputra. The escaping men had got into a boat, which was spinning in the current, but was rapidly going away from the shore. They fired a couple of shots, by which time the other guards had caught up with me at the edge of the water. I was the only one who fired at them, the others reluctant to do so, which was not at all surprising because if a poacher got killed, the guard would be booked for manslaughter. We returned to the pit, where the rhino had died by then. The horn, then worth ₹92,000 a kilogram in the black market, had to be removed. Only then, did one of the guards notice that my left boot was filled with blood. The LG slug had got embedded in my shin. Quickly lighting a fire and heating up a knife, the guards took out the lead ball. Back at the post, they applied the white of two eggs and told me I would be right as rain. Though it hurt like anything, by the time I got back to Delhi, it was hard to believe I had actually been shot.

Teesta had given up her job at the Taj and I went to drop her at 5 Mall Road which was now our residence in Jalandhar. I asked my father if I could make a quick trip to Amritsar, from where I planned to fly back to Delhi. There I ran into Shekhar Gupta who was making one of his multiple trips to the Golden Temple. I tagged along, keeping a few paces behind, and was amazed to see how well Shekhar had developed his contacts. He had been in *India Today* for barely a year himself, but he had spent half-a-dozen years as a reporter with the *Indian Express* and his coverage of the entire Khalistan movement and that of Jarnail Singh

Bhindranwale had been sensational. Though the fortification of the Golden Temple had not yet taken place, I had been amazed to see the number of weapons that were being carried around openly.

I had until then never been to the Golden Temple, so I broke away and walked around the entire complex. When I came back to where I had last seen Shekhar, he was not there but a group of men were standing together. Someone asked me if I was also from *India Today*, and when I nodded my head, I was told to follow him. Bhindranwale asked me what I was doing there, and I told him I had come to drop my sister. '*Piyo tera Fauji hai?*' (Your father is an army man?) and when I said yes, the others seemed to find that funny. We spoke for two or three minutes, then I left. By then everyone had lost complete interest in me.

Sometime in April 1984, out of the blue, when I responded to some urgent knocking on my door, I was amazed to see my Nirmal Uncle standing there. Brushing past me, he made himself comfortable, and made some small talk. He then opened his briefcase and handed me a file, which bore the legend, 'SBI'. 'Do not show it to anyone, just study it. I will be back in the afternoon.' And he was gone.

To me the papers said nothing, despite the fact that I had graduated with a B. Com degree from college. In the evening Nirmal Hoon picked me up, and we drove to New Friends Colony in his Ambassador which he was driving himself. I was then introduced to a couple who had recently returned from Dubai. It was a really fancy house that was full of antiques, which when combined with some dim lighting, gave the place a very spooky look. The file obviously contained some extremely explosive information, but I think it was by then obvious to both Nirmal Hoon and Mr Puri (I think that was his name) that it was way beyond my capability to understand not only what was happening, but they had picked a dud who actually had no say in the working of the magazine.

After a conversation between themselves, Nirmal Hoon called up Aroon Purie and they spoke for a minute or two. I caught the words 'my nephew' and my name, but other than that I had no clue what was said. While driving back to drop me at Pragati Vihar, Nirmal Hoon said, 'You will give the file to Aroon Purie. Do not under any circumstances give it to anyone else, not even his secretary.'

As instructed, still not sure if I understood what was happening, I handed over the file to the boss in his office, who then growled at me to take a seat. Once or twice, he whistled through his teeth after turning a sheet. He then got up and from his door called out to T. N. Ninan, the business editor, to come into the office. Ninan glanced at me sideways, and then started perusing the file himself. I was letting my gaze wander around the room, and it came to rest on a placard that said, 'News is What Someone Somewhere Wants to Suppress!' or words to that effect.

I played no further part in the story, but it was not only big, it was obviously huge. While it was in the process of being sub-edited, even though I had no idea what had been written, I saw the byline which said, 'T. N. Ninan with Kunal Verma.' Even within the office, there was a lot of secrecy about what was going on, and quite frankly, I had no idea how to react myself. Nirmal Hoon had simply disappeared. And there were whispers that a chartered aircraft had landed in Delhi with a relative of Aroon Purie acting as a mediator between SBI and *India Today*. Then, abruptly, there was no story—not only that, there was nothing. No trace at all. In the next issue that came out in the end of April, there was some small story about Maruti or something and I had been given a joint byline with Ninan.

The SBI episode had been a distraction. Mr Puri and his wife, I was told by the same voice that had informed me of the secret parleys, had met with an accident on the Jaipur Highway and were either dead or crippled for life. I had no idea where Nirmal Hoon was, so there was no further information available, and I couldn't possibly walk up to Aroon Purie and ask him. Somehow, the realization that people purporting to hold such high moral values actually had feet of clay, came as a major shock. I had no choice but to just live with it, but once the process of cynicism sets in, it's like a cancer. It takes time, but eventually you either become the system or you survive by walking away.

Somehow, in the entire SBI affair, I got the feeling Suman Dubey had been kept in the dark. As far as he was concerned, he had me on notice, and I then blundered big time. There was a well-known jazz group that was playing in Delhi, and since Kavita, Anita Kaul and her husband Siddhartha Basu all wanted to go, I rang up Suman Dubey's lawyer friend whose name I now forget, who was distributing the passes. I brazenly said to him Suman had requested for four passes, and he in turn promptly sent them. The next day, Suman called me to his office, and let me have it. He didn't sack me then, but for all practical purposes, I knew I was on borrowed time. At a very basic level, I felt I had let Suman down, but then one can never roll back time. The magnitude of my lie may have been nothing in comparison with other things that had happened around the same time, but just as I never forgot the thrashing I got from my mother for bullying a beggar, I was to never forget the jazz episode either.

At 23, I felt I was standing at the crossroads. During my second trip to Ahmedabad, Kavita's circle of friends had expanded at the National Institute of Design (NID) with the arrival of Brinda 'Pia' Datta. Having finished her schooling from Lawrence School, Sanawar, Pia was a 'tea garden kid', her father, Rajat 'Butch' Datta, being one of the doyens of the trade. She was extremely sporty, and I spent a few hours in NID playing table tennis with her and discussing the ground in Assam where major battles had been fought during World War II. Since then, we had been in communication, and when she said an ambulance belonging to the Goodricke Group needed to be driven from Calcutta to the Amgoorie Tea Estate in Nagaland, I had offered to drive it up. Her brother Ronojoy, who was only obsessed with golf, was to join us and Pia had then worked out an elaborate itinerary for us to stay at various gardens en route, plus also visit both Manas and Kaziranga as well.

After a two-day stay with the Datta's in Calcutta, when to my horror Pia almost defeated me in tennis, we set off on our epic journey. I soon got the hang of the Matador van's steering wheel, and then we were on the road for the next two weeks. Ever since I was a baby, I had intermittently been in and out of the Northeast, but my real fascination for the region as a whole began to take shape during this period. There were two parallel subjects that were obsessing me at that time; Zorawar Singh's conquest and the early history of Ladakh, and in the east, the role of Subhas Chandra Bose's INA.

Even before we returned to Calcutta, it was obvious that Punjab was heading towards a major flashpoint. When I finally got through to my father in Jalandhar, he was extremely guarded about the situation on the ground, but he said there were repeated messages from Western Command in Chandigarh asking where I was. Shortly after I had disconnected, he called back again saying that come 'hell or highwater' I was to catch the Calcutta–Delhi Airbus 300 flight that very evening. I would be met at the airport and would receive further instructions.

Hell was not far away, but the highwater point sure struck home with whosoever it concerned, for it began to rain. There was at least four feet of water around the Datta flat on Loudon Street, but somehow Pia got me across to Dum Dum. To my utter amazement, I was the only passenger on the aircraft as we took to the wing and landed at Palam. I was met by a captain from the Corps of Signals, who gave me a curfew pass issued by the Ministry of Defence (MOD) and then took me in his vehicle to the IAF dispersal area. I had already been manifested and I was flown in an IAF Avro 748 to Chandigarh.

Lieutenant General (later General) K. Sundarji was a man in a hurry. 'Where the hell have you been?' he asked as I was ushered into the army commander's presence at his house. He looked at his watch and said he had fifteen minutes and that something 'big was about to happen' in the next 36 hours. He asked me when had I last been inside the Golden Temple complex and he seemed disappointed that I was not cued up on the latest situation. I told him there were plenty of weapons inside, including LMGs that some of the people were carrying. 'Oh, you journalists, you always exaggerate. Once they see the army coming at them, they'll be shitting in their pants.' He then left, and I sat for another fifteen minutes with Mrs Vani Sundarji, after which I was taken to a guest room for the night. The conversation with the army commander had been so brief and so off-the-cuff, I wondered why had he bothered to get me there. On the army exchange I spoke to my parents. Obviously, there was no reference to any of the above, but my father said to me, 'Be careful. He is my boss. Don't open your mouth unnecessarily.'

The next day, a jeep dropped me off at the Ambala Railway Station, where I boarded a diesel locomotive that took me to Phagwara, which was just short of Jalandhar. The curfew across Punjab was absolute and there wasn't a soul to be seen anywhere. Another Jonga from 11 Corps that had been detailed to pick me up, after a brief stopover at home, then drove me to Amritsar. At Beas, Hodson Horse tanks were beginning to deploy on either side of the bridge. I knew most of the officers, so I stopped and took a few photographs. Then as darkness settled over the city of Amritsar, the fireworks started.

Op Blue Star was a botched-up exercise in planning right from the word go, and one man was responsible for the entire fiasco. Two days previously, Major (later General) Vijay Kumar Singh had accompanied his immediate boss, the director general military operations (DGMO), Lieutenant General C. M. Sommana and the chief of the army staff (COAS), General Arun Shridhar Vaidya to Indira Gandhi's residence. The situation in Punjab was critical but both the senior officers were clear, a frontal attack on the Golden Temple complex by the Indian Army was out of the question. Just then, driving in from Chandigarh, obviously at the prime minister's direct invitation, the Western Army commander, Lieutenant General Sundarji had arrived, and other than throwing the mandatory salute to acknowledge the army chief, had blatantly taken a stance contrary to that of his own boss and the DGMO, and told Indira Gandhi he would clear up the complex in a few hours[11] if she ordered. The moment General Sundarji decided to pull the carpet from under the COAS's feet, military logic had been compromised and each subsequent decision was then guided by political rather than military compulsions.

Sundarji was like that, brilliantly overwhelming, and always full of bluster. Arun Vaidya, Maha Vir Chakra (MVC) and Bar, as his boss, failed to stand up to him when it mattered the most, and the end result was absolute chaos. My father had once commented, 'Sundarji is like a man who opens the bonnet of a car, looks at all the wires, and pulls them all out saying they are all wrong, but then he himself has no clue how to put them back!'

Even from a couple of kilometres away, from the sheer volume of gunfire that refused to subside, it seemed things had gone terribly wrong.

---

[11] 'Of political blunders and faltering generals,' *Hindustan Times* (Bathinda), 8 November 2013, https://www.pressreader.com/india/hindustan-times-bathinda/20131108/282226598486286

The city shook with the blasts of grenades and, as the night progressed, the rumble of armour followed by the thunder of their 155 mm main guns suggested that the tanks had opened up, the sounds magnifying even further in the confines of the built-up area. By the time dawn started to light up the sky, there was a deadly silence, punctuated by the odd burst of small arms fire, and the smoke and the smell of cordite that hung over the temple city. Bhindranwale himself had been among the last few to be killed, gunned down as he made a dash from the completely destroyed Akal Takht towards the sanctuary of the relatively undamaged Harmandir Sahib.

I hung around for a couple of days, trying to gather as much information as possible as to what had happened. It was all extremely chaotic, but a clear picture of what had transpired was beginning to emerge within the army circles. The facts were horrific enough, but as I left Amritsar and moved further away, almost everyone I met believed the damage and casualties were at least ten times worse. The situation in the *India Today* office was much the same, and after briefing Suman Dubey and S. Venkat Narayan, I asked if I could also file a story to go with Shekhar's somewhat dramatic cover story where he had artillery guns opening up from Jallianwala Bagh for added affect.

Ever since I had flown out of Calcutta, I had yet to make it to my flat in Delhi and was literally surviving on cigarettes and cups of coffee and tea. Nevertheless, I rolled up my sleeves and hammered out a fairly detailed report in which I put the army dead at 89. This promptly brought Dilip Bobb into play, who seemed determined to make me look like an idiot. He even lay down on the floor, rocking like a seesaw on his belly, and threw cryptic words around, saying in his cultivated manner things like 'fixed-line of fire' and 'Shahbeg and Amrik Singh knowing their job', etc. I also had, as yet undeveloped, exposures of a photograph that showed Bhindranwale lying dead next to the Dakshini Deori. Requesting Bhawan Singh, the affable senior photographer to have my rolls developed, I started to head for home.

I was promptly called back by Suman who said news was just coming in that there had been a mutiny at Ramgarh, the Sikh Regimental Centre and that the commandant had been shot. He asked me to fly to Ranchi and see if I could get the details of what had happened. Brigadier R. S. Puri had been my father's coursemate, and by the time I got there the next day, most of the troops left in the Regimental Centre had surrendered. It was quite pathetic to see them, all bewildered recruits and men, who were in a dazed and shocked state, torn between their loyalty to their religion and also to their country. Those who had set off towards New Delhi in a convoy of thirty-five vehicles were also then intercepted and disarmed by other army units. I finally went home and slept for the next 48 hours.

When I woke up, the next few days were like a blur. The flat in Pragati Vihar was temporary, and I had to move out the next day. Kavita came over in the evening with some food, and after a quiet dinner, she told me it was over between us, saying her parents just refused to reconcile to our being together. There was nothing to be said, so I dropped her off at her Defence Colony residence and after I came back to my room, started to pack up the flat. I had hired David Devadas's mother's flat in Munirka, but it needed work, and so I moved in temporarily with Leslie George and Manju who were living in one of the government blocks in Lodhi Colony.

If a horoscope accurately depicted a person's life, I wonder what my 'month that was' would have looked like. Not surprisingly, *India Today* had not carried my report, preferring to stay with Shekhar Gupta's version where he claimed the army casualties were much higher. I was back at work, but after the SBI story, was never comfortable with the environment. Beginning of July, *India Today* carried another story on the Blue Star action, and though it may have been a coincidence, much of what I had said in my report was now a part of Shekhar's second version. Upset and angry, I headed for the roof to smoke a cigarette, but had instead stumbled upon Pramod Pushkarna duplicating my negatives, particularly the shot of Bhindranwale's body. When I asked him what he was doing, he had simply shrugged and said, 'Don't blame me, I'm just following orders.'

I came downstairs, took a sheet of paper, typed out Suman Dubey's address, and wrote a cryptic two-word resignation letter. After signing it, I gave it to my now former boss and started to walk out of the office. I think everyone in the office by then knew I was leaving. Aroon Purie was leaning against the door to his office, and he drawled out, 'Stay in touch

Kunal. I may want you to do some stories on mahseer fishing.' I just looked at him and swore to myself I would never come back.

Panwar Saab was much older than I was, but by then he was almost like a mentor to me, and he kept telling me to stay focused on wildlife and conservation issues 'because that is where your heart is.' Perhaps to cheer me up, he included my name as a delegate in an international cat conference that was being held at the Kanha Tiger Reserve. Once I got there, he gave me a jeep, and told me I had the run of the park, and yes, if I felt like it, I could attend some of the sessions. I then only had my trusted Pentax K1000 and a fixed 200 mm lens, but Kanha being Kanha, I got some really good wildlife shots, especially that of swamp deer and bison. A solitary male tiger sitting under a tree I then blew up and put up in my Munirka flat. That one photograph made me feel as if I had arrived on the wildlife photography scene.

Hardly had I returned from Kanha I got an urgent message from my father to come immediately to Jalandhar. At the time, Ramu Gaur who had made quite a name for himself as a bird photographer in Ladakh, was on General Sundarji's staff in Chandigarh. I suspect it was due to his prompting the army commander that my father along with a coursemate of his, Brigadier (later Lieutenant General) Baljit Singh, were tasked to hold a wildlife workshop at the Sariska Tiger Reserve. Sundarji had told my father to 'involve me, so I didn't waste my time behaving like an armchair general' (whatever that meant), so would I please get back to Delhi and with the help of all my 'wildlife friends' get cracking!

There were others waiting for me to get back to Delhi. In the last few months, especially since he was living in Pragati Vihar as well, Kishore Rao, a senior wildlife official, had been added to my list of 'wildlife friends'. He asked to get across to Guwahati by the morning flight as five rhinos were to be airlifted to Delhi the next day. The animals—two males and three females—had been brought in wooden cages on trucks from Kaziranga and the Government of India had chartered an Aeroflot Il-76 to transport the animals. When the plane landed in the evening, I was gaping at its sheer size. By mid-morning, the rhinos, watered and fed and partially tranquilized, were loaded onto the aircraft. No one had realized that the rhino could spray its urine metres away and soon the place was smelling to high heavens.

The Russian pilots arrived after a while, and the captain had a cigarette hanging from his lips and he was soon down to his vest. I was standing in the cockpit of the giant plane when I realized the crew was asking for a flight plan so they could fly over Everest. Soon we were rolling down the runway and it seemed like a miracle that the 96-tonne aircraft with its super heavy cargo could lift off with such ease. More to avoid getting splattered by the spraying animals, I spent most of the flying time in the navigator's bubble and as a result had a fantastic view of the Everest and Lhotse peaks from there. I joined the navigator in a swig of vodka to celebrate the occasion for I don't think too many people would in their lifetime fly with rhinos over Mount Everest.

By the time we landed in Delhi it was evening, and as the crates were offloaded, a fire engine was detailed to help cool the animals down. Somehow, I found myself standing on top of the first crate that had a big male rhino, and the fire hose was thrust up to me. When the water started, I almost got thrown off by the force of the jet stream but somehow held on. Later that night, the visual of me hosing the rhino was part of the national news as Doordarshan cameras had also arrived to record the historical moment. The rhinos were then transported to Dudhwa by road and released in specially cordoned off areas. The translocation effort was done not only to reintroduce the rhino back into its former habitat (they were very much still there in Nepal's Chitwan, which was across the border) but also create an alternate gene pool in the event of a pandemic wiping out the population in Kaziranga and other parts of the Northeast. It was one of the many successful conservation programmes initiated in the 1980s that has stood the test of time.

Teesta, in the meantime, had gotten engaged to Captain Sudesh Kumar 'Micky' Yadav, who was the ADC to General Vaidya. Being from the Deccan Horse (which was also the chief's regiment) he was most unlike her, and though everyone seemed to have serious reservations about his character, no one said anything. During this period, most of the ADCs to the President of India, Giani Zail Singh, had become good friends, and so had the others who were with the chief. As a result, I used to often go down to Rashtrapati Bhawan and play squash, or swim in the pool. Those days security was not much of an issue, and on occasion one even played a game with the air chief, Air Chief Marshal Lakshman Madhav Katre, who incidentally was also from the Doon School.

Teesta then introduced me to Captain Ajai Shukla, who said he was coming to Delhi to play in the Services Tennis Tournament. My sister promptly told Shukla he could stay with me in Munirka, an offer he quickly accepted. Shukla was then either engaged to Maneka Gandhi's sister or was just going around with her, I don't recall, but he was also the brother-in-law of Suman Dubey and Arun Shourie. I knew none of this of course, but after a couple of days of his staying with me, he was picked up by Suman Dubey from my Munirka address. When I opened the door, the look of surprise on Suman's face was obvious. 'What are you doing here?' he asked. 'I live here!' I said. Simple answers to simple questions!

Though we planned to hold the wildlife conference only in December, I wasted no time in preparing for it. Dilip Mathai, from the earlier batches of the Doon School was the president of the WWF and he was delighted at the thought of getting the army involved in conservation. Much to my glee, he then loaned me WWF's movie projector, which in turn started me off on a film collecting spree. I was struggling under a load of film cans that I had managed to get from the Canadian Embassy when I ran into Vicki Graham. She was an attractive 30-plus-year-old chief of bureau of AP. I spoke to her for five minutes, and once she learnt I had been with *India Today* and in Punjab during Op Blue Star, she gave me her card and said, 'Come see me at my residence tomorrow at 11, I may have something for you!'

The next day was a Sunday and Vicki was on the first floor of a Mediterranean-looking house which had bougainvillea growing all over the place. As I parked my scooter, she leaned over from her balcony and told me to come up the side steps. She was in a dressing gown, which made me feel I was a bit overdressed in a scarf and a blazer. 'You'll have coffee,' she drawled and told me to make myself comfortable. After a pleasant chat she told me I could not only join AP from tomorrow but do any offbeat stuff that I liked. 'No restrictions,' she laughed. 'I like the way you talk. Just write like that! You're not a wire-service guy, and I doubt if you ever will be. So just be yourself.'

I had no clue what a 'wire-service guy' was, but I couldn't have cared less. My heart was singing its own song—I had just been given a virtual dream job. We shook hands and I left. The next day I was given an accreditation card and just like that, I was a correspondent with one of the largest wire services in the world.

The next two months, Vicki almost drove me to the ground. She wanted me in Amritsar almost every second day, and as a result, I quickly learnt the ropes. Samuel, the hub around whom AP functioned, after a while said you might as well live there. I told him I had the option, for Jalandhar was just an hour's drive away. Going up and down, almost like a commute, I did get to spend some time in Jalandhar as well, especially on days when nothing would happen at the Golden Temple which was where all the anti-Indira Gandhi and anti-India speeches were held almost on a daily basis.

It was around then when I met the Grewal family for the first time. Listed as the New Delhi correspondent of *Sanctuary Asia,* I had called up Royina and fixed a time, with a vague idea of wanting to publish an article on the wildlife of Ladakh. Even as I walked in, the entire family—Royina, Ajit, Misha, Ayesha, their labrador Raja, their cat Missy, and even the grandmother, Mima—all behaved as if I had always belonged there. The lead of course, came from Royina, with whom I was to subsequently share a particular bond that is hard to describe. It would later transpire that Ajit's father had been on my grandfather's staff in the Central Provinces, but that was just one of the six degrees of separation that seemed to exist with just about every person I met.

7

Trial by Fire: The Sikh Riots

Rashtrapati Bhavan had a wonderful bunch of ADCs. Captains Minhas and Joe Mathew were both from the army, Squadron Leader Akhilesh Kumar was from the air force and Lieutenant Satyendra Singh 'Benu' Jamwal was from the navy. In addition, President Giani Zail Singh was also waited upon by four junior commissioned officer (JCO) ADCs. Both Benu's and my fathers, then lieutenant colonels, had been instructors at the Defence Services Staff College. Benu, a year senior to me was from the Lawrence School, Sanawar, was a good friend ever since we used to raid his mother's kitchen and polish off chunks of chocolate fudge that had been prepared for the Ladies Club meet. By the time we linked up again in Delhi in 1983–84, Benu had developed a major passion for body building, as a result of which he was perhaps one of the fittest naval officers one would ever meet. With his Dogra lineage, chiselled features, he looked a bit like Clark Kent, the human avatar of Superman. We would often joke that instead of the ceremonial blue patrols which the ADCs wore, Benu would be equally at home if he was to wear a blue jump suit with a red underwear over it along with a red cape with an 'S' stitched on it!

Benu's father was a year or two senior to mine and as luck would have it, after commanding the Amritsar-based 15 Infantry Division, he had taken charge of the Delhi Area. With his handlebar moustaches, he was quite an imposing figure and would subsequently command quite a few Republic Day parades. 'He probably had the best salute in the Indian Army,' recalled Captain Amarinder Singh, the chief minister of Punjab, when I met him in September 2021. Major General Jagdish Singh Jamwal was also extremely soft-spoken and every time I ran into him, he would be most affectionate and would always address me as 'son'.

On that fateful 31 October evening in 1984 when Delhi was beginning to see the beginning of attacks on Sikhs in the aftermath of Mrs Indira Gandhi's assassination, with the stolen papers from Vicki Graham's table burning a hole against my chest, I was not quite sure what I wanted to do. Driving my scooter almost instinctively, I turned from Parliament Street towards Cathedral Church of the Redemption and then went up the slope towards Rashtrapati Bhavan along North Avenue. Usually, there were at least two police pickets there, but no one challenged me. Even at Rashtrapati Bhavan there was not a soul, so I parked and went into the imposing building, literally walking in without being stopped or questioned by anyone.

I entered a long room where a JCO ADC was sitting at a desk, but he either did not see me enter or he just ignored me. Benu's room was not too far away and as I stood there wondering what to do, the JCO ADC got to his feet and Giani Zail Singh wandered into the hall. I had twice before met the President of India and had been quite taken in by his spontaneous warmth. Taking the sheaf of papers out of my jacket, I walked towards him and wished him. The president did not respond. He just seemed to look at me with a blank, bewildered look. I started to say something, but I felt the JCO ADC's hand on my shoulder. I turned to look at him, and he indicated with a nod that I should leave the president alone. I looked again at Giani Zail Singh ... his face and eyes were blank. It was almost as if he was seeing nothing, hearing nothing. He turned and went back from where he had come. It was unnerving, to put it mildly.

In Benu's room, I sat down on the bed and looked at the stack of cards on the side of the room that read '1 minute left' ... '2 minutes left' ... and so on. Obviously, they were slipped to the president when he was making a speech and was nearing the end of the allocated time. I started to go through the sheets in detail, but after a few minutes felt a wave of exhaustion. I must have dozed off, for I was woken up by Benu who asked me, 'What the hell are you doing here?'

Benu listened quietly as I quickly updated him, telling him I had stolen the papers from the AP office and then come straight to Rashtrapati Bhavan. I told him there were no police personnel on the roads and that no one had challenged me on my way in. He knew I had tried to talk to the president—presumably the JCO ADC had told him—and explained that Giani Zail Singh was almost in a state of deep shock and that he was being sedated. It was around 9:30 in the evening by then, and we both knew that the clock was ticking. Benu told me that the rioting was spreading slowly and that there were reports of tempos coming in from the direction of Gurgaon with drums of kerosene and old tyres, and widespread arson was anticipated. The voter's list now left us both with no doubt as to what was being planned.

'Kunal, you go to my father. He's in the Delhi Area Ops Room monitoring the situation. I'll call my sister and she will meet you outside Flagstaff House. Get going ...' I was already halfway out of the door and ran down the imposing courtyard where so much history had been scripted. My trusted Vijay fired at the first kick, and I was again racing along, down South Avenue, right, then left, Teen Murti, through to Kautilya Marg ... all these areas were completely deserted. Not even a stray dog was visible. Even Sardar Patel Marg was deserted, as was the police post at Dhaula Kuan. I turned in at Pratap Chowk and reached the Mandir Marg–Mall Road intersection, where on the left was General Jamwal's residence.

Benu's sister, Vandana, was standing at the gate and she climbed on behind me. HQ Delhi Area was just a stone's throw away and after parking, we both half-ran into the GOC's office. The staff there recognized Vandana and after a few minutes the general came into his office. He greeted me in his usual 'hello son' manner and said he had received a call from Benu as well telling him I was on my way. 'Where's the fire?' he asked.

I told him it was spreading and even though the South Delhi roads were still clear, there was already a pall of smoke around Ring Road. I handed him the sheaf of papers without comment. The general sank into his chair and started to glance at the sheets ... putting aside the page he had already seen. He probably ran through a dozen pages after which he looked up at me and said, 'Where did you get this?'

General Jamwal knew I was a journalist, but for some reason I felt I could not implicate AP. I said I could not tell him where I got the papers from, but they seemed authentic enough.

The general looked at a few more pages, then called in his ADC. 'Take Vandana home ... take my car.' Vandana in turn looked at me, nodded and left.

General Jamwal sighed and leaned back in his chair. He was looking at me, and I presumed he was working out what course of action to take. When he spoke, I couldn't believe what I was hearing ... 'I cannot do anything. I do not have the mandate, or for that matter the troops.'

I looked incredulously at him. He collected the papers, and deliberately folded them back into their original shape. I extended my hand expecting him to return them to me, but he instead opened his drawer and put them away. 'Leave these with me son ...' he again shook his head, 'I simply have no troops in Delhi.'

This was too much for me. I said that was not true, for I had seen at least two infantry battalions come down Ring Road earlier in the evening. Besides, 35 Infantry Brigade was in Delhi and 9 Infantry Division was in Meerut ... get them ... I implored ... then I added, there are enough *sevadars* in Delhi Cantonment who even if armed with sticks can stop any rioting by just their presence. 'Just stage a flag march in Trilokpuri sir ... whoever these guys are, they will think twice once they see the army.'

Jamwal was now clearly irritated. His entire body language had changed. 'There are no troops in Delhi under my command,' he said, his voice still measured, 'Son, you've had a long night. You've got the papers to me, now go home.' He then got up and left his office, leaving me to find my own way out.

I was devastated, not quite knowing what to do next. I thought of going back to Rashtrapati Bhavan but that would serve no purpose. I reached Dhaula Kuan and turned onto Ring Road, with the intention of going back to my place in Munirka. As I turned onto Rao Tula Ram Marg, my heart gave a jump, for a house in Shanti Niketan was on fire and a group of men, some carrying burning *mashaals*, were moving along the service lane. The Grewals were in the inner lane and I felt a wave of panic. Though Ajit was not a practising Sikh, his name was enough for there to be trouble. I turned into Shanti Niketan, went past the burning house, and banged loudly on the Grewal's gate which was barricaded from inside.

The ground floor housed some high commissioner, while the first floor was occupied by the family. After I had identified myself, the gate was opened by the lone watchman who seemed terrified. They are coming, he said, as I parked my Vijay inside the driveway, after which I ran up the stairs two at a time. Ajit was a large man, perhaps 6'2" or so. He had two double-barrelled guns in the house and was busy making little piles of ammunition. Two pistols were also lying on the table. He looked at me and said, 'Thank God you're here! They have set fire to the house down the road. We have to get the girls out of here to Mima's.'

Mima's house was in neighbouring Vasant Vihar. Though it was not far from Shanti Niketan, under the circumstances it might as well have been on the moon. Misha, the elder daughter was then 14 and Ayesha 11. While one of the weapons was obviously a shotgun, the other, an over and under, was a rifle. Unlike the 12-bore cartridges, the ammunition for this looked lethal. I suddenly realized it was a Franz Sodia 500 Express elephant gun. Royina in the meantime had entered the room, and even in that tense atmosphere she gave me a reassuring hug. 'I've told the girls we are getting a taxi to take them to Mima's, and I've hidden them as best as I could,' she said. 'How did you get here?'

'I saw a house on fire and some goons ... what taxi? There are no ...'

Royina hushed me up, just in case the girls could hear us. Ajit had loaded one of the pistols, a Beretta 9 mm, and he handed it to me, holding it from the barrel. I took it and looked at the mechanism. After pressing the button to eject the magazine, I pulled the lever back to make sure there was no round in the chamber. Then I reinserted the magazine and slipped the pistol in my jacket pocket where it fitted rather neatly. I looked up and my eyes met Ajit's. He was himself then 37, Royina a year younger. Somehow, we all knew what we would have to do if the mob broke in. There was no emotion, nothing ... just a very calm realization that none of us may not make it through the night.

There were some isolated shouts from the street below and through the slats in the balcony one could see the glow of the mashaals. As I headed for the door, I was surprised to see Royina reach for the elephant gun, and I wondered if she could handle the recoil. I came down the steps and was then again in the driveway. Three men were trying to clamber over the gate, and they were shouting, '*Khoon ka badla khoon se leynge!*' (We will avenge blood with blood!) It was terrifying, and I reached for the pistol in my jacket pocket. There was no sign of the watchman.

I walked the last few steps towards the gate. Seeing me approach, the three men on top of the gate froze. One had one leg on my side, while the other two had their torsos visible. The shouting had died away. ... Five metres short of the gate, I took out the pistol, slipped in the magazine and cocked it. In the silence of the night, the pistol's mechanism sounded deadlier than a rifle shot. I was tempted to look back over my shoulder and see if Ajit and Royina were covering me, but I didn't. My hands were shaking, my knees were threatening to collapse and for a second I could not speak.

'*Theek hai ... aap log aage aa jao ... mere paas das goliyan hai ... mein aap mein se saath aath ko toh apne saath le jaoonga*' (It's alright ... you keep coming ... I have ten bullets ... I will take at least seven or eight of you with me). To make matters worse, I had no idea if the mob on the other side of the gate was armed. But I was surprised to hear my own voice ... despite everything that was happening inside my own head, I sounded amazingly calm. The leg straddling the top of the gate was quickly withdrawn and the two torsos also disappeared. Somebody then hurled a *mashaal* over the gate, but it just hit the wall and landed in the driveway. I closed the gap with the gate and thanks to the hammering it had taken, there was a two-inch gap through which one could see some faces trying to look in. I stuck the pistol into the gap and with the gun less than a foot from the man's face, said, '*Phir se aisi harkat ki toh mein aapko nahin jane doonga*' (You try a stunt like that again and I won't let you go). The language from my end was extremely polite, but I was getting some pretty vile threats from across the gate. But I knew instinctively that these thugs had lost the initiative and would back off. There was no point in hanging around the gate, so I picked up the mashaal which was just a kerosene-soaked cloth tied to a stick and threw it back over the gate. There were more curses and threats but then after a few minutes, they went away.

The watchman who had opened the gate for me earlier came out from the shadows and said in a quivering voice, '*Bach gai saab*!' (We've been saved sir!)

It was past midnight. The danger of the mob returning was real. I don't remember if Misha and Ayesha were whisked off to Mima's, but I was by then completely exhausted. Royina said I should get some sleep while she stood guard, but I felt it was worth my while to take the scooter and see what was happening outside. I drove up to Moti Bagh, and near the Railway Museum found two army vehicles standing near the roundabout. There was a captain sitting in a jeep and after I told him I was Brigadier Ashok Verma's son, he said he was looking for a place to park for the night, but he had no idea where to go. I told him to follow me, and we drove to Shanti Niketan where the corner house was still smouldering. There was a park opposite the Grewal's gate and the captain said it was the perfect place for him to billet for the night.

With even the small detachment of the army camped outside the gate, the entire equation had changed. With the Grewals breathing easier, I still had the pending problem of the Sikh gentleman whom I had left at Leslie and Manju's place. However, Royina would have none of it, and after she gave me some bread and butter to wolf down, she insisted I sleep for a few hours, promising to wake me up at 4:30 in the morning with a cup of coffee.

It was still dark when I wheeled the scooter out of the Grewal residence. The captain was standing near his jeep talking to someone on the radio, but when he saw me, he walked across and offered me a cigarette. He said they had evacuated a few people from the burning house and had taken them to Safdarjung Hospital but he felt they were much too badly burnt to survive if they had any life in them at all. I thanked him, fired up my engine, and set off once again. The trucks from the previous evening were gutted completely, and in the headlights, one could still see some smoke emitting. Either the men killed earlier had got completely incinerated or someone had pulled out their charred skeletons, there was no sign of any remains. I could feel the nausea setting in again, so I turned left off Ring Road and went off towards Sarojini Nagar. The sky was turning grey by then, and I must have taken a wrong turn because I suddenly found myself almost colliding with a bunch of people who were bunched up outside a Mother Diary milk booth. One man, who had a shawl over his head and a vessel in his hand to collect milk, jumped back as I braked, and the shawl slipped from his head. The full glare of the scooter's headlight lit up his face. He was the same man who had turned and faced me with a spear when I had approached the truck. I felt a cold wave of fear travel down my spine.

I had to bang on the door for a while before Manju cautiously peeped out and let me in. The Sikh, he said his name was Balbir, was a lot calmer now but he kept looking towards the door over my shoulder. Balbir said he lived in Kotla which was not far from where we were. I told Manju to give Balbir a shawl which he was to wrap around his head, and I said I would drop him home for he could not endlessly stay here. I then turned to Leslie and told him I needed him to be with me for the rest of the day, and would he please get ready. I was unslinging my camera bag even as I spoke, when I suddenly realized I still had the Beretta in my jacket pocket. Balbir was looking terrified at the prospect of stepping out, so I showed him the pistol and told him not to worry. That seemed to calm him down, for he quietly climbed on behind me, after which I dropped him at the Defence Colony–Kotla Market intersection. The moment Balbir got off the scooter, he disappeared among the timber beams which were piled up outside the shops. I then realized that the market, the shops of which were mainly owned by Sikhs, had also been vandalized. Anyway, there was nothing to do but turn around and go back to Lodhi Estate.

It was Manju's turn to insist I get some more sleep, something which Leslie also seemed to endorse, even though he had dutifully gotten dressed. I also had no idea as to how much fuel I still had in my scooter, so Leslie said I should go to sleep while he would siphon off some petrol from the two or three bikes parked next to his entrance. 'They won't be needing it anyway,' he said.

It was around 9 a.m. when I walked into the AP office with Leslie trailing along behind me. The camera bag was strapped across his chest while I still had the pistol in my jacket pocket. The gun made me feel a bit more secure, but there was nothing I could do for it wouldn't have fitted in the bag which was just big enough to carry the camera.

I gave the roll of exposed film to Samuel, who seemed to want to ask me something, but he didn't. On seeing me Vicki came out of her office, and I told her about the cold-blooded murder and the burning trucks on Ring Road, about the arrival of an army column, the subsequent drama in Shanti Niketan and the smouldering shops in Kotla. I didn't say anything about Rashtrapati Bhavan or the president and the complete lack of security around him. I pushed the timing of the events in Shanti Niketan up by a couple of hours for it gave me an alibi should Samuel decide to ask the one question that was bound to be bothering him.

'Okay ... good,' said Vicki. 'Get across to Teen Murti quickly. The prime minister's body is in state and people will be paying their last respects shortly. See if you can shoot that but don't worry too much about photographs ... we have enough people there for that. Give me a report on the atmosphere there ...'

Minutes later Leslie and I were once again on our way through the still deserted streets. Teen Murti was just a few kilometres away and the magic word 'press' on my scooter allowed us in. Strangely, despite the curfew-like situation, there were almost two thousand people queued up along the driveway. I parked and with Leslie in tow approached the main building from the back.

'What about the pistol?' asked Leslie in a hushed voice.

I had once again forgotten about it, for it was nestled neatly inside my jacket pocket that almost felt like a holster by now. 'Oh damn!'

But it was too late ... we were already among a crowd of people, almost all of them in white kurta–pyjamas and Gandhi *topis*. I recognized H. K. L. Bhagat and Sardar Buta Singh, plus a few more faces. Major Generals Jamwal and G. C. Bhandari were obviously in charge. Jamwal loudly said 'hello son' and Bhandari, who was from the Rajput Regiment also acknowledged my presence. No one stopped us, and I went and stood at the top of the line, with Leslie squeezing in behind me. My black jacket was so conspicuously out of place, but I guess no one was looking at it. Mrs Gandhi's body, on an elevated and tilted platform, had obviously just been placed there and everyone was waiting to start filing past. I could see Rajiv Gandhi, the assassinated prime minister's elder son, standing on the other side to meet the mourners. A Films Division camera was placed on one side and their lights had lit up Indira Gandhi's face. It was perhaps fitting she should be placed there, for she had moved into Teen Murti in 1947 and lived there till 1964.

'Ok, move,' somebody said, and I was propelled forward. Simultaneously, the 'public' was also allowed to file past, but they were in the porch outside, from where they could get a glimpse of Indira Gandhi. Almost everyone was crying, or had tears streaming down their faces, for the moment was poignant in the extreme. I went past, and Rajiv, though he obviously had no idea who I was, accepted my hand in both his. 'I'm so sorry ...' I had barely said the words when there was a loud commotion in the porch. A group of Nirankari Sikhs, their spotless white attire and dark blue turbans tied in a distinct manner, had reached there and suddenly the crowd erupted ... '*Khoon ka badla khoon se lenge*'. In a second the entire situation had become ugly, and it looked like a riot would break out as some people tried to hit the Nirankaris.

Rajiv Gandhi left my hand and went past me, plunging straight into the crowd, saying '*Nahin nahin ... aise nahin ... aise nahin*' (No ... no ... not like this ... not like this ...). Seeing him amidst them (I am not sure if he had already been sworn in as the prime minister or not) the crowd immediately cooled down. The Nirankaris—there were at least a dozen of them—then walked in a group towards the gate, making a dignified exit. I had followed Rajiv into the crowd, and I decided to follow the Nirankaris. Leslie had handed me the Pentax. By then a crowd had built up outside Teen Murti as well, and the moment the group came out of the gate, the crowd started baying for their blood again. A hail of stones rained down on them.

Courage under fire is one thing, but the group of Nirankaris were stoic in their reaction, looking straight in front and walking purposefully. Stones and broken bricks were hitting them on their head and bodies, and some of them were splattered in blood, but not one man broke ranks or tried to run. I believe it was their dignity that saved them—had one person tried to run or even fallen for that matter, the mob would have been on them, and they would have been lynched. The group turned onto Willingdon Crescent (later Mother Teresa Road) and thankfully the hail of stones died down.

By the evening on 1 November, the killings had taken on a completely different complexion. Sikhs were being hunted down and systematically lynched all over Delhi. There were hushed whispers about what was happening in Trilokpuri, but it was obvious the killings were far more widespread. With Leslie I watched in horror as the area outside Azadpur Mandi was littered with charred bodies, almost all of them having been murdered with burning tyres tied around their necks. A lot of corpses were still in a sitting position, their hands and feet bound together. There was not a single policeman in sight, or an ambulance or a fire engine. In some alleys, bodies were piled on top of each other and were being doused with kerosene by small groups of men, so that there would be no evidence of the massacre in a few hours. Watching all this helplessly, one couldn't help but recall stories of what had happened during the Partition riots. Just how systematic the killings were can be gauged from the fact that there were no large mobs going wild, just small groups of about a dozen men who were going about the gruesome business. They seemed to have divided areas amongst themselves and knew exactly what they were doing.

No one was spared. Even army officers, those travelling on trains were chased and butchered on railway tracks. Mostly it was the menfolk who were hunted down and killed. Hundreds of Sikhs had frantically cut their hair and shaved off their beards, but frankly that made no difference for it was easy to make out who had just gone under the razor. For my generation, the Sikh riots of 1984 were undoubtedly India's darkest hour.

The emphasis shifted to the Mrs Gandhi's funeral which was on 3 November. I didn't cover that, for by the end of the previous day was just too exhausted, both physically and emotionally. With the embers of Mrs Gandhi's funeral pyre dying out, the killings also seemed to stop ... perhaps because there were no longer any identifiable targets left. On the afternoon of 4 November, Vicki called me into her office and said I was to fly to Amritsar the next day. 'It's the first flight into the city after Mrs G's assassination. See what kind of reactions you can pick up.'

Samuel gave me my air ticket, and then asked me, 'Did you come to the office on the 31st evening?'

'Heh ... what was that?' I had been waiting for him to sooner or later ask me that question.

Before I could say anything more, Vicki called me back to her room. 'Maybe you can get an interview with one of the head priests of the Golden Temple. That should be interesting.' She handed me a Walkman-type tape recorder and a Sennheiser mike. She then smiled, 'Kunal, you've got to decide if you want to be a correspondent for AP, or a journalist. It's our job to report things. Our emotions have no place in this business.'

I kept a straight face, or at least I thought I did. Come to think of it, both Vicki and Samuel would have known the papers had to be taken by me. Nevertheless ... one thing I had learnt at the Doon School ... never admit anything. Just follow the mantra—Who Sir? Me Sir? Oh No Sir!

IC 433 to Amritsar on 5 November had the strangest manifest. All the passengers were male, and with the exception of Dilip Ganguli and myself, everyone was a Sikh who had that look of a freshly shaven face that went with unevenly cropped hair. Quite a few had injuries on their faces, some had broken arms, but almost all their eyes had a sad, humiliated look. It was almost as if they collectively wanted the earth to open up and swallow them up. No one was talking, each man acutely aware that he was extremely lucky to be alive.

I had met Dilip briefly once before. He was with Agence France-Presse (AFP) and on the flight he was getting hysterical. He was convinced the moment we landed, all the Sikhs on the flight would be on their 'home turf' and would beat him up. He obviously hadn't volunteered to go to Amritsar. He then kept telling me how his elder son was also named Kunal and hence we must stay together.

I had a car waiting that had been fixed by Samuel from Delhi. It was a half hour drive to the Hotel Mohan International. After checking in, I told Dilip I was off to the Golden Temple to meet Sahib Singh, who was the head granthi and would catch up with him at the hotel later. Dilip, however, was determined not to let me out of his sight and insisted on coming along. I tried to shake him off, but he was a determined soul. In the temple complex, we were ushered into Sahib Singh's quarter in the area near the rebuilt Akal Takth, where he graciously received us. He only spoke in Punjabi, which created a problem. Though I had grown up listening to my maternal grandmother speaking to me in Punjabi, I had never as such spoken the language. Nevertheless, I took out the recorder, plugged in the Sennheiser and pressed the 'record' button.

Sahib Singh was a smallish man, wearing a kurta with a cross-belt holding a small *kirpan*. Before I could ask him any question as such, he decided to address the entire 'Sikh *kuam* (community)' through the good offices of AP. He spoke crisply, without any show of emotion, but his words were chilling. In effect, he was telling Sikhs across the globe that reports were coming in of the horrific things that had happened to the Sikh community in Delhi, and it was the sworn duty of every man to avenge what had happened. The statement was about two minutes long, and after he finished, he seemed to lose interest in us.

Dilip had no clue what had been said. At first, I thought I was getting Sahib Singh wrong, but then I knew that I had understood him perfectly well. My glance fell on a black telephone, and I asked the granthi if I could use it. Fortunately, I knew the civil number for the military exchange and luckily the operator at the other end of the line put me through to the GOC 15 Division's residence without any fuss. Hearing a familiar voice at the other end, I said in a hushed tone, 'Winnee Aunty ... this is Kunal Verma. It's an emergency ... can I speak to the general ...'

Major General A. K. 'Chicky' Dewan had been the deputy GOC of the division during Op Blue Star. He had taken over command from General Jamwal when the latter had moved to HQ Delhi Area. I heard Mrs Dewan call out to him ... 'Chicken ... it's Kunal. He says it's an emergency ...' I could hear his footsteps approach and then he was on the line. 'Sir, I won't be able to answer any questions ... I am in the Golden Temple with one of the granthis and this is his telephone. I have just recorded a statement by him asking Sikhs across the globe to avenge the Delhi riots. I am heading back to Mohan International now with another journalist. Sir, please have the police meet us there and forcibly confiscate the tape.' The general just said, 'Copied!' I hung up.

My mouth was dry, and my heart was racing by now. We left Sahib Singh's quarters and made our way out ... I deliberately stalled for time, pointing out key features of the temple complex to Dilip. The tape recorder was in the bag with the camera, and together it felt like they weighed a tonne. We got our shoes, then found our car. It was barely two-and-a-half kilometres from the temple to Mohan International and all I could do was now hope the cops had been scrambled.

Leaning against the reception was Superintendent Sheetal Das, an Indian Police Service officer who used to wear his pistol with the butt pointing outwards. Half-a-dozen armed policemen were standing around and they converged on us as soon as I identified myself to the receptionist and asked for my room keys. Sheetal Das caught me by the nape of my neck and slammed my face into the counter. 'Where is the tape?' he hissed in my ear, then let loose a string of profanities in chaste Punjabi. I could taste the blood in my mouth. He yanked my head back, and with his pistol he hit me again. In all the ruckus, I heard Dilip scream as he too was being worked over by the cops. I opened the bag and took the recorder out. Sheetal Das took it from my hand, ejected the tape and put it in his breast pocket. Then he deliberately smashed the recorder on the floor.[12]

The cops were abruptly gone. Dilip was on his knees, and he was violently throwing up. Luckily for me, though there was blood on my spectacle lenses, they were still intact. The beating and the smashing of

---

[12] Sheetal Das would be in the news a few months later. One of his own informers had turned on him, grabbed his pistol butt, yanked it out of the holster and shot him dead.

the tape recorder had come out of the blue and I wondered how on earth was I going to explain this to Vicki! Someone helped me pick up the pieces and the telephone operator and the reception staff were applying wet towels to our faces. Someone said, 'call a doctor' and we were escorted to my room. It seemed one of the policemen had hit Dilip in the stomach with his rifle butt. Cops in the Punjab had their own set of rules.

I had lost a tooth and Dilip was soon being seen to by a nursing orderly when the phone rang. It was someone from the United News of India office, and he asked to speak to Dilip, for they had a tie-up with AFP. I told him he was being attended to, so the caller said to me in Punjabi, 'Get out of Amritsar and Punjab as soon as you can. It has leaked out that you deliberately informed the army about the tape. Your lives are at stake, so please get out immediately. Even the police will not help you.'

Putting down the phone, I had a tremendous feeling of helplessness. Not only had I got both Dilip and myself into a terrible mess, the drama, it seemed, was just about to begin. I didn't tell Dilip anything, just ordered him to pick up his bag and follow me. Groaning, limping and protesting, he followed me down. His eyes widened when he realized we were checking out, but I was in no position to tell him anything. Getting into the car, I told the driver to head for the Amritsar Cantonment.

We drove into the Flagstaff House just as General Dewan was about to leave for the Wagah border. I told him we had been compromised and that the word was out that I had called him and asked him to have the tapes confiscated. I now had two choices, somehow get to Jalandhar where my family was, or get onto the afternoon flight that linked Srinagar with Delhi via Amritsar. With Dilip in tow, the first option was not too appealing for then I would still have to get to Delhi.

General Dewan then dropped a bombshell. He said he was getting late, and he drove off. Just when it seemed we were doomed, Winnee Aunty aka Mrs Dewan, who was from Goa, came into her own. She first told Dilip to stop snivelling and be a man. Poor Dilip, his brain was still trying to decipher what was happening, but he actually stopped making the funny noises he was emitting. Roma, the general's daughter handed me a mug of tea and then we watched in awe as we were treated to a lesson in 'command and control'. Calls were made, crisp instructions given, which included 'holding the aircraft' till we got to the airport and then we waited. After twenty minutes two open Jongas pulled up, each with eight men in it. They were wearing black patkas and they were all carrying weapons. A captain who was in command jumped out and saluted the GOC's wife.

Winnee Aunty told the captain the ATC had been told to hold the aircraft and that he was to flank our car with the two escort vehicles and make sure we were on the plane. 'Now get moving,' she said, 'and if anyone tries to stop you ... anyone at all ... even if they are cops ... shoot them!' I could have kissed her feet!

We didn't have tickets or boarding cards, and the Jongas escorted us right up to the ladder. Obviously, whosoever Winnee Aunty had called, had cleared all obstacles. There were just two or three passengers on the Boeing 737 which quickly closed its doors and started to taxi out. Only once the aircraft unstuck from the runway and we could see the green fields below shrinking as we gained height did I start breathing again.

I would hand over the smashed recorder and the Sennheiser mike to Vicki the next day with the official version of police brutality, and all else. But from the little twinkle in Vicki's eye, I knew my journalistic days were all but over.

8

Bhopal Gas Tragedy: The Great Escape

Things had continued to happen at a breathtaking pace. With his clean-cut and youthful looks—Rajiv Gandhi was just 40 at the time—the entire country seemed to be behind him, willing him to steady the ship after his mother's tragic demise. The day the official mourning period for Indira Gandhi was over, the new prime minister, who had also assumed the role of the Congress (I) president, announced that his government would seek a fresh mandate in December 1984, almost a year before the general elections were otherwise due. Perceived to be a reluctant politician despite his lineage, people had been extremely impressed by his dignity and poise. Almost everyone believed Rajiv Gandhi was the messiah who would now lead India into a new dawn of good, clean governance.

The elections were to be held between 24 and 28 December. The immediate fires had died down but the wounds left by the Sikh riots were festering across the country. Rajiv Gandhi, instead of trying to distance himself from the violence unleashed by his party, first put his foot in his mouth when on 19 November, while honouring his mother on her birthday, stated in relation to the violence unleashed on the Sikhs, '*Jab koi bada ped girta hai, toh dharti thodi hilti hai*!' (When a big tree falls, the earth shakes!) I remember reading this the next morning and was suddenly acutely aware that the new Indian prime minister was indeed a novice who was completely wet behind the ears. I remember David Devadas, my flatmate saying, 'He's just exonerated all the murderers in one sweep. Now they'll never be brought to book.'

Rajiv Gandhi's next big test wasn't long in coming. On the night of 2/3 December, in a horrific accident, deadly methyl isocyanate gas leaked out from the Union Carbide pesticide plant in Bhopal, killing thousands of people in their sleep who were in the vicinity. Many more would die subsequently, making the Bhopal gas leak one of the biggest industrial accidents on the planet. As the day progressed, the number of casualties kept mounting.

In the afternoon I collected my airline ticket from Samuel who was feeling quite pleased with himself for he had managed to get me a room in a small hotel overlooking the Bhopal Junction Railway Station. As the railway line headed towards the north, it ran along the eastern boundary of the Union Carbide plant, which was the main scene of the disaster. In the evening I called up my father in Jalandhar and asked him if he knew anyone in Bhopal. He said his former deputy commander in 70 Infantry Brigade, Navin Saini, now himself a brigadier, was posted in the city. He said, 'Be careful, you have no experience of something like this, so don't just wander around unless the area is declared safe.'

In the morning I checked in for the flight which to my dismay turned out to be a hopper. It would first land in Gwalior and then proceed to Bhopal. Hardly had I gotten past security, I heard someone call my name. Seeing Dilip Ganguli bounding in my direction, my heart sank, for I was quite sure by now he would have put two and two together and I was in no mood for a scrap, that too in the departure hall of the airport. But Dilip showed no signs of rancour—on the contrary, he seemed delighted to see me. 'Kunal ...' he said, slapping me on the back, 'Man, we killed it. My story on police brutality in Punjab topped the charts in France.' Instead of lowering his voice because he was by then virtually right in my face, he continued, 'When we get back to Delhi, you have to come home. I've told everyone how you saved my life.'

Dilip was riding a high, obviously. It seemed ever since he filed his version, he had been catapulted to instant stardom. He even joked how over the last fortnight he had not had to pay for drinks at the Press Club.

On the plane he booted out the passenger next to me, exchanging seats so we could go over the details of the Amritsar incident. Before we took off, since we were landing at Gwalior, I asked the captain if he could relay a message to the Gwalior ATC to inform the air officer commanding (AOC) the base that I was on the aircraft. Then, as the aircraft doors were shut and we got airborne, to divert Dilip's attention from 'our heroic deeds' in Amritsar, I began to tell him about the last time I had flown on this particular sector. I told him how from Bhopal I had gone to Jabalpur, then Mandla, and how I had been in Kanha just a few months earlier for the IUCN Cat Conference. Soon he was hooked, and I spent the next half hour talking of dholes, or the Indian red dogs that hunted in packs and could even kill a tiger.

'Kill a tiger!' repeated Dilip, his eyes getting wider and wider.

'Yeah ... you know a tiger has only a ten, maybe twenty percent chance of success when he stalks his prey. Dholes ... Ha ... that is a different story. The victim is doomed the moment the pack zeroes in on it. They sometimes start disembowelling and eating the animal even while it is still running ...'

'Still running ...' short of taking notes, Dilip was lapping it up. 'Son of a bitch! You're kidding me!' The first part of his sentence was true, the second false. They were indeed deadly killers, and the moment dholes came into a certain patch of forest, even the birds seemed to go quiet.

At Gwalior we landed, and the crew asked me to come down to the tarmac. Air Commodore (later Air Marshal) Denzil Keelor had driven across from the IAF side where the two Mirage 2000 squadrons were located. Till a year ago, we had been immediate neighbours in Raksha Bhavan. I told him I was on my way to Bhopal.

'I guessed,' said Denzil. 'Now you be careful. Reports are coming in that there are hundreds dead. Just remember to wet a cloth and tie it across your face when you get into the affected area. Just remember that ... and don't be a hero. If the area is sealed off, stay clear.' This little bit of advice was to literally save my life.

Another short flight and we touched down in Bhopal. I had a car arranged by Samuel and Dilip asked me if he could bum a ride till the UNI office. I was a bit surprised for I thought like me Dilip too would want to see the affected area and talk to the survivors. Anyway, after dropping him I went to the hotel where I found a message from Brigadier Saini, saying he would meet me in the next half hour. In those days, we did not have water bottles, so I went to the room, and after asking for a sheet, tore it into strips. These I soaked in water, and then came back to the reception just as the brigadier's Jonga pulled up. 'Your father called me,' he said. 'I am going to the area that has had the maximum number of casualties ... I thought we can go together, and I can request you to take a few photographs for me as well.'

Saini said he had been there the day before and had taken out over three hundred dead or dying people. With my car following, we drove to the Nishatpura D Cabin, and then decided to walk from there along the Union Carbide factory wall. I gave one cloth to the brigadier and tied the other around my face, covering my nose and mouth.

As we approached, the terrain ahead looked like it was covered with about two or three inches of snow. Even the couple of trees and shrubs were covered by the white powder. There was a dead crow and a dog, both also partially covered. The brigadier was looking puzzled. 'This white stuff wasn't there yesterday,' he said. He had not tied the cloth around his face, but was holding it in his hand, having folded it like a handkerchief.

Our boots were now leaving a trail, almost as if we were walking through a snow field. We came to a few houses ... more like a shanty town at the edge of the railway track. Strangely, this area did not have the white covering. House after house, room after room was deserted, and there was not even a fly buzzing around the place. There was an eerie silence. I took a few photographs and kept moving further, hoping to find someone there. After a while, drawing a complete blank, I started back, but could see no sign of the brigadier. Again, I waded through the white powdery patch and reached my car. The army Jonga had left, and the driver of my car told me shortly after we had gone in, the brigadier had returned and was throwing up violently. His driver had quickly got him into the car and rushed him off. Having no idea of where I was, the driver had just sat and waited for me. According to him, I had been there for close to two hours.[13]

After checking out a couple of overflowing hospitals and a cremation ground where bodies were being brought in thick and fast, I returned to the hotel. That was the day Raghu Rai had taken one of the most haunting images of the tragedy, where the half-buried face of a young girl was visible just before she was fully covered. The sheer magnitude of what had happened had as yet not fully dawned on most of the country. That one photograph taken by Raghu, a reflection of the man's genius with the camera, would subsequently make it to the cover of *India Today*. Just as the image of Kim Phuc Phan Thi, also known as the Napalm Girl, had become the defining image of the Vietnam War, the unknown little girl with her eyes wide open in eternal sleep, would define the Bhopal gas tragedy forever.

That night I couldn't sleep, so I just sat in the balcony, stared at the railway tracks glistening in the reflected light of the station and smoked cigarette after cigarette. In the morning, I went back to the same area, parking near the Nishatpura railway cabin and walking from there. There were, however, maybe half-a-dozen cars parked in the area. The patch of the white powdery stuff had vanished, probably blown away by the wind.

I saw Sondeep Shankar, another outstanding photographer who would later work for AP as well, and waved to him, after which I once again walked along the deserted row of huts, or houses. Unlike the previous day, there were quite a few foreigners hanging around, almost all carrying a battery of cameras. I recalled Dilip had mentioned a chartered flight with journalists was on its way from France, and I presumed most of them were from that group.

Finally, in one of the huts I found a middle-aged woman. She had returned to her hut but was just sitting there at the door, surrounded by what had been her home, but now completely bereft of any family. There was something so tragic about the one lonely woman, I couldn't even get

[13] Brigadier Saini, who had been in the thick of things even on the previous day, was later declared to be an affected person. After a few months, despite all efforts to save him by army doctors, he, like thousands of others who survived the first few days, would become yet another statistic in the casualty list.

myself to lift the camera and take a shot. It just felt like I would be violating her privacy. By then Sondeep had also drifted into my line of vision, and I could see that even with a camera in his hand, he too was not wanting to intrude on the lone woman's grief.

We started to move away when there was a sharp sound—almost a yelp. One of the European photographers had come upon the lady. What he was trying to do God alone knows, but he was taking some close-ups, towering over the woman with his camera right in her face. His auto-winder and shutter were making quite a racket, and it seemed to me he had actually pushed or hit the woman to evoke a response. Having taken his shots, he had reached into his pocket and was trying to thrust some dollars at the bewildered lady, whose face was now streaked with tears.

I think I hit him with all the force I could muster, sending him sprawling in the dirt. He obviously seemed to have no idea I was there, for even though he was a big fellow, he quickly grabbed his camera and took off at top speed. The woman, had gotten up and fled inside her home, locking the door behind her. There was nothing I could do there, so I walked back to the car and decided to again see what was happening at the hospitals. There too, quite a few foreigners were moving around. I spoke to one of them. He said he was a lawyer who had come in on a chartered flight. He said he was unable to communicate with the survivors and could I help. If he could get a client, then they could sue for millions of dollars. My hand was hurting from having belted the photographer. Now I just felt a wave of nausea, just looking at this eager beaver wanting to make quick bucks.

It had been a terrible morning, where amidst all the tragedy, the cynicism of the human race had hit me squarely in the face. I got back to my hotel near the Bhopal junction and told the driver to get something to eat, after which he should return for me in an hour or so. The man at the reception, however, on seeing us had come out and he said there was an urgent telegram for me. I told the driver to wait and ripped open the pink envelope. I could hardly believe my eyes at what was printed in strips on the telegram form.

'To APC Bhopal from chief of bureau Delhi STOP Reuters, AFP others carrying stories of wild dogs from Kanha eating dead bodies STOP Check and confirm STOP Vicki STOP.'

'What the ...' I jumped back into the car and told the driver to head for the UNI office where we had dropped Dilip the previous day.

Not surprisingly, Dilip was hunched over one of the machines, hammering away at the keys, no doubt describing the gory scenes he had not witnessed since his arrival. There were two or three other people on the other machines, and they too were equally busy filing their respective despatches. I went and stood behind Dilip and held the telegram in front of his eyes. The paper was probably too close to him to focus on and he tried to push it away with his right hand. I grabbed the hand and twisted it behind his back. 'Ow,' he said, 'you are hurting me!'

'I'll do a lot more than that,' I growled in his ear, 'read the blasted telegram. Where did this come from?'

The others had by then realized something serious had happened and they had stopped typing and were looking at us. To make sure he read it properly, I twisted his arm further and said, 'Read the telegram aloud!' He did. He faltered when he came to the word Kanha so I twisted his arm even more. He cried out in pain again. He feebly said others including Reuters had also carried the same story.

'Now you interrupt your despatch and type what I say ... type that you are a goddam liar and that Kanha is twelve hours by road and more than 450 kilometres from Bhopal.'

Dilip was in tears by then, and he said if he did that his career was over. He said I was his friend and he never thought other agencies would follow his lead. He was of course extremely sorry but pleaded against being made to write what amounted to a written confession. By now the others had all crowded around and I let go his arm. Someone suggested a correction could be put out saying it had been erroneously reported that the dogs had come from Kanha and were in fact the street dogs of Bhopal who were eating unclaimed bodies. This itself was a lie, for most of the dogs in the area were dead too. I had by then made my point, and since others were now excitedly looking for a way out, I just turned around and left. The stray dog fallacy was shortly put out, though even years later when the subject of the Bhopal gas tragedy came up, someone or the other would always bring the stray dogs into the narrative.[14]

On 6 December, after filing my daily report with Samuel over the phone, I had just settled in for the night when Vicki called and said that in all probability, Warren Anderson, the chief executive officer of Union Carbide would be landing in Bhopal the next morning. Sure enough, the white-coloured King Air 200C (VT-EID) that belonged to the chief minister, Arjun Singh, landed at Bhopal in the morning and a few passengers, including some foreigners, got off the plane. Vicki had said Anderson was easily identifiable because of his height. Four white Ambassador cars then headed out of the airport and headed for the Union Carbide guest house. Other than my car which was chasing them, surprisingly, there were no other journalists on the scene.

Vicki was herself reporting on Anderson's visit from Delhi and she had asked me to just track his movements, and if I got a chance, get a quote from him if he did happen to visit the accident site. From the American point of view, there was obviously a lot of interest around Anderson who had shown considerable courage by first coming to India, and then proceed to Bhopal with the stated objective of visiting the plant and seeing for himself where the leak had occurred. There was absolutely no security at the guest house, and after giving Anderson 15–20 minutes, I walked in. An IPS officer, Superintendent of Police, Swaraj Puri, asked me who I was and then apologetically he said Warren Anderson could not be spoken to as he had just been placed under house arrest. The orders, he said, had come from the CBI headquarters in Delhi and had taken the state government completely by surprise. After talking to the police officer for another few minutes, I got into my car and dashed back to my hotel.

By the time I got through to Vicki, she already knew Anderson had been placed under house arrest. She then said the US Embassy was

---

[14] Dilip Ganguli would move from AFP and join AP in 1986, shortly after I left journalism altogether to shoot the Project Tiger TV series for Sanctuary Films. He made quite a name for himself during the Iraq War. I met him only once after the arm-twisting incident at the UNI office, and that too many years later. We had shared a quiet smoke together and did not talk about Bhopal. He died prematurely at the age of 57 in 2007.

talking to people at the highest levels in the Government of India and there was a good chance Anderson may be flown out of Bhopal in the same aircraft that had brought him there. She told me to hightail it back to the guest house and if they moved Anderson, just follow him.

While driving back, we crossed Arjun Singh in his car, his familiar face easily identifiable, with just the two escort vehicles. Last few days, I had not seen the Madhya Pradesh chief minister even once but now he seemed to be buzzing around ever since Anderson landed. We had probably been away for 30 minutes, and all the four cars were parked exactly as they had been. Swaraj Puri was still standing near the reception, looking extremely bored. 'Are they flying him back to Delhi?' I asked.

'Who, Anderson?' He seemed genuinely surprised at my suggestion.

'Where is he?'

'In his suite ... he's been on the phone ever since we got here, and he was told he was under arrest.'

After a while some more officials arrived and there were a lot of mini conferences going on, everyone talking in hushed voices. By then two more local journalists had also arrived, and they were standing to one side, looking quite uncertain, for no one seemed to know what was going on. Suddenly the door opened, and Anderson walked out, flanked by Puri and a few others. They promptly got into the four cars that had brought them from the airport and the convoy shot out of the gate, with my car in hot pursuit. Not too surprisingly they headed back towards the airfield. We stopped near the perimeter and watched as the cars came to a halt near the chief minister's King Air. Without any further ado, Anderson and his entourage went up the foldable steps and a few minutes later the aircraft had roared off the runway.

I immediately started for the hotel so as to immediately update Vicki. Standing about 200 metres from where we had been parked, was the chief minister's car. Arjun Singh had also made sure he saw the aircraft depart with his own eyes. 'Wow,' I remember thinking, 'someone pretty high up has him jumping like a trapeze artist.' I scribbled that line down, thinking I'd use it in my despatch to Vicki.

Standard trunk dialling was not working, so I got Vicki on a 'lightning call' ... I think the tariff was ₹183 a minute or something exorbitant like that ... and told her the plane had taken off and the chief minister had watched it go. She chuckled at my 'trapeze artist' bit and said unless I wanted to stay on, I could now return to Delhi the next day.

A week or ten days after my return, Vicki invited me to her place in Jor Bagh. She was pleased at the traction her own coverage of Anderson's trip had got in the Western press, and she told me what had happened before and after Anderson's short sojourn in Bhopal. She had met Anderson in person and said he was determined to take the rap as he felt he was morally responsible for the disaster. The US Embassy, she said, had told him repeatedly that he would be lynched by angry mobs, or worse, be arrested and then 'rot in a rat-infested jail'. She had thought that the plane that took Anderson to Bhopal had been leased by Union Carbide, but when I had told her the chief minister's aircraft was ferrying Anderson and the other officials, she said it was obvious the Indian prime minister was involved.

'We'll never know for sure what transpired behind closed doors, but the US sure brought a lot of pressure on Gandhi. The order (to release Anderson) had to come from him. Though I'm glad Anderson got away, I think India missed a trick.' After reaching Delhi, Anderson was allowed to leave the country after paying a surety of ₹25,000 and signing a bond that he would return if ever he received a summons. 'Gandhi sure has shot himself in the foot,' mused Vicki. 'Now the Bhopal case will drag on and on. He just let the big fish go!' In my diary where I had recorded the details, I had put an asterisk and written: 'He's (Rajiv) an idiot!!!' I am not sure if that was what Vicki had said or if it was my opinion at that time.[15]

Gandhi's popularity was then at its zenith. Twice I got to accompany him to the Punjab, and both times we flew in a fleet of four Mi-8 helicopters,

[15] As per our estimates and subsequent government data, the immediate death toll was approximately 2,259, but quite frankly it was impossible to tell.

all of them sporting the blue and grey markings of the IAF's VIP Communication Squadron. The first time around, as the AP correspondent, I reported in the morning at Safdarjung Airfield and was amazed to see commandos in black dungarees all over the place. Gandhi then arrived with a large entourage, that included Arun Nehru, his large-sized cousin who was initially the minister of state for energy and was then shifted to the home ministry where he was in charge of internal security. Nehru was rumoured to have been one of the key people behind the orchestration of the Sikh killings, and his entire body language was that of a man completely in control of the situation.

Walking a few steps behind was Arun Singh, the other key adviser of Gandhi. Hailing from the Kapurthala family, he was not only the prime minister's contemporary from the Doon School but had also been with him in Cambridge. Appointed as the minister of state for defence, Arun Singh occupied the adjacent bungalow which then made up the entire 7 Race Course Road (now Lok Kalyan Marg) complex. All political bigwigs accompanying Gandhi were mirroring their leader's white kurta–pyjama outfit, while the accompanying bureaucrats were in safari suits. The security personnel were in black dungarees, and I realized to my discomfiture, there were only three journalists present and we were the most casually turned out. At one level that was fine—people always expected members of the media to be indifferent to what they were wearing.

Everyone was assigned to their respective helicopters, and we took off amidst a lot of noise. While we were being manifested, I had lost track of the prime minister and had no idea which of the three choppers ahead of us was carrying him. The only information I had managed to garner was that we were headed for Jandiala, where Gandhi was to address an election rally. This was to be the first of four stops, after which we were to return to Delhi. After being airborne for 30-minutes, suddenly the helicopter seemed to be landing. I looked out of the window and could see the others had touched down already. We were then quickly reshuffled and now I found myself flying in the second helicopter. Seated next to me was Arun Nehru. I asked one of the commandos just what exactly had happened. 'Security,' he said. From his body language, it was obvious I had already asked one too many questions.

We landed at Jandiala, situated not far from Phillaur and Jalandhar. From the ground it must have been an impressive sight as the four Mi-8 helicopters landed in a swirl of dust and like a rockstar Gandhi emerged to address the sea of turbaned faces. The organizers had made an elevated platform which had steps leading up to it from behind. Three sides were protected by bulletproof glass while the top had just a canvas covering. Standing inside the platform, the prime minister addressed the gathering, speaking in his own brand of Hindi. The three journalists who were part of the entourage, were then allowed to join the prime minister inside the bulletproof platform and take a few photographs. In the confined space, there was obviously no room to manoeuvre, and after taking half-a-dozen shots, I came down, already bored at the prospect of having to repeat this charade at another three locations. I also couldn't help wonder what the others like Arun Nehru and Arun Singh were doing there. No one seemed to have anything to do but just hang around near the elevated platforms. It appeared as if everyone had come on a day-long jamboree.

On the return leg, I found myself in the same Mi-8 with Gandhi, seated next to him. He seemed to be dozing. I had not been particularly impressed with the three-sided bulletproof platform and to pass the time had been doodling on a paper napkin, sketching out what I thought were the obvious flaws. 'What's that?' Gandhi was leaning across from his seat and looking at the sketch, which by then was an elaborate blueprint for his assassination. 'Do you mind if I look?'

'Not at all sir ...' I hesitated for a second, then interpreted the doodles on the napkin for him. 'This is the platform ... three sides are protected ... back is open, so is the top.'

'So?' Gandhi was leaning even closer, obviously I had his full interest.

'Anyone with a press pass can have a remote control fitted inside his camera lens. An accomplice launches an aircraft model loaded with explosives from the fringes of the rally, and for good effect he can even trail a banner saying "Vote Congress (I)". Once you're in the box speaking, you're a static target and the aircraft model zeroes in. Since the top is open and not protected ... bang! You are history, sir!'

'Indeed! Can I keep this?' I nodded, and Gandhi folded the napkin and put it in his pocket. We landed at Safdarjung shortly and that was the end of that, or so I thought. From my perspective, it had been a complete waste of a day. The one chance I had of doing a brief interview with the prime minister, I had thrown away, choosing instead to get into a theoretical assassination scenario. I was feeling like a complete idiot!

Next day I got a call from Samuel. 'I don't know why, but someone wants you on the Punjab circuit again tomorrow. This time you've been asked for by name.' I said I wasn't keen to go, but Samuel said there was no choice. He said AP had suggested someone else to go cover the rallies which was to be held in and around Batala, but it had been turned down.

We took off on schedule in the morning and once again we had quite an assorted crowd of bigwigs. Once again after our land and change tactics, we reached Punjab and Gandhi scooted up into the elevated bullet proof platform. When my turn came to go up and take the photographs, the prime minister was holding forth on some farming issues. However, he had a half smile on his face and with his eyes he indicated that I needed to look up. Sure enough, the roof had been sealed off, presumably by bullet proof glass. I couldn't help but think of the amount of people who would have been scrambled to get the additional roofing put in place at such short notice. I couldn't help but think that the words Gandhi was mouthing off had actually been written by someone else, and at that moment, the entire set up seemed to be a massive tamasha where everyone was going along for the ride. That evening back in Delhi, I wearily recorded in my diary, 'Gizmos and toys! That's what governance is to Mr Gandhi and his pals!'

After the two quick trips to Punjab in the lead up to the elections, on the eve of the polling, I was handed an air ticket to Patna and told by Samuel to 'go get briefed by Vicki.' With the elections coming, all chief of bureaus, regardless of who they worked for, always seemed to completely loose the plot. Maybe it's just the massive scale of the elections in India that are too much for any one person to handle. Looking extremely harried, Vicki told me to get some photos of 'booth capturing'. The manner in which she said it, I was supposed to know what booth capturing was, and second, it was as simple as buying bananas in Bihar. Anyway, not wanting to look like an ignoramus in Vicki's eyes, I collected enough film and sauntered off.

Though the term 'booth capturing' is self-explanatory, just what or how on earth was I to photograph it? There was no point fretting over it, so I dozed off on the flight and after checking in at my hotel, I called up Farzand Ahmed, *India Today's* long-standing Patna correspondent. Farzi landed up soon enough, and when I asked him in a roundabout sort of way, how do I photograph 'booth capturing', he gave me a strange look. By the time Farzi called it a day, I was still not any wiser!

Unable to sleep, through the night I had vivid thoughts. Gangsters in jeeps roaring up to polling booths, firing in the air, chasing away and shooting people. At some point I even imagined the goon brigade charging in on horses. The voting for India's 8th Lok Sabha started in the morning, and I plonked on in a suitable spot where I would neither get run over by jeeps or trampled by horses. There were some ten people in the line, three of them with beards. They were all men, so I figured the women would be coming along later in the day. Half asleep because of my overactive mind, I soon started to doze off. I must have been asleep for a good half hour, for when I woke up, things were much the same. 'No women,' I thought, 'that's strange.' Since we had still not been attacked, I started to drift off again ... in the distance was the polling officer's monotonous voice every 20 seconds or so ... 'Shrimati Sheila Devi'.

In school we used to call dimwits 'tube lights' for it always took them a while to figure out 'stuff'! Well, I was suddenly wide awake as it dawned on me the booth was not only captured, it had been the case ever since I had arrived. The same ten people were standing in line and the same people would cast the vote repeatedly as the polling officers ticked various names off. The irony of the situation was that the polling booth staff were following the laid down protocols to the last letter. As the farcical exercise continued, one character was being called '10 per cent'. It seemed he was casting votes for the other candidates at random, for a 100 per cent vote count would bring the matter to the notice of the election commission. The entire lot were least concerned when I started taking photographs, instead they were joking for my having been around (even if I was dozing) for a couple of hours, I was one of them. It was much the same story in all the polling stations that I visited. In the evening, after Farzi had filed his story and I had sent in my despatch, he put everything in perspective, 'It's just a matter of which candidate can capture more booths.'

9

Wildlife on One: Man-eaters and Intrigue

Back in Delhi after the events in Bhopal and Patna, I had to blank out the last few days and focus on the wildlife workshop that had to be conducted for the army. My father had left almost the entire planning to me, and with the COAS himself taking interest in the proceedings that was a huge responsibility. K. L. Saini was the field director of the Sariska Tiger Reserve, and together we did a quick reconnaissance trip which was an eye-opener. Getting off the main road on which most tourist traffic existed, Saini took me into some of the most beautiful and spectacular country I had ever seen. With H. S. Panwar and other wildlife top brass offering advice, I felt we had a pretty good plan worked out.

About twenty officers had been detailed by various formations in Western Command to attend the 'Wildlife Preservation Camp' and officers were told to drive down in their open jeeps and caravans that were parked in the vast grounds of the Sariska Palace that was to be our week-long camp. In the evening there was a campfire, and as by then almost everyone had reported in, each officer was asked by my father to introduce himself and also articulate what he thought was the reason why he had been sent to Sariska. It was pretty obvious no one had any clue, and it fell on the lot of a bullet-headed captain sitting in one corner to take the lead. After giving his name, rank and number, the hapless prisoner of circumstance then lost it completely. 'I'm a vegetarian,' he said ruefully, 'I don't know why my CO sent me here. I suppose he wants me to learn how to pickle wild boar, nilgai and partridge for mess parties.' Poor bullet-head, he just could not understand why everyone burst out laughing.

Joining me in running the camp was Ramu Gaur's nephew, Sharad, who was then with the WWF. We would screen the various wildlife movies I had managed to collect from various embassies every evening, and then senior officers from various wildlife habitats would talk about their regions, and the environment-related problems they faced. Crack of dawn would see the multiple jeep engines come to life, and with Saini's foresters as guides, they would be out for most of the day. Lunch, I insisted the officers ate with the guards at their posts, and the staple fare of bajra rotis with just salt and an onion, had more discussion around it than the fate of the tiger.

On the last evening, General Krishnaswamy Sundarji accompanied by Brigadier Baljeet, arrived at the camp and I think he was quite taken aback to see just how in a week, those who thought nothing of shooting down 'game' for the mess, were willing to lay down their lives to protect any moving creature. There was a Major Mehta who had a Kodak Hot Shot Polaroid camera and just his luck, he had run into this majestic tiger earlier that morning. The fixed wide angle inbuilt in the camera, ensured that in the photograph the tiger looked like planet earth when looked at from the Milky Way or some far off galaxy. Insisting on showing everyone the tiger individually, the conversations went something like this. 'There!' 'Where?' 'There there ...' 'Ah, I see ...' but of course, no one did see, but then they were all officers and gentlemen!

General Sundarji had brought some Black Label whisky which soon had everyone making all kinds of suggestions for reversing the fate of the tiger and other wildlife to the future army chief. After a while it transpired that he too was from MCC and after that I could do no wrong in his eyes. We passed a resolution that evening, that would have a far-reaching impact; the greening of the Mussoorie Hills by the ecological Territorial Army (TA) battalions that had been created a couple of years ago. 'You write me a report with the help of all your wildlife friends, and I'll make sure those things happen. Think utopian!' Since almost everyone at the camp had links with the Doon Valley, there was unprecedented passion on display to 'take on the limestone quarries' that had ravaged the entire area. The work done by the TA's task force during that period has today converted an area that was scarred and bleak into a verdant forest.

Towards the end of February 1985, Hindu–Muslim riots had gripped the old city of Ahmedabad. As the violence escalated and people started killing each other, the army was called in. 11 Infantry Division was then being commanded by Major General Afsir Karim, who had just taken over the division a few months before. The old city was divided into Hindu and Muslim *pols* which were not only cheek-by-jowl, they were all interconnected over the rooftops which made it very difficult to pin down the perpetuators of the violence. When it came to Punjab and Kashmir, Vicki would have her tail up, but she was surprisingly lackadaisical in her response when I suggested I head off to Ahmedabad and see if I could spend some time with the troops operating there. Had I suggested a day trip, she would have probably acquiesced, but somehow unless it was a wildlife story, she was always a bit reluctant to give the go-ahead if it meant spending four to five days.

That evening I met T. V. R. Shenoy, who was then the Delhi chief of bureau for Malayala Manorama's *The Week*, which was then perhaps the only weekly newsmagazine of substance (*India Today* was a fortnightly). Shenoy promptly asked me to do the story, saying he would even consider running it as the cover.

At the divisional headquarters, Afsir Karim was candid in his briefing. In the built-up *pols*, he said it was extremely hard for the troops to know where the fire was coming from and both sides were being ruthless, even targeting infants and little children who were soft targets despite the curfew. Fortunately, there were not too many firearms in the *pols*, but stabbings and bludgeoning people to death with boulders was the other preferred hit and run methods being adopted. I was to attach myself with Bravo Company of 14 Bihar, which was being commanded by

Captain (later Major General) Ashok Mukherjee. The battalion mainly consisted of Adivasis, and during the next three days that I was with them, I had developed an extremely healthy respect for them.

There were various acts of terrible violence that would turn anyone's stomach, but it is not my intention to describe those events. The problem was, when the evening count of casualties would be totalled, for any casualties that had occurred due to army firing, it was imperative that there would be an equal balance between 'Hotels' and 'Mikes'. This, I was told, was even more imperative, because the GOC himself was a 'Mike', so there should be no charges of 'favouritism'. It was bizarre, but when I looked at the casualty figures in the past few days, somehow that balance seemed to have been maintained. 'How do you do that?' I asked Mukherjee, as we sat in an open jeep, watching a potentially dangerous corner. He just grinned, and said that the army knew where all the goondas were.

The next day a staff officer from the divisional headquarters along with the CO of 14 Bihar came by. We even had camping with us on the first floor, a magistrate who as per protocol had to sign an order authorising the army to open fire whenever the need arose. Almost jokingly I said to the staff officer, why bother with the goondas, just make a list of the near and dear ones of the leading political big shots on either side and tell them that to maintain the scales of justice, these would be the names that would make it to the list. I left a couple of days later and true to his word, T. V. R. Shenoy gave me the cover (which was a photograph of Ashok Mukherjee sitting in his jeep). Years later, after Afsir Karim had post-retirement emerged as a strong voice in intellectual circles, I met him and he told me, my 'suggestion' had been taken. He added with a wry smile, '*Shukar hai Allah ka, samajdaro ko ishaara kafi hota hai*' (Thank God, sometimes even a hint is good enough). The day after the army called the two warring leaders and gave them the 'hint' that their kin would be picked up, it seems the killing in their area of responsibility (AOR) literally stopped overnight.

Teesta by then had got engaged to Micky Yadav and the wedding was to be held at a club that was administratively under HQ Delhi Area. My father called me and told me to go and meet the GOC, and though he had spoken to Jagdish Jamwal, I was to pay him a courtesy call and make sure everything was in order. I had not met or spoken to the general ever since our meeting in the dead of the night after Indira Gandhi's assassination and by then the Trilokpuri massacre had become infamous. My father was aware of the sequence of events because I had told him, and before I could say anything, he said, 'You be careful. Jamwal has been telling people you are too big for your boots. If he says anything provocative, just keep quiet. Remember, a trout only gets caught when it opens its mouth.'

The general was grace personified when I met him: '*Teesta toh hamari hi beti hai* (Teesta is also my daughter!) Nothing to worry about, I have already told Ashok.' He beamed from behind his desk and his moustaches. After a cup of tea, I rose to leave, but that's when the general fired his shot. 'You know Kunal,' he said conversationally, 'that night you had lost your head, and you wanted me to lose mine too. Luckily, I stayed calm.' I stared at him, wanting to actually catch him by his shirt and scream at him that had 'he lost his head' many people may have survived. Instead, I lowered my gaze, and mumbled something, said goodbye and fled. When I got to my scooter, I just sat there for a while, wondering what was the compulsion on General Jamwal's part to say what he did. To my surprise, I found my hands were trembling.

Not surprisingly, it was again Panwar Saab who drew my attention to the 'Widow's Village' stories that were making headlines in the Bengali newspapers. This time, Vicki had no hesitation in giving her approval, so I landed in Calcutta shortly after Teesta's wedding was done and dusted. I was glad to get away from Delhi, and quite looking forward to the visit to the Sundarbans, where, if the vernacular press was to be believed, tigers were killing a human every ten minutes. Since I had vague directions on how to get to the Sundarban Tiger Reserve, with my red North Face rucksack that also housed my camera gear, I walked across to the West Bengal tourism counter at the airport arrival hall and politely asked the 30-plus, slightly balding gentleman how and where to proceed.

The 'School of Politeness', from where the gentleman had got his diploma that qualified him to be behind the counter, was in full display as he flashed all thirty-two teeth at me, since I seemed to be the only person heading towards his booth. 'Sundarbans!' he exclaimed in a half-gasp, half-scream. 'Why you want to go there! Royal Bengal will eat you!' He was obviously an avid reader of all the vernacular papers. I was also to learn, very quickly, that the word 'tiger' to describe the striped feline was rarely, if ever, used by self-respecting *bhadralok*, the term 'Royal Bengal' having a more appropriate ring to it. For added effect, he added, 'You are too young to die!' Then, his professionalism coming to the fore, he pushed some pamphlets at me, 'There are many beautiful places in West Bengal ...'

I finally got it out of him that I needed to get to the Sealdah Railway Station, and then I was in this local train heading for Port Canning, crammed in between a sweaty mass of humanity. It was hot, and where in the compartments once there were gadgets to help cool you down, were the stencilled words 'Fan Stollen'. Considering there wasn't a single fan in the entire bogey and probably the train, there must have been quite a market for them outside. I found myself wondering how long a new bogey would last before the man with the stencil and the paintbrush came along.

Ninety minutes later, staggering off the train, I walked down to the Project Tiger office. By then it was nearing midday and I was beginning to understand why the British, when they lorded over India, were so obsessed with their *solar topee*! There was no one at the office other than a sleepy clerk, who told me I was indeed expected. I was to walk along the river (what river?) and go on board the launch that was at Jetty No. 32 and I was to wait there till the crew arrived which would be as soon as the high tide started coming in. I walked along the bund, a glistening mass of mud that the clerk had mistakenly called a river, and found the 10-tonne launch. Tilted at an awkward angle, lying almost on its side in the silt, there was a plank I had to traverse to get on board. There was not a soul around, so I went into the boat, found a bunk and immediately fell asleep.

My bunk was at the water level, and when I woke up the launch was chugging along the Matla River, and with the tide having come in, everything around me looked and felt like a regular river. The boat would be 'home' for the next four days and nothing had quite prepared me for what was to happen during this period. There was the Project Tiger research officer—it was *his* boat actually—and he spent the afternoon giving me a brief on the problems being faced by everyone, be it honey collectors, fishermen or just forest staff. 'It's not just the Royal Bengals that kill people,' he said, 'we also have the saltwater crocodiles, sharks and a huge variety of poisonous snakes.' I would be meeting Pranabes Sanyal, the field director of the Sundarbans Tiger Reserve the next day. To dissuade the tigers from going after humans, he had put into place various innovative schemes. Even the forest guards did not get off the boat without first wearing a spiked breastplate, some sort of neck protection and a helmet, plus of course they were armed with rifles or shotguns.

Some Royal Bengals had 'jumped over' (another Bengali euphemism) more than 250, or in one case, 370 plus people! Tragically, in the morning itself, I would get to see for myself just how difficult the situation really was. As our launch came around a bend in the channel that connected the Bidyadhari and the Matla rivers, the boat crew seemed to go hysterical and suddenly two or three guards quickly started putting on their breastplates and other protective gear. The sundari trees are more like elongated shrubs, but the vegetation is fairly thick and from within, one could hear a lot of screams. The Project Tiger launch revved up its engine and literally ran itself aground into the wet mud, where a fishing boat was also moored. The guards were off the boat with the research officer and immediately there were gunshots, with a lot of snarling juxtaposed with shouts. A male tiger had grabbed one of the fishermen when they had stepped ashore and was trying to drag him off. I was told later that all six fishermen were brothers, and showing tremendous courage, they had refused to let go. It was purely by chance that we had stumbled upon this gruesome and desperate scene.

Though I wasn't sure what was happening, I had also jumped off the launch and promptly sank into the wet mud, unable to extricate myself. Stuck in that position, I could see very little but after four to five shots were fired, the tiger had retreated. The wounded man was brought onto our launch, but the canine marks were near his jugular and blood was coming out in spurts, which suggested the artery had been severed. As we tried to race back up the channel towards Gosaba, the man gurgled and the research officer who was trying to stem the blood, closed his eyes.

Later, after we handed over the body to the police and the crew had washed the deck to get rid of the residual blood, the research officer dutifully recorded in his register, 'Royal Bengal jumped over Mr Mondal' whose details were then entered in minute detail for compensation.

What was striking was the abject poverty. We were still in the periphery of the Sundarbans Tiger Reserve whose boundary officially only started from Sajnekhali where an elevated rest house had been built, heavily barricaded to keep any adventurous Royal Bengal out. The villages on either side of the water channels were teeming with naked sunburnt children, and the women were so poor they did not even have blouses to cover their breasts. To make a living, the fishermen would head out in low open boats, hoping to catch giant prawns and crabs that thrived in these waters. Others who ventured into the area were honey collectors, who went after the hives of rock bees. Unable to protect themselves from the marauding tigers, the casualties were naturally extremely high.

Back in Delhi, the man-eating tigers of Sundarbans, when put out as despatches on the AP network, hardly created a ripple. I was a little taken aback, and disappointed. The Grewal family by then had packed up from New Delhi and shifted to Bombay. I talked to Royina on the phone about the lack of response to the Sundarbans story, but then *Sanctuary Asia* was also not quite the platform. *The Week*, she suggested, continued to be my best bet. If another opportunity came up, I should speak to Vicki and Shenoy, she added. In the meantime, there were some reports coming in that Hazaribagh District in Bihar had been plagued by an outbreak of man-eating wolves. This had been going on for a couple of years and as per reports, more than seventy children had been killed and eaten. I asked Vicki if I could file despatches for AP and simultaneously do the feature story for *The Week*. With T. V. R. Shenoy also in agreement, I wondered why I hadn't handled the earlier Sundarban assignment in the same way.

I landed in Ranchi and as I stepped out of the airport terminal, two men in cowboy hats fell in beside me, took my rucksack and asked me to get into their car. I had absolutely no idea as to what was happening, and it seemed neither did I have a choice. Strangely, the two men and the driver did not seem like thugs, but they were not particularly communicative either. After a fairly long drive, we pulled into a driveway of a large house. Outside, in a paddock, a bare-chested man in a Texas hat was exercising a black stallion. As the car pulled up, the man, perhaps in his sixties, walked up and introduced himself. 'I'm Tootoo Imam,' he said, 'Thank you for accepting my invitation.'

By then I was convinced I had been kidnapped and this was a case of a mistaken identity. 'Oh no, Mr Kunal Verma. I know who you are. You are free to leave if you wish, but you are my honoured guest.' I was more puzzled, for no one other than Samuel and Panwar Saab's staff in the Project Tiger office was aware of my travel plans. Tootoo Imam then said he was a big-game hunter, and that he was aware that I had come to Bihar to do a story on man-eating wolves. He was extremely polite, apologising if his men had conveyed any impression other than the fact that I was an 'honoured guest' and he asked one of his staff to show me to my room.

It was just Tootoo Imam and myself for dinner. He still had his Texas hat on which had a thong that was held by a clasp. He talked of killing man-eating leopards, tigers and rogue elephants, and his passion for cars and motor racing. After we had had coffee, he asked me what I knew of the man-eating epidemic in Hazaribagh so far. 'Nothing as yet,' I said, 'Hopefully I'll find out in the next day or so what is going on for myself. With over seventy children ...'

'Seventy-one,' interjected Tootoo.

'With seventy-one children killed, if you are a big-game hunter, why haven't you done anything about the wolves?'

Syed Askari Hadi Ali Augastien Imam, alias Tootoo, exploded! 'Wolves!' He was almost shaking with rage, his face turning red in anger. 'There are no wolves! Stop perpetuating a lie. There are no wolves ...' He then seemed to calm down.

I was completely and absolutely bewildered by now. I was also getting a little fed up with Tootoo Imam's histrionics and his pompous ways where he seemed to believe he was the centre of the universe. 'No one has seen any wolf.' He was talking extremely calmly, reasonably. 'Forest officers are all swine. They have to protect tigers and leopards, so they are creating a myth about wolves being behind these killings. The only evidence they have is that the pugmarks found in villages have nails.' Tootoo now called for his staff, and a servant arrived with a large wicker basket that was placed on table in front of Tootoo. In the basket lay a black cat, whose name I cannot now recall. The cat was old, very old. It tried to raise its head and look at me but it had cataract in both eyes and its head fell back in exhaustion onto a small pillow.

Tootoo Imam took one of the cat's paws and showed it to me. 'With age, it cannot like all cats, retract its claws anymore. That is why the nail marks. This is the work of an old man-eating leopard, and I have moved the Supreme Court to grant me a licence to get a client who will not only kill it but pay $100,000 for it.'

I finally knew what Tootoo Imam was up to. Anyway, two could play the game, so I made a big fuss of thanking him for his incredible hospitality and nsisted on going back to my hotel where I was booked. The next three to four days were spent in visiting Hazaribagh, where I spoke to the forest officers, and then visited some of the villages where the killings had taken place. A perusal of the Hazaribagh District Gazetteer also threw up two interesting facts. The area was not only rich in wildlife earlier, it also held the record for the best chital and sambar heads ever recorded. Second, there had been an outbreak of man-eating by wolves some seventy years previously.

I also read S. P. Shahi's wonderful book, *Backs to the Wall: Saga of Wildlife in Bihar*. On the third day, I got a message that there had been another killing. Hardly had I received the message, I was out of the door running to my car. It was at least a two-hour drive, and as we approached the village where the report had come from, I couldn't help but notice how depleted the neighbouring forest undergrowth was. On the right side of the track, for the last kilometre or so, there was a ravine. At some point of time it must have had teak trees growing there, but thanks to constant pruning for fodder, they had been reduced to the size of shrubs.

The body was lying on a charpoy and the dead 8-year-old girl's name was Farzana. When I got there, the sheet covering the corpse was removed and she had been eaten below the torso, and the upper half of the body, including the purple shirt that she was wearing, was completely untouched. It was almost as if she had been sliced in half. There were flies buzzing around her extremely serene face, and after taking a couple of photographs, I asked the people collected around to put the sheet back over the child. The wailing of the women present had gone up when the body was uncovered, while the menfolk stood around with a dazed look.

The huts in the village were all bunched together, with a small mosque in the centre. The wolves—there were at least three of them—had easily jumped over the wall and picked up the sleeping girl. The Indian wolf (*Canis lupus*) found in the plains is not a very large animal, and if it wasn't for the obvious yellow eyes, could so easily be mistaken for a stray dog. We traced the drag marks and found bits of clothing stuck to thorny bushes. The three men accompanying me showed me the spot where the chasing party had recovered the rest of the body, which had been eaten even as it was dragged. At one place, the tracks of the wolves were clearly imprinted in the wet mud, the nails protruding beyond the front toes very, very distinctively.

When we walked back to where the villagers were with the body, or what remained of it, there was another jeep standing there. The local shikari, hired by the state government to track down and kill the wolves, had arrived from Hazaribagh. He had with him a 12-bore shotgun, and a .30 bolt action rifle, which had a damaged and cracked butt tied up with wire. According to him, at first there were seven animals, but he had managed to shoot two while one had disappeared on its own. The pack now had four animals, and since he was constantly chasing their kills, though he had seen them often, they were always too far to get a shot.

My gaze was constantly travelling to the ravine. Since the wolves had obviously been in a feeding frenzy where they had devoured bits and pieces of Farzana, chances were they would be laid up in the ravine, digesting their prey. The shikari agreed with my appreciation of the situation, but he said if he was to try and walk them out, they would as usual get away. I offered to handle his spare weapon and suggested instead of trying to flush them out ourselves, why not organize a *hakka* while we manned the likely exists on the other end. The shikari shrugged his shoulders and spat on the ground, 'These people! They will not cooperate. They get ten thousand rupees as compensation for each victim. They secure their goats at night and put the children in the courtyards.'

The three men who had helped track the wolves confirmed the ravine had two exit points, but one of them then said the menfolk of the village would not beat the ravine. Incredulously I asked, 'Why not?' I got my answer almost immediately as an open jeep with the great big-game hunter came down the track and stopped next to the two parked cars which were some 60 metres from where we were standing. Four to five men immediately got up and approached Tootoo Imam, who did not even bother to disembark from his vehicle. Heads then bobbed attentively, and before one could decipher what had been said, the jeep roared off. He completely ignored the shikari and me.

The ravine was not too broad, even twenty men and women walking abreast would serve the purpose, forcing the wolves, if they were there, towards the two exits. But the trouble was not one person was willing to do a hakka. The shikari shrugged his shoulders and started to walk towards the car. Impulsively, I reached for the sheet covering little Farzana's body, and picked her up. Addressing the women, I said to them that this is your daughter, or at least what is left of her. The wolves are most probably lying in the ravine for they have eaten, and they owed it to the safety of their children to help flush them out. As usually happens, one person has to take the call, and in this case, it was the mother of Farzana. Within minutes, the entire lot of village women had stepped forward. The three men and the shikari then took over, quickly barking out orders.

We placed the two cars on the track so the wolves would not break that way and put people in between. The shikari said he preferred to use the shotgun, so he covered the main exit while I was the stop for the one further back. I had a magazine with five bullets but did not expect to come into play unless the animals broke past the shikari who seemed to know his job, judging from the speed with which he organized the people.

The line of humans started to move in the ravine, banging tins and utensils and drums, and almost immediately there was a shot. There were some shouts, then the line that had stopped started to move again. I was trying to familiarize myself with the rifle and set the sight at a hundred metres. After five minutes there were again two shots, and then silence as the hakka party once again stopped. Once again there were some shouts, and I was trying to see what had happened when one of the men with me pointed excitedly. Two wolves were standing there looking back over their shoulder as well, almost as if they two were trying to see what had happened behind them. The first wolf dropped as the bullet hit him on the head (I had actually aimed for the chest) and the second now broke into a straight gallop towards us. Working the bolt, I fired twice more, the second shot hitting the animal when it was barely 20 metres from me.

All four wolves were brought to the place where Farzana's body was being prepared for burial. Taking an axe from one of the men, the shikari gutted the animals. Both feet and other chunks of the legs, partly digested, spilled out of the wolves' stomachs. It was a gruesome end to the wolf saga, but it was proof before the people that they were indeed the killers. I told the shikari I did not want to get involved any further, for with Tootoo Imam around, the last thing I wanted was a police case against me.

Back in Delhi, it seemed Tootoo Imam's aggressive stance in the Supreme Court was more related to the Sundarbans, where his claim that all tigers were man-eaters and that the government was depriving him of a living was actually admitted. It would drag on for a few years. I couldn't help thinking of Tootoo Imam's cat. At least it had cataract that blurred its vision. What could one say about the man himself and the learned judges and our legal system where a petition such as this could be admitted. There would be an interesting fall out to the wolf story. A few months later the Australian Embassy got in touch with me, saying a woman who had lost her 3-month-old baby while out in the bush with her husband, had always maintained it had been picked up by dingos. She had been arrested and convicted for murder, but the Hazaribagh man-eating story had given her grounds to file an appeal. I had to give a recorded statement giving the brief facts of what had happened. I don't know what happened to that case subsequently.

The second Army Wildlife Workshop was being held in Dachigam, the home of not just the *hangul* (Kashmir stag) but also the black bear, with Brigadier Ramu Gaur at the helm of affairs. After the success of the first, there had been more resources made available for the workshop and the invitee list had been expanded considerably. This time Sharad Gaur, Ramu's nephew had to do most of the groundwork, and I was one of the delegates. The WWF was being represented by Dileep Mathai, *Sanctuary Asia* by Bittu Sahgal, and quite a few others including members of the Bombay Natural History Society. Sharad and I were joined by Mahendra Vyas, a good friend who had done yeoman service in the re-drafting of the Indian Wildlife (Preservation) Act. Giving the three of us company while swimming in the icy and crystal-clear Daghwan stream, were trout the size of my forearm, I also realized that once the scope of the conference was increased manifold, doing things at the grassroots becomes that much more difficult, for a lot that was discussed in the conference never got implemented.

Until the Dachigam conference, all my interaction with Bittu Sahgal had been through Royina. I was contemplating doing a feature for *The Week* on elephant poaching in South India and figured I could go via Bombay. Bittu was full of enthusiasm about various projects that we could do, so on my return I started researching various aspects of elephant behaviour and also what was there in the vernacular press pertaining to the sandalwood and ivory trade. When I presented my plan to Vicki about the South India run, she promptly said yes, but then she said before that there was a short assignment in Punjab for me. Somehow, there was something about her body language which suggested this was not going to be a run-of-the-mill Punjab story.

On the face of it, Indira Gandhi's assassination seemed to be a simple open and shut case, where two Sikh members of her security detail, shot her for having defiled the Golden Temple by sending the army into the complex in June 1984. The two guards, Satwant Singh and Beant Singh, after having shot the prime minister, had dropped their weapons and surrendered, but both were shot in a scuffle thereafter. While Beant Singh died, Satwant Singh survived to stand trial after which he was hung to death in 1989.

The very fact that the two assassins were shot after they had surrendered seemed a bit strange, but at the time there was very little information coming out about the shooting. Years later, in 2013, Karen McKay who we had got to know quite well during our Fort Benning stay in 1969, finally visited India and spent two weeks with my parents at our home in Bandrol, Kullu. In the early 1980s, she had been a key player in setting up the Mujahideen to fight the Soviets in Afghanistan. Working closely with William 'Bill' Casey, President Ronald Reagan's CIA chief between 1981 and 1987, Karen had been in and out of Pakistan but had never, ever been to India. After her stay, she had caught the overnight Volvo from Manali, and I had picked her up from Connaught Place early in the morning on 5 October.

I was driving back to Gurgaon with Karen gushing about her stay in Kullu. At the time I vaguely knew about her stint in the CIA (she had also served in the Israeli Army where she had risen to the rank of a colonel) but when she said something about Pakistan, I asked her, 'How come you never visited India?'

'I wanted to but I couldn't,' she said in a matter-of-fact manner, 'your intelligence people had linked me to Mrs Gandhi's assassination.' After President Joe Biden pulled the US troops out of Afghanistan in August 2021, she sent me an anguished e-mail about the 'American betrayal'. I wrote back to her a month later, gently suggesting that since US interests in our part of the region were now compromised, what could she tell me about the assassination. Though in her mid-80s by now, Karen deftly avoided the topic in her subsequent replies and when I finally asked her yet again, she said it was the ranting of her rivals in the CIA.

In the shadowy world of intelligence, it was hard to tell who was who. Sometime in September 1985, Vicki called me into her office. Most Sikh leaders under detention had been released by the Government of India and the much-vaunted Punjab Accord had been signed between Rajiv Gandhi and the Akali leader, Harcharan Singh Longowal on 24 July 1985. 'Beant Singh, Indira Gandhi's bodyguard who shot her and was killed ... his widow, Bibi Bimal Kaur, was released from detention recently. She has become a bit of a cult figure in the Khalistan movement. She is setting up the women's "commando force" and is trying to recruit people from various militant groups from tomorrow in Punjab.' Vicki gave me a paper with a phone number on it. 'Contact this number. Bibi Kaur is on a field trip for four days. She has agreed for you to accompany her. *Try and get photographs of everyone she meets.*'

I looked at Vicki, not particularly keen to go back to Punjab especially on an extended field trip. I had told her an edited version of why we had to leave Amritsar in such a hurry in November 1984, and she on her part had not sent me back into the state immediately, except for the two helicopter forays with Rajiv Gandhi. Grateful for small mercies, I knew she couldn't keep me away from the state indefinitely especially since the situation continued to fester, with the demand for Khalistan and Pakistan-backed insurgency refusing to die down. Vicki smiled, 'This time, for Christ's sake, you stay out of trouble.'

Bibi Bimal Kaur, freshly widowed, was the mother of three children and all of 34 years at the time. She was a nurse working at a hospital in Delhi at the time of the assassination and had been immediately picked up and detained by the authorities. Later records suggested she was officially still under detention, but obviously there were other forces at work that I was not aware of. I caught up with her the next morning in a village near Ropar. As per my brief, the vehicle that had brought me to her location from Chandigarh was dismissed and I put my rucksack in the boot of the white Ambassador, which was her car.

Bibi Bimal Kaur was as fluent in Hindi and English as she was in Punjabi. She always wore a white dress but would wear a pastel shade yellow or peach *chunni*, with which she often covered her head. A cross-belt held the symbolic Sikh dagger. She barely acknowledged my presence at first and seemed to be in a world of her own. We went from one village to another, and always there was a motely group of people, mostly young men in their late teens and early twenties, waiting to meet her. Though she was supposed to be raising a women's commando force, I never saw a single girl or woman amongst the people waiting to meet her. My presence, almost akin to being her personal photographer, seemed to be taken for granted. Every time, after each short meeting, I would tell the youngsters I needed to take their mugshots 'to hand over to the Punjab Police'. Everyone without exception seemed to love my sense of humour, and they would pose with their pistols or AK-47s, stroking their newly formed moustaches and fondling their scanty beards.

We were literally travelling and living off the land. Nights we would pull up near some house or the other and they would put charpoys out for us and serve us hot chapatis with dal and lots of onions. Nights were pleasant and we slept outdoors, while the driver would curl up in the car itself. I think his name was Balbir, but it was soon obvious to me he wasn't just a driver. He rarely if ever spoke, and I would often catch him looking at me in the backseat in the rear-view mirror. What was more, it seemed to me Bibi Kaur was scared of him, though the interaction between them was also minimal. We were like three people who were thrown together for four days but who instinctively did not want to know anything about each other.

Bibi Kaur never said a word about her husband. Sometimes she talked of her life as a nurse, but at no point did she ever talk about her beliefs. She would hold forth about the threat to the Sikh Panth and the atrocities unleashed by the Indian government on the people of Punjab, but that was all reserved for when she had an audience. By the fourth day, I had around a hundred photographs of gun toting individuals, and without much ado, we parted company around lunch time. I was dropped off at a *dhaba* and hardly had Balbir and Bibi Kaur left, the car that had dropped me four days ago came to pick me up. Just who was coordinating all this, I had no idea. This driver too, like Balbir, seemed extremely tight-lipped. As we approached Chandigarh, he pulled up near a poplar plantation, leaned across and opened his glove box, and gave me a thick envelope into which he asked me to place the exposed film roles. I did as I was told, and we drove into the well laid out city with its various sectors.

Pulling up outside a house, the driver asked me to keep sitting and taking the package of films, he got out and went into the bungalow. He rang the bell and the door opened. The film was handed over and the door closed. Leaning back and trying to see who it was, I had a fleeting glimpse of the person. It was the wife of an intelligence officer with whom I had interacted frequently during my Tiger Top days in Ladakh. Just what the US connection was with Mrs Gandhi's assassination would always remain a mystery to me. Back in Delhi, not once did Vicki ask me about these four days or refer to the photographs. It was as if four days of my life had never happened. I never saw Bibi Bimal Kaur again. She was elected to the Punjab state assembly but was killed in a domestic accident quite mysteriously in 1991.

With the Bibi Kaur episode behind me, I found myself on the Delhi–Bombay flight in the last week of September 1985. Strangely, until then, I had never been to India's commercial capital. Ajit and Royina had shifted into a sea-looking building, Ashoka, in Colaba. Plonking down in their flat, I was happily surrounded by the familiar faces of Ayesha and Misha, and their new dog, Badmash, who was an incredibly big Irish setter. At that time, I knew virtually no one in Bombay other than Aditya (AD) and Ayesha (AY), who were N. P. 'Nirpoo' Singh's children. AD was even then on his way to becoming a Page 3 celebrity and would go on to make quite a name for himself in the restaurant business subsequently. AD and his twin brother, Arjun (AR) who were exactly a month younger than me, were to have joined the Doon School with me but had failed to turn up at the last moment, much to my disappointment.

On 5 October, I flew from Bombay to Cochin and the flight even today is etched in my memory, for the beauty of India's west coast was right there below us. In Cochin my classmate, Sanjai Banerji, lived with his parents who were both doctors. Though I had never met them before, and had arrived at their house unannounced, even though Sanjai was yet to return from work, I was soon happily ensconced with his family for the evening. As the evening wore on, there was still no sign of 'Banjo'. Having peeled off to watch a movie, he finally arrived, and seeing me sitting there amidst his family, there was absolutely no change of expression on his face. 'Oh, hi Fauji,' he said, 'I was just thinking of you. By the way, happy birthday!' I guess when you live cheek-by-jowl with each other for half a decade, these things become second nature.

The next morning, I boarded the train at Ernakulam, and as we started to move, I reached into my bag and gave Banjo some rolls of Ektachrome 100 ASA film. We would meet again later that month in Dehradun, by which time Banjo was well on his way to becoming a fairly proficient photographer. As the train headed further south, I looked at the backwaters and the endless coconut trees. This time, though I had been extremely cocky about the idea, I knew I had probably bitten off much more than I could chew. I had been fantastically lucky so far, for wherever I had gone, because of the contacts I had with the likes of H. S. Panwar, S. K. Mukherjee and Kishore Rao, I had been in the thick of the action. The ivory trade was much too big, and I honestly simply did not think I had the bandwidth to unearth a worthwhile story.

I got off the train at Kottayam which was also the headquarters of *Malayala Manorama*. After a quick meeting with the editor, I caught the bus to Periyar Tiger Reserve where I got plenty of opportunity to photograph elephants over the next couple of days. Being familiar with the Nilgiris, I loved every minute that I got to spend in the Western Ghats, after which I dropped down to Mudumalai, Bandipur and then Kabini, which was then being run by Tiger Tops in conjunction with the Karnataka government under the banner of Jungle Lodges & Resorts. My good friend, Sundar Raj was then the chief naturalist at Kabini. A former poacher, he was perhaps one of the best anglers in the country, for he knew the waters and what lay in them better than anyone else. He told stories of 'monsters' that grew to more than a hundred pounds, so we promptly made a plan to fish the Cauvery sometime in January.

My elephant story was received well enough, but it only dealt with the poaching of elephants in general terms. I had quite rashly promised my two chiefs of bureau much more when I had set off for Bombay a fortnight before. They were much too polite to say anything, but I was always careful after that in making any promises that I could not keep.

It was a packed year, 1985, and far from over when in October I was once again called into Vicki's office. 'I've got something for you which I think you'll enjoy covering. I'm sending you to Dehradun to report on the Doon School's Golden Jubilee ...' Her eyes were twinkling, for Vicki knew I would be going in any case. I must have looked alarmed, for I had no intention of filing despatches in what promised to be a giant party with my batchmates, most of whom I had not seen since leaving in November

Top: My father (extreme right) with his siblings in Kashmir in 1945
Bottom: The family in 1955. My aunt Meera is holding Ammaji's portrait

Top left: My mother's photograph that was published in the *Illustrated Weekly of India*
Top right: Usha Hoon during her college days in Dehradun
Bottom: My father, then a captain, firing a Lee Enfield .303

Top: The two families meet in 1958. My grandmother, Saraswati, is sitting in the middle
Bottom left: The two grandfathers meet on 11 June 1959
Bottom right: The wedding being held at the Doon School

Top left: The parents after their wedding
Top right: Captain Ashok Kalyan and Usha Verma in Sabatoo
Centre left: As a two-week baby at 1 Balbir Avenue, Dalanwala
Bottom left: My mother and me in Dehradun
Bottom right: Riding on my father's shoulders shortly after the house in Clement Town was bought

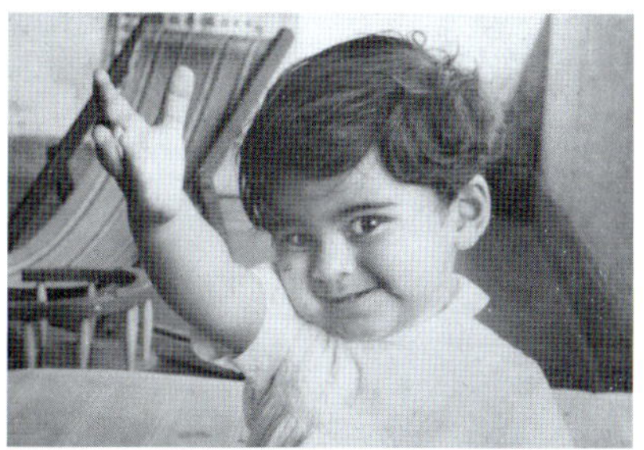

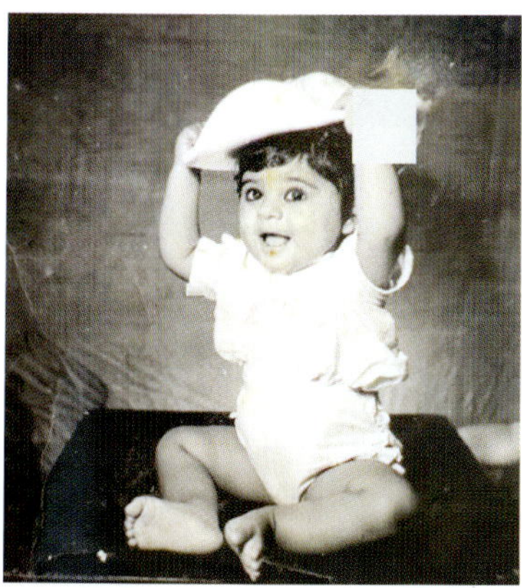

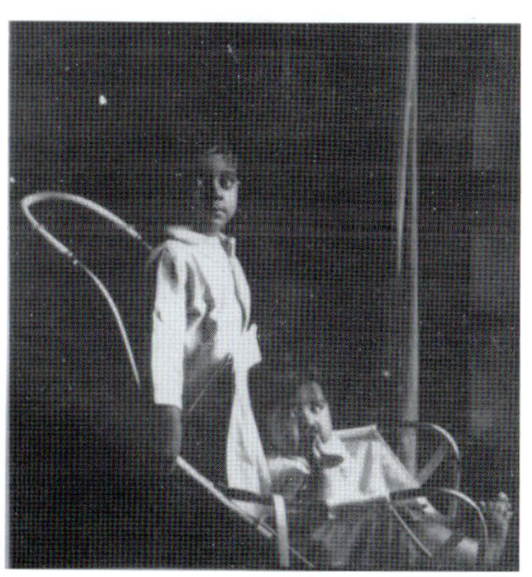

Top: In 38 Inder Road, Dehradun
Centre left: Trying on a hat
Centre right: My first first haircut
Bottom left: With Teesta at the IMA in 1963
Bottom right: Tipu retrieving a black partridge

Top left: With mom and Teesta in Dehradun
Top right: Mom, Teesta and me in 1965
Bottom left: With Teesta in Mussoorie in April 1965
Bottom right: In Dehradun Cantonment in 1967

Top left: In Alabama United States in 1969
Top right: With mom and Teesta and the Louvre Museum in Paris
Bottom left: Major Bill Curtis, Dr Mac Molnar, Jean Molnar, Sue Curtis and Major Ashok Kalyan Verma at Fort Benning
Bottom right: With my father at Panama Beach in Florida

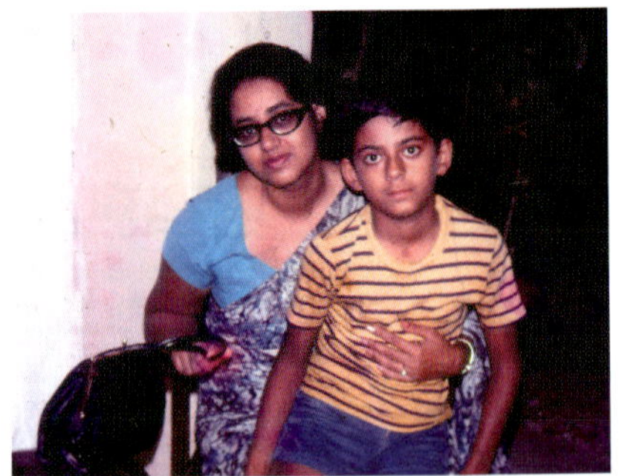

Top left: With my mom, Teesta and Sona in the special train travelling from Nasirabad to Agartala
Top right: With my Daisy air gun in 1970
Bottom left: With Teesta and Sona, one of the first Labrador retrievers to be brought to India
Bottom right: With my mother at Mhow on my way to joining The Doon School

Top left: As a C former at the Art School
Top right: With my cousins, Veer Vikram holding Tipu the dachshund, Vijit, Teesta and Suniti, holding Rita, in Clement Town
Bottom left: The Doon School play at the Rose Bowl in 1976
Bottom right: From left to right (standing): Sanjay Banerjee, Rajeeva Swarup, Sanjeev Sethi, Hari Krishan Dhar, Nakul Bubna, Hemant Kumar Jain, Shiv Kunal Verma; (sitting) Abhiram Bahadur Singh, Janardhan Kapur, Bankim Chaddha, Dr S. D Singh, Dhruv Khanna and Vipin Malhotra. 1976 Batch Hyderabad B

Top: The Madras Christian College tennis team in 1979; Murali Padmanabhan to my right was my vice-captain
Centre left: All MCC team captains; K. P Achutan the hockey captain is sitting next to K.C David the physical director
Centre right: With mom, Sherkhan and Missy in Wellington
Bottom left: Missy at Pratap Chowk in 1980
Bottom right: Sherkhan photographed on special Ektachrome 25 ASA film

Top left: The Chenab River in the Kishtawar Valley in 1981
Top right: Setting up camp at 17,000 ft on Umasi La
Centre left: The snow field between the Rewa and the Zanskar side of Umasi La
Centre right: Training with the Himalayan River Exploration on the Trishuli in Nepal
Bottom left: Working as a naturalist the Tiger Tops lodge at Chitwan in 1982
Bottom right: With K. K Gurung, the chief naturalist

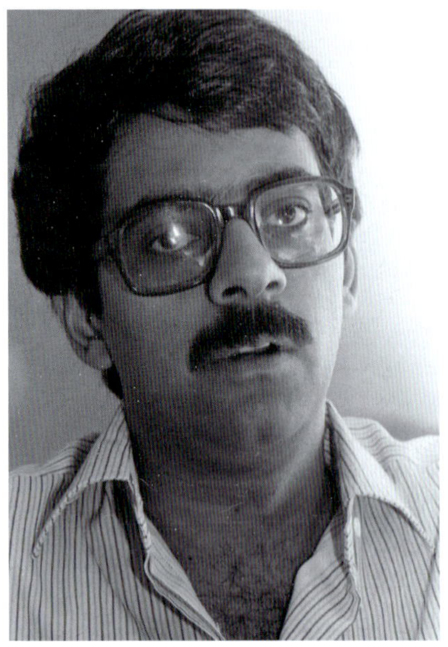

Top left: My days at the Associated Press in 1984
Top right: Sharda, with Missy and Sherkhan at Raksha Bhawan, 1983
Bottom left: Missy, Leo and Sherkhan in Jalandhar, 1984
Bottom right: With Leo, the son of Sherkhan, at 5 Mall Road, Jalandhar Cantt

Top left: Lieutenant General Adi M. Sethna
Top right: Prime Minister Rajeev Gandhi addressing a rally in Punjab from a bullet proof enclosure
Bottom left: Captain Ashok Mukherjee from 14 Bihar during the Ahmedabad riots in 1984
Bottom right: Flanked by Janardhan Kapur and Deepak Mansukhani during the Doon School Golden Jubilee in 1985

Top left: The first Army Wildlife workshop held at the Sariska Tiger Reserve in 1985
Top right: A herd of Chital at the Kalighati water hole
Centre left: The first ever appearance of a *dhole* (Indian wild dog) at the Slopka water hole in 1986
Centre right: Shooting at the Sariska Tiger Reserve
Bottom left: Filming from a boat at the Sunderbans Tiger Reserve in 1986
Bottom right: At Kanha Tiger Reserve. My assistant, Naik, is on the right

Top left: Dipti recording a "Ladakhi' song in Chushul while a Rebo shears a sheep
Top right: Filming at the Chushul airstrip. I was to lose a jeep shortly after that right under the nose of the PLA
Centre left: The son of Noon chewing on a sambar head at Ranthambhore Tiger Reserve
Centre right: Filming a herd of sambar at the Sariska Tiger Reserve
Bottom left: Shooting elephants from a boat at the Periyar Tiger Reserve in 1988
Bottom right: 'Red' elephants at Periyar

Top left: Rohit 'Bobby' Tandan during Dipti and my wedding in Bombay in June 1992
Top right: Colours being bestowed to three Rajput battalions in 1991 at Fatehgarh
Centre left: Leo, all grown up, at Topi Bungalow, Jammu in 1987
Centre right: Tara, also in Jammu
Bottom left: Taking a break while shooting in Gulmarg, 1991
Bottom right: Dipti handling a Hassleblad camera in Gulmarg

1976. 'Don't worry ...' she laughed, 'I'll have Seema Sirohi also cover for you in case you're too intoxicated to file anything. Go on ... have fun!'

Since I was on assignment, I had the option of catching the Vayudoot flight from Delhi, which was a Dornier-228, a twin-turboprop aircraft that carried nineteen passengers and a crew of three. I was delighted to see the familiar small, somewhat frail figure of India's 'Birdman', Dr Salim Ali, who was also on his way to the Doon School having taught there in the earlier part of his career. Though pushing 90 at the time and a little hard of hearing, he had quite a spring in his step. By the time we landed at Jolly Grant an hour later, the little man seemed most annoyed for the flight had obviously not quite agreed with him. 'What a horrible bird,' he said in a fairly shrill voice standing on the tarmac. I quickly guided him away from the aircraft, just in case the pilots came out of their cockpit and heard him.

The Doon School was riding a high ... Rajiv Gandhi, batch of 1959, was the prime minister and he was the chief guest, smartly turned out in an old boys' tie and blazer with the lamp of knowledge emblazoned on it. He started off by telling the gathering how he landed up in Trinity College at Cambridge wearing the blazer. An English master who was coming down the corridor asked him what the badge represented. 'That,' said Gandhi haughtily, pulling himself up to his full height, 'is the lamp of knowledge.' The master wasn't impressed, and retorted 'pity, they didn't light it in your time ...' His speech was superbly scripted, drawing all the sophisticated laughs, and as the AP correspondent on duty I got some superb shots of him in various moods.

But then as it happens, the prime minister was forgotten, and endless bottles of beer catapulted various batches into a different zone altogether. There was endless laughter and general bonhomie. Then, through the haze of it all, I saw Gurdial Singh, stride past the main building. Guru was perhaps the most iconic master who had taught us all geography, and in 1985 he was the deputy headmaster. He had also taught Rajiv Gandhi, Sanjay Gandhi and just about everyone else who were now superstars in the government.

In 1965, Guru had been an important member of the first successful Indian Everest expedition. We had all grown up listening to the sound of his crampons breaking the ice on Nanda Devi, Trishul and then on South Col as he made his way up the forbidding icy slopes towards the summit. Guru was part of the second summit team, trailing behind Major H. P. S. Ahluwalia. Four hundred metres short of the summit, he ran into Ahluwalia who had run out of oxygen. Without a second thought, Guru had unclipped his own cylinders and given them to Ahluwalia, selflessly giving up a chance to write himself into the history books. Not only was that typical of Guru, somehow, we all believed it was typical of the Doon School too. As far as we were concerned, Guru epitomised life—every mountain, every river, every bird, every flower—carried his imprint. 'Well hark,' he would say, cupping his ear with his extra-large hand, 'what is that bird that is calling?' And we would know it was a coppersmith or a cuckoo or a distant lapwing.

Now seeing him stride along, I started sprinting after him, tape recorder and mike in hand. I was joined by a gaggle of other reporters who were hanging around waiting for something to happen. We soon had him surrounded, and shoving my mike towards him, I asked him the million-dollar question: 'Sir, you've taught Rajiv Gandhi, Sanjay Gandhi, Piloo Modi, Dinesh Singh ...' Others threw in some other names while I caught my breath. 'What was the common factor that defined them in school?' Guru was obviously not liking the attention, and he tried to move on, but his path was firmly blocked by the gaggle. 'Well, well ...' he took his time, then he held up his hand and delivered a priceless quote, 'they were all duffers!' and he strode off majestically while I burst out laughing.

A year later I gave all the negatives to Sheel Vohra, who wanted to store them in the school's archives. Tragically, the photographs got misplaced and I never saw them again.

BOOK II

10

Project Tiger: The New Kid in Town

By the third quarter of 1985, my father had finished his tenure as brig adam in Jalandhar and had moved to Army HQ in New Delhi as additional director general mechanized warfare. Having picked up his rank and become a major general, this posting was by itself extremely surprising because he was an infantry officer. Allotted a house in Dhaula Kuan Part-I, which was adjacent to the Defence Services Officers Institute, I was only too happy to say goodbye to Munirka and shift in with my parents. Though I was paying David Devadas's mother rent for the place, he had asked me if he could shift in and share the flat. Hardly had David moved in, the elbowing had started, and our friendship had started to turn sour. Outwardly we remained polite enough, but I was only too delighted to flee from the flat.

By then, we had another addition to the family. Leo was Sher Khan's son and was the absolute opposite of his father. Darker in colour and smaller in size, as he came of age, the two males fought some terrible battles, leaving them both scarred. Sher Khan had also met with a bad accident while the family was in Delhi for Teesta's wedding in May. His hip had required major surgery that entailed inserting an aluminium rod, and I had flown down from Delhi to Halwara (Ludhiana), just in time to bring him back after his operation.

Micky Yadav and Teesta were by then stationed in Ahmednagar, so I flew to Pune and took the detour and visited them. The officers and their wives were performing a play at the Armoured Corps Centre, *There's a Girl in My Soup*. The next day I returned to Pune where I spent a night with Captain (later Major) Rakesh Wahi, who was a year senior to me in Doon School and was also from Hyderabad House. The two social visits out of the way, I touched down in Bangalore, where my friend Sundar Raj was waiting for me at the airport. Being ex-Tiger Tops, I had a special status, for Jungle Lodges & Resorts, that ran the Kabini Lodge and the Cauvery Fishing Camp was at the time a joint-venture and most employees were ex-colleagues. As we drove along on the Bangalore–Mysore road, Sundar couldn't stop talking of 'these monsters' and by the time we reached the fishing camp at Bheemeshwari, it was dark. After a quiet dinner, that night I went to sleep in my tent, dreaming of big mahseer that were just waiting to be caught.

I was suddenly awake as I could feel someone shaking my foot. 'Sssh ...' said Sundar, who had lit a lantern that was throwing the faintest of light. 'Elephants ...' he whispered. 'Get into half pants and come quickly.'

I followed him outside. The Cauvery was flowing silently in the moonlight, the deep pools that housed the 'monsters' making no sound at all. Sundar slipped into the water, so I followed him, and we then swam silently from one exposed rock to the other. Not having seen the river during the daylight hours, I was literally swimming blind, and the current was quite strong in places. Then I heard them, and it was obvious some of the elephants were also in the water. It came as a shock that they were in fact all around us. It was surreal, almost unbelievable. They were gliding around like dark shapes, enjoying the fact that they were weightless in the water. We sat there for some twenty minutes, not making a sound. Then Sundar slipped back into the water, and I followed, swimming back the way we had come. Once ashore, I could see his white teeth as he grinned from ear to ear. 'How you like? Now tomorrow, we catch the monsters!' If one was to go with the phonetic spelling of the word, Sundar pronounced his favourite word as 'maunstars'!

I was up at dawn, and the Cauvery was stretched out in front. One of the boys came and gave me a cup of tea and deposited a black steaming ball of what looked like elephant dung in front of me. After a while, Sundar put in an appearance and showed me how an open-faced Abu Garcia fishing reel was operated. If you were not careful with the cast, the reel ran the danger of unspooling out of control, creating a 'bird's nest' which effectively ruled one out of the days' contention for it would take hours to straighten the line. After a couple of practice casts on the shore, and after freshening up, we got into a coracle, which was a circular basket-like boat made from buffalo hide and cane. With a shikari propelling us along with a single oar, we got to some rocks downstream where we settled down with our balls of 'elephant dung', which were actually ragi that had been steamed much in the manner in which *idlis* are cooked. Tearing off a chunk the size of an egg, one wrapped it around a single hook, and then with the weight of the ragi providing the impetus, one cast the bait into the water.

Almost immediately, as the ragi settles at the bottom, one can feel the fish nibbling. Usually it's the small ones, and one has to wait till there is a run, after which it is important to strike upwards and backwards with the rod, hoping that the hook will catch the fish in the mouth. Apart from mahseer, there were also plenty of catfish in the Cauvery, plus pink and Carnatic carps, all of whom were killed for the pot. The mahseer, on the other hand, were strictly to be released.

In the afternoon I thought I had a mahseer on the line, but after fighting it for half an hour, I realized it was a Carnatic carp. Once it was weighed on the portable scale, Sundar and the shikari started dancing around with joy. I wanted to let the fish go, but Sundar would have none of it. At eleven-and-a-half pounds, I wondered why he was calling it a monster. At the camp in the evening, there was a lot of excitement, for the Carnatic carp had broken a 101-year-old record. That night it was served as fish cutlets, and everyone congratulated me. I, on the other hand, felt miserable. We had snuffed out a beautiful creature's life for fish cutlets! I was once again in that space where I had a Daisy gun, and the sheer power that I could kill, just kept me going. I hated myself, for I also did not have the courage to stop myself despite knowing what I was doing was wrong—at least to my way of thinking. I felt I was as bad as the poachers who put nails in the hollow of trees to kill jackals. That night I just could not sleep.

The next day again I drew a blank as far as mahseer were concerned. I quietly released all the other fish, and then watched a masterclass as Sundar hooked and landed a 35 lb golden mahseer towards the end of the day. It was nearly dark when we released it, and then the three of us decided to build a small fire and sleep out in the open on the other bank. We selected a sandy patch next to the river that was protected from elephants by huge boulders, and then, sleeping in a triangle around the fire, we wrapped ourselves in our solitary sheets and slept. The next morning, there were tracks of a leopard that had circled us umpteen times, before he or she decided it wasn't worth attacking the sleeping figures. Even the normally unperturbable Sundar's hands were shaking when he realized how close we had been to corrupting the leopard's dietary habits!

Shortly after I returned to Delhi, I got a call from Royina, who said Bittu Sahgal had a surprise lined up and was flying down to Delhi to see me. She also added that he would like to spend the night at our place, so could I prepare the guest room for him. This seemed like a strange request, for Bittu had never met my parents and I wondered why he wanted to do that unless he wanted to talk to the family. Next day I picked him up from the airport, and then sat back and watched as he soon had everyone eating out of his hand. The natural exuberance and affection that he radiated, he could do no wrong in the eyes of my folks.

Soon my father was telling Bittu how distressed he was because I (his son) had not joined the army and was now masquerading as a journalist who was either running around the country doing wildlife stories, or worse, floating around Punjab, where anything could happen, anytime! All that was still alright, but twenty days in a month I was playing cricket with all the kids in Dhaula Kuan, and that he had never seen me 'go to work' after I had 'fought with everyone' and exited *India Today*. Even as I rolled my eyes and prayed my father would stop crucifying me, he then requested Bittu to take me 'under his wing'. I could have died that night, but fortunately the hour hand on the cuckoo clock also had had enough and it was time to sleep. Since my uncle Ravi Hoon was also staying with us (and had been nodding along with what my father had said), I told Bittu he was to sleep in my room while I would sleep on a mattress in the living room with Sher Khan and Leo.

Bittu would have none of that, and he went into this song and dance about sleeping in the open under the stars and that, as a wildlife person, a bed meant nothing to him. So, Bittu Sahgal, having charmed every one without breathing a word about why he had come to Delhi, finally retired and went to sleep. However, unknown to him, two pairs of watchful eyes had been on him through the night. Sher Khan was by then 11 years old, but Leo was a budding 2-year-old and he had plans of his own. Around two in the morning, Leo did something he had never done before, and nor would he ever do it again ... he piddled on the sleeping Bittu!

After being initiated by 'dogmutra', I guess there was no way Bittu could not have got his wish. In the morning he took me to the nearby Taj Man Singh Hotel for breakfast and once there, he finally spilled the beans, 'Hindustan Lever has decided to sponsor a thirteen-part television series on Project Tiger and another one called '*Rakshak*' for kids, which will cover other areas in a story format. Sanctuary Films has already signed up all the technical crew—cameramen, sound recordists and editors who were all graduates from the Film and Television Institute of India (FTII) in Pune—and I would be very happy if you will come and direct some of the films.' He then went on to make me an offer which was so ridiculously low, I actually burst out laughing. Then amazingly, I heard myself say, 'Alright. Let's give it a shot. What do I have to do?'

In Bombay, I was to again stay with the Grewals. Just as I was leaving Delhi, on an impulse I bought a squash racquet for Misha, who would soon be turning 16. She would subsequently not only excel in the sport but go on to win the Indian National Championship on four occasions and be honoured with the Arjuna Award. Two of the Project Tiger films were to be put together by Dipti Bhalla from existing footage that had been shot by Tejbir Singh and Valmik Thapar, while Aruna Raje was to edit and weave an episode from the footage put together by Brijendra Singh. The Periyar episode was to be shot by the herpetologist Romulus Whitaker and Shekhar Dattatri, while the rest of the episodes were still to be worked out.

My first task was to take one of the shortlisted cameramen, Sukumar, for a short reconnaissance trip to Manas Tiger Reserve. Apart from meeting Sanjoy Deb Roy and fixing up the logistics for a future date,

Bittu asked me to take a 16 mm ST camera and see if I could get some initial footage for curtain raisers and background material. Sukumar, having featured in the Godrej shaving cream advertisement, was a familiar face, and a very pleasant person. Next thing he knew, he was transported from the environs of Bittu's living room in 'Jaldarshan' on Pedder Road in Bombay to the red ant infested jungles of Assam.

Deb Roy was delighted a film was to be shot on Manas (combined with the Buxa Tiger Reserve) and he promptly made arrangements for Sukumar and me to be taken for a ride through the jungle on a female elephant the next morning. I think she was called Ram Pyari. Sukumar was just getting used to the deadly stinging sensation of the ants who drop down from their nests stitched together among the leaves, when we ran into a tusker in *musth*. Before the mahout could realize the randy male was around, he had seen us and he ran as only elephants blinded by lust can run towards the poor female. In blind panic, our relatively tiny elephant took off in the opposite direction, with three humans on top, who would have most certainly been collateral damage had the tusker succeeded in closing the gap. To say it was touch-and-go would be to make an understatement, but Sukumar now only had one ambition in life—somehow get back to the safe confines of Bombay.

Not having been a party to the morning drama, Deb Roy had a hearty chuckle and, in the afternoon, gave me a Project Tiger jeep. 'Check out the grasslands. You might get some buffalo herds, hog deer most certainly. There is one problem though ...'

'What?'

'You'll have to drive yourself as I don't have a driver and the jeep has to be handle-started if you switch off the engine.'

In the passenger seat Sukumar's nerves had just about settled when lo and behold, we ran smack into a large male tiger walking along the track in the Manas grasslands. He was magnificent and with the grass a golden colour on either side of the track, it was a shot to die for. 'Shoot Sukumar shoot,' I hissed, not wanting to take my eyes off the big cat, who had stopped and was looking coldly back at the jeep. In neutral, the diesel vehicle was shaking like an old man having a coughing fit, so to give Sukumar a steady platform, I switched off the engine. Then I looked sideways, and to my horror, he was not where I thought he was. The camera was lying on the seat, so I picked it up and never having handled a movie camera in my life, I focused on the tiger and pressed the trigger to activate the camera's motor.

After a few seconds, the tiger got bored with us and carried on walking. I had forgotten about the jeep's hand-crank start mechanism, but now to close the gap again, I had no choice but to leap out and do the needful. Sensing I had got out, the tiger again stopped and looked back, while I tried to get the handle in the slot by matching two perforations, also trying to watch the tiger behind my back. This happened twice more, by which time I was a nervous wreck. When the tiger departed, the grass finally swallowing him up, Sukumar's head popped up from behind the seat, 'Is he gone?' That was the end of Mr Sukumar's short, happy life as a wildlife cameraman. The footage I had shot was a disaster, for it was much too shaky to be used. Only consolation for me, Bittu too was tearing his hair out when we saw the developed film a week or so later. He held his head in his hands, shaking it from side to side and said, 'Hey Ram!'

I had every intention of keeping my AP links alive, so within a few days of the disastrous Assam trip I found myself in Batala in the middle of an armed bank robbery. As usually happened, once again the Babbar Khalsa and other underground groups like the Khalistan Commando Force seemed to know all about our movements from the moment we landed in Amritsar. I was to interview the local kingpin of one of these groups, a young chap barely in his twenties, who seemed to have the makings of a future politician, should he survive that long. The Punjab Police under Julio Ribeiro had launched their bullet-for-bullet counter-campaign a year ago and the results were beginning to show. 'The people here love me,' said the 'future politician', trying to stroke the beginnings of a beard, obviously punch-drunk with the power of an AK-47. People would often ask me if the separatists were religiously motivated. Quite frankly, I thought most of them had no clue what religion was all about. Everyone seemed to be in it for a lark, and at times it seemed with good reason.

'We need some money,' the 'future politician' said, and after some time we strolled into a branch of some local bank. I was perhaps naive or just plain stupid, for I expected him to write out a self-cheque and withdraw some money, but instead we, along with his three to four armed escorts, walked into the cabin of the manager, who outwardly seemed delighted to see our mutual friend. '*Baitho ji, baitho ji*' (Please sit, please sit), he kept saying, asking if we would like tea, or coffee or *sharbat*! By now I felt the 'future politician' was indeed the son of some bigwig who probably owned half of Batala. Now that we were seated, the welcoming chant had turned to '*Dasso ji, dasso ji!*' (Tell me, tell me!)

Future politician was a modest chap, and he said he needed thirty- to forty-thousand rupees. The manager was horrified, and said, '*Eh ki ji ... tussi toh sannu sharminda kar rahe ho ji*' (What is this, sir ... you are shaming me). He promptly called one of his sidekicks and asked him to get two lakh rupees. By now it was dawning on me that this was a bank robbery. The money arrived, was counted, and put in a bag which was given to one of the 'future politician's' minions. Everyone shook hands, more offers of tea, coffee, *sharbat* ... then we were outside, and I was thankful the place hadn't been surrounded by cops. Next day I read in the papers the bank had been looted by 'armed masked insurgents' and rupees five lakh had been taken.

Another trip to the Golden Temple, which would be my last assignment with AP in September 1986, is equally illustrative. Reuters (the chief rivals of AP) had got this six-footer female correspondent who went by the name of Maggie. She was brash, aggressive and impatient, and would always get ahead of the queue using every trick in the book. It was a typical, boring afternoon, and speeches were being made to honour the assassins of General Arun Vaidya, who had been shot dead in Pune a month previously. There were a lot of flies buzzing around, and frankly everyone was half asleep. Suddenly, I saw Maggie in earnest conversation with three boys, all teenagers and I saw her give them some money. Fifteen minutes later, there was a flurry of activity as all journalists present ran towards the southern entrance of the Golden Temple Complex. There, on the piled-up debris that dated back to Op Blue Star, the three boys were posing—one with a sword, the middle one with an improvised triangular orange flag that had 'Khalistan' written on it with a marker pen, and the last one with an AK-47. Camera shutters were working overtime and the iconic photo then made it to the front pages of the *Times of India, the Hindustan Times* and the *Indian Express*. I think it was then I decided I had had enough! By then, in any case, I was fully involved with the shooting of the Project Tiger series of films.

The first film where I was given charge was on the Sariska Tiger Reserve. The cameraman assigned for this episode was the large-sized Prashant Desai, who was an easy-going, laidback character with an extremely friendly disposition. When we reached Sariska he sauntered into my room, lit a cigarette and said conversationally we had met before. Since I had no recollection, he said it was at Kavita's house two years ago and that at the time, he too was dating a classmate of hers from the NID. We had apparently spoken and had at some point in the evening said we would shoot a film together. He then asked if his ex-girlfriend could hop, especially since Sariska was a stone's throw from Delhi. Not quite being up on the dynamics of human relationships, I consented, and with my friend Leslie George also wanting to come, I told him to get in touch with the lady and bring her along if she so desired.

The lady friend was of a voluptuous build, and the close proximity of being jammed with her in the seat of a bus had reduced Leslie to a quivering lovesick mass by the time they reached Sariska. Shortage of accommodation meant Leslie, Prashant and the lady had to share a room, which had terrible ramifications for Leslie, who was scarred for life psychologically by the time the sun crested the horizon a few hours later. Prashant was too tired to shoot during the next couple of days and would start snoring at the drop of a hat. My start as a film director was in absolute shambles.

Things would only get worse. The field director, K. L. Saini who was my good friend ever since we held the Army Wildlife Workshop at Sariska, suggested we pack off Ms Voluptuous who was beginning to affect other members of my crew. However, by then, the local staff in the nearby hotel had been contacted by my 'Bombay lot' and there was obviously a steady supply of marijuana flowing, which needless to say further reduced our output. And yet, when Prashant was awake, he was getting some extremely good footage, for he was undoubtedly an excellent cameraman. In the final analysis, the Sariska film when it was edited, not only passed muster but left everyone even more frustrated with what it could have been.

Two events would stand out. We were cramped inside a stone hideout at a waterhole called Slopka, about five to six kilometres further inside from the forest post at Kalighati. I had figured if we settle into the hide early around 3 p.m. and stop all other movement in the area we may get a tiger or a leopard around dusk. I had brought a book along to read, but hardly had Prashant fixed the camera, pre-focused it and did his fancy light readings, there were a series of sambar calls which were then taken up by the langurs. We literally dived into the hide but in the process, Prashant went in the wrong way. Though we had the SR III 16 mm camera covering the waterhole, we were actually minus a cameraman. The poor fellow would remain stuck in that position for almost all of the ensuing drama.

By then the place was exploding with alarm calls. It was almost deafening, and it was obvious whatever was spooking the place, it was moving rapidly towards the water hole. Unlike video, the 16 mm film was extremely expensive. A 400-feet magazine gave us ten minutes of footage. Barely able to see through the narrow aperture of the hide, I instinctively told Prashant to switch on the camera, but he could not move as he was facing the wrong way and I had to reach out and switch it on. The red light behind the motor came on just seconds before three dholes came scampering into the frame and ran into the water, which was about 60 metres from where we were.

I was incredulous. There had been no reports or sightings of '*soan kuttas*' in the region and I also knew I'd be murdered by Bittu if I shot off half a roll on feral dogs. But there was no mistaking what I was seeing. Red in colour, the tips of their tail black, these lean and lanky canines were dholes alright. I even managed to poke my 200 mm lens out of the crack and take a few stills.

Standing in the water up to their chest, the dogs drank their fill and equally hurriedly exited the area much in the manner they had come. My hands were shaking. Prashant, who by then, after contorting this way and that, had managed to get his eye to the eyepiece, had no idea as to the significance of what had just transpired. He had seen the dogs just as they were leaving and he told me we had blown three minutes of film on some *paltu kuttas* ... domesticated dogs, adding somewhat ruefully ... *'Tiger aye toh kuch maja waja aye ... yeh kya bakwas hai!'* (If a tiger comes, then it's worth our while ... what is this rubbish!)

The jungle had gone absolutely silent, not a sound. I told Prashant to pack up and he looked at me as if I had gone completely loco. It wasn't even 3:15 in the afternoon, but the arrival of wild dogs meant the entire area was most likely spooked and I figured it was now a waste of time sitting all cramped up in the hide.

I got through to Mr Saini on the wireless network from Kalighati at 5 p.m. I told him about the dogs and asked if there were any reports of their presence. There were various guards on the network, and they all reported back in the negative. Mr Saini also didn't say anything. He said we would 'discuss it' when I got back, obviously not wanting me to make a laughing stock of myself. He was convinced all the marijuana being smuggled in for the 'Bombay Wallas' had been smoked by me after all.

Later that evening I was to join Mr Saini for dinner at Sariska Palace Hotel after which he was to leave for Alwar. I walked in and found him with some 20–30 young people who were hanging on to every word he was saying as he held forth on his beloved Sariska. But he had reserved the best for my arrival, for no sooner had I walked in he introduced me to the group saying, *'Inse miliye ... inko toh Sariska mein soan kutte dikhte hain!'* (Meet this gentleman, he sees wild dogs in Sariska!) and went into peals of laughter. Luckily, no one in that group had any idea what he was talking about. Unlike video, it would be at least a week or ten days before the film was processed. Until then, I just had to grin and bear it.

The arrival of the dogs from nowhere created a stir and after that the dogs were seen regularly as they established their territory and settled down. Prime Minister Rajiv Gandhi, curious to see the dholes that were by then being widely reported in the press, scheduled the next cabinet meeting in Sariska as a result of which the entire Alwar–Sariska road got a major facelift. The dogs were around for a few years, but they never did litter, and one by one they died. I would film them a number of times, but that first afternoon was quite something else.

Kalighati used to be my base inside the park. The forest check post was teeming with red vented bulbuls, jungle babblers, tree pies and a host of other birds, some of whom would come and eat out of my hand. I would often just sit around playing with the birds, who would hop all over me. Without my being aware of it, one afternoon Prashant ran some film on this cosy little scene.

Sariska had been the shooting preserve of the Maharaja of Alwar, and there were some stone buildings in various stages of disrepair that overlooked water holes. Saini sent me a message saying a sambhar had been killed in one such location, that the tiger had probably been disturbed and so the sambar was not as yet eaten. We had a grandstand view from the old shikar lodge of the kill, and we settled down for the night, equipped with a powerful light connected to a car battery that would illuminate the sambar once we detected any movement. I was almost certain the tiger would put in an appearance, so was alert to every little sound, while Prashant was dozing intermittently. I was hoping he wouldn't snore, when I first heard the sound of a bone being snapped. Prashant had heard it too and he was wide awake. As soon as he was ready with his eye on the camera's viewfinder, I switched on the lights. Instead of a tiger, we were amazed to see a rattle (also known as a honey badger) feeding on the kill. This was rare stuff, and as shots go, perhaps was far more valuable than had it been a tiger. The SR III started to whirr silently, and I watched the red blinking light with satisfaction. The rattle too, seemed least perturbed by the light, its eyes blazing gold every time it happened to look in our direction.

Having failed to load film in the camera's magazine, Prashant had blundered big time. To make matters worse, he simply kept quiet about what he had done, for there was no way he would not have known what had happened. Subsequently all the exposed film was duly deposited at Adlabs in Bombay and when the negatives were processed and the prints made, there was no footage of the rattle. This drove Bittu and the editors crazy for no one had figured that such an elementary mistake could be made by an experienced cameraman. That was then the end of Prashant Desai, and we were now looking at a fast-dwindling list of directors of photography (DOPs).

The next shoot was earmarked for the Sundarbans. This time around, when I reached Bombay to collect my crew, I had shifted from the Grewal residence to Bittu's flat, where apart from his wife Madhu, his two daughters Miel and Tara, there was the loveable High Brow, the boxer who could steal your heart with just a glance of his marble-like eyes. With all the equipment sorted, I was clock-watching waiting for the cameraman when Bittu's phone rang in the study. The film actor, Kamal Haasan, was sitting with Bittu in the living room, so I picked up the phone, only to be told by the designated cameraman that he was not coming.

When I told Bittu we were without a DOP, his eyes became as round as High Brow's, but since Kamal Haasan was sitting there, he couldn't say or do what would have been perfectly justifiable 'stuff'. Time was running out, so Bittu gave me the keys to his precious Land Rover, asked me to drop Kamal Haasan at the Bandra–Western Express turn off, and head for the airport. He would follow, pick up an alternate cameraman and meet us there. To make matters worse, I had never driven a vehicle in Bombay, and from the side of the road, the number of cars looked scary. Anyway, it was hardly the place or the time to nit-pick, so I pointed the Land Rover in the general direction of the airport and took off.

Bittu arrived in a taxi just as we offloaded our equipment, and the mother of all surprises, he was alone! He put his hand on my shoulder, and with the look reminiscent of so many generals who in the past committed their troops to a certain death in battle, said, 'Kunal ... buddy! You'll have to shoot yourself. All the best!' I looked at Shankar, 'the' camera assistant. He was now 'my' camera assistant, and more importantly, elevated instantly to the status of Dronacharya. Two-and-a-half hours later, we had touched down in the city of Calcutta. My trial by fire had begun.

Who needs film school? It's a joke, the teaching of all the technical stuff over three to four years. Having seen Prashant shoot, I knew how a camera had to be clamped onto a tripod and 'stuff', so with a few tips from

Shankar, I started having a ball. I had my still camera, so I figured out what the light was like and then nothing escaped my attention. From sunsets where the sun travelled along in the water with the boat, to mudskippers, various types of crabs, the vegetation, the birds, the people, the deer and the rhesus monkeys foraging on the tidal flats, I got it all. Only thing that eluded me was the tiger!

Just as well, for had I got the tiger also, I have no doubt that Bittu would have killed me, for everything I had shot was an unmitigated disaster, being horribly overexposed. Having returned to Bombay, I had handed over the film cans to Adlabs and returned to Delhi. Four days later, Bittu, along with Dipti Bhalla were watching the footage as it was being projected in the mini theatre. I am told the conversation went something like this as Bittu held his head in his hands: 'That ... that ... that ...' he could not get himself to say my name, and his Bishop Cotton School, Shimla, upbringing was restraining him from using other invectives. 'Just look at that shot! If only he had his exposures right!'

It soon dawned on Dipti that I was actually shooting without a light meter. It was her turn to look incredulous, while Bittu then looked sheepish. Subsequently, for years Dipti would claim she saved me from being lynched and her appreciation of my camera angles, whatever could be seen, gave me a second chance. I was then dutifully called to Bombay, and Bittu handed me a fancy-looking German made light meter and said cheerfully that I was to leave for Palamau in Bihar in the next couple of days. I insisted on watching the Sundarbans footage that evening and made a mental note that I was approximately three to four stops over in all the shots. As we packed up that night and pulled down the bunk bed that folded into his study wall, Bittu was in a very upbeat mood. He had spent eighty thousand bucks on the meter, and with that fancy thing, I would have no more excuses. After Bittu left, I looked at the gadget, and for the life of me, could not figure out how it worked. No worries, I thought, Shankar would know how to use it.

During all my previous trips to Ranchi, it had not occurred to me to get in touch with Major General K. S. Pannu, who was the GOC of 23 Infantry Division. As a battalion commander, he had led the 2 Para Group drop at Tangail during the 1971 War and he was a close friend of my parents, who affectionately called him 'Peter Pan'. Considering I had been virtually kidnapped by Tootoo Imam the last time I landed in Ranchi, I sent General Pannu a message through my father saying I would be arriving by the afternoon flight along with a camera assistant.

I was kidnapped yet again at Ranchi airport, this time by the general who himself was waiting at the airport. The flag staff house had a well-appointed annexe, into which I was settled. Maps were then called for and the western extreme of the Chotanagpur Plateau, where Palamau was situated, were studied in detail. A caravan, a 1-tonne with a mess detachment, and an open jeep were to be part of my support team, and two officers who had been tasked to make a 'presentation' on the Tiger Reserve filled me up with whatever background information they could garner. Palamau had been one of the nine original regions that had been brought under Project Tiger. With all this out of the way, the general then bellowed for his mess waiter and in his booming voice, said the magic words, '*Saab ke liye whisky lao*' (Bring some whisky for sir). That it was still bright sunshine outside didn't seem to matter.

General Pannu was considered to be a 'madcap', and rumour had it that he had been commanding 23 Division for an unprecedented six years because the army did not know what to do with him. Mrs Gandhi, who had visited Ranchi twice during his perennial tenure, had remarked at the airport, 'General, haven't you been the GOC here for a rather long time?' and Pannu, in his own words had responded, 'Madam, haven't you been the prime minister for an even longer time?' By midnight, we were toasting the Oscar-winning documentary I was to shoot on Palamau, and by the early hours of the morning, the conversation had veered around to 23 Division's formation sign, which was a fighting cock in a round circle.

Adjacent to the GOC's house was the Doordarshan tower, and at 4 a.m., the general decided Ranchi needed to wake up and see the divisional flag fluttering on top. With a Gorkha JCO who was the guard commander saying '*Shaab Shaab ... aap mat chado shaab*' (Sir, sir, you please do not climb), Pannu, myself and the hapless JCO following, we were on top of the tower when the sun came up. Being a paratrooper, Pannu wanted to jump down, but the JCO by then had had enough and refused to let go of his general's leg until the fire brigade guys arrived and got us down. By then, my little convoy of vehicles was all lined up, and after dunking my head under the tap so I could focus on the moving objects around me, I left for Palamau.

My arrival at the headquarters of R. C. Sahai, Palamau Tiger Reserve field director, with an entourage of a nawab created quite a stir. After the madness of the previous day, everything in Bihar seemed nice and orderly, and at the field director's suggestion, we set up our camp next to the tourist lodge in Betla. The canteen manager, Mr Dubey, eyed my mess detachment as they went about the business of cooking dinner with some disapproval as they impacted his 'business'. However, since he was of a friendly disposition, he soon filled me up with the local 'gen', especially about the elephants of Palamau, who he said, did not particularly like humans. 'What about tiger sightings?' I then asked the question which everyone sooner or later asks compulsively.

Dubey-ji immediately had a philosophical look on his face, the look which sages have when they are asked the ultimate question. 'Luck by chance!' I had to admit I had never heard that one before, but it was quite a catchphrase.

The Palamau Tiger Reserve had an interesting history, for the area designated as the core area of the reserve had earlier been used to extract timber and bamboo by the forest department. Though it had a rich and diverse density of wildlife, the elephants were said to have been a feral population that had over the years returned to being wild. The proximity of villages meant the elephants were constantly at loggerheads with people, as a result of which, there was no love lost between either side. With Sahai offering to drive me around himself, finally it seemed we were ready to roll.

I had simply not had the time to figure out the light meter, so in the morning, as we waited for Sahai to arrive, Shankar and I were figuring out how it worked. With the camera mounted on the field director's jeep, we then headed into the forest. I had yet to take my first shot when we came to a small water body, and I decided to look into the water to see if there were any fish, when ... *plop!* My light meter fell into the water! It was retrieved soon enough but it was completely ruined. Logic suggested I eat crow, pack up the shoot, and head back to Bombay, but then, what the heck, who needed a light meter because I knew I was off by three stops the last time around. So once again I started reverting to the exposures I was getting, arriving at what I thought should be the aperture, and then stop it down three times. It was inverted math at best but then, there had to be a Plan B and I couldn't think of anything else.

The next three days around Betla were extremely productive, with elephants not only charging us, but chasing us long distance every time. Sahai was cool as a cucumber, weaving in and out amidst the bad-tempered pachyderms. Apart from elephants, we also got some good shots of gaur. We then shifted location and moved into the core area of the reserve. Sahai had some excellent Adivasi trackers, and they said a tigress was lying up near a water hole. Even though it was getting late, and the light was running away from us, we entered a grassy patch next to the water. A herd of gaur were approaching, and suddenly a tigress came out of the grass and faced the bovines. A fascinating stand-off then ensued, with four of the younger gaur forming a defensive wall, while the rest of the herd bunched up around the calves. The drama was still going on when it became too dark, so we left the area. Since there was no kill in the area in the morning, obviously the gaur had won that round.

Amazingly, the footage I shot in Palamau had perfect exposures, so I never bothered to tell anyone that the light meter was damaged. After coming back from Palamau I had been spending time at the *Sanctuary Magazine* office with the editorial team that was headed by Gita Vasudevan. *Sanctuary* had a children's edition called *Cub* and I wrote a couple of articles for it, which included a sanitized version on the wolves of Hazaribagh. Summer was just setting in, and I was now wanting to return to the Sundarbans to re-shoot that episode. In addition, I also wanted to go see Butch Datta in Calcutta and find out where Brinda was. Almost a year had passed since Kavita and I had broken up, and I often found myself thinking of the Assam trip. Unfortunately, ever since I had said goodbye to Brinda at the airport, in the rush of subsequent events, there had been no contact whatsoever.

Bittu, however, was keen that I go to Kashmir and Ladakh with the team shooting the *Rakshak* series, insisting I had to shoot the wildlife part of the docu-drama that revolved around a city boy tackling conservation issues. However, since there was a gap before we departed for that shoot, he suggested I return to Delhi for a while, and join the team directly from there. I had no clue what was brewing and had no clue that even Bittu was a party to it.

11

The Reluctant Goose & the Gander

When my uncle Ravi Hoon wore his polka dot aquamarine bow tie, it usually meant he was out to impress some people, with his 'England-returned' lineage. I was told we were going to the Raj Bhawan to meet the lieutenant governor of Delhi and that I should not dress as if I was coming from the jungles of Bihar. I for one had no desire whatsoever to meet anyone, so did my best to wriggle out, but then I got the cold stare from my father, which meant that I was to shut up and do as I was told.

We still had our trusted Fiat with the TRA 1111 registration number, and I drove my parents and my uncle to Old Delhi, with no one saying anything, which was a bit strange. Ushered into the august presence of the lieutenant governor, Air Vice Marshal Harkrishan Lal Kapoor, I was surprised to see a fair number of people, who were all introduced as members of his extended family. Among them was also Bittu Sahgal's brother and his children. Seated in a corner were three or four young girls, all very pretty. Until that moment, I had actually convinced myself that I had been dragged along only because my parents needed a driver, but then to my absolute shock, it dawned on me I was the victim of what in Delhi's Punjabi circles was known as 'matchmaking'.

Panic comes in all forms and sizes, and this one was a tsunami. The events as they unfolded, it was almost a caricature. The first young lady was Bittu's niece, but she very expertly, while giving radiant smiles to everyone, told me from the corner of her mouth, 'Please say no. I have a boyfriend!' *Yippee, one down! How many more to go?* The matchmakers had also decided since cupid and cold coffee were both spelt with a 'c', I would be given a large glass which would see me through the allotted audition time with each 'candidate'. The next one I found myself with was Simrita Kapoor, who seemed even more terrified than me. The choreographers for the evening had ensured we would get ten minutes together alone in a side room, and the Raj Bhawan bearers plonked two large glasses of cold coffee in front of us. 'So ...' I said, wondering what on earth was I supposed to say. Simi, for that was the shortened version of her name, looking more and more like a frightened rabbit, spoke up instead: 'I hate wildlife!'

I think I burst out laughing, which was taken by all the others watching from the living room as a sign of how well we were getting along. I don't know if high-fives were exchanged, because by then I desperately needed to get to a loo and get rid of the two jumbo-sized glasses (without ice cream) of toned milk. The only saving grace was that the other girls (if they were indeed there for that purpose) were not subject to this utter nonsense. Then the lieutenant governor was showing my father an engraved shotgun to that had been presented to him by President Mikhail Gorbachev and after a few pleasantries, we were driving back home. And I was fuming! I don't think there was any ambiguity in what I said.

Two days later I flew to Srinagar to join the crew that had reached directly to shoot two of the *Rakshak* episodes. The fairly large team was being headed by Vikas Desai, who was a reputed name in Bombay, especially in the ad film circles. Also waiting for me was Sanjay Monga, a naturalist who Bittu wanted me to take on as an understudy. Considering I had barely shot the Palamau film, that was one heck of an ask! We moved to a camp with some wooden cabins just outside the gate of the Dachigam National Park, where the first episode was to be shot. As actors were involved in the shoot, I was to delink and shoot the background material, which included landscape shots and whatever wildlife I could get.

I had not met any of the people before, but I soon realized I had walked into an extremely hostile environment. If I walked into a room, the conversation would stop, or if I sat on a table, the others would actually get up and sit elsewhere. It was, to put it mildly, disconcerting but there was nothing I could do about it under the circumstances. The only exception was one of the assistant directors, Sumee Hathangadi, who smiled at me when she walked past. Sure enough, the next morning I was told the vehicle was full and it would return for me and my assistant after dropping the others. Not wanting to miss out on the light, I started walking with the camera while Shankar carried the heavy tripod and batteries. We took some shots on the way, but by then I realized no vehicle was coming for us.

By the time we reached the place where the shoot was being held, it was lunch time. The van was parked nearby, and the driver was fast asleep in it. Having walked 10 kilometres, I was in a nasty mood. I saw Vikas Desai standing on a wooden bridge, so I went up to him and caught him by his shirt, bending him over the railing. 'Listen, I'm here to do a job. You do yours and I'll do mine. Just don't cross with me again.' Vikas said there had been a misunderstanding, so I let go of him. After that we had a frosty and stand-offish relationship, but no one interfered with my work. A couple of days later I got a chance to speak to Sumee and I asked her why the crew was so against me. She looked at me frankly and said, 'Vikas and the crew are all from FTII. They feel you are a general's son and Bittu is humouring you because he needs you to open doors here in Kashmir and later in Ladakh. Also, it's a well-known fact that you've taken the place of an FTII cameraman.'

To make matters worse, the trip was fairly long. From Srinagar we then flew to Ladakh where the forest department was planning to release a snow leopard that had been trapped earlier by them. Bittu had promptly tweaked the script to include the moment, which I duly filmed. Then having shot their scenes, the Bombay crew departed, and I was quite happy to see them go. Ramu Gaur (now a major general) was at the time commanding the newly raised 28 Infantry Division, which was based at Nimu, and he had promised Bittu logistic support, so I could proceed to Chushul and shoot the black-necked crane and also the kiang (Tibetan wild ass) that were found in abundance on the old Chushul runway.

An open jeep was a rarity in Ladakh, for almost all army vehicles were winterized. I had also been assigned Captain Sawhney, who was from the Punjab Regiment, and we set off over Chang La with a 1-tonne and 3-tonne with support staff. At that time of the year, the 17,688 feet (5392 m) pass was a lark, but we got held up as the army was in the process of inducting the BMPs for high-altitude trials. Taking armoured vehicles across on roads that were not designed to handle such heavy trailers was requiring a lot of manoeuvring, and both Sawhney and me had to pitch in to guide the inexperienced drivers through the night.

In Chushul we got the mandatory footage of the stately, black-necked cranes and their yellow-coloured chick. According to wildlife authorities, only three pairs used to come into Indian territory at the time. Then we headed for the Spangur Gap that was to the south of the majestic Pangong Tso where the kiang roamed the deserted airfield on the Indian side. Since November 1962, when IAF An-12s had flown AMX-13 tanks to take on the Chinese, the area was a sort of no man's land. The runway was littered with the debris of the war, for no one had ever ventured into the area. Since the Chinese ate the kiang, the herds used to stay more or less on the Indian side. One of the most endearing qualities about these animals was their tendency to race along vehicles.

One of the first movies I had seen as a kid was *Hatari* in which they capture wild animals by noosing them from vehicles. With the wind flying through my hair, I was perched on top of the seat, filming the racing kiangs in much the same manner when suddenly, the Chinese post on the flank of the Spangur Gap started to wave a red flag. 'Oh shit!' said Sawhney, reluctantly bringing the jeep to a halt. 'What's their problem?'

The flag, some 3 kilometres from us, was waving even more vigorously, so we figured we better head back. The kiang had also stopped and were looking at us, their tails twitching, for they too were enjoying themselves by the look of it. We were still 500 metres short of the dirt road on our side when I said to Sawhney, 'I think we are sinking!' We barely managed to get out with the camera equipment, before the jeep disappeared into what was a freezing cold swamp. On the surface the ground looked firm enough, other than the fact it seemed to have a whitish look.

Watching the jeep disappear, our support team in the 1-tonne immediately decided to come to our rescue, and promptly started sinking themselves. Fortunately, the heavy vehicle didn't go all the way, but the tyres were no longer visible. Caution not being part of any army's ethos, the 3-tonne now rushed forward. Fortunately, Sawhney managed to stop them from also committing hara-kiri by yelling and flapping his arms like a madman from across the 'swamp'. I have no idea how the loss of a jeep was explained by 28 Division, but we were told later that the 'white patch' had claimed umpteen vehicles, including a couple of bulldozers. Since the 3-tonne could not pull the 1-tonne out, I requested the officer in charge of the BMPs to winch it out. The presence of the armoured vehicles was supposed to be a secret from the Chinese, so we could only recover the 1-tonne in pitch darkness.

After dumping the footage in Bombay, I returned to Delhi in the first week of June, thinking all the 'matchmaking' drama had been settled. I was told that the 'family' had approved of the girl, who was from Welham Girls' School and was four years younger to me, that the 'engagement' had been fixed for 12 June and that I was not expected to make a scene! Simi and I were allowed to meet once at her house in Faridabad, where neither of us knew what to say to each other. I again protested, but was told the invitations had been issued, and why was I posing to be a problem. Anyway, came the date and we were betrothed!

Now that the suckling pig had the apple in its mouth, Bittu became extremely cooperative about doing the Sundarbans shoot and Shankar and I were soon back in what was fast becoming familiar terrain. Pranabes Sanyal by then had become a close friend and we got some very good footage of the various initiatives being taken to encourage the 'Royal Bengals' to change their habits and even more importantly, their diet. Though twice we saw a tiger in the distance, they were much too far to get a shot, so I decided to construct a machan supported by stilts near one of the freshwater ponds where animals used to come and drink. After it was prepared, I climbed onto it with a camera and a shotgun and told my launch to return in a few hours. Sitting about 4 metres above the ground, barely camouflaged by some scanty branches, I was hoping to get a few good shots. However, after half an hour I realized I was down to 3 metres, then after another half hour, barely a metre and a half above the ground.

I was by then fervently praying the 'Royal Bengal' did not turn up, for even the shotgun was loaded with bird shot and not LGs. By the time the launch came back, I was sitting on the ground, a complete nervous, but fortunately, alive wreck!

I was badgering Sanyal to take me to Chaimari, which was where the Sundarbans met the Bay of Bengal. The beach was teeming with a million red-coloured ghost crabs that ran away from you like a wave as one walked along the beach. The tidal flats had a series of tree stumps, the ground all around covered with tracks of the Royal Bengal. Chital, with their tails up at the sight of humans, let out a few alarm calls, then ignored us, allowing me to take some languid pans that involved moving the camera around a full 360 degrees. We had also brought along some olive ridley turtle hatchlings, and since the eggs had been collected from the same beach, they were released about 50 metres from the water. As the little fellows used their flippers to propel themselves towards the ocean, I couldn't help but wonder what lay ahead of them. If they survived, they would come back here maybe a decade later and lay their eggs on the same beach. Standing at Chaimari, it really felt one was where the land met the sea, and in the process of evolution, this was where life had begun.

Back in Bombay, Bittu told me Dipti Bhalla was going to edit all my films, which at that point of time were Sariska, Palamau and Sundarbans. Though she had often been talked about, I was yet to meet Dipti. From the 1984 editing and direction batch of FTII, given my experience with Vikas Desai and the other alumni of the film school, I expected her to be equally cold and aloof. On the contrary, she was vivacious and friendly, and suggested I accompany Bittu in the evening to Badhwar Park where her sister Niti was getting married to Gagan Sharma, he being of the 1972 batch of the Doon School.

I obviously did not know this then, but Dipti had already started sorting the Sariska footage a couple of days earlier and had come across the small clip that Prashant Desai had shot of me laughing and feeding the tree pies at the Kalighati forest check post. On an impulse, she had clipped that section of film out and taken it home, where she stuck it to her dressing table mirror. She then showed it to Niti and mentioned 'that's the guy I want to marry' or words to that effect. Then she added quite ruefully, 'but he's just got engaged'. Niti, the wise one, replied, 'How does that matter!'

The next couple of days along with Bittu, I sat at the back of the room watching Dipti cut the film on a Steenbeck editing table. She would sing Hindi songs aloud while she worked, and she obviously knew her job. After the rough cut was done, I was to fly back to Delhi. At that time, my father's brother, Vijay Dhruv was also posted at the Bombay and Maharashtra Area Headquarters and his labrador retriever had littered. My father asked me to pick up a female pup and bring her with me to Delhi. On my way to the airport, I had to stop at Famous Studio where Bittu and Dipti were editing, and in the semi-dark room, I handed the puppy to Dipti for a minute.

Those days the airlines were a lot more easy-going, and I had Maggi (named subsequently) in my lap throughout the flight. She was barely seven weeks old and was loving the attention she was getting from all the air hostesses on board the Airbus 300. After we landed and I disembarked, I let her loose on the tarmac and she promptly squatted under the ultra-massive engine of the Airbus and piddled and piddled, the patch getting bigger and bigger!

Simi and I were married on 10 October 1986 at the Air Force Officers' Mess next to India Gate. That night, for the first time we actually got a chance to talk, and it was pretty obvious to me I had been married to a person whose expectations from life were completely at odds with me. At breakfast I told my father it was not going to work, and he sagely said give it time and don't rush things. The next day we were packed off to Goa, where the Corps of Signal's Mess had reserved a room for us. There we spent a miserable night, swatting mosquitoes, after which I decided we needed better digs. Fortunately, we got reservations at the Taj Aguada at the last minute and moved into a fairly comfortable cottage.

The coconut trees swaying in the breeze, the sea, and the Taj ambience seemed to mellow Simi down, but only for a while. She now confessed to me how she dreaded the arrival of the Portuguese from the sea, which was one of her childhood nightmares. 'Then why did you agree to come to Goa?' I asked in despair. At my wits end and my father's wise words ringing in my ears about rushing things, I decided to go for a walk. The Aguada Fort overlooked the bay, which was empty except for one solitary figure who was bobbing around with the waves. I stood there, thinking 'it cannot get worse', and at that point, the figure in the bay, some 200 metres out, turned in my direction. In what would have killed a Bollywood scriptwriter with unbridled joy, the person was Brinda.

From Goa we flew to Bombay where Bittu fussed over Simi and then grandly announced I would be shooting not only the Manas and Buxa films in Assam and West Bengal respectively, but also the Namdapha episode in the extreme eastern corner of Arunachal. Dipti also came and met my new bride and they seemed to hit it off, at least on the face of it. Ever since I had got hitched, everyone seemed to roll their eyes at me—first Brinda when she heard I had just got married and was there with my wife, then Dipti when she made eye-contact with me, and then even Gita Vasudevan in the *Sanctuary* office. *You! Arranged marriage!* Everyone was behaving as if I had let my entire generation down!

Back in Delhi I took a loan at some ridiculous interest rates from a finance guy and bought a Maruti Gypsy duly registered as DID 7523. Simi by then seemed resigned to her fate and had stopped indulging in histrionics about the Portuguese and other equally bizarre characters, and we set off on quite an incredible drive. The first stop, I was told subsequently, was a blunder—never take your wife to the Taj Mahal, after which we proceeded to Kanpur and then Patna via Arrah. After the Gypsy's first servicing was done, we then proceeded to Allahabad and then drove through endless banana plantations to Purnea, and then finally reached Siliguri. I now had a new camera assistant, Naik, who joined us at Bagdogra and then we went and set up base at Alipurduar, which was the headquarters of the Buxa Tiger Reserve.

Though the reserve itself had some of the most spectacular forests on the banks of the Sankosh River, there was very little wildlife to be seen. After a few days in the area, we then drove through Bodo country to Barpeta Road, where we linked up with Sanjoy Deb Roy again. Initially we set up our camp at Mathanguri, which overlooked the Manas River that acted as the International Boundary between India and Bhutan. The course of the river itself was fascinating—it entered India from Tibet at Khensemane as the Namgyang Chu, was joined by the Namka Chu a couple of kilometres downstream, then almost doubled in volume when it met the Mago or Tawang Chu that flowed in from the east near Lumla. It then entered Bhutan, skirted the Se La massif and continued southward, being joined by many other spectacular rivers. After it re-entered India at Manas, it braided into two main channels in the plains, and then joined the Brahmaputra as the Bwrsi and the Bholkaduba. 'The mahseer are running,' said Deb Roy, seeing my fishing gear in the Gypsy, 'try a few casts just before sunset!'

One could see the fish, and they were some huge specimens coming to the surface every now and then. On the second day, just as the sun was about to set, I walked across to the river. Giant hornbills were flying across the river, their wings going *woosh-woosh*, and I tried a few casts using *chilwa* as live bait. Not getting a strike, I decided to walk back, with the intention of filming the sunset. There was a small branch of the river that one had to ford, and just as I entered the water, I heard a tiger calling behind me. I spun around and to this day, it has to be the most majestic sight I have ever seen. Framed perfectly against the setting sun, the tiger was standing on the very rock I had just vacated, and perhaps it was my lingering scent that triggered it off, he was calling *aaah-oooo, aaah-oooo*! The tragedy was, I could see Naik walking down from the other side with the tripod and the camera, but then some moments are better left imprinted in one's mind's eye alone.

While we were at Mathanguri, His Majesty Jigme Singye Wangchuck, better known as K4 arrived at his lodge across the Manas. I had crossed the river to try and film the golden langur (*Trachypithecus geei*) which was found on the Bhutanese side. I promptly ran into K4 who most graciously invited me to have a cup of tea with him, and for the next two hours we had a long chat about conservation measures being adopted in India, especially the concept and the setting up of tiger reserves. By the time I took his leave, the sun was way too high for any worthwhile shots, so I returned minus the golden langur, without which the film on Manas would be incomplete.

Manas was perhaps one of the richest reserves in the country when it came to biodiversity, but it was difficult terrain to negotiate as the roads were nothing but overgrown jeep tracks and streams had to often be negotiated. So, we decided to shift to the forest post at Bansbari, which was in the Central Range and close to Deb Roy's headquarters at Barpeta Road. By then Simi was also getting into the act, a far cry from her 'I hate wildlife' statement when I first met her. I kept postponing the shooting of the golden langurs, and eventually time ran out as I had to return to Bombay with the masses of exposed film cans. Leaving Simi and Naik with friends in Guwahati, I flew to Bombay and returned in a few days after having seen the rushes. The golden langur would have to wait, for we now had to go and shoot the Namdapha film.

The park's headquarters were at Miao, from where we had to drive along some of the wildest rain forest country on the eastern side of the Noa-Dehing River. The cane and banana vegetation, the incredible size of the trees that seemed to reach for the skies, it was simply awe inspiring. 'Oh look,' said Simi who first spotted a troop of hoolock gibbons (*Hoolock hoolock*), the only ape species to be found in the Indian subcontinent. We sat in the Gypsy watching the black-coloured males and golden females leap from incredible heights, going from one tree to another. Having spotted the gibbons, Simi felt exhilarated, and during this leg of the filming, she was extremely involved in the shoot.

The road was cut by a landslide 3 kilometres short of Deban, where the circular, elevated guest house was situated. An elephant was waiting for us at the spot, so the equipment was transferred, and we walked the rest of the way. Sharma-ji, the cook-cum-caretaker had just settled us into our rooms, when he came and said I was needed in the wireless room. After a lot of clicks and hisses, Bittu was patched in from Bombay. The thought that we were in the pristine rain forests was driving him insane with excitement, and he went on and on about shooting everything that existed, from the rotting vegetation on the ground to the middle and top canopies. 'And of course, see if you can get the tiger.'

We soon realized the going was extremely tough and that we were not really equipped to handle the vegetation. For starters, the ground was crawling with leeches, while the larger tiger leeches dropped on you from the shrubs. Despite having worn protective gear over our boots and doused ourselves in diesel, both Naik and me were a bloody mess in a matter of minutes. Besides, the vegetation was so thick, light hardly penetrated to the ground. With an increasing sense of panic, I came to the conclusion we were going to get very little worthwhile footage unless I did something drastic. When confused, I'd go fishing, and so I took my rod in the afternoon, and after crossing the aqua green waters of the Noa-Dehing, decided to reconnoitre the area across the river.

I caught two black mahseer, both identical in size, weighting approximately 20 lb each and had just started to walk back towards the boat that would take me back across the river when a vehicle arrived and two men carrying a rifle started to walk towards me. One of them asked me if I was Kunal, and then he introduced himself as Rajen, the son of the Tai Khamti chief, Chow Khamoon Gohain, my father's old friend who had shot buffalo with him twenty-five years previously. They had come from Chaukham to invite me and my wife over for a couple of days to visit their family. While we talked, Rajen also said the family owned a sawmill, and sure, I could film it if I wanted to. One of the biggest problems, Deb Roy had explained to me on an earlier occasion, was the felling of the hollong trees whose veneer was then stripped to make plywood. Not an easy tree to cultivate, most of the 40-metre-high specimens in the wild had been harvested.

Though Chaukham was not very far from the other side of the river, I had no choice but to drive all the way back to Tinsukia and then loop back. Since it was also obvious to me that no matter how hard we tried, filming Namdapha was not going to be possible, I decided to first go to Dinjan, where thanks to the GOC 2 Infantry Division, I loaded my Gypsy with three crates of rum. Then we carried on to Chaukham, reaching well after sunset.

As we entered the compound of Chow Khamoon Gohain's house, I was surprised to see elephants milling around. Lavished by Tai Khamti hospitality, the next morning I filmed the saw mill, where huge boles of hollock, perhaps three to four metres in girth, were loaded onto machines by elephants, and then the veneer was taken off almost like an endless saree to make plywood.

Back in Deban, I told Sharma-ji to get hold of the *gaon burah* and spread the word in the villages that I would give a bottle of rum for any animal or bird species, so that we could film and release them in the wild. The Project Tiger headquarters had a mini zoo, and two slender lorises had arrived to be filmed and returned. By the time I did that and deposited them back in Miao, it was late in the evening. By the time I got back, the entire garden of the rest house was covered with sacks, some emitting snarling sounds, some hissing and some lying there in a sulky silence. Sharma-ji explained that most of the animals were used to humans as they were pets, but since I had not specified wild or otherwise, he had given each person a bottle of the promised rum. After releasing half-a-dozen terrified dogs that had been trussed up in the sacks (you'll find scamsters wherever you go), I decided to open the rest of the sacks only in the morning.

We got some wonderful shots; the star of the show was a thirteen-foot-long reticulated python. One hoolock baby was a menace, for she insisted on sitting on my shoulder and peering through the viewfinder of the camera when she was supposed to swing from a vine instead. We had a pygmy rhesus that ran away with the lens cap and all sorts of birds that refused to be 'released in the wild'. By the evening, we had dozens of species on camera, but not one of the characters of the ensemble cast was willing to leave the scene. One by one their drunk owners straggled by, collected their wards, and sanity returned to the situation. The reticulated python, of all things, became great pals with Simi, who was handling it with absolute ease. It was perhaps the only creature that finally slithered off to its 'freedom'.

We now needed a break, so again we left the Gypsy in Guwahati and while Simi flew to Delhi, I came back with Naik to Bombay, and then proceeded to Delhi having left the exposed footage with Adlabs. Sher Khan had passed away while we were away and had been buried outside the house in Dhaula Kuan, but the parents had moved to Jammu by then as my father took over the reins of 26 Infantry Division. All my belongings had been packed in cartons and had been deposited at the

Noida flat in Arun Vihar. We were just beginning to unpack, when the doorbell rang.

I had not seen Nirmal Hoon ever since the SBI episode. Now, two-and-a-half years later, almost as if it was the most natural thing in the world, he opened his briefcase and placed a large file on my table. Even before he could say anything, I told him I no longer had any active links with any newspaper, magazine or even the AP for that matter. From my uncle's tone, I knew he was in one of his moods, so I just shut up and listened. I was aware Nirmal Hoon had fallen out with Ashok Jain, his old bosom buddy and Chairman of the Bennett Coleman Group (*Times of India*) over what he considered a personal betrayal over the acquisition of his company, Turner Morrison.

'Rajiv Gandhi has said in Parliament that if any evidence of black money stashed abroad is presented to his government, he will take immediate action. Ashok and Alok Jain have ₹700 crore stashed away in Barclays Bank in the UK and other European countries. All the records and papers you need are in this file. Can you get it to him?' How on earth did he expect me to, and besides, how could I check and verify anything? 'You'll think of something,' he said. 'I'll contact you. Three days from now, same time.' After fussing over Simi for a couple of minutes, Nirmal Hoon was gone.

Once again, I couldn't make head or tail of most papers, but it was highly unlikely that the papers did not carry gravitas. In the morning, still not sure if I wanted to get involved, I went and met Vicki at her residence and showed her the file. She leafed through it and every now and then said 'wow'. Then she said, 'Kunal, it looks genuine enough, but AP doesn't, cannot do an investigative breaking story. It's not our mandate.' She was holding the file out to me, but then she seemed to change her mind. 'Tell you what, leave the file with me for 48 hours. I'll get the documents verified and authenticated. Then it's your baby!'

Two days later Samuel returned the file. 'Vicki must really like you,' he said. 'It cost AP a bomb to check these out. They're all authentic. Good luck!' That was also the last time I ever went to the AP office. I stood outside and looked back at the yellow barrack-like building. I knew it was the end of yet another chapter in my life.

Lieutenant Colonel Ajay Narayan Mushran was two years older than my father and they had grown up together in Jabalpur. After serving in the army, he had sought voluntary retirement and successfully created a place for himself in Madhya Pradesh's political scene, even serving as the finance minister in Digvijay Singh's cabinet in the early 1980s. Considered to be an upright and clean politician, at the time he was the chairman of the National Ex-Servicemen Congress. From the AP office I went straight to his house and even though I had arrived unannounced, he saw me immediately. I told him I had some vital information for the prime minister, and could he facilitate a meeting. I showed him the file, and after flipping the first few pages, he got up and locked his study door. For the next two hours he then read every scrap of paper in the file, while I just looked at him. He then picked up the phone and dialled a number, speaking in a hushed voice, so much so that even I could not hear him clearly. Putting the phone down, he said, '10 o'clock you come here sharp. Rajiv-ji has agreed to meet us.' As I was leaving, I handed the file back to him. 'Sir you keep it. I don't feel safe carrying it around.' He nodded, and locked it in his drawer.

In the evening, bang on schedule Nirmal Hoon was standing at the door. I briefed him about what had happened and told him the meeting was fixed for the morrow. My uncle then took his visiting card, and wrote a number at the back. 'Give this number only to Rajiv if he asks for it. No one else!'

We drove in Ajay Mushran's car to 7 Race Course Road and walked into Arun Singh's residence, which I think was part of the same complex that housed Rajiv Gandhi. Dressed in his trademark white kurta–pyjama, Arun Singh started reading the file while he was still standing in his living room. Four or five pages later, he let out a whistle and in an exaggerated manner fell on the sofa, 'This is killing stuff!' He handed the file back to Ajay Mushran, after which we walked across some manicured gardens and into the prime minister's presence inside his spacious office.

The room was heated and Rajiv too was dressed like Arun Singh. There was an off-white telephone on his table, but other than that, nothing else. There was no sign of recognition, which was not surprising, and it was his turn to start reading the file. I was watching his face carefully, and there was not a hint of emotion, just the same pleasant demeanour which never seemed to change. After five minutes, having perhaps read ten or twelve pages, Rajiv Gandhi shut the file and gave it back to Ajay Mushran. Looking straight at me, he said, 'Your source? Can I speak to him?' He nudged the phone towards me. I took the card out of my pocket and dialled the number. After the first ring, it was picked up immediately. 'Ram Jethmalani here,' said a voice. I asked if I could speak to Mr Hoon who immediately came on. 'I'm with the prime minister. He wants to speak to you.'

'Give it to him,' said my uncle. I handed the phone to Rajiv, who then spoke to him for three or four minutes. The prime minister was speaking in monosyllables. He then put the phone down and was then all charm. He told Ajay Mushran that we should proceed to South Block and meet his personal secretary, whom he referred to as Sarla-ji. He had asked him to give her the file and she would take the matter forward. He thanked me for all the trouble I had taken but did not get up to shake hands. His face was smiling, but his eyes were cold.

I think even Ajay Mushran was caught by surprise when we met Sarla Grewal, for her tone was hostile and her body language downright rude. Mushran was quiet when we left South Block, for he was probably astute enough to realize what had happened. I then said goodbye to him and went home. The next morning, we shut down the Noida flat, and I flew to Guwahati, while Simi went to Faridabad to spend a few days with her parents after which she would fly to Jammu. In the evening, there was a call from her. She then said that in the afternoon papers, there was a photograph of my uncle, Nirmal Hoon. He was handcuffed to a hospital bed, where he had been shifted after he had complained of breathlessness after being arrested earlier in the day.[16]

[16] A couple of months later, I was asked by the executive editor of the Indian Express, Arun Shourie, to come and see him. He then asked me if I had any clue as to what was going on. He then showed me a subsequent report that had been tabled in Parliament where Nirmal Hoon started the narrative by addressing the prime minister and saying,' My nephew Kunal Verma had met you ...' Shourie then said, whose money do you think was being laundered? 'Don't get yourself killed in the crossfire.'

12

Wild Buffalo & Naked Women

There were more serious matters afoot, than to worry about Nirmal Hoon, who was in any case resourceful enough to deal with the entire Rajiv Gandhi government on his own. Despite his disastrous handling of Op Blue Star, General Sundarji had taken over as COAS in February 1986 from Arun Vaidya, and by November he had put into place Op Brasstacks, which amounted to virtually deploying the entire Indian Army on the Western Front. Sundarji's confidence and mannerisms were such that he could bulldoze his way past just about anyone, and by the end of the year, war with Pakistan seemed to be around the corner. Naik had been replaced by Mathew, who had arrived full of trepidation, for after returning to Bombay, the former had been telling tall tales about how difficult the shoots were, about elephants and buffalo, and leeches and more leeches, and of course what a horror I was for I would have him up at 4 a.m. every day and walk and walk in jungles that were so thick you could not see your hand in front of your own body. I wrapped up the loose ends in Namdapha and after a quick trip to Bombay around Christmas, reviewed all the footage with Bittu and Dipti that we had shot. Bittu said he wanted me to now exit from the Northeast, finish Sundarbans and then go on to Simlipal in Orissa. From there I was to come into Madhya Pradesh and shoot the film on the Indravati Tiger Reserve as well.

In another time and space, according to the Ramayana, Ram's *vanar sena* had been led by golden langurs and these were turning out to be my biggest headache. With Mathew in tow, I drove to Barpeta Road with the intention of filming the monkeys on the Bhutan side and had tentatively given myself two to three days to do so. As we sat down for lunch at Deb Roy's residence, the All India Radio news was extremely grim, and it seemed a matter of hours before war with Pakistan would break out. Impulsively, I said I had changed my mind about filming the langur and would make an overnight dash for Calcutta which was around 700 kilometres, from where I would fly back to Jammu via Delhi. As we were leaving, Deb Roy said, 'Just short of the Sankosh River, there is a patch of forest. If you are lucky, you may find the golden by the side of the road. Very few people know they exist there, so keep it to yourself.'

I almost missed the langurs. Clipping along, I had forgotten what Deb Roy had said when I saw a dead monkey on the road. Thinking it was the usual Hanuman langur, I went past, intent on getting to Siliguri where I planned to refuel. Three kilometres later I stopped, reversed and came back. The golden were supposed to be arboreal, but there was no mistaking the carcass even though it was partly squashed by a passing vehicle. Then I saw some movement in the trees and realized an entire troop was watching me, some of the langur sitting on branches fairly close by. Telling Mathew to unpack and load the camera, I then spent a couple of hours filming these wonderful creatures, even as trucks and other heavy vehicles thundered past every now and then.

Driving through the night, I crossed the Farakka Barrage at sunrise, and stopped to watch thousands of ducks wheel around in the sky. Further down the road, every few hundred metres, men were selling cotton and common teals, pochards, mallards and an assortment of other water fowl. Again, we stopped to film this blatant violation of the Wildlife Act, coming to the sad conclusion that laws in India, even if they did exist, meant nothing. The ducks were easily caught by the local populace who would enter the water with an earthen pot over their head and swim slowly into an unsuspecting flock. One by one, they would grab the birds by their legs and pull them underwater. These live birds would then be sold to passing vehicles in their hundreds.

Bittu's nephew, Arjun Katyal, looked after *Sanctuary Magazine's* office in Calcutta. I had a quick shower, and leaving the Gypsy in his care, got to the airport where Mathew was put on the Bombay flight. I got to Delhi late in the evening and since the Jammu flight was early in the morning, I curled up and slept at the airport itself.

In Jammu, no one knew I was coming, and since the army area was closed to civilian traffic, I had to walk to Topi Bungalow which was the GOC's residence. By then I looked like something the cat brought home; I was stopped by the guard commander at the entrance. I said to him I was the general's son, but he said, *'Hanji. Jaroor honge. Aap peeche se aiye, waha aapko Subedar Saab milenge'* (Oh yes, you must be. But please come from the back where you can meet the Subedar Saab). Topi Bungalow is perhaps one of the most sprawling estates in the Indian Army, having been the abode of the British Regent at one time. Fortunately for me, just then I saw Leo, Tara and Maggi being taken for a walk at the far end of the driveway. The moment I whistled, Leo went berserk, tore himself free of the leash and came running into my arms. The guard looked most sheepish, but he was only doing his job.

Op Brasstacks meant everyone was on high alert, but at another level, life was fairly normal outwardly. Captain (later Major General) Anil Rai, who was from 15 Rajput, was my father's ADC. He was about a year older than me, and we were to become good friends over the years. But there was nothing much for me to do in Jammu, so after a while as the tension at the border also seemed to cool down, I flew back to Calcutta. Until then, Simi was enjoying being the daughter-in-law in the environs of Topi Bungalow, but the moment I left, she started saying she wanted to be on the shoots as well.

Shankar was back as my camera assistant, and I headed off into the Sundarbans yet again. This time around I also had Indrajit Neogi, who was an FTII trained sound recordist, and when Arjun Katyal also decided to join the gang, the film crew had more than doubled in size. Sound was such an important part of a film, and it was an education watching Neogi at work, for he also had to try and get matching tracks for our earlier shoots. He had this elaborate list given to him by Dipti Bhalla, that for once we, the camera crew, were in a supporting role. Arjun, on the other hand, discovered a cockroach on the boat and letting out a yelp, climbed up the boat's exhaust pipe. Since at night I also had to do my share of lookout duty in case a tiger tried to clamber on board, I used to sit on the deck with a canvas thrown over my head, a shotgun in my lap, and a torch stuck to my shoulder while I read Carl Sagan's *Cosmos*. All I had to do to connect with the subject of the book was to throw the canvas off, and the entire Milky Way and the Universe used to smile down on me.

A day before we were to return to Port Canning, we ran into a terrible storm. The lids on the water tanks on the deck were accidentally left open, as a result of which salt water got into them as the waves washed over the boat. The next day, Shankar despite being told not to do so, drank from the tidal creek and by the time we got to Calcutta, he was violently sick. Arjun Katyal and Indrajit Neogi rushed him back to Bombay, but I learnt later that the brave soul who had been with me now for all my Sundarban shoots, sadly failed to make it. Naik, flown in as a replacement, now had a chance to add to his stories as ahead of us lay uncharted territory for I was not familiar with this part of the country.

A fair chunk of the Eastern Ghats that stretch from north to south running parallel to the Bay of Bengal are a part of the Simlipal Tiger Reserve in Orissa. Surrounded by Santhal and Ho villages, the wildlife was completely spooked because of the regular practice of *akhand shikar*, where villagers slaughtered anything that moved. As a result, the entire wildlife in the region had become completely nocturnal. Simi was back with me, and I was also concerned about anyone picking up the deadly cerebral malaria, which was rampant in the area. On the flip side, Simlipal with its hills and streams was perhaps one of the most beautiful reserves I had seen. Three days of driving around and not seeing even a mouse during daylight hours was a huge problem. I also wanted to film the rituals around the *akhand shikar*, and so I drove to one of the Santhal villages late in the evening, with the intention of meeting the village elders. However, within seconds we were surrounded by an extremely hostile crowd, who felt we were 'government agents'. With some difficulty, we managed to extricate ourselves from the mob, who seemed even scarier in the headlights of the Gypsy.

From Baripada in Simlipal, one had to go along the coastal road via Balasore to Bhubaneswar, a six- or seven-hour drive. Bittu had made contact with the director of the Nandankanan Zoological Park and messaged me to go and see him. I needed to service my Gypsy, so we stayed for a couple of days in the city, then headed back to Simlipal with a leopard, a sloth bear, a pangolin, a hyena and a few more assorted creatures loaded at the back. The leopard, whose handler promptly let him out of his cage, had his head stuck out of my window like a dog for the entire duration of the drive back to Baripada. At the Simlipal Tiger Reserve gate, the guard almost had a heart attack, and to make life even more exciting, the leopard insisted on sleeping on my legs at night while Simi sat bolt upright.

Two days later, after we had finished with the animals, a van from Nandankanan came and took them away. I was sorry to not only see the leopard go, but also the sloth who took great delight in twisting my foot this way and that. The pangolin too had spent the better part of its stay clinging to Simi, while the hyena had followed her around like a puppy. Hardly had the van departed that an Ambassador car came along with a surprise visitor. Toby Sinclair, who was 'Papa' John Wakefield's son-in-law, arrived with a skinny looking lady. Since I had the guest house allotted to me, I had Naik give his room to them, while he slept in the car with the driver. The conversation in the evening centred around the animals that had just departed, with Toby, who acted as a coordinator for BBC and other film crews, asking a lot of seemingly innocent questions. A few days later, a very damning article was to appear in the *Indian Express*, tearing into Bittu and me for using 'captive' animals. Considering it was never meant to be a secret and even the film titles acknowledged the help provided by the Nandankanan Zoo, it was hitting way below the belt.

From Simlipal I knew I had to drive 850 kilometres through isolated country including the drought-hit district of Koraput to get to Bastar, which in turn was Naxal country. Winter had receded and the temperatures were beginning to soar by the day, and the incident in the Santhal village had underlined the dangers of filming in remote areas.

Simi wanted to stay on for the next leg, but I had to put my foot down and escorted her back to Delhi from Bhubaneswar. After the usual diversion via Bombay, I returned and then with Naik and the camera equipment packed in the Gypsy, I initially followed the coastal road south, and then after Chilika and Chatrapur, turned west towards the heart of Central India, getting to Rayagada before entering the district of Koraput. The trepidation I had felt, now hit me as mile after mile of country had been completely stripped of vegetation. I felt like I was driving into a nightmare, for the landscape looked like it had been devastated by a nuclear explosion. No trees. No grass. No cultivation. Nothing.

Going past villages in a Gypsy with the foot on the accelerator, one was simply closing one's eyes to the children who stared at us with lifeless eyes, their naked bellies swollen like those of pregnant women. It was around 4 p.m., the heat of the day abating, when I stopped at a village *hat bazaar* where they were selling tribal drums along with other things. The man wanted twenty rupees for a pair of drums, and I realized there was no concept of money in a place where there was no food to buy. Though the granaries in the rest of India were overflowing, what was happening in Koraput and some other districts of Orissa, was nothing short of criminal. As I walked back to the Gypsy and handed the drums to Naik, all hell broke loose. People started rushing towards us, some thrusting their children, some even pushing teenage girls at me, begging I take them with me, in the hope that they would somehow live long enough to see another sunrise.

The moment we entered Madhya Pradesh, the vegetation was back, and the horror of the drought-prone areas started to recede with every passing kilometre. At Jagdalpur, I spent the night at the IG Police's residence, a tough looking cop who looked like someone you didn't want to mess with. At breakfast Mr Modi (I think that was his name) said the Naxals were very active around Indravati Tiger Reserve, whose boundary separated Madhya Pradesh from Maharashtra. He also asked me not to venture into the Abujhmar region for if something went wrong, even the police would not be able to get us out. I said, *why would I go there?* I was only there to shoot the wildlife. Mr Modi gave me a strange look, after which he saw us off.

The daytime temperatures at that time of year were in the high forties. Even though the sun was nowhere near its zenith, the road itself looked like a shimmering mirage. Fitted around my Gypsy were *chagals*, canvas bags in which I used to store drinking water. The breeze generated by the moving vehicle used to keep the liquid cool, and I remember stopping to drink endless amounts of water every half an hour. The park headquarters were at a place called Kutru. I was delighted to see Bittu Sahgal waiting for me at the guest house—the first and only time he came to one of my shoots. Bittu had already been appointed to the steering committee of Project Tiger, and it now seemed he had been given charge of the relocation of villages from the designated core area of the Indravati Tiger Reserve. By the very virtue of the fact that he had a steering committee member as his guest, the field director was also present.

The heat was getting to Bittu and he said he was returning to Bombay early the next morning. He was obsessed with the Bastar buffalo and he kept asking the field director, who was fairly reticent and quiet, 'I've been here for three years sir,' he said, 'and though there are regular signs of them, I have not been able to see them.' Bittu then told me to make contact with Dr Prakash and his wife Manda Amte, who were both doctors and ran a hospital at Hemalkasa, where the tribal population were treated free of cost by them. 'We need shots of the Gond and Maria tribes as well,' added Bittu, hoping the field director would not say he had never seen them as well.

'You will need to get the Naxals to take you to their villages. Prakash-ji is the best person to help you with that.'

The track from Kutru towards the Indravati River barely qualified to be on the map, being more like an alignment for some future road that ran through a dry deciduous forest consisting mainly of *sal*, some teak and bamboo, with an occasional *mahua* and *ber* tree. However, I wasn't looking at trees, for even though it was still fairly in the morning, the scorching heat was already building up. There was hardly any shade anywhere, and looking at the profusely sweating Naik, I was worried both of us would go down with a heatstroke. I remember counting the 86 glasses of water that I drank through the day, my *chagals* coming in most handy. I was on the verge of turning back when we suddenly came across an extremely odd sight. There was a hand pump in the middle of nowhere, and next to it was a gigantic watch tower made out of wrought iron. There were about half-a-dozen bees buzzing around the sliver of water that had accumulated at the base of the boring pump. The lower half of the ladder to get onto the watch tower had eroded and fallen away, so the only way to pull ourselves up on to the platform was to park the Gypsy directly under the remnants of the ladder and then clamber up.

The heat was almost unbearable, and I think I was almost semi-conscious when I heard a grunt. There was no point telling Naik to check because he was out cold, so I propped myself up and looked down on a herd of some ten buffalo who were standing near the boring pump. The massive sweep of their horns, which were even more in girth than what I had seen in Kaziranga, had my heart racing. There was no point trying to wake Naik, so I grabbed the camera and started filming. The heat was forgotten, and my heart was pumping madly. There had been no photographic record of the bovines since 1956 and I knew this was a godsend opportunity. The angle from the tower was restricted, so I decided to swing down and shoot from the ground.

Going down without help with a 16 mm camera was tough, but I managed. By then the buffalo had seen me and were looking at me most curiously. From the Gypsy, at ground level, I shot off some more footage. Then, unable to resist the temptation, I did something extremely stupid. I jumped off the Gypsy and walked up to the startled animals who were by then staring at me in disbelief. I actually managed to get two extreme close-ups, before one of the young bulls finally let out a grunt that sounded like an alarm. Fortunately, the buffalo, which have a terrible reputation for being aggressive, turned en masse and thundered off. Though I was shooting without a tripod, the shot of the buffalo galloping away would come out extremely well.

That evening a very tired and distraught Arjun Katyal arrived at Kutru. Bittu had told him to get to Jagdalpur from Calcutta, where he would find 'thirty buses' that would take him to Kutru. After waiting and searching for a day, he finally had found one, which broke down twice. At one stage, he was sandwiched between two Bastar beauties who were topless, which was hard on his Calcutta-bred nerves. He had only one ambition, which was to find 'Bittu Mama' and kill him! I told him he would have that opportunity soon, for not wanting to store the exposed film cans in the extreme heat, I was despatching him for Bombay with the precious footage of the buffalo. Katyal was a real sport, for he cheerfully set off the next morning. The pleasure of plunging a dagger into his mother's brother's chest outweighed all the other discomforts in his mind.

The Gonds were the dominant tribe in the area with various sub-castes that included the Muria. There were hardly any men visible, only women. They had a loincloth wrapped around their waist sometimes, but other than that there was no vestige of any clothing. The most noticeable thing about them was their erect bearing, which gave expression to the term 'ramrod straight!' Every village or settlement I came to, often driving cross-country following walking trails, we would find totem poles and a gate at the entrance where stuffed animals had been hung. The presence of Naxals in the area had put the fear of God in all outsiders. If anyone so much as tried to exploit the women, justice would be swift, often resulting in the loss of a limb or two.

By then, I was getting used to the heat. It was time to pay a visit to Dr Prakash Amte, the son of Baba Amte, whose rehabilitation of leprosy victims made him a legend in his lifetime. To get to Hemalkasa, I had to cross the Indravati River near what was referred to as the 'junction', where another stream came in from the north. Prakash Amte's location was across the border, in Maharashtra, but the area was contiguous with the Abujhmar region, home of the Abujh Maria and the Bison-horn Maria. At the junction, I found a small boat to load all the camera equipment, followed by Naik, who announced he could not swim but knew how to pray. Leaving the Gypsy behind, I half waded and half swam across the river, somehow manhandling the boat and its cargo. Naik's chanting of religious mantras may have contributed greatly in getting us across.

Along with the hospital, Prakash also ran an animal shelter, where he provided a home to a variety of birds and animals who had been orphaned. He had leopards, hyenas, deer and an assortment of creatures, for whom he was everything. He then sent word to the Naxals that I wanted to film in Abujhmar, after which all that we could do was sit and wait and play with his leopards and hyenas. Every time Prakash caught the hyena by the scruff of its neck, it would come out with a sound that resembled human laughter.

At night we slept outdoors, with a mosquito net over my bed. In the middle of the night the Naxals came, and I was woken up and asked what and why I wanted to shoot in Abujhmar. Obviously satisfied with my answers, some more Naxals appeared, and soon Naik and I were walking along village trails, part of our equipment being carried by them. I had charged batteries that at best would last me three days. After a few hours, with the sun beating down by then, we finally walked into an Abujh Maria settlement. The Naxals carried rifles and they all had black cloths covering their faces. By that time, much to my shock, I had realized that the leader of the group was a woman. She settled us into a hut and told me to be ready to film in an hour. She then wandered off to make the necessary arrangements.

The rice husking sequence was breathtaking stuff. Women were lined up inside a longish hut that was a granary of sorts, and while I filmed, I told Naik to keep his gaze on the camera and not look left or right. He was so terrified of what the Naxals could do to him, he for all practical purposes was still in the boat, praying away! In the evenings the few men that were present and the women would line up and dance. I was often dragged in but had been told by my Naxal lady friend that if I so much as smiled at any woman, she would consider me that woman's 'property'. Not sure if my leg was being pulled or not, I also started following Naik's example. The footage we got, later would give Bittu the heebie-jeebies, for he felt Doordarshan would object to the nudity. I told him if you put clothes on the women, they would actually look vulgar. They were so much at ease with themselves, it communicated itself even on camera.

By the time we started on our return journey for Hemalkasa, the Naxal lady had become quite friendly with me, though she was extremely careful about not saying anything that would compromise her identity.

She was obviously highly educated and spoke fluently in English and in Hindi. We were sitting under a tree taking a break, so I told her since I would be on my way in an hour or so, what was the harm if I saw her face. She laughed and made as if to untie the cloth, then paused and said in a dead serious voice, 'Sure, I can. But then I will have to cut your throat.' Trouble is, when the other side holds all the weapons and the cards, you are never sure where the Rubicon flows!

The Abujh Maria, Bison-horn Maria and the other tribes were a proud people with a culture and lifestyle of their own. There was no way one could or should judge them by standards that do not apply to them. Ironically, the fallout with Bittu would happen over the Indravati film subsequently. Though Bittu was the first person who would endorse the above sentiment, for some strange reason he asked Shabana Azmi, the popular film actress, to do the narration for the Indravati episode (different film stars were handling each episode). The actress was at that time the flag bearer for the rights and welfare of Bombay's slum dwellers, and somehow the tribals of Bastar, seemed to get equated with them. To make matters worse, the Indravati Tiger Reserve then, and perhaps even so now, remained a large area demarcated on the map with almost no real management whatsoever. It wasn't just the forest department, almost all other agencies that are required to enforce the writ of the government, simply did not exist, or if they did, they were completely ineffectual. Unfortunately, Bittu was also made the steering committee member for Project Tiger and was asked to oversee the relocation of 56 villages from the so-called core area of the reserve. I had been allowed to film in the Abujhmar area mainly because I believed the Marias and the other tribes were as much a part of the ecosystem as any animal, bird or insect. It was a Catch-22 situation and eventually the tipping point came when, with the help of Sanjoy Monga, Bittu put in a voice-over on the locked commentary tracks that purportedly put out the establishment's point of view. I somehow felt that by putting the voice-over, my position had been compromised and I had betrayed the trust, especially of my Naxal lady friend. This led to a complete break in communication between Bittu and me that lasted for almost two decades.

I think the brother-in-law duo of Tejbir Singh and Valmik Thapar were originally slated to shoot the Kanha episode, for I drove back to

Noida from Bastar after canning the Indravati footage and sending Naik back to Bombay from Raipur. Driving alone, I had complete confidence in the Gypsy that had performed valiantly and had never given me even an iota of trouble. Parked in the garage after getting back home, when I raised the shutter after a couple of days, in what was almost symbolic, three of the four tyres were flat!

I flew back to Bombay with Simi to review the Indravati footage and to sit in with Dipti on the Simlipal edit. Technically, the shooting for Project Tiger was over, and only the post-production work was left to be done. I had by then worked with Dipti on half-a-dozen films and we had found we not only worked reasonably well together, but we also got along fairly well. We were sitting on the roof of Famous Studios taking a cigarette break, when Simi suggested Dipti and I should look at working together. I remember laughing and telling her that if we did that, she would be the first one to have a problem; if not in the immediate future, sooner or later it would be the case. The very next day, Bittu asked me if I could now shoot the Kanha film as well. 'You kidding? I practically drove past it while coming back from Bastar. I'm not driving back all the way!' Bittu then suggested Dipti also accompany me for the shoot, adding that all logistic arrangements would be handled by the *Sanctuary* representative who lived in Jabalpur.

After dropping Simi in Delhi, I flew to Jabalpur, where I rendezvoused with Tanaji, my new assistant, and Dipti, who had earlier directed a few episodes of *Rakshak*. The three of us were received by Mr Rekwar, who ran a travel agency called Shakti Travels, a largish individual who seemed hell bent on treating us as 'foreign tourists', insisting we try the 'local lentils with a local bread called roti'. Rekwar also announced he had 'stones' and could only drink beer. Leaving him behind to guzzle the crates of beer, we started filming one of the most photogenic sanctuaries. By and large, I always preferred to drive myself, and on one occasion went over a wooden bridge that straddled one of the small streams. As the wooden beams made a noise, a large tiger cooling off underneath came bounding out. He would glare at us, then go back for his siesta, only to have the jeep go over the bridge in either direction, which would send him scampering out again. After three such instances, I decided to leave him alone. Later I was told the tiger's name was Hauwa and he had this thing about red cars, which he would chase sometimes for kilometres. As far as sanctuaries go, one can hardly go wrong in Kanha, and after a week of intense filming, we returned to Bombay to finish the edits on the Indravati and Kanha films.

With the end of the Project Tiger series in sight, Simi's family was getting extremely concerned about our financial future. Bittu had been great to work with, but other than clearing my loan for the Gypsy, I had little cash to show for my efforts for I don't think we ever sat down and discussed payments as the series progressed. It was extremely ad hoc, for as the producer, Bittu's style of functioning was such that almost everyone was clamouring for money at the end, and no one was sure who had been promised what. Anyway, I had just returned to Delhi when I received a message saying the lieutenant governor, Simi's uncle, desired to see me. Air Vice Marshal Kapoor met me in his study, and he asked me of my future plans. Before I could say anything, he said since the Delhi Administration was under him, maybe he could pull a few strings and 'fix me up' somewhere decent. I told him I was deeply touched by this magnanimous gesture, but thank you sir, no thank you! It sure was a come down from my last visit to Raj Bhawan when I was being asked to choose between his nieces.

In early 1988 Dipti flew to Delhi, and we decided to form a partnership firm of our own. As usually happens, we could not decide on a name for the company. However, having driven to Delhi from Noida, we found ourselves standing in front of a vendor who was to sell us the stamp paper on which the agreement was to be drawn. '*Baap ka naam?*' (Father's name?), he intoned, and we gave our respective details. '*Company ka naam?*' (Company's name?), he asked, not even bothering to look up. Dipti looked at me and said, 'KaleidoIndia!' which was one of the names bandied about and then that was that.

13

KaleidoIndia Takes on Wings

The first break we got, was a small scratch-budget 10-minute film on ITDC's Kovalam Ashok Hotel. Shooting manicured gardens and hotel rooms was a far cry from the rough and tumble of Project Tiger. To make matters considerably worse for me, this kind of shot takings usually involved lighting the subject, which I was not only useless at, but also least interested in. On the flip side, both Dipti and I had exquisite suites that opened out on the Kovalam Bay, where we sat drinking cocktails while wondering what to do with ourselves in the immediate future. Not yet 28, both of us were broke and at that point of time, for the first time in my life, just to keep our heads above water I was having to make films on subjects that I wouldn't otherwise touch.

Hemant Gupte was a senior officer in the department of tourism, and it was his job to commission short films that were then showcased at embassy parties and screened on government-controlled platforms like Air India. Gupte usually dealt with people from the advertisement agencies, for whom films like these were bread and butter. In all probability, he found both Dipti and me to be different, for we had walked in and asked him if the department would like to commission a five-part series on Indian wildlife. 'Write a proposal, and I'll try and push it through.' We were halfway out of his office when he asked us if we would like to shoot a video film on the Nehru Cup, which was to be held in Alleppey two or three weeks later. The film had a modest budget, and if we could put up ten per cent as earnest money, he would commission the film there and then. Though Dipti had worked on a music video on the Betacam format when she had gone to the Australian Film School in Sydney for a few months four years previously, I had no idea how a video camera worked. And also, we did not have the twenty-thousand rupees between the two of us to meet the procedural requirement of earnest money. 'We'll do it,' I heard myself say.

No one was willing to believe that I actually had no funds to put up the earnest money. Dipti had returned to Bombay to set up the logistics for the shoot. Eventually, a family friend of Simi who was in the business of 'finance' stepped in and gave me the loan that was to be repaid in three months with the agreed interest. At that point of time, I had no idea what the repercussions of this transaction would be, for it seemed a straightforward deal on the face of it. Nevertheless, with the film commissioned, Dipti and I rendezvoused in Trivandrum, where she had roped in her classmate, Santosh Sivan, to shoot the boat race along with me. Even at that point, Santosh was considered to be a class act, and his enthusiasm and skill with the heavy-duty video cameras was all too evident. As the snake boats, or *chundans*, got going, Santosh would think nothing of plunging into the backwaters to get various angles on tape.

The sheer spectacle of the boat races and the energy around it, one couldn't go wrong. The short 20-minute film was a visual delight, and more than anything else, it had considerably strengthened Hemant Gupte's hand to fast-track our wildlife mini-series proposal. Everything went smoothly at the post-production stage as well, and within three weeks, the film was ready.

However, on the personal front, events had taken the most bewildering turn. When I flew back from Bombay with the edited film after a gap of fourteen days, I was surprised to find the door of the flat in Noida locked from the outside with a note from Simi saying she was at her parent's place and that I could fetch her from there on my return. Taking the key from the neighbour, I had opened the door and got the shock of my life, for the house had literally been cleaned out. Except for the Gypsy that was standing where I had left it in the garage, everything from my scooter to my aftershaves were gone. I had been speaking to Simi from Bombay and she had not said a word. My neighbours said two days after I had left, Simi's father had come with a tempo in tow into which everything had been loaded, including the scooter.

Even more bizarre was the fact that when I went to Faridabad the next day after handing over the film to Gupte, Simi seemed genuinely happy to see me and was packed and ready to return home. There was a brief interaction with her parents after which we started driving back, when I asked her what was going on. Adopting the voice of someone who has been coached, Simi said since her family had 'arranged the loan', it was felt that the money that would accrue from the boat race film would be kept with her mother who would make sure there was no 'useless expenditure' since after having shot the Project Tiger series I had squandered away the lakhs I got from Bittu. I started to laugh and then as we crossed the Jamuna barrage, I pointed out to Simi that Dipti was a fifty per cent partner in KaleidoIndia, and why would she agree to any such ridiculous plan. Why on earth would I?

The *Alleppey Boat Race* film was viewed the next day by the tourism secretary, S. K. Mishra and the director, B. K. Goswami. They immediately ordered the release of the money due to us within 48 hours and the first two films of the *Call of the Wild* series were approved by the end of the day itself. I called Dipti and told her to take the first flight to Delhi as we had our plates full with the upcoming wildlife shoots. Besides, I also felt, Dipti would be able to drill some sense into Simi's head. Twenty-one days after having taken the loan for the earnest money, we returned the principal plus interest plus penalty for returning the money before the stipulated three-month period. Just when I thought the loan business was behind us, Simi in the evening dropped a straight-faced bombshell by suggesting KaleidoIndia should be a three-way partnership, since she had first come up with the suggestion of forming the company.

Our successful foray into video notwithstanding, we decided to fall back to 16 mm for the *Call of the Wild* series. Once it dawned on everyone that a series commissioned by the Government of India would bring in a corresponding amount of money, even some of the stuff taken from my flat started to reappear. The first film to be shot was on Rajasthan and the Gir Forest in Gujarat. Dipti had gone back to Bombay and struck a deal with Govind Nihalini to hire the French Aaton XTR camera, which duly arrived with her and Rajender, our assistant and the third member of our crew. I received them at Palam, and after loading the reliable Gypsy to the gills, we set off for Sariska just as the sun was setting in a red ball of fire.

K. L. Saini and the forest staff received us with open arms and for me it felt like a homecoming, especially after the uncertain period of being stuck in Delhi, wondering if we were doomed to spend the rest of our lives shooting hotel rooms. The dholes were still around, but they were by then no longer a novelty. For Dipti, who had edited the Sariska Project Tiger episode, places and people hitherto on celluloid came to life, including the tree pies and babblers who were by then also among my close friends. The manner in which the films were structured, we did not need to shoot the park in great detail, so after three or four days, we moved on to Ranthambore, where we were given the suite in Jogi Mahal by the field director, Fateh Singh Rathore.

In the morning, as we drove around the Padma Talao, we ran into Fateh who was driving his jeep wearing his trademark hat. He told us the resident tigress Noon and her two grown cubs were feeding in the grass not too far off the road, and if we were lucky, we could get behind them and film the cubs demolishing a sambar stag. The male cub, almost a fully grown 2-year-old, was chewing the ears of the stag, the head having been decapitated. While the Aaton ran the film in a near silent mode, Dipti leaned across and managed to get a few good stills while at the same time recording the sound. The old hunting preserve of the Jaipur maharajas, the park is dominated by the spectacular Ranthambore Fort that had been laid siege to by the Mughal emperor Akbar in 1568. The fiercely fought 40-day campaign that saw extensive use of cannon, eventually saw the Rajputs under the command of Rai Surjan Hada surrender. Local folklore in the park placed the location of Akbar's personal tent under the massive banyan tree that existed right next to Jogi Mahal.

Upbeat at having got the male cub in almost perfect conditions, we returned to Jogi Mahal only to find quite a few DOSCOs led by Gajendra Singh of the 1974 batch playing tennis ball cricket, using the steps of the red-coloured Jogi Mahal as a wicket. Gajju, who was an excellent squash player in school, was walking up to his bowling mark when he suddenly realized Noon was standing under the banyan tree, watching him at close quarters. That was the fastest I've ever seen an entire lot, batsman, bowler, fielders, et al, disappear.

Dipti knew the topography of Ranthambore fairly well, for not only had she edited the Ranthambore episodes, she had also visited the park with Valmik Thapar and Tejbir Singh, who had spent a considerable amount of time in the park. The next day, I was as usual at the wheel and we were driving to Bakola when she suddenly said, 'Tiger!' Neither the forest guard with us, nor Rajender nor I could see what she was looking at, but we clamped on the camera, and I got into position at the back. Then suddenly I saw the huge fellow, sitting virtually in the open, invisible because of the play of light and shade. As the Aaton started to roll, the male got up and started to briskly walk away. To my delight, even as I watched through the viewfinder, a female also got up and followed.

The guard was now gurgling with excitement, 'Mating! Mating!' he said in an excited whisper. Dipti said there was a side track which should bring us face-to-face with the pair, so I shot off that way, the guard by then having expanded his vocabulary by a hundred per cent, 'Enjoying! Enjoying!' Sure enough, the pair were sitting just ahead, and as I vaulted back over the seat and the camera came on, they copulated. It was short, brief and extremely aggressive, the female snarling and turning on the male almost instantly. Then for a few minutes, the two tigers, seemingly exhausted, just sat there looking at us. Then again, they got up and in the brisk manner started to move again. We followed, and they entered a rocky nullah, where they again mated. This time, without breaking the silhouette of the Gypsy, I shot the scene with the camera on my shoulder, from in front of the Gypsy. It was surreal, two tigers mating, both their yellow eyes fixed on me not more than 10 metres from them.

Word that we had captured mating tigers on film got around like wildfire, with even Fateh Singh Rathore driving across to congratulate us on having got the tigers 'enjoying'! It only then dawned on me what the guard had been going on about, for until then I was under the impression he was talking about himself. Combined with 'luck by chance', we sure had the beginnings of a wildlife thesaurus.

Ranthambore is a haven for tiger photography and our luck continued to hold over the next few days as we continued to get some good behavioural shots, especially among the cacti covered rocks around Bakola. The month of February also meant that the grass had turned the landscape into a sea of gold, and some of the sambar shots in particular were exceptional. Though loath to leave, we then moved on from Sawai Madhopur and on to Jodhpur, where we had decided to film the Bishnoi who as a people had opened their hearts and their homes to the black buck and chinkara that shared the land with them. We checked in at the majestic Umaid Bhawan Palace, which had been converted into an ITC hotel, and were hosted by Maharaja Gaj Singh. Most of the recruitment for the Rajput Regiment being from this area, during our brief stay, I met an incredible number of people who knew my father.

The final port of call was Jaisalmer, that was 280 kilometres from Jodhpur. Dipti, having again directed an episode of *Rakshak* there, wanted to film and record folk music for our own background tracs. We then moved to the Desert National Park (DNP) at Sam, the home of the great Indian bustard, and also known for the large flocks of the imperial sand grouse that visited the water holes. Having obtained a caravan from the army, we then set up our camp among the sand dunes. The next morning, hidden in a hide covered with thatch, we first watched one, then another of the two long-legged beauties make their way to the water. Then, the bustard would fold their legs underneath them and drink from a squatting position. Almost on cue, the sand grouse also started to arrive. Not only would they drink, but just before they got airborne, they would step into the water, letting their chest feathers soak up the moisture, presumably for their chicks waiting back at their nesting grounds.

Having canned what we wanted from the DNP, the plan was to send the caravan back and for us to drive overnight to Jodhpur from where Rajender was to fly to Bombay by the early morning flight with the equipment and the exposed footage. After dinner, we set off to cover the three hundred odd kilometres to the airport. By the time we reached Jaisalmer, there wasn't a soul on the streets. With no signs to go by, and completely disoriented in the dark, we hit the road going south towards Barmer instead. After covering 40 kilometres, finally a milestone showed up. It was a scramble after that to make it to Jodhpur in time, and with minutes to spare we watched Rajender dash into the airport terminal.

Even though we had taken the decision to edit the first film at Mike Pandey's Riverbank Studios in Old Delhi, we still needed to view and sort out the footage before embarking on the Gir Forest leg of the shoot. After depositing the Gypsy and the winter wear back in Noida, we then arrived at Bombay and were delighted with the quality of the rushes. Two days later, we landed at Rajkot, from where we then set off for Gir, the home of the Asiatic lion. The hired vehicle, a Tata Trax, was quite a disaster, for it sometimes wouldn't start. I realized then just how close we had been from Gujarat when we returned to Delhi from DNP. Later I would often regret not having done my homework, for the route via Barmer would have allowed us to film the Rann of Kutch too. More importantly, without the reassuring platform of the Gypsy, filming was never quite the same thing.

At Sasan, the divisional forest officer (DFO) had welcomed us but left us perplexed by announcing that we could only enter and stay in the park if we were accompanied by a 'cheat', that too if only provided by him. There had been the usual whispers that if we wished to get around the prohibition orders, there were 'ways and means', but honestly I hardly expected the top ranking forest official to be involved in such a scandalous manner. To make matters worse, everything I asked for, I was told, 'no problem', the 'cheat' would handle it. It was only when he reached into his drawer at the end of our meeting, took out a pad and wrote on it, that I realized he was referring to a chit! I felt like a prize idiot, but the DFO was right, the chit virtually gave us a carte blanche to shoot where and how we liked. As we entered the park, we realized Gir was not only a beautiful forest, it was also determined to rain cats at us. As we drove in, we saw two leopards, one literally dropping out of the trees. But they were gone in a flash, giving us not the remotest chance of a shot even with a still camera.

In the evening, still not quite ready to start filming, we just stepped out in the Trax when we saw a dozen peacocks and peahens in a circle. I came to a halt near them and to my disbelief, realized there was a jungle cat kitten in the centre of the rapidly closing circle. It was snarling and fighting back, but the slashing spurs of the big birds was going to cut it to pieces. Before I could do anything, it made a dash for the Trax and literally stood on its hind legs, instinctively begging to be saved. Without thinking, I scooped it up and shooed off the aggressive peacocks. By then the little horror, had forgotten how close he was to death, and I became enemy number one. Holding him firmly by the scruff of his neck and by grabbing his four tiny feet, I then scouted around for its mother, but she was nowhere to be seen. In the morning I handed over the kitten to the DFO, who held his head in his hands and said he now had three kittens, all of them rescued in similar circumstances.

Dipti unfortunately went down with a severe case of gastroenteritis and with extremely high fever. As a result, filming with the lions was somewhat restricted, though our luck continued to hold when it came to getting some unique behavioural shots. Late in the afternoon, we chanced upon a solitary male that had killed a sambar stag and having dragged the deer some 30 metres into the vegetation, he was feeding on it while keeping a wary eye on our Trax. Unable to restart the vehicle without pushing it, I couldn't change my angles, which was extremely frustrating, but nevertheless, the young male was in his prime and gave us some wonderful moments. Later that evening, I ran into Ravi Chellam, who was an expert on the Asiatic lion. While playing a game of table tennis I described the scene of the kill to him, and to my surprise he got most worked up, saying a male lion was highly unlikely to kill a sambar on his own. Since the footage was on 16 mm, I obviously could not play it back to him, and strangely the matter seemed to take on personal overtones. Having obviously propagated the theory that a male would not on his own kill large prey, Chellam was just not prepared to accept what I was saying to him.

We returned to Delhi after having processed the Gir footage at Adlabs and then edited the film at Riverbank Studios. However, it was obvious the Rajasthan and Gir film would be a one-off experiment for all 16 mm related post-production work still needed to be done in Bombay. Having handed over the first completed film to Gupte, then Dipti and I embarked on the second film, which was on South India. We had just landed in Coimbatore and were checking into a hotel when the Indravati episode of Project Tiger started playing on the television screens. The hotel staff must have thought we were wildlife fanatics, because we promptly pulled up chairs and started watching it.

Shabana Azmi had been tempered down and she was careful not to link the slum dwellers with the tribal communities. Bittu had been most apprehensive about Doordarshan clipping out the Abujhmar sequences because of the nudity, but there was not a single frame missing. Then came the moment of truth, for suddenly the soundtrack was lowered and there was a voice-over which said it was Project Tiger's view that the 56 villages inside the core area of the park had to be translocated. Having made the point, the film then played itself out.

We reached the Periyar Tiger Reserve and were allotted a boat that would remain with us over the next few days. I met the range officer (RO), who said though we were to initially stay at the Lake Guest House, a BBC film team had arrived, and the place had been allotted to them. He was very apologetic and said we had been booked into the main lodge near the jetty instead. The boatman, Kannan, had been with me two years previously when I had done the elephant poaching story and he was all gung-ho about filming the next day. In the early morning light, while it was still dark and the semi-submerged trees looked like ghostly silhouettes, we cast off. Dipti was wearing a white shirt and a khaki skirt, and as usual her job was to take still pictures and record the sound. Rajender and I were more concerned about steadying the boat, and we were carrying a rope which we felt could be used to tether ourselves to the submerged tree stumps should the need arise. As the sun rose in the sky, we were having a pretty good morning, having filmed elephants that were feeding in one quiet corner along one of the many branches of the lake.

We were then chugging along the lake when Kannan saw some dholes near the edge of the water and immediately set course to get close. Another boat was already there and as we got close; I realized it was the

BBC crew who were filming the dogs who had killed a chital. Their boat was at a flank, so we took up position at the other end, and Kannan and Rajender quickly moored us to a tree stump. With the boat steady as a rock, I started filming the dogs who were tearing away at the carcass. Intent on looking through the viewfinder as the camera ran, I was taken aback when the BBC boat not only drifted into my frame, but with clear intent, placed itself so that I was cut off. I was so taken aback, I forgot to switch off the camera and as I straightened up, I could see a boy sitting on the pilot's cabin roof, throwing stones at the dogs.

Dipti and I were too stunned to react. Even though Kannan was cursing the BBC crew and getting most worked up, we quickly untied ourselves from the tree stump and tried to take up a fresh position, only to have the other boat cut us off again. The stones having disturbed them, the dholes abandoned the kill and went and stood some hundred metres away. By then I had lost my temper, for this was not only boorish, it was criminal for the boy to throw stones at the animals. Expecting to see foreigners, I was further taken aback to see an Indian with a scraggly beard, who yelled across, 'Call yourselves wildlife filmmakers.' Pointing at Dipti he accusingly added, 'That woman is wearing a white shirt!'

By then Kannan wanted to ram the other boat, for he seemed more upset than the rest of us, who were more bewildered than angry. I had managed to get some footage of the dogs, so rather than get into a full-blown altercation, I told Kannan to head towards the dam where I hoped to get some more elephant footage. Again, we were incredibly lucky, for a herd of around forty elephants decided to swim across. It was a majestic sight, and we got some amazing footage as well. By the time we returned to the jetty, it was dark, and I was surprised to see the RO waiting for us. I hadn't even got off the launch when he waved a piece of paper and said a complaint had been filed by the BBC crew against me for disturbing wildlife. This was too much for Kannan, who hitched up his lungi, jumped ashore and let loose in Malayalam. By the time he finished, the RO was a changed person, and he was apologizing profusely. I then asked him who this BBC team was because I had not seen any foreigners. It seemed the person who had yelled across at us was a well-known wildlife filmmaker and the boy on the roof was his son.

The RO got onto his motorcycle and departed. As we unloaded our equipment, I asked Kannan what did he say to the official that had brought about such an abrupt change in his behaviour. Kannan, whose English was limited in the extreme and who did not know a word of Hindi, adjusted his lungi and said, 'I told, Saar has video ... of bugger throwing stones!' Well, it wasn't video, but the 16 mm clip is still there in Adlabs. It never ceased to amaze me as to just how 'cut-throatish' the competition was between the various wildlife filmmakers. It was a huge pity because the person was actually an outstanding filmmaker. He was also Dipti's senior from the FTII, and otherwise seemed like a soft-spoken person and had even been awarded the Padma Shri subsequently. The sons too, in later years, did some outstanding work.

We would then meander through to Munnar where we filmed the Nilgiri tahr. We then drove to the Blue Mountains, and I was happy to be back in the familiar environs of Coonoor, Wellington and Ooty. Wanting to film the shola grassland habitat, we then moved to Pykara Lake where it was my turn to fall sick. The local doctor who came to see me then asked Dipti to give me red rice, an exercise by itself, for it took Dipti and Rajender half the night to get it to an edible state. We then dropped down to the Moyar Valley, where we spent some time filming in Mudumalai and Bandipur, getting repeatedly charged by elephants. The hired jeep we had did not have a starter, and the driver would start giggling every time we had an elephant thundering down on us, while he flicked two wires together to get the engine to fire.

The Project Tiger authorities gave us special permission to drive through the core area of the park, following a jungle road that would take us directly to Kabini. I have rarely seen such pristine forest, but the surprising thing was that the core area had very little wildlife. Animals too seemed to prefer being closer to human habitation, a phenomenon which 'Papa' John Wakefield endorsed later that evening.

At the lodge I was delighted to meet up with Sundar, who took me fishing to the reservoir the next day, where we caught a 10 lb *mullee*. In the evening we again filmed herds of elephants that had come down to the lake, and Papa John told stories of the old days when this was the venue of the great elephant khedas. Giant stockades would be built, into which selected animals were driven, and then broken to serve the will of man. It struck us that if we could lay our hands on some of the kheda footage, it would be a welcome addition to the film. Papa John said he remembered having seen some footage with the Karnataka Forest Department that had been shot in the 1940s by the American filmmaker, Robert J. Flaherty. On the way back to Bangalore, we also decided to visit the village of Kokrebellur where storks and pelicans were nesting on trees among the village itself. Human beings, when they decide to open up their hearts to animals and birds especially as a community, witness a bond that is unique and extra special.

With the help of Dr Ullas Karanth, one of the leading zoologists who was then developing scientific methods to arrive at accurate tiger counts, we amazingly managed to trace and obtain the kheda footage. After finishing the film in Bombay, I flew back to Delhi and handed over the second film to the department of tourism. Hemant Gupte held a special screening for his immediate superiors and they in turn, promptly cleared the rest of the series.

My father had in the meantime finished his tenure in Jammu and by May 1988 had moved to Mhow as the commander of the Higher Command Course. The year-and-a-half in Jammu had been eventful. During my brief visits, we would often go shoot partridge along the Indo-Pakistan border. On the Indian side, cultivation was not allowed while the Pakistanis would cultivate right up to the jeep track. Teesta had also moved in to be with my parents for the birth of her first child and delivered Dhruv on 25 December 1987. Maggi, the puppy that had flown with me from Bombay, unfortunately ate a stone and had died and was buried next to one of Sam Manekshaw's dogs.

After a brief stay in Mhow, Simi and I returned to Noida but by then it was obvious the marriage was on the rocks. I was getting more and more frustrated having to be tied to Delhi, and after a fairly ugly fight when her brother had come to stay, we decided it was time for us to split. Dropping

Simi off at her parent's place, we spoke for the one last time standing at her gate, where we both agreed we had no major problems with each other but were simply not meant to be. Her last words to me were, we must exchange birthday cards every year.

However, life is seldom uncomplicated, and within a few weeks the balloon had gone up. My father was on his way to Nagaland on 23 January with an overnight halt at Delhi. Simi's uncle, Air Vice Marshal Kapoor, in the meantime had said the two families had to meet. Since Micky Yadav's sister was also getting married that evening, we could only meet at 2 a.m. at the governor's daughter's house in Vasant Vihar. Since he had a 5 a.m. flight, my father was back in uniform when we walked in. The governor and his wife were sitting on a sofa, and my father and I took seats facing each other in front of them, while Ritu stood near the door, leaning against it. The governor took out a small piece of paper and then started reading ten charges against me, that ranged from throwing Simi out of a moving vehicle to having paraded her naked in Noida or words to that effect. At first, I protested as each point was read out, but then I just kept quiet, for there was no point repeating like a pet parrot, 'But this is not true ...' After a while, one even starts sounding stupid to oneself!

If the idea was to make me look like a pervert and a sadist, the governor was doing a fine job of it, and I was wondering why this meeting had been called. Having hurled his ten accusations at me, the governor now took out another chit from his pocket. I can only presume there were a similar ten charges against my mother, for after the first round of allegations, my father had reached out for his cane and cap and curtly said to me, 'Let's go!' As we got into the car, I said to my father, 'You sure sat through all the charges against me. The first one against mom, you get up and leave.'

Two weeks later, my father received unusual orders from Army HQ that he was to fly to Bombay from Indore on the Indian Airlines flight. He was to fly in civilian clothes, and he would receive further instructions by and by. Perplexed by these rather hush-hush orders, he was given his boarding card at the airport and on the Boeing 737, he occupied the aisle seat on the front row. The seat in between was unoccupied, but at the window seat, there was a man reading a newspaper. The plane took off, and the newspaper was folded. Gopi Arora from the PMO introduced himself and handed my father an envelope that had a return ticket to Indore and a voucher for the Centaur Hotel for the night. 'We've been having a lot of trouble with your brother-in-law, N. S. Hoon,' he said, 'please ensure your son does not get involved any further. You do know he had barged into the prime minister's office with a file.' Nothing more was said as the newspaper came back into play. I had had nothing to do with the case since the meeting with Rajiv Gandhi, but obviously the wheels were still churning.

I was called to Mhow and got a rocket from my father, who refused to believe me when I said this business with Rajiv Gandhi was old hat. Since I was gearing up to shoot the North India wildlife film, I was told to prepone the shoot and get out of Delhi, otherwise my uncle would invariably rope me in yet again.

Dipti's father had retired as general manager, west from the Indian Railways and had been re-employed as the chairman of the Railway Recruitment Board. As a result of which Dipti was shifting house in Bombay, her family moving to a large and spacious flat in Janjira Chambers that was located right opposite Regal Theatre in Colaba. Loath to miss out on any of our own shoots, she decided to come to Dudhwa but would have to truncate the Corbett leg.

North India in winter, with the fog and the cold, has a charm of its own. The Terai region, with endless sugarcane fields, often had tigers straying into these areas to litter, as a result of which, cases of human attacks were not uncommon. We stopped at Tiger Haven, Billy Arjan Singh's legendary farm where he had raised the tigress Tara, but he was extremely bitter and disillusioned with the authorities who he claimed had declared the tigress a maneater and shot her. Pouring me a Peter Scot whisky, Billy said to me, 'Remember Kunal, the day you fall afoul of any official, high or low, you cannot fight him. No matter who is right or wrong, the system then just closes in on you.'

At Dudhwa, one got to meet my old friends, the rhinos, who were now running wild and thankfully breeding. We also got some reasonable footage of the barasingha or swamp deer (*Cervus duvauceli duvauceli*) which was not surprising considering the fact that Dudhwa is perhaps the biggest stronghold of this graceful deer. Though there was plenty of tiger movement, we did not run into any of the big cats.

Some moments in life get etched in the mind's eye. 8 March 1989, I was driving back from Corbett, the equipment all packed. Dipti had already returned to Bombay and the plan was for Rajender and me to also catch the afternoon flight for we had technically finished shooting the North India film. After leaving Dhikala, we were held up by elephants as a herd was moving back into the forest from the Ramganga River. The light was streaming in and sometimes it's good to just drink in the scene without always trying to capture it on film.

There was a slight gap in the elephant herd and Brijendra Singh, who had not only shot the Corbett episode for Project Tiger but was also the long-standing honorary wildlife warden, cautiously came through from the other side. Rajender had quickly loaded film in the magazine and Brijendra told me to get to the base of a large tree and sit there motionless because the resident tusker invariably crossed from there. Grabbing the Aaton, bent double I sprinted across and did as I was told. A little out of breath, I was sitting cross-legged with the camera in my lap, with an extended eyepiece which allowed me to see through the lens. It then struck me I was in no position to run should the tusker turn on me.

It was too late anyway, for the huge hulk was already standing there, and he was not more than 4 metres from me. There had been no sound, no indication, as the jumbo had just glided into position. He was so close to me I could only frame his head even with the lens in a fully wide mode. The hair on his chin were glowing as they caught the sunlight. With one eye on the view finder, with the other I watched the tip of his enormous trunk as he got a fix on my position. He knew exactly where I was. And I was entirely at his mercy. Through the lens, my gaze shifted to his reddish-brown eyes. It was a miracle my hands were not shaking, for at one level I was frightened ... more appropriate would be to say terrified ... but at another level, I felt a tremendous sense of calm and what is a contradiction of sorts, an absolute lack of fear.

The tusker took three steps forward and stepped on the road. He paused again, almost wondering if he could turn his back on me, and then, with the arrogance that only an elephant in his prime can have, he sauntered off, unhurried, majestic, supreme! If I had to pick a moment in my life when time stood still and I came closest to attaining nirvana, this was it. From the technical point of view too, everything was perfect ... the exposures, the framing, and the rock steady frame which did not reflect the jumping of my heart. Later that evening in Bombay, as I described the scene to Dipti, I found I was so overcome with the emotion of the encounter, I was actually crying.

14

The Price of Idealism

Apart from the personal front, things had so far gone smoothly, to a large extent because of the support I had from my friends who were occupying important positions in New Delhi. H. S. Panwar had moved from Project Tiger to the Forest Research Institute in Dehradun to take up a fresh assignment, while some of the others too had been posted out. Come May, our plan was to shoot Dachigam in Kashmir and then move up to Ladakh and film as many areas as we could. Mir Inayat Ullah had been replaced by Mr Wani, who I had met in Jammu, for he always made it a point to visit my father at Topi Bungalow whenever he was in town.

His office was at the Tourist Reception Centre complex in downtown Srinagar and I was staring at him incredulously. Having met Dipti and me graciously, Wani was telling me since we had come 'from India', we would have to pay filming rates that were applicable to 'foreigners'. I felt a surge of anger. During my time in Srinagar earlier, one would on occasion come across the odd person who would ask if we had 'come from India', but I had never encountered a senior officer so openly make such a provocative statement. At that point of time, though there was simmering discontent in the valley, the situation had not as yet turned ugly. The Jammu Kashmir Liberation Front, though, was doing its best to make itself relevant.

I told Wani he was being ridiculous, but he then said he had to make sure 'his people' were not 'robbed of revenue due to them'. At that point we got up to leave, for obviously there was no meeting ground, when Wani again said something about 'my people'. I pushed his rather large table into him, and frankly I wished I had hit him then and there. He was by then shouting, saying I had assaulted a government officer when we moved out, and fortunately no one tried to stop us even though I could hear Wani making an infernal racket.

We were staying in an ITC houseboat on Nagin Lake, which was reserved usually for their senior staff, but there was no point going there. Instead, I told my driver to head for Badami Bagh, and we went straight to the residence of Lieutenant General D. S. R. Sahni, GOC, 15 Corps. I told him what had happened, and he in turn telephoned Jagmohan Malhotra, the governor, who promptly called us to Raj Bhawan. I repeated the sequence of events, after which the governor said we should go to our houseboat and wait there. He would find out what was happening and revert to us the next day.

That evening we were having dinner with Omar Nedou at his residence when there was a deafening blast not far from where we were. Everything in the house shook with the shock of the explosion. Subsequently, we would find out that the bomb had gone off by accident and that there were no casualties. The next day, we were called to Raj Bhawan. The governor suggested we proceed to Ladakh and finish shooting there, after which we could come back to Srinagar and film in Dachigam. He said he was ensuring no false cases were filed against us, and we would not be harassed by the forest department either. Since we still had two days before we moved on to Leh, we bummed around in shikaras and took a few shots around Gulmarg, but eventually Kashmir itself had to be dropped entirely from the film.

For Dipti, it was her first trip to Ladakh. From the moment we landed at Leh, everything had been taken care of. Apart from messages from the governor and the corps commander in Srinagar, Major General P. C. Puri who had just taken over 3 Infantry Division in Leh, was also from the Rajput Regiment and our families had been together at Wellington as well. A JCO from the Ladakh Scouts was detailed to be our liaison officer and a cheerful bunch of soldiers from a Mahar battalion were to be with us for the duration of the trip. For the Kashmir and Ladakh shoot, we had hired an Arriflex ST camera that had come all the way from Cuttack in Orissa. The person happiest to have half-a-dozen people around was Sahu, the camera assistant.

Dipti wanted to record traditional Ladakhi music. She had a professional Walkman recorder and a Sennheiser mike that was so sensitive it even picked up her own heartbeat if she was not careful. We spent the day recording and filming at the Phyang Gompa, after which we set off for Durbuk the next day. Despite it being June, the weather started to pack up the moment we started to climb up Chang La from Karu, forcing us to spend the night at Zingral. The last time I had been on this stretch was two years ago when we had been hauling BMPs across the 17,585 feet (5360 m) pass. In the morning, the entire area was covered with snow and using the large format Hasselblad camera, we captured in a single frame the entire Zanskar Range that lay to the south of us.

Durbuk in Ladakhi means the 'gateway to hell', which was a fairly apt description for the terrain was not only extremely difficult, the altitude was constantly increasing. The road then forks off to the north where it meets the Shyok River Valley or turns left to Tangtse which was the headquarters of 114 Infantry Brigade. After spending a sleepless night (a rat kept jumping on Dipti) we then made our way to the expanse of the majestic Pangong Tso. More photographs, and then we reached Chushul where we set up camp. A large flock of sheep were grazing near a Rebo camp and much to Dipti's delight, a Changpa herdsman was shearing his flock, singing through his nose in the shrill manner of most Ladakhis. While I filmed the sheep shearing, Dipti was sitting like the Buddha, holding her breath (at that altitude!) as she recorded song after song. After spending close to an hour, she felt she had enough music for a multitude of films, so out came the notebook and pencil. She rewound the player and played back the first song and reverently asked the Changpa for the title.

'Mohammad Rafi ... *philum* (film) *Pratigya*!' said the sheep shearer, who even added who the composer was. And so forth! I was laughing so hard by the end of it, I almost developed HAPE (high-altitude pulmonary edema) and was lucky I didn't end up falling into the stream flowing nearby.

The black-neck cranes were very much there, bringing up a solitary chick with all the paternal care in the world. While we filmed them, the river terns that were also breeding nearby dive-bombed us repeatedly. We filmed the kiang in the vicinity of the Chushul runway, being careful not to stray anywhere near the white patches that had swallowed up our vehicle the last time around. I wanted to proceed on the Yankee-1 axis to Demchok, and then follow the Indus back via Nyoma to Chumathang and Kiari. However, bad weather resulted in our returning the way we had come, after which we approached Kiari from the direction of Leh.

Being back in Kiari, memories came flooding back. Nothing had changed, other than the people. From there we proceeded to the relatively smaller Tso Moriri, crossing the Indus River at Mahe near Chumathang. Even the curtains in the guest rooms at Chumathang were the ones selected and bought by my mother eight years ago. Fairly satisfied with the overall footage we had got, we then returned to Delhi, where we needed to take a call on the next shoot. With the monsoons around the corner, we had to decide if we wanted to head off immediately into Central India. After a lot of discussion, we figured it would a risk worth taking for it would give us a completely different look altogether, even though filming may not be that easy.

The film on Central India was to be shot in Bandhavgarh, Kanha and Palamau. Once again, the Gypsy was back in play as we headed out from Delhi along the familiar road to Kanha. We stopped in Mandla where we stayed at the Government Rest House on the banks of the Narbada River, and I kept thinking there was something oddly familiar about the place. Sure enough, when I described the exact location to my father, it had indeed been my grandfather's residence four decades previously. It was strange, because I myself had never been there, and yet it felt as if I knew exactly where every room was. The next day, after driving on to Kisli and unloading our equipment at the Bagheera Camp, I got all the local information about conditions in the park from the camp manager and decided we would start filming from the Sauf Meadows the next day.

Kanha, apart from being one of the best tiger reserves in the country, was barasingha country. The deer were, at that time of year, in full rutting form and Dipti got some superb calls as stags threw back their heads and called out to the females. I was languidly sitting in the Gypsy, letting her record sound, when Tanaji, who was the assistant this time around, said in a whisper, 'Sirji look ...' As I vaulted to the back, I could see the dholes every now and then stand up on their hind legs and peer over the grass, before going to ground again. There were three of them, in a 'V' formation, and they were obviously the jaws of the carefully set trap. Suddenly, from close to a mile out, one could see the chital running for their lives, as the rest of the dholes herded them straight towards their waiting companions.

It was our presence that saved the lone chital stag. With less than 20 metres to go before he ran into the first waiting dhole, the deer turned like a motorcycle in a Grand Prix and made a beeline for the Gypsy. Just when I thought he would collide with us at full tilt, the chital literally, in a gravity defying leap, sailed over our heads, his flailing hooves actually hitting me on my shoulder. To dogs who had followed the stag, came to a halt next to the Gypsy and gave us the most exasperated look possible. Though I was glad the stag had gotten away, we had probably come within a hairs breath of recording an actual kill on the run by dholes, for I had been perfectly placed. But then, that's what wildlife filming was all about. Being at the right place at the right time!

During the day we ran into the principal chief conservator of forests (PCCF), Purushottam Lad. He insisted we join him for breakfast, and he took a real shine on Dipti, so much so I might as well have not been there at all. Most of the senior forest officials one met were, by and large, very dedicated and knowledgeable people, and one learnt a lot from them in even casual conversations.

We got plenty of exciting footage, in fact eleven different tigers in four days. Then we set off for Bandhavgarh, the second leg of our trip. The roads, I had been warned, were in a very bad state and with the onset of the monsoons, they would become even worse. Instead of taking the route via Jabalpur to Katni and then Umaria, I decided to cut east before Mandla and get to Bandhavgarh via Shahpura and go directly via Umaria. The 300-kilometre drive became a nightmare, for at places the highway didn't even exist and one just navigated along what looked like an alignment for a road.

I was looking forward to shooting in Bandhavgarh for two reasons; first, I had never been there before and second, the field director was Dr Rajesh Gopal who had been H. S. Panwar's assistant director. We were to stay with K. K. Singh who had a beautiful bungalow-cum-resort just outside the park, and since the rains would soon be upon us, there were not too many tourists around. However, when we reached Bandhavgarh, I was told that Rajesh Gopal was on leave, so I needed to see his deputy director and do the necessary paperwork for the next few days. The deputy, I think his name was R. P. Singh, met us at his home. He was extremely polite, all the while talking about his interest in photography, and saying how expensive the 'hobby' was for a 'poor forest officer'. Finally, since I was refusing to take the hint, he then bluntly asked me for six rolls of Ektachrome.

Perhaps we had led a sheltered life, but neither Dipti or I had ever been asked to pay a bribe, either in cash or kind, until that moment. The cost of six rolls was negligible, but here was an officer from the Indian Forest Service, with his hand extended. I felt a tremendous sense of shame, and frankly did not know how to react, but it was soon evident to the man that he wasn't getting anything from us. There was an immediate change in his demeanour, for he now produced a file with all the forms that needed to be filled before we could enter the park. Taking it upon himself to fill in the details, he ticked off the various boxes, finally coming to the part which asked what format we were filming in. 'The charge for 16 mm is ₹150 a day and 35 mm is ₹5,000,' the deputy helpfully added.

'16 mm,' I said.

'But is there proof that you are not shooting 35 mm,' added the deputy slyly.

'You can inspect the cameras and check the raw film,' I said.

'Ah, but I am a poor forest officer who cannot tell 16 mm from 35 mm. You will have to pay 35 mm rates I am afraid.' The expression on his face seemed to indicate he was genuinely sorry for us. 'At my level, there is nothing that I can do. You please get me a certificate that you are shooting 16 mm, then we will see.'

Later that night, with some difficulty I managed to trace Rajesh Gopal's number and through the Umaria telephone exchange, got him on the line. After I explained the entire thing to him, Rajesh said that I need not worry, that I should report in the morning as planned at the entrance gate, take a guard with me and go in. When we were back in the evening, we could meet the deputy and do the required paperwork.

In the morning, we were the only vehicle approaching the check point at the entrance when one guard armed with a rifle came tumbling out and took up a firing position. Two others without weapons also came out and stood next to him. I was incredulous, so telling Dipti and Tanaji to stay put, I got out and walked up to the armed guard and took his rifle from him. I then told the guards I had spoken to Rajesh Gopal and that they should open the gate. Turning to the owner of the rifle, after making sure there was no round in the chamber, I handed him his weapon and told him to get in at the back with Tanaji. Fortunately, he did as he was told, and so did the others, and we then went about the business of filming in the park.

When we got back, things seemed normal enough until I walked into the deputy's office. 'You have filmed with 35 mm cameras. You are a criminal.' Again, after a considerable effort, we got through to Rajesh Gopal, who was now singing a completely different tune. The deputy, he said, had put it in writing that we needed certification from a higher authority. Please go to Bhopal, and get the PCCF, Purushottam Lad to certify your camera is indeed 16 mm. It was a small matter of detail that Bhopal was 500 kilometres from Bandhavgarh!

Since we were losing precious time, we drove through the night and got to Purushottam Lad's residence at 10 a.m. on Sunday. I remember that because the television serial *Ramayan* was on, and we had to wait for it to finish before we met the PCCF. He was delighted to see Dipti and introduced her to his entire family while I was given a cup of tea and had to sit glumly in the outer room. For Dipti to get the required certification out of Lad was child's play, for he signed without even looking at the camera, and then we were on our way back.

The next few days we were allowed to shoot the park, but since it had begun to rain, sightings were extremely poor. I was cleaning my camera in the afternoon when K. K. Singh walked into the room and said that the six rolls of Ektachrome were back to haunt me. 'The sub-divisional magistrate (SDM) is here,' he said wryly. 'Whatever happens, don't lose your temper.'

The deputy had been busy as a beaver. The SDM, after introducing himself, said the forest official was insisting I be arrested for having obstructed government officials from discharging their duty. I had also kidnapped the forest guard and then entered the park with a rifle, since I had disarmed the guard in front of witnesses who had given a written statement to that effect. The SDM had taken the trouble to drive down because he did not want the situation to get any worse, especially since we were shooting the film for the Indian government. He also said he had heard of my grandfather, and though he sympathized with us, we should leave Bandhavgarh immediately. That would mollify the deputy who was on the warpath, and they could try and ensure no formal case was filed against us. An hour later, the Gypsy loaded up, we were on our way to Palamau, leaving the nightmare of Bandhavgarh behind. Officialdom, when it turns against you, causes everyone to become a mute spectator, even those who know what is happening.

The 500-odd kilometre drive got even longer for the roads were cut off by rivers, but we followed the forest belt which underlined the fact that the entire Palamau–Bandhavgarh belt was linked, which made these reserves even more important. With R. C. Sahai around, we were quickly into the groove of things and would get some spectacular footage, especially of charging elephants. Aggressive females would cut us off by effortlessly knocking a tree down across the road, and while the rest of the herd crossed, would come at us full tilt. Once again, it was Sahai's steady nerves that allowed us to film, for despite having his back to the unfolding drama, he would only hit the ignition switch when I yelled 'go!' Being familiar with the area, we also succeeded in getting some extremely good rumbling sounds made by communicating elephants. Sitting in the open Gypsy under the canopy of stars, surrounded by wild elephants, one couldn't ask for more.

We drove back to Delhi via Lucknow. My classmate, Captain (later Major) Mohit Whig was the ADC to Lieutenant General Faridoon Bilimoria, who was then the Central Army commander, and we spent the night with him. Mohit had joined the army along with two other of my batchmates, Group Captain Sanjiv Singhal and Major General Jagatbir Singh, and had been commissioned into 2/5 Gorkha Rifles. His father, Brigadier M. L. Whig had commanded the famous 121 (I) Brigade in Kargil during the 1971 War and had been decorated with the MVC. Mohit had two Dobermans who were extremely aggressive, and one of them even snapped at Dipti. Mohit not so apologetically told her his dogs only bit civilians!

Both the North and Central India films had fallen short on their original wish list, but except for ourselves, nobody else knew what we had missed. The edits were completed and the films handed over, which now left us with just the one film on East India. Our biggest problem was the Manas Tiger Reserve. After I had shot the Project Tiger episode two years previously, there had been absolute mayhem let loose in the area. A violent ethnic agitation calling for Bodo political autonomy had rapidly spread through the region, and the Manas Tiger Reserve had been one of the biggest casualties. Weapons had poured in and the reserve itself became a haven for armed rebels. Nothing was spared–tigers, elephants, rhino, buffalo, sambar and hog deer were all but wiped out. Six forest guards had been killed, some of them beheaded, and even the domestic elephants had been slaughtered. I spoke to Deb Roy, who sounded completely devastated and he said under no circumstances was I to go anywhere there, especially with Dipti in tow. He also added that during the build-up, he had repeatedly warned the intelligence agencies, and though they acknowledged his warnings, nothing had happened on the ground.

With Manas out of the reckoning, that left us with the Sundarbans, Kaziranga and Namdapha. Jaldapara was an option, but that too fell in the Bodo and Mech areas. Instead, we decided to add the Loktak Lake in Manipur, where even if we failed to get the rare sangai, also known as the thamin or the Manipur brow-antlered deer, we would at least get the habitat and the wetland birds.

Taking Dipti to the Sundarbans was not feasible, for the boats would afford her with no privacy. It was decided I would shoot for a week, after which she would join me in Calcutta on New Year's Eve, and then we would fly to Dibrugarh and film the Namdapha Tiger Reserve. Accordingly, I flew off again into 'Royal Bengal' country, which by then I was extremely familiar with. With dame luck and my old friend Naik by my side, I got excellent footage, and then was heading back to Port Canning on the 31st morning, sitting on the deck of my launch watching the countryside go by. The channel was almost a kilometre wide, and the only other thing on the water was a small craft that was called a *phut putty*! I have no idea what happened, but somehow, as excited voices in Bengali rose to a crescendo to the point of them becoming shrieks of despair, the *phut putty* came and hit us smack on the side, and then dutifully sank!

The four men on board were first fished out of the tidal creek, and then every member of the crew came, looked at them with contempt and slapped them while they guiltily looked at their feet. I was wondering if I should also join the queue, when our boat pulled up and dropped anchor. 'Accident! Police case! We wait!' All my ranting and stomping of my feet had no effect, and by the time we pulled into Canning, it was almost time for the last local train to leave. A mad dash began from the jetty, our expensive equipment loaded on cycle rickshaws called *bhans*. Most sewage channels were bridged by just three sticks, and in the dark, somehow the *bhans* negotiated them at top speed. Sprinting after them, I was not so lucky and fell straight into a drain. We made it to the platform with a minute to spare, but since I was stinking to high heavens, the guard who was watching the drama, said he would hold the train for two minutes while I was shoved under a hand pump.

Just in case I had got held up, my two cousins, Vijay Dhruv's sons, Arjun and Arun, who lived in Calcutta were to have met Dipti and taken her home. Being young men about town, and it being New Year's Eve, they both had abrogated the responsibility to each other, and as a result, by the time I got to their house, the servant told me there was no Dipti and the two baba log were out 'dancing'. The taxi then rushed me to Dum Dum where a very, very distraught and angry Dipti was sitting with a black cloud hovering above her head. There was no point leaving the airport, for the flight to Dibrugarh was to take off in a few hours anyway.

We got to Namdapha and were greeted most effusively by Sharma-ji and the *gaon burah* who was hoping for more dole-outs of rum. Also occupying a room in the guest house was the research officer, whose name I have forgotten but who had a big moustache. The state of communications was so pathetic in those days, a telegram informing him of the passing away of his sister had taken a week to get to him. To make matters worse, he had expended all his leave and the government regulations refused to let him go home. He had arrived in Deban a few hours ahead of us, bringing with him a cannister of pure alcohol which ostensibly was meant for preserving specimens.

He also had a tranquilizing rifle and a supply of darts loaded with the extremely potent M-77 drug which carried the clear warning 'For animal use only'. A combination of the alcohol and the power of the rifle to back him up, he decided to 'sort out Naik' who, poor chap, was not being 'respectful enough to Kunal Saab!' I had never seen Naik take off with such alacrity, and it took quite an effort on the part of Sharma-ji and me to disarm him and put him to bed, where he slept calmly for 72 hours.

Namdapha afforded some spectacular views, especially of the Noa-Dehing River, but the going was always tough. We decided to spend the night at Bulbulia, a forest outpost on the other side of the Deban Nullah. At one stage, we were literally walking on a moving mass of leeches. The conditions under which forest guards and their officers operated were extreme, and we could only admire them for their absolute dedication to the job. Sometimes up against poachers who were armed with sophisticated weapons, most of the field staff would be out patrolling and just quite simply doing their job.

A quick break in Bombay, then we were back in Calcutta, this time around on the eve of Republic Day. The flight to Imphal was, as usual, at the crack of dawn, so half asleep we landed up at the check-in counter, only to be asked if we seriously wanted to go to the Manipur capital. We were told we were the only three people on board, which was us, as the underground groups had called for a complete shut down on the occasion of India's 39th Republic Day. However, since the pilots and the crew had also reported for the flight, I found myself looking down at Kangla Fort as we circled the city, and apart from some greyish-blue vehicles of the Central Reserve Police Force, there wasn't a soul visible down below.

An army Jonga came and met the aircraft. We had to wait for a ladder, after which we were dropped at the hotel where we were booked. In the evening people had started coming out on to the streets, so we too wandered down. I was buying some cigarettes across the road when Dipti let out a stifled shriek. She had walked across to a vendor who was selling munchies. Thinking she would pick up some, she had looked closely at what the stuff was, and to her horror, found herself staring into the roasted eyes of locusts, cockroaches and other exotic delicacies.

The next day we drove to the Loktak Lake and it was like nothing we had ever seen before. The Manipur River, coming in from the direction of Senapati, fed the massive body of water that covered a substantial part of the Imphal Valley. The largest freshwater lake in Northeast India, the Loktak has a unique ecosystem, perhaps the only one of its kind globally. *Phumdi*, a heterogenous mass of vegetation, soil and organic matter at various stages of decomposition, appear as floating islands, on which not only the sangai but even humans can walk, or even build small shelters. This large waterbody extends up to Moirang on the southern side of the Imphal Valley.

The place was teeming with whistling teal and other water birds, which we spent a fair amount of time filming. Having experienced Loktak, Dipti had to fly back to Bombay, while I stayed back with Naik. We were filming standing on a floating mass when Dipti's flight went over us. Though we had prepared a floating base for the camera and the tripod, both Naik and I had to be extremely careful as to where we chose to plant our feet on the wobbly mass. Perhaps losing my concentration for a fraction of a second, I stepped on a section that could not take my weight and down I went into the dark depths, clothes, shoes and hat et all. As I swam towards daylight, I inadvertently got a good look at even the submerged part of the unique vegetation.

The sangai were found in the marshy grasslands of the Keibul Lamjao National Park which was on the southern side of the lake. Twice we came close enough to hear the deer, but they ran off without so much as offering us a glimpse. It was fun chasing them around nevertheless, but without specialized equipment, I was only endangering the camera in what was fast becoming a wild goose chase. *No luck, no chance*! It was a pity though, for the sangai were perhaps among the rarest deer in the world, with their numbers in the wild down to just a handful at the time. In Manipuri folklore, the deer is said to bind the soul between humans and nature.

The next and final port of call was Kaziranga, so we packed up in Manipur and got to the grasslands of Assam by the first week of February. Memories of my last horrific visit five years ago were still fresh in my mind, and Naik turned pale when I took off my boot and showed him where I had been shot. There was a state-run ITDC hotel in or around Kohora where we had our rooms, and soon we were running around the park filming everything from rose-breasted parakeets to swamp partridge to rhinos to large herds of elephants. The eastern range in particular, had the largest *bheels* and we were in danger of running out of film, as hundreds of pelicans and a variety of animals lit up in the camera's viewfinder. Shooting mainly on foot, accompanied by a solitary ranger with a rifle, I was having the time of my life.

15 February would be our last day in the park, and I was sitting on a mound, partly hidden by the grass as I watched a herd of approximately seventy elephants feeding in the bheel, first uprooting, then swishing and cleaning the grass. A huge *makhna* (tuskless male) was quite close to us, while some females were on a grassy embankment some 150 metres away. Suddenly, a tusker, obviously in *musth*, appeared and started chasing one of the females. The makhna, seeing the intruder, got mad and through the

water he rushed towards the male who ran off into the grass. While the makhna was venting his anger on the embankment, all the other elephants started to congregate in another corner, and they seemed to hem in the female that had been at the receiving end of the tusker's attention. Sensing something spectacular was about to happen, I was filming the entire scene, when the tusker came out of the grass and without any preamble, mounted the female who seemed to be held in place by a dozen or so other elephants. The copulation was fairly brief, but during that moment, almost every elephant including calves (except the angry makhna) trumpeted loudly. Apart from the camera, I was also handling the Walkman recorder, and doing a fair job of it, even though an IAF An-32 decided to overfly us around the same time.

That night I packed my bags and the equipment and went to bed with mixed feelings, for the *Call of the Wild* shoots were over. Dipti was to fly in to Dibrugarh from Delhi the next day, and Naik and I were to embark on the same plane that would take us to Calcutta and then onto Bombay. All the exposed film was sealed, the cans marked, and I could hardly wait to see the rushes. Hardly had I gone to sleep when there was some urgent banging on my door. I opened the door and found myself staring into the barrel of a pistol. There were five men, and they were drunk silly, for they could not stop giggling. The pistol part, they explained to me, was a joke, and the gun was replaced by quarter bottles of whisky.

They said they were a part of Alpha' which made no sense to me, until I realized they were saying 'ULFA' (United Liberation Front of Asom). I knew that the separatist group had been founded about a decade ago by Paresh Baruah and had its main bases in Burma and perhaps South China. Just what did they want from me, I knew I had to be patient, for they would tell me soon enough. As it is, it's hard to deal with drunk individuals who are all armed and in an emotional state of mind, where their professed love for you can turn into murderous hatred at the blink of an eye. 'You,' the leader of the group kept jabbing me in the chest, another arm across my shoulder, 'great friend of Asom and Ahom people!' This statement would repeat itself three to four times, before his soaked brain finally articulated the next sentence. 'You come ... you come with us. We show you something!'

The cold winter air should have sobered them down, but it seemed to have little effect. The leader drove the jeep for half an hour, heading eastwards until we came to the Bokakhat Police Station, from where we turned south into the sleeping cluster of houses. A left and a right, we came to a halt and spilled out of the vehicle and entered a house that had three more armed men guarding it. Inside, lined up in crates, wrapped in oil seal paper, were AK-47s. 'We will liberate Asom,' said the leader, again putting his arm around me. '200 guns.' I am not sure how accurate the number was, but there were enough crates stacked up to the roof to substantiate that claim.

'Why are you showing these to me? I will report the matter, you can be sure of that.'

'Ha! Nobody can touch us. Not the police. Not the army. They will soon know what Alpha is.' There was some more swearing of eternal friendship, after which I was dropped back in my room. It was already getting to be light outside.

My mind was in a whirl. I kept thinking of what Deb Roy had said and the fate of Manas in two short years. I called Naik to my room and handed over the exposed film, telling him to repack quickly, after which we left for Dibrugarh. At the airport I decided not to board the flight, sending Dipti the message that I would follow in a day or so. As the plane took off, I had no clear plan of action, just this desperate feeling I needed to do something.

All taxis had left the airport, including the vehicle that had brought us from Kaziranga. I went to the ATC and requested the people there to let me put in a call to the GOC of 2 Infantry Division at Dinjan. Major General Ravi Eipe was the GOC and not only was he originally from 2 Rajput, he had taken over 18 Rajput from my father as well. After some delay I got him on the line, and he immediately said he was sending a vehicle to pick me up. By the time I reached his residence and was shown to my room, it was close to dinner time. It was the general's fiftieth birthday, and we were joined by Captain (later Lieutenant Colonel) Sanjeev Oberoi, his ADC, who was also from 2 Rajput.

I told Ravi Eipe about the weapons, and that the crates had Chinese markings and according to the comments I had been privy to, they had been routed via Bangladesh. Even while I spoke, I had this feeling of déjà vu, and kept thinking of General Jamwal on that fateful night in Delhi.

'But we have a treaty with Bangladesh!'

'Sir, I'm telling you what I saw myself. I think these guys showed them to me because now that the weapons have arrived, they at a subconscious level do not want to take on the army, hence the bravado. I think we just need to walk into Bokakhat and though there may be some resistance, we can get the entire lot. They may have already moved them, but if we move now, we can ambush them in the early hours.'

I could see Ravi Eipe was in a quandary. First, the area was not in his AOR, and second, I just felt he didn't believe me or simply did not want to believe me. He said something about not being able to just rush in like that. He also made no move to inform 4 Corps, which was headquartered across the Brahmaputra at Tezpur.

The general got up to go to the washroom. Sanjeev Oberoi, who had been silent throughout, now said to me, 'Sir, forget it. The general cannot do anything. He will not do it. You are wasting your time.' We finished dinner in silence. There was nothing more I could do, so I rebooked my flights and followed Dipti to Bombay. When I told her what had happened and why I hadn't boarded the flight the previous day, she just looked at me and said, 'You're an idiot! You will never learn!' I guess I finally had to admit she was right.

15

Where Natives Walk Sideways

I was beginning to toy with the idea of writing a detailed script for a series of films that would document the history of the Indian armed forces. Not quite sure where or how to start, I was reading up whatever matter I could lay my hands on. In the meantime, Dipti chanced upon a small snippet in the papers that talked of a resort called Bangaram in the Lakshadweep Islands that was being developed by the Casino Group of Hotels in Cochin. We had stayed at the Casino after we had shot the Alleppey Boat Race, so I wrote to the owners, asking them if they wanted to consider doing a film on the resort and the islands per se.

We were promptly invited to come and do a reconnaissance trip. We landed in Cochin on 18 September 1989, where we spent time with the Dominic brothers, especially George and Jose, who were running the island resort. I had invited my cousin Vineeta Hoon to join us as she was at the time doing research on coral reefs and energy use of island communities. From Cochin we flew in an HS 48 Avro to the tiny island of Agatti whose entire breadth seemed to be the width of the runway itself. A Pawan Hans orange and white-coloured Dauphin helicopter was parked nearby, and we were introduced to the two pilots, one of whom was Wing Commander Raeburn 'Ray' Demonte, who had flown Hawker Hunters with my uncle, Group Captain Dolly Yadav. 'Hang on guys,' said

Ray, turning around to us as the helicopter lifted off, 'I'll show you what it's like to fly a Hunter!'

Our first port of call was Kavaratti where we were the guests of Wajahat Habibullah, who was the administrator of the Lakshadweep Islands. An Indian Administrative Service officer, he was from the 1961 batch of the Doon School, and he generously shared with us his vast knowledge of the archipelago. After loading us up with seafood cooked in the Kerala style, it was time to take his leave. Noticing a number of paintings of women sitting around, all holding their head, Dipti asked who the artist was. 'My sister,' said Wajahat, 'I call them the *hai phuti kismet* (my lousy luck) series!'

The next day we flew to the islands of Kiltan and Ameni, marvelling at just how small and tiny the islands were. These were short 20-minute helicopter hops across, but they were giving us a wonderful idea of the layout of the archipelago. In the evening, the Pawan Hans pilots threw a party, and Ray announced grandly that tomorrow we would set foot on Bangaram, an experience he said that would change our lives. So, on the morning of 21 September, we said goodbye to Wajahat Habibullah and strapped up yet again. Our first hop was to Agatti, where we picked up two other passengers who were dressed in immaculate white shirts and the traditional Kerala lungis.

With Ray and his co-pilot in an aerobatic mood, it was one hell of a ride. We had the door open and that considerably added to the experience. The blue lagoon and white beaches gave way to first aquamarine and then a deep purplish sea, as we skimmed along barely five or six metres from the surface. Even from the chopper we could see the bed of the sea, the shoals of fish and the occasional manta ray gliding along under water. Twenty minutes later, we were approaching Bangaram, which had a massive lagoon around it, the reef breaking surface thrice to form the atolls of Thinnakara, Parelli I and Parelli II. Short of flying upside down, the pilots had done everything to make the trip memorable. However, our two co-passengers shot off the moment we landed, swearing they would never come close to a helicopter again. They kept rolling their eyes and saying 'Pilot mad! Pilot mad!' long after the Dauphin had taken off and disappeared over the horizon.

We spent three languid days on the island. There was a German diving instructor on the island, Andreas, and I got to do a practice dive with him inside the lagoon, also discussing with him how best to film underwater. As the sun set, we decided to take a boat out into the lagoon and catch some red snappers. We were using small *minyan* (oriental sweetlips) for bait and the plan was for me to teach Dipti the nuances of handline fishing. Unknown to me, the blasted red snappers were all sexist, for they ignored my juicy baits and kept hooking themselves on Dipti's line. An hour later, she had eight snappers, while I had none. Keeping a straight face at times like this becomes quite an art, and I was lucky it was pitch dark. Then, the largest snapper of the evening mistook my bait for Dipti's, and after a short, breathless fight, I had a fish that was a teeny weeny larger than any of the fish caught by my so-called pupil.

Back in Delhi we got busy preparing for the shoot. We had a limited budget and since 16 mm was too expensive and cumbersome a format to shoot the Bangaram film on, we switched to Betacam for the first time. After landing I got a hang of the new camera system at the Casino Hotel where we shot lobsters being grilled on open fires. Sanjai Banerji, my Cochin-based classmate, had gotten married in May 1989, so after filming the shellfish, we then proceeded to demolish them as well with Banjo and his wife Sanjukta.

The Bangaram film had all the elements. We got some fabulous aerial footage of the lagoons and the islands from the Dauphins, and using an underwater camera housing, we got reasonable shots of a variety of coral reefs and colourful fish. The film got its title *Where the Natives Walk Sideways* from the crabs that were literally everywhere. The film done and dusted, we returned to Delhi wondering what were we to do next.

The *Call of the Wild* series had been very well received across the board, and our style of film making allowed us to make inroads with the department of tourism who until then had by and large only been dealing with advertising companies in this regard. What was even more important, they had become extremely receptive to any ideas we put across to them. On the flip side, we were expected to be equally open to suggestions from them. Hemant Gupte, who had a Spanish wife, had become a good friend by then, and over dinner at their place, I had convinced him to start the paperwork that would allow us to make a 30-minute film on fishing in India. The next day, even the ring on the phone had sounded urgent, and Gupte asked me to come to his office post haste. Wondering what on earth could have gone wrong, I was immediately taken to B. K. Goswami's office. The director tourism was looking quite grim, and as I walked in, without any preamble, he said, 'What do you make of the term "Incentive Travel"?'

I had no clue, so I said it sounded like an award for good performance or something. It transpired that Madhavrao Scindia, the union minister for civil aviation had called S. K. Mishra, secretary tourism, to make a film on Incentive Travel. Mishra couldn't possibly ask the minister what that meant, so he called Goswami and said much the same thing. Goswami couldn't ask Mishra, so he called Gupte who at that stage called us. Goswami agreed with me about the generic meaning of the term, 'Yes, but how do you make a film? What do you show?'

'You show whatever you want,' I said tongue-in-cheek, 'shoot some exotic locations and call it Incentive Travel.' Goswami looked at Gupte, and some message must have passed between them because KaleidoIndia got the film. Trouble was, in those days when there was no internet, finding the exact meaning of the term that had been used by some marketing whiz kids in the minister's presence, was quite a nightmare. A few days later we were still clueless as to what exactly Incentive Travel meant, so we decided to shoot in four fairly exotic locations, which we felt would be enough incentive for people to travel. Since we had recently shot in Bangaram, I suggested we start the film from the Lakshadweep Islands, then film the Windsor Manor in Bangalore, the Lake Palace Hotel in Udaipur and finally close with the Taj Bengal in Calcutta.

We romped around the country, shooting whatever caught our fancy. It was a freewheeling film, and we further expanded the envelope by filming underwater on the outer side of the Bangaram reef. In Bangalore we filmed the races, shooting from a speeding vehicle keeping pace with the horses, while an assistant held my legs so that I didn't fly out of the open Gypsy. In Udaipur, we sat drinking cocktails, watching spectacular sunsets in between taking tracking shots of the lake and the Rajasthani architecture, before winding up in Calcutta where we filmed the recently inaugurated Taj Bengal. All this while I kept thinking what Madhavrao Scindia would say, and just how easily this film could backfire on us.

When the film was edited and delivered, Hemant Gupte asked me to accompany him to the aviation minister's residence. The film was screened and the 'wow' factor carried the day, though the minister did remark that it looked like a promotional film for the Taj Group. After the screening, Madhavrao looked at me and asked the million-dollar question, 'What exactly do you mean when you say Incentive Travel?' Before I could reply, Gupte quickly piped up, 'Incentive to travel, Sir!'

The minister had obviously completely forgotten that the term had originated from him. We promptly added the word 'to' so it now read *Incentive to Travel*. The film was then cleared to be screened on all inbound Air India flights, and both Dipti and I heaved a sigh of relief.

In the meantime, the approval for the fishing film had come through and the planning for that started in real earnest. The options were manifold, but I preferred to film in areas I was familiar with, and I also decided on getting my father to be the person who would do the fishing. For trout, there was nothing more scenic than the upper lakes of the Nilgiri Mountains and for Mahseer we wanted to film both in North and South India, so it again narrowed down to the Ramganga in Corbett and the Cauvery at Bheemeshwari. The most exciting part was the deep-sea fishing angle that we wanted to bring in, for it meant yet another trip to the Lakshadweep Islands.

Just around then my father had been posted to the NDC as the senior DS (army). I was only too happy to shut up the Noida flat and move back with my parents, who were allotted the bungalow at 75, Lodhi Estate. My father had two months annual leave, and the prospect of fishing in all these areas was enough to get him all excited. In November 1987, he had also taken over as the Colonel of the Rajput Regiment from Lieutenant General Ranjit Singh Dayal, after which whenever he had time, he would visit Rajput battalions deployed all over the country. However, before we could head off on the fishing trip, he was extremely keen to visit his old formation, 26 Infantry Division in Jammu, and also 2 Rajput that was then deployed on the Line of Control (LOC) in the Rajouri Sector. Another Rajput battalion was deployed in Pathankot, so a five-day trip was worked out wherein we would also get a crack at jungle fowl in Rajouri and partridge around Pathankot. Dipti hadn't been to these areas, so the three of us flew in to Jammu on 1 January 1991.

Konsam Himalay 'KH' Singh was from Thoubal in Manipur. He had just been commissioned into 2 Rajput (Kali Chindi) in 1980 when we had visited the battalion in Poonch, and for all practical purposes, he had literally been adopted by my father as his second son. As the youngest officer in the battalion at the time, the CO, Colonel Thomas Mathew, had detailed him to go find 'narcissus' flowers for my mother and the entire battalion had gone into a tizzy until it dawned on them she wanted the daffodils that went by the name of *nargis* in Hindi, which were growing all around them. KH and I had become close friends and were in regular correspondence ever since. A die-hard infantry soldier, he would write to me in MCC ... 'I hope you are not wasting money smoking and drinking. If you are, it will reflect very badly on 2 Rajput ...' KH was now a major and having just finished his Staff College course had rejoined the battalion as a company commander. He was at the airport to receive us, and we were of course, delighted to see him again.

The shoot literally on the LOC was an experience by itself, with people telling us repeatedly not to expose ourselves because various areas were bracketed by Pakistani guns. For Dipti in particular, it was an eye-opener, for she got to see firsthand what life was like for the officers and men on the LOC. KH had us in splits when he narrated how, contrary to orders, the men at a particular post had decided to sleep under the stars because it was hot and sultry in the bunker. Lying side by side, five of them had got bored and felt the need for a smoke. The man on the extreme right had lit a beedi that was then passed onto the man on his left. Number 5 forgot he was the last man and passed it on to number 6, which was a black bear who had come and laid down with the men. The tranquil scene was history as the bear, not liking the idea of being poked by a burning beedi, went berserk. The minutes of the resultant court of enquiry would have made for extremely interesting reading.

However, the real drama on the trip was yet to unfold. We moved from Rajouri to Pathankot where Brigadier (later Lieutenant General) Tejinder Singh 'Maun' Shergill was commanding 16 Independent Armoured Brigade. Maun had organized a partridge shoot near Pathankot and even as we reached the area where the bandobust had been made, I noticed one of the members of the shooting party, the second-in-command (2 I/C) of 63 Cavalry, being a little too exuberant about life. The safety protocols that individuals followed were ingrained into everyone, but the 2 I/C was letting it rip left and right without hitting too many birds. Dipti and KH were following the shooting party, and once or twice I mentally checked to see that they were not in range or line of fire of our local Clint Eastwood!

There was a large patch of sugarcane and as per the norm, we had all taken up our positions. My father was to the left of Maun while I was in position to his right. Taking to wing that day were both black francolins that tend to initially climb above sugarcane height, and also the grey partridges that went past relatively lower to the ground. As per the procedure, every time a gun fired, the *hakka* (beaters) party would pause so that the individual could reload, and then they would move forward again, forcing the birds to break cover. There was a brief period when suddenly both blacks and greys got up together, and as there was a volley of shots, I suddenly saw Maun bend double, one hand clutching at his face. Major (subsequent rank or fate not known) 'Boota' Gill, the 2 I/C had just shot his brigade commander! The pattern that had peppered Maun had miraculously missed his eye, for he had shot on either side of his eyeball. Maun, in typical armoured corps style, asked if the shot had also hit the 'bloody bird' but he was indeed extremely lucky that day not to follow in the steps of Moshe Dyan, the former one-eyed Israeli defence minister. That also prematurely put an end to the shoot that day.

Lieutenant General Adi Meherji Sethna had been the commandant of the Defence Services Staff College when my father was posted there. Our residence, Mansarovar, was part of the trio of houses that faced the commandant's gate and very often, I would walk down to the Madras Regimental Centre memorial with the general and his golden cocker spaniel, Scamper. While at the time I was just passing out of the Doon School, Adi Sethna had preceded me by more than three decades. Commissioned into 5 Rajputana Rifles (Napiers), Adi Sethna had, like all officers of his exalted rank 'been there and done that' before he retired as the vice chief of the Indian Army. Entrusted with the task of running the Asian Games in New Delhi in 1982, he had worked closely with Rajiv Gandhi. Post-retirement, he had been the chairman of ITDC, and it was in his spacious office at the Ashoka Hotel that we were meeting in the second half of 1990.

I had just offered him a job, which was tickling him pink. As the chief consultant of KaleidoIndia, he would receive a cheque of ₹5,000 at the end of each month. He would be a part of the three-member core team (the other two being Dipti and me) that would work towards producing a 15-part film series called *India's Fighting Man*. The first film would start with the division of 1st Punjab in the immediate lead up to Partition, after which we would progressively tell the story of all the three services. My plan was to write three scripts, and then with a bit of luck, we would see how to further develop things.

My father being back at the NDC once again gave me access to the library, and I was getting more and more fascinated by the Great Game and how the geopolitics of the early-1800s had not only impacted life but continued to do so. My father apart, Lieutenant General Sushil Pillai was the other person I would spend time talking to. Not only was Sushil Pillai (he had been a platoon commander with my father at the IMA) from the Assam Regiment, he started making me look more and more to the east as well. Almost every morning at the breakfast table, my father and I would talk about various things—and there were a million questions that needed answers, and some of them started falling into place, or at least, there were plausible answers that seemed to emerge. I also kept searching for the Meinertzhagen Papers, but there was no trace of them anymore. It was almost as if they had never existed.

By then the first script was completed, and Adi Sethna felt we needed to make three copies. The first copy he gave to N. N. Vohra, the defence secretary; the second he gave to Rajiv Gandhi, who was out of power but widely tipped to come back as the prime minister. The third copy he gave to Air Marshal N. C. Suri, who was then the vice chief of the air force. The first one to be returned was from Rajiv Gandhi, with a yellow paper clipped on, saying 'Nice!' He also had given time for a meeting.

The three of us trooped into his office, this time at 10 Janpath. If Rajiv had any recollection of the earlier meeting four years ago, he showed no signs of recognition, and I wasn't going to remind him either. His equation with Adi Sethna was obviously very good, for he seemed genuinely pleased to see him. Dipti, who knew about these things, would say subsequently that Rajiv was wearing make-up, so obviously there was a television crew waiting to record with him. It was obvious he had at least scanned through the script, if not actually read it. He wanted to know why we wanted to start the series with the division of the British Indian Army. 'Considering that the Indian Army's history goes back almost two hundred years, wouldn't it be better to have an episode that encapsulates that period as well?'

Adi Sethna started saying something about not wanting to get into the political aspects of things, but I felt I needed to elaborate on this point, so I cut in, 'Well, sir, actually we wanted to start the series from World War I, especially 1919.' Rajiv Gandhi was looking at me intently, obviously I had his interest. 'We don't have any documentary proof as yet sir, but we have reason to believe that the India Office had actually prepared a detailed plan for the partition of India into three separate states—Hindustan, Pakistan and Princesstan. I don't think they were serious about the Princesstan bit but had included it as a bargaining chip to counter any opposition from the Congress Party to make Pakistan a reality.'

'Go on,' Rajiv Gandhi said quietly.

'After the performance of Indian troops in World War I, especially in Europe, where the Garhwalis for example were instrumental in breaking the deadlock over trench warfare, our people had returned to India with the tacit understanding that Home Rule would be granted to India in recognition of their loyalty. At least that was what the general perception seemed to be. The India Office, which was tasked to prepare a strategy, took into consideration a 1857-like scenario where a massive uprising would force the British to leave the subcontinent. The document was prepared and submitted to the House of Commons, but it was rejected. In the meantime, the Jallianwala Bagh massacre happened, and the British invoked the Rowlatt Act and things just fizzled out ... However, the seeds of creating Pakistan primarily to serve British interests in West Asia and to counter the Russian threat from the direction of the Pamirs, the plan became the unofficial document that guided British policy and eventually led to the creation of Pakistan,' I said in a rush, getting a little breathless at the end of it.

'The concept of a Muslim state was first advocated by Iqbal in 1930. The very word—Pakistan—only came into play three years later,' Adi Sethna added, 'it was first mentioned by Rahmat Ali in 1933.'

'How do you know any such document was prepared? And how can you pin it down to 1919?' asked Rajiv Gandhi.

I said I had seen the document in the NDC library in 1983 and now that my father was on the staff, I was looking for it but could not find it.

'That is the main problem,' said Dipti, who until then had been sitting quietly, 'though it is completely in keeping with the way the British War and Colonial Offices worked, the trouble is we don't have access to the papers. For all we know, if they did exist, they could have been destroyed.'

'But they weren't,' said Rajiv Gandhi dramatically, at the same time getting to his feet, smiling broadly, 'The document you are talking about was indeed prepared at that time and it was declassified some years ago. I have it here ...' Incredulously, the three of us followed him, as he moved to his left towards a shelf lined with leather-bound documents. He was running his finger over them, leaning back and reading the various titles ... 'Here it is ...' he started to remove it when there was a loud knock at the door. Captain Satish Sharma, a close confidant of Rajiv Gandhi came into the room and took him aside. He was still holding the leather-bound file in his hand. Rajiv Gandhi then addressed Adi Sethna: 'I am sorry general, but something important has come up. May I suggest we meet again shortly to discuss this further?'

The meeting was over. We were so close, and yet so far! We shook hands and started to leave his office. Captain Sharma stood aside for us to pass. In his hand was a telex message in which the words 'Bofors' had been highlighted with a fluorescent marker a couple of times.

Two days later, Adi Sethna, Dipti and I met again. The general was pressing hard for a second meeting, but wasn't making any headway with Rajiv Gandhi's Secretariat. 'He won't see us,' Dipti the pragmatic one put into words what we were not wanting to articulate even to ourselves, 'Rajiv's reaction when you talked about the 1919 file was spontaneous, but he'll have time to think about it and he won't want any of this to be made public.'

Adi Sethna sighed loudly, leaned back in his chair and shut his eyes: 'She's right, dash it! If this comes out in any form whatsoever, the entire Congress Party at the time of Independence look like a bunch of novices who were led up the garden path held by their noses. Still ...' he reached out for the phone and started dialling Rajiv Gandhi's number again.

We had never succeeded in getting through to him again. A few months after that, in May 1991, Rajiv Gandhi was assassinated by the Tamil Tigers at Sriperumbudur while attending a public meeting.

Like the proverbial spider that refused to give up, the energy brought into play by Adi Sethna was incredible. He fixed meetings with whoever he thought could help get the series of films underway, and if we drew a blank, which was mostly the case, it would hardly ever faze him. Some of the meetings would have made it to a stand-up comedy show! Shortly after the Rajiv Gandhi meeting, Adi Sethna and I found ourselves sitting in the office of Lieutenant General Ravi Mahajan, who was the deputy COAS. By then I think we had the synopsis for episode 2 and 3 also ready, and as was our wont, we were enthusiastically holding forth on the structure of the proposed series. After hearing us out, Ravi Mahajan helpfully suggested, 'Very nice, but you need to bring in the love angle? Without some cleavage, nothing works!'

Earlier, one of the first meetings we had, was with the naval chief, Admiral J. G. Nadkarni. Of all the offices occupied by four-star officers, that of the chief of naval staff (CNS) was the most imposing. Lieutenant (later Captain) Kabir Vasudevan, whose bass voice added to the majesty of the admiralty, sat just outside the chief's door and was known as 'the flag'. He was from the Doon School, albeit Tata House, and as he flung open the massive door leading into the inner sanctum of the office, I for one felt the full impact of what the British called the 'majesty of governance'.

The CNS had listened intently, then he asked a question that we should have anticipated. 'Out of the fifteen, how many episodes will the navy get?' I opened my mouth to answer, but quick-draw Adi left me far behind in his wake ... 'Five!'

Nadkarni was happy with the response, so he expanded the envelope further. 'We must show computerization in the navy.' Again, I was outgunned, for Adi Sethna had already endorsed it, 'But of course ... By far the most advanced service of the three...' The CNS then wanted to show us his latest pride and joy, for as he explained, his office had just graduated from XT to AT computers. Making the right ooh and aah noises, we moved to his side of the table and with a flourish, the CNS pressed the 'on' button. We got a glimpse of how Ali Baba would have felt if his command '*khul ja sim sim*' had not had the required result.

'Flag!' bellowed Nadkarni, and Kabir was in like a flash. 'Sir?' he said very crisply.

'Flag, the computer is not working. Call able-bodied seaman Tiwari.' Or words to that effect!

'Sir!' said Kabir, and he went looking for Tiwari, who it transpired was missing from his Crow's Nest having decided to go walkabouts for reasons unknown. By then the SO (staff officer) and the NA (naval assistant) had also realized the reputation of the blue water navy was at stake but their jabbing at the computer had no effect. Even a couple of admirals poked their head in but decided the situation needed to be handled by a technical guy. By now able-bodied Tiwari's immediate whereabouts had taken on the character of a national emergency.

Finally, Tiwari came scampering in. Poor fellow had gone to have a samosa and a cup of tea when the heavens had fallen! One look at the transformer connected to the mains, he pressed a red button, and the AT computer sprang to life. The navy's honour was redeemed. Adi Sethna could still claim it was the most technologically advanced service of the three. And able-bodied seaman Tiwari did not have to walk the plank!

My father's office at the NDC was right opposite Birla House on Tees January Road where Mahatma Gandhi had been assassinated. As the colonel commandant of the Rajput Regiment, he convened a meeting, asking both Dipti and me to attend. There for the first time, I was introduced to Pushpindar Singh Chopra, whose father had also served in the Rajputs. 'Pushy' was also from the Doon School and had done or was doing a pictorial book for the IAF, while he was also publishing *Vayu* which was a magazine dealing with aviation issues. Also present were Major General R. S. 'Munna' Taragi and Brigadier Bhup Singh, the Rajput Regimental Centre commandant. Taragi, who was not only my father's schoolmate from Nainital, was also a close family friend. He was then perhaps the senior most Rajput officer after my father.

Three relatively new battalions, 25, 26, and 27 Rajput, were getting their colours at Fatehgarh and for the regiment, it was a historic moment. My father wanted us to film the event, for which some basic funds were required. Pushy, larger than life in these matters, promptly said he would raise the money. Just the cost of raw film, camera hire, and cost of travel amounted to rupees three lakh. The rest, editing and post-production, we were to absorb. Dipti had her reservations about doing the film because I was my father's son, but she was told by all it did not matter.

After the meeting, Munna Taragi had stayed back in the office along with us. He was quite soft-spoken and sometimes one almost missed what he was saying. My father, who after the 1971 War had a hearing problem, asked Munna Taragi to speak up. 'You've given the film to your son,' he said, 'give the brochure to my son-in-law.' The inference was obvious, but my father missed it completely. He said, it was not possible because Atanu Roy was already working on it.

Dipti had flown down from Bombay for the meeting, and in the evening during dinner, she again expressed her reservations, especially in light of Munna Taragi's remark. There was a virtual explosion, and she got a 'stern' lecture about ethics and the Indian Army, about army officers not being like civilians, and how an officer was a gentleman and how, in future, if she had such a narrow vision of life, she could 'lump it'!

Anyway, when it came to his regiment and 'his people', my father was impossible to talk to. Since it mattered so much to him, I told Dipti we would film it anyway, so there was no point in saying anything. Pushy, of course, did a disappearing act, though he kept telling my father on the phone that the required money was 'pouring in'. He even got me to edit *Vayu* for him for a couple of issues, during which time I researched and wrote a piece on the siege of Poonch.

We drove to Fatehgarh, while the camera and Indrajit Neogi, the sound recordist, flying in from Bombay. The highlight of the event was to be the Colour Parade, that was commanded by Bhup Singh. General S. F. A. Rodrigues, the army chief, was to present the colours and the moment he landed, he sent for me. 'What's happening to your army series?' he asked. 'Don't waste your time with the IAF and the navy. Come see me when you get back to Delhi.' He went on to say he had read the script, which N. N. Vohra had passed on to him, and it was riveting stuff. 'Roddy' had been my father's immediate boss in Ladakh when he was commanding 3 Infantry Division, and then again, he was the corps commander in Nagrota during his tenure in Jammu. Roddy's two sons, Neil and Mark, and his daughter Susan, were good friends of mine, and though I had often shot partridge and gone fishing with the general, I was always a little wary of him.

However, the trip to Fatehgarh was beginning to turn into a nightmare. We were busy filming the various ceremonies but time and again Munna Taragi would position himself close to us and while maintaining a smiling exterior, would go on and on. 'Who are you fooling? There is no film in the camera!' Initially I thought he was just being funny in an avuncular sort of way, but after a while it started to get to us. It was all very covert, and when I told my mother what was going on, she simply said, 'You should have listened to Dipti. Your father will never believe

Top left: Strapped into a Mirage 2000 for my first fighter sortie
Top right: The Battle Axes (7 Squadron) in Gwalior. Wg Cdr Nandu Jog is next to me second from right
Centre left: With the CO of 5 Squadron, Wg Cdr 'Ike' Iyer, after a Jaguar sortie while Dipti and others look on
Centre right: The 12 Jaguar formation that attacked Nal having taken off from Ambala
Bottom left: A Cheetah from 114 Helicopter Unit landing at Zulu Post
Bottom right: The 75-km long Siachen Glacier photographed from an An-32

Top left: The Salt of the Earth crew posing in front of an An-12 at Chandigarh
Top right: A MiG-25 Foxbat takes off from Bareily
Centre left: T-59 tanks depicting the Pakistani armoured thrust at Longewala advancing
Centre right: Filming with Madras Regiment troops at Salur enacting IPKF related scenes
Bottom left: Low-level maritime strike off Mumbai having taken off from Pune
Bottom right: With Wg Cdr 'Tiny' Kumaria and pilots from 6 Squadron after the sortie

Top left: INS Ganga, INS Godavri and INS Gomti (Godavari Class frigates) off Mumbai
Top right: INS Ranvijay, the Russian-built SNF destroyer
Centre left: An OSA Class missile boat preparing to launch a missile off the coast of Vizag
Centre right: Communication sorties in a Chetak helicopter
Bottom left: RAS (Replenishment at Sea) as warships are refueled
Bottom right: The carefully worked out shot of seven ships in formation, with INS Delhi in the middle

Top left: Windsong being completed at Bandrol in 1995
Top right: My father while the house was being constructed
Centre left: Relinking with the army after spending a few days with Mujahids in January 1995
Centre right: With an officer from 13 Kumaon drinking tea sitting on a Jonga
Bottom left: Fishing the upper reaches of the Kaveri in 1995
Bottom right: Holding a Carnatic carp which was then a record fish

Top left: Dipti with a year-old Vallika in 1995
Top right: Vallika in Reston, United States
Centre left: Dipti with Vallika at Borobodur, Indonesia
Bottom: Filming at Yogyakarta with Vallika by my side

Top left: Vallika at NOIDA in 1996
Top right: Reading the 3-D version of National Geographic
Bottom left: Mother and daughter at Kodaikanal in Tamil Nadu
Bottom right: Vallika with me

Veeha is born at New Delhi in May 1998

Top left: 155 mm Bofors howitzers being towed across Zoji La
Top right: The 3 Infantry Division Ops Room during the Kargil conflict
Centre left: 105 mm guns engaging targets in the Batalik Sector
Centre right: 17 Garhwal Rifles displaying captured ammunition and weapons in the Drass Sector
Bottom left: 155 mm Bofors firing
Bottom right: Pakistani artillery fire bracketing the area around Kargil town

Top: Maj Gen 'Viru' Budhwar being briefed by Col K. K. Sinha about the impending attack on Chorbat La
Centre: Flying in an army aviation Cheetah with GOC 3 Infantry Division in the Yaldor Sector
Bottom left: Major Rajiv Dua, Brig Devinder Singh and Maj Gen Budhwar at Ghanasok, the 70 Infantry Brigade's TAC HQ
Bottom right: Refueling at Mughalpura just before flying to Srinagar

Top left: The Bison Road Tigress in Kanha Tiger Reserve
Top right: Barasingha (swamp deer) and a chital stag
Centre right: A tiger cub on a chital kill provided by its mother
Bottom: Gaur or Indian bison in the meadows of Kanha

Top left: Vallika and Veeha in Noida**Top right**: A fast growing Veeha on her favourite horse
Bottom left: Veeha and Dipti at Bandrol in 2000
Bottom right: Vallika and Veeha with Dhruv Yadav who was then at the Doon School

Top left: Strapping into a MiG-29 cockpit during the filming of Aakash Yodha
Top right: Over-flying the glacier on the northern side of Umasi La
Centre left: With Wg Cdr P. K. Singh in Adampur after a MiG-29 sortie over Zanskar
Centre right: Debriefing Wg Cdr Anil Tharani, my liaison officer during most of the filming
Bottom left: Preparing to take off for a strike towards Kargil from Ambala
Bottom right: Crossing Rohtang. Note the over-wing missiles

Top left: Approaching Sonam Post on the Saltoro Ridge, which flanks the western side of the Siachen Glacier
Top right: Another view of the Siachen Glacier, looking north towards Indira Point that borders the Shaksgam Valley
Centre left: The moraines on the glacier itself. For all its claims, Pakistan has no presence on the glacier itself
Centre right: With the helicopter crew at the Siachen Base Camp
Bottom left: At the opposite end of the spectrum, Indira Point at the southern-most tip of the Greater Nicobar Island
Bottom right: Flying in Su-30s over Pune. These were the first batch of Sukhois that were inducted into the IAF

Top: Cadets being drilled at the National Defence Academy
Centre: Preparing for the Passing-out-parade
Bottom left: Gp Capt Johnson Chacko taking off in a Super Dimona at the NDA
Bottom right: During the premier of the Standard Bearers at Habibullah Hall

Top left: The Passing-out-parade at the Indian Military Academy
Top right: During the filming of Making of a Warrior
Centre left: Gentlemen Cadets (GCs) marching onto the drill square
Bottom: 'The Soul is Immortal'... Honouring their fallen predecessors at the War Memorial

Top: My father with Manavi, Veeha and Vallika
Bottom left: Veeha, all dressed up, with her Dadimom and Vallika
Bottom right: My father with his two granddaughters in Kullu

Munna will do this.' She added that my uncle, Vijay Dhruv, who was Munna Taragi's classmate, had also been saying the same thing to people.

Anyway, the parade was filmed, and we flew to Bombay where the rolls were processed by Adlabs. The event, with all the glitz and sparkle, was terrific and the colour presentation was as good as it gets. Meanwhile, Bhup Singh had handed over command of the Rajput Regimental Centre to Brigadier (later Lieutenant General) H. S. Bagga. With nothing further happening on the film, he dropped by to 'resolve' the issue. Since there was no further response from Pushy Chopra about the funds he was raising, Bagga said he could approach the MOD to sanction the funds, but for that I first needed to fly Munna Taragi to Bombay and 'show him the footage'. I politely refused and that was the end of that.

We were in Bombay when the news came that my father had not made the cut for lieutenant general. Though he was most taken aback, the news was not surprising for he had repeatedly fallen on the wrong side of Roddy who was his superior officer. The first instance was during Exercise Chequerboard in 1987, when a sand model exercise was held to anticipate Chinese reactions. General Sundarji had been the chief then, and my father (GOC 26 Infantry Division) was appointed the Chinese commander while Lieutenant General B. C. Nanda (the Northern Army commander) and Roddy (GOC 16 Corps) were the Indian commanders. To add pressure on the Indian side, during the sand model appreciation, the 'Chinese commander' activated the Northern Areas (Gilgit-Baltistan) as well. This was not in keeping with the Indian belief that the Gilgit side was dormant, and they were caught napping. As a result, to put it mildly, the sand model did not go well for the Indians. Roddy later gave my father a mouthful, telling him he had made him and Nanda look like idiots.

The next instance was at Mhow in the previous year, when Roddy as the vice chief had come to address the Higher Command Course. While speaking to the colonel-level students on the operations in Sri Lanka, in the question-answer session that followed, Roddy was repeatedly cornered by some of the officers who had themselves commanded units as part of the Indian Peace Keeping Force (IPKF) operations in Sri Lanka. Roddy had been the DGMO, which made the situation even worse for him, and after a while he abruptly stormed out, leaving a stunned audience behind. The Higher Command Course had been the brainchild of Lieutenant General Eric Vas, who had designed it in a manner where officers attending the course were not graded, allowing them to have a free and flowing discussion on various subjects without the fear of getting a negative report.

Roddy, who was in line for chief then, told Lieutenant General N. S. Narahari that he not only wanted the heads of the officers who had been 'impudent', but he wanted officers to be graded in future as well. This led to quite a situation, with both Narahari and my father also getting onto Roddy's wrong side. However, despite what happened in Mhow, Roddy then appointed my father on the Reorganization Committee that was to suggest restructuring the army in order to streamline the teeth to tail ratio and called him to his office and said he was a 'Gujarati peanut' implying he need not worry about stepping on toes as he would be cleared for the next rank anyway.[17] Roddy probably meant it, but then again, during the colour presentation in Fatehgarh, they again clashed, this time over Bhup Singh, the centre commandant. A hostel for the children of Rajput war widows had been set up, and to get around the red tape, Bhup had allegedly taken a few decisions that had been reported to Roddy via an anonymous letter. Roddy wanted to sack Bhup and hold an enquiry, but my father said while an enquiry was his prerogative as the chief, sacking Bhup was out of the question.

Anyhow, what was done was done, but it meant that my father would now retire in a few months at the end of October 1991. Somewhere along the line, I had all but forgotten that Simi existed until I received summons for a divorce hearing at the Tis Hazari Courts. My 'go-to' person in any legal crisis was my friend and classmate, Arvind Kumar Nigam, who was a leading lawyer practising at the Delhi High Court. Nigam got a friend of his, Sanjay Aggarwal, to represent me, and so along with my mother we trooped in on the appointed day.

Simi, who had shortened her hair, was present with her father, and I think she had decided to represent herself. The judge, the moment he entered, asked both Sanjay and me to approach the bench and he said

---

[17] Gujarati peanuts were genetically improved and double the size of a normal peanut.

please listen carefully to what I am saying. 'I am distantly related to the petitioner, but if you move for me to recuse myself, I will.' Sanjay looked at me, but I said I was fine with the judge presiding. 'Are you sure?' I was asked again. I just nodded.

Asked to go first, Simi went into an elaborate 'your honour this' and 'your honour that' routine, after which she virtually repeated the ten charges the lieutenant governor had hurled at me two years previously in the middle of the night. In fact, even the catchphrases were much the same. She then switched her attack to my mother, and this time she got to a few more points before the judge stopped her. 'All of you,' he said, 'come into my chamber.' There he addressed Simi, 'Beta, you think I was born yesterday. Everything you said in there is a lie, it's obvious.' Simi then started to say something about 'external influences', obviously referring to Dipti, but the judge had already made up his mind. He turned to me and said, 'My family used to watch Project Tiger every Sunday morning. You did a good job. You are free to go ...' I couldn't believe my luck and shot out into the corridor where Simi's father was standing with my mother. He started to say something, but I was sprinting, for the tension had got to me and I just had to get to a loo. I made it with a fraction of a second to spare. I never saw Simi again, or for that matter, asked about her.

Towards the end of May 1991, Adi Sethna called and announced Air Marshal Nirmal 'Nimmi' Chand Suri, the vice chief of air staff wanted to see us. 'Wear the Doon School tie,' he said mischievously, adding that since the air marshal was from RIMC, we might as well have some fun! Nimmi Suri was from the 1st Course JSW and he was not only my uncle Dalbir Yadav's coursemate, he knew my family well from his pilot officer days when they were training in Hakimpet in Hyderabad. As expected, he ribbed us about being 'from the other side of the wall' and then, in the most inoffensive manner, he told us we were unlikely to make any headway with the film series. 'Pardon me, general,' he sighed. 'You guys are wasting your time. It is impossible to get the three services on the same page.' He let that sink in.

I had never seen Adi Sethna at a loss of words, but Nimmi Suri had all three of us staring at him with our jaws hanging. 'As you know, sir,' he then added, '1992 is the diamond jubilee year of the IAF.' Shifting his gaze to Dipti and me, he said, 'Consider doing a standalone film on the history of the IAF. Once you do that, then the army and the navy will also follow.'

Two months later, as luck would have it, Air Chief Marshal Suri would take over as the 15th chief of air staff (CAS). 'The IAF will give you every possible support,' said the chief in the first meeting with him after his elevation. 'But, don't ask us for any money. That has to be raised from outside sources.'

Within Air HQ, three individuals, would play key roles in the making of *Salt of the Earth*. Air Vice Marshal (later Air Marshal) D. R. Nadkarni was a Jaguar pilot, who was the assistant CAS (ops). 'Natty' was a man of few words, and meetings with him always followed a set pattern. We would troop in, Dipti and me, accompanied by whoever else was required to be there, and lemon tea would be asked for. Until it came and it was served, Natty would smile at everyone, maintain eye-contact but never 'talk shop' till everyone had their tea. Then, I would list out my requirements, and the meetings would be over in less than 90 seconds. Natty's deputy, the additional ACAS (Ops), was Air Vice Marshal C. S. Doraiswamy, who was for all practical purposes the main point of contact between us and Air HQ. A Mystere pilot, Doru had flown a number of ground-attack sorties in the 1965 War, including the final runs during the Battle of Dograi. Like Natty, he was quiet and unassuming, and extremely quick to take decisions.

Working closely with us was Wing Commander Leslie Springett, who threw himself into the project with all the enthusiasm in the world. An Anglo-Indian, he was a second-generation officer whose father had also been in the IAF. Large-hearted, gregarious and always in trouble with the entire world, Leslie Springett was one of a kind. The one thing that struck Dipti and me at the very outset, was just how passionately all the air force officers loved their service. They not only lived on their bases in a world of their own, the interaction between them was very different from what one had seen in the army. Even those who had been passed over, as Springett had, bore little ill-will and continued to create chaos in their own merry ways wherever they went. For example, since a lot of information was required from various corners of the country while we developed the script, Leslie Springett promptly got himself an STD phone allotted at his residence in Princess Park. Next five days, all his friends—sex, caste, colour—were sitting at his place calling all their loved ones. When someone realized what was going on, Air HQ threw the kitchen sink at him and gave him a bill of ₹35,000. Needless to say, all friends were nowhere to be seen then.

The script would take time, for it required an endless amount of research. During that period, there was little or no information on anything. Squadron histories were non-existent, for even those that had been created as part of the RIAF during World War II had at best, one para write ups. The only published book at the time was Air Chief Marshal P. C. Lal's *My Years with the IAF*, and most of the events had to be pieced together by correlating them with army records.

The big debate was whether to shoot on video or go with 16 mm. There was no precedent, so we had no idea what problems we would face once the shoots began. Betacam cameras were extremely bulky and sensitive, and again we had no way of knowing if the signals were not affected by radar. The more one got into the theoretical aspects of aerial photography in particular, the more complicated it seemed. There was talk of gyro-stabilizers on the one hand, while on the other it was suggested we try using bean-bags. The other problem was related to battery packs. These were heavy and cumbersome, and even on the ground, would at best pull about 15-minutes or 600 feet of film.

Since we were looking at a docudrama, the other big decision pertained to who would play the characters. In the case of actors playing the roles of air force officers, somehow their body language never felt right. But while serving IAF officers had 'the look', they were not actors and would become self-conscious the moment the cameras began to roll. We decided on opting for the latter, after which Leslie Springett abrogated to himself the role of casting director. He and Dipti would pour over the entire air force list, get the photographs of just about everyone in uniform, and then try and see who looked like the person they would have to play.

Air HQ too had a bunny on its back, which was the MOD. Getting the air sorties sanctioned amounted to staff officers writing essay after essay on how the camera team would be integrated with 'routine training sorties and every time an aircraft, be it a fighter, helicopter or transport aircraft got airborne, it would be at 'no cost to the Government of India'. Just how that was possible, beats me, but the line was so often repeated, they might as well have made a rubber stamp and saved themselves the trouble of typing it each time.

The decision to go with 16 mm was taken by October 1991. Natty was asked by the MOD to personally ensure that those who would fly fighter sorties were fully briefed about each aircraft. On my part, I had to demonstrate, to Natty's satisfaction, that in the event of an emergency, I could pull the handle between my feet, then in the mini-second that I would have between my canopy blowing off and my seat firing, jettison the camera and eject from the cockpit. A MiG-23 UF trainer was positioned at the Air Force Station Hindon, and I duly strapped up and demonstrated how if the command to eject was given, I would swiftly disconnect the camera from the battery, throw out the camera and pull the ejection handle.

Driving back from Hindon in his staff car, the air vice marshal's pennant on the bonnet, Natty was in a thoughtful mood. As we were reaching Vayu Bhawan, he said, 'Kunal, you know with all that paraphernalia in the cockpit, it will be impossible to get out in an emergency.' What the air marshal did not know was that I was actually planning to fly with four or five cameras. The standard 400 feet magazine in most 16 mm cameras fitted either on top or behind, which made it impossible to use. The only alternative was to use internal 100 feet spools, which roughly translated to two-and-a-half minutes' worth of footage. Given the fact that film invariably had pinholes in the beginning, this effectively meant two minutes of actual run time. Since reloading magazines in the air was also out of the question, taking extra cameras was the only alternative. Natty didn't expect me to reply, so I didn't. The note for MOD was duly prepared, signed and sent.

For us, it was a Catch-22 situation, for unless the MOD gave the formal nod, we could not approach any sponsor for funding. Even though the air chief himself was pushing the project, things were moving at their own pace. We could hardly stop working on other projects as well, but then each film took a couple of months to shoot at the very least. Even though our equation with the IAF was extremely good, most of the other projects were continuing to run into trouble. The fishing film had been commissioned and part of the funds had been released which allowed us to start shooting in January/February 1992. The balance payment for the Incentive Travel film was pending, which was surprising for by and large the department of tourism had been extremely efficient with us, often the payments being cleared in a matter of a few days. Wondering why there was a delay, I went across to the accounts department where I met the person concerned.

It was soon obvious that the file had deliberately been put into a loop, and the man blatantly asked for a bribe—of all things, he wanted a Barbie doll for his daughter. Once again, I was faced with a Hobson's choice; for if I didn't play ball, I would most probably be in a Bandhavgarh-like situation once again. I told myself being rigid in a situation like this would only create problems for me, so I might as well just get on with it. But then again, a part of me kept arguing, what the heck, it wasn't the quantum of the bribe, it was the principle of the matter.

I walked into Hemant Gupte's office and told him what had happened. 'I have been receiving complaints from all the others ... HTA, Lintas ... others. In their case he keeps demanding a car to take his wife shopping. Here he's asking you for peanuts!'

Gupte pushed a blank paper at me, 'Write it down! I will ask the others to do so as well.' Two days later Gupte called and said none of the others were willing to put it in writing. What did I want him to do? If my complaint stood, it would go up the chain of command first to B. K. Goswami and then S. K. Mishra. He would have no role to play in the matter after that. There was no choice as far as I was concerned. To cut a long story short, we never got the final payment—which was about a lakh and a half—and it also spelt the death knell of our relationship with the department of tourism. The fishing film was shot, but never completed. When combined with the losses incurred on the Rajput film, I am surprised we didn't have to fold up then. More importantly, even though

Dipti was as badly affected, not once did she ever say I was a stupid idiot! Just about everybody else, however, had no qualms in telling me that!

I think it was sometime in October 1991 when I asked Dipti to marry me, forgetting the age-old dictum of 'once bitten twice shy'. Two days later my father again asked me to come to his office, and since he was retiring from the army at the end of the month, he had got his 'financial file' together. 'Don't bother to read the entire thing,' he said offhandedly, 'just read the flagged pages!' The only plausible explanation for what was staring me in the face was that it had never occurred to my father that he would retire someday. 'We can't live separately from my folks,' I told Dipti ruefully later that evening, 'I've just seen my father's financial file, and it's a disaster.' The pension he would draw was virtually non-existent. The main saving grace was that at the age of 56, he was fit as a fiddle and was capable of starting a second innings should he choose to do so. Apart from the flat in Noida which gave everyone a roof over their head, he had also invested in a one-and-a-half bigha plot in a village called Bandrol, in Kullu District. But before we could build on the land, his domicile application had to be processed.

The script for the IAF film had been completed and to the collective relief of everyone concerned, MOD gave the go-ahead by mid-February. We had extensive discussions on who we should approach for the funding of the film, and Adi Sethna prepared a list of a dozen potential sponsors. I was of the view we should ask only one person at a time and wait till we were turned down before approaching the next person on the list. I remember cutting out all the other names, until there was just one person left on that list. 'You know, I'm almost certain we will not need to look at this list again,' I said. That night, sitting with Dipti, I drafted the letter to Air Commodore (Honorary) J. R. D. Tata (JRD).

However, the fishing film had yet to be shot, so we decided to get that out of the way. My father having retired, he was to star in the film. On 13 March 1992, we flew to Bangalore from where we proceeded to the

Kaveri River at Bheemeshwari where Papa John was waiting for my father and us to arrive. While they were catching up on old times, I had already hooked on to a 20 lb golden mahseer. After landing the fish, we decided to put Papa John in a coracle, and he was to land the fish again on camera. As the fish was reeled in, he had to say a two-word dialogue ... 'Ah, it's a golden mahseer!' After half-a-dozen failed takes (he kept calling it a silver mahseer) we let both our actors off the hook! I am not sure who was more relieved ... Papa John or the mahseer! Point a camera at someone and their world comes apart!

There was a massive jinx on my father as well. Try as he might, the fish disdainfully ignored whatever he had to offer as bait. Meanwhile, I was having the luck of the devil. Hardly would I cast, the line would sing out as fish after fish took the ragi balls and ran with them. After two days, Sundar also arrived at the camp, and we decided to move further upstream of Dodamakli. The Cauvery flowed through massive volcanic rocks, and it had a completely different feel altogether. Deep pools with frothing water were a far cry from the placid environs further downstream. Ragi as bait in these circumstances was of no use, so I quickly caught some *chilwa*, threaded a hook on it and started casting into the rapid. I was standing on a large rock and the first pull almost yanked me into the water, but before I could strike, the fish had let go.

The camera was next to me, and while I kept an eye on my father, I diligently stuck to the same pool, casting the *chilwa* again and again and again into the same place. For more than an hour, nothing happened; and then came the pull again. This time I was waiting for it, and I struck upwards with the rod at just the right moment, and the fish was hooked. For the next forty-five minutes, it was gut-wrenching stuff, as the mahseer used every bit of the terrain to fight me. Dipti had started filming the entire sequence and after a while Sundar and my father also came up and watched the drama unfold. 'It's not a golden,' said Sundar, impressed by the fish's tactics. The narrowness of the gorge was acting like a funnel for the water to rush through, and I had to leap from rock to rock to counter some of the moves. Finally, with the light beginning to fade, I got the exhausted fish to the side, where Sundar got hold of it. The fish weighed in at 40 lb and as we photographed it, Sundar said it was a rare grey mahseer. Not wanting to traverse across the rocks in the dark with the cameras, we quickly revived the fish and let it go. With a powerful flick of the tail, it was gone.

After fishing the Kaveri, we made our way up to the upper lakes of the Nilgiris. Some of the trout were released but some were brought back to the Ooty Club where I cooked them in butter on an open fire. This brought out the culinary critic in Neogi, who would declare with the passion of a satisfied Bengali that he had never had anything better before, forgetting he had said the same thing the previous evening as well. All this while, we were constantly in touch with Adi Sethna, and in each call, we asked the same question, 'Anything from JRD as yet.'

On 21 March we flew to Agatti from Cochin and then went on to Bangaram by boat for the deep-sea fishing leg of the film. Dipti and I were old Lakshadweep hands by then, and I was watching my father drink it all in. At Bangaram, the boats had been modified for fishing and the next few days we trawled the waters just off the reef. Strikes were frequent, but the fish would initially fail to get hooked, until we realized we needed to let the fish run with the bait just a bit longer, for then sea fish would invariably hook themselves. We caught some giant trevally and barracuda, and even hooked onto a reef shark. On the way back we would catch some snappers inside the lagoon itself, and these would then be barbequed on the beach in the evenings.

There was a wireless on Bangaram Island and we were sitting on hammocks drinking cocktails, when Dipti and I were summoned by the radio operator. It could mean only one thing, and we soon had Adi Sethna excitedly saying we had a meeting with JRD the day after in Bombay. The next day we just made it in time to Agatti to catch the Dornier to Cochin. While my father got a connection for Delhi, the earliest available flight to Bombay would land at Santa Cruz just three hours before the scheduled meeting in Bombay House on 29 March. Adi Sethna was also flying in around the same time from Delhi, and I asked him to pick up a copy of JRD's biography, *Beyond the Last Blue Mountain* that had been written by R. M. Lala.

JRD was just short of 88 and he along with his designated successor, Ratan Tata, welcomed us into his office. With Adi Sethna around, breaking the ice was never a problem. We were seated on deep-set chairs and were served tea on individual silver trays, a tradition that was meticulously followed in Bombay House. I was seated next to Ratan Tata and was watching him dip his glucose biscuits in his tea with great fascination. JRD then decided enough small talk, so he said, 'You know Kunal, in your letter to me you addressed me as an air commodore. I think there is a rank higher than that!' Even before we could start apologizing, he continued, 'Firstly, you have asked for twenty-one lakh rupees for the film ... yes, we are giving that to you. However, I have only two conditions. One, if you want more money, ask for it now. Do not come back to us for more. And second, make a film that makes the air force feel nine feet tall!'

'We intend to do that sir. And no sir, we have arrived at the figure after due consideration. It is enough for what we have in mind.'

'How,' Ratan Tata was still dipping his biscuits, 'do you plan to depict 1962 in the film? It was a terrible defeat!'

'We plan to look at things as they happened, sir,' I replied.

'I think we should leave 1962 out.'

'Erm ...' the last thing I wanted to do was to get into an argument with Ratan Tata. 'Sir, it's a historical film and we cannot ...' Much to my discomfiture, it was becoming a minor argument.

Adi Sethna felt the need to cut in after a while, 'You know Kunal gets emotional about 1962 ... his father's battalion was at Namka Chu ...'

'Which battalion?' JRD asked. Without waiting for an answer, he went on, '2 Rajput? I think more than 280 men were killed on that morning.' I think we were all gaping at him, for I don't think there would have been more than a dozen people in the country who could have rattled off that information. Also, fortunately for me, Ratan Tata let the matter rest there.

Adi Sethna had managed to pick up just one copy of Lala's book, which he had handed over to me. As the meeting was over, I asked JRD if he would autograph the book for Dipti and me. JRD looked at it, and asked his personal secretary to come in. '*Mera almirah mein se woh doosra kitab leh kar au*' (Get the other book from my cupboard). I cannot recall the lady's name, but I think it was Mrs Britanniawallah or something like that. Mrs B stood her ground, and said there was only one copy left, which implied she wasn't going to let him part with it. '*Aare baba, leh kar au na*' (Oh ho, go get it). Reluctantly Mrs B then brought the book *Aircraft and Engine Perfect: The Story of JRD Tata Who Opened Up Skies for His Country* that had been authored by Murad Fyzee.

JRD then sat down to autograph it for us. He just couldn't wrap his head around Dipti's name, calling her Dip-sy repeatedly. After putting that down on paper, his eyes sparkling mischievously, he put the pen down. 'This book is about the air race from London to Karachi,' he said. 'As future aviators, who will fly with the air force, I will ask you a question. I was flying my Leopard Moth and I had my map on my lap. I should by all reckoning have been over the Dead Sea (Dip-sy having triggered off the story) which was rectangular. But the sea below me was more oval in shape. Why?'

I knew the Dip-sy was not going to hazard a guess, and nor was I. But I could see Adi Sethna about to say something, so I nudged his shin in the age-old manner under the table, politely suggesting he keep quiet! While the general gave me a hurt look, JRD came up with his punch line with great glee, 'I was lost!'

Lala's book was signed for Adi Sethna's grandson, so we all came out of the office very happy. Adi Sethna, however, was not going to let me get away with my impudence. 'What the heck did you kick me for?'

'You were going to say something about the ozone layer, weren't you?'

Lieutenant General Adi Sethna, former vice chief of the Indian Army, grinned and let bygones be bygones! 'Dash it!' he said. 'How on earth did you know that?' Dipti and I came down and, on an impulse, jumped into a horse-drawn Victoria buggy and clattered off towards Marine Drive. Two days later we walked down to Nimmi Suri's office in Air HQ. Everyone seemed to know we had got the money from JRD and already there was a spring in the step. 'Go for it now,' said the air chief, who was affectionate as always. The one person who was not only delighted but was also promising to pay off all his creditors was Leslie Springett. As we walked into his office, Dipti and I heard him on the phone saying, 'JRD's given the money na, I'll pay you back as soon as the cheque arrives!' Yeah sure!

16

Salt of the Earth

With the MOD approval and the funds in place, everything seemed to go into overdrive. The amount of background research that was required to be done was phenomenal. Apart from finalizing the cast for the film, getting old uniforms stitched, medals, wings and ribbons ordered, Dipti had her hands full with finalizing the shooting crew. Even though I probably had more field experience in the actual shooting of films, my previous work had all been around the Project Tiger series, and I was not confident enough to assert myself at this stage and let the FTII culture seep in. The tendency to discuss scenarios and shots ad nauseam tends to complicate the situation, and before one knows it, there are more crew members added on than perhaps necessary. We soon had three or four assistant directors, camera assistants, light boys, trolley pullers, and God knows who else. Not counting the cameraman, Dipti and myself, we already had fifteen people!

In between all this, the wedding date was finalized for 27 June in Bombay and Dipti was running around (with her same set of FTII advisers) also looking at *lehngas* for herself. Since it was felt that I should restrict myself to direction and some aerial photography, the search for a cameraman was on, and we settled on Alok Upadhyay, who among other things, was the nephew of Wing Commanders P. Gautam and P. Ashoka.

The former was a famous Canberra pilot who was a double MVC and Ashoka was a test pilot of considerable repute. Alok had an extremely good resume and he was also Dipti's classmate. His twin, Bharat, was also a friend of mine, having been a part of Kavita's circle at the NID.

During this period, we were constantly talking to retired officers, their inputs being most helpful in adding little flourishes to the scripted sequences. We met Air Chief Marshal Arjan Singh at his residence, and it was impossible not to be affected by his charm and warmth. He pulled out a letter an 8-year-old had written to him during the 1965 War, in which he offered his services to the air chief, finishing his letter with the punchline 'I have gun!' This letter was later read out by the officer who played Arjan Singh in the film. Quite naturally, the conversation revolved mainly around the events of 1965. Very little was known about what had actually happened at that point of time, so I asked him what had prompted him to use the Vampires in Chhamb on 1 September when Pakistan launched Op Grand Slam in that sector. He seemed to want to say something, but he didn't. Instead, he started talking about the Rann of Kutch incident which had taken place five months earlier. 'Air Marshal Asghar Khan was the PAF chief at the time. When the trouble started in the Rann area, he had called me and on the telephone we had agreed to keep the two air forces out of what was basically a border skirmish. We had served together in World War II and this agreement held till the PAF bombed both the Amritsar Railway Station and the prison at Jodhpur.' He added somewhat ruefully, 'Air Marshal Nur Khan had replaced Asghar Khan when the war in Punjab broke out.'

It was fairly obvious Arjan Singh wanted to stay with what was known about the war and did not want to get drawn into any detailed discussion. He called the Kalaikunda raid by Pakistan a 'sneak attack' and did not mention the subsequent air battle in which Flight Lieutenant Alfred Cooke took on and shot down two F-86s and would have perhaps got a third as well if his aircraft had not been loaded with practice ammunition instead of the required high explosive 30 mm cannon rounds. Of the publicly known events and characters like the Keelor brothers, Denzil and Trevor, Pathania, Nebb, Rathore ... the former chief spoke most glowingly of all of them, but when we tried to dig deeper, he just smiled and spoke of other things.

Driving back in the car, it was Dipti who articulated what all of us were thinking. 'How could an air chief have a private agreement with his counterpart? It just does not make any sense.' Adi Sethna, who was silent until then, weighed in, 'That's the trouble with the IAF. They behave as if they have nothing to do with the army.' This sentiment would be echoed repeatedly in the days to come. IAF officers on the other hand, would laugh and say, 'just remove the north arrow from the army maps and watch the fun!' The gulf between the services is a real problem and it continues to show up repeatedly.

I got a call from the ADC to General Rodrigues. 'Chief wants to see you. Army House, 6 p.m.' Roddy was sitting in the garden, and he had obviously been drinking. Jean, his wife, quietly emptied the glass by his side into the grass when he got up to greet me; then she left us and went indoors. 'How's Ashok taking it?' The question wasn't about my father's post-retirement life, but the fact that he had been denied his next rank.

I wanted to tell him to ask him directly, but instead I said, 'He's having a ball. Been fishing in the Cauvery, Nilgiris and Lakshadweep. And he caught some real big ones!' Nothing kills a fishing enthusiast more than having to hear of other people catching the big fish!

'What is this I hear; you are calling the air force film *Salt of the Earth*? That's not an air force title. It's more appropriate for the army.' I was wondering if the chief had lost his marbles. He had specifically asked me to come and see him and he was complaining about the title of a film that was yet to be shot. I waited for a while wondering if he had something more to say, then took my leave and left.

Adi Sethna had been on the general staff of Lieutenant General Jagjit Singh Arora during the 1971 War, and with some difficulty he had fixed an appointment with Air Marshal Hari Chand Dewan, who had been the C-in-C Eastern Air Command during the war. We met him in Defence Colony, Delhi where we sat on the terrace, and he spoke at length of the air operations in 1971. I knew he had flown with 7 Squadron in the Arakans during World War II, and after asking him a few questions about that period in his life, we decided to pack up the Walkman recorder. 'Wait,' said Dewan, stopping Dipti from putting away the Sennheiser mike, 'You know, I was the ACAS (Ops) during the 1962 War with China ...' This should be interesting, I thought to myself, as the air marshal went into a diatribe about Lieutenant General B. M. 'Bijji' Kaul and B. M. Mullick, the intelligence chief at the time. 'When it comes to the Sino-India conflict, everyone talks about Bijji Kaul and Mullick, but what they do not know is that I was often invited by the prime minister (Nehru) to Teen Murti as well. It was I who dissuaded Pandit-ji from using the air force fighters, otherwise it would have been an even bigger disaster.'

I was gaping at Dewan, not quite believing what I was hearing. In 1992 the prevailing belief was that the decision not to use the IAF had been a political call and the top brass had not been consulted. 'But sir, why not?' I asked. 'Surely the IAF would have had a major impact on the war.'

Dewan cut me off with a wave of his hand, 'Young man, you obviously know nothing about fighters flying in the mountains. Here, let me show you ...' He flipped open his logbook that was lying by his side and he went back to his days in the Arakans. 'I flew 171 photo reconnaissance sorties, and not once did I spot the Japanese, despite the fact that they were there all over the place. I told the prime minister it was impossible to spot the Chinese, especially since we then had aircraft that were flying even faster than the Hurricanes that I flew in World War II. It would have been a useless exercise and would have resulted in the Chinese getting an excuse to bomb Calcutta ... maybe even Madras. I had briefed Aspy Engineer (the CAS in 1962) and he agreed with my assessment.'

'So, it wasn't Nehru's decision?' I asked. Adi Sethna, Dipti and I were looking intently at Dewan.

'Oh, it was his decision alright ... he was the prime minister and also the defence minister during the war. But yes, I convinced him.'

Back in Air HQ, Doru (Air Vice Marshal C. S. Doraiswamy) heard the tape. 'Damn,' he said, getting extremely agitated, 'As young pilot officers at the time, we were often accused by army officers of chickening out and I think we had countless bar fights over this. This is killing stuff.' He went off to meet Natty, and five minutes later I was called in.

'Well?' asked Natty.

'Mr Ratan Tata wanted us to bypass 1962 altogether in the film,' I said. 'We can hardly script this in and create a huge hue and cry, especially since it makes the IAF top brass look bad. It will also overshadow everything else, the role of the transport pilots and even the Mi 4 helicopters. We already have a scene scripted where Hunters and even Sea Hawks are lined up in Gorakhpur waiting to get airborne in support of our troops in the NEFA and Ladakh. We'll say the orders never came.'

'Ok,' said Natty.

On 27 June 1992 Dipti and I got married at Badhwar Park in Bombay. Apart from my parents, my uncle Vijay Dhruv and my classmate, Sanjiv Singhal, were the sum total of the *baraat*. There was a last-minute flap in finding someone who could conduct the ceremony, so it seems an actor who was a 'filmi priest' presided over the event. Dipti's entire FTII crowd was present in strength though, as were her close friends Sarika and Kamal Haasan, the South Indian superstar. Even during the ceremony, much to my father's irritation, Dipti was looking at equipment lists. Talk about multi-tasking! In the evening there was a reception, where Royina, Ajit, Bittu and Madhu also swung by.

Since we were shooting on 16 mm, the entire crew other than the assistant directors were from Bombay. I don't think we had even a moment to ourselves as equipment lists, crews and the paraphernalia was sorted out. Back in Delhi, on 6 July we entered Air HQ, where almost everyone, in a repeat of the aftermath of our successful meeting with J. R. D. Tata, came out of their offices to wish us. Leslie Springett, had in the meantime, worked out the itinerary for a 15-day reconnaissance trip that was to start on 24 July and finish on 8 August. We had also decided that all coordination with army units would be done by me on a one-to-one basis, for if we involved the MOD, the 'no cost to the government' factor would no longer be in our control and would endlessly delay things.

With our three assistant directors in tow, we lifted off from Palam in a Dornier 228 that belonged to 41 Squadron and set course for Jodhpur. Captaining the plane was Squadron Leader Akhilesh Kumar, who had been one of the ADCs to President Giani Zail Singh along with Benu

Jamwal during the Sikh riots in 1984. Before the Air Force Academy shifted to Dundigal in Hyderabad, Jodhpur had been the hub of the IAF. While Dipti and the others got busy with working out the details of the shoot, I headed off to meet Lieutenant General Moti Dhar, who was commanding 12 Corps. We were meeting after eleven years, having done some photography in Ladakh when he was commanding 114 Infantry Brigade at Tangste. I briefed him about the IAF film and told him one of the key sequences in *Salt of the Earth* would be the enactment of the Battle of Longewala. For that, I needed at least two troops of tanks, preferably T-59s, which would have to be painted with Pakistani markings.

'You want these in Longewala? And when?'

'No Sir. I'm flying to Jaisalmer tomorrow and we are looking at doing the enactment in Pokhran in the second week of October. Hunters will be coming down from Kalaikunda and will be firing live ammunition. I'll also need a detachment of sappers to simulate explosions on the ground.' Moti Dhar, who had the heart of an artist disguised in an army uniform, called his staff and dictated a request letter from me to him, asking for everything I had listed. As soon as it was typed, I signed it.

'Anything for the air force,' said the general. 'They are a terrific bunch of chaps. You need not worry about anything from my end. The tanks and the Engineers will be there.'

The old disused WW-II airstrip at Nasirabad had been activated just for us, and in the afternoon, we landed bumpily not far from the old house where I used to shoot pigeons with Jimmy Abraham. The CO of 23 Punjab looked at me as if I was nuts. I had just finished telling him how I was determined that the troops on the ground for the Battle of Longewala should be from his battalion, which had been holding the position under Major Kuldip Singh Chandpuri when the Pakistani armoured thrust developed. 'I don't have transport to take my men all the way to Pokhran,' said the colonel.

'Oh, don't worry about that,' I said airily, 'We'll airlift your boys both ways.' I was beginning to think like the IAF. We had also planned that once elements of 23 Punjab were moved to Pokhran towards the end of September, my father would join them there before we arrived, just to make sure everything was ship shape.

Dipti had in the meantime figured out the what and when to shoot in Jodhpur, and the next morning we landed at Jaisalmer. Leaving one of our assistant directors and the Dornier crew behind, we jumped into a Chetak and flew back the way we had come to Pokhran. We were flying fairly low and could see flocks of sheep scattering below, while the herdsmen in their oversized turbans would throw themselves to the ground. I was sitting in front in the jump seat and asked Wing Commander P. Singh who was flying us, 'Why are they doing that?'

'They think we are gods coming from the skies ... they are prostrating in front of us,' he replied deadpan. I wasn't sure if he was pulling my leg or not, but the phenomenon continued to repeat itself below us.

At Pokhran there was a range safety officer's (RSO's) tower next to the helipad, and nothing else for miles around. It was perfect for what we had in mind. We drove around the area in a jeep that belonged to the RO and selected the area where the 23 Punjab defences would be dug. Then back we went over more prostrating individuals, and after a meeting in Jaisalmer to work out the logistical support that would be required, we flew to Ojhar, which was a Hindustan Aeronautics Limited (HAL) airstrip dedicated to 23 Base Repair Depot where MiG-21s, 23s and 27s were overhauled. Waiting for us there was Wing Commander (later Air Marshal) Simhakutty Varthaman, who had been chosen by Dipti and Leslie Springett to play the role of Wing Commander P. Gautam in the film. Since 'Vartha' was a test pilot, he could also fly the Canberra which was an added bonus. Also, he hailed from Tambaram, which in a way made us brothers for life!

Vartha's wife, Shobha, was away on a UN assignment, but he nevertheless invited us home for dinner the next day. Since he was busy with us the entire day, his 8-year-old son, Abhinandan, had taken it upon himself to arrange everything, and we were all very impressed by Abhi. Ten years later I would run into him again as a NDA cadet, and then, of course, he would shoot to fame when he engaged and downed a PAF F-16 while flying a MiG-21 Bis, before he himself got shot down.

While at Ojhar, we drove down to the artillery school at Devlali. One of the biggest challenges was to get DC-3 Dakotas to fly, and since the Poonch landing in 1948 was to be enacted, we needed to also show 25 lb guns being loaded onto the aircraft. There was an old airstrip at the artillery school, but after much consideration, it was declared unsafe to land a Dakota on it. We were also in touch with the JK Tyre Group who still had an operational aircraft, and eventually it was decided we would film the scene at Palam in New Delhi itself. The ceremonial battery that fired the 24-gun salute during the Republic Day Parade was then used, while troops from the Sikh TA battalion were also brought there, their uniforms and weapons matching the period. Subsequently, when the shooting began, after the guns were loaded, we decided to fire them as well. Delhi ATC in the meantime had directed an Airbus 320 to use the taxi track where we were filming, and suddenly the pilots came face-to-face with two arty guns that were literally firing at them at point blank range! I've never seen a big aircraft like an Airbus literally turn on its tail and vamoose from there. What the pilots must have said to the ATC is any one's guess!

From Ojhar to Pune was a relatively short hop. We needed to select six NDA cadets to play the role of the first cadets who had gone to the Royal Air Force (RAF) Academy at Cranwell in 1932, which was officially being considered to be the beginning of the IAF's history. The idea was to film the young men horsing around on a ship, and for that INS *Magar* had been selected. To meet the Western Fleet commander, we had to go to Bombay and the meeting took place on INS *Viraat*. The navy, too, was extremely cooperative and the dates for the filming were fixed. One of my assistant directors, however, was sitting in such an insolent manner in front of the admiral, I fired him from the crew the moment we got off the ship.

The next port of call on 28 July was Sulur. The Gnats had been mothballed and stored there and work was on to somehow make them operational again. It had been a long flight from Pune, but much to my delight, a Mi 8 helicopter was already starting up for an aerial reconnaissance of the Nilgiris as we landed. Leaving Coimbatore behind, we flew along the eastern side of the Blue Mountains, and then from Mettupalayam, we followed the railway line. For me, it was a special flight, for every inch of the terrain was familiar. We crested the ridge near Coonoor (the site of the most unfortunate crash that took so many lives along with India's first chief of defence staff, General Bipin Rawat later) and there before us was Wellington. The Mi 8 was too big a helicopter to land outside my old house, but we hovered over it nevertheless, and had everyone in the neighbourhood come tumbling out of their residences. We then turned and flew along the road to Kotagiri, from where it was then a straight drop to Bhawani Sagar. That evening, sitting in Sulur, we were loving the breeze that we were told was due to the Palghat Gap. That same breeze would create major problems for us when we subsequently shot the briefing for the Battle of Boyra, for it kept blowing one of the pilot's false moustaches away!

At Bangalore we met Air Commodore (later Air Marshal) Philip Rajkumar who was commanding the Armament & Systems Testing Establishment. One of India's best test pilots, Philip Rajkumar had been the tail-end Charlie in the famous daylight raid on Sargodha during the 1965 War and would go on to play a key role in the manufacture of the Light Combat Aircraft (LCA), now known as the Tejas. The IAF put Dipti and me up in a special suite that had been prepared for the president of India and in the evening, at Philip's suggestion, we roamed the streets and had ECBs (extremely cold beers) and sizzlers at Caesars.

By now life had taken on a frenetic pace. The next day we landed at Begumpet in Hyderabad, the very airfield where my father used to watch Dolly Yadav and Nimmi Suri fly four and a half decades previously. After a quick briefing, we then landed at Hakimpet, which was where the advanced jet training was done and where also the helicopter pilots were trained. In the afternoon, Dipti and I did our first-ever sortie in a Cheetah, which was the HAL version of the French designed SA 315B Lama. It was the first of hundreds of subsequent sorties, and we just fell completely in love with the highly manoeuvrable and versatile machine. From the filming point of view, it was an ideal platform, though I would have to find ways and means of minimizing the shake. In the sortie at Hakimpet, the pilot demonstrated how they were trained to 'auto-rotate' and land the chopper should the single engine flame out mid-air. It was scary but at the same time also exhilarating. In the evening, we then touched down at Dundigal, which was the home of the IAF's Air Force Academy ever since it had been shifted from Jodhpur in 1969. With three airfields in close proximity, and lots of trainee pilots in the air, the joke was there were lots of unguided missiles in the airspace around Hyderabad.

On 31 July, we were fitted out in flying overalls and briefed by Wing Commander (later Group Captain) Rajesh Chidambaram who was going to fly me, while Squadron Leader Rao was detailed to fly Dipti, an event which had every one's attention for at the time, very few ladies had flown in a Kiran Mk II. Rao's briefing to Dipti was classic, 'If I say, ezect, ezect, ezect three times ... madam, you ezect!' As we taxied out, I had forgotten all about the rest of the world and focused on the calm instructions being given by Chidambaram over the RT. In the Kiran we were seated side by side, but right from the start, I was being allowed to handle the aircraft. The roar of the engine and the exhilarating feeling as we unstuck from the runway, was something that then gets imprinted on the brain. Not only did I get to fly the circuit, I was also talked through doing loops and rolls in the sky. When we finally landed, there was Dipti also taking off her helmet, and fortunately she did not have to 'ezect'. She had also taken to the skies like a duck takes to wing! Pleased as punch, we then flew back to Delhi in the evening, landing at Palam just as the sun was going down. The first leg of the reconnaissance was over.

After a four-day break, we were again allotted another Dornier, with Squadron Leader A. Verma and Flight Lieutenant R. Bakshi as our two pilots. This time we flew east, and after refuelling in Patna, we landed at Guwahati. We were to proceed to Barapani from there, for a meeting with Air Marshal Dushyant Singh, who was the C-in-C Eastern Air Command. However, bad weather over the Khasi Hills meant the rest of the day went by waiting for the sky to clear. Finally, at 1600 hours, with the light beginning to fade, we were loaded onto a Mi-8 and flew through lots of spectacular streaks of lightning to Shillong. There we were received by the SASO (senior air staff officer) and another air vice marshal, who then rushed us off to meet the C-in-C. What followed was a scene out of Tom and Jerry, as we 'crept' around corners as the offices by then were deserted and no one wanted to run into the big man, and it was soon pretty obvious Dushyant Singh had his subordinates living in a state of abject fear. Once the two air marshals realized their boss had got fed up and also gone home, they cheered up considerably and brightly asked the bemused Dipti if she'd like to go shopping. 'The C-in-C,' they said sheepishly to me, 'he should have been in the army!' I had half a mind to tell them Dushyant Singh was indeed my father's coursemate, and he was in the army, but then why ruin a perfectly good cartoon strip with unnecessary facts.

The next morning, we finally met Dushyant Singh and he told us how in the Congo he had bombed the daylights out of a post office while flying his Canberra. 'Finest moment of my life,' he boomed, and the two air vice marshals accompanying us nodded vigorously with every 1,000 lb bomb that their boss recalled dropping on the hapless postal employees. We went through the various things we planned to do in the Eastern Sector, and the C-in-C issued crisp and precise directions. 'Anything else?'

'No sir. I think that covers it.'

'Very good. Since you are Ashok's son, you will have my personal aircraft ferry you around while you are in my command.' I was of course flattered, but had I known then we would be flying around in an Avro HS 48, then I would have begged to have been spared the honour. In Dushyant Singh's aircraft, while Dipti and me lorded it in large-sized seats, the rest of the crew were so miserable I almost had a mutiny on my hands. In an An-32, at least we were all equally happy or miserable! Besides, with all the equipment we carried, loading and unloading an Avro was a regular headache, especially since airmen, unlike soldiers in the army, considered it below their dignity to extend a helping hand.

The same afternoon, we then flew from the Barapani airstrip across the Brahmaputra and landed at Tezpur on the North Bank. Apart from 30 Squadron (Bisons), the base was also the home of the MiG Operational Flying Training Unit, and we had quite a fair number of scenes scripted around them. Even as we went over the details with the concerned people, the constant thunder of MiGs taking off would shake the buildings to the core. Part of the reconnaissance trip was also to meet the people who had been shortlisted to play designated roles, so while Dipti and the assistant directors did that, I went across to HQ 4 Corps and met Lieutenant General Ajai Singh to ask for troops who would be airlifted by Mi 8s on to some of the islands on the Brahmaputra to depict the Narsingdi heli-lift. Ajai Singh, who was from 17 Poona Horse, was also a coursemate of my fathers and we had done plenty of partridge shooting together. 'Stay a day longer,' said the general, 'we'll go shoot some ducks.' But we had big game lined up for the next few days.

We took off from Tezpur in the morning and headed off to Kalaikunda on the eastern coast. 20 Squadron (Lightnings), which was flying Hunters, was based there and they were pivotal not only for the Battle of Longewala but were also required to fly extensively for the film from Kalaikunda as well. Wing Commander (later Air Vice Marshal) Keshav Gopal Bewoor, who was commanding the squadron, was also supposed to play the role of Squadron Leader S. D. L. Tully, who was a part of the Jaisalmer-based No. 122 (Ad Hoc) Squadron that had played merry hell with the Pakistani armour in 1971. Keshav Bewoor, who was the son of the former army chief, General G. G. Bewoor, seeing I was smoking Benson & Hedges cigarettes, slyly suggested he practise Tully's mannerisms that included blowing smoke rings in the air.

Sticking to his own brand of cigarettes was one of the most likeable characters that we got to interact with in the air force. Group Captain (later Air Commodore) Biswajit 'Bonny' Mukerjee was the chief operations officer (COO), and he had everyone eating out of his hand in a matter of minutes. A former CO of 20 Squadron, he had been a part of the original aerobatic team of the IAF, the Thunderbolts, that had wowed thousands of people before the Surya Kirans came into being. Strangely enough, neither Bonny Mukerjee nor Keshav Bewoor, who had been on Hunters most of their lives, talked about Flight Lieutenant Alfred Cooke. Or maybe we never asked the right questions then. It was such a pity, we missed what was perhaps one of the greatest air battles ever fought right over Kalaikunda itself. It was a bad miss!

The next morning it was a two-hour haul to Allahabad, where we refuelled our Dornier. The aircraft had changed at Tezpur and now we had with us Flight Lieutenant Raghvendran, who after another two hours in the air, turned to me and said we could not land at Gwalior because the weather was extremely bad. Agra being the only option, we spent the night there, and then early in the morning on 8 August 1992 we approached Gwalior where both the Mirage 2000 squadrons were based. As we circled in to land, I could see the Scindia School. 'The white building on the edge,' Raghvendran said, 'is the headmaster's residence.' I knew my former housemaster, Dr S. D. Singh was heading the school. It was extremely useful to know where he lived. The little devil in my brain was rubbing its hands with glee!

Air Commodore (later Air Marshal) Adi Rustomji Ghandhi was AOC 40 Wing and he knew my father very well. He was waiting for us, and after a quick briefing, he turned to me and said, 'Ok Kunal ... this is it. Kit up. You're flying in a Mirage 2000.'

Flight Lieutenant (later Air Commodore) Harpreet Singh Basra graciously presented me his spare flying overalls that had the 7 Squadron formation sign, the *Battle Axes*, sewn on it. I would wear that throughout subsequently with great pride, regardless of which squadron I flew with, and I would fly with them all. I was briefed by Wing Commander Vijay Prakash 'Nandu' Nandrajog, the CO of the Battle Axes, and then with my heart in my mouth, my helmet under my arm, we walked to the aircraft.

In the Mirage 2000 trainer, as in most fighter trainers, the cockpit is so designed that you cannot see the pilot in the front, for he is sitting slightly lower. Once airborne, we climbed up and up, the sky a brilliant blue without a speck of cloud. We levelled out at some incredible height, when Nandu Jog's calm voice filtered through to me in my lonesome cockpit. 'When you write your autobiography,' he said, 'remember this moment. Alright Kunal, you have control.'

For thirty-five minutes, I did loops and barrel roles, gut-wrenching turns and all sorts of things, all the while Nandu Jog's voice guiding me and telling me the technical terms used for the manoeuvres we were doing. Then with our fuel running out, we were on finals, and though my approach was a bit wobbly, I seemed to be doing fine when Nandu took over and put the Mirage down on the runway. With the tail parachute deployed, we came down to taxiing speed, and then after jettisoning the chute, we came back to the 7 Squadron dispersal area.

While I had been busy with my sortie, Dipti and the two assistant directors had been busy tying up all the other details. Gwalior too would be a major filming base for us and there were a few scenes to be enacted. On that day, we still had a meeting lined up with the Para Training School in Agra, after which we returned to Palam. The reconnaissance was over and now the filming would begin in right earnest. We had a week to get everything sorted out.

The first glimpse we had of 'our' Antonov An-32, tail number K 2730, I felt a real thrill go down my spine. After almost a year of preparation, we were ready to roll. The An-32 was the workhorse of the IAF in those days, and even though it wasn't designed to be the most comfortable aircraft when it came to ferrying passengers, it was perfect for our requirement for we simply opened up the back hatch and rolled our equipment out. After a refuelling halt at Ahmedabad, we touched down at Bombay on 14 August where the full complement of our crew joined us two days later. Shooting inside INS *Magar*, I just hung around watching as Dipti and Alok Upadhyay got to work. Lighting up interiors and working out camera angles in confined spaces was not my forte, but it was exciting as shouts of 'lights ... camera ... action ...' took centre stage as Ritu Kapoor, Sarita Joshi and Varsha Dewan, the three assistants, ran around with clapper boards. The six cadets from the NDA that had been selected to play the roles of the pioneers, were driving their escorting officer bananas as they would disappear into some former squadron mates' cabin for a quick smoke, but the opening scenes went off reasonably without a hitch.

The next day our entire crew bundled into the An-32 for the short hop to Pune, where boxing and riding scenes had to be shot. I was down with fever, so was isolated in my room at the Bombay Stadium. I had been looking forward to exploring the Academy, but that was not to be. With the required Cranwell depictions canned, we then headed off to Dundigal, where the real flying sequences were to be shot. Until then, I was quite redundant, but now I had to pull every resource together for I was aware of the fact that the entire success (or failure) of the film would hinge on the aerial sequences.

Once again, I strapped into the cockpit alongside Rajesh Chidambaram, but this time I had the ST camera with me, and we would have other aircraft flying with us that I had to film. Sitting on the right side, it's always hard to contort one's strapped body and shoot, and in the sortie, I found myself struggling a bit. This was also my first experience of flying wing tip to wing tip with other aircraft, and one couldn't but help being impressed by the level of flying skills on display. As we came in to land, I could see Dipti and the rest of the crew filming on the ground. As I walked across to see what they were shooting, Alok Upadhyay chuckled, 'Yeah, yeah! You're having all the fun while we do the donkey work!'

I had another equally interesting sortie lined up in the HPT-32 Deepak that was the propeller driven primary trainer used by the IAF at the time. These aircraft did not have ejection seats, so the parachute was strapped on and you sort of sat on it. My pilot laconically briefed me as I got into the tiny plane, 'If we get into trouble, slide open your canopy and release your seat belt. I'll turn the aircraft upside down and you'll fall out. Or, if I give the word, get out of your seat, step on the wing and jump.' Just as well none of that happened, because after we landed, my instructor realized he had failed to brief me on how to actually deploy the parachute!

At Hakimpet, the focus shifted to the filming of Cheetahs and Chetaks, and it was fun flying in large helicopter formations. In addition to flying Kirans with the Advance Jet Training establishment, I also got a sortie on the Polish-built PZL TS-11 Iskara, which the IAF was using as an advanced trainer. Fairly satisfied with the shots we had managed to get at Dundigal and Hakimpet, we again bundled into our An-32 and headed off to Sulur, where we hoped the mothballed Ajits (Gnats) would have been souped up for us to film not just the enactment of the Boyra incident, but also get enough shots to be able to talk of the epic battles that the gallant fighter had fought with the F-86 Sabres in 1965. By the time we arrived, a detachment of pilots drawn from 2 Squadron had also reached from Kalaikunda.

During the next three days, we filmed whatever we could with the Gnats. The Boyra briefing, ground crews arming the aircraft, pilots on ORP (operational readiness platform) scrambling, the aircraft lined up at sunset—just about any angle we could get on the diminutive aircraft, it was taken. Though the Gnats could be started and taxied, racing them down the runway was proving to be extremely hazardous. Though the pilots as usual were gung-ho, I did not want to push it beyond a point. The Mi-8s based at Sulur also came into extensive play, allowing for the filming of enactments that depicted the IPKF operations. We also took three helicopters and first flew west through the Palghat Gap, then turned south along the coast towards Cochin to film the terrain that was similar to the topography of Sri Lanka.

Squadron Leader (later Air Vice Marshal) Ashwini Kumar Nabh, with whom I had flown a sortie in the Kiran in Hakimpet three days earlier, also arrived in Sulur with his aircraft. I cannot now recall what we were trying to do with the Kiran on that particular sortie, but we flew north till we hit the Kaveri River. Once we located the fishing camp at Bheemakali, getting into the spirit of things, Nabh did a barrel roll and a loop in honour of the mahseer fish down below.

From Sulur we made our way to Ladakh, stopping en route in Dundigal to replace our An-32 (it had run out of flying hours) and then in Bombay to drop off the exposed film cans. While the entire crew sat in the aircraft, Dipti and I dashed across to Adlabs, where the exposed film was to be processed. It was then a three-hour non-stop flight to Chandigarh. The long haul from Sulur had taken its toll, for a couple of the light boys and a camera assistant reported sick and had to be left behind. Early the next morning on 27 August, we were probably the first aircraft to get airborne and much to my delight, after crossing the Great Himalayan Range at Rohtang, we were soon above the stark trans-Himalayan region interspersed with glaciated valleys. Standing behind the pilot's seat as we approached the runway, I could see the Stok Palace across the river. As we disembarked and loaded our gear onto the waiting air force vehicles, the officer who had come to receive us said word had got around Leh that a film was being shot, and a motely crowd was lining the road outside the airfield, hoping to catch a glimpse of Sridevi, the actress. Since Dipti was wearing a hat, dark glasses and a scarf around her neck, she looked the part and even waved from the open vehicle at some of Sridevi's ardent fans, who then went home deliriously happy.

We were to stay with the 114 Helicopter Unit, and after the rest of the day for acclimatization, we were to fly to Siachen the next day. I briefed the crew, telling everyone that at 10,800 feet (3292 m) their bodies needed to get used to the rarefied air, and I wanted no heroics from anyone. Before retiring to our room, we were given a quick briefing by the CO of the unit. I was acutely aware of the fact that 24 hours was nowhere near adequate for acclimatization, especially since the next day we would be operating at even higher altitudes

At dawn, seven Cheetahs, each with two of our crew on board, got airborne. Dipti and I were in the lead helicopter, and we could see Leh town just beginning to awaken as we flew past the imposing Ladakh

Palace on our left. All the while we were climbing sharply and after a while, we crested the Ladakh Range at Khardung La, which at 17,582 feet (5359 m), was then the highest point on any motorable road in the world. We then dropped down to confluence of the Shyok and the Nubra Rivers, turned west and landed at Thoise. There we were given a quick briefing. A couple of weeks previously, our anti-aircraft guns deployed on the glacier had brought down a Pakistani Mi-17, after which our own choppers had been avoiding flying in the area. Before we headed out on the main central Siachen Glacier, a Cheetah underslung a snow mobile to a post called Rewari, with Dipti and me trailing behind. Rewari was on the southern part of Siachen, but in effect it was our first real glimpse of the highest battlefield in the world.

When we returned to Thoise, the remaining helicopters were all lined up. An army major who was in transit himself, was threatening to arrest all my crew because they had no 'identification papers' on them. He calmed down when I walked up to him and asked him, 'Seriously? How the hell do they think the whole lot got here past multiple layers of security?' After quickly refuelling, we then led a formation of seven Cheetahs. Crossing Partapur, we came to the confluence and turned north along the Nubra River. After fifteen minutes, we got a glimpse of the mouth of the 75-kilometre-long massive chunk of ice. We then touched down one after the other at the Kumar Base, where we were greeted with hot tea.

Once again Dipti and I led the way in the first helicopter, which seemed to climb almost vertically along what looked like a virtual ice wall. We then reached the top of the Saltoro Ridge and about 2 kilometres ahead of us, we could see a helipad perched on top of an ice column, looking a bit like a giant mushroom. Displaying incredible flying skill, the pilots landed on the platform. Ghostly figures, in greyish hooded overalls, then ran towards the Cheetah and opened the door on Dipti's side. Unknown to us, Zulu Post, which was situated at 18,500 feet (5368 m), was occupied by a section from 3 Rajput. The officer who gallantly opened the door found himself staring at a lady, which by itself was an event. 'Ma'am,' he exclaimed, 'I know you! You're General Verma's daughter-in-law!

Alok was in on the second helicopter, and we quickly positioned his camera on a heavy-duty tripod, while I took up a position on the flank with my camera, shooting off the shoulder. One after the other the rest of the crew arrived, where once again they were served hot tea as they landed. Inside the bunkers, my crew was staring at everything open mouthed. The beds had been made on piles of dry fruit, and the walls were lined with Cadbury chocolates. 'Frozen chocolate,' the men explained, 'is ideal protection for bullets just bounce off them'!

After filming for thirty minutes, the helicopters started to come back and started pulling out the crew from Zulu. Alok Upadhyay and I were in the last Cheetah and even as we turned sharply to go back the way we had come, the area was beginning to get covered in mist.

'It's a whiteout developing,' said the pilot, and we literally began to spiral downwards in near zero visibility. On the glacier itself, there was no problem and we landed at Kumar without any further ado. One of the assistants came running towards me and said the crew had left the main tripod up at Zulu.

The pilots had a quick chat and then they said to me the situation in a whiteout changed by the second, so we should try and get back to Zulu, especially since the weather for the next few days was unpredictable. I told Alok Upadhyay to get off, and we lifted off again. The corkscrew climb up Saltoro cliffs was terrifying, for the pilots were literally flying by the seat of their pants. 'One thousand one ... one thousand two ... one thousand three ... turn ...' Then we could see Zulu and in the swirling mist landed on the tabletop helipad. The 3 Rajput major yanked the door open and yelled something. The door had hardly shut, we had lifted off, turned and then began the equally frightening return leg. I had no idea what was happening, and only when we were back on the ground at Kumar, did the pilots turn around to me and say the tripod had been found after we had taken off and the information had been conveyed to the Zulu post commander. Those twenty-five minutes remain etched in my mind as perhaps the most dangerous in my entire life.

While Zulu post on Saltoro was battling severe weather conditions, on the main glacier the skies were an electric blue! A Mi-17 1V had already started up by the time I landed, and as I got on board, the large-sized helicopter lifted off. Dipti had positioned Alok Upadhyay at the back, so I went forward to shoot the glacier over the pilot's shoulders. The sheer size and scope of the glacier below us was stunning and we got some incredible footage of some of the major landmarks, including the northern most point, Indira Col. After a breathtaking forty minutes in the air, we landed back at the Kumar Base. 3 Rajput was being replaced by 17 Rajput on the glacier, so officers from both battalions hosted us a biryani lunch. Then the formation of Cheetahs again took to the skies, and we made a beeline back to base, overflying Khardung La and dropping down to Leh, a total flying time of an hour.

My crew was thankfully holding out. I think they were probably just awestruck at what was unfolding around them for anyone to feel they should be suffering from the effects of altitude, which just goes to prove that more often than not, ninety percent of the problems are in the head. The next morning, everyone was in sparkling form as we again lifted off in a formation of helicopters and instead of heading north, we flew east along the Indus River till Karu from where we overflew Chang La and landed at Tangtse for refuelling. Another thirty minutes of flying time, and we landed at Chushul, from where we went by surface transport to the abandoned airstrip near the Spangur Gap where the IAF in 1962 had landed An-12 aircraft that had airlifted AMX 13 tanks to counter the Chinese moves. The airfield, rarely visited ever since, was covered with debris from the war. While we were shooting, a herd of kiang trotted across to see what we were doing, and I couldn't help but laugh for the last time I had come calling, I had lost a jeep while chasing them around. I walked across to where I thought the vehicle was, and showed Dipti the ground, even stepping on the white crusted surface to demonstrate how it could open up and swallow whatever ventured into it. In the process, I wet my shoe and had to fly back to Leh with one frozen foot.

Even though this was Dipti's second trip to Ladakh, I had not as yet been able to take her to Stok. The next morning, we were to return to Chandigarh, but before that I asked for a Cheetah that would fly us first to the Hemis Monastery and then come back to the airfield via Ladakh Sarai. As we overflew the camp, people came tumbling out of the yurts, some of which I had constructed a decade previously.

The waiting An-32 that had come for us in the meantime was from 25 Squadron, which had some real old-timers on its rolls. The Sikh wing commander who was captaining the aircraft, had a young flight lieutenant as his co-pilot and the plan was to exit Leh by literally hugging the ground through valleys which the old pilot was familiar with. Standing at my usual place behind the captain's seat, I watched in awe as we scraped past ridge lines with barely any clearance, or flew through narrow gaps that seemed to be barely wide enough for a Cheetah, let alone a big aircraft like the An-32. It was fascinating, and as we entered a particular valley, I somehow knew what lay ahead and told Dipti that once we crested the ridge, there would be some stone huts on the other side. Proved right, the pilot, who had overheard our conversation, spun around in his seat to look at me while I kept pointing ahead as it seemed we would fly into the fast-approaching cliffs.

Later in the afternoon, the gigantic Mi-26 Featherweight started up. These heavy-duty Soviet machines were something else, and while Dipti and Alok Upadhyay clambered on board to film from within, I got airborne in a Cheetah which felt like a diminutive and pesky gnat hovering around the big bird. After demonstrating its heavy lift capability by flying around over Chandigarh with a 5-tonne underslung load, the Featherweight set course for the Sutlej and then flew along the river up to Kinnaur. At one point, we were flying directly above its rotors, and some of the shots I got were almost surreal. On the way back, we overflew Kasauli and the Lawrence School at Sanawar.

Early the next morning, I got airborne in an An-32 to film a drop over the Kumar Base on the Siachen Glacier. It was a three-hour ten-minute round trip, so I climbed onto the parachutes that were fitted on the drop crates and went off to sleep. Even though the body of the aircraft was pressurized, long-haul flights used to get quite cold. My assistant, however, was most concerned for my safety, and he spent an anxious hour wondering what would happen if I got jettisoned with the load. Once we crossed the Indus below, the aircraft started to prepare for the drop. I clambered down from my comfortable perch and we quickly secured all the pieces of equipment. Then the hatches started to open, and the roar of the aircraft engines combined with the blast of cold air was exhilarating stuff. Looking down from twenty-odd thousand feet, the view of Siachen was simply breathtaking. There was a flurry of activity inside the fuselage, and various coloured lights and alarms kept going off, until we were over the drop zone and the crates were released.

The drop having been executed, I got to the edge of the An-32, and with just a monkey belt attached to my waist, sat there with my legs dangling over the glacier, filming virtually vertically downwards. The aircraft turned languidly, giving me a wide sweep of the entire region. By then, I was fast beginning to freeze to death, so on the headset I gave the order to shut the hatches. Once again, there was a lot of noise as the various sliding panels went this way and that, until we were once again sealed into our little cocoon up in the sky.

By the time we landed back in Chandigarh, Dipti and Alok Upadhyay had finished the ground sequences and they, along with some of the crew, were on board an Antonov An-12 waiting for my arrival. I literally ran from one aircraft to yet another An-32 that had already started up and the two planes then taxied out together. The plan was for the An-32 to lead, and once we crossed over from the Kullu–Manali axis into the glaciated region beyond the Great Himalayan Range, the four-engine An-12 was to 'feather' it's two starboard propellors. This was an important sequence depicting Squadron Leader (later Air Marshal) Chandan Singh's epic flight in 1962 when Chinese ground fire had damaged two of his engines.

At the designated point, my aircraft opened the back hatch, and I was perfectly positioned to execute the shot as the An-12 was flying steadily 200 metres behind us. I had a headset, so was in communication with both the aircraft, and at my command, the An-12 was to perform the manoeuvre. 'Papa Yankee ...' I said, switching on my camera, 'feather now!' Nothing happened. I asked my pilots what was happening, and they replied that the An-12 though in communication, was not responding.

On board the An-12, a bizarre situation had developed. The Soviet aircraft, that had been designed in the late 1950s, had been in service with the IAF since 1961. Although used to ferry passengers to and from Ladakh and other remote airfields in the east, the main body of the aircraft was not pressurized. Dipti, Alok Upadhyay, the camera assistants and the three assistant directors, were all breathing with the help of portable oxygen cylinders while the camera was focused on the port engines from within the aircraft through one of the emergency windows. Around the time the aircraft crossed Rohtang, the captain of the aircraft decided to go 'check on the film crew', handing over control to his lesser experienced co-pilot.

As he exited the pressurized cockpit, the pilot literally collapsed. Dipti and the three girls who were closest to him, managed to grab him and lower him to the floor, but between the four of them, they could not move him immediately back into the cockpit. The rest of the crew, strapped onto their oxygen sets further away, either did not understand what was happening, or they could not get to the semi-conscious pilot. This was around the time, sitting with my legs dangling out of my aircraft at 28,000 feet (8500 m), I was giving the command to feather. Without oxygen and beginning to freeze myself, after a while I reluctantly gave the call to close our back hatch, and we watched with mounting anxiety as the An-12 continued to steadily fly along behind us. Quite a few minutes ticked away, then much to our collective relief we heard the captain's slightly shaky voice on the RT, 'Breaking contact.' Watching the An-12 turn in the sky, we followed suit and tucked in behind it all the way back to Chandigarh. Seeing all the fire engines and ambulances lined up by the side of the main runway made me realize how close to a major disaster we had been. Fortunately, no one was severely hurt but I think the wing commander who as at the centre of the drama was properly chewed out by the air force.

It is not in the nature of the air force to let you take a step back and ponder over what could have or could not have happened. The next morning, 1 September, we boarded the massive Ilyushin Il-76, aptly named the Gajraj by the IAF. The aircraft was being flown by Air Commodore (later Air Marshal) Ashok Kumar 'Raja' Goel, the AOC of 12 Wing. There was a slight miscommunication in the timing, so we landed up ten minutes late, which led to some frowns all around. Capable of airlifting even T-72 tanks, we watched in awe from within as we thundered down the runway and set course for Leh. 'Get down into the navigator's cabin,' Raja Goel said to Dipti and me, 'the view is something else.' Fifty minutes later, we were on finals, having shot almost vertically downwards all along the way. Being with the navigator, the advantage was we knew exactly what was below us, though between Keylong and Upshi, I don't think there were any human habitations visible.

Raja Goel, after off-loading us and allowing us to position cameras at various ends of the runway, did a quick take-off and landing for our benefit, then back we flew to Chandigarh, this time around filming the route in reverse order. We had started our descent over Gobind Sagar when Raja Goel turned to me, 'You're going to DBO ... the An-32 is starting up and waiting for you. Switch planes the moment we land.'

'Yes, sir,' I grinned. I just loved the pace at which the IAF worked. I went back to my crew and asked them if they wanted to do the DBO sortie. A collective groan went up. They had all become dedicated land lubbers, including Dipti.

In the An-32 I took my position behind the pilot's seat. It is funny how quickly one becomes 'an experienced hand' and learns what to expect and look for. We flew just to the west of Tso Moriri and could see small flocks of bar-headed geese taking to wing, which meant the goslings were ready to enter the adult world. After crossing the Indus Valley, the navigator drew my attention to the large expanse of the Pangong Tso to the east, and then we were in the Shyok River Valley, flying past Galwan and entering the Depsang Plains. Below us was the Chip Chap River, the headwaters of the Shyok, but by then we were ready to drop, so I had to scramble to the back and film the crates with their orange-coloured parachutes as they went out. Below us was the air strip of DBO, the runway, amidst the desolate wilderness marked by bleached human bones that were at least a hundred years old if not more.

DBO was the last campsite before the Karakoram Pass and it was situated at a height of 16,700 feet (5100 m). Set up as the northernmost outpost in 1960, one could still see the crashed remains of a Mi-4 helicopter. The IAF in 1962 had modified the C-114 Fairchild Packet by fitting an additional jet engine on to the aircraft and had landed at DBO, an amazing feat by any standards. With the An-32's hatches open, I was once again sitting at the extreme edge, and filmed the terrain as we made multiple passes over the runway. To the north the land sloped up to the KK Pass which led to the Shaksgam Valley just a few kilometres away. We then turned and flew back, filming important landmarks. The expanse of the Qara Qash and the Aksai Chin was on our port side, and though it was tempting to try and get a glimpse of the G-219 Highway that the Chinese had built, we set course for Chandigarh. In terms of sheer starkness of terrain, this was to be one of the most dramatic sorties ever.

17

Salt of the Earth-II (The Boys in Blue)

It had taken months of preparation to work out all the details for the IAF shoot. The logistics involved were tremendous, and more importantly, every aspect had been worked out so that we could optimize on the effort being put in. Some sequences, however, were completely off-the-cuff, for there was no way one could anticipate what we would get on film. While the itineraries were being worked out, I had walked into Natty's office, and after the usual routine of drinking lemon tea, had asked him, 'What about the "Foxbats"?'

'Who told you we had them? They are top secret!' replied Natty, with an impish grin.

'*Jane's Defence Weekly*!' I also thought of adding the Fiza'ya (Pakistan Air Force) but decided not to push it.

'I'll check with the chief,' said Natty, picking up the phone. Thirty seconds later, the necessary orders had then been passed. Accordingly, on 3 September, the entire crew bid adieu to Chandigarh, and we set course for Bareilly. The previous day we had once again taken off in the An-12 and done the feathering exercise, but this time it was shot only from within the aircraft even though we had flown all the way to Zanskar for the exercise. For all practical purposes we might as well have shot it on the ground itself, for without the external perspective, the shot was a damp squib. I was sitting in a corner making my notes on the An-12 sortie when the engineer came and said I was wanted in the cockpit.

We were about fifty miles short of Bareilly but were turning back, because fire warning lights had come on. On the ground in Chandigarh, the aircraft was checked and once again we took off, only for the problem to repeat itself, as a result of which we had a forced landing at Hindon. By the time we touched down at Bareilly, a good part of the day was over.

102 Squadron was known as the Trisonics, for the MiG-25R, NATO codename 'Foxbat', could fly at altitudes of over 120,000 feet (36575 m) and hit speeds of 3 Mach. It was so fast that most conventional missiles fired at it would be unable to catch up. Three aircraft were lined up on the tarmac and they were massive in size, almost as big as the An-32 itself. Wing Commander (later Air Vice Marshal) Jagdish Singh Grewal was the CO, and he welcomed all of us with a quick briefing about the aircraft and its capabilities. It was too late in the day to launch a sortie, so we busied ourselves with the fitting of a camera on the belly of the MiG-25R, and later Grewal was filmed looking at the huge A-3 size negatives with Squadron Leader (later Group Captain) Johnson Chacko. The latter also apparently had to suit up for the camera, after which Dipti made him walk to the aircraft a few times, something which Chacko continues to complain about even today.

Just for this sequence, we had hired a 3,000 mm lens, which was almost like a bazooka. It was so heavy and so difficult to operate, that Alok Upadhyay had not used it even once. I was adamant that we would use it to film both the take-off and the landing the next morning, so in the evening we figured out how best to execute the shots. Accordingly, we picked up Jagdish Grewal as he lined up at the other end of the runway, and the effect of the powerful lens was amazing, for the runway looked like a shimmering mirage. Once we had him framed, I told ATC to let him roll. The take-off would subsequently become the title shot of the film, while the equally spectacular landing also found a place in the film. Though we could not see the actual shots until the film was developed later, I knew the shot was spectacular. Since Alok was unable to pick up the subject easily through the lens, we considered improvising a gunsight kind of a contraption, but somehow it was not to be, and though the lens was carried around religiously in its wooden crate-like case, it was unfortunately never used again.

The next port of call was Agra, where some major enactments pertaining to the airlift in 1947 and Canberra raids over Pakistan in 1965 were to be shot. As mentioned earlier, Alok Upadhyay was the nephew of Wing Commander Padmanabha Gautam, who had been one of the most celebrated Canberra pilots in the IAF, having been awarded the Mahavir Chakra twice over. His daughter, Usha, was married to my former colleague in *India Today*, the well-known journalist, Raj Chengappa. With Simhakutty Varthaman playing the role of her father, it made sense to cast Usha in the role of her mother. The scene that had been scripted was a conversation between Vartha and Usha, but somehow, everything went terribly wrong. No one realized it, but there was a glaring continuity jump, with one party speaking on the phone in blackout conditions at night, while the other was talking in broad daylight. It just underlined the fact that no matter how much effort is put into any scene, one stupid mistake is enough for everything to come apart at the seam. This blunder was, of course, only realized much later on the editing table.

The shooting in Agra was jinxed at another level, for the other scene involving Padmanabha Gautam also had to be dropped despite it having been shot perfectly. During the 1971 War, the IAF had decided to drop the Y-bomb on the Mianwali airfield. This involved loading a drop tank with quick drying glue and nails, which if dropped from a height of 50 feet (15 m) over the runway, would shatter in such a manner that it would effectively deny the use of the airfield to the Pakistanis for a much longer period. The usual payload of 1,000 lb bombs filled with TNT, only created craters that the Fiza'ya ground crews could fill with quick drying cement fairly quickly. Needless to say, we were all very pleased with the scene until someone pointed out that the Pakistanis had filed a case against us in the International Court of Justice, saying that by using glue as against TNT, India had violated the rules of engagement. A Pakistani F-104 'Starfighter' was supposedly lost on take-off and the pilot had been killed, something that had upset our western neighbours immensely. No one was sure if the case existed or not, but once the objection was raised, we decided to drop the scene altogether.

The shooting in Agra had used up three valuable days, after which we landed at Adampur on the morning of 8 September. Alok Upadhyay had been bitterly complaining that he had not yet been given a fighter sortie, so he now had his big chance. Both of us strapped into MiG-29 trainers, and then along with another three fighters from 223 Squadron (Tridents) flanking us, we got airborne. Flying in a tight configuration at low level, we executed some sharp turns that resulted in the occasional pull of 4 to 5 G, which though not enough to cause a momentary blackout, made it impossible to shoot, for the camera automatically dipped as its weight increased manifold. After about thirty minutes in the air, one by one the five aircraft were recovered.

I had been flown by Squadron Leader (later Air Commodore) Thinide Kumar 'Tinkle' Nair, who was the senior flight commander. Dipti and the crew were in splits, for after Tinkle had finished his sortie, he had hopped onto a bicycle and nonchalantly cycled off. From one of the most sophisticated technologies in the world to the most elementary! In the evening, we met again at the bar, where Alok was reliving his sortie earlier in the day with whoever was present. Using his hands to depict his aircraft and the others, he was having the time of his life. 'And then we turned hard ... 5 G ... maybe 6 ... I kept the camera focused on the belly of the aircraft next to me ...' The more I listened to Alok's descriptions, the more I was getting depressed, because I had not been able to film anything after we crossed the threshold of 4 G. Luckily, Alok needed to get rid of the beer he had been guzzling and he briefly left the room.

'He's talking rubbish,' said Tinkle Nair quietly. 'I was watching him. He wasn't shooting!'

After a while I took Alok Upadhyay outside for a walk. 'Seriously,' I asked, 'were you comfortable shooting?'

He looked at me for a while. It takes courage, especially if you are the nephew of one of the greatest pilots that the IAF ever had, but he levelled with me. 'Man,' he said, 'I was terrified. I cannot do it. It's your baby!' I told him not to fret over it, but in that case, I would have to take the SR-II camera up myself the next day, for we were scheduled to fly a formation of MiG-23 MFs over the Siachen Glacier. I told him to use the Arriflex ST for the ground sequences.

The MiG-23 UB was the trainer version and as I strapped in, I found I could not close the canopy with the SR magazine. I asked the COO if I could fly without the helmet, with just the inners on. He looked horrified at the thought but conveyed my request to the AOC, Air Commodore Inder Jit Singh Boparai who exploded on the walkie talkie. 'Don't be an idiot, Kunal!' To add to my discomfiture, we were flying with drop tanks attached, which would give us the endurance to get to Siachen, buzz the glacier with a formation of accompanying MiG-23 MFs, and then return to Adampur, which meant being airborne for twice the duration of a normal fighter sortie. 'As it is, you'll have a sore arse from being strapped in for so long ... you don't want a smashed skull to boot!'

As luck would have it, the entire Himalayan region was under a blanket of thick clouds. Looking for a gap, we hung around for a while after which the other aircraft peeled off for base. One valley was visible, which happened to be Spiti, so we dived down there and went zooming along the river on a 'sightseeing' visit, hit the Sutlej near Baspa and then returned to Adampur.

Two Mi-25 Hind helicopter gunships had arrived from their base at Halwara and the entire film crew was embarked waiting for my arrival. Once again, in what was fast becoming the pattern, I was whisked from one cockpit to another, and we lifted off the moment I was on board. The plan was for the gunships to fire RPG rockets and their machine guns at the SK (Sidhwan Kalan) Firing Range near Ludhiana, while Alok and I filmed each other's helicopter. The Mi-25 attack helicopters overflew the Jalandhar Cantonment and I could immediately pick out 5 Mall Road. The bottlebrush I had planted at the entrance eight years previously was a reasonable sized shrub by then. The ground-attack helicopters had played a major role in the IPKF operations in Sri Lanka, and once over the range, we opened up with rockets, and the spectacular chin-mounted twin-barrel 23 mm cannon that was firing thousands of rounds per minute. Back in Adampur, I asked for a vehicle and took Dipti to see the bottlebrush on the ground as well. The house had different occupants, but it was still a part of me, for it had been 'home' in the not-too-distant past.

10 September 1992 will be etched in the minds of many people. In the morning, we took off in our allotted An-32 and did a short hop across

to Ambala. We were received by the COO, Group Captain (later Air Vice Marshal) Donovan Eric Jonas, who drove us across to 5 Squadron (Tuskers) that was being commanded by Wing Commander (later Air Marshal) Venkataraman Ramamurthy 'Ike' Iyer. In the briefing room, it looked like the entire city of Ambala was present, for there were quite a few Jaguar pilots from 14 Squadron (Bulls) also present. 'Gentlemen,' Ike soon had everyone's attention, 'we are today going to launch a 12-aircraft strike at Nal. It's a historic day for us, for we will have the pleasure of flying Mrs Dipti Verma, and of course Mr Kunal Verma and Alok Upadhyay. Mrs Verma will be the first lady to fly in a Jaguar today.' I threw a quick glance at Alok, but I need not have worried, for he was modestly giving a thumbs up to some newfound friend.

Dipti was strapped in and was flying as No. 12 in the formation with Donovan Jonas, who also gave her the standard 'eject ... eject ... eject ...' briefing. I was in the first formation of 4 aircraft with Flight Lieutenant (later Group Captain) Ashutosh Chandra 'Choppy' Chopra and the RT was buzzing with call signs as multiple aircraft were positioned around at the top of the runway waiting to get airborne. It was a sight as afterburners started coming on and Jaguar after Jaguar unstuck from the runway. In the sky, they quickly grouped up in fours, and Choppy weaved around to give me the shots I wanted. Apart from the Arriflex ST, I also had two more 16 mm cameras that belonged to the Armament & Systems Testing Establishment (ASTE), but these had a fixed focal length and were actually designed to be used in pods fitted to the wing tips.

Nal was the air base at Bikaner and as we got further from Ambala, the landscape changed dramatically, giving way to a scrub-like desert. The Jaguar formations were hugging the ground to avoid being detected by radar, and we soon flashed past the runway below us. The formations now split, and Choppy and I were on our own. I could see villages, women in colourful *dupattas*, standing around wells and looking at the horizon for our sound was way behind us. 'You know Choppy, a partridge gets up, we'll get hit!'

'Hang on,' he responded, bringing the aircraft even lower. For twenty seconds or so we were at bush-top height. After that, even the 50 feet we were otherwise maintaining seemed relatively high enough.

In Ambala, the IAF made a big fuss around Dipti, presenting her with a certificate. In those days sexual discrimination was not such a buzzword, but after someone whispered something in Ike's ear, they produced two more certificates which were then presented to Alok Upadhyay and me, obviously as an afterthought! After parity had been restored, we were back in our An-32 on our way home to Adampur. When we landed, Boparai was waiting for me. One of the MiG-23s that had flown as part of the formation with me on the previous day had crashed. Fortunately, the pilot had ejected and had been picked up by the SAR helicopter shortly thereafter. Boparai had brought his helmet along for me to see, for it was smashed and dented almost beyond recognition. 'That could have been your skull,' said the AOC. I never even dreamt of making another such suggestion ever again.

After a brief stop in Ambala for some ground shots, we landed at Hindon, which was then a fighter base on the eastern bank of the Jamuna. 9 Squadron (Wolfpack) had been commanded by my uncle, Dolly Yadav in the mid-1960s, and also by his brother, Karan Yadav who was in command during the 1971 War. At the helm at the time was Wing Commander (later Air Marshal) Krishan Kumar Nohwar[18] and the squadron was equipped with both the MiG-23 UB and the MiG-27 MF. While I was briefed by Nohwar on the planned aerial sorties for the day, Dipti was in discussions with Air Commodore Ravish Malhotra[19] who was commanding the base.

The maximum number of officers that had been selected by Dipti and Leslie Springett to play bit roles were from the Hindon Air Base. Among them was Air Commodore (later Air Vice Marshal) Saravjit Singh Hothi, who was cast as the legendary Air Commodore 'Baba' Mehar Singh. Jovial and extremely helpful, Hothi was a natural film director, for he had perfect advice for all his subordinates as to how to perform in front of the camera, but when it came to him, he got hopelessly tongue-tied!

---

[18] Later Air Marshal K. K. Nohwar was on the Board of Air India. He was C-in-C Eastern Air Command when I happened to meet him again in 2010. He told me I had been flown by all the C-in-Cs who were then in office.

[19] Air Commodore Ravish Malhotra was the standby cosmonaut for the first joint Indo-Soviet space venture that took place in April 1984. Squadron Leader Rakesh Sharma was to make the historic flight.

While the crew got busy with the enactments, I had my hands full. The first task was to get airborne with five MiG-27 MFs who were to do a simulated air attack on the Hapur Railway Station. Situated on the Delhi–Moradabad Highway, the little township would get shaken to the core as fighter after fighter rolled in for an attack. By now I was getting fairly used to the MiG-23 BN, but hardly had we landed, I was airborne again with another formation, this time flying over the Ganga at Garhmukhteshwar. By the time we finished, I was getting cross-eyed with fatigue, for the concentration levels one had to maintain were sapping. Nohwar grinned happily, 'We're giving you a break. Next sortie will be a night run over Delhi. Take-off will be after last light!'

I caught up with the crew who were shooting the Arjan Singh scene where he reads out the letter from a boy in Bombay, then headed back. The sun had set but there was still a slight residual orange glow in the sky when we lined up with another aircraft. The afterburners coming on in the dark, the rings being formed and the blast as we got propelled forward into the night sky was surreal. As we gained altitude, the horizon was still bright, and one could see a vertical greyish-black haze over the city of Delhi. 'What's that?' I asked incredulously.

'Pollution,' replied Nohwar, who was flying with me. 'From this altitude it is clearly visible this time of the year.'

After we touched down and taxied to the dispersal area, I could see Dipti and Ravish Malhotra standing there with my parents. Getting out of the cockpit and walking across in soaked overalls, that moment gave me a tremendous kick. Later that night we shot the bonfire scene, where Hothi could not get to say, 'Carry on chaps!' without a dozen takes. With more scenes scripted with him over the next few days, we all knew we were in serious trouble!

After three days of shooting, we moved, *by road*, to Palam! It was such a unique experience not to fly from point A to B that the bus journey stood out. All sorts of scenes were shot in Delhi Cantt, but the highlight for us was Adi Sethna acting as Abdul Motaleb Malik, the last governor of East Pakistan, who resigned on 14 December 1971 when the IAF put some rockets in from the window at Government House where he was holding a meeting. There were enactments galore, from 1 Sikh embarking on Dakotas to 1 Squadron being photographed with the Wapiti in the background, the photograph being taken by the Mahattas who dug out the original camera used in the 1930s. *Hindustan Times*, getting into the spirit of things, ran the press with the newspapers carrying photographs of M-48 Patton Tanks that were photographed by IAF Vampires as they advanced into the Rann of Kutch. In all, we were well disciplined penguins for a good eleven days, after which it was time to fly again.

On 23 September we took off from Palam and landed at Gwalior, where there were more ground scenes planned. The next day, we took a mixed formation of six Mirage 2000s from both 1 Squadron (Tigers) and 7 Squadron (Battle Axes). I was flying with the CO of the Tigers, Wing Commander (later Air Marshal) Anil Chopra while Dipti was being flown by Squadron Leader (later Group Captain) Rajan Bhasin. The Tigers, being the oldest squadron in the IAF, were also celebrating their diamond jubilee. While the Battle Axes were trained more for interdiction, the Tigers were the interceptors, but for filming purposes, Anil Chopra had wanted his aircraft to be filmed low level as well. After a few passes over the airfield and then the Chambal River, we were in the process of executing a 'scissor' manoeuvre when the aircraft came within a fraction of colliding in mid-air. All aircraft had to pull close to 7 G to pull apart, and it was obvious it had been a narrow shave.

Heading back, my aircraft was the last in formation to land, while Bhasin and Dipti were leading the way. The Gwalior Fort was tantalizingly visible down below and I asked Choppy if we could 'buzz' the headmaster's residence. Nothing brings out the evil streak in pilots more than a good heart-rendering 'revenge on the housemaster' plea, so we peeled off, corkscrewed high into the air and then zoomed down and broke the sound barrier just over Saand's house. After that, we went in for finals, and with an absolute look of innocence we touched down.

There is no fun in doing something if you cannot visit the scene of the crime and see for yourself the havoc unleashed. Since I had to look up Mrs Avasthy as well, and just in case I needed a human shield, we drove over to Dr Singh's house in the evening. He was so hopping mad at the IAF, so much so that he hardly noticed that I had visited him. Every third sentence he wanted to lynch the pilot who had 'cracked every window in his school'. I shook my head and tut-tutted and said 'very bad' a few times in sympathy. Next morning Anil Chopra and I got hauled up by Adi Rustomji Ghandhi.

'Kunal, this is not expected of you! Anil, I will deal with you separately, but you! Dr Singh is almost having a heart attack!'

'Who is he, sir?' I asked innocently.

The AOC glared at me. Anil Chopra had said to deny everything, and I stuck to the 'who sir, me sir, no sir' routine like a limpet mine. 'Listen you liars! Three-fourth of Gwalior's population saw you guys and *you are denying it*! Now get out of my office ...' [20]

The next day, the crew moved ahead to Agra while I did yet another Mirage 2000 run with Nandu Jog and a formation of Battle Axes in the morning. Since Dipti had also stayed back, we got into a Cheetah helicopter and flew to Agra later in the day. En route, we flew along the Chambal River for a while, and it was quite a sight to see the gharials and marsh muggers basking on the banks. One huge mugger did not slither back into the river when we went over, so we came around to see what had happened. Almost seven or eight feet long, the reptile's head had been blown off and it was just lying there. One of the pilots, Flight Lieutenant Mehta, said it was a common sight as poachers would leave explosives inside a dead animal's carcass by the river for the crocodiles, and then they would come and skin them.

We landed at the Para Training School, where Alok Upadhyay and the crew had already been embarked on An-32s with the paratroopers. Dipti quickly joined them while I was to stay with the Cheetah and get the men as they dropped in sticks of 16. There was a flurry of activity as three An-32s got airborne, followed by my helicopter that then waited near the drop zone. It was quite a spectacular sight as the paratroopers came hurtling out, but somehow the helicopter was not the ideal platform for me to shoot from, as we had to maintain a safe distance from the deployed parachutes. Flight Lieutenant Mehta, who was flying me, turned

---

[20] Thirteen years later while shooting the film on the Gnat, Air Marshal Adi Rustomji Ghandhi said he knew all along why we had buzzed Dr S. D. Singh's residence. He said he would have happily done much the same, but he had to do his job and chew us out!

to me and said on the RT, 'Sir, message from Dipti Ma'm. She wants us to land back at the airfield.'

'You're wasting your time in a chopper,' shouted Dipti over the roar of the engines, pulling me aboard the An-32 which had embarked the next lot of paratroopers. Since I was comfortable shooting from the edge of the aircraft, she suggested I position myself there and shoot the men as they plunged past me into thin air. I quickly tied my monkey belt to a bar near the exit and tucked myself in. It was scary, for as we took off, there was nothing between me and the ground, but then as we came in for the drop, everything else was forgotten. The men took up the cry, '*Chatri Mata ki jai*' and as the lights turned green, out they went like tumbling sacks. It was fantastic stuff and as shots go, it was one of the most breathtaking scenes in the film subsequently as it was used to depict the 1971 Tangail para drop. Indrajit Neogi, who was a gutsy character, had also moved up right next to me and the sound he got of the paratroopers going out was top quality. Very often we take the sound for granted in a film, but sometimes it takes even more effort to capture the real thing.

That night we returned to Gwalior, and as had been promised by the commander-in-chief (C-in-C) Eastern Air Command, we were given an Avro HS-48 the next morning for the three-hour flight to Kalaikunda. By the time we reached, the entire crew was looking bedraggled and exhausted, but it didn't take long for Bonny Mukerjee to have them all perked up. As far as I was concerned, having grown up listening to stories about the Gnat and the Hawker Hunter, another dream was about to come true. Strapping in beside Squadron Leader (later Group Captain) Rakesh Anand, we took off on a low-level reconnaissance cum familiarization sortie. Unlike the supersonic fighters like the MiG-23s, Mirage 2000s and the Jaguar which I had until then flown in, the Hunter was a completely different cup of tea, and she handled beautifully in the air. After we flew along the coast till Puri, we gained height, flipped the aircraft on its back and flew back to Kalaikunda upside down, then did a few loops over the airfield and then came into land.

The next few days for me were Hunters, Hunters and more Hunters, as I filmed various aircraft formations in various configurations, including firing 30 mm cannon over the sea. After a sortie with Squadron Leader (later Group Captain) Balbir Singh Nagra, one of the flight commanders with 20 Squadron, I was formally presented with a logbook, which helped me keep a fairly accurate record of my various flights during those tumultuous days. The logistics behind some of the sorties were mind-boggling, but everything went off like clockwork. MiG-21s coming in from Hashimara flew escort for the Hunters at low level, which I filmed from a Jaguar[21] that had come down from Gorakhpur and was flown by Squadron Leader (later Wing Commander) Girish Kumar.

On 29 September, after doing one last Jaguar sortie with the Hunters around the Eastern Ghats, we again loaded up Dushyant Singh's Avro HS-48 and took off for Chabua in Assam, another three-and-a-half-hour flight. The airfield was one of the oldest air bases in the Northeast and had served as the main base for DC-3 Dakotas that had kept the Chinese supplied during World War II by flying over 'the Hump'.

Early the next morning Dipti and the rest of the crew took off for Tuting in an An-32 while I followed in a Mi-17. After lift-off, one could see the endless expanse of tea gardens after which we crossed the Brahmaputra. At Pasighat, the Siang River came in from the north and joined the Lohit that had already considerably increased in volume after the Dibang debouched from the Mishmi Hills and their waters merged at Sadiya. We flew along the Siang, which was a massive body of water by itself, and eventually could see the Tuting runway that was partly made up of strips of perforated steel plates where the An-32 was parked. After completing the filming on the ground, I wanted to see the Dibang Valley as well, so after consulting the maps, the Mi-17 entered Mishmi country by overflying Andra La, from where we then followed the course of the Dibang River back to the plains of Assam and onto Mohanbari, which was just five minutes flying time from Chabua.

That evening we met Flight Lieutenant (later Squadron Leader) Farhat Samiullah 'Sid' Siddiqui[22] and Flying Officer (later Flight

[21] Of all the aircraft, the Jaguar was proving to be the easiest platform to film from, so Girish would later be drafted in to shoot the Hunters at Jaisalmer as well.

[22] Sid would fly extensively with me when I was filming with the Indian Navy subsequently. After the Kargil War, I got the tragic news that his Cheetah had crashed beyond Manali, killing him and his co-pilot, Flt Lt Sanjay Kumar Pandey.

Lieutenant) Amardeep 'Birdie' Bhardwaj[23] who were to fly us to Vijaynagar the next day. Dipti and I were to go with them in a Cheetah while the Mi-17 would take Alok Upadhyay and the rest of the crew. Since it meant overflying the Namdapha Tiger Reserve, we got a map and showed the two pilots the layout of the area.

Since we only had one headset at the back, Dipti was on RT with the pilots. We flew along with the Mi-17 and soon had left Deban behind. The Noa-Dehing was flanked on either side with some of the most pristine primary forest, and it came as a bit of a shock as to how little ground we had actually covered earlier when I had shot the *Project Tiger* and later the *Call of the Wild* films in Namdapha. Dipti was in the meantime giggling and tugging at my sleeve, and she shared the headset with me. Birdie, peering down into the endless canopy of trees was saying, 'Sid, if we go down here, you think anyone will bother to even look for us?'

'They can look all they want,' replied Sid, 'but they'll never find us.'

The area below then opened into a valley where Gandhigram, locally known to the Lishu tribe as Shidi, was situated. We overflew the settlement and then arrived at the Vijaynagar airfield, where there was an Assam Rifles post. The Mi-17 also landed and with the weather being a bit uncertain, we quickly filmed a casualty being evacuated, after which the crew headed back to Chabua almost immediately. Fifteen minutes later we followed suit, flying back the way we had come. Desperately low on fuel, the Cheetah just made it back to Chabua for hardly had we touched down, the engine flamed out.

After the Mi-17 had landed, Alok Upadhyay and the rest of the crew had wandered off to the mess for lunch, leaving only Indrajit Neogi behind. The COO, however, was waiting with the message that troops from a Madras battalion were waiting for us at Mohanbari for the Narsingdi enactments. We quickly refuelled the Cheetah and did the short five-minute hop to Mohanbari, where three Mi-17s with the troops on board were already started up. I only had the Arriflex ST camera and was pretty low on film. Squadron Leader (later Wing Commander) Malkiat Singh Bains was in command of the detachment of helicopters,

[23] Birdie was killed in a Mi-25 attack helicopter crash in 1994 while flying with his CO, Wing Commander Rajbir.

and I asked him to lift off and drop me on one of the islands on the Brahmaputra. He was to then circle around and one by one, the three Mi-17s would then come in and disembark the troops.

The island was fortunately covered with fairly tall grass and as Neogi and I dropped down from the helicopter, where the down draft from the rotors was creating a terrific, swirling effect. Using hand signals, I then asked Bains to come in. Since the original heli-lift on the Meghna River in 1971 had been done using Mi-4 helicopters, I had to avoid showing the Mi-17s as such. The entire operation went off extremely smoothly and was perhaps one of the most spontaneous scenes in the film. Indrajit Neogi also got excellent sound recordings. Sometimes just shooting with the flow results in terrific cinema. Later I was looking at the scripted scenes for the enactment of the heli-lift and felt it was a blessing in disguise that Alok and the crew had gone missing at that very moment.

On 2 October we moved from the Dibrugarh area (Chabua and Mohanbari) to Tezpur. By now it had almost become the pattern for the crew to move by An-32s while Dipti and I would move by the Cheetah. This gave us a greater understanding of the terrain, and since I always flew with the Arriflex ST by my side, one could film if an opportunity presented itself. After taking off from Chabua, we flew along the South Bank and at some point, the An-32 overtook us high in the sky. Then we were above Kaziranga, and in the eastern range we could see small herds of elephants and the odd rhino in the bheels. We swept over the grasslands where I had been shot eight years previously in the run in with poachers, and from the air I was showing Dipti the various landmarks.

Sid had taken control of the chopper and he moved in close to a rhino that was feeding in the bheel. The downdraft of the rotors and the noise of the Cheetah strangely did not seem to bother the animal at all, who sort of looked around but never looked up. I was by then leaning out and literally standing on the skids shooting downwards.

We then saw some elephants and moved in over them. A large makhna was out in the open in the water, and we got the shadow of the Cheetah go past him as we circled just 20 feet (5–6 m) above him. On the RT, I was constantly adjusting the helicopter's position, for Sid was having to look past Birdie and the last thing we needed was for the elephant to pull us down, for sooner or later the big fellow would look up. Having got some unique shots, I said, 'Ok, let's get out of here ...'

But Sid had seen a rhino with her year-old calf in the grass, and as we came close the grass literally parted, taking away whatever semblance of cover the female had. The rhino began to run and we stayed with her, flying sideways, filming. It was a tremendous shot and though it was tempting to hang around and film animals from this unique perspective, I did not want to disturb the area any further.

We crossed the Brahmaputra, and it was Dipti's turn to reminiscence for down below was the bridge that was built by Larsen & Toubro, which she had filmed in 1984. We landed at Tezpur and were received by Group Captain (later Air Commodore) Parvez Hamilton Khokhar who was commanding the MiG Operational Flying Training Unit. 'You guys been buzzing Kaziranga?' Khokhar had been the air attaché in Pakistan and obviously knew a thing or two about extracting information. Immediately I had put on my 'who sir, me sir, no sir' expression. Khokhar grinned and told Sid and Birdie, 'In that case you guys better get rid of the grass stuck to your helicopter's skids!'

Khokhar conducted the briefing the next morning. I was finally going to fly in the MiG-21, something I had been waiting for. Inducted into the IAF from the Soviet Union before the 1965 India–Pakistan War, the delta-wing MiG-21 with its multiple variants had been the backbone of not just the IAF, but also of many other air forces in the world. There were two sorties lined up that morning, the first a five-aircraft formation that would fly at mid-level over the Brahmaputra, and the second was to be with 30 Squadron (Rhinos) in which we were to rendezvous with two MiG-21s coming from Chabua who were to fire their rockets at the Dollungmukh firing range that was on the Assam–Arunachal border.

The first sortie was a lark, and as we unstuck, I could see Dipti filming the take-off from runway's side. Though relatively cramped for space, I found the MiG-21 quite comfortable to shoot from. After we landed, I moved across to the Rhinos, and after a detailed briefing, strapped up in the Type 66 once again. I was being flown by Squadron Leader (later Wing Commander) Navindra Nath Verma, and we headed east towards the confluence of the Subansiri and the Brahmaputra.

The MiG-21 had a unique characteristic. The air conditioning used to kick in only after the aircraft gained an altitude of 6,560 feet (2000 m). My overalls damp from sweat, I was looking forward to the blast of cool air, but instead we started getting roasted by a jet of hot air. 'Damn,' said Navindra Verma, 'the air conditioning has got jammed on full heat.' We debated what to do, for we could call off the other MiGs, stay low level to stop the air conditioning while we expended fuel, or just go on and finish the task. Since getting range clearance was a problem, we decided to push on. Soon the two other MiG-21s had linked up with us and they fired their rockets, which I dutifully filmed. They then peeled off and returned to Chabua while we set course for Tezpur.

We had climbed up to 10,000 feet (3500 m) when it occurred to me that we were in a shallow dive. I could also suddenly see Navindra Verma's helmet as his head seemed to be lolling over sideways. I called him on the RT, but there was no response, so I shook the stick violently which resulted in the aircraft jumping around but him leaving it. I quickly pulled back to regain the lost altitude and then called Tezpur ATC. 'My pilot is not responding,' I said, forgetting to give my call sign.

'Who is this?' asked the voice cautiously at the other end. 'What do you mean pilot is not responding? What is your call sign?'

'Screw all that,' I said, 'just get the COO on the air.' A few seconds later, obviously someone who knew what we were doing up there was on the RT.

'Ok Kunal, what's the problem.' I said the air conditioning was jammed and we were roasting in the cockpit and that the pilot seemed to be unconscious. I was holding course and could see the Kameng River and the airfield. As the situation developed, I started to lose height and circle around as instructed by the voice, but just when everything seemed to be heading for a climax and a possible ejection, I heard Navindra Verma's calm voice saying he had control. He must have been out for almost three to four minutes, during which time my entire life had flashed before my eyes. We landed without any further fuss, but once again the ambulances and fire engines lining the runway were a stark indication of just how lucky we had been. Parvez Khokhar[24] would tell me later he had been

[24] Parvez Khokhar was the chief test pilot when I shot the LCA film in 2003 and we would fly together on a few occasions.

with the COO when the emergency call had come in and he was impressed by the fact that I had not panicked, and my voice had been calm and in control. I told him frankly I was crapping my overalls. He laughed and said that was but natural.

Having had enough excitement in Tezpur, we then moved to Bagdogra, which was yet another picturesque IAF base situated amidst the tea gardens of West Bengal. The next day was my 32nd birthday and I knew something was up, but what exactly, I had no idea. We were up at the crack of dawn, and in a stream of Cheetahs we took off. From the Coronation Bridge we turned into the Teesta Gorge and after a forty-five-minute flight, landed at Gangtok. It was cold and misty, but nevertheless we sat in garden chairs near the helipad and had omelettes and cutlets. We then took off for Nathu La pass but frankly, were not quite equipped for it. The Cheetah was flying without doors and Alok Upadhyay who was with me and Dipti, started to freeze in the extreme cold. We had climbed up to the Baba Harbhajan Memorial when it seemed Alok was going to pass out, for he was turning a distinct shade of blue. I told the pilot to abort the sortie and drop down to Gangtok. It took a while for all of us to stop shivering from the cold, after which the entire formation of Cheetahs flew back to Bagdogra. I was, however, in for a special treat, for instead of flying south, my helicopter flew north along the Teesta River till we came to Lachung. From there we turned back, flying over the Dzongu area that is inhabited by the Lepcha community at the base of Kanchenjunga.

We briefly touched down at a tea factory at Darjeeling and a small sack of tea was shoved inside the chopper, after which we landed back at Bagdogra airfield. The crew was all embarked in the An-32, ready to leave, and we promptly set course for Hindon, which was three-and-a-half hours away. I was in for a surprise for waiting for us were my parents, Adi Sethna, Ravish Malhotra, Hothi and just about every pilot in Hindon who had acted in the film. They all sang happy birthday, and after a lavish lunch, we got airborne again, this time for Jodhpur. By the time we touched down, the sun was setting over the desert, and once again I was welcomed with a birthday cake. I never felt so popular across such a large geographical bandwidth again in my life. It had been one heck of a day.

10 Squadron (Daggers) were flying the MiG-23 MFs, and the next morning we flew four of them over Umaid Bhawan Palace. Meanwhile, since 23 Punjab and the armour had all moved into position at Pokhran for the depiction of the Battle of Longewala, Dipti and I took a Chetak and flew across to meet the people on the ground and also check the arrangements that had been made for the filming. Everything seemed to be in order, so we flew back to Jodhpur, where I went in the evening and thanked Moti Dhar for his help.

On 7 October the crew shifted by An-32 to Jaisalmer, after which the aircraft flew me to Palam where the Air Force Day parade was to be held the next morning. The impressive parade was commanded by Air Marshal Nanda Cariappa and all the squadron colours were being paraded, which gave me some excellent footage from my vantage point just above the saluting base. The moment the parade got over, I jumped into a Dornier 228 and headed back to Jaisalmer where Dipti and the rest of the crew were waiting for me. There was a lot of excitement in the air, for the next morning the Hunters were due to fly in from Kalaikunda.

Keshav Bewoor, along with four other pilots, landed in the morning, while an An-32 ferried the ground crew. Another aircraft came in from Hyderabad, carrying the rails and rockets that needed to be fitted on the Hunters, and by afternoon, everyone was quite tired and had retired for some well-earned rest. Dipti and the crew had already left for Pokhran, while I was half asleep in the room when the COO burst in excitedly. 'Come quick,' he said, 'you've got to see this.' I followed him to the gate of the Officer's Mess and was amazed to see women in colourful sarees with pots balanced on their heads followed by men in the typical large turbans marching towards the main gate of the air base. The DSC guards, completely thrown by this massive congregation, were trying to take up firing positions but it was obvious the crowd was not going to stop.

'*Khol do*' (Open the gate), the duty officer at the entrance gave the command and the congregation breezed past, the momentum of their forward movement carrying them through. There was a second gate which was also thrown open and soon the *jatha* reached the parked

Hunters. No one knew what was happening but there was nothing anyone could do. Coming up to the first aircraft, the lead women promptly started doing an aarti and someone made the mark of the swastika on the aircraft's nose. One of the men then started to move forward presumably with the intention of smashing a coconut on the nose as well, when someone from the air force finally found their voice and stopped the man, who then smashed the nut on the tarmac in front of the aircraft itself. By then Keshav Bewoor and all the pilots had also arrived and they were garlanded and also had aartis done. Having paid their homage to the 'saviours of Jaisalmer', the congregation turned on its heels and went back the way they had come.

Days of preparation were finally going to be put to test. On the morning of 10 October, I strapped into a MiG-23 UB that had come in from Jodhpur, and with two Hunters, took off from Jaisalmer. Against the desert backdrop, with their camouflage paint, the Hunters looked deadly in the sky. Approaching Pokhran, we dropped down to low level and though we could see the RSO's hut, we just could not get a fix on the tanks. A few days earlier, Pokhran had witnessed some unseasonal rainfall as a result of which, the entire desert had bloomed with tiny little yellow flowers. The abundance of vegetation meant tank tracks were not visible from the air, which meant we were flying blind. We made some half-a-dozen passes, and each time we drew a blank. On the final run, we lined up with the target area and discharged the 30 mm cannons and then headed back to Jaisalmer. After my MiG-23 landed, I opened the cockpit and was getting some fresh air as we taxied back to the dispersal area, when I suddenly noticed a pair of painted sandgrouse flying along beside me. It was the most unusual sight.

During the debrief, both the Hunter pilots confirmed that they had been unable to see the tanks. 'Go in a bit higher this time,' said Keshav Bewoor to Rakesh Anand. So again, we got airborne, Andy armed with rockets and the MiG-23 UB flying alongside. Again, we made multiple passes, and yet again drew a blank. On the final run, Andy fired off his rockets and we again returned to Jaisalmer.

A Mi-8 had started up, so I jumped on board along with Bewoor and Andy. Landing at the helipad, I could see Dipti running towards the helicopter. I was a bit alarmed and made my way towards her bent double to avoid the still swirling rotors. We had been in radio contact during the day, and she was aware that we had missed the tanks altogether. 'Listen,' she panted, 'whatever you do, do not tell the tank crews you could not see them from the air. They were doing such a fantastic job of being hit and dropping off from their turrets every time you guys flew over, it'll break their heart if you tell them you couldn't see them!'

In the RSO hut, we once again went over the problem of locating the tanks from the air. It was suggested that expended oil be used to light three fires a kilometre apart on the ground, and that the Hunters would then align themselves accordingly. The tanks would do the same thing on the ground, as a result of which we would get the aircraft and the armour in the same alignment. The sapper detachment would also place their explosives accordingly. The Mi-8 was promptly despatched to Jodhpur to requisition the oil. The rest of the day was spent watching the ground sequences being shot, which included two RCL jeeps roaring in and opening fire at the 'Pakistani' armour.

A Jaguar from 16 Squadron had arrived all the way from Gorakhpur. Squadron Leader (later Wing Commander) Surinder Singh Chahar was flying with me, while the solitary Hunter was again armed with rockets. Somehow, overnight the oil had been procured and the smoke was going up in perfect vertical plumes. All we had to do then was go dead straight and zoom over the tanks, which strangely we could see quite clearly now. A second sortie with two Hunters in tow shortly thereafter completed the sequence, after which we got some exquisite medium level shots as well. After landing, I said goodbye to the Hunters and the Jaguar, who after refuelling, thundered off back to Kalaikunda and Gorakhpur respectively. The station commander, Group Captain (later Air Commodore) Narendra Minocha was standing with me as the Hunters lifted off. 'One thing is for sure,' he said wistfully, 'that is the last time we will ever see Hunters at Jaisalmer.'

The ground filming at Pokhran would continue the next day as well. In the meantime, I had to film MiG-23 MFs and Mi-8s also firing at the range. In the morning, I took off from Jaisalmer and rendezvoused with two fighters from Jodhpur. My aircraft was the first to line up and fire. As we approached the triangular target made up of sandbags, I suddenly saw a man dart in behind. 'Abort ... abort ... abort ...' I called on the RT and my pilot, Flight Lieutenant Srivastava, banked away sharply in response.

'What happened?'

'There's a man on the target ...' I said incredulously.

On the RT, conversations are by and large extremely cryptic. We were already turning hard to get into formation with the second MiG-23 that was to fire. 'Ignore the guys below' was the response to my plea, so we came in not once, but three times and plastered the target area with 32 rockets at a time. The other two aircraft then went back to Jodhpur while Srivastava and I touched down at Jaisalmer. It seemed it was normal to have villagers hanging around the target for they picked up the lead from the exploding shells that fetched a good price in the market. Sometimes someone got killed while others lost limbs, but for the air force, it was an occupational hazard.

The MiGs were to fire again in the afternoon, and so were Mi-8 helicopters. I flew back to Pokhran where Dipti and Indrajit Neogi were having a raging argument. Having observed my earlier three-aircraft assault on the target and also seen the villagers sheltering behind the sandbags, Neogi, probably eying an Oscar for the 'most innovative sound recordist', wanted to sit on the target and record the impact of rockets. Dipti was telling him he was positively loco when I arrived.

Obviously 'sitting on the target' had to be treated as a figure of speech, but Neogi could get behind the sandbags if he was so keen, I suggested. The argument settled, Neogi trotted off to get his posthumous citation, while Alok and I took up our camera positions. A few minutes later, the three aircraft came in and saturated the area with their armaments. Neogi survived. But the interesting thing was the sound he got. There was first the impact of rockets hitting, then the wooosh ... then the sound of firing, and finally the roar of the MiG-23s. In effect, everything was in reverse order, and the irony was, in the final film, to match the visuals, we had to play it backwards as well.

Sunsets in the desert are always spectacular. The Battle of Longewala done and dusted, the other firings filmed, we still had one little thing to do. A detachment of the elite 10 Para Commandos had arrived and with the setting sun behind them, we had them slither down from Mi-8s. It was a spectacular and fitting end to the Pokhran/Jaisalmer leg of the film.

From Jaisalmer we flew south the next morning on 13 October in our An-32 and landed at Bhuj. While the rest of the crew moved by Mi-8, Dipti, Sarita Joshi and I took off in a Chetak and flew to Banni in the Rann of Kutch where a troop of T-59 tanks from 63 Armoured Regiment were waiting for us. Since we did not have access to operational Patton tanks, the plan was to film the T-59s from the ground in the Rann and also from a helicopter. Again, even though Flying Officer (later Wing Commander) Utpal Barbara in 1965 had done his aerial reconnaissance in a Vampire, our plan was to use a Canberra to overfly the tanks.

I quickly returned to Bhuj and strapped into a MiG-21 Type 69 with Squadron Leader (later Group Captain) Sashi Kumar Nair. A Canberra had already taken off from Jamnagar and we were to locate it, then fly formation with it so as to film the aircraft as it went over the tanks that were deployed below. As we unstuck from the runway, there was a loud noise and the aircraft lurched sideways. My hands flew to the ejection handle, but there was no command to eject, but the slight sideways movement continued even as we gained altitude. 'Damn!' Sashi Nair's voice came over the RT, 'I think the undercarriage has not retracted!' I glanced at the three green lights on the control panel and could see they were flickering.

Nair called the ATC and asked them to do a visual confirmation. We orbited around and buzzed past the tower. 'Affirmative. Undercarriage has not retracted!'

Nair coolly told me I better put away the camera and sit straight, for if he said eject, I must get out without any hesitation on my part. However, he said he would make a few passes of the runway and we would pull 7 or 8 G and see if that would bring the wheels down. We could hear the Canberra calling for us, so he was told by ATC to abort the sortie and go back to Jamnagar as the MiG-21 had an emergency. On the third pass, as we pulled up in yet another stomach lurching effort, there was a noise and the aircraft nose straightened. The wheels were down, and we could breathe again. Nair said it was going to be touch-and-go, for hopefully the undercarriage would hold when we landed. After expending our fuel, we then landed without any further ado.

Every time there was a crisis or a near close shave, no one in the air force seemed to want to dwell on it, and it would be business as usual. I was also quite getting used to taking these things in my stride, so it was perfectly natural for me to strap into a MiG-23 UB the next day. We had flown across the Gulf of Cambay in the morning in the An-32 and on arrival at Jamnagar, I had received my briefing from Squadron Leader (later Air Marshal) Angad who was then a part of the very prestigious Tactics and Air Combat Development Establishment (TACDE). We were to first fly with a single Canberra over the Rann of Kutch, and then later in the day do another sortie with a pair Canberra flying formation.

Even as we were roaring down the runway, Angad had retracted his undercarriage and he proceeded to put the MiG-23 through the paces. Having twisted my guts in every possible direction as we turned and corkscrewed this way and that, thankfully Angad settled down and we sedately flew along with the Canberra which had by then linked up with us. The Canberra, like the Hunter, was a real beauty, and though it was a relatively large aircraft, it seemed to fly like a ballerina in the sky.

However, the real dance in the sky was yet to come. The second time we got airborne, we linked up with a pair of Canberras and after we had completed our filming task, I just sat back and enjoyed being a part of the formation which then performed every possible aerial move. When we landed, Dipti said everyone at the Jamnagar base had stopped doing what they were doing and had watched the three aircraft. 'It was languid, and it was surreal!'

The shooting was beginning to wind down, and we were now on the last leg of our trip. After a two-day stop over at Ojhar, we landed at Pune for what was going to be the grand finale for me. Wing Commander (later Air Marshal) Dinesh Chandra 'Tiny' Kumaria was commanding 6 Squadron (Dragons) which was flying the Jaguar-IM, which was the maritime version. Alok Upadhyay was filming us, as the three pilots and me walked to the aircraft, went up the ladder, and started to strap up. We started up, closed our canopies and taxied out, and then with the afterburners coming to life, we were airborne.

The three Jaguars quickly got into formation over the lush Western Ghats, and we crossed the coast near the fortress of Murud Janjira. We flew past some oil rigs and then dropped down to just over a metre, skimming over the sea! The aircraft were so low that the Jaguar felt more like a supersonic speedboat. We shot past two Indian Navy Rajput-class destroyers (SNFs) and then languidly turned back towards Bombay. A few more oil rigs and then we were gaining height, and soon the Air India building, and Marine Drive were visible below us. We then waltzed through the Ghats to Pune, orbited on finals, and touched down. As the parachutes deployed and we slowed down on the runway, the realization hit me ... the shooting for *Salt of the Earth* was over! That night we said goodbye to our crew in Bombay, deposited all the exposed film at Adlabs, and on 18 October 1992, Dipti and I flew back to Delhi in an otherwise empty An-32.

Now that the filming was over, we had a pretty good idea of what the gaps were. We had been looking for existing stock-footage and much to our chagrin, we had made very little headway with either Films Division or the Sena Chitra Prabagh. Since most of the required footage pertained to the British period, I sent a query from Nimmi Suri's office to the RAF's historical section that was based at RAF Hendon in the UK. Within a few hours, the RAF sent us a long-winded telex with film after film listed. However, the catch was that they also had listed the prices, which even included 'viewing charges'. Just to get through the material on offer, we would require a budget that was more than what we had for our entire film. We obviously could not go back to J. R. D. Tata, and Nimmi Suri flat refused to ask the RAF to waive the charges.

Two nights later, I received a phone call. The voice was very accented and initially I had no clue as to what was being said. The person said he was calling from the UK and had seen the request we had sent to the RAF. He said he was an old man now, but he had been in charge of the RIAF film records before Independence. The previous year he had visited India as part of the War Graves Commission and he said in his old office in the

'H' Block Hutments, there was a wooden box that was being used as a seating arrangement by the person whose office it was now. In the box, he said, we would find a lot of silent 16 mm films that pertained to the war.

I still wasn't sure if someone was pulling my leg. 'All the original films were shot on celluloid, and since the nitrate element in them was extremely inflammable, they were stored in Simla. Then came 16 mm which was made from non-combustible acetate plastic, so we converted some of the stuff and shifted it back to Delhi. Quite a bit of what you want is still there. I tried to tell the official last year, but he had no clue what I was talking about. My guess is, it's still there.'

It was well past 1 a.m. If this information was correct, we would hit the jackpot. I called Nimmi Suri. The air chief picked up the phone and growled, 'Kunal, this better be important!' I told him briefly about the call from the UK and asked him to come to the 'H' Block Hutments at 0700 hours. 'You know, you're asking the CAS to break into a government office! Ok, I'll be there.'

The 'H' Block Hutments had been the old Air HQ before Vayu Bhawan had been built. DSC guards were doing their *daatun* when I reached there in my Gypsy. Three minutes later, star plates and flag in place, Air Chief Marshal N. C. Suri had the whole place on fire. '*Taala toro*' (Break the lock) was the command and the DSC guys did the rest. Sure enough, the wooden box was packed with cans of film, the Eastman Kodak yellow, black and red labels neatly marked. The film was all loaded in my Gypsy, and I shot off from there like a jackrabbit. Some other air force officers had arrived, and they were told by Nimmi Suri to get the office fixed 'quietly'.

I went and collected Dipti, who had slept through the entire drama, and we headed for Palam. There an An-32, which had modified An-12 engines, was waiting for us. In the crew room, Philip Rajkumar gave us the look. 'Oh, it's you two! We were told to pick up some precious cargo from Delhi.' I grinned and told him 'the precious' was the film, not us.

The box of film was loaded and Group Captain Ajit Keshav Agtey, the co-pilot, filled us in. 'Tomorrow being Diwali, we were picking up all the ASTE boys from various air bases. We were diverted to Delhi to pick you up. Anyway, welcome aboard.' We then got airborne and set course for

Jamnagar. Three technical crew were picked up, and after refuelling, we set course for Bombay, where one more airman was waiting. Late in the evening, we landed at Bangalore and taxied to the ASTE dispersal area.

'You guys are incorrigible,' said Philip, 'Always working. I'm told you need to be dropped in Madras tomorrow. But since it's Diwali, and I think you need plenty of ECBs, as commandant ASTE and with the powers vested in me, I am ordering you off for three days on a second honeymoon! All arrangements have been made. See you here on the morning of 26 October. Now buzz off!'

We had dinner at Caesars, and then Dipti had a brainwave. 'Listen, we are in Bangalore. I have an idea!' I groaned inwardly, for wives getting 'ideas' usually meant trouble for husbands. 'We should get Wing Commander Rakesh Sharma to do the narration for the film. He's a recognized face and he will be brilliant on camera.' From the restaurant we called Leslie Springett. He was most enthusiastic about the idea. 'Galloping wild horses! Why didn't I think of that!'

Despite it being a holiday the next day, the various wheels were set in motion, and we met Rakesh Sharma and his wife Madhu at their residence on 25 October. The film's edit was yet to start, so we figured it would be a couple of months before we would be ready to record with him. Rakesh Sharma then decided to show us a film in which he, along with other cosmonauts and astronauts, talk of the earth from outer space. Suddenly, boundaries seemed to have such little meaning, and the earth took on a completely different meaning when looked at from above. As we were leaving, from a little notebook, Rakesh pulled out a piece of paper, which he gave to Dipti and me.

'Who else has seen the rainbow's end ... The real reason why birds sing ... Because I fly ... I envy no man!'

I could never find the origins of the poem and suspected that the wing commander had written them himself. Nevertheless, they would be used as the opening lines of the film, spoken as the MiG-25 Foxbat unstuck from the shimmering runway at Bareilly.

The next day, true to his word, Philip Rajkumar gave us an Avro HS-48 to fly us from Bangalore to Tambaram. At ASTE, test pilots are supposed to be able to fly any type of plane, and it was soon obvious to us that neither of the two flight lieutenants at the controls had a clue about the Avro, for both were reading from manuals in their laps. Seeing our worried looks, they promptly put on their most reassuring smiles and gave us a thumbs up, the universal sign in the IAF that says 'I haven't a clue but you need not worry'. We then took off and wobbled all the way to the east coast, and somehow the two pilots between them managed to bring the Avro down on the runway. After a quick diversion to show Dipti MCC, we reached Prasad Labs where they had the facility to telecine the stock-footage from film to video tapes.

The process was extremely expensive, so we had to be extremely selective. RIAF related footage apart, I was intrigued to see the film coverage of the Royal Indian Navy (RIN) and even some of the battles fought by the 14th Army in Burma. Though all the footage was silent, one had a fair idea of what one was looking at. For the purpose of *Salt of the Earth*, we had adequate material. The cans of film were then packed up and sent back with the air force to Delhi, where it was put back in the box. However, by now the cat was out of the bag and the footage was then duly transferred to Sena Chitra Prabhag's custody under the MOD. Later, when we did the *Naval Dimension* films and I wanted the RIN footage, despite the navy's best efforts, we could not get past the red tape involved.

Another Avro HS-48 flew us back from Tambaram to Bombay, where we settled down to view all the rushes of the film. After two weeks all the footage was moved to Delhi, where it was then entirely Dipti's edit. Finally, on 20 January 1993 we were ready to record with Rakesh Sharma, which was done in the Bangalore Planetarium over the next two days. We then drove to Madras where we got the news that Niti, Dipti's elder sister, had delivered a baby girl. After a two-week break in Bombay, we then returned to lay the commentary tracks on the final film.

Doordarshan continued to have a complete monopoly even then. K. P. Singh Deo was the information and broadcasting minister, and we now had to get the film to be aired on the National Network. Having served in the TA, the minister was extremely gung-ho about the film as well. Along with Adi Sethna, we found ourselves sitting in his office when the director general (DG) of the television bemouth walked in.

'We'll give you a slot from 11 p.m. to midnight,' said the DG generously.

'Sorry, sir,' I found myself saying, 'We will only give the film to Doordarshan if we get the hour-long slot between the Hindi and English News!' The DG looked at me askance, for he knew we had no other platform to air the film.

'We cannot lose revenue.' The DG was adamant. Then he slyly said, 'Ask J. R. D. Tata to pay the advertising money and we'll give you the slot.' That was a tactical blunder on the DG's part. K. P. Singh Deo now got into the act and with the minister holding forth about how money was not everything, the DG had to beat a strategic retreat.

On 21 March we held the premiere at the Taj Man Singh Hotel in New Delhi. The hall was packed with people and there was no room to even sit. I wandered back to the bar and poured myself a whisky and found myself standing next to Natty. After a couple of minutes, Doru too joined us, and the three of us stood there alternately staring at the ice cubes in our glasses and then occasionally looking up at the film as it ran on the screen. Natty then looked at me, raised his glass and said, 'Here's to you and Dipti!'

J. R. D. Tata had wanted us to make the IAF feel nine feet tall. That evening, I think we more or less had achieved that objective. 'Here's to the boys in blue, sir!' Two days later, on 23 March 1993, after almost a year's slog, we all sat down to watch the film come alive at Prime Time across television screens all over India. It was magical!

The next morning the DG called us at home. He was almost incoherent. 'The air force film outstripped Chitrahar's viewership.' As far as Doordarshan was concerned, that then seemed to be the only yardstick to measure the success or failure of any programme. 'Can we re-run the film again tonight?' My business sense kicked-in, and I said sure, but Doordarshan would have to pay us a royalty for that. 'How much do you want?' Like an idiot, I asked for a lakh! 'Done!' he said.

18

The Naval Dimension & Green Flash

It was only in February that we realized Dipti was expecting. However, shortly afterwards, disaster struck as the water bag burst and we lost the baby. The doctors promptly put the blame on all the flying, but frankly there was little likelihood of that having been the case. For both of us, it was a major traumatic setback, but life had to go on, and since the edit of the film was at a crucial stage, we got down to the grind.

After the screening of the film, two VHS copies were sent to J. R. D. Tata who expressed his desire to meet us. Dipti needed a few more days before she was fit enough to fly, so the meeting was fixed for 30 April 1993. The first thing JRD said when we walked in, 'Why have you sent me two copies?' We promptly responded saying one copy was for Mrs Britanniawallah. 'Ah,' he said, 'that was thoughtful of you. For a while I thought I had given you too much money.'

JRD knew about Dipti's miscarriage, and for the next ten minutes he spoke to both of us and the importance of having a family. He then showed us the window leading to his office that had been broken into and much to his horror, the prized model of his Leopard Moth had been stolen. He then asked me to brief him about the Siachen problem, which I did in some detail. We had been with him for more than an hour, and as we prepared to leave, he took Dipti's hand and said, 'I don't usually encourage these things, but someday maybe you could make a film about me.' Five months later, JRD would pass away. Maybe someday, one will be able to honour his memory for he had played a pivotal role in our lives.

There had been a change of command in the army, and General Bipin Joshi had taken over as COAS in June. Shortly after taking over, he asked me to see him, and he said that the army was willing to pull out all stops and we should start planning on making a series of films. The next day the media was being taken to Srinagar for a press conference as a large number of Kashmiri youth had been caught by the army while they were being taken to Pakistan for training. The general said both Dipti and I were manifested on the flight, and that he wanted us to help them streamline the newly set up army liaison cell. So, on 10 August 1993, we both flew in an An-32 to Srinagar, and watched the army put up a show for the press, especially the foreign media. The whole exercise was ham-handed, and no one was impressed or fooled. The army had blown it the moment we landed, for there was a big banner at the airstrip itself that proudly proclaimed, 'Media Management Team welcomes you to the Kashmir Valley.'

We landed back at Palam late in the evening, and the next day I briefed Bipin Joshi. 'You don't "manage" the media,' I told him. 'Just ensure the free-flow of information and people who can help interpret what is being put out because very few journalists are cued up on matters military.' The general, whose vocabulary in Punjabi would have made media headlines, was extremely earthy and quick to grasp what I was saying. He issued some directives then that were to stand us in good stead even during the Kargil War six years later.

The Indian Navy too had seen the impact of *Salt of the Earth* and they too reached out to us. Vice Admiral R. B. 'Bunny' Suri was the chief of personnel (COP) and I was introduced to Commodore Arun 'Sacchu' Sachdeva. 'Work out a three-part history of the navy,' the admiral said, 'the CNS is all for it.'

'The script for the IAF took almost six-seven months,' I said. 'I need time to understand what we need to do.'

'Well, you have carte blanche,' said Bunny Suri. As I was getting up to leave, the admiral added, 'There's one more thing. We'll give you all the support you need. Ships, helicopters, aircraft ... submarines ... but you'll have to raise the money.' I grinned. I had heard that one before. But then I had a secret weapon up my sleeve, which was Adi Sethna. We did a few reconnaissance trips mainly to Bombay, where we met submariners and visited a few ships. Despite having grown up in the army, I realized the navy was a completely different ball game and I started reading up whatever I could on maritime issues.

We started working on the scripts, but it was time-consuming and tedious work. On 24 December we decided to go visit Dipti's sister and brother-in-law, Niti and Gagan Sharma in Dubai. On the morning of the New Year, the *Khaleej Times* carried a large feature on the making of *Salt of the Earth*. In India too there had been, and continues to be, a reasonable amount of coverage, which then allowed Adi Sethna the leverage to generate the funds for the army and the naval films relatively easily. Rather than a single sponsor for the films, the general roped in half-a-dozen companies that included Coca-Cola, Ashok Leyland, SAIL and Kirloskar Pneumatic. To make matters easier, apart from a quick trip to meet Atul Kirloskar in Pune, neither Dipti nor I had to do any follow up. Also, the funds raised were not for any specific film but for all six that were being planned for the army and the navy.

Unfortunately, despite the IAF experience, and partly because the other two services had a different ethos, in the planning stage there was no one playing the role of a Leslie Springett. The grassroots coordination would always be a little shaky in relative terms. By March 1994, we had the rough plan worked out for the navy. The three-part series would be titled the *Naval Dimension* and would eventually need to be shot across the globe. At Naval HQ, there was a lot of apprehension about shooting on video, for it was felt that radar signals being emitted by the ships would play havoc with any electronic system. The navy also categorically refused to let women on board the ships, so it meant I would not only have to shoot myself but do all the backend work as well. Since lighting up interiors was not my strong point, at a subsequent stage Alok Upadhyay or someone else would join me. Accordingly, with a crew cut down from 18 to 4, armed with a 16 mm camera, I flew to Cochin, where we embarked on INS *Ganga* on 2 April 1994.

Sailing out on a naval warship for the first time is a heady feeling. We moved out slowly from the harbour, past the Chinese fishing nets and then we were out in the open sea. By early afternoon, we had our rendezvous with INS *Vikrant*, after which we took off in a Chetak and landed on the aircraft carrier. The ship was in the midst of recovering half-a-dozen Sea Harrier jump jets, so from the moment one hit the flight deck, it was all action.

A short while later, a Sea King helicopter landed and disgorged a tall strapping figure. Admiral V. S. Shekhawat looked every bit the wizened sailor as he strode across the flight deck. Seeing me standing there, he turned to me, 'You must be Kunal. Your father and I shared a cabin in JSW. We were both Easy Squadron. After the air force, I am glad you are doing this for the navy.' He disappeared into the ship after that.

We kept buzzing around between INS *Ganga* and *Vikrant*, and after the CNS left in his Sea King, we were shown to our cabins where we would be staying for the next two nights. The next morning, I was flown to the Rajput-class destroyer, INS *Ranveer*. Last time I had seen the warship was when we had buzzed it with maritime Jaguars. The SNFs (standing naval forces) were of Soviet design and were extremely low-lying. Standing on the helipad, one felt the sheer awesome power of a warship. That evening I had dinner with Captain (later Rear Admiral) Ravi Kochhar on *Vikrant*, and the next day after disembarking at Cochin, we flew to Bombay by the evening flight.

Dipti was in Bombay with her parents, who had by then shifted to Lokhandwala. Though the signs had been there for some time, she had got formal confirmation that she was expecting. This would change the equation quite dramatically, for apart from everything else, it shifted Dipti's base to Bombay and reduced her involvement in the navy and army projects considerably.

Working with the navy, my social circle began to include retired naval officers as well. I had started playing golf, initially with my father and his friends at Noida, but then had begun playing at the improvised air force links at Race Course. I soon became part of a group that included Commodore Vimal Mohindra, a naval architect who had taken premature retirement from the navy. Vimal, a thorough gentleman, was a graduate of the Indian Institute of Technology and was extremely tech savvy, and he mooted the idea of producing an encyclopaedic CD-ROM on India's wildlife. Those were the days when computers were just beginning to come into our lives, and it was obvious technology would sooner or later completely change the way we functioned. Quite enthused by the idea, I met Sharad Gaur at his WWF office, and he reacted with such enthusiasm that whatever misgivings I had, literally evaporated. A meeting was held at Vimal's makeshift office over his garage in Defence Colony, and Meta Media Indica came into being. Sharad resigned from WWF and took charge of the project and before we knew it, we had a rapidly expanding staff.

To meet my half of the expenditure, I had to expand the scope of my own work. It was obvious by then that the *Naval Dimension* series was going to be a long-haul project, for unlike the IAF, it was not possible to move large ships around just for a film. As a result, when Sacchu called me to Naval HQ and asked me if I'd like to make a 20-minute film on INS *Shivaji*, that was located at Lonavala, I jumped at the offer. Though the film had a relatively low budget, it would at least help meet the staff salaries for a few months.

INS *Shivaji* housed the Naval College of Engineering and with Indrajit Neogi recording the sound while I handled the Betacam video camera, we had a wonderful time exploring the Western Ghats as well. Being a shore establishment, the film was deceptively easy to shoot, and since Dipti was in Bombay during that period, I did the edit with Sunil Rai at Kay Videos and handed in the film. INS *Shivaji* was promptly telecast on Doordarshan and it was extremely well received, so I was completely unprepared for what was to follow shortly thereafter.

Vice Admiral Vishnu Bhagwat was then the deputy CNS. Known to be a man of strong likes and dislikes, he was extremely put out by a series of films made by Wing Commander Bedi that were, to put it mildly, quite indifferently made. On 3 August 1994, having flown to Goa with a four-man crew, we had just embarked on INS *Godavari* and were being allotted our cabins when the ships internal public address system boomed out, 'Kunal Verma to the bridge. Kunal Verma to the bridge.' The ship was preparing to cast off, and the captain was holding a message in his hand looking most perplexed.

'I've been told to disembark you ...' There were no explanations, just a quick scramble to get off the ship and then we were standing on the dock watching the warship head off. Next three days there were a series of conflicting messages from Naval HQ in Delhi, which had us going around in circles. No one had a clue what was happening. Back in Delhi nine days later, I asked Sacchu what was going on. Looking extremely sheepish, he put his finger on his lips and whispered, 'Bhagwat!' In the evening, Sacchu dropped in at my place and told me his version of what had happened. 'It doesn't matter if you have nothing to with Bedi. Bhagwat at present hates all filmmakers and his office deliberately played this childish game with you. Just keep a low profile and don't react. I'm trying to sort things out. Trust me, please!'

I had no other option, but I was wondering what kind of a circus the navy was. Everyone seemed to be terrified of Vishnu Bhagwat and we were supposed to be shooting the navy's history over the next few months, if not years. In the meantime, I had to go to Dubai to purchase an underwater housing and a Sony video camcorder that would also be used for aerial filming. I was received at the airport by Niti and her husband Gagan, who then promptly went missing for a couple of nights. When Gagan returned to his by then hysterical wife, he refused to give any explanation. I would later find out he had passed out at an acquaintance's place for 48 hours, which was roughly half the time I was to spend in Dubai. It was obvious there was serious trouble brewing at that end.

Sacchu in the meantime, was being true to his word. A major shoot was being planned in Madras (later Chennai) at the end of August that involved not just the navy but the army and multiple other agencies as well. To depict the early history of Fort St. George, we had got hold of a massive Union Jack from the British High Commission. On 29 August, with the film crew in place, the flag was hoisted and it could be seen for miles around. It was also then lowered symbolically, after which we prepared to shoot a Gorkha battalion driving down Mount Road in the early hours of the morning, on their way to Madras Harbour where they were to embark on the Shipping Corporation's MV *Tipu Sultan* and onto an LST (landing ship, tank), INS *Cheetah*, as part of the IPKF depictions. Gorkha troops, who by nature are terrified of water, looked so grim at the prospect of boarding a ship as if they were indeed going to war. With all this action happening around, there were some fairly interesting snippets published in the local press that claimed the British had returned and were being fought off by Indian troops in 'pitch battles'.

From Madras I moved with the crew to Cochin, where it was yet to be seen if the 'Bhagwat syndrome' would kick in again. Sacchu had obviously been working overtime, for I was given a few sorties in Sea King B helicopters that allowed us to film the Malabar area from the air fairly extensively. This was followed by a low-level run all along the coast in a Britten-Norman BN-2 Islander that the Naval Fleet Arm operated. This extremely light aircraft was ideal to shoot from, for I could just open the door and sit there comfortably as the coast whizzed past on camera and otherwise down below.

We then hired a medium-sized vehicle and drove along the coast to Goa. At almost every corner, there was something or the other that was of historic importance. We covered the 750 kilometres over four days, not only shooting Portuguese forts and churches, but also getting a feel of the Zamorin's kingdom and an understanding of who the Kunjali admirals were. Sitting in Bombay, Dipti would be researching the route ahead of us, and I would connect with her every few hours from local STD booths as cell phones were still nowhere on the horizon at that stage.

This time around, INS *Hansa* was our base for the next eight days. I was given Chetak helicopters to film the coast up to the Anjadip Island off Karwar in the south, and then we were flown onto INS *Vikrant* that was exercising Sea Harriers off Goa. On 14 September, a large number of troops from the Maratha Light Infantry Centre at Belgaum arrived at

Goa for the depiction of Op Vijay in 1961 when India had liberated the last remaining colonial enclave on the west coast from Portuguese control. The military action, given the green signal by Prime Minister Jawahar Lal Nehru, had angered the Western countries, with President John F. Kennedy saying sardonically that Nehru's action was akin to finding a priest in a whorehouse. Pleased with the results of our first round of shooting, I stopped briefly in Bombay and then flew back to Delhi where by then, work on the wildlife CD-ROM was progressing in full swing.

Golf, as P. G. Wodehouse and so many others will tell you, is an obsessive game and I was pushing myself to the limit whacking that white ball around. On 2 October, I had one golf shoe on at 0430 hours in the morning when the phone rang. 'What are you doing?' asked Dipti's voice.

'Nothing, I was sleeping,' I lied. Golf does that to you!

'Liar ...' wives also know that, 'you picked up the phone on half a ring. You were off to the golf course. Anyway, listen, forget about the game. Get to Bombay. The baby is coming ...'

The earliest plane I got was the early evening Sahara Boeing 737/200. I rarely ever wear a watch, so turned to the person next to me at some point during the flight and asked him the time. '1746,' was the reply. Call it what you may, but it was the exact time when Vallika was born. When I landed at Bombay, I was told on the phone that the baby had arrived. I had a Sikh taxi driver and I told him to drop me off at the nursing home in Lokhandwala and then go drop my bags at the residence of Dipti's parents.

There were three newborn babies cocooned and placed in a cot. Dipti's father said, 'Guess which one is yours?' and honestly, I had no clue. Luckily, the guessing game was not persisted with, and I was handed over my 'package'. It had been a near thing, for the baby's umbilical cord had got wrapped around her neck. Dipti was looking worn out but happy and we spent a long time just sitting together. My parents were in Kullu staying at the Indo-Tibetan Border Police officers' enclave, having started work on

Windsong Cottage, and that evening I got through to them but could hardly speak. Fortunately, they had already been informed.

After a short break of ten days, I had to fly back to Delhi and then proceed to Jammu for the army film's reconnaissance. The main area I wanted to see was the Akhnur–Jaurian–Chhamb sector where Pakistani armour had made considerable progress, first during the 1965 India–Pakistan War and then again in 1971. Major General 'Binny' Shergill was commanding 10 Infantry Division, and since we had done plenty of partridge shooting together, he took me around the entire sector himself. After we had crossed the Munawar Tawi and moved up along the Chenab towards the International Border, Binny looked at his watch and said, 'In five minutes, the first shots will be fired.' Sure enough, on the stroke of 1800 hours, the firing started, and continued intermittently until there was a long burst of light-machine-gun fire from the Indian side. We spent the night in a guest house at Jaurian where the then Major General (later General and President) Yahya Khan was reputed to have broken the bed with his mistress.

Having tied up the details for the impending shoots in Rajauri and Poonch as well, I flew to Srinagar and met with the local commanders. In autumn the Kashmir Valley was at its most picturesque, and I knew by the time I returned towards the end of November, it would be a completely different ball game. Apart from going over the ground, I was also looking at going to Hong Kong and picking up smaller Hi-8 professional cameras that would be easier to handle, as against the bulky Betacam units that would make me a sitting duck in case we got involved in a firefight. Given the nature of the filming, I had already decided to go in with just a single assistant, and for the task had recruited Havildar Deen Mohammad, who had retired from the army a year previously. A devout Muslim, he had served with 15 Rajput and had also been on my father's staff. Deen Mohammad was to be an ideal choice for he was completely devoted to me and would constantly pick up little bits of information that helped understand the situation from both perspectives.

In Delhi, Sacchu asked me to quickly make a short film titled *Victory at Sea*, which focused on the navy's contribution to the 1971 War. Work on the CD-ROM had exposed me to various new technologies, so I decided to use a combination of paintings and real footage of INS *Vikrant*. Once again, the film was an instant hit, and even more importantly, Vishnu Bhagwat loved it. Since he was also moving to Bombay as the flag-officer-commanding-in-chief, this would prove to be a huge boon. Suddenly Bhagwat was waxing eloquent about how his father too had served in the Rajput Regiment, and in a subsequent meeting with Adi Sethna at a high tea at Rashtrapati Bhawan, the admiral had exclaimed, 'That boy is a genius. Tell him the navy is at his disposal.'

The exact amount of foreign exchange that had been drawn for the trip was entered on the penultimate page of my passport. I reached Hong Kong in the last week of November and was to stay with my aunt Molly. At the immigration there was a long queue for Indians and Pakistanis, while all the other counters serving other nationals were more or less free. I was standing at the end of the line when a policeman of Chinese ethnicity came and rudely asked me, 'You Indian! How much cash are you carrying?' I told him it was none of his business and within seconds the situation turned extremely ugly. Unclipping his baton, he jabbed me in the chest with it and again demanded to know the amount.

I did not want to get into a fight with the policeman but rightly or wrongly felt I was representing my country, especially since the yellow sign with black lettering saying 'Indians & Pakistanis' was directly over my head. Fortunately, seeing the fracas developing, a tall policeman of European origin, wearing the rank badges of a superior officer, came across and politely said to me the policeman was within his rights to ask me the question. I just opened my passport and showed the amount that was entered at the back. Immediately, I was told that I was eligible to move to a 'business line', but I politely refused, saying I rather stand in the queue where I was. The cops moved away, and the man in the line ahead of me said, 'They can deport you, you know! Don't let your pride get in the way.'

Throughout my three-day stay in Hong Kong, I ran the risk of getting into a fight. My aunt Molly's apartment overlooked a busy shopping street in downtown Kowloon, and all the camera shops I needed to visit were right below. 'They don't like Indians,' my aunt explained, 'mainly because the Air India crew come around in *chappals* and are always looking for cheap deals. Mostly, they never buy anything!' Sure enough, the first few shops I visited the next day gave me the 'You Indian! No touch! No see!' I finally bought what I required and frankly was extremely glad to get back to Indian shores. At Bombay airport, the customs people were more interested in the pampers I had bought for Vallika, and hardly seemed interested in the camera equipment.

Things were moving at an incredibly fast pace. Forty-eight hours after returning from Hong Kong, I landed in Srinagar on 30 November 1994 with Deen Mohammad in tow. As anticipated, temperatures had plummeted since my brief reconnaissance trip in mid-October. A quick reaction team (QRT) had been allocated to me by HQ 15 Corps, that comprised two 1-tonne vehicles and a Jonga. The team was waiting at the airport and without wasting any time, we set off for Pattan where I was asked to report to HQ 192 Mountain Brigade.

I had covered Punjab fairly extensively a decade ago, but nothing had prepared me for how bad the situation was in the Kashmir Valley, which was nothing but a war zone. The first battalion I filmed with was 2 Garhwal Rifles who were conducting 'cordon and search' operations in the villages scattered among apple and other fruit orchards. As the troops closed in following their age-old standard operating procedures (SOPs), it was obvious that the initial dice was loaded in favour of the insurgents who could be hidden anywhere within the civilian populace. As the village got surrounded, the men, women and children came out of the houses and as per instructions given over a megaphone, they formed little groups and sat down in the open. Just then I came face-to-face with a 'spotter' and it sent a chill down my spine. The man was covered from head to toe, with just two slits for his eyes, and he was escorted by two soldiers, one of whom was tied to him. He was asked to scan the faces of the crowd which he did with field glasses from his hidden position on a flank.

Nothing moved. The people just sat on their haunches, probably aware they were being scanned by the informer, for they had obviously been through the drill on a fairly regular basis. After what seemed an eternity, the 'spotter' gave the nod, which meant there were no insurgents among the people. Small, designated groups of soldiers then darted forward and entered the nearest houses. 'Usually this is when the first shots are fired,' whispered the officer who was escorting me. 'Stay down, and do not expose yourself under any circumstances.' As houses got sanitized, we moved in as well. Even then, each house was a potential death trap. The entire operation, which yielded no suspects, took almost five hours. Even extracting from the area was a painfully slow business.

I made my way via Baramulla to Sopore where the situation was even worse. Both 2 and 27 Rajput were deployed in the area, with the latter being inside the main town itself, which prior to the battalion moving in had been brazenly flying Pakistani flags from various rooftops. The urban scenario was even worse, for one could come under fire from a sniper who would be difficult to detect. Sopore itself was in a state of perpetual curfew, with no one daring to venture out on the streets. In the battalion headquarters, the civil telephone line would ring every now and then, with young college-going girls asking for officers by name. The adjutant, Captain Saini, was among the most popular. 'They are a major source of information. If explosives are planted anywhere, Saini gets to know through his network of girlfriends,' one of the officers jokingly explained. 'We really wonder how he has time to run the battalion as well!'

Sopore and the surrounding areas had been a nightmare and would continue to remain in a virtual state of siege for months to come. The situation on the ground was explained to me: 'Everything is under control until an IED goes off, or a shot is fired. The very nature of this kind of fighting is that we have to take casualties, but then we have to make sure anyone firing at us pays the price and cannot get away. With civilians all around, we also have to ensure there is minimum collateral damage. In the end, it's all about getting the right intelligence inputs.'

Sometime later, I crawled into a tiny attic on top of one of the 'safe houses' where an Intelligence Bureau (IB) operative was holed up. He was intercepting messages which were being passed using a numerical code.

There was occasional static but otherwise the voice transmitting from somewhere in Pakistan was quite clear. The IB man was writing down the numbers ... something something 31 ... something 31 ... again and again, after every two or three numerical 'words' the number 31 would be repeated. I was filming the scenario in the near dark room, making sure the IB operative's identity was not compromised. Finally, I asked, '*Yeh 31 kya hai?*' (What is the significance of 31?)

'Kill!' It was the shortest, most chilling answer I could have got.

10 Bihar had been with 18 Rajput in the Battle of Ashuganj during the Bangladesh War in 1971. The day before I had reached Srinagar, the battalion had got embroiled in a firefight with four Afghans at Dajipura. The CO, Lieutenant Colonel Harsh Uday Singh Gaur had been killed in the exchange. A message was received from HQ 15 Corps that I should proceed to the area immediately. Dajipura was situated on the flank of the Wular Lake and when I got there, we rendezvoused with a platoon of troops who came in from the other direction. With my QRT also joining them, our party of some fifty men began to move through the village towards the location where the firefight had occurred. Walking amidst the group, was a 'spotter', who was once again covered from head to toe in his eerie outfit.

Major Kashmir Ghosh, who was officiating CO 10 Bihar, had sent a platoon with an officer who started to brief me in detail about what had happened. 'This was an ammunition party of sorts, who were moving on the track above the village. Colonel Gaur and his QRT was passing when they saw these suspicious looking people, and without waiting for reinforcements, he rushed up the slope. 10 Bihar had not lost a single man in operations until then, and they used to say if we take casualties, the CO was going to be the first, for he was always leading from the front.'

Just then, there was a strange sound, quickly building up to a crescendo as women started to emerge from the houses all around us. Mostly in the 40s and 50s, they came out with their *phirans* held up, exposing their swinging naked breasts. Safety catches on weapons were switched off and our entire party came to a halt under this bewildering onslaught. There must have been close to sixty-odd women and they were all hollering at the top of their voices. 'What the heck ...' I was so stunned

I forgot to reach for the camera, instead instinctively reaching for my own weapon, which I also had to carry for my own protection.

The 'spotter' saved the day! Holding up both his arms, he stepped forward and shouted something in Kashmiri. As the hollering stopped, he repeated what he had said again, which promptly led to the women dropping the *phirans*, regaining their modesty and going back into their houses. In two minutes, there was not a soul visible, just some children and young women looking at us from open windows. I turned to the spotter and asked him what had he said.

'I told them we were not looking for militants but were making a film. They do this when the army moves in ... they warn everyone in the area that the soldiers are coming.'

'It's the SOP,' said the officer. 'They do this if any prisoners are also taken. Our men do not know how to react, and in some cases, they have been killed by having their testicles crushed. If the women of a village don't do this, their men are pulled out by the militants and shot in front of them subsequently.'

From Dajipura I moved to Watlab, where I spent time with 26 Punjab that was being commanded by Colonel S. M. Chib. The two days I was with the battalion, I shared the room with Captain Devashish Sharma, the battalion's medical officer. He had been with the battalion for almost a year, having earlier served with 10 Garhwal Rifles. Devashish talked late into the night, reliving countless operations, where he had seen so many casualties, he could not even remember them. 'It's a joke sir,' he said, 'this entire militancy. No one is interested in solving the problem. It just goes on and on. How many more lives will we lose, I wonder?' The next day, during another cordon and search operation at Watlab, I filmed him treating the villagers as well. That footage would become his memorial, for he was killed 72 hours later in a similar operation at Dangarpur village. Shot in the thigh during an intense firefight, the young doctor in his twenties would refuse to be evacuated until he got all the other casualties out. By the time they got him to the Base Hospital in Srinagar, he had bled to death.

On 8 December, Deen Mohammad and I flew to Jammu for the second phase of filming. The two weeks we spent in the region, mostly around

Poonch, were dedicated to enactments we had to do that mainly pertained to the fighting in 1948 and 1965. Poonch is situated in a valley that is overlooked by Pakistani positions. It had valiantly held out during the siege 46 years previously, and as part of the filming, we spent one morning around the Betar Nullah enacting foraging parties going out under escort looking for food. Using gun cotton explosive slabs, we were depicting artillery shelling. At 1200 hours I got a message from HQ 25 Division asking me to stop the explosions as a helicopter was coming in to evacuate the local MLA who had had a heart attack. Since we had finished in any case, we also packed up and came back to Moti Mahal, where I was staying.

That evening, we received intelligence intercepts from our side of the border where a lot of Pakistani operatives had reached out to their handlers and claimed the explosions were acts of sabotage committed by them, with serious casualties on the Indian side. The MLA's entourage and his evacuation further added colour to the unfolding running commentary. We were at the bar in the evening when Radio Azad Kashmir announced gleefully that a 'Major Kunal Verma' had been killed by the brave Mujahids. The news had me spill my beer all over the place.

We then climbed up to Raja Rani where the epic battle fought by Lieutenant Colonel N. N. Khanna's 2 Sikh had taken place in 1965. Our plan was to use a platoon of Border Security Force (BSF) jawans as Pakistani troops on the leeward side of the feature, but as luck would have it, they failed to turn up and we soon received a radio message that they had to turn back for some reason. I'm not sure now, but I think it was 8 Jat that was deployed there at the time, and the JCO said to me, why don't you ask the Pakistanis to play the role of Pakistanis? The officer who was with me just shrugged his shoulders, so we moved along the crawl trench to a particular spot and the JCO shouted, *'Saathi, Saathi!'* and soon there was a Pakistani soldier with big moustaches looking over the wall. *'Yeh saab apse baat karna chahate hain ...'* (This officer wants to talk to you).

We did some hard negotiations and the Pakistani agreed that his men would be at my disposal provided they were 'adequately compensated'. I offered him three bottles of rum, but he slyly upped the stakes and asked for a case. Four, I said. Eight, he said. Six, we agreed! In advance, he said, underlining the fact that we were enemies after all! Half in advance, half later, I said. Next half hour there was a flurry of activity, and suddenly both sides were openly standing around. Twenty Pakistani troops with their rifles then came across and for the next three to four hours we all had a great time, setting off gun cotton explosions with men running this way and that firing off live ammunition. Deen Mohammad made a few friends, so did the Jats, who were otherwise lousy actors, for they would freeze every time I swung the camera in their direction. The Pakistanis then went back and by the evening, everyone was back in their bunkers, their weapons sited in each other's direction.

Dipti and Vallika had moved from Bombay to Noida by then, so from Jammu I flew back to Delhi for four days. Then on 26 December, once again Deen Mohammad and I landed in Srinagar for the third phase of the shoot. My QRT was there at the airport, and everyone was very happy to see each other again. However, the landscape had changed considerably. Not only was it much colder, as we approached Baramulla, the entire area was covered with snow. We were issued snow boots, army parkas and AK-47s, so that we did not look any different from the rest of the party.

Once more we were back to the routine of cordon and searches, road opening parties and getting into the odd gun fight. After a while, one gets habituated to the environment, to the extent that you stop even noticing the human suffering and start viewing everything purely in tactical terms, which boils down to 'where will the next shots come from?'

I had moved to Manasbal where the newly raised 13 Rashtriya Rifles was sharing the camp with 10 Bihar. I was happily digging into wild boar pickle with some good whisky with the CO, Colonel R. S. Jamwal, when a message came from the GOC 8 Mountain Division, Major General Sarabjit Singh Grewal, that I needed to meet Major Kashmir Ghosh, who would brief me about an 'opportunity' that had come up. I went across to the neighbouring battalion headquarters where I was given a full briefing. A senior militant was in the process of negotiating his own surrender with 10 Bihar and the pro-India group, the Ikhwan-ul-Muslemoon, under Mohammad Yusuf 'Kuka' Parray. Kashmir Ghosh said I could spend four to five days with one of the Hizbul Mujahideen groups that was operating in the area. Of course, the major added, the choice to go or not to go was entirely mine.

It was three in the morning on a pitch-black night on the eve of the New Year, the temperature was further plummeting, and the sides of the road had over ten feet of snow. Wearing a straw-coloured phiran over my jacket I had the Canon video camera with four spare batteries, a small tripod, half-a-dozen tapes and a slightly damaged 10-year-old identity card that said I was from the AP. Making me even more uncomfortable was a 9 mm Beretta tucked away in the waistband of my trousers, with two fully loaded magazines. The pistol was a last-minute addition to my gear, handed to me by Ravi Jamwal after I had got out of his Jonga at Milestone 7. 'It's a captured weapon,' he had said, 'throw it away if you don't need it.' Before I could protest, he had driven away. He had spent the last few hours trying to convince me not to accept the Hizbul Mujahideen's offer to film with them, but the meeting had been arranged and though I was terrified at one level, I had decided to go ahead with the rendezvous anyway. '*You're crazy*,' had been his mantra. At that moment I guess I agreed with him.

It was so cold there was no ambient sound, no crickets, no cicadas, not even a whisper of a sound. An hour seemed to be a lifetime and then out of nowhere someone had grabbed both my arms and a sack was put over my head. A voice told me to start walking, and with two men holding me from either side I was frogmarched roughly along. First, I tried to count ... twenty-five steps to the right ... fifteen to the left but it was useless, so I gave up within the first minute itself. We must have been walking like that for half an hour, though I suspected we were still pretty close to where I had originally been picked up. We went up a stairway, and finally the sack was yanked off my head and my arms freed.

The room was carpeted with mattresses, and it had about a dozen men, all wearing the trademark *phirans* looking at me. Each man had an AK-47, those who had come in with me were holding theirs, while those who were sitting there from before had their weapons by their side. A mild-mannered man with a bald head, whose voice I recognized as the one that told me to start walking, introduced himself as the 'Peer' and for the next four days he was rarely more than two feet away from me.

A young girl, her head covered in a floral *hijab*, handed me a cup of tea that I gratefully accepted. Then the 'Peer' started to introduce the others, starting with one man who had a pock-marked face and obviously was their kingpin. Meet Lieutenant General so-and-so ... (I didn't catch his name, but I think he said Saibuddin or something like that ... *'Yeh yeha ke army commander hain ... inhone army ka teen head shot kiya hai ... aur baiaasi aurto ka balatkar kiya hai'* (He is the local army commander, and he has shot in the head three army personnel and raped eighty-two women). I couldn't believe my ears! I stopped the 'Peer' and asked, 'Can I film the introduction?' Amazingly he said yes, so I put the camera on the tripod and started rolling ... the introduction was repeated while pock-marked grinned hideously.

As I bent down to look through the viewfinder, the pistol popped out of my waistband and fell with a 'thunk' on the thick rugs. My heart was in my mouth, and I was grateful I was wearing a *phiran*, for I sank down and groped around for the weapon like a pregnant duck. I was feeling quite pleased with myself for having recovered the situation without anyone having noticed.

I had to conserve battery, so I was filming selectively. I was asked to sit and make myself comfortable and drink my tea. Then the 'Peer' said in his soft voice, *'Kunal saab, aap woh pistaul ko side mein rakh do. Chub rahi hogi'* (Why don't you put the pistol away? It must be poking you). All the men in the room, obviously in on the joke, burst out laughing. It would transpire later that they had been observing me the whole time with a night vision device. They were better equipped than most infantry units, even their communication systems were superior.

In the morning we went into a mosque. All the menfolk from the village were sitting inside. Armed with a mike, the 'Peer' started his monologue ... *'Hindustan ki hakumat'* (the Government of India) was getting it in the neck in lavish doses, so was the BSF and the army, who according to the 'Peer' believed in the mantra—if it moves, rape it! The red recording light was blinking, but this propaganda stuff was getting on my nerves. I got two or three quick shots of old men, the stubble on their chins white, listening and nodding in rapt attention. I stopped filming and did something very stupid—I interrupted the 'Peer' and asked him for the mike. I think he was a bit taken aback, for this was not in the script, but he gave me the microphone. I probably didn't need it, but it gave me the authority to speak. 'How many of you believe this nonsense?' I asked.

No one said anything, they were all watching me. At one level I was scared, and my voice sounded as if my throat needed lubrication, but then I started to tell them what I knew was the background to Pakistan's invasion, the loot and the mass murders in Baramulla, the abduction of women by the tribal *lashkars*, the Deed of Accession, the fighting at Shalateng, Patan, Baramulla and Uri. Even the guys with the guns standing at the windows were listening. But no one was reacting, no nods of the head ... they were just fixatedly looking at me.

How and when this finished, I don't remember, but as I was leaving the mosque walking a step behind the 'Peer', an old man with cataract in his one eye stopped me by tugging at my phiran. '*Hum kya karen janaab,*' he said loudly and clearly, he then let his gaze travel to the armed men around me, '*aap ki baat sach hai, lehkin inke haath mein AK hain*' (What can we do sir? There is truth in what you say, but they are the ones holding the guns). The entire congregation behind the old man nodded their heads in agreement. The 'Peer' said nothing, just turned and walked away and I followed him.

At this point of time, we were six years into the reign of terror, part of Op Topac, unleashed by General Muhammad Zia-ul-Haq, his master plan based on the principle that to wrest control of Kashmir, Pakistan must make India bleed by a thousand cuts. As time passed, I got to know the group of chaps around me reasonably well. They all thought I was a part of the Western media, and they obviously had their instructions to ensure I wasn't harmed.

During those four days, I kept probing, trying to understand why young men in their early twenties could be enticed to live a life that would sooner or later meet a violent end. Religion? Not particularly, though on the face of it all the superficial trappings were visible. Ideology? Apart from the local politics of the immediate area they were in, they seemed to have little idea or interest in the larger picture. Economics? Perhaps in the case of a few. The majority seemed to be there simply because it was perhaps the only way to protect their own families. And of course, the language of the gun, which gave them unbridled power. It seemed incredible that this motely crowd and others like them could so easily hold a state to ransom! I kept thinking of Devashish Sharma, his life snuffed out, and his words that no one in power were in the mood to stop the militancy.

After their ham-handed attempt to blame the army for the rapes and the loot, the Hizbul Mujahideen guys didn't even bother keeping up that pretence. Next 72 hours were crazy ... gunfights, killings, dragging screaming women out of their homes holding pistols and carbines against their children's temples to force them to go with them, the wailing, the breast-beating, the misery, the terror ... and the constant lament, *'kya karen janaab, unke haath mein AK hai!'* became a blur in my mind. We were also hiding from army patrols, sometimes in lofts, sometimes in dark chambers dug below the floorboards. This was rural Kashmir, and the horror was endless. With no electricity to recharge my batteries, I kept shooting little snippets.

How exactly I got back to the army's side I don't remember. I was told to discard my *phiran* and start walking and was quickly intercepted and whisked away in a vehicle. That night I was with 13 Kumaon, my feet in hot water, my hands shaking with what I had seen. There would be some more filming, with both 3 and 4 Grenadiers around Kupwara but everything was a blur after the days spent on the other side of the fence ... the moment I took off from Srinagar for Delhi on 4 January 1995, it felt as if I had crawled out of my shell as a new me. It was all so unreal ... a different world which was hard to comprehend ... and yet, there was the film. Neatly labelled tapes ... thirty-odd days of hard shooting. Everything one had seen and felt, quite a bit of Kashmir's reality was stashed away in those tiny cassettes, without which I myself would have thought I had just had a bad dream.

19

Across Seven Seas

Back in Delhi, the army chief, General Shankar Roychowdhury saw the tapes, and so did Prime Minister Narasimha Rao. Lieutenant General (later General) Padmanabhan was director general military intelligence (DGMI) and we screened the four tapes shot with the Hizbul Mujahideen, unedited, to a select group of ambassadors and military attaches and newspaper editors. The *Times of India* which was writing sanctimonious editorials about the army raping people suddenly changed its tune. And yet, we sat with that footage, not knowing exactly how to use it.

Until then, all my naval shoots had been restricted to the western seaboard. There were no direct flights to Vizag (Vishakhapatnam), so after spending a night at Hyderabad, I reached Eastern Naval Command on 2 February 1995. During the 1971 India–Pakistan War, the Indian Navy played a significant role. Perhaps the most successful and daring acts had been the missile boat attacks on Karachi harbour. The OSA-class boats of Soviet design had only just arrived in India before the outbreak of hostilities and were primarily meant for harbour defence. The boats had, however, been towed all the way to Bombay, which gave those at the helm of affairs the idea that they could be taken across to Karachi and Gwadar, the two main Pakistani ports, and be let loose to create havoc. To add to the drama, until that time, missiles had rarely been fired in anger against any maritime targets.

The next morning, I landed on the INS *Savitri* in a Chetak. The ship was an offshore patrol vessel and had extremely comfortable cabins. Two missile boats, INS *Prabal* and *Chatak*, were scheduled to fire P-15 missiles, and my task was to film the launch. After a short gap, I was airlifted to INS *Dunagiri*, which was flying the flag of Rear Admiral (later Vice Admiral) Harinder Singh. The Eastern Fleet commander told me I was to position myself on INS *Savitri* a kilometre and a half from the missile boat and film the launch from there. I was incredulous, for not only was the distance too great, the sea state was also fairly choppy, which would make it almost impossible to shoot.

I stated my case and asked if I could position the helicopter just above and to the side of the missile container. There was a discussion on the bridge with gunnery officers who said we should be safe enough. As the countdown for the firing approached, I got airborne from INS *Dunagiri* and we quickly closed in on the relatively tiny fast attack craft, INS *Prabal* (K-93). The target was 40 kilometres away, and the missile was to be tracked by a Tu-142 aircraft that also had to be overhead at the time of launching. I was literally at a handshaking distance from the container. Since we were firing with a tailwind, keeping the Chetak steady was proving to be quite a task. Then, there was a wisp of smoke, followed by the missile propelling itself out of the container with a lot of fire and fury. I was holding my breath, trying to capture the spectacular moment as best as I could. The missile then 'wooshed' away, and I was wondering why there was a terrible smell. We veered off, our job done, and headed back to the flagship. As we touched down on *Dunagiri*, I suddenly realized that the smell was of burnt hair. Part of my moustache had got singed. We viewed the launch of the missile on the bridge, and then prepared to do an encore with INS *Chatak* (K-96) which was beginning to line up to fire.

With two missile firings safely filmed, the next two months were spent editing the Jammu and Kashmir footage. Port Blair in the Andaman Islands was next on the agenda in April. Since I was carrying my underwater housing, I was hoping to capture some reasonable footage of the marine life as well. Unlike the diving sets that we had used in the

Lakshadweep Islands, the ones being used by the navy were twin-cylindered and required breathing within a face mask. Both Jolly Buoy and Red Skin islands were a part of the Mahatma Gandhi Marine National Park and for the first time, I was able to use the underwater housing that I had bought in Dubai effectively at these two locations. Later in the evening, while heading back to Port Blair, we saw what looked like logs lying on the beach. Moving closer I got a shock, for the entire beach was littered with sixty to seventy dead sharks, their fins having been sliced off presumably for 'shark-fin soup'.

An amphibious landing had been planned, and I embarked on INS *Cheetah* and set off for Havelock Island. The LSTs had a very shallow draught and could come right up to the beaches, where they disgorged troops and even armoured vehicles. There was a lot of coloured smoke and machine-gun fire to battle inoculate the troops, but after the exercise was over, I just walked along the white-coloured sand and the tall trees, and it was the most serene setting in the world. Not surprising that in subsequent years it would become a major tourist destination.

A Chinese merchant vessel had caught fire and it had been abandoned between Port Blair and Ross Island in fairly deep waters. Someone suggested we film naval divers placing limpet mines underwater on the submerged hull of the ship, which could be used to depict similar actions that had been undertaken during the Bangladesh War. Accordingly, we set off in Zodiac boats, the naval commandos in wet suits while I was to dive with my 'buddy' using the twin-cylinder apparatus, operating the camera in its underwater housing. Diving in open waters was quite scary, for one had no references to orient oneself with. I was struggling with the camera as the naval commandos approached the hull of the ship, when I felt (rather than saw) a shadow glide past me. Ignoring it, I filmed the mines being placed, when again there was the same sensation of something large gliding past. This time I looked at my buddy, who was three or four metres from me, and even though the visor of the mask, I could see the look of terror on his face.

Willing hands pulled us onto the Zodiacs as we surfaced, and my buddy was actually trembling with fear. It took a few seconds for him to calm down and speak coherently. A large saltwater crocodile had appeared as we were filming and had started circling us. At first, none of the three sailors had seen the reptile, but then suddenly he had literally swum through us, coming face-to-face with my buddy. That explained the 'shadow' and having filmed these dangerous creatures in the Sundarbans, I knew just how big they could be. I think we were incredibly fortunate not to have been attacked that afternoon.

I also spent a fair amount of time at the Cellular Jail. Since I was shooting for the navy, the Andaman administration had given me a free run of the place. There was not a soul around and I just sat there for a couple of hours, just getting a feel of the place. After a while, one can see haunting images that come to the fore from within one's own being, and the screams in one's head get louder and louder. Though I would visit the Andamans again, this was the only time I spent time inside the Cellular Jail. Any apologist for the British Empire and colonialism needs to be sent there, just to see for themselves what happened in the confines of those solitary cells that were designed to mete out the harshest penal treatment day after day.

Framed on the wall, was also an old photograph of Netaji Subhas Chandra Bose visiting the jail after the Japanese had overrun the islands.

On 19 April I landed back in Calcutta from where I had to catch the connecting flight to Delhi, an Airbus 300. The large lumbering aircraft took off after sunset and almost immediately it was obvious that there was something seriously wrong as the air pressure built up inside the cabin as the aircraft climbed. It felt as if the eardrums would explode, but then the aircraft levelled out and for a few minutes it seemed as if things were normal again. I was sitting right in front and could see the city of Calcutta lit up below, when, out of the blue, the lights flickered and there was complete darkness inside the plane. Some people started screaming in fear, but they calmed down quickly enough. After a while, the captain came out of the cockpit and said there had been an electrical failure and we would be landing back at Dum Dum, but only after we had expended another half hours' worth of fuel. He had to shout and reassure passengers as the public address system was also not working.

We must have flown over Victoria Memorial at least fifteen times before we started our landing approach. The aircraft touched down, after which it seemed to be having trouble braking. There were a few loud bangs, which I presumed were tyres exploding, and then we came to a halt just near the boundary wall. Then there was complete silence. Not a whimper as everyone held their collective breath, waiting for instructions. In pitch darkness we waited, then some emergency vehicles with their yellow lights flashing approached the plane and people were evacuated one by one. I was impressed by the absolute calmness that prevailed, mainly thanks to the Indian Airlines air hostesses who were in complete control. A replacement plane was then flown in from Mumbai (as Bombay was henceforth to be known) and by the time we landed in Delhi, the sun was way up in the sky.

My parents had by May 1995 moved to Dochi, where Captain Amarinder Singh had a small cottage from where my father was to help manage the Maharaja of Patiala's mushroom farm, while at the same time completing the formalities that would allow him to be a domicile of Himachal Pradesh. We spent a few days with them at Dochi, after which Dipti and Vallika proceeded to Mumbai, from where they planned to visit her brother Gaurav in Reston, Virginia, with his wife Dilnavaz and daughter, Panah. I saw them off at Delhi and caught the flight to Calcutta, from where I proceeded to Jorhat and Dimapur. Until now I was fairly well versed with militancy in Punjab and also Kashmir but had little idea of how precarious things were in the Northeast as well.

Lieutenant General K. M. Seth was commanding the then decade-old 3 Corps and he himself gave me an extensive briefing regarding the situation in Nagaland and Manipur. I listened, incredulously, for the national media by and large had little or no coverage of what was happening in the Northeast. Originally, we were to move by helicopter to Leimakong, but the brigadier general staff (BGS), Brigadier (later Major General) A. J. B. Jainy said he had come from Imphal and there were no roadblocks by the Nagas on the road. Besides, he argued, that to get a real feel of the situation, I needed to travel by road. Major G. D. Singh, from the intelligence corps (formerly from 4 Rajput) was to be my liaison officer and the next day we set off for Leimakong in Imphal via Kohima.

GD, being an intelligence officer, seemed to know every Tom, Dick and Harry and progress was excruciatingly slow. First, he chatted up all the girls selling pineapples near Ghaspani, then he stopped to have 'tea and gup-shup' with every Assam Rifles and army unit en route, as a result of which the three-hour journey to Kohima took close to seven. Not too surprisingly, GD declared it was too late to proceed, and that there was a coursemate of his who would be delighted to see us. We spent the night at the post, and the coursemate who was from the Punjab Regiment proved to be the most delightful host.

The next day we left the post at Kohima in the morning. Our departure coincided with the arrival of two Naga boys in their mid-twenties, who had come to meet GD's coursemate with some 'important information'. We were travelling in a hired civil Ambassador and our driver was a Manipuri, but if you went by his looks, he looked more like a Bengali. We then took the road that linked Nagaland to Manipur, the only other approach at the time being from Silchar in Assam. 'If this road is blockaded by the Nagas, Manipur is at their mercy.' GD was explaining the internal political structure of the underground Naga movement when we crossed Zakhama, picking up speed as we moved through a densely forested area.

Though I saw the roadblock from afar, the driver initially somehow missed seeing the black flag draped obstructions and we just missed colliding with it. As we came to a screeching halt, we were surrounded by eight or nine heavily armed men who dragged all three of us out of the car. My face was slammed against the bonnet of the Ambassador, while the driver was hit a few times by a particularly vicious-looking character who GD would refer to as the 'half-breed' later. With a bayonet stuck against my throat, my head was yanked up and I could hear GD saying he was an army officer and that we were on a special mission to Imphal. The half-breed asked GD to produce papers. Just then there was the sound of shots being fired, and one of the Nagas was obviously hit. Fortunately for the three of us, the survival instincts of the group came to the fore and they literally jumped off the road into the dense vegetation and were gone.

As we had departed from the Assam Rifles post, GD's coursemate had turned his attention to the two Nagas who were standing quietly waiting for us to leave. They in turn had come to warn the coursemate of the roadblock. Our Ambassador was still in visual contact, so after the mandatory 'Oh shit!' and a few other Punjabi expletives, coursemate had barked out orders for the men to jump onto vehicles and take off after us. Their arrival had literally saved our skins, for the driver, who understood Nagamese, said the half-breed had been saying that they should cut our throats and leave the bodies around the makeshift barrier.

Too shaken to carry on, we retraced our steps back to Dimapur where Seth gave Jaini a right royal tongue-lashing for having endangered our lives. The next day, GD and I flew in a Cheetah to Leimakong. A couple of days later we flew to Imphal and then headed north along the Naga–Patkai to Tousam Post. GD pointed out the various features, emphasizing on the remoteness of the region. 'Each post has to be capable of withstanding a major attack. This area is all part of the demand for a Greater Nagaland.' To our east lay Myanmar, the entire border not manned. 'The trouble is, many tribes in the region are settled on both sides of the boundary, so weapons supplied by the Chinese through the Kachin Hills can hardly be intercepted.'

From Tousam Post we flew to Ukhrul, which was home to the Tangkhul Nagas, who though well within the boundaries of Manipur, provided most of the leadership that was spearheading the Naga movement. The helicopter left me at Ukhrul, which allowed me to meet and film some of the leaders of the Greater Nagaland movement. Plain speaking, simple people, there was a touch of naivety about the entire exercise. 'The Indians,' lamented one senior spokesman, 'they do not love us!' I couldn't help thinking that there was a complete gulf between people outside the Northeast, but also within the region. In Manipur, the Kuki did not trust the Naga, while the Naga tribes of various hues did not trust the Meiti who dominated the Imphal Valley, to say nothing of the people from plains, be they Assamese or from any other part of the country.

My Manipuri driver had driven up to Ukhrul from where I made my way to a fortified camp just outside Kangla Fort in Imphal. GD was waiting there and we had just settled down when suddenly there was the sound of distant small arms fire. Telephones started to ring, and the firing seemed to draw closer and closer. We sprinted across to the wall to see what was happening and could see civilians parking their two-wheelers and lying down by the side of the road as the sound of gunfire got closer.

The guards at our gate had their weapons at the ready when a convoy of three 3-tonne army vehicles came tearing down the road. The gates were thrown open and all the vehicles turned into our camp. In the leading truck, a soldier was bleeding profusely, having been shot in the thigh.

GD being the senior officer in the camp took charge of the situation and the wounded soldier was quickly evacuated to the nearest medical post. By the evening, just what had happened began to emerge. 'One minute everything seems to be completely normal. Then suddenly, there is a shot fired, and all hell breaks loose. At first, the JCO commanding the convoy claimed they were fired at by Gypsy-borne militants, but it then transpired it was a random shot fired from a hidden position just as the vehicles were entering Imphal from the direction of Thoubal. Instead of stopping and flushing out the hidden sniper, these idiots panicked.' GD fished out a paper from his pocket on which he had scribbled a figure. 'The army fired close to eleven hundred rounds in response and peppered the area. Thank God they didn't hit anyone!'

Two days later we headed to the Myanmar border at Moreh. I was surprised to find that the local population at the border post was predominantly Tamil and controlled the flourishing market across the border. The army had recently been given the responsibility of keeping the Pallel–Tengnoupal–Moreh road open and GD had grumbled about it endlessly, 'The only buggers who use this road are the smugglers! Imagine, we have to deploy ROPs every day just to protect them.' People were coming and going across the border post with the most perfunctory frisking. About a hundred metres on the Indian side, an open army Jonga with its windscreen down was parked, with four bored men from 6 Raj Rif sitting in it.

After spending two weeks in Nagaland and Manipur, I flew from Imphal to Dimapur where GD got off the plane, while I carried on to Calcutta and Mumbai. Ever since Vallika had been born, I was hardly getting any time with the baby, and six days later I saw them leave for the United

States along with Dipti's parents. I hoped to follow in a month's time, but before that, I had an eleven-day shoot in Ladakh and also had to tie up with the navy the planned shoots in Europe.

My entire focus during the Ladakh trip was on the Shyok River Valley. Unfortunately, promised helicopter sorties failed to come through, as a result of which filming on the Siachen Glacier became a non-starter. However, moving westwards along the Shyok, I got to explore the Chalunka and Turtuk villages, which had been captured by the Indian Army in 1971 and for a change, had not been handed back to Pakistan. Climbing up to a post held by 5 Sikh that overlooked the Pakistani approaches to the Southern Glacier, one could see the valley opening up and not too far away was Skardu. I was sitting out in the open looking down and reliving the horror of what had happened there in 1948 when the Pakistani commander had gleefully sent a telegram after the garrison had held out for months saying 'All Sikhs shot! All women raped!' when my small group came under machine-gun fire. I had to wait till it got dark before extricating myself from there and climbing down to the road below.

I arrived at Dulles on 7 August 1995 and was looking forward to spending some uninterrupted time with my then 10-month-old daughter and wife. Gaurav lived in what was a predominantly white suburb, and though he terrified everyone else in his family, I had a fairly easy relationship with him. Wearing trousers in the summer, for example, was a strict 'no-no' and even my father-in-law, Har Dyal Bhalla, turned out as was expected rather than face the wrath of Gaurav. I had hardly recovered from my flight when Dipti's father said we needed to talk. We went and sat on the wooden patio outside and at first, I thought I had completely misheard what was being said.

'Dipti has been through an extremely traumatic period. She feels motherhood has now completely shattered her dream of pursuing her film career. She feels you are not doing enough to support her and has of late said she wants to file for divorce.' Mr Bhalla was speaking in his usual, soft manner and I was completely thrown for I had absolutely no idea anything like this was in the offing. Before I could react and say anything, he continued, 'If the subject comes up, don't react with anger. She needs to express herself, so try to be understanding. Motherhood is a full-time job, and she is beginning to come to terms with it. You must realize she needs your support.'

As it happened, the subject never came up again. Ten days later, with the in-laws, we flew to Orlando where we spent six days at Disney Land, doing all the things tourists did. From there Dipti and I with Vallika branched off to Atlanta where Dr Mac Molnar was waiting for us at the airport. We would stay with them for a week at their home in Columbus, from where we also visited Fort Benning. The old house was still there, as was the Wilbur Elementary School.

After five days with my family's former sponsors, we headed back to Reston. After spending two months in the United States, Dipti and Vallika and the in-laws flew back to India, while I flew to Lisbon via London where I planned to film the early Portuguese history when Vasco da Gama set sail for India 'on a voyage of discovery' in 1498 on board *St Rafael* and *St Gabriel*.

The Indian ambassador to Portugal was on leave, but he had most thoughtfully placed his official Volvo along with his German driver at my disposal. The maritime museum at Lisbon had some wonderful paintings and records which I recorded on camera. In the afternoon I walked to the seafront and filmed the Padrão dos Descobrimentos, the monument built to mark the 500th death anniversary of Henry the Navigator and from where da Gama had set sail for India. With my video camera slung on my shoulder and the tripod in my hand, I started back for my hotel.

Walking on the cobbled streets of Lisbon, I was marvelling at the sheer beauty of the city which seemed like a giant art museum by itself. I was not paying much attention to where I was going, so did not realize I had walked into a bunch of fifteen-odd skinheads that included some half-naked girls in filthy rags. They quickly surrounded me, hissing in the most menacing manner and chanting 'Paki Paki!' One or two had flick knives and they closed in, hands outstretched saying 'Money! Money!' I backed up against the wall and was wondering if I should try and dodge past and make a dash for it or stand my ground and fight when two policemen on horseback entered the street. The skinheads promptly flopped to the ground in one ugly mass, and I walked away from what was undoubtedly an extremely dangerous situation.

The next day the Ambassador's driver Michael, while driving me past the presidential palace asked me if I'd like to take a chance and see if we could have a cup of coffee with the president of Portugal, Mário Soares, who he claimed was with him at Lisbon University. I thought he was pulling my leg, but the car had already swung past the white-plumed ceremonial guards. There were no obvious signs of armed guards though they were there, and we walked across to Soares who was most welcoming, even pouring the coffee himself. After spending twenty minutes with the president, where I grandly invited him to come to India, we walked back to our car and drove off.

After four days, I flew back to London, where I continued to film various landmarks that were of relevance to the naval film. I was staying with my aunt Roma, who though estranged from Nirmal Hoon, ran an open house as far as the family was concerned. Since I had a Schengen visa, I decided I might as well film Paris and cover the French angle too. Accordingly, I booked myself into a tiny hotel near the Eiffel Tower and flew into Charles de Gaulle Airport on 16 September, where I went through the immigration formalities. The next three days I was busy shooting on the streets of Paris, after which it was time to fly back to London. As per protocol, I presented my passport at the immigration booth which was next to the British Airways gate from where one was to board the flight to Heathrow.

The policeman took my passport in the usual bored and detached manner and stamped me out of France. Then, still looking at my passport, his eyes widened and he got extremely agitated and excited, addressing a string of French words at me. I had no idea what was happening, but by then the ballistic cop had picked up the phone and soon some more policemen wandered over, peered at my passport and got equally agitated. Soon there was an internal shouting match, as one faction of the policemen seemed to be fighting another. They seemed to have lost complete interest in me, so I picked up my passport and walked past them to the British Airways counter, where the airline crew were watching the developing riot at the immigration booth with a great deal of interest. They grinned at me, then tore the boarding pass stub off and waved me into the vestibule.

'Bloody wogs!' said the person at the gate, 'You're on British territory now!' I grinned back at him, and with no idea what had happened, boarded the Boeing 767 with a huge sense of relief.

It was only when I got back to India that I realized what had happened. My Schengen visa was a single entry that had officially expired when I exited Portugal. The French immigration officer had stamped me in without noticing the technicality, but the eagle-eyed policeman at the exit counter had picked up the error. I just heaved a sigh of relief, for inadvertently, I could have been in a lot of trouble.

Back in India, it was business as usual, with one naval shoot following the other. After a quick trip to Goa, I was again in Vizag with the Eastern Fleet. After a couple of days that were spent flying around the eastern coast and filming Foxtrot submarines, I embarked on INS *Savitri* and headed out to sea to join the fleet that was being commanded by Rear Admiral (later Admiral) Arun Prakash, who had replaced Harinder Singh as the flag. In the Ward Room, I was pleasantly surprised to find Flight Lieutenant Sid Siddiqui, who was on deputation with the navy. Soon we were catching up on all the flights we had done together in the Northeast, including the filming of rhinos in Kaziranga.

Arun Prakash was on INS *Kirpan* and the next morning I was ordered to report to him. With Siddiqui was Lieutenant Rajesh Vishnu, and we lifted off in a Chetak to do the short hop to the flagship. On the bridge, Arun Prakash looked at me coldly. 'You are here to film the missile firing. I am told you have done this before.' I told him how we had placed ourselves next to the missile containers and had filmed the two previous launches. Siddiqui also weighed in saying we had discussed the task the previous evening and could possibly place ourselves another few feet forward, so we could see the missile emerging as well. 'Well, if you two hotshots have it all figured out, go ahead. But I'm not risking two pilots. You fly solo, Siddiqui.'

Siddiqui was flying the helicopter from the right seat while I was facing backwards in the jump seat. INS *Chatal* was all set to fire, and we were completely focused on the task when two seconds before the launch, there was an electronic disturbance on my viewfinder. Instinctively, I told Sid to pull away, but it was too late, for the missile came out of its

Top left: Vallika and Veeha at Bandrol, 2001
Top right: First day at school for Veeha. Both girls studied at the Sri Ram School, Aravali
Bottom: Trying to teach Vallika how to cast for trout in the Parvati River

Top left: Elsa at Bandrol
Top right: Vallika next to an oil painting I made of the Bison Road Tigress
Centre right: With the girls in Shimla at the Annadale Golf Course in Shimla
Bottom: Veeha in Beverly Park

Top left: After winning the Doon School Old Boys' (DSOBs) golf tournament in 2007
Top right: Both girls were trained to ride by Beeya Vohra at the DLF Golf & Country Club
Bottom left: A golden mahseer caught in the Ramganga, Corbett
Bottom right: Veeha's first tiger in the wild at the Kanha Tiger Reserve in 2005

Top left: Shooting with the Angami Tribe in Nagaland in 2009
Top right: Along with the 3 Corps and assam Rifles books, work started on the Northeast Trilogy
Centre left: Myanmar in the background. At Moreh in 2009
Centre right: Dipti with a Naga child
Bottom left: The President of India, Pratibha Patil releasing the Assam Rifles book in New Delhi with Lt Gen Karan Yadava
Bottom right: The 18 Rajput memorial at Agartala that was constructed after the 1971 war

Top left: A red panda in Darjeeling
Top right: Shooting in the streets of Kalimpong
Centre left: Aerial view of Nathu La where 18 Rajput and 2 Grenadiers clashed with the PLA in 1967
Centre right: The bunkers that flank the pass on either side
Bottom left: At Nathu La with the Chumbi Valley behind me
Bottom right: Meeting a Chinese soldier at the pass half a decade after the Barbed-wire clash

Top left: The Tawang Monastery as seen from the road going to Bum La
Top right: Monks offering prayers in Tawang
Centre left: Gaon Buras out in their traditional red coats at Taksing
Centre right: Nah-Tagins, a remote tribe that inhabits the Upper Subansariregion
Bottom left: Tagin dancers at Daporiji
Bottom right: Presenting a case of rum to the Tagin dancers

Top left: Idu Mishmi's affording me with a traditional welcome at the Anini helipad
Top right: Dancers pose for a group photograph
Centre left: The versatile Cheetah helicopters that flew me to various locations to wrap up the aerial coverage for the Northeast Trilogy
Centre right: At Kibithu, where the Lohit enters India from the Tibetan Plateau
Bottom left: Women from the Adi Tribe perform at Miao
Bottom right: Cooking Maggi noodles on the Roing-Anini Road

Top left: The northern face of Kanchenjunga, the shot having been taken from well over 20,000 feet
Top right: Dividing Nepal from India, the Singalila Ridge. The Tibet Plateauis also visible
Centre left: Landing on the Sikkim Plateau at over 17,000 feet so that pilots could switch
Centre right: With the pilots of the two helicopters during a refueling break, March 2011
Bottom left: The Yoggyap La, which was crossed by Captains Morshead and Bailey in 1913 to survey the watershed
Bottom right: Andra La, the traditional pass that linked the Dibang and the Dihang River Valleys

Top left: Blaise as a four-year old in Bandrol
Top right: Pasha (to my right) was from the litter as Blaise
Bottom left: My mother in her garden at Windsong. For her it was all about the flowers
Bottom right: The girls at Bandrol. Vallika then was in her first year in St Stephen's College

Top left: Signing a copy of The Long Road to Siachen for Rajiv Sarin, who was my school captain in 1974
Top right: Lt Gen M.L. Chibber speaking at the book's launch at the India International Centre
Centre right: Gen Vijay Kumar Singh, Col 'Bull' Kumar and my father
Bottom: Krishna Kumar (KK) Candeth, who taught me English and Sheel Sharma, my former maths teacher

Top left: Barkha Dutt, Gen VK, Subramanian Swamy at the launch of 1962: *The War That Wasn't* in New Delhi
Top right: Ayaz Memon, Wg Cdr 'Jaggi' Nath and Ashli Varma launching the 1962 book in Mumbai
Centre left: With Captain Amarinder Singh at the Delhi Gymkhana Club Literary Festival
Centre right: My mother's 80th birthday. She is flanked by Vallika and Pushee Bhalla, Dipti's mother
Bottom left: Filming in West Sikkim with Sanjay Aggarwal
Bottom right: The pilot episode for Epic Television would fail to get off the ground

Top left: Presenting a copy of the Tamil Nadu & Puducherry book to the President of Taiwan, Tsai Ing-wen in Taipei
Top right: Standing next to a statue of Chiang Kai-shek during the NATO Conference in 2018
Centre left: Returning to Taipei from Kinmen, also known as Quemoy Island, which is just 3 km from mainland China
Bottom: Living life king-size with Vijay Maharaj (who was from Johannesburg) in Vietnam

Top left: DG Sudesh Kumar, Lt Gen Rakesh Loomba and Lt Gen K. J. Singh at the annual Military History Seminar in Welham Boys, Dehradun in 2019
Top right: The long-standing chairman of Welham Boys' School, Darshan Singh
Centre left: With Bittu Sahgal at Welham Boys' discussing the 'Enemy Within'
Bottom: All Rajputs; with Air Marshal 'Nanda' Cariappa (Gen Cariappa was 1 Rajput) and Lt Gen K.H. Singh

Top left: After moving to Kullu, the first puppy to find her way in was Kaali
Top right: The next day Bhuri would arrive, and both were named by my mother
Centre left: Romeo was abandoned, and he was welcomed with open paws by Bhuri and Kaali
Centre right: Bhondu, another large male who just decided to move in
Bottom left: The most intelligent dog I have ever seen, the mother of all the pups
Bottom right: Bagheera, Tipu and Akela, who were brutally poisoned along with Kaali in September 2022

Top left: Book signing session for both the 1962 book and also 1965: A *Western Sunrise* in Dehradun
Top right: Talking about the 1965 War with Maj Gen Jagatbir Singh, my classmate from school
Centre right: With Dr Pariksith Singh and Anirudh Chakravartty, two major players in the Value Education Program
Bottom: In conversation with Lt Gen Satish Dua at the Puducherry Literature Festival

Top left: Windsong under snow in January 2022, my second winter in the Kullu Valley
Top right: In many ways the winter is a lot less severe up in the mountains
Centre left: The apple tree and the gazebo
Centre right: Sana Durrani outside Hyderabad House
Bottom left: In a conversation with Air Chief Marshal RKS Bhadauria and Admiral Karambir Singh at the 6th Military History Seminar hosted by Welham Boys' School in Dehradun on 28/29 October, 2022
Bottom right: Back at the Doon School in 2022

container in a blinding flash and with the help of a booster rocket, initially gained some height, before dropping down and setting off towards the target. But then, for no apparent reason, it plunged into the sea some two miles ahead of us. While we were still circling around the missile's splash point, we were ordered to immediately land back on INS *Kirpan*.

On the bridge, Arun Prakash was looking extremely grim, and the look he gave me almost suggested I had caused the missile to malfunction. 'Why did you ask Siddiqui to pull away before the launch?' I realized then that our RT communication on the helicopter was being monitored.

'There was a disturbance in my viewfinder, the sort of thing that happens when radar interferes with the signal,' I answered. We all looked at the footage of the firing on the small black and white playback screen, but the disturbance had not registered on the tape, though there appeared to be some minute sparking. INS *Prabal* then lined up to fire its missile and again Siddiqui and I took up our position, staying a little further to the aft than before. Once again there was the disturbance just seconds prior to the launch, and once again after getting airborne, the missile crashed into the sea.

Back we landed on INS *Kirpan*, and everyone crowded around the camera's playback screen. One could barely make out the sparking, but it was there. 'The navy fires these missiles after they are past their shelf life,' grumbled Siddiqui, who was getting tired of having to fly without a co-pilot, especially since we were holding position with a tailwind which made flying very difficult. A third firing was then planned, and this time the flagship was to do the honours. This missile was either of a different type or vintage, for it launched off beautifully, giving me a terrific shot from a slightly higher perspective for INS *Kirpan* was a Khukri-class corvette, which though a small warship, was almost two-and-a-half times the size of the relatively tiny missile boat!

The next day I lifted off from INS *Vindyagiri* in a Sea King 42 C helicopter, and from Vizag flew back to Delhi via Hyderabad. Vice Admiral Sushil Kumar Isaac, later CNS, had taken over as the COP and Commodore Arun 'Sacchu' Sachdeva called the same night saying I needed to see the admiral first thing in the morning. I was asked to bring the camera and the footage of the tapes pertaining to the twin missiles that had malfunctioned. Plugging the output onto the large television screen, the electronic disturbance was evident. Two senior scientists were also present in the office. I never could figure out the technical jargon, but it seemed the filming of the missiles from so close, had given the navy a clue as to how to extend the shelf life of missiles that were otherwise fired as they neared the Russian manufacturer's stipulated shelf life.

By then, there was virtually no let-up in the shooting. A week later I landed at Port Blair where I was assigned a BN-2 Islander to take me to Campbell Bay in the Nicobar Islands. I was standing near the aircraft when an army Jonga pulled up, and the CO of 8 JAK LI, Colonel P. S. Khangarot stepped out and asked if he could fly with us as one of his companies was deployed at Campbell Bay. It was a two-hour flight, and since Subedar Bana Singh of Siachen fame was then still serving with the battalion, I jumped at the opportunity of spending time with the colonel. At Campbell Bay, one of the LSTs, INS *Guldar*, rendezvoused with us, as a result of which we had quite a mixed bunch of officers with us in the evening. Around midnight, we all piled onto what was perhaps the only Jonga with the army and set off further south to a beach that was supposed to be the nesting grounds of leatherback turtles.

Within minutes of our departure, it started to rain heavily and in the open vehicle, all of us were soon drenched, cold and miserable. The rain, slanting-in in the headlights, felt like pellets and was extremely painful. After a couple of hours, we reached a large beach, where we disembarked. It had stopped raining, and we had half-a-dozen flasks of coffee which we were all looking forward to. Two naval officers, who were still shivering and not wanting to walk, promptly selected a large rock and sat on it, while the rest of us headed off looking for the gigantic turtles. Every few hundred yards, there were deep furrows in the sand that looked as if a tractor had gone that way, but there were no signs of any nesting females dropping eggs.

When we got back, the two naval officers were incoherent and in a deep sense of shock. It took a while to figure out what had happened. They were both sitting on the 'rock' when it started its journey back to the water, and though there was no reason for them to be terrified, they both froze and went along perched on top till the water knocked them off.

Luckily, after a fair amount of searching, the six flasks of coffee were found in the surf.

The next morning, we made contact with the indigenous Nicobar tribe, the Shompen. At the time, there were reputed to be around 300 individuals, but their numbers were fast dwindling. Primarily a hunter-gatherer tribe, I filmed them harvesting honey. Unfortunately, since we had to rendezvous with INS *Guldar* off Indira or Pygmalion Point, we had to leave for the airstrip where the Islander had already started up. We flew along the eastern side of the island until we came to the lighthouse, which was the southernmost part of India's territory. After photographing the ship and the lighthouse from up in the sky, we set course for the two-hour haul back to Port Blair.

The sheer spread of the Andaman and Nicobar Islands is mind-boggling, as a total of 572 islands extend from Landfall Island, north of Cape Price in the Northern Andamans, all the way to Pygmalion Point (also known as Indira Point). I moved up to Diglipur the next day on INS *Cheetah*, but then was picked up by a naval helicopter which brought me back to Port Blair. The same evening, Sacchu called up from Naval HQ and said the navy wanted a film made on naval hydrography as INS *Investigator*, a survey ship, was leaving for Malta to participate in an international convention of hydrography. Sacchu then said the COP wanted to speak to me. Sushil Issac, who himself was a hydrographer, then discussed what we could do, to make the film special. Drawing on my earlier Lakshadweep experience, I suggested we shoot the hydrographers at work around Bangaram and Minicoy and pull out all stops so as to showcase our coastal region and islands as well. As we were very short of time, instead of returning to Delhi, I would have to fly to Madras and then onto Cochin where I wanted another survey ship assigned for the task.

We sailed out on INS *Sujata* from Cochin on 6 November. The ship had just returned from sea and the crew had to turn around and head out again for the waters around the Lakshadweep Islands. The next four days I had a whale of a time, filming hydrographic activity off Androth, Kavaratti, and then Minicoy. Using the ship's Chetak, I landed at Minicoy, where there was a small naval detachment that was being commanded by a lieutenant commander but was being run by Humsa Koya, an islander who was originally not from Minicoy, but Kavaratti. From skimming up a tree to get a green coconut to arranging a place on the tuna fishing boats, he was the 'go-to' man.

Humsa quickly improvised a 'spinner' by wrapping a piece of coconut leaf around a hook, and he suggested after I had filmed the skipjack tuna that were caught by the pole-and-line method, I should trail the handline out and see if I could hook onto some yellow fins. Not quite knowing what to expect, I tucked the wooden slat with the fishing line wrapped around it in my camera bag and then hung on for dear life as the boats cast off into some fairly choppy waters. In the distance, I could see INS *Sujata* as it patrolled up and down, staying clear of the island for fear of damaging the corals near the harbour entrance.

After half an hour, the boat I was on, spotted some gulls skimming over the water. We immediately headed in that direction, and it was almost unbelievable as the fishermen then took up position on the flanks and started hauling in fish that were literally plucked out of the water onto the slanting deck, which was soon a massive mass of five- to eight-kilograms fish flapping around as they slid into the cold storage below the deck. After I had filmed the skipjack carnage, I did what Humsa had suggested, letting the landline trail out. Hardly had the palm frond hit the water, that it started to rotate like a propeller, and it got taken when it was about 80 yards out. The initial strike was so strong I almost got yanked into the sea, but after the line had sung out till there was hardly anything left to play with, I started to establish some control. By then, all the other fishermen were by my side, and I was getting an endless amount of advice.

The yellow fin, after I had brought it in and it was gaffed, was around 30–35 kilograms. Out went the palm frond again and within the hour I had four almost identical fish on the deck. On a commercial fishing boat, the concept of catch and release would have made me look like a complete idiot, so even though I was loath to kill the yellow fins, they were soon despatched off by the bevvy of pole fishermen who had nothing to do until they ran into the next shoal of skipjacks.

Back on Minicoy, Humsa was delighted with my handiwork. A man with an extremely practical bent of mind, he improvised a rope, that was strung through the gills of the fish and then wound around the wheel of the Chetak helicopter that had come to take me back to INS *Sujata*. We lifted off with the fish dangling below, and once we had approached the flight deck of the ship, the helicopter hovered above it, allowing me to release the rope. Once the fish disappeared into the pantry below, we came in and landed. That evening, each member of the ships' company got a large, fat juicy tuna steak. The crew, who until then were not too happy about having been sent back to sea at short notice, now eagerly wanted me to stay on longer and catch fish for them daily.

The next day, when I landed at Minicoy, I took a carton of Benson & Hedges cigarettes for Humsa, who was over the moon at receiving such a gift from the ship. After shooting on the island, in the evening as I got into the helicopter, I looked around for Humsa but since there was no one around, we took off. Hardly had we cleared the tree line, I could see a lone figure cycling madly to get to the helipad, which was at the extreme end of the slim island. We circled around and landed again, by which time Humsa had reached the helipad. The downwash of the rotors blew his dhoti away, but that did not stop him from running across to me and shoving something wrapped in a newspaper into my hands. 'For Vallika ...' he yelled, and then backed off allowing us to take off again. In my cabin, I opened the package and in it were twelve large-sized cowries.

Back in Delhi, Admiral Sushil Kumar rather ruefully said the MOD had shot down the proposal of sending INS *Investigator* to Malta, so the film too was on hold. After a month's break in Delhi, I headed off again to Mumbai in January 1996 where various warships were exercising. For the next two weeks, I was virtually living on INS *Godavari*, hopping between various ships, including INS *Shakti*, the tanker that replenished INS *Kuthar* with both ships moving along at over 20 knots. Just for the heck of it, I got to jackstay from one ship to the other. Looking at the frothing water in the narrow gap between the ships and the sheer power being generated by the propellors of the two ships, I for one was very clear in my head—I much rather go by helicopter from one ship to the other.

Since the *Naval Dimension* films were not limited to just the navy but also the maritime history of India, we planned to shoot extensively for a month in Southeast Asia. In February 1996, with a year-and-a-half old

Vallika in tow, Dipti and I headed off to Cambodia. The Tamil Chola kingdom had extensive links across the Bay of Bengal and their influence was clearly visible in the temple architecture and carvings at Angkor Wat. However, the situation in Cambodia was extremely volatile at the time, as Pol Pot and the Khmer Rouge were still a fairly cohesive force. Even as I planned the trip, my father said I was out of mind contemplating filming in the region with my wife and daughter in tow.

In Phnom Penh we stayed at the Ritz where most AP correspondents had been stationed during the Vietnam War years. There were still plenty of signs of the collateral damage, with veterans without limbs sitting along the Mekong River waterfront, where we went walking in the evening with Vallika in a stroller. Two days later we boarded a Royal Air Cambodge ATR-72 aircraft and flew north across the expanse of the Tonle Sap to Siem Reap, where we checked into a comfortable hotel that also had a sprinkling of US Marines that were on deputation with the United Nations. In the evening, as the sun set, we climbed up to the highest point in Angkor Wat. Watching Vallika playing on the steps, I wished she had been a bit older. I looked across to Dipti who was also obviously thinking much the same thing.

The next day we found ourselves at Angkor Thom, which literally translates in Khmer as 'Great City'. Built around the remnants of earlier monuments, it was established in the twelfth century by Jayavarman VII and at the centre of the city is the imposing Bayon temple. Given the disturbed conditions in the country, there were not too many tourists around, but just a few UNESCO people who were restoring some of the temples. Someone suggested we also film the small temple in the ancient area of Hariharalaya, also known as Roluos, which was the first seat of the Khmer Empire. There was a relatively small temple called Preah Ko, which we set off to film on our third day at Siem Reap. We were driving back along an elevated unmetalled road when suddenly a T-72 tank with armed soldiers on top, loomed in front of us. I had no idea if we were looking at government troops or the Khmer Rouge. Luckily, the tank was not interested in us. The next day, as we boarded the return flight to Phnom Penh, there seemed to be some sporadic gunfire from the vicinity of the airfield's perimeter. Fortunately, Dipti was more interested in feeding Vallika barbeque-flavoured wafers, and she didn't notice the unfolding drama. At the Ritz the next day, the owner told me our flight had lifted off minutes before the fighting had spread to the airfield.

We would proceed to Jakarta and then on to Yogyakarta, where we filmed the largest Mahayana Buddhist temple in the world, the nine-layered Borobudur. Built in the ninth century, the temple structure reflects art from the Gupta period and is suggestive of the links that existed with the subcontinent. Despite being abandoned in the fourteenth century when the decline of the Hindu kingdoms in Java coincided with the advent of Islam on the island, the restoration work done between 1975 and 1982 was indeed most remarkable. With over two and half thousand relief panels and multiple statues of the Buddha in perforated stupas, from a filming perspective, it was a dream. Next, after filming in Bali, we moved on to Bangkok where we had been given permission to film scenes from the Ramayana that adorn the main Thai Grand Palace.

On our return to India, Vimal Mohindra dropped a major bombshell, saying he was opting out of the wildlife CD-ROM project. This created virtual havoc for a lot of work had been done and there were over a dozen people on our payroll. Until now, I had been supervising the content with the belief that Vimal would work on the marketing and distribution after the development period was over. At this stage, I should have abandoned the project, but then I felt particularly responsible towards Sharad Gaur who I had pulled out of WWF.

Faced with a Hobson's choice, I decided to complete the wildlife CD-ROM on my own. While the *Naval Dimension* films were shaping up well, work on the three *Green Flash* films was falling behind. Unlike the IAF where we could plan actions and execute them, shooting with the navy was a completely different ball game. For starters, most older ships like INS *Delhi* had been decommissioned, or as was the case with INS *Vikrant*, had been modified to operate completely different aircraft, though the helicopters remained much the same. One of the most exciting acquisitions had been the gigantic anti-submarine and maritime reconnaissance Tupolev-142 MK-E (NATO code name Bear F/J) aircraft and within a month of returning from Southeast Asia, I found myself driving from Chennai (as Madras was now known) to Arakkonam where the newly commissioned air base, INS *Rajali* was located.

I almost failed to make it. At Sriperumbudur, work was on in full swing on a memorial for the former prime minister, Rajiv Gandhi, who had been assassinated there by a suicide bomber. I was sitting at the back of an Ambassador car when a truck coming out of the memorial site hit the car from the left side. Just before the impact, I had thrown myself towards the right and that saved me from being crushed. I was lucky to get away with minimal bruises and a badly swollen foot, though no bones were broken. Getting to the naval base, I was horrified when the navy doctor on duty refused to look at my foot, saying he hadn't joined the service to treat 'bloody civilians!'

The Tu-142 sortie apart, in May 1996 I finally got to fly with the Sea Harriers from INAS 300 (White Tigers) though I could not do a deck landing on INS *Viraat*. There were endless sorties to and fro from ships, and I also got to fly in and film the Ilyushin-38, which more or less wrapped up the naval inventory of aircraft. By the end of 1996, I probably had ample footage of missiles being launched from various ships, rockets being fired and even torpedoes being launched. One also got to film the offshore oil rigs off Mumbai,

With the wildlife CD-ROM sucking up funds at tremendous pace, I simply had to step up the pace at which I was working, just to pay the salaries of the staff. Three additional films commissioned by the navy in 1997 succeeded in keeping our heads above the water. First, the hydrography film got the nod again, and off I went to the Lakshadweep Islands. Once again, I had a survey ship, INS *Jamuna*, that served as my base and the film, *Charting the Deep*, would not only have a tremendous impact in Malta where it was screened at the Hydrographic Meet, India also edged out Pakistan to land the contract to chart the waters off Oman.

At this stage, with Vallika requiring Dipti's full attention (the 'terrible twos'!), the naval edits also had become my responsibility. After a concentrated ten-day edit culminating with the handing over of the hydrography film, I headed off to Binaguri, which was the headquarters of 20 Infantry Division that was being commanded by Major General (later Lieutenant General) Tom Mathews who was from 2 Rajput. Situated in the Duars in West Bengal, the terrain and area to the immediate south were very similar to what one expected to find across the border in Bangladesh for depictions of the 1971 War of Liberation. Ideally, I wanted to film PT-76 tanks but had to make do with T-59s, and the footage was indeed quite spectacular as the tanks moved through villages and river beds.

End of March it was still fairly cold. To get a feel of the conditions I then moved up to Sikkim for the next ten days. Nathu La was the first port of call, and I was surprised to see no mention of 18 Rajput at the post, though 2 Grenadiers had their memorial right there. I was told there was a plaque with the names of the Rajput dead at the Baba Harbhajan Singh shrine near the helipad which was a couple of kilometres on the Nathang-Zuluk-Rhenock axis. While I was filming at Nathu La, some PLA soldiers came up to the boundary on their side, and we swapped cigarettes. The one common factor that was affecting Indian and Chinese alike was the cold, as sweeping winds from the direction of the Chumbi Valley swept across the gap at 14,140 feet (4310 m).

Moving 4 kilometres further south on the Dongkya Range, was Jelep La, the original pass that linked Tibet and Kalimpong through the Silk Route. There was a Gorkha battalion holding the posts in the area, which was covered in snow. Here the PLA positions were not visible, so I filmed our troops and then returned to Gangtok. Even though I had a fair idea of the topography of Sikkim, I frankly had very little idea of the lay of the land. After spending two or three days at Lachung, I returned to Bagdogra from where I flew to Guwahati with the intention of familiarizing myself with the lay of the land vis-à-vis the 1962 clash with the Chinese. Even though I had access to all the senior officers in XXXIII Corps, I realized that other than their own immediate AOR, few people had any idea about what existed around them—be it geographical, historical or anthropological.

At Guwahati, I was given a QRT, for by then the ULFA and other militant groups were quite active. As we approached Tezpur on the North Bank (of the river Brahmaputra), the level of security personnel seemed to increase exponentially. My liaison officer said a serving JCO had recently been gunned down just outside HQ 4 Corps, as a result of which everyone had his finger literally on the trigger. I kept thinking of that fateful night in Kaziranga and the weapons that I believe we could have so easily captured. I had dinner with the GOC, Lieutenant General (later COAS) N. C. Vij, who on a map gave me a fair idea of what was happening in the region.

The next morning, I set off for Bomdila via Bhalukpong. The moment we entered the foothills, the road along the Kameng River became a muddy track which had vehicles slithering this way and that. At Sessa, an army convoy had come to a halt, for falling rocks had ripped through the canvas top of a 3-tonne vehicle and grievously injured a soldier. Since I had the relatively lighter Jonga, we transferred the profusely bleeding man to my vehicle. My driver also seemed to have completely lost his nerve, so I took the wheel and somehow slithered and skidded my way to Tenga which was the headquarters of 5 Infantry Division. Much to our collective relief, the soldier would survive, though I was told it was touch-and-go!

Bomdila had fallen to the PLA in November 1962 with hardly a fight, but no one seemed to know what had actually happened. Though I was filming the various landmarks, I had very little information to go on. It was almost as if nothing had happened thirty-five years ago, and if it wasn't for the occasional stone slabs with the names of dead men that had been put up by their respective regiments, even those who knew would feel it was just a bad dream. It was almost as if the history books had been wiped clean; and to make matters worse, it felt as if no one cared either.

It was much the same story at Dirang Dzong. I particularly wanted to know where Lieutenant Colonel Bramhanand Avasthy had been killed, so I backtracked across the Mandala Heights, but the road conditions were so bad we had to return after a few kilometres. As we approached Se La, I tried to memorize the terrain, for dozens of soldiers had been killed between Sapper's Camp and Senge. After crossing the 13,700 feet (4176 m) pass, there was Nuranang by the edge of a medium-sized lake. The old headquarters of 77 Infantry Brigade where my father had been the brigade major lay abandoned, and I realized with a start that as a 36-year-old, I was probably three- or four years senior to what 'my old man' would have been then.

We followed the crystal-clear waters of the Nuranang River as it dropped down sharply towards Jaswant Garh, where 4 Garhwal Rifles had put up a brief, but determined fight. The old bunkers were still intact, and I went and sat in one of them, trying to visualize what could have happened. Directly below us was the village of Jang, and across the Mago Chu one could see Tawang. Even to my non-tactical eye, it seemed the Indian positions at Jaswant Garh were most defendable. I just could not understand how the PLA had got past the defences in just a few hours. The only word that repeatedly suggested itself was 'panic'. There was simply no running away from the hard reality of it—the Indian side, in all probability, the senior commanders had simply lost their nerve.

I could not proceed beyond Tawang, as the road towards Bum La and Zimithang-Khinzemane were yet to be opened post-winter. In the evening, after filming the Tawang Monastery, the brigade commander took me to an open-air theatre where he claimed there was a 'Sound & Light' show on the 1962 War. I think we were the only audience, and after a while, the cold crept in and our bottoms were getting stiff. The physical discomfort was only a miniscule part of the torture, for the entire hour-long 'show' alternated between jingoistic 'one Indian killed 300 Chinese' kind of stuff, and some serious breast-beating about 'how we were stabbed in the back' narratives repeated ad nauseam. Whatever the logic behind the show, it certainly failed to tell anyone anything about the clash!

Ever since we had returned from the US trip, we had hardly had any time together as a family, so with Dipti's sister Niti and her daughter Manavi in tow, we spent a week in Diu. The wildlife CD-ROM was at a stage where we felt we could show it to *National Geographic* and work out a marketing collaboration. After a presentation to WWF India, it was gratifying to see that they too felt the project was in a class of its own and were quite willing to sponsor a trip to Georgetown, Washington, D.C. where the National Geographic Society's headquarters was located. A meeting was fixed for end-November, which gave Sharad Gaur and the rest of the team ample time to get our presentations together.

As soon as I got back to Delhi from Diu, Sacchu called and said Vishnu Bhagwat, who had taken over as the CNS, wanted to see me. Wondering where and how I might have wronged someone, I walked in to find a smiling and extremely happy CNS. 'Your film on hydrography,' he said, 'was seen by the Sultan of Oman. We were not even in the running as it was between the Royal Navy and Pakistan which is a member of OIC (Organisation of Islamic Cooperation) countries, but he decided to give the contract to the Indian Navy. Just for your information, this will result in the construction of four more survey vessels.'

Bhagwat then said the chief scientific adviser to the government, Dr A. P. J. Abdul Kalam wanted to see me. Putting on his hat, the naval chief exited his own grand office and headed down some corridors in South Block with me at his heels. Kalam had no visible trappings in terms of PAs or PSs, so the chief knocked on the door and entered. The future President of India was at his desk in a vest, his shirt on a hanger. Least concerned about the contrasting attire, he warmly shook my hand. 'Ah the film on hydrography!' he exclaimed, when I was introduced. Admiral Bhagwat had settled into a chair, and I was also asked to sit down.

'We want you to do a film on all the work that is happening within India. There are multiple projects that involve defence, but we will focus on indigenization and the navy in particular.' Kalam went on to talk about various projects, including aircraft design and development, the air defence ship and more particularly about INS *Delhi* and INS *Mysore* that were being built at Mazagaon Docks. Kalam's enthusiasm was almost childlike, while interestingly, Vishnu Bhagwat just sat there and listened to him quietly.

I had been planning to edit the army films, but once again I found myself on the move. The next month and a half were as hectic as they get—starting with Garden Reach in Calcutta, I was waking up in a different part of the country almost every day. I could understand why Dr Kalam wanted the film to showcase only naval-related work, for the sheer scope of what was happening across the board, was impressive. The Defence Research and Development Organisation had not had much success with the army and the LCA programme was still in its infancy. However, when it came to the navy, there were not only the two Delhi-class ships, but an assortment of other work that included submarines, an air defence ship, and all sorts of weapon systems.

INS *Delhi*, then commanded by Captain (later Vice Admiral) Anoop Singh, had already been put to sea and in October I was told to shoot a small film that was to be shown to Prime Minister Atal Bihari

Vajpayee when he would formally launch the ship. Benu Jamwal, then a commander, was the executive officer of the ship, and I looked forward to seeing him again. Since the shoot was off Mumbai, Dipti and Vallika flew with me to Mumbai on 21 October 1997 with the intention of spending a week with the grandparents. The next day I sailed out on INS *Ranvijay* and for the first time got a glimpse of the Indian Navy's latest ship, which was a massive warship. I got airborne in a Chetak and took various angles from above and the side, after which we sailed back to Mumbai.

By the evening I was back in Lokhandwala, still recovering from the morning's filming. Dipti had not been feeling too bright and I drove her across to get an ultrasound done. I was sitting in the car making notes on the morning's filming, when I saw her walking back, with a big smile on her face. I had absolutely no clue, and for that matter until then nor did Dipti, but she opened the door and slid into the passenger seat. 'I'm expecting,' she said simply. The yet-to-be-born Veeha had made her magical way into our lives!

20

The Great Betrayals

The meeting with National Geographic was getting closer and work was getting fairly hectic. With over 4,000 images, hundreds of bird and animal paintings and 4 million words of supporting text drawn from various unheralded sources across the country, it was an extremely comprehensive work. We decided to call it the *Golden Bird* and all my spare time was spent making navigational screens. Apart from detailed sections on the habitat types, the CD-ROM covered not only mammals and birds, but reptiles, amphibians, insects, invertebrates and also listed all types of marine species that existed in the subcontinent.

While text hardly took up space, photographs even in reduced low resolution were heavy. Film clips were extremely space-consuming, but without them, the entire product would be incomplete. What also gave me a lot of satisfaction was the fact that we had to an extent succeeded in reaching out to scholars who had done some incredible work on wildlife and conservation across the country, but their work was buried somewhere because they did not know how to position it. Toward this end, Sharad Gaur had had a major role to play, and under him, the small team had done quite a remarkable job over the last three years.

I had decided not to as yet embed the movie clips, which had been edited and set aside for the CD-ROM. There was plenty of choice of high-class footage, for our *Call of the Wild* series, shot after Project Tiger, had been extremely comprehensive. Our problem was what to remove, for at best we could carry a total of 45–50 minutes of digitized video. To show the selected film clips to National Geographic, I had to convert the video from PAL, which was the global standard, to NTSC, which was the video format that played in the United States. The conversion was to be done in a studio in South Delhi the day before I was to fly out, but at the last minute, Dipti had some pregnancy-related issues, as a result of which I sent Sharad Gaur to do the needful. He was to meet me with the film clips at the airport. It was a simple enough task.

I flew out on 21 November and landed at Dulles Airport, where I was met by a representative of the WWF USA and put up in a comfortable hotel in Georgetown. Sharad Gaur had failed to turn up, so I called him from Paris. He gave me some story about getting the timings of my flight mixed up and was extremely apologetic. In any case, there was nothing I could do, so I told him to properly pack the tape and be ready to courier it to National Geographic. I would let him know the address and the name of the contact person once my initial meeting was over. Sharad then said please call your father, who was urgently trying to speak to me. 'Your mother has been coughing, and she has double pneumonia. You better come back immediately.'

The meeting with National Geographic could not have been better. I explained the delay with regards to the film clips and said the VHS tape would be couriered to them from India by FedEx the next day. The meeting ended with the head of the CD-ROM division, Bob, saying they would respond to me as soon as they had seen the film clips as to how to take the project forward as an India-specific joint-venture. A week later, I was back in Delhi, feeling the entire exercise had been worth the risk and expense. My mother's mysterious double pneumonia had turned out to be a minor sniffle, and all it did was to have me scuttle back as soon as I could, having cut short a planned visit to the west coast. Sharad Gaur said the tape had been despatched, but for a second I felt he was being evasive. At that stage, I had no reason to suspect any foul play. I hired another four girls to expedite the large volume of work but began to notice that Sharad was beginning to behave extremely erratically.

Weeks became months, and still, there was no news from Bob or anyone at National Geographic. At some point, I got a brief message from him with a photograph of the flimsy packaging in which the VHS had been received. Even queries by WWF USA evoked no response. To put it mildly, I was completely baffled by what was happening.

To make matters worse, though the text had been edited by our staff, I still wanted a professional editor to give it the once over. I had known Tarun Tejpal as one of the people who used to be in David Davidar's circle of friends. He had joined *India Today* shortly after I had moved to AP and I had been impressed with his command of the English language. He was at the time with *Outlook* magazine, and though Vinod Mehta was still the editor, Tarun was de facto running the magazine. We met in his office and I asked him to go over the entire text. It would take a year to complete, and I offered to pay him ₹3.5 lakh. We shook hands and I wrote out a cheque for ₹35,000, as an advance payment.

The next day, instead of Tarun, his wife Geetan showed up at our Noida office. 'Tarun's too busy,' she said sweetly. 'He's asked me to read through the entire matter.' Not wanting to be rude to Geetan, I called Sharad Gaur and asked him to insert half-a-dozen not-so-obvious errors into a 2,000-word chapter. I doubted if Geetan would pick out the flaws, so I told her to take it home, correct it and revert to me the next day.

The next day, not a single error had been detected. I showed Geetan the embedded flaws and told her the deal was off. I called up Tarun on the phone and told him to refund the money paid in advance. Suddenly, the mask was off and there was a string of profanity on the phone. 'My wife,' he said in between the abuses, 'has been to Noida twice.' Not wanting to extend a pointless conversation any further, I told him to subtract the taxi fare. 'She's there, isn't she,' he said, 'what about her time?' I hung up and told Geetan to leave. Needless to say, the money never was returned. The ramifications of this interaction would even impact the coverage of the subsequent Kargil War.

All around us, at the personal level, the situation seemed to be coming apart at the seams. My sister Teesta, who had at best had a tumultuous relationship with her husband, was bringing matters to a head and it seemed a matter of time before she stormed out of her marital home with Dhruv and Vidur. My father, who never quite knew how to react to a crisis within the family, typically declared 'once a girl is married, her place is in her husband's home!' He then went off to Kullu with my mother and a few days later, with the two boys in tow, Teesta had moved into Noida. I prophetically told Dipti that evening, 'Now that Teesta has moved in, we'll soon be out!'

Around this time, I was also getting extremely perplexed by Sharad Gaur's behaviour. He would be absent from work for hours, and it wasn't in my nature to quiz him about it, especially since he was running the CD-ROM-related work. In any case, with Dipti not available, I was either editing various films at the studio or sailing with the navy, when Sharad's wife Nupur called a couple of times and harangued me about making him work from dawn to dusk. Finally, when the situation seemed to get worse, I asked him what was the matter. We were sitting in my Esteem, and I was certainly not prepared for his answer.

'If I had stayed with WWF, I would have been at least a vice-president today. You are a B. Com ...' he paused to let that sink in, 'and I can have 300 people with qualifications like yours working under me. You know how humiliating it is for me to get a pay cheque from you!'

'Last four years it didn't seem to bother you ...' I couldn't think of anything else to say. 'I thought we were all working towards completing the wildlife CD-ROM together.'

Sharad had this deep voice and mannerisms that made people automatically trust him. Even though he was my friend, I had seen him transform as he wrestled with his demons over the last year. I was told by a Dutch lady who also worked for WWF that Sharad had left the organization and joined me in 1994 because there had been some issues at one of the camps held at Corbett. More importantly, when Vimal Mohindra jumped ship, I had kept the project going mainly because I felt a sense of loyalty that I had pulled Sharad out of a set job. 'I have already fixed you,' he blurted out, 'you will find out one day.' He opened the car door and was gone. Just like that! I would see him a couple of years later when he was back to working with WWF. We never spoke, nor did I acknowledge him, for by then I knew what he had done. And it was absolutely unforgivable!

National Geographic had gone cold on us because the tape sent to them had deliberately included shots from Nat Geo films, which amounted to plagiarism. One of the points that had come up for discussion in the Georgetown meeting had been India's lax, if not non-existent, copy and intellectual rights laws. It would not have taken anyone more than a few seconds to identify any of their own shots and slam the door in our face after that.

Veeha was born on 19 May and her arrival completed our cup of joy.

The naval films were finally reaching completion. Before putting the final soundtracks and mixing the film, I wanted the navy top brass to view the final cut while I physically read out the narrative. Admiral Bhagwat promptly said that the session would be held at Navy House and a four-hour session was scheduled. About a dozen admirals were invited, and we all got started on the first leg of the marathon session. The TV monitors had been set up in front of which the CNS and I were sitting, while behind us were the others. Commodore Sachdeva was right behind me.

Reading the script along a running track is the most difficult thing under the sun. To make matters worse, each admiral in the rows behind was busy making copious notes, presumably as to what was wrong with the film. The sound of their pencils on paper was like gunfire to my ears. After the first film got over, Bhagwat said we will have a five-minute break and reserve our comments until the end of all three episodes.

By the end, I was completely exhausted. The notebooks behind me were brimming with 'stuff' and once one admiral started, the others would undoubtedly let loose too. However, Admiral Bhagwat stood up and then made a brief speech. 'Gentlemen, what we have just seen is four years of dedicated slog work. Kunal, on behalf of the navy, I cannot convey our appreciation. The narrative is perfect. I have no points. Gentlemen? Any of you?' I always marvelled at how the notebooks mysteriously disappeared. I looked at Sacchu, who grinned and rolled his eyes. I wanted to shout—'Long live Bhagwat! Long live the navy!' But the ambience at Navy House did not encourage slogan shouting, thankfully!

Lieutenant General Adi Sethna by then had been appointed to the Minorities Board. Sometime in September, he asked me to come and have lunch with him and Keki Daruwalla, who was heading the Kashmir Cell under the Ministry of Home Affairs (MHA) after having retired as the head of the Intelligence Bureau. *Green Flash* one, though not as yet telecast, had been seen by Daruwalla who wanted us to put an Urdu narrative to it so that it could be widely circulated in Pakistan through the existing covert channels. This was done with Shammi Narang doing an excellent job with the voice-over.

Three to four sessions with Daruwalla followed in quick succession where we talked about Kashmir and the existing situation in the valley in quite some detail. Daruwalla wanted me to make a film on Sufism and how 'Kashmiriat' was influenced and spawned by the Saints. I was least interested in that aspect, for beyond a point I believed the entire issue had nothing to do with idealism, Islam or anything other than realpolitik against the background of geopolitics. Gradually, Sufism went off the table and I found Daruwalla listening more and more to my theories pertaining to the 'why's' of history. 'This was not our war,' I repeatedly said. 'It was first a play-off between the British Empire and Tzarist Russia ... but post World War II, the dynamics have shifted and it's now the US versus China. The people of both India and Pakistan have just got sucked into it, and unless we look at that, there can be no end in sight.'

The idea of a film on those lines was germinating in my mind, tentatively titled *An Airfield at Gilgit*. Daruwalla and Adi Sethna were my sounding boards. We did some rough back-of-the-envelope calculations. I would need rupees one crore thirty-five lakh. 'Slush funds, not traceable. I need a British crew to shoot in the Northern Areas and POK (Pakistan Occupied Kashmir), while I shoot the Indian side.'

'Let's do a presentation for MHA,' said Daruwalla. A week later, he kept his word, and I briefed some bureaucrats who listened without any interruptions or questions. 'Put it on paper now. Address it to the Kashmir Cell.'

I sat down and hammered it out. I had done five pages and all the essential information was there. I read the proposal and then read it again. Dipti made a few corrections, and so did Adi Sethna. I then quite unnecessarily added a sixth page. After chewing on it for a while, I typed out the heading, 'The Future'! I made it bold and then underlined it. Then virtually predicted the Kargil conflict!

By November the *Naval Dimension* was edited and ready for telecast. Sacchu called and said Vice Admiral Sushil Kumar, who had moved as C-in-C Southern Naval Command wanted me to see him in Cochin. Navy Day was on 4 December. 'Let us do a Sound and Light Show here,' said the admiral as we drove around the naval base on Wellington Island. We selected a spot near the water and decided to do a three-screen historical depiction with live performances interspersed. We even planned to position anti-aircraft guns within the audience that would open up from within. Back in Delhi, everything was put on hold as I got to work on the three film tracks.

The governor of Kerala, Justice Sukhdev Singh Kang, the select crowd, just about everybody, were on their feet by the end of *Changing Horizons*. When the guns had fired from within, almost half the crowd had jumped into the sea. 'We must do this at Mattancherry Harbour every evening,' said His Excellency. I flew back to Delhi, only to be told by Sacchu within a few days I was wanted again in Cochin. Thinking the governor had got the civil administration hooked on the idea of doing the sound and light show, I was surprised when on landing I was told I was being taken to the C-in-C's residence, my bag and all. Admiral Sushil Kumar, usually very cool and collected, was looking positively agitated.

'Am sorry Kunal to hustle you down like this, but I need some advice,' said the admiral. I was quite taken aback, for though Sushil Isaacs had been a DS with my father in Wellington in the 1980s, I only knew him as the COP which was his previous appointment. Even then, we had not interacted at a personal level. The Raksha Mantri, George Fernandes had asked the admiral to fly to Delhi later in the day. It seemed the CNS, Admiral Bhagwat, had 'lost his marbles and was busy threatening the elected government of the day'. I was still wondering what I was being asked, when the admiral said, 'I just wanted to know what you and your father would think if I agreed to take over as the chief of the navy.'

The loneliness of command! There are few friends at the top of the pyramid. My father was not around, so that was obviously just a euphemism of sorts. I had no idea what had happened or was happening, between Admiral Bhagwat and the Government of India. Shortly afterwards, the admiral left for Delhi in a RAW An-32 aircraft, telling his staff to make sure I was comfortable. I followed by the evening flight back to Delhi via Mumbai, getting in fairly late at night. Once again Sacchu messaged to say I should see Sushil Isaacs in the morning at Kota House. Wearing a black woolly cap, the admiral was sitting huddled next to the fireplace, and he was shivering from the cold. 'Bhagwat has gone mad! M ... A ... D ... mad! He has threatened the prime minister.' I still was none the wiser about what was happening and was astute enough to realize I was just a sounding board.

Next couple of days the media was full of all sorts of stories, with some intrepid pen pushers even suggesting INS *Viraat* was sailing up the Jamuna to wrest control of New Delhi. Bhagwat was replaced by Sushil Kumar, but he was still in Navy House packing his belongings. I called the admiral and spoke to him for eight minutes or so, wishing him all the best. Though he had given me a tough time initially, I had found him to be extremely well-read and extremely frank in his opinions. Once again, I was called to Kota House. 'You called Bhagwat,' said Sushil Kumar, 'that was good of you. But you realize we will now have to remove his name from the film's credits?' A naval chief had been sacked, and a new one had taken his place, and here we were discussing the credit roll of a film. I think I said as much to Sushil Kumar, who also chuckled. I then said I would not remove Bhagwat's name from the acknowledgements of the *Naval Dimension* for all this had nothing to do with the internal politics around the navy. Sushil Kumar did not say anything, but the CNS's eyes were not laughing.

That night I told Dipti the Naval Dimension would now never get telecast.[25] All the hard slog would go down the drain, but I could not agree to removing Bhagwat's name. 'Just do what you think is right,' she said simply, turning around and going off to sleep.

For the last one month or so, the proposal relating to *An Airfield at Gilgit* was fermenting on my desktop. Adi Sethna was livid with me. 'Keki Daruwalla has the MHA extremely excited about the film, and you are sleeping on the proposal. Damn the navy and get on with this ...' The next morning, I printed out the six pages under the KaleidoIndia letterhead

---

[25] A couple of months later, Admiral Sushil Kumar asked me to make a single hour-long film, for which the navy would make funds available. This film simply did not carry any acknowledgements.

and drove across to North Block. Keki Daruwalla had said to deliver the proposal by hand to the Home Secretary, B. P. Singh. After I was ushered in, I handed over the papers and asked for a copy to be signed as an acknowledgement. The stamp on the front page had the Government of India's Ashoka Lion on it, and the date, 14 January 1999.

The flat in Beverly Park-II was to have been handed over to us by DLF Universal Limited in 1996, but at that stage, they had not even started working on the complex. To add insult to injury, they then escalated the price by fifty per cent, which made no sense whatsoever. I turned to my classmate, Arvind Nigam, who was a leading lawyer in the Delhi High Court and we along with a few others filed a case against DLF demanding expediting of the delivery and also challenging the increase in the price.

Not too surprisingly, towards the end of 1998, Teesta's domestic issues had impacted us as well. My father's reactions were typical, for he promptly blamed me for having precipitated the crisis by allowing her to come back 'home'. He had come down from Kullu to handle one of her periodic crises and was heading back on 2 October which was a day prior to Vallika's fourth birthday. I had gone to drop him at the airport when he started talking about Teesta's situation. 'I had specifically told you not to let her leave her marital home. Look at what you've done.' He then angrily started to walk away with his bag, but then he stopped and came back. 'You were such a bleeding heart. Now you solve the problem. She needs space, so you find alternate accommodation.'

I just sat there and stared at my father's figure as he went into the terminal. Since my parents were due to shut down Kullu for the winter and drive down in a fortnight, I came home and told Dipti to start packing. We had a small flat that was our office in Ram Vihar, and we moved there in the next few days. The four of us would stay there for two months, after which we moved to Beverly Park in Gurgaon, as DLF Universal had to, under orders of the Supreme Court, give us possession. This episode would have a deep lasting impression on Vallika in particular, who just could not understand why her home had got disrupted by the arrival of her aunt and her two cousins.

We had just entered our new home and I was sitting on the floor with Veeha while Dipti was pottering around elsewhere in another room. Though she was standing with support, Veeha had not 'walked' until that moment. Suddenly, she set off while I watched in amazement, doing over twenty tottering steps before she plopped down on her bottom. I excitedly called Dipti, who refused to believe me, for Veeha just sat there and refused to move after that. It would be a while before she reached the twenty-step mark again.

Spring gave way to summer, and the parents moved back to Kullu. The unfortunate business of being 'booted out' needed to be buried quickly, and so we set off to spend time with the parents by the second week of May itself, which was when they themselves had moved up from Noida. It was Veeha's first trip into the hills, and I was quite looking forward to spending an extended amount of time with the girls and also Elsa, who then was the reigning queen of Windsong! By then there had been a considerable amount of talk on the media channels about some Pakistani infiltration in the Kargil Sector, and I remember watching the news on 9 May, when artillery shells from across the LOC set fire to the ammunition depot.

The house in Kullu overlooked the Beas River, and the highway to Manali passed in between. Army convoys with troops started moving up towards Rohtang and suddenly there were banners everywhere wishing the soldiers godspeed, while people lined the streets with flags. Overhead, the constant drone of An-32 engines brought home the reality of the fast-developing situation. I couldn't help but look up every time a plane went past, and my father noticed my growing restlessness. 'You're not in the army or the air force. It's not your job.'

Doordarshan was soon broadcasting regular reports on the 'war'. To my surprise, they started opening the national news with a clip from our recently edited *Green Flash* film, where the colours of the IMA were paraded past Chetwode Hall with Shammi Narang's voice extolling Arjun to take up arms and fight, for it was his dharma. I was in Kullu market on 26 May when news came through that we had lost two MiGs in quick succession, both presumably shot down by shoulder-fired surface-to-air missiles. Next, a Mi-17 met with a similar fate while attacking Tololing in the Drass Sector. My attempts to get through to both army and Air HQ on the phone was proving to be futile, and so I bundled up the kids and Dipti in the Maruti Esteem, said bye to my parents and drove back to Delhi.

I look back now, and I really wonder how things happened so fast. It was almost as if I was expected to come knocking on the doors, and before I knew it, I was cleared to fly with the IAF and film the designated target areas. On 30 June, I boarded an An-32 that flew in from Agra to take me and my assistant, Sahu, to Srinagar. The only Digi-Beta camera I could get was from Bhubaneswar, for none of the Delhi camera units was willing to rent me equipment to be taken into the 'war zone'. We had started up and were heading out towards the main runway when we were called back to the IAF's technical area. A vehicle from Air HQ was waiting and I was told the CAS, Air Chief Marshal A. Y. Tipnis wanted to see me.

At Air HQ, I was straightaway ushered in to see the CAS, who asked me what angle of attack did we need to fly in to film potential targets on the ground. I said one would have to be steady and put in a fairly smooth run for I would be filming manually with a hand-held camera. 'We have already lost three aircraft,' said Tipnis thoughtfully. 'With shoulder-fired Stingers on the ground, you might not stand a chance.' Then, amazingly, the trip was off ... just like that! I was staring at the CAS, but he had already lost interest.

Not just the CAS, but everyone else had also disappeared, for after all there was a war on. I had no idea what to do next, so I wandered down after a while. I had managed a call to Colonel (later Brigadier) Rajiv Williams who was waiting for me outside Air HQ. 'Air force chickened out?' He grinned.

'Yeah!' I was still in a state of disbelief. 'I'm going back to the airfield. Hopefully, Air HQ would not have thought of standing down my An-32. I'm going anyway.'

'You do that. Get in touch with HQ 15 Corps and wait there. I'll talk to Arjun Ray (Lt Gen) and let's see if we can push your case with MOD. In that case, shoot the war from the army's perspective.'

Sure enough, my aircraft was waiting where I had left it. We took off from Palam, with Sahu and me the only two passengers on board. The crew were positively nervous about flying into a 'war zone' and it didn't do their morale any good when two MiG-21s suddenly appeared when we crossed Banihal and escorted us in. Hardly had we touched down, the back hatch was opened, and we were evicted onto a remote corner of Srinagar airfield, after which the An-32 turned like a motorcycle and took off leaving a trail of black smoke.

Even at the best of times, no one wants to be standing at the Srinagar airfield, and that too without any papers whatsoever. Luckily, the CO of 51 Squadron, Wing Commander 'Tiny' Tandon, sent his Gypsy and soon I was drinking a cup of tea in his office. I told him what had happened with the CAS and spent the rest of the afternoon filming the MiG-21s going and coming from Kargil. By then there was a message from Army HQ that I should move to the Transit Camp at Badami Bagh. Colonel (later Major General) Raj Kapoor was colonel Q and I was to contact him. This was a stroke of unexpected luck, for Raj was married to Mala Bhasin, who had been one of my closest friends when I was in MCC.

On 1 July I was given a white Sumo with a local Kashmiri driver and a JCO for liaison purposes. We set off early in the morning and crossed Zoji La along with an artillery regiment that was towing the Swedish 155 mm Bofors howitzers across the pass. Eighteen years ago, I had spent the night stranded on Zoji La surviving on Scotch and 'Fruit and Nut' Cadbury chocolates. We reached Gumri on the northern side of the pass and watched as a Mi-17 helicopter came in to evacuate a couple of casualties who were suffering from HAPE. An anti-aircraft gun crew which was covering the approach to the pass watched the proceedings from where they were deployed.

HQ 8 Mountain Division was at Mughalpura, which despite its grand-sounding name was just a helipad and some well-concealed bunkers. Since I had no papers worth the name, I was getting a cold shoulder from the G-1[26], when Major General (later Lieutenant General) Mohinder Puri returned from a walk. He was dressed in a tracksuit, and

---

[26] General Staff Officer – 1, or GSO – 1

he cheerfully greeted me. I spent a day at Mughalpura and was impressed by Mohinder Puri who was at all times a picture of complete calm with his headquarters working with quiet efficiency. Once the extent of Pakistani ingress into the area around Drass had become clear, 8 Mountain Division had moved up with its two brigades from the valley immediately. 79 Mountain Brigade, with five battalions, had deployed in the Mushkoh Sub-sector while 56 Mountain Brigade with four battalions had taken charge of the area around Drass itself. In between phone calls from the DGMO and the COAS, General Ved Malik, Mohinder Puri talked in detail about clearing the heights along the main Srinagar–Kargil National Highway 1A (commonly known as One Alpha).

Despite the fact that the well-dug in Pakistani infiltrators had the advantage of occupying the heights, almost all initial objectives including Tololing had been captured, even if in the process the division had taken some heavy casualties. 192 Mountain Brigade, with whom I had operated five years previously in Pattan, had also moved up, and they would be responsible for the capture of Tiger Hill and the Zulu Spur in the next few days.

As I prepared to move further east towards Drass and Kargil, Mohinder Puri had offered just one piece of advice: 'Be careful, there are sections ahead that are under Pakistani observation, and they can call in fairly accurate artillery fire. Don't take any unnecessary chances.' [27]

I got to Drass without incident, stopping to film both 105 mm and 155 mm howitzers deployed along the route in action. 56 Mountain Brigade's headquarters was on the right side of One Alpha and I was met by the deputy brigade commander, Colonel David, who was from the mechanized infantry. He immediately wanted to know which news agency I was from, and he seemingly lost interest in me when I said I was just filming for the navy. He waved me to a bunker, saying if the shelling started, I should jump into it.

The next couple of days I spent moving around the area, driving into the Mushkoh Valley where medium and heavy mortar batteries were deployed. The quantum of fire we were belching out at that stage, must

[27] Writing in the *Sunday Guardian* two decades later, Mohinder Puri would comment: 'During the War, he (Kunal) had wandered into my headquarters and spent some time with me, before heading off nonchalantly to film the troops in action all along the front, operating later mainly with the neighbouring 3 Infantry Division.'

have been keeping the Pakistani gunners awfully quiet, for there was hardly any retaliatory fire. The Mushkoh Valley was known for brown bears, and while driving back from the mortar positions, I saw some bear droppings. I was busy examining them when a very irate colonel coming from the other side in his Jonga shouted at me, 'You idiot! This entire area is under Pakistani observation. Get the f*#k out of here ... now!'

I then noticed we were in a valley with a few partially destroyed stone structures. I jumped into the Sumo and had hardly gone 50 metres when the entire earth seemed to erupt behind us as Pakistani artillery shells zeroed into what until a few seconds ago was a nice, static juicy target! Despite shrapnel flying around everywhere, I grabbed the camera and jumped out of the vehicle, telling the driver to keep moving. The stone shelter provided ideal cover, and I started to film the incoming fire, which was, earthshakingly terrifying! That day I was probably born under a lucky star, for the shelling abruptly stopped. I waited for a while and then headed after the Sumo, which was waiting for me a kilometre away in what was a designated 'safe zone' that was marked with flags.

Every now and then, hired vehicles from Srinagar would ferry in a journalist. In some rare cases a few exalted personalities (mostly from the English-speaking television channels) would arrive by helicopter and as per the SOP laid down by MOD, would be disgorged at Drass. With nothing else to occupy him, David had taken it upon himself to be the single point of contact, and it was amusing to see how he would lay out the 'one-man' red carpet if the incoming was a lady. By the evening of 3 July, after I got back from Mushkoh, I was introduced to Star TV's (forebear of NDTV) Vikram Chandra by David, and as the sky over Drass darkened, we watched the Indian guns hammer away at Tiger Hill. A couple of 155 mm Bofors howitzers were positioned fairly closed by, firing almost continuously. In the dark, one could follow the red-hot shells as they propelled forward like red-hot tracers, and every time they hit the target area, there would be a huge explosion. Intermittently, there would be some retaliatory fire, but that was almost non-existent.

We were sitting out in the open under the stars and I was pointing out to Chandra how to distinguish between 'ours' and 'theirs' artillery fire when suddenly a phone rang. I nearly jumped out of my skin for until that moment, I had never seen or heard of a 'sat phone' and watched in awe as Chandra pulled out the folded aerial and took the call. I realized he was talking to Lieutenant General Arjun Ray, and I asked if I could speak to the general. Chandra handed over the phone to me. The line was crystal clear, and I asked Ray to call up Dipti and just inform her I was doing alright. Arjun Ray said my helicopter clearance from the MOD should be out by the next day, and that Rajiv Williams was pursuing the case on a 'war footing'.

After another fifteen minutes of watching the fireworks display, it suddenly occurred to Vikram I could speak to Dipti, and he offered me the phone again. The Bofors next to us was creating an infernal amount of noise, and my inquisitive wife wanted to know if I was at a 'safe distance from the action'. She also gave me a rocket on the phone for asking Arjun Ray to call her, for when he did, she had presumed the worst. 'Do you realize,' she said in all seriousness, 'if you get yourself killed, I'll have to keep a full-time maid with two kids to look after!'

The next morning, Vikram Chandra left and in came his colleague, Barkha Dutt. Seeing her, David got all excited and was soon leading her around the brigade headquarters holding her hand. I had other things to do than watch the unfolding Mills & Boon romance under fire, so moved up to the 18 Grenadier location where unfortunately there had been some casualties during the night. An ANI TV crew was filming some men coming down from Tiger Hill carrying the body of a soldier who had been killed the previous night. The body was unwrapped at the battalion headquarters as others gathered around. The dead Grenadier was a Naik, who had a gunshot wound on his head and he was leaving behind his parents, a wife and three daughters. It was heartbreaking and extremely hard to film. In the end, for all the grandstanding plans made on maps in distant headquarters, the price is paid by simple people on both sides who are there just doing their job.

When I got back to HQ 56 Mountain Brigade, it was obvious the main attack on Tiger Hill was being planned for the night. I didn't at the time know Barkha, even though her mother had been my colleague in *India Today*. I thought of walking across to her and saying hello, but she was being led by David towards the brigade's Ops Room. I took my equipment and walked across to the main road, where the Sumo and my motley crew were waiting. I had received a message that my helicopter sanctions had come through, and under the cover of darkness should move to HQ 3 Infantry Division at Kargil. I planned to stay and watch the initial bombardment of Tiger Hill and then leave.

The light was beginning to fade when Barkha and her cameraman came walking towards the main road. She had borrowed a helmet from a soldier, and she stood there and started filing a report. She had in her hand a mike and a sat phone, an instrument that I recognized by then. The light on the camera had come on to illuminate her.

My JCO almost went berserk. '*Saab ... CB ayega ... CB ayega!*' He literally pushed me into the Sumo and told the driver to drive. I had no idea what he was talking about but was whisked away. We had gone barely a kilometre when the ground seemed to shake. I presumed the guns had opened up and the attack had begun. I was feeling most peeved at the JCO who had made me miss the opening salvos. At the time I had no idea how close we had come to being killed. I owed my life to the JCO. CB was 'counter bombardment' and the moment the light had come on, it was obvious that Pakistani observers would direct their guns to open up.[28]

3 Infantry Division was being commanded by Major General V. S. Budhwar. Originally, it had 121 Independent Brigade under its command as well and the fact that the initial ingress by the Pakistanis had not been detected, the blame was being laid at the division's doorstep. Budhwar's AOR since the outbreak of hostilities was to cover the territory east of Thasgam that has Drass to its immediate west. 3 Infantry Division was also responsible for the Kaksar and Kargil Sub-sectors. 70 Infantry Brigade, which my father had commanded in the early 1980s in Kiari, was under the command of Brigadier Devinder Singh. The brigade had been inducted into Batalik, with the Yaldor Sub-sector stretching from the Indus to the Chorbat La–Handdangbrok–Hunuthang line. 102 Brigade (also known as the Siachen Brigade) had the responsibility of Sub-sector West which extended from Chorbat La to the Shyok River and Sub-

---

[28] Later, according to Barkha, though she had filed her report using a sat phone, there was no 'live broadcasting' facility available and the call to air her report almost real time was taken in New Delhi. She would also claim that David had tried to get 'funny' with her in the Ops Room, but she had managed to dodge past him. She would also write later that there were heads of Pakistani soldiers displayed at the 56 Brigade gate. If they were there, I for one had missed seeing them.

sector Hanif that extended from Turtuk to a point some 10 kilometres southeast of the Southern Glacier in Siachen. To put it mildly, it was a huge area.

HQ 3 Infantry Division was a huge bunker close to the helipad. 'Viru' Budhwar, unlike Mohinder Puri, did not believe in keeping his own counsel and would always be loudly proclaiming how he was going to 'be sacked'. His deputy was Brigadier Ashok Duggal and his colonel, general staff (GS) was Colonel Avtar Singh, who like Budhwar, was also from the Kumaon Regiment. Brigadier C. P. Nayar was the commander arty, and he would occasionally pop by from his neighbouring bunker. I found a place for myself and settled down next to the deputy GOC. In addition, there were three more officers who sat together at the far end, with a battery of telephones to keep them company. To sleep at night, I was allotted a stone hut near the helipad, which was the official residence of a doctor. The medical teams were so busy with casualties, I was told I was highly unlikely to be disturbed.

I felt Budhwar was unnecessarily getting influenced by the media reports. The focus until now was on the 'victories' that had primarily been achieved by 8 Mountain Division, mostly against features held by the Pakistanis that overlooked One Alpha. On the other hand, most of the battles being fought by 3 Infantry Division were in regions that were completely isolated. 70 Infantry Brigade had been given the responsibility of the Yaldor Sub-sector but in reality, at the outbreak of hostilities, there were simply no troops under this brigade. Subsequently, eleven battalions were inducted into the formation, and the commander fought an incredible war, sometimes not even being able to put a face to the name on the other end of the telephone line.

Unlike 8 Mountain Division, 3 Infantry Division was fighting a battle of attrition, trying to cut off the supply lines of the Pakistani intruders. The terrain in Batalik also meant that the heavier 155 mm Bofor guns of the artillery regiments that were lined up all along the road from Mughalpura to Drass were far fewer, the main armament being the 105 mm and 130 mm guns which were supporting the troops. Some extremely well-fought actions, therefore, went unreported and in the final analysis, the absence of the media from this region resulted in 8 Mountain Division being in the limelight far more often.

My helicopter sanction allowed me the freedom to fly around everywhere. The MOD had stipulated that I could only fly when an officer of the rank of a brigadier or above would accompany me. This suited me, for I found myself in the company of General Budhwar on most occasions in the next few days as we visited some of the far-flung sectors that included Ghanasok and Chorbat La. To use the Cheetah as a filming platform, I needed the doors to be removed, which did not seem to unduly bother him, even though at times it got bitterly cold.

70 Infantry Brigade was fighting in the Batalik Sub-sector and the brigade's TAC HQ was located amidst some rocks that were marked as Ghanasok on the map. With equipment, it was a three-day haul from the roadhead at Dah. Getting to these locations for journalists was an impossibility unless movement was facilitated by helicopters. The first time we landed at Ghanasok, Brigadier Devinder Singh was at the helipad to receive Budhwar. An artillery officer, he was also a paratrooper, which accounted for his maroon turban. As the two officers reviewed the situation, I filmed them surrounded by maps under camouflage nets and then also took a few still photographs.

Just then an IAF Chetak came and landed, and a group captain walked up to where we were sitting. Budhwar wanted to know if the larger Mi-17 1Vs could be pressed into service, as there were a large number of casualties. Cheetahs could evacuate a single stretcher case at a time, or at best take out two sitting casualties to the Kargil Hospital. The group captain was extremely polite but firm: 'No, sir ... Mi-17s cannot come in low. There simply is no clearance on the sides for them. Unless the heights around Yaldor are cleared by the navy, we cannot be of any help.' The Chetak then flew back the way it had come.[29]

---

[29] Four days later when the heights around Yaldor were cleared, an IAF Mi-17 came to Ghanasok. Showing amazing flying skills, the IAF pilots came in hugging the ground, turned the huge helicopter around and in a swirl of dust, landed. There were many incidents like these that created an undercurrent of hostility between the army and air force.

From Ghanasok we flew north to Chorbat La where Colonel K. K. Sinha received us. An attack was being planned for the occupation of the pass the same night, and I watched as the captain who was to lead the attack was given a 'pep-talk' by the GOC.

We were back at Ghanasok when news came in that there was a serious chest wound at Yaldor. Without waiting for Budhwar, the pilots with me at the back took off. As we landed at the improvised helipad, the badly injured soldier was put inside the helicopter with his head in my lap. I handed my camera to the men on the ground and grabbed the wounded and unconscious soldier. The flimsy field dressings were soaked in blood, and I could even see his heart pumping as we flew desperately towards Kargil. I took off my shirt and with it tried to stem the flow of blood, and to some extent, I think I did succeed. At the Kargil helipad, the medics were waiting, and it was all go ... go ... go! Still minus a shirt, we went back to collect my camera and the GOC. I was told later the man had pulled through. No wonder then that the men on the ground looked at the Army Aviation pilots as 'Angels from the Sky'!

In the post-Kargil War scenario, the witch-hunt to pin the responsibility on someone fell on the shoulders of 3 Infantry Division. Though it obviously makes inordinate sense to look at both your successes and failures, from whatever I could make out, the performance of this division was in no way inferior to that of 8 Mountain Division. Unfortunately, our system is such that both Major General Budhwar and Brigadier Devinder Singh along with a host of battalions that had performed superbly were not adequately recognized and were given a raw deal. As we look at the area even further to the immediate north towards the Haneef Sub-sector, the troops who fought there were not even talked about at the time; the capture of Pt 5700 by 27 Rajput being a case in point!

On 6 July, three days before the Pakistani troops in the Yaldor Sub-sector were to finally implode, I was to once again fly to Chorbat La. The helicopter that was to take me there arrived from Srinagar, with Brigadier Bhagat on board. As was my usual practice, I asked the ground crew to remove the doors and went off in search of a jacket for the brigadier. I borrowed Major General Budhwar's parka and after removing the rank badges I was walking back to the helicopter when there was a shout from behind me. I turned to find Colonel Avtar Singh, the colonel, GS of 3 Infantry Division, waving a piece of paper at me.

"This signal has just arrived," he said, "all journalists are to be kicked out of Kargil!" The previous day, Major General Budhwar's ADC, a young captain and the colonel had been involved in a verbal scrap with Raghu Rai, India's foremost photographer. My intervening on Raghu's side had made me a marked man in the colonel's book!

"Why?"

"Chief's orders!" barked the colonel. He then pointed a finger at me, "Especially you!"

Leaving Sahu, the JCO and the Sumo with the driver behind, I had the doors put back on the helicopter and told the pilots to take off for Srinagar, with a refuelling halt at Gumri. When we landed at Badami Bagh an hour-and-a-half later, I saw General Ved Malik and the corps commander, Lieutenant General Kishan Pal in the small hut which served as the waiting-cum-rest room. Arjun Ray, who continued to head the Media Cell in Delhi, was also there, and I walked across to him and asked him why the eviction orders.

"The old man's hopping mad! Barkha Dutt of Star TV had aired an attack on Tiger Hill live a few days back and we lost quite a few guys," he answered.

I didn't get a chance to speak to the chief who left with the other two general's shortly, but I did tell General Ray that this was a ridiculous decision and all the good work done with the media bringing the war live to the world would be undone. 'Besides,' I pointed out, 'the problem was at the navy's end. The fact remains no one should have been privy to the attack plans.'

"I'll see what I can do," was General Ray's parting comment.

Fifteen minutes later the phone in the hut rang. The JCO in charge said the caller, General Ray, wanted to speak to me: "The order's been revoked. Some journalists had been asked to leave but they will be stopped at various check posts and allowed back," he said curtly. "You can fly back to Kargil."

My pilot, Major Rajiv Dey said it was too late to do that, and suggested I get myself a bath as I was looking like something the cat had brought home. So, I spent the night in Srinagar, and in the process filed an article for *The Statesman* titled the 'Mouse Trap'. Early the next morning, as we were preparing to take off, a Cheetah with Kishan Pal landed. The corps commander was in a very upbeat mood and had with him a captured shoulder-fire surface-to-air missile launcher. 'They are withdrawing, they are withdrawing! The Pakistanis are abandoning their posts in Batalik. We have won!' There were tears streaming down his cheeks. I congratulated him and he danced with me and the other pilots in sheer joy! As soon as he got into his vehicle and left, one of the pilots grinned and said, 'It's bloody Bill Clinton! He gave Nawaz Sharif a right royal spanking. Now, we will have all the conquering heroes emerge from the woodwork.'

My crew was waiting for me anxiously at the Kargil helipad. It was amazing how quickly signs of the fighting disappeared. Gun positions were abandoned overnight and suddenly the silence was deafening. The 'war' was still some days from officially getting over, as battalions deployed along the Line of Actual Control continued to jostle with the Pakistanis to capture and hold terrain that would help dominate their sectors. I asked Viru Budhwar if he would like to summarize the operations on camera and got from him a complete overview of what had happened as an uninterrupted monologue.

The helicopters were flying almost without a break, as casualties were being ferried out. Almost without exception, men with limbs blown off, had stoic expressions as they were stretchered out. It all seemed so unreal, for all that had really happened over the last two months was that Pakistani soldiers, perhaps as bewildered and completely unaware of what was happening, had occupied heights that hitherto had just been markings on maps in their higher headquarters. Once the Indians had called their bluff and thrown themselves into the fight, men on both sides had fought and actually died for nothing, for nothing would change on the ground. All the fire and fury had resulted in killing and maiming individuals who were just doing their job and perhaps had little or no animosity towards each other. But then the more senseless it is, the more we try to glamorize the actions.

I started to move down, stopping to film with 8 Sikh that had fought the Tiger Hill battle. Everyone was on a high, but there was also a subdued air for all units had lost men. At Mughalpura, it was the turn of Mohinder Puri to summarize the operations. The next morning, we came down Zoji La and after reaching Badami Bagh, I went straight to Mala and Raj Kapoor's residence, wanting nothing but a homecooked meal. 'Shut up yaar!' said Mala, handing me a towel and soap. 'First you go have a bath. You're filthy!'

At the Srinagar airfield, I ran into Ayaz Memon, the sports writer and commentator who had flown up from Mumbai (as Bombay was now known) to see what was happening for himself. There was an artillery captain who had been a Forward Observer and even though he too was all freshly bathed and in civilian clothes, Ayaz walked up to both of us and offered to treat us to a cup of coffee because 'we were obviously coming from Kargil'.

'That obvious, is it?' I asked.

'Yes, you both have the look!' Seventeen years later, Ayaz would moderate the launch of my book, *1962: The War That Wasn't* in Mumbai. He laughed when I reminded him of our meeting. 'You guys just smelled of soap, so it was easy to pick you out!'

Back in Delhi, I worked closely with the Army Liaison Cell (ALC) during the immediate aftermath of the Kargil War. Most networks and channels had footage of the Indian artillery guns in operation, but as I said before, they were hampered by their inability to go beyond Alpha One. We evolved our own techniques of functioning; a TV network would approach the ALC for footage and they in turn would direct them to me. I never refused, be it Zee TV or CNN, but would insist on giving them an edited clip where we controlled the narration as well. Basically, we were only interested in keeping the typical 'anti-Indian' twist out of the reporting which most Western channels would subtly resort to, referring to Jammu and Kashmir as 'Indian occupied Kashmir' and so on. Since I was completely independent, they couldn't howl and say we were censoring their reports.

General Ved Malik, the Indian Army chief, was the victor, yet he too was cropping criticism starting with his visiting Poland at the time when the first reports of Pakistani ingress were being reported. Ironically, General Pervez Musharraf, his Pakistani opposite, who had been vanquished, was to become the president of his country! Personally, I felt that General Malik was much too sensitive to media reports, both during and after the war. I had gone to see the chief in connection with the Kargil film, which at that time was in the process of being edited. As one approached the COAS's secretariat, everyone seemed to be running around in circles. It transpired that *Outlook* magazine had printed some report on the war which was a blatant case of biased reporting. I scanned through the offending piece while I was waiting to go in. After discussing the issue at hand, I was about to leave when the chief asked me if I had seen the *Outlook* article. He was looking positively distraught and personally hurt. Replying in the affirmative, I suggested to him that he just ignore the article, for quite frankly, in my opinion, any response from Army HQ would only fan the issue. General Malik asked me if I knew Tarun Tejpal, the editor. I said yes, but also added that he was no friend of mine as he had swindled me of some money a year ago.

Ved Malik asked me to speak to Tejpal and see if I could set the record straight. Against my better judgement, I called up *Outlook* from the COAS's office and got through to Tejpal who obviously had an incoming number identification facility for he immediately asked me if I was calling from the chief's office. I told Tejpal that I had seen the article in the magazine and that I could easily rubbish it, for not only had I been present in the area but also had both the film and the photographs to back up what I was saying. Tejpal let out a stream of obscenities in Punjabi, most of them aimed at the chief, finally saying that enough had been written on the subject and the matter was now closed. So much for objective journalism!

Pre-determined perceptions were also hard to change. Amarinder Singh, the Maharaja of Patiala, along with my father had once again set off to do a book together on the Kargil War.[30] In his notes, Amarinder Singh had rubbished the IAF's claims and even questioned the number of sorties launched. I found that hard to stomach, so invited His Highness

---

[30] They would both write their own separate books in the end. *Blood on the Snow* by Major General Ashok Kalyan Verma was published by Manohar; while Amarinder would write and publish *A Ridge too Far* under his own banner. Their earlier attempt to collaborate had also resulted in two different books—Rivers of Silence and Lest We Forget!

to come and see the entire IAF-related footage that I had shot on the first day. Amarinder would sit at my residence in Beverly Park where the equipment was set up and go through the entire footage that I had shot, but in his book, he stayed with what he had written earlier. The day Amarinder Singh launched his book, he most graciously invited me on stage and presented me with a copy. General Ved Malik, who was also present, signed it with the comment that what I had done for the cause was invaluable.

Another surprise visitor to our home was J. N. Dixit, the then national security adviser (NSA) to the prime minister. After viewing the rushes, there was another meeting with Jaswant Singh, the foreign minister. Apart from generously giving footage to whoever wanted it, I had initially made a short 17-minute version with Rajiv Williams doing the narration. The minister then said the US president, Bill Clinton was visiting India in March 2000, and would I make the film that could be screened for him and his team. We talked for a while, and I suggested we expand the scope of the film to cover the events from 1947 to 1999. Accordingly, the title would be 'From Baramulla to Kargil'.

Meanwhile, I got a call from Rajiv Williams who asked me if I wanted to film the eight Pakistani prisoners of war (POWs) that were in our custody. We discussed the ethics, and I spoke to the NSA who said since the Pakistanis were doggedly saying they were not regular soldiers even now, it made sense to see what they had to say and put it on international television. 'Otherwise, the poor chaps will remain disowned by their own army and languish in our jails. I think it's a good idea.'

It was raining when I got to Base Hospital where four of the prisoners suffering from snow blindness and frostbite were being treated. They had been shifted to the VIP ward, and there were flowers on the side table and copies of the Koran placed there as well. A senior officer from the Army Medical Corps had lined up all the nurses on duty and was as per his discretion, selecting the 'pretty ones'. I stood there watching while smoking a cigarette. Then after the officer had finished his selection, I walked up to him and said, '*Subedar Saab ... Mera naam Kunal Verma hai.*' I stuck out my hand, '*Aap ko milke ...*' There was an explosion, and the officer tapped his rank badges and said he was a senior officer and the trouble with bloody civilians was they did not recognize or respect rank. 'Oh, I do,' I said pleasantly, 'my father is a general. But you are, sir, if I may say so respectfully, giving a completely wrong message to your people!'

The man turned red in the face and for a moment I thought he would hit me with the swagger stick in his hand. I turned to the nurses and told them they were not required and barked out orders to shift the men to the general ward and to take away the flowers and holy books. No one moved, not the nurses, nor the orderlies. The officer suddenly broke into a huge smile, 'Good Lord ... what was I doing? You're right ... carry on everyone. Do as he says, he knows what he is doing!' Williams rolled his eyes and said there were more diplomatic ways of handling the situation.

The Pakistani soldiers too had been given some spin that I was from the Red Cross, and they could talk to me. I wasn't going to let that pass either, so I frankly explained to them that I was not from any organization but would be happy to put out what they wanted to say for in my opinion, that was the only way their country would acknowledge them. What then followed was incredible stuff, for the men began to open up completely. Three out of the four prisoners were from the Northern Light Infantry, and they spoke so simply and earnestly about what had transpired, there could be little or no doubt that they were telling the truth. By the time I finished with them, it was late in the evening. The second batch of four was at the Rajputana Rifles Centre, where we set up lights in a single room with just two chairs facing each other across a small table which had on it an ashtray. The camera would be on the prisoner talking to me, and the glare of the powerful lamps created the perfect setting.

The first man to be brought in was Naik Inayat Ali. He was a simple soul who was headed for retirement the day he was captured by Indian troops, and he was more concerned about passing a message to his wife that he was alive, and she should not marry someone else in the meantime. Gradually, Inayat began to open up, and then suddenly he said he was part of the ground party that tried to apprehend the pilot of the MiG-21 who had successfully ejected from his stricken aircraft after it was hit by a shoulder-fired missile. The pilot (Squadron Leader Ajay Ahuja), according to him, had clambered in among some rocks and had kept them at bay with his pistol, but it was soon obvious he was down to his last round. It had become obvious to the Pakistanis by then that Ahuja was not going to allow himself to be captured alive. '*Ham ne unko kaha, Saab, kuch nahi hoga. Aap haath oopar kar do*' (We told him, Sir, nothing will happen. Put your hands up).[31]

By the time we reached the last POW, it was 2 a.m. and everyone was fed up. I was out of cigarettes and the intelligence people with us said the remaining prisoner was a real '*kattar*' who refused to give away anything other than his name, rank and serial number, implying we might as well pack up and go home. Just then, someone produced a solitary unfiltered cigarette, which cheered me up considerably and I decided to carry on with the filming. Unlike the others, this prisoner was blindfolded, handcuffed and attached to his SLR-toting sentry with a dog chain. 'Release him,' I said and though the sentry looked uncomfortable about doing so, the man was released. After I asked him to sit down, the prisoner glared coldly at me while rubbing his wrists.

I stared back at him and lit the cigarette. The prisoner's gaze had got fixated on the tip of my cigarette, so I put it on the ashtray and pushed it towards him. He picked it up, and holding it almost like a chillum, he took a deep drag. This promptly brought about a fit of coughing, which resulted in him putting the cigarette back on the ashtray. Still looking at him, I reached out and after taking another pull at it, stubbed out what remained. The prisoner had got his wind back, but he was looking at me differently. Suddenly, he stood up and his chair fell. The sentry, standing at the door started to raise his rifle but I signalled him not to move. Taking two steps toward me, the Pakistani sank to his knees and buried his face on my knee. His entire body was shaking, and he seemed to be sobbing.

For almost a minute the prisoner stayed in that position, and then he looked up, his face streaked with tears. No one in the room had moved, and I gently told him to pick up the chair and sit down. After a while, he collected himself. '*Saab*,' he said, '*hum ko humari fauj mein bataya jata hain ki Hindustan mein sab buzdil hai aur jaati jaati ek doosre ko haath nahi laga sakte. Lekin aap toh meri muh lagaye cigarette bhi pi rahe ho*' (Sir, we are told in our army that all Indians are cowards and men from different castes

[31] The suggestion that Ahuja had shot himself rather than be captured would lead to a sharp reaction from some senior retired IAF officers. 'Don't even entertain the idea,' I was told by a former chief,' as far as we are concerned, the Pakistani soldiers killed him.'

cannot touch each other. But you are smoking the same cigarette I smoked). The dam had broken, and Prisoner No. 8 was singing like a canary. I had to twice or thrice restrain him from naming his officers.

By the next evening, the footage of the Pakistani POWs was being aired on multiple television channels. It was a matter of time before the Pakistan government threw in the towel and agreed to send a Pakistan Air Force aircraft to New Delhi to collect 'their men'. Our entire objective had been to get the eight soldiers back to their families, and when after some diplomatic delays the plane took off for Pakistan, both Rajiv Williams and I felt we had succeeded in our objective.

The Kargil film was edited, telecast and it was made into a VCD. There were two sub-sections that included the edited interviews with the POWs and another on the handing over of Pakistani bodies in the Mushkoh Sub-sector. A few days later, Adi Sethna called to say that L. K. Advani, the home minister who was also the deputy prime minister wanted to meet in his office in the Parliament building. Since the general was not particularly involved in the shooting around the Kargil War, he asked me what was going on. I honestly told him I had no clue.

When we walked in the next morning, there was a thick file lying partly open on the minister's desk. I recognized the KaleidoIndia letterhead, and knew the meeting related to the proposal for making *An Airfield at Gilgit*. The Kargil VCD was also lying next to the file. The minister got up and came around his desk to meet us. Adi Sethna started to introduce me when Advani picked up the jacket of the film and asked me, 'Who is this Dipti Bhalla?' He then asked what was her *gotra*. I honestly replied I had no idea, only that her parents were refugees from Lahore and Sialkot in 1947.

Moving back to his table, he then picked up the file. It was open on the sixth page of the proposal, and I could see the heading 'The Future' typed in bold and underlined. 'How did you know this would happen?' I had almost forgotten about this aspect of the proposal, and for a moment I felt I was about to be arrested. Adi Sethna was looking at me, completely unaware of what was happening.

I found my voice quickly enough and thankfully my voice sounded even enough. 'The analysis in the first five pages suggested that might happen, Sir ... I think what the Pakistanis tried to do in Kargil, validates what I am saying. It was mainly nothing but a spoiling action on their part, and it didn't work out for them.'

'Yes,' said Advani, and suddenly the atmosphere in the room was more relaxed. The minister flipped the pages and slowly read the title of the film aloud ... 'An Airfield at Gilgit!' He was engrossed in the file for a few seconds, then he shut it and said, 'The film must be made.' He then changed tack. 'Who paid for the Kargil film?'

'No one sir ... the fighting broke out and I offered to go up.'

With his fingers interlocked and his hands just below his lower lip, the minister said I must be compensated the money that I had spent from my own pocket. He then wrote two numbers on a piece of paper and gave them to Adi Sethna. 'Go to North Block directly from here. This gentleman will initiate the process for you to be compensated the money you spent on the Kargil film. This other number, you please call me at 11 tomorrow. Do not speak to anyone else but me. We will work out how to fund the Gilgit film.'

Things from this point onwards were going to get extremely bizarre. In North Block we were directed to a joint secretary (JS) who promptly pushed a blank sheet of paper and asked me to write an application to the honourable minister asking to be reimbursed for the expenses incurred while filming in Kargil. Including post-production costs and the edits, the actual costs were around ₹8 lakh or so. 'Listen,' I said, 'I am not asking for this money. I'm not writing any application. If bills are required for what has been paid, I can make those available.'

'It's just a formality,' said the JS, looking extremely bored at having to go through with the entire business. Going against my instincts, I wrote a one-liner saying further to the meeting with the home minister, I was putting on record the amount that had been spent on the Kargil film. 'You will hear from us in two or three days.'

The next day, as per instructions, Adi Sethna sat in his basement office at F-17 Hauz Khas and started dialling Advani's 'hot line'. Nothing! After an hour, the general gave up. Four days later, I received an official-looking envelope. Inside was a 'show-cause notice' saying I had supplied/

given footage of the Kargil War to nineteen television networks. If 'my case' for reimbursement was to be considered, I was advised to get signed affidavits from all concerned that no money had been paid to me or KaleidoIndia. I had never felt so insulted in my life. I never bothered to answer the letter.

The year flipped, and we entered the year 2000. I was with Dipti, Vallika and the 2-year-old Veeha in Corbett and we watched the last sunset of the millennium from a ridge above the grasslands. I was then 39 and it had been quite a ride so far. I looked at my daughters and my wife and felt my world was quite complete.

Twenty-six days later, K. R. Narayanan, the president of India, held the 'At Home' in the evening at Rashtrapati Bhawan. Adi Sethna saw the deputy prime minister of India, L. K. Advani advancing toward him. 'General Saab, what happened to that film?' Sethna said nothing had happened despite the fact that he had tried to repeatedly call as instructed. Taking out his Ashoka embossed visiting card, Advani wrote a number on the back and gave it to Adi Sethna, saying 'call me at this number tomorrow at 11'. No major surprises there, for the next day we had an encore with there being no response to the ringing telephone.[32]

However, it seemed the project wasn't quite still born even then. Rajiv Williams and I had a long meeting with an IAS officer, Anurag Mathur on the subject. A few days later, once again much against my will, we were directed to go to Doordarshan and collect the money for the film. When we got there, Rajiv Williams in uniform, we were first made to wait for a few hours, and then finally called in by some medium-ranking official. We had been told that Doordarshan would be making the funds available for the project in its entirety, but instead, they offered us a quarter of the stipulated amount and that too on the condition that we pay them a reasonable percentage to look after 'their people'. I was appalled and asked to speak to someone senior. The official promptly got the deputy director general (DDG), Harish Awasthi on the line and handed me the receiver without even taking my name. It was almost as if

---

[32] Two years later, when shooting the film on the LCA (Tejas) programme, I found myself seated next to L. K. Advani on a flight to Bangalore. Not surprisingly, the former deputy prime minister did not recognize me, but once I reintroduced myself, he promptly asked what happened to the 'Gilgit' film. I told him what had happened, and he listened most carefully. He then fished out his visiting card, which now had 'Leader of the Opposition' written below his name.

the DDG was waiting to speak to me, for he launched into a long monologue about how I had created a lot of trouble for Doordarshan with my coverage of the Kargil War. There was no point in talking to Awasthi any further, so we left Mandi House and drove straight from there to the information and broadcasting minister's office where we met Arun Jaitley, repeating the conversation verbatim. The minister heard both Rajiv Williams and me most patiently and made all the right noises, but neither the navy nor I ever heard from any of them again.

BOOK III

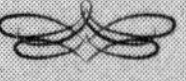

21

Aakash Yodha: Afterburners on Again

Even though the *Naval Dimension* had been scuttled for the time being, I was functioning as Admiral Sushil Kumar Isaac's 'go-to guy' every time he wanted something done. During the Kargil War he had asked me to include a section in the film on the navy.'All the attention is on the air force and the army,' he said to me, 'but the navy has effectively blockaded Karachi harbour.' , the CNS would call up and say he was coming to the studio. He would then just sit and watch us edit in the darkened studio. At first, the arrival of a serving naval chief at Kay Video in Mayfair Gardens created quite a stir, but after a while, everyone got used to it.

Admiral Arun Prakash had by then moved as the COP, and he was seen as the man who would take over the CNS's mantle in a couple of years. Every year Navy Day used to be celebrated with a lot of pomp and whatever the function was, it would culminate with *Jai Jai Bharti* and the national anthem. Sushil Kumar was keen I cut a four-odd minute montage that would run on the screens when the band played the navy tune. The film was easy to make, but it had a lot of cross fades and multiple tracks. Those rendering was a complicated and expensive business, so I wanted the tracks approved before we took the final step. Arun Prakash was asked by the CNS to do the needful, and he said he would drop by at the studio two days hence, which was a Saturday.

Hardly had this been decided, I started getting an endless stream of phone calls from Naval HQ. The assistant COP, Rear Admiral Ravi Kochhar, whom I had known since I landed on INS *Vikrant* half a decade previously, kept insisting on setting up the machines in Arun Prakash's office. The studio's switchboard logged seventeen calls, and I finally agreed to do the needful. Security clearances were required, and the multiple Digi-Beta players had to be set up the previous evening.

The process was so innocuous and simple that it was ridiculous to go to such lengths over it. Anyway, Arun Prakash had been requested to come to his office by 8 a.m., and the studio boys were there half an hour before him. I set off from Beverly Park at 6:30 in the morning and ran into a thick blanket of fog. I was on the Gurgaon–Mehrauli road, where a traffic jam started to build because a bus overturned after it had hit the kerb in what was zero visibility. Somehow, with great difficulty, I managed to make a U-turn and by the time I got back to Beverly Park, it was already 8! I called Naval HQ and was told by the COP's naval assistant that Delhi was crystal clear, and I should better get to Naval HQ as soon as I possibly could.

After I crossed the Palam runway, the weather indeed cleared up completely. I was in Arun Prakash's office by 9:15, and the moment I got there, the multiple tracks making up the film were played. In five minutes, we were through, and Arun Prakash nodded his approval. The equipment was dismantled and taken away, and I got up to leave when the COP said coldly, 'Sit down!' He then blasted me, saying that I was a liar and that the weather was crystal clear and what the hell did I want him to believe ... 'that you were flying in on a Jaguar?' He then asked why had I put his staff to so much trouble when he himself had said he would come to the studio to approve something as trivial as the four-minute film.

I was staring at Arun Prakash in disbelief. I now turned to Ravi Kochhar and said, 'Tell him! You asked me to come here. You kept ringing me up at the studio ...'

'No sir ... I never called him!' Kochhar's words were stunning. Arun Prakash then added what he thought of spoilt brats who thought, because they were senior army officers' sons, they could get away with anything. I was fast losing my temper, but there was not much you can do when up against a room full of senior brass. Commodore Sachdeva, my lone ally in the room could say nothing.

I drove back to Beverly Park in a daze. At home I sat down and wrote a letter to Arun Prakash, saying people without the moral courage to tell the truth were not fit to be called officers. I printed the one-page note on my letterhead, signed it, and drove back to Naval HQ. I used my morning pass to get in and gave the sealed envelope to the duty officer. Having let off steam on paper, I sort of cooled down and forgot about the incident.

Monday morning, I had gone to buy provisions in Khan Market (Gurgaon then was a virtual village) when my mobile phone rang. It was the CNS, who in a hushed voice said, 'What have you done? Come to my office right now!' I told the chief I was in flowery shorts and bathroom slippers, but he said it did not matter. Feeling like an idiot, I flip-flopped into the mecca of Naval HQ where the chief, Arun Prakash and Ravi Kochhar were sitting facing each other across the desk. 'You cannot write a letter like this,' said Sushil Kumar. 'You should have come to me instead.'

Some sort of a compromise was thrashed out, and like errant school boys, we had to shake hands while the CNS acted like a headmaster. But I knew then those years of hard work which had resulted in a wonderful relationship with the Indian Navy were over. I had been asked to do the photography for the navy's coffee table book, the cover of which eventually had my shot of seven ships. Titled *The Indian Navy: A Photo Essay*, the cover title was given to Vice Admiral Raja Menon and my name was removed.

The Naval Fleet Review was held in 2001, and the MEA sanctioned a budget for a film that was ten times what we had been working with. Needless to say, I was by then persona non-grata and the film was given to Nandan Kudhyadi, a Mumbai-based film producer. The film, in the words of the CNS, was a complete disaster and in what would be the final curtain call with the navy, I was asked to see the new assistant COP, Rear Admiral Ajit Tiwari. The admiral put a blank cheque book in front of me and said, 'Fill in the amount!' I ignored it.

One of the first editing assignments Dipti had done was for Nandan. 'Sir, if Mr Kudhyadi asks me to do it, I'll do so in a matter of a few hours. And I don't need any money for it. But as a filmmaker, I cannot do it if the navy asks me to do so. It would not be ethical.' That was the last time I ever set foot in Naval HQ.

On the flip side, with the main Kargil film done and dusted, discussions with Air HQ were on for the making of a film on Op Safed Sagar, the code name given by the IAF to the Kargil conflagration. Air Vice Marshal Satish Kumar 'Sakka' Jain was the additional ACAS (Ops) and Group Captain (later Air Commodore) Ashok Dhar was my main point of contact. The first meeting towards the end of 1999 was an unmitigated disaster. The air marshal had leaned back in his chair and grandly suggested I make a film that showed how the IAF had won the Kargil War virtually on its own. I had burst out laughing and told him to find someone else to do the air force's bidding. When Sakka Jain didn't say anything, I got up and left his office. I was halfway to the elevator when Ashok Dhar caught up with me. 'Aren't you overreacting? You're shooting yourself in the foot behaving like this.' Fact of the matter, I was fast heading towards getting a doctorate in axing my own feet. It's an art, the ability to self-destruct. But from where I stood, I really had no choice. There were certain things one just could not shut one's eyes to.

The US president, Bill Clinton, finally visited India in March 2000. The Kargil VCD was presented to him and the entire US press corps along with a handwritten covering note written by Jaswant Singh. The NSA, J. N. Dixit, had asked me to be present at the press conference and I was amused to see one American correspondent look at the VCD, and then throw it in the trash can. I walked across and retrieved it. In the subsequent reports that covered the presidential visit, *Time* magazine carried a box item where they talked about the film and featured the cover of the VCD.

'Kunal,' the voice on the other end of the telephone had a warm, friendly sound, 'This is Inderjit Badhwar here.' From the 1959 batch of the Doon School, he had been one of the most successful editors of *India Today* in the mid-1980s and 1990s. Two of his brothers, Brigadier 'Nippy' and Lalit, I knew reasonably well, the former having served under my father in Mhow. 'Listen, I am coming to meet you with Xavier Collaco. We have a proposition for you.' Then Inder chuckled and said they both drank only single malt whisky, so I better stock up.

Off and on I used to write for *Discover India*, which was a part of Kuku Uberoi's Media Transasia Group. Within the hour, Inder with the amiable Xavier was sitting in my living room, holding forth about how the Kargil film needed a wider platform which through their enormous network of magazines in India and other countries, they could easily provide. Inder was currently the editor of *Swagat*, the Indian Airlines magazine, and he talked earnestly as to how he wanted to transform it from a collection of high-paid advertisements into a serious inflight *National Geographic*. The conversation then shifted to the soon-to-be-completed wildlife CD-ROM, and Xavier said his organization would help market that as well.[33]

I had scrupulously avoided getting into a tie-up with any organization in the past, but at that point in time, my boat with the navy after the clash with Arun Prakash was as good as sunk, and the interaction with Sakka Jain meant the IAF film on Kargil had crashed even before it could take off. *An Airfield at Gilgit* was a non-starter and the much-needed marketing tie-up with *National Geographic* was obviously not going to happen. Even though Sharad Gaur was no longer there, I was still paying the salaries of half-a-dozen people. Dipti, completely tied up with Vallika and Veeha, was no longer available even to edit the films which perforce had to be done by me.

Now there was this Trojan Horse with Inder the cheerleader telling me to take opportunity as it comes. A dinner was held at Inder's residence where Kuku Uberoi met me, and the talk was all about raising the bar for not just *Swagat* but *Discover India* as well. I was appointed the Group Features Editor, and a private limited company called Canvas Media with Dipti and me as 50 per cent stakeholders was launched. I was given half the third floor at K-35 Green Park where all the staff working on the wildlife CD-ROM were shifted. For the first time since Vimal Mahindra had mooted the idea in 1994, I did not have to worry about salaries.

Working with Inder was uplifting, for he was in my opinion, one of the best editors in the country. Within months, the change was obvious.

[33] At that point of time, the Media Transasia group, especially Swagat magazine, had been under fire. The inflight Indian Airlines monthly magazine had been with the Bangkok-based U. C.'Kuku' Uberoi for twenty-one years. It generated nearly a crore a month by carrying advertisements and advertorials. Retaining the contract year after year, involved all sorts of stuff behind the scenes. When starred questions were raised in Parliament, Xavier had turned to Inderjit Badhwar and was desperately looking for something'nationalistic' to hang the hat on. The Kargil film fit the bill perfectly.

Swagat, for example, carried a twenty-one-page feature titled *Ocean to Sky*, which was all aerial photographs of India. This was a far cry from the one- or two-page articles that were being allotted to topics earlier. Apart from finishing the *Golden Bird*, we also started work on an interactive CD on the Taj Mahal. As part of the shoot, my good friend Ashok Dilwali and myself found ourselves squeezed into the narrow minarets of the Taj. The thousands of unhatched pigeon eggs we crunched over as we climbed those narrow stairs, indicated no one since Shah Jahan's days, had been up that way.

True to their word, Media Transasia started to bring out full-page advertisements plugging not just the Kargil VCD, but also the *Golden Bird*. At first, there was no reaction to the Kargil film, and to be honest, that came as a huge surprise. A few months later, a grinning Xavier walked into my office and handed me a cheque for a few lakhs. 'What's this for?' I asked.

'Kargil film!'

I listened incredulously as Xavier explained what had happened. 'Those who fly in planes are the ones who are indifferent, even sceptical, and rarely will they buy the film. *Swagat* being a glossy magazine then goes to a lot of street vendors. Orders are coming from people who do not even have computers. They take the CD to a shop and see it there. It took me some time to understand what was happening.' No marketing teams making fancy projections on whiteboards would vector in this audience. It was an important lesson for us.

Air Marshal Sakka Jain had been posted out of Air HQ shortly after our meeting. However, I was surprised to get a call from Group Captain (later Air Marshal) Rakesh Jolly who asked me to swing by the next day and meet the additional ACAS (Ops). Expecting to meet someone new, I was greeted by Sakka Jain who was back after a brief stint elsewhere. He wasted no time, getting straight to the point: 'We started on the wrong foot. Let us wipe the slate clean. How do you want to make this film?'

I had obviously and finally got out of the right side of the bed that morning. I could hardly believe my luck. 'Sir, for a start, let's call in COs from squadrons that flew during the conflict ... Mirages, MiG 21s, 23s, 27s, 29s ... Jaguars, Canberras, Helicopter units. Let us see what they have to say and how we should project their roles.' Sakka Jain reached out and spoke to Air Marshal Vinod Patney, the vice chief. After a minute he put his hand on the mouthpiece and asked, 'When do you want to do this?'

Nothing gets the air force going as does crisis management. The more difficult the task, the more they get fired up. 'How about tomorrow? 11 o'clock?' I said with a grin. There was a mini explosion at Patney's end, but amazingly, the debrief began dead on time. Just who was dragged out of bed where and flown post haste to Air HQ, I will never know, but it sure was impressive.

We still had to raise the money for the film. Sakka Jain said the air force would cover it, so I told him what had happened with the Kargil VCD. 'There is no point making an hour-long film that is hardly seen by anyone. Let us also put the film out as a VCD. We can share the proceeds. Base money put in by the air force will partly get recovered, and we will also make our share of the money.' Everyone thought it was the ideal way to make the film, and an elaborate contract was drawn up. Part of the stipulated clauses also dealt with the sale of footage to any third party. I would have a veto, but if we both agreed to let another filmmaker use my footage, we would share the proceeds in that case as well. At rupees three or four thousand a second, I doubted if there would be any takers. But it felt good to put it down on paper.

When I reached home, I told Dipti about the proposed financial agreement. 'Are you loco?' She was incredulous. 'They offered you the money and you took just a part of it. Listen, right now it's all "hail fellow well met" but tomorrow you will have different people in that office.'

The other person who was equally upset was Rakesh Jolly for he was having to sit with the legal branch and draw up the contract. No self-respecting air force officer likes additional paperwork: 'My name is Jolly!' He sighed, looking as morose as a Labrador Retriever who watches you eat his favourite dish without giving him a bite. 'But I am anything but jolly! Anyway, I think we have all angles covered.' Sakka Jain signed the document on behalf of the IAF, while I did the same for KaleidoIndia. Now the file had to be pushed through the MOD. What that did to the Group Captain's good nature, I, fortunately, was not around to see it.

The sanctions came through a lot faster, perhaps because there was the precedent of *Salt of the Earth*. There was also a huge change in our own shooting profile. I was equipped with video cameras, which made life so much easier. The crew was reduced from one-and-a-half dozen to just half-a-dozen people, with Beena Rehman acting as my main assistant, whose job was to keep detailed notes. Rajendra Janglay, Dipti's classmate from FTII, also came on board for some of the legs. He was based in Bhopal and was a very competent cameraman. He had his own assistant, Suresh Dixit and was accompanied by Sanjeev Datta, a photographer. Others who were working with me at Canvas Media were also to be taken along for the experience and were allotted specific tasks. Dipti, who should have been an integral part of the shooting, though manifested for all the trips, eventually did not come for any of the shooting legs as both Vallika and Veeha were too young to be left with anyone else.

The shooting of *Aakash Yodha* finally got underway on 10 July 2001. Wing Commander Anil Kumar Tharani was to be my liaison officer and once again, the shoots were a complex maze, with the entire country our virtual canvas. We took off in a An-32 from Palam for Tambaram, picking up Rajinder Janglay and the other two on the way from Bhopal. The next morning, we flew to the IAF base at Car Nicobar where we fixed the heavier cameras at the rear, so that shots could be taken with the hatches open. I planned to shoot as many of the islands as possible, and with video no longer restricting us in terms of batteries and rolling stock, we had a virtual ball in the sky, often shooting down almost vertically. The aquamarine colour of the lagoons and the green of the islands made for some dramatic footage, as we crisscrossed the skies above. On the first day, we flew north, covering the Andaman chain including the volcano at Barren Island that was spewing lava. The sky was filled with ash, which made it difficult to get a vertically downward shot impossible. Back in Car Nicobar, in the evening, as the sun set, we headed into a lagoon and just floated around on our backs. The two pilots, Squadron Leader (later Wing Commander) Prem Singh Bajia and Flight Lieutenant Raj Kumar were talking amongst themselves.

'The AOC was pissed. He was hoping we would fly in some fish.'

'Fish? In Car Nicobar?' I asked, incredulous.

'Yes sir,' said Bajia, who was an experienced Andaman hand. 'In Nicobar you cannot buy fish. The locals go out, catch what they want for themselves and their families, and then put the rest back into the sea. That is their custom and no amount of money will get them to change their ways. So, we have to fly in fish from either Vizag or Tambaram.'

Heading south the next day, landing the An-32 at Campbell Bay was a tricky business on the short runway. We switched to the colourful, orange-coloured Mi-8 helicopters and clattered along the coast, before landing at the helipad near the lighthouse. The footage we shot was extremely valuable because in December 2004 when the earthquake with its epicentre just off Sumatra triggered a massive tsunami, major sections of the islands were severely damaged and the geographical profile of some islands including the Greater Nicobar Island were considerably altered.

For the next few months, the filming was almost continuous. From the Andamans, we returned to Delhi and then landed at Adampur on 15 July 2001. 223 Squadron (Tridents) was equipped with the deadly MiG-29 (NATO code name Fulcrum) which had been commanded by Wing Commander P. K. Singh. Equipped with BVR missiles, during the Kargil conflict they had been maintaining a constant vigil overhead, following a figure-of-eight patrolling pattern. For the next few days, I flew extensively from Adampur not only with MiG-29s but also the MiG-27s and Mirage 2000s that had taken on the task of ground attacks. Each time the routing was more or less the same, for we would leave the Punjab plains with the Dhauladhar Range to our west, cross over into the Kullu Valley, and then get into the Zanskar area to the north of Rohtang. Keeping the Great Himalayan Range to our left, we would then sweep across towards Kargil, before making our way back. Each sortie, sometimes with as many as four other aircraft flying formation with my MiG-29 trainer, was spectacular. Looking at the terrain below, having filmed the war from the ground and earlier having walked most of the valleys during my Tiger Tops days, I could relate to almost every feature.

While we blazed around in fighters, Janglay and Suresh Dixit were positioned in a An-32 to the north of the Great Himalayan Range. On our return leg from Kargil, we would then twist and turn around in the valleys while we were filmed. After spending five days at Adampur, we flew to Ladakh in a An-32 and landed at Thoise. After switching to a Mi-17 1V helicopter, we proceeded to the Siachen Base Camp. My entire crew by then were green in the face, for the air force had not catered at all for acclimatization while making the shooting schedule.

Letting them rest at Base Camp which was at around 15,000 feet (4752 m), I took off in a Cheetah to film the Sonam Post, which at 20,000 feet (6096 m) even by Siachen's standards, was one of the few examples of extreme endurance by the Indian Army. Named after a soldier from the Ladakh Scouts who had helped establish the post in 1984, I also wanted to see Bana Top where Subedar (later Honorary Captain) Bana Singh had earned his PVC. The rotors of the Cheetah barely getting any traction in the icy cold air, we literally climbed up along a vertical ice wall and landed at the post. A photograph I took on the approach would later be the cover of my book, *The Long Road to Siachen: The Question Why*. Brigadier Rajeev Williams, then a major had been the company commander at Sonam in 1987 when Bana Singh had captured Qaid Post.

Back at Base Camp, Sanjeev Datta was looking positively unwell, so we switched to a Mi-17 1V and flew back to Thoise. After a quick lunch, leaving the others behind, Janglay and I headed back to Base Camp and then flew along the entire length of the 75-kilometre glacier as we got to Indira Kol on the extreme northern side. The Shaksgam Nullah was visible, flowing northwards, when we turned around and returned to Base Camp. Once again, the footage we had obtained was spectacular, for we were also blessed with extremely good weather.

Unfortunately, back at the airfield at Thoise, Sanjeev was continuing to find the going difficult and was by then constantly throwing up. A night at Thoise was the last straw for him, so he was put on an aircraft that was flying back to Palam from where he had to make his way back to Bhopal, while we boarded our An-32 and headed for Srinagar. Frankly, I was hugely relieved that we had had only one dropout. Even though Janglay was struggling himself, his dedication to the task had seen him through.

51 Squadron was still being commanded by 'Tiny' Tandan and he had worked out some ambitious sorties for me. We finished briefing and

within an hour of having arrived in Srinagar, I was strapping up in the MiG-21 Bis trainer. A flight lieutenant had climbed up the ladder and as I started to put on the helmet, he handed me a 9 mm Beretta pistol. 'Just in case, sir,' he said with a grin, 'in case you eject in hostile territory. Remember six rounds are for the enemy and two are for yourself.'

I thought of Naik Inayat Ali and his version of events as they closed in on Squadron Leader Ahuja. Then the canopy was down, and the engine roared to life, and with our afterburner on, we lifted off from the Srinagar runway. We were immediately joined by two MiG-23 BNs that had gotten airborne from Avantipur, and together we then overflew Zoji La and struck simulated targets in the Kargil area. Returning to Srinagar, I switched to another aircraft, and this time around we took off with two other MiG-21s. I had wanted to film the pair against the backdrop of Nun and Kun, the two largest peaks in Zanskar. As we languidly circled what looked to the eye like a giant ice cream cake, I hoped there were no mountaineering expeditions on the mountains for the roar of our engines could well trigger off the odd avalanche below.

The next day we tried to get to Kargil but could not cross Zoji La due to inclement weather. As we landed back at Srinagar, news started trickling in that there had been a horrific massacre when terrorists had opened indiscriminate fire on pilgrims on their way to the Amarnath shrine. Janglay immediately took off in a Mi-17 1V for Pahalgam and they came back with a couple of bodies shortly. One of the victims was a middle-aged Gujarati lady in a saree, and it was horrific to see just how ruthlessly she had been shot. After the ambulances had taken the corpses away, the pilots and I together hosed the chopper's interiors down. The blood running on the tarmac past our feet seemed to flow endlessly.

After flying around and filming helicopter operations all across the Kashmir Valley, on 25 July we moved to Ambala. I was to fly in a three-aircraft Jaguar formation from Ambala the next day and we planned to get to Kullu where we were to do a loop over Bandrol before we proceeded on to Kargil. After doing all the intricate calculations, I called up my mom and briefed her in detail. TOT (Time over Target) which was Windsong, was 0827 hours and I told her both she and my father should be outside to see their son streak overhead.

'*Le ... satte naa maar ...*' (Don't pull fast ones!), was the response I got.

'Listen mom ... I'll call you from the top of the runway just before I close the cockpit ... we'll be overhead in seven minutes ...'

Everything went like clockwork the next day. We got airborne, the other two Jaguars flying with over-wing Magic missiles. We kept a mid-level profile, and over Bandrol, which was 9 kilometres upstream of Kullu along the Beas Valley, we pulled back on the stick and executed a perfect formational loop, then engaged afterburners to gain height, crossed Rohtang and carried on. Later, I would learn my parents had missed the aerobatic display altogether, for they were still finishing breakfast. Only when the house almost came down in the roar of the aircraft, did they scramble out but by then we were far gone. We returned to Delhi the next day, having completed the first leg of shooting for *Aakash Yodha*.

Unlike *Salt of the Earth* that had been shot in one continuous stretch, the shooting this time around was to be staggered. The next leg was almost a month later. After getting to Chandigarh on 23 August which was spent flying around in the humungous Mi-26 (Featherweights), I was airborne early the next morning for one of the most dramatic sorties of my life. I was particularly keen to film Sesar Kangri massif and the Rimo Muztagh which were the two dominating and defining features in the Karakoram region. Flying in a non-pressurised aircraft with the back hatches open, I knew it was going to be extremely difficult. I asked Janglay, who had returned from Bhopal after the break, if he wanted to stay back, but he was as always game for it. We had four oxygen cylinders with us, but after taking off, we realized they were quite useless. A second An-32, flying in from Chandigarh, lined up and flew behind us. The temperature was plummeting, and we were struggling to breathe, which gave a literal meaning to the 'landscape below us taking our breath away'. Janglay was beginning to turn blue, so I gave the command to shut the hatches. However, we still had to drop the load we were carrying on board at DBO. With the hatches again open, almost all of us were struggling to breathe, and the cold was getting to everybody. The fifteen or twenty minutes that it took for the aircraft to touch down at Leh were the most agonizing, for one could almost feel the marrow in our bones beginning to freeze, and the pain in the limbs would linger for a few days.

Shortly thereafter, we took off from Leh in an Il-76 for Chandigarh. I had gotten into the navigator's cabin which was literally below the nose of the giant aircraft. Lying on my belly, holding the camera steady, I filmed the terrain as we lumbered along the runway, then lifted off and left the Spituk Gompa below. The glistening waters of the Indus were joined by the Zanskar, but by then we had turned south. It was perhaps one of the most spectacular flights and I continued to film continuously until we overflew Keylong and Rohtang, after which we entered the Kullu Valley.

Rajendra Janglay had done a very good job, but the flying was proving too much for him as well, and I reluctantly bid him and Suresh Dixit goodbye. With the abrupt exit of Janglay, even though other cameramen were considered, none fit the bill and the entire shooting was now my responsibility. More than the lack of a second camera team, I was feeling the absence of Dipti, who was not willing to leave the two girls behind in anyone else's care. As for the work related to Canvas Media, Dipti was not involved with the wildlife CD-ROM which was at this point being finalized. At one level, I desperately needed to decentralize, but the nature of the work was such that I found even the simplest of tasks would have to be redone if they were not supervised minutely. If one had to do that, then one might as well do it oneself. Anyhow, I was not complaining, for I always told myself no one had ever died of a work overload, and what was more, I was quite enjoying the pace at which things were moving.

I cut the crew down even further, with just Beena Rehman accompanying me and Tharani mostly. We took off in a Dornier from Delhi to Bagdogra on 28 August, which was a fairly tedious three-hour flight. True to style, the moment we landed, I was given a sandwich and a cup of tea by the IAF, and promptly took off in a Cheetah along with a Chetak to film the accompanying helicopter flying along the Teesta from the Coronation Bridge. By the time I landed back at Bagdogra, 8 Squadron (Pursoots), commanded by Wing Commander (later Air Vice Marshal) Tejinder Pal 'TP' Singh,[34] were all set to get airborne. Equipped with the MiG-21 FL variant, we planned a three-aircraft formation that would take off from Bagdogra, gain altitude and then overfly the summit

[34] TP had acted in Salt of the Earth while he was posted at Hindon earlier and was therefore an old friend.

of Kanchenjunga. We would then do some low-level formation flying below the Teesta Barrage and then land back. As we walked towards the aircraft, an officer came running and said that information was just coming in that a MiG-21 had crashed near Tezpur and Flying Officer Amit Bansal had been killed.

TP had just taken over the squadron, and I was watching his reaction. He promptly asked all aircraft be readied; the entire squadron would fly as soon as we got back. We then proceeded to our trainer, where I hesitated at the base of the ladder. It was TP's turn to watch me now, and he softly said, 'It's OK. Just shove your hand under your thigh and get to the first step.' I clambered up, and once I started strapping up, I had forgotten all about the crash, at least for the time being. We started up, taxied out, lined up and with that thunderous roar which had become a part of my DNA, we lifted off from Bagdogra. Flying in formation, we gained altitude over the Teesta River and then turned into the huge Kanchenjunga massif, which was partly under cloud. With the summit below us and the other two aircraft in formation just above it, I lined them up in the viewfinder and started filming. I took a deep pull at the oxygen and looked around me. Beyond the Singalila lay Nepal and as we banked sharply north, the Tibetan Plateau was stretched out below us. From the air, it all seemed so ridiculous ... boundaries that separated India from Nepal, Tibet, or Bhutan for that matter.

The next day, we again decided to overfly Kanchenjunga, and once again the massif was partly under cloud. 'I don't know what it is about Kanchenjunga,' said TP, 'if you take a camera up, it's always partly under cloud cover.' There was a major standing nearby, and he added he had just come from Lachung where he had been posted for two years. An amateur photographer, he said he had tried almost on a daily basis to get the mountain minus clouds from the northern side.

'You have to have the gods on your side, sir,' he said ruefully, 'I wasn't so lucky.' I would remember his words exactly a decade later.

It was evening when we had landed at Kumbhigram in South Assam. The next morning, with Reena and Tharani following in a Chetak, I took off in a Cheetah for Kamzawl. As the Lushai Hills rose up from the plains and merged into the Naga–Patkai, we overflew Vairengte and Aizwal, the capital of Mizoram. We then overflew Champai and Lunglei and refuelled at Kamzawl. During this one sortie, I had covered most of the areas where 18 Rajput companies had been deployed after the Bangladesh War in 1972. My father used to take five days to cover the circuit which had taken us just two hours to do. The advent of helicopters in particular had completely changed the dynamics. 'Another decade,' I told Tharani, 'these places will be as accessible as any other part of India.'

We were joined by a Mi-8 helicopter, and we set off for Parva which was the southernmost post held by the BSF. The Mi-8 had some technical problem, so he returned to Kamzawl, while we continued to Parva. Situated some 50 kilometres south of Lawngtlai and Siaha, the post kept a watch over the 3 Country Point, where the borders of India, Bangladesh and Myanmar meet. For the men stationed there, the sense of isolation was tremendous, and to make matters worse, the area was notorious for cerebral malaria. To the west, lay the ports of Chittagong and Cox's Bazar. One could not help but wonder at the absolute idiocy of the situation. For the Mizos to get to a port, they had to travel thousands of kilometres to get to Calcutta, whereas the Bay of Bengal was within shaking hands distance from them. But then, that was perhaps the biggest tragedy of India's Northeast.

On the return leg, after refuelling at Kamzawl, we flew along the Bangladesh border for a while and then set course for Silchar where we landed at Kumbhigram. The next day the An-32 deposited us at Guwahati from where we flew back to Delhi via Bagdogra in the gigantic Il-76. Once again, I spent the entire time lying on my belly in the navigator's cabin, filming the Brahmaputra Valley down below.

The role of the Mirage 2000 during the Kargil conflict, where laser-guided bombs (LBGs) had been used with relative precision, had been one of the highlights of the war for the IAF. Taking off in a Dornier from Palam for the hour-long flight to Gwalior, I was looking forward to flying with not only the Mirages but also with TACDE and the Electronic Warfare Unit. Considered to be the equivalent of the USAF's Top Gun programme, I was wondering how to capture some modern-day aerial combat on film. Rajan Bhasin, who had flown Dipti in 1992, was by then a group captain and the COO at Gwalior. He had climbed up the ladder and watched as I strapped into a Mirage 2000 cockpit. 'You sure are a lucky chap,' he said, 'you sure as hell have someone's hand on your head!' I grinned back happily, and then along with another two fighters, we were starting up, taxiing out and after the mandatory last-minute tyre checks, we were airborne. The planned sortie was a ninety-minute simulated air strike against Jodhpur airfield, and we went in low level which gave me some fabulous angles on the other two Mirages who were from 1 Squadron (Tigers).

This was followed by a sortie with TACDE pilots. Though the manoeuvres that were executed were stomach-churningly exhilarating in the extreme, from a filming point of view it was a disaster. After a while, I just put the camera away and concentrated on the roller coaster ride. When we landed, Tharani, who was watching us twist and turn in the sky from the ground, said that he was surprised I hadn't thrown up all over.

We then flew from Gwalior to Agra, a short twenty-five-minute ride in the Dornier. The COO, Group Captain Paul held a detailed briefing that included pilots from not just the An-32 squadron and Para Training School (PTS) but also the Canberra crews. Suggestions and ideas were flowing from all directions, for no one wanted to miss out on being part of the film. The next morning, we were airborne at first light and by the end of the day, had been in the air for upwards of nine hours, mostly filming with the back hatches wide open. We dropped 1,000 lb bombs at a range somewhere near the Chambal River, dropped sticks of paratroopers, flew formation with other An-32s, dropped flares and even flew formation with a Canberra for an hour or so.

By the end of the day, half of my crew was running a fever or was suffering from extreme fatigue. The next day was to be as hectic with multiple sky dives and more para jumps scheduled. I suddenly found myself without a crew, and I needed people to hand me cameras and take notes as the day progressed. I asked Tharani to pull out the sanction letter from the MOD which allowed people who were members of my staff to be manifested on flights. The only names mentioned were Dipti and me, while the others had been left to my discretion. One of the flight commanders at PTS, Wing Commander Anirudh Shreekanth Pednekar, said that in his entire service life, he had never been able to fly his wife. He suggested if rules permitted, she would be only too happy to volunteer. Group Captain Paul, the COO, shrugged his shoulders and said he had no problems, so it was decided that Mrs Pednekar would be my assistant the next day.

With the back of the An-32 wide open and serious-faced paratroopers going past you into thin air, my entire focus was on the shots I was getting the next morning. Mrs Pednekar, draped in a saree, though somewhat inappropriately dressed for the task, was doing a fine job, handing me different cameras as per the pre-arranged signals. After a while, we landed back, and as we were taxiing back to pick up more paratroopers, the door of the cockpit briefly opened, and I saw Pednekar's son standing behind his father's seat. I instinctively knew that this would mean serious trouble, but at that moment was much too busy to do anything about it.

After lunch, I rounded up my still unwell crew and herded them into the Dornier. At Bhatinda, Squadron Leader (later Group Captain) Kambhampati Nachiketa was waiting for us. 'Nacchi' flying a MiG-27 in a ground-attack role had been hit by a shoulder-fired stinger missile, had ejected and become the first and only Indian POW. He was part of the UAV TETTRA School which was flying an Israeli variant of the unmanned 'eyes in the sky' and we spent an interesting afternoon looking at what was then literally cutting-edge technology at work. By the time we wrapped up in Bhatinda, it was fairly late, and we took off well after it had gotten dark and set course for Ambala where we were to spend the night. One of the two pilots who was flying us was Flight Lieutenant Karishma Bhalla, who around midnight, as we approached Ambala, turned to me and asked me what my mobile number was.

It seemed that ever since we had taken off from the Agra Air Force Station, there had been chaos on the ground. From what I could subsequently gather, while we were up in the air dropping sticks of paratroopers, a delegation of air force officers' wives had marched to the office of the AOC, Air Commodore Suryakant Nijanand Bal and demanded that if Mrs Pednekar could 'fly', so must they. The AOC, who was until then pondering on issues related to the higher direction of war, had no idea what they were talking about and he in turn called the COO who nonchalantly said all the paperwork was in order. But then leadership qualities in the IAF are not necessarily restricted to only those who fly and one of the leaders of the delegation had demanded, 'But what about Pednekar's son?' Both the COO and the AOC were stumped, for that was news to them also.

Anirudh Pednekar, after landing back at Agra, had realized he had crossed the thin red line. The co-pilot, the navigator and the ground crew were sworn to silence, but by then the wheels were turning furiously. Nijanand Bal wanted the 'truth, and nothing but the truth' so everyone was interrogated in different parts of the base and were told they might as well become 'approvers' as the others had 'spilt the beans!' All this had culminated with Karishma Bhalla getting a series of urgent messages while we were still in the air, asking for my number. Hardly had we landed, all groggy and sleepy, I had Pednekar pleading on the line that the 'sanction' letter be faxed immediately. The COO in Ambala, who was either Pednekar's coursemate or soulmate from a previous birth, was equally worked up and had half the air base on standby to send the fax. Tharani, pragmatic fellow that he was, summed it up in one line: '*Sab saale khiske huain hai!*' (All these fellows have lost it!)[35]

On 10 September, after a short break, Tharani and I flew from Palam to Bidar via Nagpur in North Karnataka. Despite all the fighter sorties that I had done by now, I was apprehensive about the flying the next day, for I would be with the IAF's aerobatic team, the Surya Kirans. Nine Kiran Mk-IIs, painted red with yellow streaks depicting the rays of the sun, were to be put through the paces while I was to be No. 10 in the formation, sometimes slipping into the No. 9 position. In the afternoon, the Surya Kiran formation took off and put up their usual spectacular aerial display above the airfield for my benefit as I filmed the various breathtaking manoeuvres from the ground.

[35] Wing Commander Anirudh Shreekanth Pednekar was tried by the IAF in a specially convened court martial where I was one of the key witnesses much after the film had been edited and aired. The wing commander was let off with a severe reprimand, but he did not progress any further in the IAF.

The next morning, I strapped in beside Squadron Leader (later Group Captain) Sanjeev Sethi and it was quite exhilarating to fly close formation with another nine aircraft. The forty-minute routine in the air gave me some wonderful shots and after executing some gut-wrenching twists and turns, we landed back at Bidar. We then boarded the relatively sedate Dornier 228 and set course for Pune. It was still daylight when Tharani and I dumped our gear in the rooms allotted to us at the Air Force Mess at Lohegaon. There was a television in the room, and it was tuned in to CNN. I reached for the remote to switch it off but then paused as I could see one of the Twin Towers of the Trade Centre emitting smoke. Anil Tharani also entered the room, and we watched as a second aircraft appeared and flew into the second tower.

That night, like most of the world, we watched in disbelief and horror as a synchronized attack on the United States unfolded on the television screen. The Twin Towers imploded, and both Anil Tharani and I decided to walk across to a nearby café for dinner. At that point of time, no one knew what was going on, or who the hijackers were. 'Like Pearl Harbour, this is going to deeply impact the US psyche. Two things will happen; a) The hijackers will be Muslims and Islam will now be viewed as a global threat and c) the Americans will lash out at any target, so long as there is a target. They cannot touch the Saudis and Iran as they have burnt their fingers in the past. Probably they will go after Iraq ... You watch ...' I told Anil. 'Somehow Pakistan will also be linked to this'—I had written this on a paper napkin as I spoke. Two decades later, it would fall out of my 2001 diary.[36]

Tharani felt it was highly unlikely, for the attack was much too sophisticated in its execution. He said it was most probably a right-wing western group. I told Tharani that this would lead to the US attacking Afghanistan, and Bush being Sr Bush's son would use this as an excuse to take out Saddam Hussain as well.

I don't think we got too much sleep that night, being glued as it were to the news coming from various parts of the United States. However, for us, it was to be business as usual, and I found myself strapping into the

[36] I had also recounted this conversation to the *Times of India's* US correspondent, Chidanand Rajghatta. In response to an article he had written at the time, in an email to Chiddu on 9/11/2006, I had also written: 'Remember Mandrake, the Illusionist of our childhood created by Lee Falk of Phantom fame. Well, replace him with a certain General Musharaff.

rear cockpit of a Su-30 shortly after breakfast. 24 Squadron (Hawks) were at the time the privileged lot, for the Su-30 was then considered to be 'arguably the best fighter on either side of the Suez Canal'. Flying in a formation of four aircraft, we got airborne and then spent an hour and forty-five minutes putting the aircraft through its paces. To say it was one of the most languidly electrifying sorties of my life would be making an understatement.

Back in Pune, we moved across the tarmac to 6 Squadron (Dragons) and once again, having done much the same thing earlier in 1992, we streaked off towards Mumbai. Flying low-level, barely a few feet above the water, we 'bounced' a couple of warships, including INS *Delhi*, and returned to Pune. Fairly exhausted by then, I slept through the nearly four-hour-long flight in the Dornier to Bhatinda where we spent the night. The next morning Nacchi (Nachiketa) flew his UAVs and after filming the futuristic-looking contraptions, we headed off for Srinagar where a bizarre situation was beginning to unfold.

To simulate explosions on the ground, I had asked for a couple of 1000 lb bombs that were to be exploded with the help of sappers at a firing range just off Kargil. An An-32 had dutifully flown two bombs to Srinagar airfield and offloaded them not far from the main runway. The airport authorities in Srinagar, always on an alert but perhaps even further spooked by the terrorist attacks in the US, started getting the heebie-jeebies about two 'live 1000 lb bombs' lying in open view of every incoming and outgoing civil aircraft.

Group Captain Ramesh Malhan was the Air 1 in Udhampur and being an avid photographer, he had been flying with me on some of the filming legs. He was now going ballistic, for the forklift that could load the two 1000 lb bombs onto the Mi-17 1V helicopters at the Srinagar airfield

---

The fortress of Xanadu, let's call it the ISI or the entire fortress of Pakistan. And Osama, well, remember Hojo, Mandrake's chef at Xanadu who is the secret chief of Interpol—just imagine Osama as the *khansama* at the Army House who slips prime minister his daily instructions with his fried eggs each morning.'

had become unserviceable. At my suggestion, we got a working party together of Sikh LI troops, and after some heavy lifting and a lot of motivational slogan shouting, one bomb was finally lifted into the helicopter. However, during the process, the Mi-17 was slightly damaged. After a lot of cajoling, the pilots agreed to load a second bomb onto another helicopter. We then heaved a collective sigh of relief when the two 'large explosive devices' were finally airborne. However, half an hour later both the helicopters were back as the weather at Zoji La had gone bad.

The next day the two bombs were deposited at Kargil, and once again there was general panic, this time the messages coming thick and fast from the army formations in Kargil, all ending with the plea, 'do something!' By then I had not only flown back to Delhi but gone on to Bangalore where I was filming with ASTE. Philip Rajkumar, still commanding the unit, wanted me to try and film a manoeuvre called 17 Alpha, which meant climbing up to an altitude of 20,000 feet in a Jaguar, then switching off the engine and dropping like a stone. The trick, it seemed, was to reignite the engine before hitting the ground. All I remember is that we hit 7 or 8G in the process, and I was so thrilled I was alive, I forgave Philip for having put me through the gut-wrenching but exhilarating ordeal.

Air HQ then literally went to sleep for three weeks, which gave me a much-needed break. Ramesh Malhan was still behaving as if I was personally responsible for the twin beauties adorning the yet-to-be-completed Kargil airstrip, and so I suggested to him, 'Just paint the bombs in air force colours and place them on either side of the base's gate ...' Finally, on 9 October, we got going again, landing at Halwara where we were joined by a bomb disposal team. After much back and forth, finally, the fireworks we needed for the film were created and the saga of the 1000 lb bombs finally came to an end with two huge bangs.

Just how treacherous things can be on the Siachen Glacier was demonstrated most starkly the next day. Asked to hop across to Thoise by Air HQ to film a forward landing ground (FLG) close to Indra Col the next day, we moved by a Mi-17 to the Base Camp. There I transferred to a Cheetah and we flew in near-perfect conditions to the FLG. I had put on a jacket but had not bothered with the down pants, as the Mi-17 was to follow five minutes later. My task was to film the helicopter as it made the approach and landed, then clamber on board from the rear and return to Base Camp.

As the 'whup whup' sound of departing rotors receded into the distance, a deadly silence enveloped the entire area. The sky was blue, and I could see the moraines on the glacier extending for miles. I settled down to wait for the Mi-17, when suddenly, out of nowhere, a whiteout started to develop, and within a minute I was in the midst of a dense cloud. The temperature started to plummet, and my teeth began to chatter. Just then, I could hear the incoming Mi-17, but it was highly unlikely that the pilots would have a visual approach to the FLG.

Barely twenty minutes had passed, and I was beginning to freeze. The Mi-17 pilots knew I was not equipped to withstand the cold, so they continued to hold just around the FLG. Finally, the visibility improved just that bit, and the helicopter cautiously entered the mist, and though I was almost blacking out, I managed to film it as it came and landed. However, by then, my legs were gone, and the co-pilot and engineer came out and dragged me into the helicopter, even as the pilot lifted off almost simultaneously.

There were more bombing sorties flown, the action shifting to Jodhpur and Uttarlai. Flying in a MiG-21, I filmed other MiGs as they dropped more 1000 lb bombs and fired rockets at ground targets at Pokhran. We got one particular shot which was extremely spectacular, but very difficult to execute. As the bomb detached from the belly of the ground-attack MiG-21, we went into a tight turn and followed it as it went all the way to the ground and then exploded in a huge fireball. What was even more pleasing was the fact that the pilot's aiming skills were excellent, the bomb hitting the centre of the target area. Judging from the craters around, it was obviously not that easy.

Back in Gurgaon, I had to take over a second apartment in Beverly Park. Both Dipti and I were acutely aware that sooner or later, the onus of looking after her ageing parents would squarely fall on us. Gaurav was in the United States and Niti was in no position to do anything should any major health-related crisis develop. The very nature of the subject was such that no one wanted to openly discuss it, preferring to behave like ostriches with their heads buried in the sand. Mr Bhalla, who was by far the most logical and balanced person in the family, had listened to me when I first broached the subject of investing in a 'family flat' which at that time was costing around rupees seventy-five lakh. We were in court with DLF Universal having challenged the illogical escalation of costs in the case of 1201-A, and I had asked indications from Rajiv Singh, whether he would lower the price by fifteen lakh as part of an out-of-court settlement should we buy 1704-A as well. We had also invested in a flat in Noida in the railway colony, that we could sell and bring another fifteen lakh to the kitty. The rest could be contributed by the in-laws and Gaurav, and Dipti's parents could shift from Bombay if and when.

I was somewhat taken aback when Dipti turned to me and said why was I getting involved in 'her family matters'. By that time the process to sell off the flat in the railway colony had been initiated, and DLF too had after some hard bargaining lowered the price as promised. Around the time the final payments were to be done, Gaurav arrived from the US on one of his periodical trips and exclaimed the flat was indeed a terrific 'investment' opportunity, and he would pay the money. In fact, he claimed rather grandly, it was worth buying five to six flats in Beverly Park. I expected Mr Bhalla to say something, but he didn't, for Gaurav was always difficult to talk to. Bottom line was that the flat in Noida got sold off for no rhyme or reason.

What was done with the best of intentions would subsequently impact our lives in the most negative manner. In 2006 Mr Bhalla sat down with Sanjay Shah, the chartered accountant who handled all our accounts and returns, and systematically worked out who within the family owed money to whom. In addition, since all electricity and maintenance bills were being paid by KaleidoIndia in the interim and would be reimbursed by Gaurav periodically from his NRI account, it was suggested that the partnership firm set up in 1988, be converted into a sole proprietorship in the name of Dipti. I saw no major advantage in this, but since it was suggested by Sanjay Shah with Mr Bhalla's approval, I went along with it. Dipti, who by and large had little to do with accounts, reacted sharply when fresh papers had to be signed. 'I hope you don't try and send me to jail!' Strangely, even then the remark of hers had rankled.

October 2001 was also the Silver Jubilee of my batch in Doon School. After a quick trip to Dehradun, it was time to wrap up *Aakash Yodha*. Considering the IAF's three losses during the Kargil conflict were all due to shoulder-fired stinger missiles, we needed to shoot similar types of weapon systems. However, we still had to shoot in the Vijaynagar salient of Arunachal and accordingly had flown to Jorhat from where we had proceeded further by helicopters.

In the evening two days later, I got a message to call ACAS Ops at Air HQ most urgently. Both Anil Tharani and I were a bit surprised, but nevertheless, since there was no cell phone cover where we were, we walked out of the Jorhat Base, crossed the railway line to the nearby market and found an STD booth. Sakka Jain asked me if I had seen the NDA advertisement in the *Times of India*. I, for one, had no idea what he was talking about, and I told him that.

The NDA in Khadakwasla wanted a film made and since the commandant was Air Marshal A. K. Trikha, the Academy had been requested by Air HQ to also allow me to bid for the film. Even some big film producers were in the run for the project, and among the names thrown at me, were J. P. Dutta and Ramesh Sippy. I was still processing this unexpected information in my head when Sakka Jain bowled what seemed to be a reverse swinging googly ... I had to make the presentation at NDA by 1100 hrs the next morning.

Air HQ, when it got into a crisis management mode was unbeatable. 12 November 2001, at 0400 hours I lifted off from Jorhat in an Avro HS-48, transferred to An-32 at Guwahati, switched planes at Allahabad, met Dipti at the tarmac at Palam where she handed me my blazer and tie, then landed at Pune from where I transferred in a Cheetah to NDA. At 1100 hours I was ushered into a conference room where around two dozen immaculately turned-out officers and their wives were seated. Each had a paper and a pencil and was obviously grading each candidate. One column caught the corner of my eye. It read 'appearance of the Director'. Considering I was feeling like something the cat had brought home, I wondered if I'd even score on that front.

I had expected to at best meet three or four people, and I was not prepared to make a presentation or a speech. Anyway, clearing my throat and speaking as slowly as I could, I started to ad lib. However, after two to three minutes, I gave up.

'Sir, this makes no sense, my standing here and saying what the film will be or won't be. I have no idea what the ethos of the NDA is beyond the basic generic stuff which everyone knows ...' I addressed Anil Trikha, 'All I know at this point in time is that I would be honoured to be given this task. I also feel I would require at least a year to shoot the Academy from within, with the least amount of enactments.' The IAF had gone the whole hog to ensure I got to NDA on time, and I had just blown the entire presentation.

Anil Trikha stood up. I am not too sure if anyone had marked their sheets as yet. The commandant took a stride towards the rostrum where I was standing. 'Congratulations Kunal,' he said, while at the same time shaking my hand. 'The film is yours!' He turned to Major General Ivor Satur, his deputy, 'Work out the details!' And he was gone. I realized with a start that I had not even quoted a figure for the film. Satur turned towards Group Captain Johnson Chacko, who was one of the four battalion commanders at the Academy and was in charge of the film.

'Johnson, work out the details!' He too made his exit with his little entourage. Chacko grinned at me, and I half expected him to pass the buck to someone below him.

'You remember me? I featured in *Salt of the Earth*. I was flying the MiG-25s in Bareilly.' Though official quotes had not as yet been asked for as yet, in the presentations made before the committee during the last few days, the budgets indicated had ranged from rupees three lakh to three crore. I sat down with Chacko in his office and did some back-of-the-envelope calculations and arrived at thirteen lakh. Chacko was looking at me quizzically. 'You sure about this?'

'Yes,' I then explained the model we were working out for *Aakash Yodha* as well. Air HQ was paying for the making of the film, but I was also talking to Kapil Chandni and P. V. Jagmohan to market the IAF film. 'We can do that with NDA as well. As a filmmaker, I want the film seen, not confined to its a few official screenings. I am talking to Bharatrakshak.com and if we have the Academy on board, we can sell the VCDs and share the profits.'

After two more days during which I also got to fly with Chacko over the nearby Sinhagad Fort in a Diamond HK36 Super Dimona, an Austrian motor glider that allowed air force cadets at NDA to get initiated to flying, I returned to Delhi. The *Aakash Yodha* shooting was over and the edits were on, shooting for NDA was to start almost immediately after that and after the completion of the wildlife CD-ROM, we had decided to do an interactive CD on the Taj Mahal.

The pace at which things were moving, I was not surprised to find myself on 6 December in the unlikeliest of places. Having arrived to shoot the Taj Mahal at Agra, we were met with the usual bureaucratic 'no photography' response, despite having previously obtained permission from the Archaeological Survey of India that regulates and controls most monuments in India. However, after a while and a couple of cups of tea, the local director was running ahead of us opening all doors, so much so that I found myself not only on the roof of the Taj but also sitting on the main dome. As if that was not enough, I was then asked if we wished to go up the minarets. Ashok Dilwali, one of Delhi's most recognized photographers, was with me and we together climbed the ever-narrowing steps, stepping on hundreds, if not thousands of unfertilized pigeon eggs. As we wound our way to the top, the officials accompanying us proudly said the minarets had never been opened from within for at least a hundred years.

On 20 December, Dipti and I presented the *Aakash Yodha* cut to Sakka Jain, who suggested we consider doing one more shoot to include the IAF's operational role. He slyly added he would throw in another Su-30 MKI version for me to fly in, and the greedy fellow that I was, I took the bait hook-line-and-sinker! Life at the end of 2001 could not have been any better.

22

Standard Bearers & Canvas Media: Triumph & Disaster

Veeha followed Vallika who was in Grade 3 into Shri Ram School, joining Pravesh Vatika (Nursery) on 7 February 2002. The IAF edits were on in full swing and Canvas Media was all poised to take off with both the wildlife and Taj CD-ROMs completed and published. A few days previously, I was in the K-35 Green Park office, when Inderjit Badhwar, the editor of *Swagat* called up from the basement where the editorial offices were located. I knew Media Transasia was in discussion with the MEA to start a multilingual magazine called *India Perspectives*, but other than just a casual interest in the matter, I was not particularly involved or interested in what was happening. One of their premier magazines, *Discover India*, had already been transferred to Canvas Media and the first edition on the tigers of Kanha had already rolled out. I was therefore a bit surprised when Inder, in his usual enthusiastic manner, said he was coming up with some people to discuss the MEA project.

'Media Transasia cannot take it on,' said Inder, lighting cigarettes for both of us. With him was a middle-aged lady who was obviously the 'fixer' in the deal for there was nothing covert about the conversation that followed. 'It's all been fixed. Canvas Media will publish the magazine in five languages.' The lady then took over while Inder and I listened. She said Director XP (External Publications), a Sikh gentleman who had handled the press briefings during the Kargil conflict, would receive ten per cent kickback while others, whom she named, would receive similar amounts. Even how the payments would be made to them was discussed and obviously with *Swagat* there were a lot of precedents.

I didn't say anything then but asked Inder to hop into my car as we prepared to head home to Beverly Park and the Media Centre in Gurgaon respectively. 'Tell your driver to follow,' I said. Taking the Mehrauli Road, I could see the sun setting in a red fireball to the west, while Inder sat in the car with his feet on the dashboard. 'You know,' I said, 'You were the editor of *India Today* for fourteen years ...'

'Fifteen ...'

'Yeah, fifteen. I guess your biggest achievement was to doggedly go after and eventually bring down the Rajiv Gandhi government on the Bofors issue. That took some doing!'

'Sons of bitches ...' It was Inder's favourite subject, so it was easy enough to get him started. 'Just imagine, you are the prime minister and you start taking kickbacks!' I think the realization hit him as he spoke the words. I had to give it to him for switching tracks without breaking a sweat or missing a beat. 'Who the hell do these MEA bastards think they're dealing with? Kickbacks! Huh!' The crusader in Inder was back, or so I thought, and even when he switched to his car at my gate, he was muttering about how he was going to 'screw them all!'

The next day I had a pre-scheduled meeting with Monika Mohta at MEA. She was at the time working directly under Director XP and I bluntly said that her boss and all the others who were salivating about how much money they would make could take a hike. It simply wasn't going to happen on my watch. I had come to talk to Monika about distributing *Aakash Yodha* to various Embassies and High Commissions, but I don't think I got around to that subject.

That night Kuku Uberoi flew in from Bangkok and we met over dinner at Inder's place. Xavier Collaco was also present. Nothing was said about the MEA project, but a Board meeting was fixed for the next day. I was the last to enter, by which time everyone else was seated. Inder was looking here and there, as was Collaco. Kuku Uberoi started to talk about the 'Corporate' structure and how one had to flow with the tide. I was by then feeling physically nauseated, and I pointedly asked Kuku if I had been approached by Xavier a year ago because, by marketing the Kargil film, it would help enhance their credibility with questions having been raised in Parliament about the endless contract Media Transasia had with Indian Airlines. The silence in the room was deafening. 'Alright,' I knew what I had to do, 'I quit! You can wrap up Canvas Media, but I want all accounts settled, an inventory of all CDs in stock and my staff paid three months' salary.'

In the last year that I had known him, Xavier had become a close friend. I walked out of the room expecting him to do the needful. The mistake I made was to call my staff and tell them we were closing down, and then I got into my car and drove off. I should have known; I was dealing with a hard-nosed businessman and had played squarely into his hands. I never got any account, nor were any payments for the wildlife CDs ever made.

What probably made the situation worse was the fact that I was constantly on the move. *Aakash Yodha*, even though one leg remained to be completed, was in the final stages of completion. My entire focus was on the IAF and NDA films and I just did not have the time to extricate myself from the Canvas Media fiasco. The case against DLF was then in its fourth year and all that had happened was one date given after the other, mostly four to five months apart. Rajiv Singh had virtually laughed in my face saying he had deep pockets and even if the case dragged for fifteen or twenty years, his legal team would ensure basic arguments would not come up. Filing a case against Media Transasia, I was advised, would also meander along much the same route.

Most of the shooting for *The Standard Bearers* began in early March 2002, even before the formal quotations had been called for. One of the annual features was the highly coveted Bakshi Cup, where NDA and IMA sporting teams fought it out on the playing fields. By then, 'Maun' Shergill had risen to the rank of Lieutenant General and taken over as the commandant of the IMA. Over a cup of tea at the Lake View Guesthouse that overlooked the picturesque Peacock Bay, Maun suggested I make a film on the IMA as well. 'I'll initiate the process when I get back to

Dehradun tomorrow,' he said, 'Swing by and meet the deputy commandant and the BGS.'

The next few months were a blur as I shuttled between Gurgaon and Khadakwasla. NDA was a dream to shoot, and I think everyone involved with the making of *The Standard Bearers* hugely enjoyed the process. Trikha gave me a free hand and with Johnson Chacko coordinating the shoots with Major Ajith Kumar, a Jat officer who was also the Divisional Officer of Juliet Squadron, everything went like clockwork. On 31 May I filmed the passing-out parade at NDA as 102 Course graduated, and exactly a week later on 7 June, the summer passing-out-parade at the IMA became the first event to be canned for *The Making of a Warrior*.

Looking back and reviewing my notes from that period, I really wonder how one managed. Dipti was busy with the *Aakash Yodha* edits, and with the heat of summer hitting its zenith, one even managed a four-day trip to Kullu, where Vallika and Veeha revelled in climbing the plum trees, playing with Elsa the Labrador, and eating barbecued trout that I cooked in the newly constructed gazebo.

By October, even though the winter passing-out parade was yet to be filmed, the bulk of the NDA film was done and dusted. Post-production work was being done in 1704-A Beverly Park and Dipti had seamlessly switched from the IAF to the NDA edits.

Especially, since all the marketing channels we had used to distribute the Kargil CD as a film had dried up with the abrupt end with Media Transasia over *India Perspectives*, I then had to look for effective ways to distribute both *Aakash Yodha* and *The Standard Bearers*. Kapil Chandni was Mumbai-based and was one of a small group of highly motivated individuals who had got together to form a website called Bharatrakshak. Though the group was partial to the air force because of their own leanings, they were fast becoming an important repository of information on matters military in the Indian context. I asked Kapil to hop across to NDA during one of my shoots, and we worked out a system wherein Bharatrakshak would globally market our films. I wanted the institutions, namely Air HQ, NDA and IMA, to also put their weight behind the distribution endeavour, so we decided on a three-way sharing of any revenue on an equal basis.

I discussed this with Sakka Jain and as the add-on shoot for the IAF was finally getting cleared by the MOD, I decided to manifest Kapil and P. V. S. Jagan Mohan as a part of my crew. Fresh agreements were signed and we were finally good to go towards the end of October. Op Parakram at the time had been in place for almost a year, so we flew from Delhi to Jaisalmer with the intention of filming the Indira and TR-68 radars. Sitting in the mobile command centres, the radar systems could even pick up vehicular movement on roads, which had us wondering how low would one have to fly now to avoid radar detection. An IAF Chetak picked us up from the radar unit and we then flew along the Indira Gandhi Canal that had literally changed the look of the desert even then. Landing at an army post, we were offered the customary glasses of water. The men had to ferry water from quite a distance and though the water was green in colour, I did not have the heart to refuse it. By the time we returned to Jaisalmer for the night, I was in severe pain and was violently sick through the night.

The next morning, we landed in Pune, where despite being extremely wobbly from the previous day's infection, I could only take shots of Sukhoi-30 MKIs taking off and landing. Jagan and Kapil were getting to see the IAF in operation from within as the entire morning was spent with 20 Squadron (Lightnings) which had finally retired their trusted Hawker Hunters and converted to what was then considered to be the best fighter 'on either side of the Suez'. Scheduled to fly later in the day, I was still not fit enough to get airborne, so we headed off to NDA instead where we discussed the marketing of *The Standard Bearers* with Satur and Chacko. The next day NDA sent a formal DO to me saying the tie-up with Bharatrakshak was definitely a novel idea and the Academy was all for it.

After a quick spin with the Su-30 in the morning, we then headed back to Delhi, moving to Ambala the next day to do a sortie with the MiG-21 Bison which was then upgraded with new Israeli avionics systems. We then finished off by filming the Pechora missiles, both in Ambala and at Arjangarh. Coincidentally, the shooting for *Salt of the Earth* had started at Arjangarh, and in the case of *Aakash Yodha*, we finally called pack up at the same location.

Philip Rajkumar was by then heading the Aeronautical Development Agency (ADA) which was entrusted with the production of the LCA, subsequently known as the Tejas. I was asked to make a short film on the LCA, *Wings of the Future,* and was given a Dornier from 41 Squadron to ferry me to Bangalore. HAL, which was contracted to manufacture the aircraft, had a small group of test pilots who were on deputation from the IAF. Landing at the old Bangalore airfield, I was given a detailed brief on the project. The first task was to film the prototype in the air from a Mirage 2000, with the intention of showing the clip to parliamentarians that made up the Standing Committee for Defence and on whose recommendations budgets were cleared, or so it was believed.

What I had seen and understood about the LCA was indeed impressive. Made primarily from compressed carbon-fibre composite structures and skins, it was a light supersonic fighter that would replace the existing MiG-21 fleet. The LCA programme, started in the 1980s, was India's second attempt at designing and manufacturing a supersonic fighter, and ADA had initially set itself three goals. These included the three most sophisticated and challenging systems: the fly-by-wire flight control system, multi-mode pulse-Doppler radar, and the development of an afterburning turbofan engine.

The LCA was the second supersonic aircraft being designed in India, after a gap of more than two decades. HAL had in the 1960s built the Marut, which was originally designed to break the 2 Mach barrier. However, there were problems with the engine and a mismatch with the airframe meant the aircraft struggled to even break the sound barrier at 1 Mach. Not surprisingly, a lot of the conversation among the test pilots was centred around the Marut saga. 'It was a shame,' I was told by Parvez Khokar, 'The entire database mysteriously disappeared from HAL.' It was also a bit of a coincidence that the Mirage III and V built by the French seemed to have incorporated many of those features.

I strapped into a Mirage 2000 that was being flown by Wing Commander 'Soggy' Krishna while Group Captain (later Air Chief Marshal) R. K. S. Bhadauria started up the LCA prototype, KH 001. Khokar in a MiG-21 was also to fly abreast while a Jaguar would be tailing the formation as well. The entire sortie was being monitored through telemetry, and all the aircraft lined up for take-off. The LCA had begun to roll and as we turned onto the runway, my mask jammed and I could not breathe out.

'Take it off and whack it against the panel in front,' said Soggy, and as we lifted off the runway, I managed to get the airflow going.

All four aircraft got into position and Bhadauria started to put the aircraft through its paces. On the Mirage's radar, I noticed the LCA was hardly painting, while the Jaguar and MiG-21 were lighting up like Christmas trees. Bhadauria then started to do a roll, when my mask jammed again. The camera was running and unable to exhale, I started to grey out. Eventually, after the roll was completed, I had a hand free to snap off the mask, but by then my vision was blurred and I was shooting almost entirely by instinct. It was a major relief when we landed and reached the dispersal area, and as I opened my cockpit, Philip came up the ladder. 'You got the shot?' He asked, took the camera from me and disappeared. By the time I somewhat recovered and groggily caught up with everyone, they had all seen the footage. No one had noticed I was missing!

Drama around the LCA continued even on our next sortie a couple of weeks later. My camera assistant suddenly became unwell and at the last minute, Sunil the studio head decided to come along with the camera instead. I told him to be properly dressed since we would be dining at the air force mess. However, the next morning at Palam, my jaw hit the ground as Sunil got out of the taxi wearing his gold-lined wedding suit. By the time we landed at Bangalore, the poor fellow was roasting and was doing a regular strip tease. As luck would have it, the Mirage 2000 and the Jaguar were unserviceable, so we called for an An-32 from the neighbouring IAF base at Yelahanka. For the LCA to fly formation with the transport plane which would have its rear hatch open, we had to carefully coordinate our respective airspeeds.

I told Sunil to secure his gold-lined coat and other woollens properly for once airborne, the An-32 would depressurize abruptly once the hatches were opened. I then tied a monkey belt around myself and settled down to film the LCA which was at that stage not in visual contact. The hatches opened with all the associated drama and sound effects, and I scanned the skies for Soggy Krishna in the LCA. Just then, to my absolute horror, I saw what looked like a man in a coat literally 'walk' past me and step into space. Before my brain could process what had happened, Sunil's pullover did much the same, and it too literally 'walked' away from the aircraft. Considering we were flying over Hunsur, at a fairly high altitude, we could only hope some farmer would have been 'blessed' with this gold-threaded mana from heaven. A distraught Sunil failed to see the funny side of it, and he even wanted to take Gypsy and go looking for the gold-lined wedding suit.

With both *Aakash Yodha* and *The Standard Bearers* completed, we didn't have to look for a platform to air the films, because Discovery Channel came calling instead. Pankaj Saxena was Dipti's classmate from FTII and he called saying as part of a new *Discover India* series, the channel would like to air both films. The overall flow of *The Standard Bearers* had been objected to by an officer's wife who had been put on the committee to 'approve' the film, resulting in fifty-plus objections to the movie. My reaction to the points sent to me by e-mail had resulted in a one-word reply to Trikha, 'Poppycock!' Being official correspondence, this created further mayhem with the commandant even accusing Satur and Johnson Chacko of being 'on Kunal Verma's payroll!' By then Trikha had been posted to Southern Air Command and he was replaced by Vice Admiral Suresh Bangara. After going through the film multiple times and my one-word e-mail as well, he was ready with his verdict. The principal of NDA, the deputy commandant, Johnson Chacko, Ajith Kumar and myself trooped into Bangara's office.

'Ever since I have taken over the Academy, I have gone over every bit of the film. The beginning is perfect ... and I love the ending. The main body of the film is also just as it should be. Though you have been acerbic in your correspondence with the Academy, the film stands approved.'

The film was screened at the Habibullah Hall and along with Vallika and Veeha, even my parents were present for the inaugural screening.

Both Air HQ and NDA were extremely thrilled that Discovery would showcase the films. For *Aakash Yodha*, Discovery held a launch in Delhi which was presided over by Air Marshal Mike McMohan, the vice chief and was attended by dozens of senior officers. In Bombay the event was conducted by Air Marshal 'Pudding' Ahluwalia. A week later we filmed a brief message from the CAS for the film, after which Air Chief Marshal 'Keecha' Krishnaswami said to me, 'Kunal, you have single-handedly solved the IAF's recruitment problems. *Aakash Yodha* is being screened everywhere, in all stations. Great job!' I was also happy that the VCDs being sold by Bharatrakshak were doing well. Last couple of months I handed over cheques in excess of a lakh to Air HQ. We were on a roll!

Just before *Aakash Yodha* was telecast, I got a call from Rakesh Jolly. The RAF's aerobatic team, the Red Arrows, were coming in from Langkawi in Malaysia and would be performing with the Surya Kirans at Hindon. The RAF was flying the Hawk, which at the time was a frontrunner for the IAF's acute requirement for an Advanced Jet Trainer. With both the teams performing, it was quite a breathtaking display. I was pleased as punch, for along with the IAF tie, I now also could wear the RAF's colours.

The telecast of the air force film on Discovery Channel coincided with Air Force Day on 8 October 2003, and it was followed a few weeks later by *The Standard Bearers*. I was at home sometime in the first week of November when there was a phone call from Air HQ. 'The shit has hit the ceiling,' I was told by a wing commander whose name I cannot now recall. 'The chief is on the warpath and your neck is on the line.'

I had no clue what had happened; bit by bit, one had to piece together what had transpired. The air chief had been on a visit to HQ South Western Air Command (SWAC) in Gandhinagar, and in the evening along with the officers in the Command Mess, he had seen a television serial which was ostensibly based on the IAF. Almost to a man all those present had said they were terribly embarrassed by what was being portrayed and wondered how Air HQ had allowed such drivel to be aired. The air chief had airily said he would return to Delhi and have the series taken off at once.

In Delhi, Keecha had yelled at all those who had cleared the series. He then asked for the producers to be called before him so he could give them a piece of his mind. With two or three air marshals also present in his office, the chief then let fly and demanded the series be scrapped forthwith. Unfortunately, the producers were the sons of a senior politician who was later also the governor of Uttarakhand, and they told Keecha exactly where he got off his high horse. Obviously forewarned about the chief's intentions, they had also come prepared. They said as per the Indian Telegraph Act of 1926, or something on those lines, the IAF was culpable of violating governmental guidelines as 'Kunal Verma's film had been telecast on the Discovery Channel which was a foreign channel'. They then demanded that all air-to-air footage shot by me should be made available to them free of cost so the IAF could then look good in their serial. Thirdly, they threatened the chief at a personal level saying they would institute an enquiry into some Sukhoi deal and link him to it.

The air chief had stared at the two brothers and then ordered them out of his office. After five minutes, he asked ACAS Ops, Air Vice Marshal (later Air Marshal) Packiam Paul Rajkumar, to come into his office and said he wanted to disassociate the IAF from the Discovery screening. Sakka Jain, who by then had moved to SWAC as C-in-C was sent for, and he categorically said it was impossible as the vice chief himself had been a part of the launch. He also told Keecha there was an agreement between the IAF and KaleidoIndia that governed the use of the footage, and if the Alva brothers wanted it, they would have to pay two-and-a-half thousand rupees per second. At this point, the air chief completely lost his cool. He accused Sakka Jain of having betrayed the IAF and said he did not care how they did it, but Rajkumar was told I was to be blacklisted forthwith for having screened the film on Discovery without the IAF's approval. He also gave orders that all sales of the film by Bharatrakshak be stopped and each VCD be accounted for.

At first, I thought this was all a joke, but then reality began to rear its ugly head. Suddenly, almost everyone in Air HQ refused to even take my calls, let alone look me in the eye. Sakka Jain was told he was on my 'payroll' and sidelined. Rajkumar, a helicopter pilot who until then was perfectly cordial and easy with me, went after me with a vengeance. Letters were written to Discovery threatening legal action. They were equally befuddled and wrote to me saying please sort out your 'differences' with the IAF.

All the hard work put together by Bharatrakshak also came to nought. Then, horror of horrors, P. P. Rajkumar got posted to NDA as the deputy commandant. Matter of time before I was hauled up to Khadakwasla. 'I have the entire power of the Government of India behind me,' he said to me, 'and I will have you arrested if I can.' He picked up the phone and asked to be connected to Johnson Chacko, who was then no longer posted to the Academy. He asked Chacko if indeed NDA had concurred with the screening of the film, and the way Rajkumar framed the question, there was no doubt what answer he expected. In a way, it was a veiled threat to Chacko as well.

There were others in the office and so confident was Rajkumar of the answer he would receive that he put the call on speaker. Chacko, sounding like the epitome of logic and patience, step by step spelt out each stage of clearances obtained at his end. Not only was everything above board, but all the necessary paperwork had been done. All through this, the Air Marshal just glared at me. Without support from Chacko, it was obvious he had nothing against me. 'Get out,' he said, 'I'll ensure you never step into the Academy again!' It was an inglorious end to what until then had been a dream run. There was a joint HDFC account being run by the Academy into which proceeds from the sales of the film used to go. Both NDA and KaleidoIndia had opened it with a deposit of ₹50,000 each and by then there was quite a lot of money in the kitty that according to the contract, was to be divided. I never found out what happened to the account. Some years later I visited Gol Market in NDA. I was asked by various shopkeepers if I wanted a copy of The Standard Bearers at half the official price.

Back in Delhi, Dipti just looked at me sadly. 'It's your fault. Who on earth gets into a contracted film and works out such a convoluted system of payments? I warned you.' I guess she was right.

It didn't end there. Rajkumar, on behalf of NDA, wrote formally to Discovery Channel, who had been fairly balanced in their reactions when Air HQ had gone ballistic. The upshot of this was that the IMA film, *Making of a Warrior*, never got aired at any level. Also, at Keecha's insistence, all VCDs that had been made were confiscated by the air force police who came to Beverly Park and literally sealed my house. He decreed the IAF would sell the VCDs for both *Aakash Yodha and Salt of the Earth* henceforth because Bharatrakshak was 'crooking the IAF' by selling the VCDs abroad at double the rate. One year later, I got a statement from Air HQ saying three VCDs had been sold at a fifty per cent discounted price by the Air Force Museum at Palam for ₹275 each.

The worse part in a situation like this was there was no one to even talk to. With the chief having issued a decree, all doors just slammed shut automatically. Years of work just went down the drain.

Frankly, I had had an overdose of the Armed Forces by then, but we were so interlocked with the services that it was hard to break free. After the *Project Tiger* and the *Call of the Wild* series, though we did visit some of the sanctuaries periodically, the opportunity to shoot a wildlife film never materialized. In 2004 I met a Swiss travel agent, Catherine Tschannon, who was extremely keen on shooting a film on Indian wildlife. Stephané Chopard was a French-speaking Swiss, and I flew to Switzerland to explore possibilities. Unlike in India, the documentary film scenario in Europe was extremely organized but the mistake we made was that we never narrowed down on any particular subject. Stephané had shot a film on foxes in his backyard, but when he came to India and we shot in Gir and Sariska just to get ourselves oriented, I found there was a huge gulf in our styles of functioning. Catherine in particular, being more in the 'coordinator' role, had just about every Indian male drooling over her. After spending a couple of weeks together, I just decided to call it off.

I continued to shoot small aviation-related films, including one on the development of the Saras aircraft by NAL. As a result, one got to interact with some of the most distinguished names in the Indian scientific community, which included Dr B. R. Pai, Kota Harinarayana and even Dr A. P. J. Abdul Kalam who was by then the president of India. Another film to commemorate 50 years of the Folland Gnat would also be commissioned by HAL subsequently and once again one got to spend some invaluable time with some of the greatest legends of the IAF.

Towards the end of March 2004, as the shooting of the Saras film continued, Dipti and the girls flew down to Bangalore. Along with Philip Rajkumar and his wife Sheila, we set off for Kabini. I was carrying with me a 2-litre bottle of Johnny Walker Black Label for 'Papa' John Wakefield, my old boss from the Tiger Tops days. Sundar Raj, my fishing buddy, was the chief naturalist and on the phone, he had promised he'd help me catch a 'maunster!'

Papa John was by then either in his late 80s or early 90s and he was still full of beans, often himself driving people around to see elephants and tigers. He was thrilled to have me over, an emotion that perhaps got accentuated by the whisky I had brought for him. After I had introduced Dipti to him, in a stage whisper that could be heard across the Kabini Lake, his eyes glinting with excitement, Papa John asked, 'Is she Kavita?'

'Good lord, no sir ... she's Dipti!'

But by then Papa John was on a roll and had come up with two to three other names that he associated with me from the Tiger Tops days. I was by then dead meat and sinking faster than the Titanic as Dipti fixed me with 'the look' which is usually the harbinger of a tsunami.

Just when it seemed all was lost, Papa John switched tracks. 'Kunal,' he reminisced, 'you remember during World War II in Burma we ...'

'He's gone loco,' I quickly told Dipti. 'Don't believe a word he says! I wasn't even born during World War II!'

Back in Delhi, I got a call from Krishna Kumar Candeth, or KK as he was known in school. 'Fauji,' he said, speaking from New York, 'I want you to find me a good cameraperson.' He went on to say that he was shooting a film on people coming to die in Varanasi. He had done some preliminary shooting himself around the Assi Ghats and now needed to shoot a pilot on the basis of which he hoped to raise the requisite funds. His main protagonist was Swami Tambe, who in the earlier part of his life, had been a bureaucrat. Since the man was marking time to kick the bucket, there was a sense of urgency around the entire business.

'I'll shoot it,' I said after looking at my filming schedule for the Saras. The next thing on the agenda was for a twin take-off by LCAs in the second week of May; so, I had a clear window.

Varanasi invoked strange emotions in me. Death, as a subject, meant we would be looking at people who were either there to die or dead already. I wasn't sure if I was apprehensive because I was scared or because beyond a point, despite having seen a fair share of combat, I knew nothing about it. Anyway, once I had said yes and KK having accepted my offer, there was no running away from it. The fear of the unknown has a strange way of drawing you towards it, almost like a moth to a flame.

On 23 April 2004, KK and I landed at Varanasi. I had hired a PD-150 camera which arrived with Vinod, the camera assistant. KK kept pulling my leg about being on a mid-term with him, and in a way he was right. He had his own misgivings, for he wanted a cameraman and not someone who was used to calling the shots in his own films as well. The fact that KK had been my mentor in school, however, made it easy for me to slip into that role. His style of shooting was completely different from mine, for KK rarely if ever wanted to cut camera. We checked into a small hotel at Assi Ghat and I wondered how could we sleep with the smell of constant cremations hanging in the air.

The next two days we just wandered around shooting all sorts of stuff. At first, I baulked at the constant stream of bodies that were constantly arriving in a rush, but after a while, like everyone else, I wasn't even aware of them. The human mind takes hardly any time to acclimatize itself to new surroundings. KK would fuss over camera framings, then the camera would do its job while I lit a cigarette and watched the world go by. 'That guy just stepped into the river and washed his arse ...' KK was in raptures, for the endless roll on the camera had captured the act for prosperity.

'Yeah ...' I hadn't noticed the earth-shaking act, 'May I cut camera, sir?'

'No ... let it run! Who knows what happens next!' I lit another cigarette. Time was eternal and we were just transient beings watching it go past.

After dark, we filmed the Aarti's that were performed on the ghats from a boat and the river came alive with floating lamps. Heading back later on cycle rickshaws I started filming the puller's feet, then tracked up to shoot life from our moving platform. At the hotel, KK was over the moon looking at the shots. After that, we struck a balance between his long shots and my independent forays!

Swamy Tambe had a small room above the ghats, and we filmed with him in the dim light, KK not really asking questions but prodding him on, every now and then. I was surprised to hear that sadhus were not cremated, but their bodies consigned to the river for fish and marsh muggers to finish off their remains. As soon as we started filming, a large male Hanuman langur entered the room and sat dutifully at Tambe's feet. From the tilt of its head and demeanour, the monkey was listening to every word that was said, and he just sat there for the entire duration of the session. Somehow, it seemed like it was the most natural thing. When we finished, the langur sedately left the room.

The next day at dawn we took a boat and crossed the Ganga to Panchganga Ghat, which is directly across. The souls of the departed were supposed to inhabit this absolutely desolate and empty landscape, and it was quite eerie, with just a solitary water buffalo grazing in the distance. Somehow, it was all very symbolic of Yamraj. KK was in a world of his own, and after we wandered around on the sand, we returned to the hustle and bustle on the other side. Getting out of the boat, I tripped and fell heavily within the boat. As I watched the blood ooze out of a couple of bruises, a small girl watching walked across and offered me a leaf which had a dollop of *chandan* on it. Applied to the wound, the bleeding stopped almost instantly. It was almost as if it was preordained ... the fall, the presence of the girl, not more than ten years old. I looked at KK. He was smiling and obviously wishing the camera had been on.

On 26 April I spoke to my father who gave me Honorary Captain Dashrat Singh's coordinates. The former JCO from 2 Rajput was one of the survivors from Namka Chu and he was then serving as the ADC to Anant Narayan Singh, the Maharaja of Varanasi. The next day KK and I went across to the palace which was in a state of disrepair but were welcomed by Dashrat Singh who was then in his 80s.

'Aapne meri godi mein bahut susu kiya tha' (You piddled a lot in my lap!), my father's former company JCO said. After a cup of tea, he then told us the story of what had happened at Namka Chu on the fateful days of 20 and 21 October 1962. What unfolded in the next one hour was one

of the most incredible stories I had ever heard in my life. Shot twenty times in the stomach, Dashrat Singh relived the long night spent drifting in out of consciousness and the arrival of a Chinese execution party the next day, which started putting both Indian and Chinese wounded out of their misery. Led by a Chinese nurse, when his turn came, she asked him in Hindi where he was from, to which he replied 'Allahabad'. Just why he said that even to that day was a mystery for he was actually from Etawah, but the Chinese nurse decided to spare his life, despite the fact that he was perhaps one of the worst casualties in front of her.

Taken on a litter to Le and then to a POW camp, he was operated on multiple times, each bullet extracted by Chinese doctors. All this time the nurse was by his side, looking after him. No words were exchanged, but when Dashrat could finally speak, he asked her why was she doing this for him. The nurse had looked at him and said that she had done her nursing studies in Allahabad. She would stay by his side till he was repatriated to India at Bum La along with the other prisoners of war, being the last to step back at the Heap of Stones, only after briefing the Indian doctors on how to keep Dashrat's remaining lung inflated. Twelve years later, when my book *1962: The War That Wasn't* was published by Aleph, this would be the opening of the book. Talk about six degrees of separation ... sometimes, things happen in a way which we cannot explain. I couldn't help but think of the girl who was sitting on the ghat the previous day, almost as if she was waiting for me to get injured.

Back in Delhi, I suggested KK step away from the film and let Dipti edit the 20-minute pilot for him. But KK being KK spent the next two to three days cutting the film and landed up with a pilot that was ridiculously long. Back in the US, he didn't get the funding he was hoping for, and by the time he returned with enough money, Swamy Tambe and his other protagonists were long gone.

Even as we wrapped up the Saras film, other developments were taking place at a rapid pace. Unable to conform to Kuku Uberoi's underhand ways, Inderjit Badhwar had also moved out from Media Transasia and had by then joined *Roli Books,* run by Pramod Kapoor. Inder was extremely keen Dipti and I do a coffee table book on aerial India, and though Kapoor was notorious in the publishing world for his unethical practises, I got talked into it. While flying with the IAF, I was generally completely focused on filming, so rarely carried still cameras. For the book to have any gravitas, we needed a few more sorties. With the IAF out of the equation post Keecha's bizarre histrionics, I asked the army for some additional sorties. The MOD gave us clearance to fly in Bareilly, Srinagar, Leh and Mhow.

In Leh, Lieutenant General Milan Naidu was at the end of his tenure as the 14 Corps commander. Over dinner he talked about the prime minister's recent visit to Siachen. 'The prime minister talked of converting the glacier into a Peace Park. That's ok ... he has said that before. But the DGMO (then Lieutenant General J. J. Singh) then made some rather strange comments which took us all by surprise. I wonder if the prime minister is even aware of the fact that Pakistan has no actual presence on the Siachen Glacier.'

I had looked at Milan quizzically. But the conversation had moved on. However, the remark rankled, especially since JJ was then definitely in the running for chief.

Milan Naidu then moved to Mhow as the commandant of the College of Combat and he asked us to make a film on the War College, which was a small, neat compact film. There I also met Major General (later Lieutenant General) Rakesh Loomba who was the commander of the Higher Command Wing, a designation held by my father a decade and a half previously. While filming with the Higher Command Course, one of the sessions was with Air Chief Marshal Shashi 'Bundles' Tyagi. On that occasion Dipti was also present and seeing me filming, the air chief started his session by saying that on behalf of the IAF, he wanted to apologise to us for what had transpired with Keecha. It was by then a bit like shutting the barn door after the horse had bolted, but nevertheless, it was awfully large-hearted of the chief to publicly apologize.

Another individual one met at Mhow at the Higher Command Course was General 'JJ' Singh, who by then had become the chief. I was filming him deliver his talk to the officers, all of whom were colonels that had finished commanding their respective battalions with distinction. JJ was aware I was shooting, and within a few seconds, I realized he had not given any thought to what he was going to say. 'Gentlemen ...' he squinted at the crowd of faces, 'Gentlemen, do you want me to speak from my head or my heart?' It was another mannerism that I noted and filed away in the recess of my head.

Maybe one could blame it on the stars, but despite continuing to do good work, everything continued to fall jam side down. After we completed the helicopter sorties, *Roli* brought out our first book, *Ocean to Sky: India from the Air*. Wing Commander Rakesh Sharma wrote the foreword and with everyone warning us not to trust Pramod, I asked him to pay the full royalty upfront which he did, though I had no way of knowing how many copies had actually been printed since the books had rolled off the press in Singapore.

Feeling rather chuffed at having our first book in print, I presented a copy to Ramu Gaur. He was leafing through the book in my drawing room, when he asked, 'Why have you assigned the copyright to Roli Books?'

'I have?'

'Yes ... it's assigned to a Roli affiliate in the Netherlands.'

Inder had by then also fallen out with Pramod and when I called him and said the copyright had been highjacked, he let loose a series of profanity. The next day he sent me to meet Raghu Rai, whose book on Sikhs among others had also been published by Pramod.

'You first-time authors,' Raghu started to lecture me, reaching out for his own book simultaneously, 'you're so thrilled someone is publishing your book, you never check. The copyright page even an idiot ...' Raghu's mouth was a round O and words just dried up. He was staring at his own book. 'Son of a bitch ...' he finally found his vocal chords again. Raghu's copyright had been highjacked as well and India's leading photographer had been clueless all this while.

Filing a complaint with the police proved to be an even bigger nightmare. No one had heard of the term 'copyright' in those days, or if they had, they were past masters at playing dumb. I was fast beginning to learn that in India, there was simply no justice for anyone. You could file a case and watch in frustration as for years there would be no movement, just a series of adjournments and fresh dates, sometimes months apart.

The girls were growing up fast. Both had settled into a steady routine at Shri Ram School and were doing fairly well in swimming and riding. Niti's daughter, Manavi, had joined Mayo Girls in Ajmer and she too had found her niche amidst her peers. Trouble started when Manavi arrived during the holidays from school and under the pretext of being exhausted from hostel life, would not awaken till lunchtime. Vallika and Veeha quickly cottoned on to this and any suggestions that they go swimming or riding soon became a no-go. Even though we had a tennis court and our own swimming pool, they just refused to step down. Any effort on my part to get them going would result in a sharp exchange of words between Dipti and me. Even the annual trips to Kullu, where we would be packed in the Maruti Esteem because Niti and Manavi would accompany us, became a cause of complaint. 'Why can't we go to Bombay instead?'

After a certain point in one's life, one has to watch the parents age, and as part of the process, handle associated medical problems. The eldest among the four parents was Mr Bhalla and given his almost saint-like existence, there were not too many health issues in his case. In 2002, my father had been diagnosed with Myeloma, which was a form of cancer that affected the body's production of blood. Fortunately, the army's Research and Referral Hospital had an excellent team of doctors, foremost among them being Major (later Lieutenant General) Velu Nair. 'We are still trying to understand the disease, and given the current level of advancement, your father has at least three to four years. Let us see how things play out,' he told Dipti and me. 'Just mentally be prepared. Your family is dealing with the big C!'

Sometime in 2005, I had taken both the fathers to Mangar where I jointly owned some land with some naval officers. Though initially bought with the intention of making small farmhouses, the society known as SAGRIKS had decided not to do anything with what was in essence a beautiful valley in the heart of the Aravalli Hills. My father was sitting near the car while my father-in-law had walked up to a stone hut that housed a generator. We were sitting on slabs taking out thorns that had gripped our socks, when mid-sentence, Mr Bhalla's eyes just seemed to cloud over, and he toppled sideways. I was barely six feet away, so grabbed him before he could roll onto the ground. Propping him up, I tried to revive him but for all outward appearances, he was in a deep sleep for he seemed to be breathing naturally. I ran across to where I could see my father and I yelled for help, but he couldn't hear me. One of the staff ran across and again we tried to shake Mr Bhalla awake. Just as he had knocked off, he came too and in fact even completed his sentence.

Seeing the look on our faces, he asked me what had happened. I told him he was out cold for more than two minutes. My father had also come up by then and we got Mr Bhalla to the car. We were at least half an hour from Gurgaon and even the mobile signal was dodgy. I got through to our family doctor, Dr Kitty Law and she said to get across to the Spinal Injuries Centre where Escorts had an emergency heart centre. Dipti and the two mothers were watching a movie and they came tumbling out, after which we got to the hospital.

The incident at the farm would subsequently result in open-heart surgery, and suddenly everyone was glad we had taken the trouble to buy and set up 1704-A as an alternate flat. Gaurav's acerbic comments about the flat belonging to him had initially resulted in Dipti's parents going back to Mumbai after getting all the woodwork done, but it seemed they were now quite willing to shift to Gurgaon. Unfortunately, once the initial crisis had abated, again some words were spoken which resulted in the in-laws once again heading back to Mumbai.

Though work was not quite buzzing the way it had in the last few years, we were motoring along quite comfortably. I had met the Chairman of the State Bank of Travancore, Om Prakash Bhatt at my cousin Arun's residence at Guwahati, and he asked me to make a film on the bank. I flew down to Trivandrum and met the Board of Directors, who were very impressed with *The Standard Bearers*. 'Make a film like you made on NDA,' was the refrain. I burst out laughing, and actually it was quite a wonderful film to shoot. More than anything, it gave me quite an insight into just how difficult it was to do anything constructive in Kerala during that period when trade unions completely ruled the roost.

In 2006, Mr Bhalla on one of my stopovers in Mumbai, said that we needed to streamline all the paperwork related to the flats. Sanjay Shah, the chartered accountant had drawn up all the papers which mainly segregated Gaurav's holdings from ours. In passing he also suggested that KaleidoIndia be made into a proprietorship as money from Gaurav's NRI account was coming in once in a while to reimburse whatever expenses were incurred on his behalf. I didn't give it a thought and signed away my entire share to Dipti. In Gurgaon, Dipti glared at me, 'You're trying to trap me or what?' I realized she had not been consulted, but from my perspective, it made no difference. Dipti at this point was completely focused on the girls and would provide all the backend support I required.

The Military World Games (MWG) were being held in Hyderabad in October 2007 and Army HQ asked us to not only make a small film on it but also produce a coffee table book. Until then, I had been only shooting on analog and had no experience with digital, or for that matter, sports photography, which is a highly specialized field. Indarjit Bansal, a classmate of Dipti from FTII was roped in as the main cameraman for the film, while another highly recommended 'India Today' photographer joined us to take stills. I was to operate as the wingman for both these shooting units, so as to act as the second camera as and when it was required. I had switched to Canon's digital platform and spent quite a few hours looking at various magazines like *Sports Illustrated* to see the kind of shots each discipline could offer. The quality of photography was such that it soon became obvious one had to pre-plan the kind of shots, and then wait for the right moment to try and freeze the action. At the speed at which things would happen, especially in track and field events, there would be no scope for any error.

By then, Mr Bhalla's health had deteriorated rapidly. Post his open-heart surgery, he had developed cancer of the prostate and it had then rapidly metastasized through his body. Initially, he was admitted to a private hospital in Mumbai as heavy rains made it impossible to get to the railway hospital and it was with growing horror that one saw just how the medical system was like vultures designed to strip a man of any vestiges of his dignity, to say nothing of his savings. To make matters worse, most of the doctors were 'known' people. A week before the start of the MWG, I met him for the last time. When I walked into the ICU, Gagan Sharma was sitting with him and as he left, he whispered to me that 'the old man has stopped talking'. However, in the one hour that I spent with my father-in-law, we had the most matter-of-fact conversation. At one point, he closed his eyes and asked me to tell him what it felt like to fly in a fighter. It was indeed most uncharacteristic of him, for he had never shown any special interest in flying before. He then talked about leaving his body the previous night, wandering around the hospital and coming back. He then pointedly asked me what did I think of death. Frankly, I had never dwelt on it until then, so I said in my opinion it didn't change anything for no matter who was born or who died, the weight of the Earth remained constant. Strangely, Mr Bhalla seemed to relate to that.

14 October 2007, I had to shoot the final days' play of the Indian Open Golf in Delhi for Canon while Dipti along with Bansal and the still photographer were to shoot the opening ceremony of the MWG. Jyoti Randhawa had just sunk an eagle putt to seal the championship on the 17th hole and the cheers were at their zenith when Niti called to say Mr Bhalla had breathed his last. At that very moment, Dipti was with the president of India, Pratibha Patil, in the VIP enclosure. I called Bansal and told him to take her aside and break the news. Later, around midnight, I reached Hyderabad, after which Dipti flew to Mumbai for the funeral. Apart from the fact that I could not be with her during this extremely traumatic period, it also meant we were without a key person for the rest of the shoot. Vallika and Veeha were in Kullu with my parents and there they were told about their grandfather's demise by my parents.

Everything seemed to go into a tailspin after that. The still photographer who was shooting with a Nikon camera, insisted on shooting everything three stops under, insisting that it gave the best results when corrected on an editing table. As far as Bansal was concerned, he had unknown to himself, developed cataract and everything he was shooting was slightly out of focus. So hard-pressed were we, I could only view random shots on his viewfinder, which is no way to measure critical sharpness. As luck would have it, it all then came down to what I was shooting. Fortunately for me, all my homework paid off, for I got some really good images. Eventually, both the film and the book were hailed as being top draw, but just how close we came to a disaster, only I knew!

23

Arunachal to Assam Rifles: Look East Policy

Our book on the MWG created quite a stir, for despite all the problems, the end result was quite spectacular. The International Military Sports Council or CISM, the Brussel-based administrative body that ran the games, had sent their own battery of sport photographers and their images were offered to us, but none made the cut. This did my confidence a world of good, especially since I had just taken the all-important decision of converting to digital photography. To top it off, we were also asked to make the film on the College of Defence Management which was in Secunderabad. As a result, I got to attend quite a few lectures that were held as a part of the Long Defence Management Course. Having similarly sat through sections of the Higher Command Course, I got a firsthand feel of both the premier courses conducted by the armed forces for mid-ranking officers.

It was in July 2008 while the layouts for the MWG book were being done that we had a surprise visitor at home in Beverly Park. The guards at the gate simply said, '*Governor Saab aaye hai*' (The governor has come) and General Joginder Jaswant 'JJ' Singh breezed in. After he had retired as the army chief in September 2007, he had become the governor of Arunachal Pradesh within three months. Until that moment, we only had a passing acquaintance, having met briefly on a couple of occasions. The governor, warm and affectionate, was apologetic for having barged in, and after a few other pleasantries got straight to the point. *National Geographic* had approached him and wanted to do a cover story on the erstwhile NEFA, now Arunachal. They had asked him, JJ, to tell them what he wanted done for his state. With such a fantastic offer, the first names that came to his mind were Dipti and mine. So here he was ....

Flattery apart, this new development seemed like the ultimate dream offer, the sort that comes up once in a lifetime. JJ offered to appoint me as his 'adviser' and asked me to meet him at Itanagar as soon as the paperwork was done. We needed to not only zero in on what we wanted done, we would also have to make a presentation that the governor would then take to the *National Geographic* headquarters in Georgetown, Washington, D.C.

I landed in Guwahati on 14 August and helicoptered to Itanagar. On the same chopper were an elderly American couple, and we landed at the Raj Niwas helipad to disembark them, as they were guests of His Excellency. Hardly had I reached my room when I was told we were heading for Tawang in the Mi-172. Since I had no warm clothes, I borrowed a shawl from the ADC's wife, and we took off in fairly bad weather. Unable to cut across directly, we came back to Guwahati, refuelled, and then routed along Eastern Bhutan. As a result, we overflew the Manas Tiger Reserve, and with the governor lapping it up, I pointed out various landmarks to him from the air. General 'JJ' Singh boasted of a photographic memory, and it was amazing how he could subsequently regurgitate almost everything verbatim.

At Tawang, the brigade commander was from the Maratha Light Infantry, which was also JJ's regiment. After taking the Independence Day salute in the morning, we headed up towards the upper lakes around Bum La. I took the opportunity to shoot as much as I could because we would need images to illustrate the governor's presentation in October. I also got talking to the American couple, who had come to Arunachal as the governor's guests with a view towards investing money in a few chalets, but by the look of it, there was no supporting infrastructure so they might as well forget about that aspect. The gentleman was a former USAF fighter pilot, who had spent most of his years flying the F-86 Sabrejets.

After two days of lording it around Tawang, it was time to head back, and since the American's were to catch a flight from Guwahati, we needed to return the way we had come. Unfortunately, heavy clouding made it impossible for the Mi-172 to land at Tawang, so in a cavalcade of cars, we headed for Lumla, a small helipad that overlooked the confluence of the Nyamjang Chu and the Tawang Chu just before the river enters Bhutan. The helicopter was not taking chances and was in orbit, so we were waiting for it to land when I noticed a television crew standing on the other side of the helipad. Rajeev Bhattacharya, the leader of the group, walked up to me and asked if they could come with us to Guwahati.

Though there was plenty of room in the helicopter, I needed to ask JJ. His eyebrows shot up, 'Will they interview me?'

The interview began then and there and continued as we flew back to Assam. At the airfield, the Mi-172 was being refuelled, so the interview went on even more, wherein the governor expounded on all his policies for the betterment of the general population. Since the Americans were leaving, I expected JJ to at least say bye, but he just waved to them in an offhand sort of way. The VIP terminal was some 500 metres away and I started to walk there with the Americans.

'So, how long have you known the general?' I asked conversationally.

'Good Lord, we don't know him,' the wife replied. 'We came through the general's son in Paris. And it's been an awesome experience. You guys sure have it good in India.'

I wasn't sure if I had heard the lady correctly. After handing the couple over to the airport manager, I walked back to the helicopter where Rajeev looked at me pleadingly to stop the endless interview. We flew back to Itanagar and since the Americans had left, was shifted to Raj Bhawan. All this while my head was in a spin. This cannot be happening, I kept telling myself. In the afternoon we went to the zoo and took some shots of a clouded leopard and hoolock gibbons.

Even though the dinner was a quiet, private affair, there was an element off grandeur as we were waited upon by Raj Bhawan staff dressed in the traditional regal manner. Finally, I couldn't take it anymore.

'Sir, I'm going back to Delhi. I'll do the *National Geographic* presentation for you because I feel it's important, but there are things here I am not comfortable with.' I think by then JJ had figured out that I knew. He made some noises about going with the times, but my mind was made up. The next morning, I flew back to Guwahati and then on to Delhi. Two weeks later Dipti and I returned to finish the shooting for the presentation. JJ was on the Dauphin helicopter with us from Guwahati to Itanagar, but he pretended he hadn't seen us. The next day we got an IAF Chetak to take us to Mechuka, and he pointedly left Dipti behind, telling Mrs JJ at the helipad to take her 'shopping' instead.

With *National Geographic* willing to play ball, I was particularly keen we get them to do the story along with an accompanying map. There were two bulges that existed on the eastern flank of Arunachal that were the result of a terrible bureaucratic blunder made by India in the 1960s when our own maps showed these two areas as belonging to erstwhile Tibet, which by then had become the People's Republic of China. These not only defied our own logic of following the watershed, which was the guiding principle behind the McMahon Line, these two areas were also traditionally Mishmi hunting grounds that were clearly defined in all the agreements that then existed between the Tibetans and the Idu Mishmi chiefs. The army maps showed these two areas as Fishtail-1 and Fishtail-2. '*Nat Geo* publishes this in accordance with the geographical features, it will undo the blunder we made half a century ago,' I told JJ. I also suggested that in our presentation, we suggest that the story be on the clouded leopard, which was one of the least studied animals in the wild. 'It should really get their adrenaline going.'

By end-September we had made a power-point presentation for the governor, and I wrote out a script for him that needed to be memorized. I wanted to leave nothing to chance, so had even put in markers where he was supposed to take off his glasses and take a sip of water. As far as the map went, we worked out potential questions that could queer the pitch. However, my two or three attempts to sit with His Excellency and get him to go over the script met with irritated responses. 'I'll read it on the flight. I just need to scan through it once. I'll do it closer to the date.'

Since I had not joined the governor's staff, I then computed the actual expenses we had incurred, which basically amounted to just the air tickets. I gave it to JJ who said it would be cleared forthwith. I was, of course, never reimbursed.

The meeting with *National Geographic* was scheduled for the early part of October and we waited with bated breath to get news from the US. A few days before that, we watched JJ get the *Sikh of the Year Award* in New York—sponsored by the Indian American hotelier, Sant Singh Chatwal—on the news. The general to me looked positively inebriated. I said to Dipti, 'I just hope he doesn't blow the presentation. He refused to read the script.'

'Come on ... he's a former army chief and a governor. Just relax, will you! You cannot macro-manage everything, and besides, as far as he's concerned, you are way past your expiry date!'

There was no news. After a fortnight I got a call from the Arunachal Bhawan in Delhi saying His Excellency wished to see us. JJ was sitting in the basement eating dry fruit, and from the look of it, he was extremely nervous. 'Your presentation,' he said without a preamble, 'was a complete disaster. None of the ideas that you put forth, especially about the clouded leopard, were of any interest. *Koi gal nahi ... meine unha nu tiger pe story karne ko kaha hai* (Never mind ... I've asked them to do a story on the tiger instead).'

Just then Mrs JJ arrived, and it was obvious there was bad blood between husband and wife. She greeted both Dipti and me warmly. JJ was by now demolishing the dry fruit in a blur of constant movement.

'Has he told you? He never read your script and at *Nat Geo* he forgot the clouded leopard ... started doing "tiger tiger" instead. I kept telling him ... read Kunal's script. But *nah ji* ... Over there he started off by saying, shall I speak from my head or my heart. He does that when he hasn't done his homework!'

Needless to say, that was the end of that!

However, General JJ had sowed certain ideas in my head. I started thinking of undertaking a major project wherein we could document virtually every corner of the Northeast. 'Nobody has a clue about the region ... it's like massive blanks on a map! It'll take a few years, but I think we can find a way of doing it,' I said to Dipti. Both the girls were sitting there, listening to the conversation, and I jokingly added, 'I think we should do it even it means selling this flat!'

Call it serendipity or whatever, but in December 2008 I got a call from Rakesh Loomba who was by then commanding 3 Corps in Dimapur. He said he was flying into Delhi the next day and wanted to see me. From the airport he came straight to Beverly Park and said he wanted me to make a coffee table book on his formation. I knew 3 Corps reasonably well from my earlier foray into the area and was aware of their AOR. Unlike any other senior officer in the services, Loomba perhaps had an open mind and was always willing to alternate suggestions. At that point, I had only briefly interacted with him in Mhow, and didn't know him that well. 'Sorry sir ... I don't think we should do it.'

Loomba laughed. 'I thought you might say that!'

'There is no point doing a book on the formation which will obviously just cover the current crop of people. Once they move out, including yourself, the book will be worthless.'

'So, what do you suggest?'

'Let's do a book on 3 Corps but let's look at the region and the people. You guys are spread across Tirap and Changlang in Arunachal, Nagaland, Manipur, Mizoram, Tripura, South Assam and Meghalaya. Let's focus also on the people ... that way the book will have some value.'

'Done,' said Loomba.

We worked out the economics on the spot. I wanted the shooting expenses covered and all the support from the army and would give the Corps HQ a ready-to-print layout.

'Whatever the costs are, work that out with the press.'

Dipti was shaking her head, for all my convoluted payment schemes in the past had been a disaster, but I was not going to let the opportunity go by.

'Sir, give me a senior liaison officer ... preferably a brigadier, who will be taken seriously. Plus, after we have finished shooting, we can use the existing and unused material for a larger project on the Northeast.' Loomba eyes were lit up. He was not only on board, he would be one of the driving forces behind the making of the *Northeast Trilogy* later. True to his word, Loomba assigned Brigadier (later Major General) Souresh Bhattacharya as our liaison officer, assisted by two lieutenant colonels, Sujay Ranjan Chaudhuri and Amit Rawat. All three were EME officers and together we made a happy team. With Dipti and the girls in tow, we started shooting in Manipur towards the end of 2008 before moving to Nagaland. Vallika and Veeha were halfway through grades 4 and 1 respectively, and I seriously thought of asking Shri Ram School to give them the rest of the academic year off.

'They'll learn a lot more if they are with us for the rest of the shooting,' I told Dipti. She seemed to consider the idea, but then we did nothing about it, and it eventually became one of the two or three shoots Dipti attended over the next three-and-a-half years.

On 11 June 2009, my parents celebrated their Golden Anniversary. Elsa, my father's constant companion, had died a year earlier and ever since, the void in the family was hard to fill. Though we had a string of Labrador Retrievers ever since 1970, my mother was then adamant that my father's medical condition would unnecessarily create a problem if he had to look after yet another dog. She just refused to entertain the idea of a new puppy, and as far as she was concerned, that was it. Vallika had spent her early years with Elsa in Noida while little Veeha only had one perennial request every year, 'Mama, can I get a puppy!' Dipti, like my mom, also had dropped a shutter, saying unless we had a bungalow, keeping a dog in the house was an absolute 'no-no'.

At this stage, my father and his childhood friend, N. P. 'Nirpoo' Singh, hatched a scheme. For the parent's anniversary, Nirpoo would present my parents with a male Labrador puppy. So, in accordance with the plan, a kennel owner arrived at my doorstep on a motorcycle with a blue bag strapped across his body. To my horror, the zip was opened and a small 7-week-old, shivering with fright, puppy was placed on the drawing-room floor. The poor fellow was so traumatized, he just created a little puddle then and there. I was so angry with the man for having transported the pup in this horrible fashion, I almost belted him. 'Just in case you do not want this colour, I have a slightly darker male from the same litter.' Giving me his card, the man left.

It was impossible not to fall in love with the little fellow. Veeha promptly named him Blaise and an hour later, since I was stretched out on a mattress on the floor, he came and curled up next to me. Our departure for Kullu kept getting delayed, and after a few days Dipti came into the room and announced that since she had been cleaning after Blaise and had already done the hard work, we could consider keeping him. Before she could blink, I had called the kennel owner and told him to bring the other puppy as well and that I would pay for him. Two hours later, this time transported in a proper cage in a car, the second, equally adorable puppy had arrived.

We arrived in Kullu a day before the anniversary. My mother by then had wind of the puppy's arrival, and she had figured she would throw a fit and ensure the fellow went back to Delhi with me. What she wasn't prepared for was two of them as they came flouncing out of the Scorpio, happy to be free after the twelve-hour drive. The second puppy, just a shade darker, was named Pasha and he quickly made Windsong his home, while Blaise stuck to the girls and me like glue. My mother was all set to murder me, but she then had no choice in the matter. It was game, set and match for all concerned. Blaise seamlessly became the third child in the house, adored and loved by everyone who came into contact with him.

By the end of 2009, the Northeast Palette was ready to be launched by the Eastern Army commander, Lieutenant General (later General) Vijay Kumar Singh who was from 2 Rajput. Dipti and I had met him in 2005 when we were shooting in Srinagar for *Ocean to Sky*, but other than that our interaction had been extremely limited. Sitting in his office at Fort Williams in Calcutta, I watched him go through the pages. 'I like the fact that you and Rakesh have highlighted the people and the region rather than focus on the army.'

That was all the cue I needed. 'Sir ... let's do three illustrated books on similar lines. Those will not be large coffee table books but will instead be windows into the entire Northeast. 33 Corps can include Sikkim, North Bengal, Assam and if we stretch it a bit, Meghalaya. 4 Corps we can focus entirely on Arunachal, while 3 Corps we can wrap up the entire Naga–Patkai region. We can call it the *Northeast Trilogy* and it will change the perception. With the army's help, let us bring it to the nation.'

VK nodded. He was also extremely decisive, for he picked up the phone and promptly called Lieutenant Generals K. T. Parnaik and D. S. Sidhu, who were commanding 4 and 33 Corps.'Am sending Kunal across to you ... he has an idea. Get back to me on how to implement this.' Shortly after the launch of the *Northeast Palette,* I then sat with the three generals, including Rakesh Loomba, and gave shape to the project. Loomba then said Assam Rifles, after having seen the 3 Corps book, was keen to do a book.

'Lieutenant General Karan Yadava is the director general. I've already told him you are coming to see him in Shillong tomorrow. Tell him you will shoot for the *Northeast Trilogy* simultaneously as well.'

Karan Yadava was from Mayo College and his father had been the brigade commander at Dalhai in 1971 when he was wounded and had to be evacuated. My father had physically helped load his stretcher on to the evacuating aircraft. From his body language, it seemed to me he wasn't particularly interested in showcasing the region but was focused entirely on depicting the para-military force under his command, which incidentally was completing its 175th year in 2010. I also doggedly continued, 'Let's divide the book into two parts sir ... the people and the region, and then the illustrated history of Assam Rifles. It will give us the backdrop against which it'll be easy to understand what the force's role has been over the years. Let us also do a soft-cover version in Hindi that can be circulated among the men. These large format books are useless ... they remain confined to guest rooms and are given to senior officers who barely glance at them.'

The general looked at me sadly.'Rakesh Loomba said you are a lousy marketing guy. You're telling me a coffee table book is useless! Ok, let's go for it, but I don't want you getting carried away with all this stuff about tribes and the region.'

'Let me shoot it and put it together. At that stage, if you feel I need to tweak it, I'll do so. But till then I need a free hand.'

I had just finished a shooting schedule in Mizoram and returned to Delhi when we decided Dipti needed to her much overdue mammary gland scan. After forty, it was being regularly advocated, but we had just not got around to it. Colonel (Dr) Chandra Shekhar Pant in Green Park was the brother of Lieutenant General J. C. Pant, who as a lieutenant colonel had been our immediate neighbour in Wellington. The check-up was routine, or so we thought, but suddenly out of the blue we were being told Dipti had grade 2 cancer. The shock of the revelation was further compounded by doctors who advocated immediate surgery, giving us no time whatsoever to even think.

Advice poured in from all directions and ninety-nine percent of it was absolute rubbish. Everyone who called up seemed intent on telling his or her story, and all that they succeeded in doing was creating more confusion. Cancer survivors think they are counselling you and giving you strength, but in reality, it all starts to sound like a long-drawn-out violin which monotonously goes on and on. Finding the right hospital where you are getting the correct advice was also a nightmare, and one hadn't quite forgotten what had happened to Dipti's father in Mumbai. I then turned to Tufan Ghosh, who was heading the Columbia Asia chain of hospitals, with a branch in Gurgaon as well. Tufan's father and mine had been subalterns in 2 Rajput together, and our families went back a long way together. The surgeon in Gurgaon was Dr Loraine Kalra, who instantly recognized Dipti from school. 'You were my house captain in Nazareth House in Loreto,' she announced, after we had gone through the initial meeting.

Even the night before the surgery, Dipti was showing no signs of nervousness. On the contrary, she just played around and danced with the girls and Blaise. Four or five days later, she was back at work, giving finishing touches to the *Northeast Palette*. However, unknown to her, the storm was still raging all around. Loraine Kalra wanted to follow up the breast removal with chemotherapy, but I was just not convinced. Once again there were endless discussions, but no doctor was willing to actually take the call. 'You decide,' was the constant refrain.

Finally, I asked the vital question. 'What are her survival chances without chemo, the post-operative treatment being just restricted to hormonal treatment?'

'97 per cent.'

'With chemotherapy ...?'

'97.5 per cent.'

'What are the chances of side effects of chemo leading to related issues?'

'20 to 30 per cent.'

Dipti's brother around that time had visited Beirut, where he met a soothsayer who read tea leaves. He was told that in the next year or so, his sister was going to die of cancer, or words to that effect. I overheard Gaurav talking to his friend, Rakesh Mahajan, whose wife Nalini was a doctor and had handled Veeha's delivery. I barely slept for the next few nights, just watching Dipti asleep with all sorts of thoughts flashing through my head. It was always going to be my call, and it wasn't easy. However, once I made up my mind and Dipti concurred, the very same doctors said it was the right thing to do. The only person who remained adamant and insisted we should have still done the chemotherapy was Loraine Kalra.

Over the years, I had always stayed clear of the Doon School Old Boys' Society (DSOBS) other than participate in the annual inter-house golf tournament and the Gibson Cup where we squared up against Mayo College. There were quite a few dedicated DOSCOs who were doing wonderful, dedicated work, but by and large there were some old boys from extended families who never seemed to have ever left school. Most of these people had nothing to do with education, yet in most get-togethers they would hardly let anyone get a word in sideways. Ankur Bahl, my classmate who was also my golf partner had just taken over as the batch representative, and I remember a conversation with him. 'You know, DSOBS needs to look outwards as well rather than all the time raise money for school. Old boys do a lot individually, it needs to be brought under some sort of banner. Public perception is most guys are just spoils rich kids.'

I was, therefore, a bit taken aback when Kanti Bajpai, the headmaster of Doon School called me up and asked me to come down to Dehradun and meet him. Kanti was at the fag end of his tenure and though our own time had overlapped briefly in school, I did not particularly know him. I didn't ask what it was about, and Kanti didn't say anything either.

Being summoned to the headmaster's (HM's) office usually meant trembling knees and I paused briefly to drink in the atmosphere before walking in. The huge doors seemed smaller, the office not as terrifying and the headmaster had shrunk in size from a twenty-foot Colonel Eric Simeon to a five foot something bespectacled Kanti who greeted me warmly. 'I'm handing over to Dr Peter McLaughlin ... but before I leave, I want to put something in place.' 2010 was the Doon School's 75th year. 'I've asked Inderjit Badhwar to edit a commemorative coffee table book on the school and I wanted you to make the film. Trouble is Inder is adamant he'll do the book if you shoot it and author it. Would you be interested in taking on both the projects?'

It was a special moment, and I nodded. 'Good then, that's settled. The appropriate bodies will soon get in touch with you.' I flew back to Delhi in a bit of a daze.

I always believed Inderjit Badhwar was one of the finest editors in the country. His grasp of any subject was instantaneous, and he was decisively quick. But Inder could not tolerate fools and he was no good at hiding his emotions. Almost immediately there was trouble as egos began to clash. Soon he was at loggerheads with half the committee members on the DSOBS. As far as I was concerned, I was working out a different format altogether for the book, more on the lines of the *Northeast Trilogy* with a built-in mechanism where we could print on demand. 'Let's keep the costs down, and make the projects self-sustaining,' I told Inder and Dipti as the former drained my stock of single malts.

Dipti exploded. 'You're a prize idiot. Haven't you learnt with the air force and everyone else your convoluted schemes where money is involved never work. What's your problem?'

My former roommate was Vipin Malhotra, who was then the president of the DSOBS. He called me and asked me what budget was I looking at for the film and the book. What I had in mind was one-fifth of what had been roughly budgeted. 'You gone mad Fauji? No one is interested in saving money.'

Inder was hounded out of the book shortly by the behind the scene 'movers and shakers'. I wanted to quit with him, but he insisted I see the project through. Accordingly, I was invited to attend a meeting at the

India Habitat Centre, where just about everybody was present. In a square seating arrangement, one row had the entire Doon School Board presided over by Analjit Singh and Peter McLaughlin, while opposite to them was the DSOBS with Vipin the kingpin. The second row had all those who were involved with various events, while the fourth side of the square had only me. I was surprised to see Suhel Seth, who was not a DOSCO present and seated opposite me. In an expansive way he waved a cigar in the air and said since it was Doon School 75, all projects being discussed must have a budget of rupees seventy-five lakh each. It was one of those silly, social comments and most people laughed.

When my turn came, I quoted the figure I had told Vipin earlier. There was dead silence for a few seconds, with Vipin sadly shaking his head. Then Dhruv Sawhney, a senior member of the Doon School fraternity, got up and started saying something about a flight he had been on to London. He said sitting next to him on the plane was Naseeruddin Shah's wife, Ratna Pathak, who twenty-five years ago for the Golden Jubilee had staged a play at the open-air Rose Bowl that had been quite a hit. He, Dhruv Sawhney had given his word to Ratna, that whoever now made the Doon School film, would work under her mentorship. I couldn't believe what I was hearing, so I just collected my stuff and got up to leave. No one said anything, except Analjit, the chairman of the board and the owner of Max Hospital. 'Stay on ... we are serving good whisky!' I just walked off, without saying what I should have in two words.[37]

In the beginning of 2010, Pratibha Patil, the president of India, launched the two Assam Rifles books with all the appropriate fanfare in New Delhi. By then I was shooting almost every week for the *Northeast Trilogy*, which was all falling in place rather neatly. Rakesh Loomba moved to Army HQ as DGMI while V. K. Singh took over from General Deepak Kapoor as the 23rd COAS. In Fort William, I met and briefed VK's

[37] The book, a large sized coffee table, was eventually made, as was the film, on budgets suggested by Vipin Malhotra. The film was a disaster and had to be pulled, as a result it was never shown after the inaugural screening.

successor, Lieutenant General (later General) Bikram Singh. For reasons I just could not fathom then, I got the distinct impression that the new army commander was hostile to the project, though, on the face of it, he made all the right noises.

Eventually, there were a total of a hundred and five shooting trips, each averaging five days. It was real slog work, and I don't think we left anything out. Some areas like Joupi in Manipur were extremely hostile and at times even I had to tuck in an AK-47 next to my camera bag for protection. There were some regular ambushes which kept us on our toes, but you cannot exactly get good, candid shots if you walk into a village with a protection party. I would usually stop short of a village and walk in alone and look for any girl or woman. Before they could react, I'd snap off a few shots, walk up to them and show them themselves, saying I was doing a book on pretty girls of India. Their squeals of delight would attract a crowd, and soon everyone would also peer at the image in the viewfinder. It worked each and every time, so much so that by the time my protection team would wander in, no one would notice them.

The army in the meantime had applied for helicopter sanctions so that we could bring in an aerial dimension to the shoots. A. K. Antony was the Raksha Mantri and though General V. K. Singh's office was pushing for the clearances, MOD was taking its own time. Design work on all three volumes had been going on simultaneously and I had Epson dummies that gave us a very good idea of how things were shaping up.

However, just when one thinks things are under control, disaster strikes and in this case fate was ruthless. In the immediate aftermath of Dipti's surgery, Niti had moved in with us for a couple of weeks and around then she developed a fairly innocuous cough. She had gone to the beach at Juhu where she lived and had drunk some guava juice after which she said the irritation in her throat had persisted. After a couple of weeks, she flew to Hyderabad to join Gagan who was conducting a course there. The cough had gotten worse, and then came the diagnoses ... Niti had cancer and it had gripped her lungs, which were filling up fluid at an alarming rate.

We just did not know what hit us, and before anyone could get a grip on the situation, she had started to deteriorate at an alarming rate. She was shifted to the Ambani Hospital in Bombay and it was then just a matter of time as we watched in horror and sheer helplessness as she literally began to fade away.

To make matters worse, the ugly side of living in a condominium like Beverly Park also raised its head around that time. There was an extremely aggressive couple living in one of the towers whose son had a medical problem. I was away in Tawang shooting when Dipti, who had taken the girls to the pool, had admonished the child's maid who had got into the water with him with her clothes on. She had promptly called Avinash Raghuvanshi who started not only abusing Dipti but followed her all the way to the flat and threatened her.

After I got back, I was taking Blaise to the other flat with the intention of giving him a bath. I was carrying shampoo and a towel when I was accosted by Raghuvanshi, who I did not recognize, and he accused me of 'swimming the dog in the pool'. At first, I didn't even know what he was talking about, but within the hour the matter had escalated to a point where the man started issuing death threats in writing. Expecting the condominium management to step in, I was instead taken aback at how others began to support Raghuvanshi, who changed tack and said I was bathing my dog in the fountains in the courtyard. The situation got so bad, one could not even head off to Mumbai until the absolute very end. Niti died shortly after that, and even to go for her funeral, I had to make sure there was police protection for the girls while we were away. Subsequently, everyone got very sanctimonious and apologized, but I could never forget the incident.

Niti's demise hit the family very badly, especially Vallika and Veeha. Her life snuffed out just like that, in many ways it shattered the family, and I don't think we ever recovered from her loss. An integral part of all our holidays, be it to Kullu or otherwise, the *Northeast Trilogy* was dedicated to her memory.

The books were mostly ready, except for the helicopter sorties that were still pending. On 15 January 2011, which was Army Day, it was decided that we would shift the chief's 'At Home' in the evening from Army House to the Manekshaw Centre, where a hundred blow-ups from the books would be displayed on stands with special lighting since we would have the president of India and the entire central cabinet present on the occasion.

The president's arrival, followed by the National Anthem, and with all the accompanying spit and polish, made it the perfect setting. Immediately after the band stopped playing, Dipti and I were introduced to Pratibha Patil by General VK and we took her and the prime minister, Dr Manmohan Singh, around the impressive display. The chief, on his part, briefed the president and the prime minister on what we hoped to do by getting the books across to schools and educational institutions across the country. The president took Dipti's hand and said, 'You will change the face of the country with this.'

We then made a brief presentation to the Cabinet, and the prime minister asked us what needed to be done next. 'We want an allocation of one crore per state sir, so we can also produce the books in the vernacular ... Tamil for Tamil Nadu, Nagamese for Nagaland, Manipuri for Manipur, Gurmukhi for the Punjab, Gujarati, Kannada, Bengali, Odiya, Hindi, and so on ... we will also give each state 10,000 sets for distribution and then take it up with them further ... these books are also as vital within the Northeast as they are outside of the region ...'

In his soft-spoken manner, Dr Singh said, 'That's less than what a house costs in Greater Kailash ... Is the English version of the books ready?' Without waiting for my answer, he turned to General VK, 'I can release these on 15 August from the Red Fort ... this will do more for National Integration than any other scheme.'

I started to say we still had a few areas left to shoot, but the chief stopped me, 'The prime minister wants the books by August.' I promised the chief as much.

Before the helicopter sorties could kick in, I had to do another ground run in the beginning of February. KK was in India on one of his visits and he promptly accepted my offer to accompany me to Roing where I still had to shoot the Idu Mishmi tribe that inhabited the area between the Siang and Lohit Rivers in Arunachal. When we got to Roing, we found there was a local Mishmi festival on and there was no accommodation worth the name available. We were wondering what to do when in a whirl of dust, the Pawan Hans Mi-172 that regularly ferried the governor around landed and out came General and Mrs JJ Singh. They were accompanied by Dr Farooq Abdullah and were obviously the chief guests at the festival. Seeing me standing there, His Excellency promptly gave me a bear hug and to all those present, it looked like he was my long-lost uncle.

After a short while, the governor took off in the helicopter and left Roing. The local MLA, perhaps overwhelmed by my apparent proximity to the governor, promptly offered us the accommodation that had been kept in reserve for the governor. We gratefully accepted the offer and got on with the business of shooting.

The next morning, we drove up to Hunli, which was on the road to Anini. Quite a few *gaon burras* were assembled there from the nearby villages. As on the previous day the governor had landed at Hunli after leaving Roing. Apart from the governor, Dr Abdullah had also made a short 'motivational' speech, and a local cameraman had shot it on video. Both KK and I watched the tape in absolute disbelief.

'Kashmir mein hum Pakistan ko kehte hain, hum par bum daalo ... goli chalao ... jab who hota hai, to Hindustan ki hakumat tokri mein paisa bhar kar bhag ke aati hai' (In Kashmir we tell Pakistan to hurl bombs at us ... shoot at us ... when they do that, the Indian government comes running with basketfuls of money). The camera at that stage cut to General JJ, then came back to the good doctor. *'Aap log bhi Cheen ko yahi bolo ... phir dekho kya kya nahi hota'* (You people should also tell China the same thing ... then watch what happens).

I wanted the tape, but the cameraman got a bit apprehensive. He obviously did not want to mess with His Excellency. He slyly said he would be back in an hour with a copy, after which he hightailed it from there. KK and I sat around for a while, drinking the local *aka* and eating pieces of mithun meat which was being served on leaves. After a while we said goodbye to the *gaon burahs*, and headed back to Roing. We then moved to the South Bank and headed off to Wakro and then on to the Namdapha Tiger Reserve. By the time we got back to Delhi a week had passed, but I told General VK about the Dr Abdullah speech. The chief told the DGMI to try and get the tape through the local army intelligence units, but by then it had probably been destroyed.

I had to almost immediately rush back to Dibrugarh for the helicopter sanctions were finally through. Dipti, who had been cleared by name for the sorties was no longer willing to leave the girls alone. 'Next year is Vallika's Board exams! You manage,' she said dismissively. I tried to argue with her, but I realized the futility of it. Unfortunately, I could not even replace her because the sanction was extremely specific.

'You have to include Fishtail 1 and 2 in the book,' said General VK, going over the maps with me on the eve of 13 February. These two areas had been erroneously marked as Chinese territory in the Indian maps published and given to the Chinese in the 1960s. I pointed out MOD had asked for flight plans to be cleared by them and we were to stay clear of the International Boundary. 'Find a way,' grinned the general, 'but if something goes wrong, I can't hold your hand.'

In the flight plan, we slyly referred to the two regions by their Tibetan names. As anticipated, no one bothered to check where exactly or what we were referring to, and I was cleared to go. All the helipads servicing Arunachal were based in Assam, and by midday, we were generally told to exit the mountainous region. It was also imperative we finish all the flying before the monsoon hit, besides which we were committed to finishing the *Northeast Trilogy* by mid-July for the prime minister to release it in August.

On 14 February we got airborne from Dinjan and flew eastwards along the southern bank of the Brahmaputra. The Lohit braids after it debouches from the hills and the islands it forms are fairly well vegetated. Visually it's a photographer's delight and I blazed away, even though I had shot the same vistas earlier. 'My father along with the Khamti Raja shot wild buffalo here before the 1962 conflict ...' I told the two pilots on the RT. They perhaps were fully convinced that I was a 'fully cracked' character, for one of them politely answered, 'That's so nice, sir!' I decided I should not try and multitask. Polite conversations in the air when you have to shoot are difficult indeed.

None of the pilots in the helicopter unit had flown into the Fishtail region, and at Hayuliang where we refuelled, we went over the maps again. The plan was to make a single pass over the fairly large Krangtui Lake, then exit the area to the west and fly back the way we had come. The Cheetah unfortunately has no fancy navigational aids, and as a result, we had no idea how the weather would be. There was a thick overhanging greyish cloud cover over the lake, and in sections, it was also snowing. The lake was spectacular but looked grim and forbidding under the prevailing conditions. Having got the shots I wanted, we then flew back.

After a gap of a week, I was back in Dinjan, and during the next six days flew sortie after sortie. Though I had on a couple of occasions flown over and even filmed supplies being dropped from An-32s in the Lohit Valley, I had never physically set foot in Walong. That night I could barely sleep, for I had grown up hearing many a story of 2 Rajput's deployment on either side of the Lohit between 1959 and the Sino-Indian war of 1962, while my mother cooled her heels at Tezu. By then I knew the geography of the region fairly well and was easily picking up the landmarks on the ground. After the mandatory stop at Hayuliang, we again got airborne and headed along the Lohit, overflew Walong and landed at Kibithu from where we could easily look river coming in from the Chinese side.

As we headed back, I could make out various features that had been so gallantly defended by 6 Kumaon and 4 Sikh and marvelled at the fact that the Chinese actually managed to get past the Indian positions. Finally, we landed on the grassy airstrip at Walong. There was a simple memorial and the wing of a crashed Twin Otter aircraft in one corner to remind one of the battles that had been fought at the very spot. Two Miji Mishmis had wandered down to look at the helicopter, and after photographing them I walked down to the edge of the Lohit River. More than half a century previously, in 1960, the Eastern Army commander, Lieutenant General S. P. P. Thorat had stood somewhere at the edge of the airfield and with my father and Subedar Dashrat Singh as his two liaison officers, had told the CO of 2 Rajput, Lieutenant Colonel (later Brigadier) Maha Singh Rikh that the Chinese would attack Walong on or around 20 October 1962. This little nugget of information in my head would play a crucial role subsequently.

At Wakro, Rohinso Krisikro ran a school by the Anu Shiksha Seva Trust that catered to the Mishmi children in the area. I had promised him we would try and overfly his institution, and on the way back, though we were stressed for fuel, I could see all the children lined up below. Dipti had in her sister's memory, instituted the Niti Bhalla trophy for the best all-round student in the school and Rohinso over the years never forgot to send us photographs of the winner every year. We orbited around twice and headed back to Dinjan.

Every day was remarkable and special. The next day we headed out to Vijaynagar, first overflying Mia where I could still see the remanets of a campfire around which KK and I had drunk whisky and eaten pork served to us by the Assam Rifles just a couple of weeks previously. As we approached Namdapha, almost the entire belt of forest where I had filmed hoolock gibbons while shooting the *Project Tiger* and *Call of the Wild* films was history, replaced instead by Chakma huts that were scattered in the deforested areas. Beyond Deban, the story was much the same, as a road was being cut through to Gandhigram. The destruction of one of the last remaining primary forests in India was happening under everyone's nose, and tragically, no one seemed to care. I had been to Vijaynagar twice before, but the emphasis had been on the air force and later the Assam Rifles. This time I photographed the Lishu tribe, which I was told subsequently used the *Northeast Trilogy* to help change their identity from refugees to a recognized tribe.

I was not at all familiar with the Dibang River Valley, or Anini which was the district headquarters. This was the route taken by the two British officers, Captains Frederick Bailey and Henry Morshead in 1913 when, as a follow-up to the Abor Expedition of the previous two years, they had ascended the Dibang River and entered Tibet by crossing the Yonggyap La. Morshead, who was a surveyor, had taken detailed readings that established the watershed that extended up to the Nyamjang Chu, on the basis of which the McMahon Line was drawn up in Simla in 1914. I spent the entire evening after getting back from Vijaynagar the previous day going over the terrain with Harish Kapadia, the editor of the *Himalayan Journal* who had led an expedition in the area. 'We had pretty lousy weather mostly. But do try and get a shot of Namcha Barwa that is visible from Yonggyap La on a clear day.'

On this occasion, we flew across the expanse of the Brahmaputra River and from Sadiya followed the Dibang River Valley. To our right, we could see Anini perched on a plateau, but we continued upstream and initially headed west towards another equally important pass, Andra La. After photographing that, we retraced our steps to the Dibang River and then made a beeline for Yonggyap La. The sky was completely blue, and I was shooting as fast as I could for we were literally flying along the snow-covered McMahon Line. Namcha Barwa, a 25,455 feet (7755 m) peak, visually almost merged into Yonggyap La even though it was more than fifty nautical miles further to the north. Quite honestly, I had never seen a more desolate country, and I even had the presence of mind to swivel around and shoot backwards, which gave me some spectacular shots that represented what the Chinese would see if they were to shoot from their side of the border.

At Anini, we were greeted by a large welcoming party who danced and sang in the Idu Mishmi manner. While the helicopter was refuelled, I took a car and quickly drove around the tiny district headquarters. One of the pilots had come along with me. 'It's a very isolated place. They say Anini has a very high suicide rate.' After we took off again, we flew along the Dree River that came in from the direction of Fish Tail 1. With all the flying in different directions, the geography of Arunachal could get extremely confusing.

Three more extensive days of flying took me to places which I had only seen on the map. Monigong lay in the upper reaches of the Bokar region and to prepare a helipad for us to land, a Sikh LI working party from Mechuka had slogged it by road taking four days to get there. After we had finished taking photographs of the Bori people and were preparing to leave, I called the JCO in charge and told him to wait at Monigong for a couple of hours before starting back. He nodded and saluted just as we lifted off in a swirl of dust. At Along (now Aalo), where we stopped to refuel, an IAF Mi-17 was busy ferrying supplies to various posts. I asked the IAF pilots if they could go to Monigong and airlift the Sikh LI boys to Mechuka. 'Sure thing,' said a smiling squadron leader. Forty-five minutes later he was back, luckily still smiling. 'You didn't tell me the helipad was so ad hoc. Instead, we just landed in a field and picked them up. They are back in the unit at Mechuka.'

Taksing was equally remote. We flew along the Subansiri River this time, following its course till it seemed barely a stream amidst deep and desolate gorges. I had photographed the Tagin, moving along the road from Daporijo but was not at all prepared for the sight that would meet us when we landed at Taksing where there was a solitary infantry battalion manning the remote outpost. A short walk from the helipad and I was amazed to see the entire village turned out in their traditional finery. It was an anthropologist's dream, for the Nah Tagins, who had evolved as a buffer between the Tagins to the south and the Tibetans to the north, were dressed in the manner of the Mahayana Buddhists. Ethnically, linguistically and even in their religious practises[38] the Nah seemed to be an extension of the Tagins, but the gaon burra went to great pains to insist that they were indeed a different group altogether.

On the way back, we landed at Daporijo, where Tagin women were lined up to perform traditional dances at the helipad itself. While I got plenty of action on camera, I kept wishing Dipti had been present for she would have naturally switched rolls with me, and I would have filmed all the action. Before we took off, for all the trouble the Tagin women had taken, I handed over a couple of cases of XXX rum. In exchange, I was delighted when the female *nyibu* gave me a bottle of *aka* that had a smell touch of orange blooms.

Flying for a sixth day in succession, we first landed at Zero, the incredible valley of the Apatanis, where in 2008 with Dipti in tow, I had photographed fish being bred in paddy fields. Though it was a fairly common occurrence in coastal areas and some Southeast Asian countries, in Arunachal this phenomenon was restricted to the Apatani tribe, who also adopted the somewhat bizarre custom of inserting nose plugs in their women's nostrils to deliberately disfigure them while also tattooing their faces, in a bid to protect them from being carried off by their relatively aggressive Nishi and Adi neighbours.

We then took off for Kurung Kumey, which in the pre-Independence days was known as Daffla country, just as the area between the Siang and Dibang Rivers was known as the Abor region. The

[38] The Nah Tagin, though they follow the Donyi Polo, also have adopted many of the Buddhist customs. For example, all their religious ceremonies are presided over by a *We entered the Teesta Valley over the Coronation Bridge*, but Buddhist monks are also present.

nomenclatures had since changed, and no one used the word Daffla anymore, referring to the people as Nishi. There was another helicopter in the area that was ferrying a local politician. The women were all turned out to perform for the big wig, but since our helicopter arrived first, we got the royal treatment instead. Not one to look a gift horse in the mouth, I gleefully shot the dances and before anyone realized we were not there to make a speech, we were on our way back to Assam.

Instead of going directly to Dinjan, we diverted and landed in Jorhat where the local pony races were on. The Jorhat Club had seen better days obviously, but as I looked around for some old trophies to photograph, there was a bit of a commotion and the head bearer walked up to me, reverently carrying a pair of riding boots that looked as decrepit as the club itself.

'John Sahib ka boots,' he said solemnly, and the one question that my generation asked our parents and grandparents as to why the British could so easily rule over us was answered. However, it wasn't my place to tell the bearer to chuck them in a bonfire, so I just kept quiet and photographed some of the races. When we got airborne, we were as much an attraction as the local horses, so we orbited around, did what from the ground would have looked like aerobatics and then set course for Dinjan.

By early March 2011, we were more or less done with Arunachal though the Kameng region still needed to be photographed from the air. Shooting the Kanchenjunga massif from the northern side was an obsession with me, my earlier attempts to shoot from MiG-21s having been only partly successful owing to perennial clouding. On 6 March, with two Cheetahs flying as 'buddies' we got airborne from Sevoke Road, Siliguri. The visibility was so poor that I was worried the chasing chopper might just telescope into us. We entered the Teesta Valley over the Coronation Bridge[39] and after we crossed Kalimpong, the visibility improved dramatically. There wasn't a single cloud over Sikkim, and everything was visible for miles around.

Before getting airborne, we had decided to prioritize the shooting of the Sikkim Plateau as getting a weather window there would be a

[39] Pilots refer to the Coronation Bridge as Alpha-Bravo. NH-31 continues eastwards from here and enters what is referred to as the 'Chicken's Neck'. To the north lies Sikkim, flanked by Nepal to the west and Bhutan to the east.

godsend. But with Kanchenjunga standing tall without even a slight wisp of a cloud, I was tempted to make a straight run for the mountain of gold. From the Namchi–Chungthang axis, the Kanchenjunga (also spelled Khangchendzonga) massif comprises Narsing on the extreme left, then Tolung with Gabru South and Gabru North to its right, with the world's third highest peak sitting in the centre, and the Simru Glacier and Siniolchu on the flank. By then we were over the Singtam Valley and town and approaching Toong. Below us was the fast-flowing Teesta and dead ahead to the immediate north lay the imposing central massif which divides north and northeast Sikkim at the town of Chungthang.

Below us, the Teesta, now barely a stream, comes down from the north and we followed its course below. To our left now was the cluster of Kanchenjunga separated by another line of peaks, dominated by Menshithang and Kishong now to our left. The CO of the helicopter unit, Colonel Saleem B. Shaikh in the captain's seat, kept pointing out each feature while guiding the co-pilot as we climbed steadily past the 14,000 feet mark, the rotors sounding different as they tried to find traction in the thin air. Down below, I could see the Thangu Valley that broadened marginally. The gompa at Thangu with its yellow windows was clearly visible below, and to our right was the Plateau, guarded by the king, Khangchengyao and the queen, Chomoyomo. Clear air turbulence and fierce headwinds were tossing the helicopters around, and the tension was quite palpable as the pilots kept looking for an updraft. At 17,000 feet, Saleem Shaikh, in between guiding the younger pilots, Captains Badal Kumar Dash and R. K. Semwal, calmly through the gap into the Plateau, told the story of the lover peaks. Khangchengyao, with a massive rockfall below, certainly looks like the masculine peak, while the massive but somewhat rounded Chomoyomo looks like a middle-aged lady.

Once we were into the plateau, conditions evened out but only marginally. The northern face of Khangchengyao has a permanent formation of ice that looks like the peninsula of India. This range forms the eastern wall of the Plateau which to the northwest extends into Tibet. The huts of the Yak herders were below us and then we could see the frozen expanse of the Gurudongmar Lake with the gurudwara the only colourful landmark in the starkly bleak landscape. That the lake never freezes over completely turned out to be a reality, for even from the air I could see a tiny spot in the middle that was still water. Beyond Gurudongmar, the Tibetan Plateau seemed to stretch endlessly into the horizon while a little ahead, under the imposing Paunhari feature, was the Kerang Bowl, the northern corner of which has the Teesta Khangtse, from where the river originates. To the left was Tibet with virtually no snow as the terrain was like a flat, curving tabletop barring the five-sister complex that had a bit of snow and ice. Beyond the Kerang Bowl, it was all Tibet and we turned back with 150 litres of fuel.

Under the Paunhari, one could now see the frozen Gyamtsoma Lake. Separating the Gyamtsoma water body and Gurudongmar was a ridge extending into the flat area. The vast frozen desert-like expanse looked awfully desolate and lonely. A few quick shots now to the left of the Gurudongmar lake, and then we were over the stone shelters of the nomads. A yak herd was being guided along by some men, but by then it was obvious we were going to land. We touched down on an isolated helipad where the second chopper flown by two younger pilots was already on the ground. I quickly got off and photographed the helicopters, and even those few steps seemed laboured. Saleem Shaikh's number two switched places with one of the pilots. Airborne again, through the gap we descended into the Thangu Valley, orbited once over the confluence of the Teesta and the Barum Chu, overflew Lachen and landed at Chatten for refuelling. The weather was holding though the glare from the snow was quite pronounced and the ultraviolet factor was increasing by the minute. Over the Plateau we had been flying along the border with Tibet, but now we were turning our attention to the Muguthang Sector that bordered Nepal and was dominated by the north face of Kanchenjunga.

We got airborne once again and headed up the Teesta, turning into the Zemuchu Valley almost immediately. Climbing all the time, we were soon over the immediate icy and rocky ridgeline and Kanchenjunga towered over us in all its majestic glory—the summit itself, flanked to the right by the Twin Peak features, the Nepal Gap, Tent Peak and the Pyramid Peak. Initially, we flew away from Kanchenjunga, turning into the Lonak Chu and Goma Chu Valleys. I was by then shooting almost continuously, while also trying to scribble the names of the various features on a scratch pad. The Dolma Sampa, a flat valley, looked like a frozen lake and then there were the various features that separated India from Nepal–Langpoi, Johnsang La, Johnsang Peak, U-Cut, and the relatively gentler slopes of Naku La. To the right and to the north we could see the flat expanse of Tibet. Just short of the pass we began to turn left, and were now flying along the Nepal border; Lungnak La, Khora Khangse, Chorten Niyma, the Chorten Niyma La and the Sentinel Peak flanked the Gomachu Valley.

By then we had crested 20,000 feet on the pressure altimeter (which is pretty much the ceiling for the Cheetah) that on the ground would correspond to around 24,000 to 25,000 feet and were directly below the north face of Kanchenjunga with the Twin and Zemu Glaciers glistening in the sunlight. The winds combined with sharp downdrafts were our biggest worry, and the choppers were getting buffeted around quite a bit. To our right was the entire spread of Sikkim and from our little glass bubble in the sky, I could see for miles all around. Across East Sikkim lay the Chumbi Valley (under Chinese control) and the Chomolhari massif, which is the second highest mountain in Bhutan. I put the camera away and looked around me ... drinking in the expanse of white below us.

We were to fly into the Lachung Valley again the next day, this time photographing the southern side of Paunhari. From there we went eastward and photographed Nathu La and Jelep La, beyond which lay the tri-junction where the borders of India, China and Bhutan met. Each peak and feature down below had a name and associated with the name were countless legends that told of caravans that struggled over these very routes linking Lhasa with Kalimpong and Gangtok in the days of yore. Having spent the last three years shooting on the ground through the entire Northeast, the aerial perspective was a wonderful bonus. After all, that is how God sees this incredible land of ours!

Back in Delhi, I spent a couple of hours with General VK going over the aerial photographs and also discussing the nuances of what we needed to put in the text. The books were unprecedented in both their scale and content and since we had only limited space for text, it required almost two to three times the effort to compress the information we needed to put out in each of the captions.

I was aware that there was some problem related to General VK's date of birth which would impact the length of his tenure as the army chief. Like almost everyone else, I too thought there must have been some ambiguity as in the 1950s and 60s, even 70s record-keeping was extremely vague. A fair number of my own classmates in Doon School, especially sons of old boys had fudged their date of birth which gave them a physical advantage over their peers when it came to sports in particular. Ironically, it was the elusive tape of Dr Abdullah's speech, that would lead to the uncovering and articulation of Op Moses.

Firstly, General VK was an army officer's son, and his father was from 14 Rajput. Whatever one did or didn't do about obtaining birth certificates then, it was well-nigh impossible for army officers to fudge the date of birth of their children. In the general scheme of things where others did it, call it an 'occupational hazard' for when an army child is born, even unit records will dutifully record 'captain or major or whatever rank so-and-so and his spouse was blessed by a baby boy/girl on such and such date'. Besides, in the army, no one does these unethical things, simply because in your protected environment, it is not done! There may be exceptions, but this applied to ninety-nine per cent service officers.

The story as it unfolded, had none other than the reputable former army chief and the then sitting governor of Arunachal Pradesh at the hub of it. His Excellency, whose ethical morality I had been privy to, was the Western Army commander in 2005 and there were rumours, call it langar talk, that the good general may be superseded. I distinctly remembered a front-page report in the Indian Express wherein the Shiromani Gurdwara Parbandhak Committee, the governing body of the Sikh faith, had written to the prime minister imploring him to appoint Jaswant Joginder Singh as the next army chief, which would then make him the first (the air force already had two) Sikh four-star appointment.

I don't want to get into the details here, but suffice to say, General JJ felt he owed his elevation to the prime minister, and he gratefully enquired what he could do in return. Maybe it was a rhetorical question, but the reply he got, either directly or indirectly, would set many a cat in motion. First, it was gently suggested that the good general support the prime minister's personal wish that India withdraws from Siachen, to which General JJ according to the then press adviser, Sanjaya Baru, replied saying it was 'doable!' Second, it was again suggested that a certain brigadier needed a leg up in a manner that the stars would fall in place for him and a path be cleared for him to also don the same mantle. This, of course, would require a mastermind who would have to look at various permutations and combinations. General JJ, by then fully initiated in the art of backroom warfare, said he would 'try'.

Having got a brigadier in MS branch on his side to clear the way for Bikram Singh, it was decided that General VK had to be the chief but could only serve for two years and not three. Not only was General VK affected, but so were another dozen or so officers whose careers had been adversely impacted by General JJ. The entire plan was so diabolical, it was amazing. Major General Ravi Arora was a case in point. He was from the same course as Bikram Singh (by then having made it to C-in-C Eastern Command) and he was a year younger plus also the winner of the Sword of Honour. To 'fix' Ravi Arora, General JJ had simply delayed his promotion board. By the time Ravi Arora filed the requisite non-statutory and then statutory complaints, the bus with General JJ as the driver had left many a time.

Everyone knew what was happening but could do nothing. Four or five coursemates of Bikram Singh then got together and met Subramanian Swamy at his residence in Nizamuddin. They were extremely vocal and frank with their views, so it was decided the entire chronology of events needed to be written down. By this time, Major M. G. Devasahayam, formerly from 17 Madras but subsequently switched to the IAS, had also reached out. He said he knew what was happening and though he was based in Nagercoil in Kanyakumari District, he felt this entire manipulative nonsense had to be fought. 'Why the heck are you getting sucked into this?' asked Dipti. 'It isn't your fight!'

'Isn't it? I think it concerns us all ...'

Devasahayam, who was quite a firebrand as a social activist, put it more aptly, 'It's not about General VK ... it's more to do with fighting for Institutional Integrity.'

I spoke to my father, who said since General JJ had cleverly played his cards and linked it to General VK's age, to refute it in the public perception would be akin to looking for a black cat in a dark room that doesn't exist. 'But do what you think is right ...'

The sordid story (at least what we knew at the time) was listed, and the only poetic licence I took was to name General JJ's master plan as Op Moses since it meant parting of the seas to clear the way for General Bikram. 'If General JJ has to take a lie detector test, at least he'll score on this one,' I told Colonel B. R. S Dahiya, another close confidant of General VK who was senior to him in school in Pilani. 'Brij' Dahiya was from the Grenadiers. An out-and-out gentleman, he was too trusting a soul. I don't know what got into him, but he sent the draft chronology to Colonel Ajai Shukla who had been his cadet in IMA. Shukla-ji, as he was subsequently nicknamed by General VK, promptly forwarded the draft to General JJ. When I found out, I was livid. '*Maine socha mera cadet hai ... angrezi check kar lega!*' (He was my cadet! I thought he'll check the English).

The three volumes of the *Northeast Trilogy* together consisted of over two thousand three hundred images spread over eleven hundred pages. The way the project had evolved, I had done the entire designing myself. The sheer scale and volume of work was driving me into the ground, but I was loving it. When in Delhi, I would work almost every day till midnight with Blaise squeezing himself in the narrow space under the study table. The work in Delhi also involved the storing of images, sorting and colour correcting each photograph, and making maps while all the time working on the text. I tried to involve Vallika in the map-making and the designing of covers but was not making any headway with her. I began to realize that for anyone to work on the *Northeast Trilogy*, they had to understand the entire scale of things that was being attempted. 'You have to decentralize,' my father would repeatedly say, but he failed to understand that to even get my own daughter to work on the project, I had to spend endless hours. It was easier to do it yourself!

For months, I would get up in the quiet of the morning and work on the other book that was long pending. Though *An Airfield Called Gilgit* had failed to get off the ground as a film, I had decided to put it down as a book. For years, I had been part of various discussions with senior officers, including my father, and we would talk about Kashmir and Pakistan a lot. We would go over minute details of what had happened not only in 1947–48 but also during the years preceding that period and the post-Independence era when Pakistan became a part of our vocabulary. And then there was the fighting at Siachen! What used to intrigue me in these conversations was that no one ever tried to get into the mind of the British, Chinese or British officers that were controlling events from their end. China of course was a different cup of tea, but when it came to Pakistan, the response always was, '*Yeh toh kattar mulle hai, pagal hai saale*' (They are fanatical Muslims. They are off their head).

Finally, the book had been completed and was published by Rupa & Co. as *The Long Road to Siachen: The Question Why*. Rajiv Williams, who was from 8 JAK LI, had worked on the Siachen section, especially the Bana Singh episode that he had witnessed as a company commander sitting at Sonam firsthand. The book was released by General VK as the chief and the launch at the India International Centre in New Delhi was attended by Lieutenant General M. L. Chibber and Colonel 'Bull' Kumar, both of whom had played a key role in what was to become a major slugfest and test of endurance with the Pakistanis. They had also spoken at the event.

I received three or four invitations to speak and promote the book at universities in March, but with the deadline for the *Northeast Trilogy* looming, had to regretfully decline. By mid-March I was back, this time operating with the Army Aviation's helicopter unit in Tezpur. It felt strange this time to fly over the Brahmaputra in the reverse direction, but our first task was to shoot the Khasi and Garo Hills of Meghalaya. After landing at Shillong at the helipad opposite Eastern Air Command, we flew to Cherrapunji, but the stream there was bone dry! Having already filmed the state on the ground with Somu Ingty as my extremely knowledgeable guide, it was easy to pick up landmarks from the air and we shot not only the Baghmara area beyond which lay Bangladesh, but also Tura, which was the capital of the Garo region.

In the Kameng area, I had already got quite a few shots of the Tawang area, even though we had always flown in from the direction of Eastern Bhutan. When we planned our route, I made a big blunder. I had not done proper homework, so decided to fly aimlessly along the Kameng River to Seppa, the capital of East Kameng, then head north into Adi country, before overflying the Tenga Valley and La Gyala Gompa where Colonel Avasthy had been killed. Later, I would repeatedly kick myself for I missed out on Se La, Tse La and Poshing La, which were such vitally important features in November 1962. Sometimes, despite pouring over maps and satellite images, we miss out on the most obvious aspects.

I flew from Tezpur to Liemakong in Imphal. The next day we took the two choppers and landed at Aizawl where we spent the night. Once again, our objective was to get to Saiba and Lawngtlai, the two southernmost townships. However, bad weather forced us to return to Imphal, and it was only in April that we could hack this leg which took us deep into the Chin Hills. The last and final sortie for the trilogy we did was to fly back from Tuting on 19 April. On the return leg to Delhi, I was changing planes at Guwahati and could see all my friends, the crew of the Mi-172 getting ready to take off for Tawang. I waved to them and they waved back. When I landed in Delhi, I got the tragic news that the Mi-172 had crashed while landing at Tawang and all seventeen people on board had died.

The shooting for the *Northeast Trilogy* was over and I heaved a sigh of relief. In a span of three-and-a-half years, using every resource that came my way, I had met all the objectives I had set for myself. Even the remotest corners of Tripura, Mizoram, Manipur and Nagaland had been covered. The text needed to be finalised and Dipti and I worked almost non-stop putting it all together. Biswajit Bhattacharjee, the coordinator for Lustra Press, then took over, and miraculously, by the first week of August, a few presentation sets were delivered to the prime minister. General VK, true to his word, was constantly reminding the PMO about Dr Manmohan Singh's promise to release the book from the Red Fort.

15 August came ... and went. Nothing happened then, nor was there any feedback from the prime minister subsequently. By October I was champing at the bit and suggested to General VK that he do the needful himself. 'I can't. I have the Raksha Mantri above me.'

'So, ask him ...'

A. K. Antony was a wonderful man, most endearing in his manner. At the Maneckshaw Centre he had blundered into both Dipti and me. In his trademark white shirt and Kerala dhoti, he had been dwarfed by the service officers in all their regalia. 'No no ...' said the Raksha Mantri, when asked to release the books, 'It is controversial!'

General VK looked at his boss, and incredulously repeated, 'Controversial?'

Antony had no objection to General VK or the other service chiefs releasing the book. This set the wheels in motion, and we started to prepare in right earnest. On 15 January 2012, all three chiefs released the trilogy of books after the Army Day parade was over. The army invited Rohinso from Wakro, Teitei Khawling from Aizawl and Somu Ingty from Shillong and presented them with the army chief's medal for their help in coordinating various shoots. In the evening the action shifted to Army House where sets of the books were formally presented to the president, the vice-president, the prime minister and also to the Congress chief, Sonia Gandhi.

The next morning, however, the balloon went up, with General VK seeking the Supreme Court's intervention in the so-called 'age issue!' Virtually every television channel was going ballistic and from the next day, newspapers led by Shekhar Gupta's *Indian Express* started having epileptic fits, as carefully worded stories started appearing ridiculing V. K. Singh and suggesting all sorts of nonsensical things. In between all this, we had formal launches of the trilogy in Hyderabad, Chennai, Trivandrum, Mumbai and Kolkata (formerly Calcutta). During the last launch in Fort William, despite being the author, I was completely ignored by Bikram Singh, who as the Eastern Army commander was next in line if General VK was hounded out. At each launch, the local press would get after General VK and his answers would be all over the media.

It was fairly obvious that the chorus against the chief was being orchestrated, and though by then the name of General JJ's former intelligence bunny was doing the rounds, there was not much that could be done in a reactive mode, especially since the man was then posted in 3 Corps that came under Eastern Command. The case, by the time it came up for hearing on 10 February, was attracting a piranha-type hysteria in the media. The two-man bench presided over by Justice R. M. Lodha, widely tipped to be the next Chief Justice of India, made a mockery of the law and when it was obvious that they would side with the government on what was a non-issue, General VK withdrew his petition. Watching the drama unfold, Devasahayam kept repeating, 'It's not about this fellow VK, I say ... they are making a mockery of Institutional Integrity!'

Should General VK have resigned? This question would sweep through the services, but I felt very strongly there was no point in having taken on the government if he was to throw in the towel. In a meeting that afternoon at Army House, almost to a man, his few gathered friends and close advisers said he should quit. General K. S. Thimayya was being referred to and some strong words were used against the judiciary. I hadn't said anything, but after everyone present had his say, General VK looked at me quizzically. We stepped out of the room and I suggested to him to stay the course.

'What does your dad think?'

'Stay put. Let them sack you, let's see if they have the guts. If you put your hand in a beehive, then expect the stings.' It is always easy to dole out advice in proxy mode.

General VK stayed on. The press and the media now got into overdrive, and it was pathetic to watch people scurry away to pay allegiance to what they thought was the emerging sun from VK Singh's shadow. But the fact that the army chief had stayed upset the apple cart and sure enough, on 4 April 2012, the country would awaken to bold headlines in the newspapers suggesting VK Singh had moved troops to Delhi with the intention of staging a coup. The principal author, not surprisingly, was Shekhar Gupta, who had been on a virtual crusade to hound General VK out of office. In his no-holds-barred attacks on General VK, he even published a nasty little story about the *Northeast Trilogy* and called me names on the front page of the *Indian Express* when I refused to facilitate a conversation between his crack reporter, Ritu Sarin and General VK.

'That son of b@#&h! To think I got the rascal married when I was the DC, I say!' exclaimed a highly agitated Devasahayam. He was so hopping mad he decided he would separately move the Supreme Court on the issue of Institutional Integrity! By then I was a complete devotee of MGD, who though he was in his mid-seventies was full of fight for social issues. Dipti kept rolling her eyes and asked repeatedly, what are you guys hoping to achieve? I spoke to Kamini Jaiswal, a senior Supreme Court advocate and explained the broader picture. She agreed to take on the case. Two former naval chiefs also became signatories to the petition, as did my father and some other senior retired generals. Then, led by the unsuppressible M. G. Devasahayam, we charged the proverbial windmill!

24

The Fight for Institutional Integrity

The coup story in the *Indian Express* was the oldest trick in the game. B. N. Mullick had first used it as a ploy to keep Prime Minister Jawahar Lal Nehru on his private leash by constantly whispering in his ear that the then army chief, General K. S. Thimayya, along with Lieutenant General S. P. P. Thorat was plotting against him. Despite the disastrous consequences of this in October 1962, subsequent prime ministers had always been wary of the army. Over the years, Shekhar Gupta had emerged as a senior journalist. We had been reasonably friendly when I was briefly in *India Today*, and Shekhar sometimes would drop in with his trademark *jhola* and sneakers for a chat with my father in Raksha Bhawan. He of all people would have known the exact consequences of the story he had put out (it earned him the sobriquet of Couptaji) and in my opinion, what he had done, amounted to treason.

On an impulse, I had driven across to Shekhar's office, and he until then was making all the right noises and taking me by the hand, had even taken me around to meet some of his other colleagues, among whom were Manu Pubby and Maneesh Chibber. I had taken a presentation set of the *Northeast Trilogy* for Shekhar, and when we had returned to his office, I gave it to him. In his younger days, the Northeast had been Shekhar's beat and I knew he would at a glance know exactly what we had succeeded in putting together. 'This is for you. It's the same *Northeast Trilogy* you reporters have been writing about on the front page, insinuating all kinds of stuff. Anyway, do go through it ...'

Shekhar mumbled something about being the people's watchdog, especially when government resources were being used. 'Really?' Shekhar was clearly uncomfortable, and I was in no mood to let him off any hook. 'Why did you do it?' I asked him point blank. 'Before you say anything, let me tell you frankly, I'm not here on General VK's behest. In fact, he has no idea I've come to see you.'

He came up with some vague rubbish about his sources and how he had to protect them. 'There are no sources, Shekhar, so cut the crap. Why did you do it?' I asked again, not really expecting an answer. 'Don't you realize what you've done? This isn't about a chief and his tenure, it is about an institution that you have always claimed to be such a fan of.'

'Don't threaten me Kunal ... I am not Arun Jaitley!'

That was least expected. 'What the hell are you talking about? Who told you that?'

'You threatened Arun,' he repeated. 'There was Arun and you in the meeting in his house, no one else, and you certainly did not tell me.'

I actually burst out laughing. I had indeed met Mr Jaitley who was the leader of the opposition in the Rajya Sabha at the time. I had presented him with a set of the *Northeast Trilogy* and then raised the concerns Devasahayam and some of us had about the fact that Institutional Integrity was being compromised. I had as a long shot, requested him if he, as a lawyer, would consider taking on the case. He had glanced at the papers I was carrying, which included the detailed brief about Op Moses. After scanning through the file, Jaitley had handed back the file to me. His eyes by then had what at best can be called a 'celebrity look' which makes it obvious to the other person across the desk that the meeting is over. He did not answer me, yes or no, thanked me for the books, and had me seen out. 'If you call what transpired between the two of us as me threatening him, then someone needs psychiatric help.'

That seemed to hit a raw nerve. 'That's the trouble with you guys, you are loose cannons. Like you, General VK is arrogant and downright dangerous. He thinks he is bigger than the system. He invited me to Army House for lunch and he insulted me.'

'What are you talking about now?' I honestly had no clue where the conversation was headed.

'It came as a shock to me, for VK had invited another person ... the editor of some ... some ... some Hindi newspaper! He had done it on purpose, to show me down. I was, and am, the editor of the *Indian Express*! He may be commanding an army, but I too head a vast newspaper empire.' I couldn't believe what I was hearing. This was the Shekhar Gupta who had his own *Walk the Talk* television programme on NDTV and who rubbed shoulders with just about everyone who mattered. He was then either the president of the Editor's Guild or would shortly take over. He was actually sitting in his own office and admitting he had a bone to pick with General VK. The only thing he hadn't owned up to was the fact that the story was completely fabricated. 'You don't move troops in the direction of Delhi in the middle of the night unless you are planning something.'

'Troops? You gone loco or what? At any given time there will be army vehicles moving on exercises, and some may point inwards towards Delhi.' But logic has no meaning in a scenario like the one that was developing. At this stage, we had been joined by Raj Kamal Jha, who had caught the tail-end of the conversation. After Shekhar had introduced us, me as his 'dear friend from the good old *India Today* days', I insisted on coming back to what we were discussing.

'Ok ... here's what I suggest. My Scorpio is parked outside in your slot. Get into it and let's drive across to Army House. Have a chat with the general, ask him whatever you want, then put out the response. After all, every newspaper is honour bound to carry a response.'

'Oh, I think it's a wonderful idea ...' Shekhar suddenly had a life buoy, which he grasped at instantly, 'You proceed ahead, I will follow in my car.' By then, my former colleague must have been desperate for my departure from what had been his den for more than a decade. His regular 'National Interest' articles, usually well-written and articulate, shaped the minds of hundreds and thousands of people.

Either I was just naive or maybe just plain stupid, but I actually waited for Shekhar to arrive outside Army House for half an hour before I drove in. The chief was in uniform and he listened when I told him what happened. He was scowling and shaking his head, and by the look of it, getting very angry with me. 'Why did you go? He will think I sent you there and interpret it as a sign of weakness on my part.'

'But I told him I had come on my own ...' My voice trailed off.

'You seriously thought he will follow you like a lamb.' Needless to say, nothing happened. Today, even after a decade of the story being published, I still meet a lot of people who insist there was a major move afoot, and they always seem to have 'inside knowledge' that no matter what you say will not make them change their mind.

With Devasahayam, there were no half measures. The petition, with Op Moses explained in detail with supporting documents, completely spelt out the modus operandi of General JJ and other vested parties to manipulate the entire system. General Bikram Singh, now waiting in the wings to take over from General VK had not exactly covered himself in glory, instead leaving a trail of misdemeanours in his wake that was normally enough to abruptly end any lesser mortals further advancement in the armed forces. Contrary to what the establishment and the media believed, it was not a backdoor attempt to reintroduce the age issue into the apex court, and that in fact, in the preamble had been clearly articulated as well.

What we did not realize at that time was the fact that we were not so much as trying to hold a mirror to the Government of India, but we were actually fighting none other than the two-man bench of Justices Lodha and H. L. Gokhale, to whom this case was allotted. The petition had been filed, and from every point of view, anyone who read it would have realized the sincerity of what was being said by the petitioners. The Supreme Court had accepted the writ, and the day of the hearing dawned.

While I do not know the backroom drama, what had transpired once the writ had gone into the system does not take much to guess. The end result was, as the *Indian Express* was delivered at various doorsteps, and Shekhar Gupta's edit page under his mighty pen was flipped open, in the name of National Interest, the petition had been ripped apart.

Couptaji's journalistic skills had indeed been tested and try as he might he could find no obvious weakness in the writ petition, so he latched onto the phrase 'langar talk' that had been used in a particular context and basically accused all the petitioners as being 'communal' since the three personalities involved were Dr Manmohan Singh, General Joginder Jaswant Singh and the then Lieutenant General Bikram Singh. Somehow, the fact that all three personalities were from the Sikh community made the writ null and void and should hence be thrown out.

I had never been inside the Supreme Court, and it was certainly an imposing place. Most of Lutyen's Delhi had been built by the British to hammer home the 'majesty of governance' and the apex court was no exception. The courtroom was packed to the gills, and I sat with Devasahayam at the back and stood respectfully when the order to rise was given and Justices Lodha and Gokhale strode in.

The Government of India was taking no chances and was being represented by all their big guns, including the attorney general. It was also obvious within minutes that the two learned judges were fully aware of the 'National Interest' op edit, for their comments seemed to be coloured by it. Nevertheless, the attorney general who had the floor was saying that there was nothing new about the incidents being quoted in the writ and that in the ACC file that was to be put up to the president of India with the recommendation as to who should be the next chief, had indeed taken note of and discussed these 'grave and not so grave charges'. Justice Lodha, in what seemed like a rehearsed one-act play to me, asked for the file to be put up before the honourable court at 1400 hrs. For two hours, until then, the court was recessed.

'What does he mean by "not so grave charges"?' I asked Kamini, besides whom quite a few other well-known advocates, including Prashant Bhushan had slipped in.

We found out soon enough. The writ had focused on three issues. First, there was a pending case in the J&K High Court that alleged that a fake encounter had been staged at Janglat Mandi under Bikram Singh who was then a brigadier. The script had gone hopelessly awry and apart from loss of lives on the civilian side, it resulted in the tragic loss of a colonel from the Bihar Regiment as well. The second was the testimony of his own second-in-command that talked of a staged incident on the LOC; and the last for which the army was actually in the process of conducting DNA tests at Meerut, involved the deployment of Indian troops on a UN mission.

Reading from the ACC file now before him, Justice Lodha said there were not three, but fifteen charges listed against the general. He rattled off some of them, including the fact that the daughters of the general were married to Pakistani nationals. There was something about a shop in Badami Bagh, Srinagar and some other frivolous stuff. Talking amidst themselves, Justice Lodha said he could see there was a 'handwritten note' by the director, IB that said he had gone through all the above listed allegations and found them to have no substance. Some other documents were quoted including the dates they were filed in the ACC report, after which Justice Lodha shut the file, waved it at the attorney general and said there was nothing to the case, made a sly dig at the communal petitioners, and dismissed the petition. Kamini Jaiswal was protesting but no one was listening and that was that.

There was complete pandemonium outside where the press was assembled, and TV channels were putting it across as 'Breaking News'. We assembled in Kamini's office, and the contradictions were soon obvious. The dates quoted by the Honourable Justice Lodha when he read out from the file only he was privy too, indicated that the list of charges and the so-called handwritten exoneration by the IB was pure tripe and had been inserted in the last hour or so. 'Besides, who the hell is the director, IB to say there is no merit in a case that is currently in the J&K High Court,' fumed Kamini.

This was blatant perjury. The dates quoted by Justice Lodha were on record, and these were so out of sync with the facts that a few days later we filed an appeal and politely pointed out the discrepancies. I do not know how the system works, for again the appeal went back to the very same learned bench. This time there was no discussion, just a wag of the finger and a clear warning that the petitioners would be in the dock if they persisted with this 'ridiculous case'. I looked at MGD, who just shrugged his shoulders. 'So much for trying to stand up for Institutional Integrity! You think anyone is bothered at this level,' said Dipti later that evening.

'You're just determined to shoot yourself in the foot. You have a family, you know, and responsibilities. Grow up, for God's sake.' MGD was on the dining table when this was said. He just looked at me, and when the lady of the house stepped into the kitchen, he just said, 'Wives, I say!'

Sometime in October 2012, the phone rang late at night. I was asleep and was slowly coming awake. It was Lieutenant General Prakash Katoch, who had served in the Special Forces, been wounded during Op Blue Star, commanded the Siachen Brigade during the Kargil War and was since retired. One of the most blunt and straight-talking soldiers, he also used to write regularly but was too forthright a person to be any think-tank's darling. And yet, Katoch had an analytical mind and the ability to put his arguments across on paper, so they could not quite ignore him either.

I moved to my study. The general was agitated and very angry. 'The PMO has all but decided to pull the plug on Siachen. It's all very hush-hush but I stumbled onto what they have been up to and am now up against a brick wall for no one is willing to listen.' What he was saying was chilling to the extreme. According to Prakash Katoch, ever since the US had moved into Afghanistan, they were desperate to give Pakistani generals something in return for their cooperation. What could be better than the Siachen Glacier? As far back as 2005, the Indian prime minister had been told or it had been conveyed to him, that if India vacated the 75-kilometre glacier, touted by the media as being the 'highest battlefield in the world', the Americans would use their clout and ensure he got the Nobel Peace Prize.

The story, as I understood it even then, was sordid enough. A retired Indian brigadier, Gurmeet Kanwal, was selected by the PMO and sent off to Ottawa, which was some Canadian or US-sponsored think-tank called the Atlantic Council. A Pakistani brigadier was sent from Pakistan and together the two worked out the blueprint for a 'withdrawal plan'.

The prime minister would have known that the army, especially the vast majority of veterans, would be up in arms if they got wind of the plan and he knew he had to tread cautiously. As an economist, he had probably always considered the deployment at Siachen since 1984 a colossal waste of money, but he would have also known that men had paid with their lives to protect the territorial integrity of the land and would not take kindly to any such scheme. However, in 2005 the then army chief had put himself 'in the bag', which allowed the PMO to move forward, albeit extremely cautiously and with the utmost secrecy. Over the next half decade, the ground work was done, and by September 2011 the PMO was ready for the big push.

India nominated 11 members, all retired personnel, of whom seven were from the armed forces, for Track 2 talks with Pakistan. On the Indian side, though Lieutenant General B. S. Pawar was officially the chair, Air Chief Marshal 'Bundles' Tyagi was the highest-ranking officer. In addition, there were two more lieutenant generals, a vice admiral, two brigadiers including Gurmeet Kanwal (since then the founding-director of the Centre For Land and Warfare Studies better known as CLAWS), a former cabinet secretary, two former ambassadors and Colonel Ajai Shukla, who was listed as a 'journalist'. Pakistan, on its part, designated General Jehangir Karamat, a former chief of the army, as the top honcho. Karamat had been the Pakistani ambassador to the United States around the time the Siachen 'study' was being conducted under the aegis of the Atlantic Council. Supporting Karamat were the two former chiefs, Admiral Tariq Kamal Khan and General Tariq Majid, who had only recently hung up his boots in 2010. Majid had also been the DGMI and in addition to him, there were two more lieutenant generals, a major general and an air vice marshal. The remaining three civilians were all retired former ambassadors.

There had been a series of meetings in different countries—after meeting in Dubai for the first time, the jamboree met again in Bangkok in February, Chiang Mai in April, Palo Alto, California in July and finally at Lahore between 23 and 25 September 2012. Almost two dozen or more big wigs on periodic jaunts should have raised the fundamental question as to who was paying for these trips. It was certainly not the Americans, so in all probability it was coming from the only agency that had unlimited resources, the ISI, but no one on the Indian side paused long enough to ask that million-dollar question.

That the entire Siachen withdrawal aspect was pre-planned and the main agenda, there can be no doubt for even though a couple of the Indian delegates objected, they were brushed aside. One of them, had contacted Prakash Katoch and desperately asked him 'to do something!'

Time was running out, as according to Prakash Katoch the PMO was on the verge of accepting the Track 2 recommendations. Every journalist he knew, he called, and even though some did lend an ear, within the hour they would politely refuse to get involved. The big brother syndrome of George Orwell's Animal Farm seemed to have become a reality. With General Bikram Singh in the saddle since July as the chief, there was absolutely no chance of any support from that end either. Finally, fairly late in the night, he thought of calling me and enlisting my support.

The next day, General VK listened in horror as I told him whatever I knew at that stage. 'The only way is to get this in print,' he mused. 'TV channels, if we do get one to carry the story, will not know the nuances involved. Call MGD.'

I repeated the entire thing to Devasahayam on the phone, as did General VK. 'Delhi, the entire media is gagged. Can you get the Hindu on board?'

'They'll get to them as well, I say. Just wait general ... I will call back in five minutes. Kunal, put it down as an article.' True to his word, he called within the specified time span. 'Anil Tyagi, the editor of *G-Files* will carry it. He doesn't give a damn farthing for these guys and they cannot buy him out.'

I hammered out the basic details, while MGD framed some key questions that needed answers. *G-Files*, a magazine that catered primarily to every bureaucrat, past and present in the country, certainly had the reach and on 12 November 2012 it was published.[40] General VK had not minced any words, and I quoted him in the article. With the link available online, we could then sit back and watch the drama unfold as veterans across the country started responding. Almost all army groups on social

---

[40] Kunal Verma and M. G. Devasahayam, 'Siachen Handout: Bartering India's Security?' 12 November 2012, https://www.gfilesindia.com/siachen-handout-bartering-

media were beginning to react but the job from our point of view was only half done. Our knowledge of what had transpired was partly speculation, so we needed to needle someone from within Track 2 to react.

I needn't have worried, for Air Chief Marshal 'Bundles' Tyagi called me almost immediately and within the hour he was sitting in my drawing room. Personally, I liked the former air chief and was disappointed to see his name, along with another lieutenant general who was a close family friend, on that list. From the way Bundles was sitting, I got the distinct impression he was recording our conversation. He then went on to say what a great initiative the withdrawal was, and how it meant all we had to do was draw a line on the ground and if any Pakistani crossed that, 'we could fight them in the air.' I was politely listening but was beginning to realize to my absolute horror that Bundles had not even thought the problem through, having just signed whatever paper was put in front of him. He had absolutely no idea what he was talking about. After two minutes I had had enough, and said, 'Sir, just one question ... tell me where Siachen is?'

Bundles looked as if I had insulted him, and said so. Then, seeing I was dead serious, he told me it was the extreme northern part of Kashmir.

'Ok ... that's fair enough. Now sir, just tell me who are we really facing on the Glacier ...'

'Pakistan, of course ...'

'No sir ... I do not agree with you. The three or four choke points on the Saltoro Ridge are held by us and Pakistan has a zero presence on the glacier. Your real threat, if you vacate the area even after demarcating the boundary which in that area is pretty tough, is also from China ...'

'China? What are you saying?'

'Sir, the Shaksgam Nullah to the east of Indira Point drains into the Shaksgam Valley. The entire area was ceded by Pakistan to China in 1963 and if anyone actually has the capability to roll down the glacier, it is the PLA. Why did you get sucked into this? You had no clue about the ground reality and General Karamat has made a monkey out of you guys.'

That upset Tyagi even more, and he started to say something but then thought the better of it. 'If what you are saying is true, then I need to take this back to the other members of the Track 2 group,' he said quietly, all bravado having evaporated.

'Do that, please!' I implored. 'You have to understand that if we do pull out of the glacier, the new line of defence will have to be along the Ladakh Range. To draw a new defensive line along this axis will suck up at least one, if not two more infantry divisions. What are you guys even talking about?'

Things were happening extremely fast. The *Outlook's* Hindi version was quick to ask me to make a map for them as they translated the *G-Files* article and published it. There was a flurry of phone calls after that and the editor-in-chief of *Outlook*, Krishna 'KP' Prasad said he was assigning one of his reporters, Toral Varia to do a cover story on the Siachen withdrawal issue. I dug into my archives and gave her quite a few aerial images of the glacier and their design teams got busy with the layouts. In the evening I drove across to their office in the Safdarjung Development Area and after looking at the pages, was sitting with KP in his office when the phone rang. From his body language, I knew the call had something to do with me, and after he had hung up, I thanked him and left. I had barely gone around the block when I got a tearful call from Toral saying could I come back please and that she would see me downstairs. Sure enough, unsurprisingly, the story had been pulled and she was crestfallen.

But the damage had been done and any amount of calls from the PMO could not reverse the situation. The chief minister of Gujarat, Narendra Modi, issued a statement saying not a square inch of Indian territory, be it Sir Creek or Siachen, would be compromised. Seeing how things were shaping up, General Bikram Singh also issued a statement saying there was no question of a compromise, and the hot potato was then duly dropped by the PMO.

That should have been that, but things started to get very interesting after that. Other than the fact that his name was on the list, none of us were looking at Ajai Shukla though it did seem strange that among such senior officers his name had been included. We would learn by and by that Shukla had not only been drafted into the team, he was the PMO's man in the Track 2 team. Brought in by Pankaj Pachauri, his erstwhile colleague in NDTV, who was the Press adviser to the prime minister,

Shukla had been promised chairmanship of Prasar Bharti if he could implement the Siachen plan. Bundles Tyagi and the others were just the window dressing and it is doubtful if they were even consulted. His carefully engineered plans going up in smoke, Shukla in a fit of pique, shot of three emails; the first was to Prakash Katoch in which he accused the Special Force's general of being upset only because 'he hadn't received the goodies' which the members of the Track 2 team got; an hour later he attacked MGD in a second e-mail; and just so I shouldn't feel left out, I got my certificate as well shortly thereafter.[41]

Fighting for Institutional Integrity and getting into a brawl over the Siachen sell-out was all very fine, but I had also succeeded in burning a lot of my bridges behind me. The year 2013 was Vallika's final year in school and she was set to graduate by the middle of the year. The *Northeast Trilogy* had become collateral damage, and as far as the PMO was concerned, there was no further talk of getting the books to the states or anywhere else for that matter. I had also rather ambitiously decided we needed to do a similar *Northern Trilogy* and had started work on that by the middle of the year. 'I'll find a way to do this too,' I told Dipti, who thought I had completely lost the plot.

Sometime around the end of 2012 I had received a call from Dereck Mountford, who was then the principal of the Assam Valley School (AVS) near Tezpur. I only knew Dereck in passing, having once before met him many years previously at the Doon School's Founders Day when he was a housemaster there. 'Why don't you come and talk to our kids about the Northeast,' he had amiably said on the phone. Having accepted the invite, I was looking at him incredulously as he poured a drink for both of us in the school's stylishly appointed guestroom.

'Have a heart. An hour-and-a-half? And the entire school, including Class 6? There is no way anyone can hold their attention for that long.

[41] Ajai Shukla would continue to vent his ire periodically at me. Using the platform he had in the *Business Standard*, he launched more than one or two personal attacks. I called up T. N. Ninan, the editor and told him it was unwarranted. Adopting the sanctimonious 'holier than thou' tone, Ninan gave me the usual answers about filing a complaint with the Editors Guild, etc.

And you want me to talk to them about the Northeast?'

'Well, it's been scheduled and announced. Of course, I can always change it,' said Dereck. Fortunately, I had all the files pertaining to the *Northeast Trilogy* on my laptop. I got up at dawn and for the next ten hours worked on a power-point based slide show. Almost cross-eyed with fatigue, at the scheduled hour I walked into the packed auditorium, the class 6 kid's feet not even touching the ground as they sat in the front row and stared at me.

I leaned across to Dereck, 'Listen, one kid yawns, I'll wrap it up.' He just grinned and proceeded to introduce me to the school, after which the stage was mine. I had no script, and in fact, had not even had the time to note down any points. All I had was the images, and once they started to play out on the big screen, all I had to do was operate the remote and keep describing the shots. The ninety minutes passed. In fact, I felt I could have done with a few more minutes for I had to wrap up the section on Mizoram rather abruptly.

During dinner, Dereck proudly said not one kid had yawned. I said I had noticed that. 'Listen Kunal, I have a strength of 900 students. I think this *Trilogy* needs to be circulated and I have spoken to my Board earlier today. We would like to order 1,200 sets if that is possible.'

Back in Delhi it was the turn of Biswajit to look at me in disbelief. 'You offered the books at this rate? There's no way we can print them.' I told Biswajit that Dereck, who seemed to know the basic economics around printing, had also said much the same thing. He had also said that regardless of what price we finally quoted, the order was a firm one.

'I don't want to change my quote. Tell me, how many books do we need to print for the figure to be economically viable, where we also make a profit?' Biswajit took a deep breath, sighed and got busy with his calculations.

After fifteen minutes, he looked up. 'Three thousand six hundred copies.'

What then followed was a whirlwind series of lectures across the

---

The press, with it unlimited supply of ink, can destroy people at the stroke of a pen and how!

country. My first stop was the St Paul's School in Darjeeling, where the Reverend Joy Haldar hosted me for a couple of nights. With the flowering rhododendrons providing a splurge of colour, looming over the school's beautiful main building was Kanchenjunga. After my lecture, I made absolutely no attempt to sell the trilogy, but AVS had set a precedent and word had got around. St Paul's ordered 500 sets. Others followed—Pine Grove School in Sabatoo, the Mann Public School, Pathways, Welham Girls, and finally Welham Boys', both in Dehradun. The only stumbling block, which by then was no longer a surprise, was the Doon School. I finished my talk there and the headmaster, Peter McLaughlin, literally took the mike from my hand. 'I personally want 150 sets ... the school will be giving you a final number in a day or so.'

'Thank you,' I said, and ironically, I was presented a humongous, large-sized book on the Doon School that had been printed as part of the 75-year celebrations.

Wing Commander Anupama Joshi was Peter's Executive Assistant and she had been a part of the first batch of IAF lady officers. In 1992, she had been one of the cadets, a real novelty at the time, while we were shooting *Salt of the Earth*. Two weeks were to pass and still, there was no word from Peter, so I called up Anupama. 'The HM? Hah ... he says something to you and does just the opposite. I asked him a couple of times and this morning he said the Doon School could not afford to buy the books. If you wish to present them, he will be happy to accept.'

The day we hit the target of 3,600 sets, I told Biswajit to go ahead and print the books. I decided to add another 400, which brought the total to 4000 sets. The books were bulky, a carton just packing in six sets, so storage of the remaining books was going to be a problem. Dipti did not want me to 'dump' the books in 1704-A, which was Gaurav's flat, but I saw no reason why the servant quarters of an empty flat should not be used for this.

The books were printed and despatched to various parts of the country, and the balance sets were stacked away in Gurgaon. A month had barely passed when the Bangalore-based Mohandas Pai asked Dipti and me to meet him in Delhi. He had been presented the *Northeast Trilogy* and now he wanted to know how many sets did I have readily available.

Having given the books to schools at one-third the listed price, I felt it would not be right to charge a higher figure from Mohandas Pai. He burst out laughing, 'You guys may have the skills to produce something as spectacular as this, but I'm afraid you have no business sense!' He picked up all 400 sets and insisted on paying the actual MRP.

Finally, the day when Vallika's final Board Exam marks were to be declared was upon us. She had always been a bit of a 'throw-away' genius who without any obvious attempt at studying had always done well. A few years earlier I had sat both Vallika and Veeha and told them two things. One, if you get 99 or 100 per cent marks without understanding what was going on, it was a waste of time. Second, I was not going to send them abroad, especially to the US, for undergraduate studies. 'Get the marks and get into a good college. After that, when you want to further study and specialize in any field, we will find the money and send you where you want to go.'

Vallika was also a reasonably good artist. She was the chief editor[42] of the Shri Ram School and had also been selected to represent the country in a SAARC group. When she was younger, to get her going, I had started painting myself and would be joined by the two girls as we dabbed away on a canvas with oil or acrylic paints. Vallika certainly had the talent to look at art as an option, but I was not sure if conventional art school was the best option for her. I felt she was a non-conformist who could sketch and play with colours, and I felt she needed to allow herself the liberty to experiment and generally just have fun with paints without being obsessed with end results.

Vallika's results as they came in, had Veeha and her jumping for joy, for she had astounding marks. Suddenly, it was obvious she could literally opt for any college of her choice in the country. Art school continued to dominate her wish list, so with Vallika in tow, I went about the business of meeting and speaking to people. Delhi College of Art was having all sorts of problems and for the last couple of years, it seemed students were just bumming around. The Mumbai-based JJ School of Art had very limited seats for students from outside of Maharashtra, while NID in

---

[42] Three years later, Veeha would also follow suit. In Shri Ram School, the chief editor was given a lot of importance, for in the annual journal, they even preceded the school captain.

Ahmedabad as an option had been shot down by Dipti even when it was suggested, mainly I suspect because of the Kavita connection. Also, almost everyone we met, all artists of repute, all said much the same thing to Vallika. *Pursue art by all means, but don't put all your eggs in one basket.* They all also hammered home the point that talent was just ten per cent of the deal, ninety per cent was sheer hard work, which in this case meant you just sketched and painted, morning, afternoon, evening and night.

With hindsight, I wish Dipti had accompanied Vallika and me for these meetings, but she would refuse to come. Vallika would report back to her, and instead of focussing on nine good things they said, she would latch on to the one negative, which invariably was about how difficult it was for an artist to make money.

Everything I would say during that period would subsequently become extremely contentious. I felt Vallika had the talent to easily make the cut for the civil services and I encouraged her to apply for either History or English Honours in St Stephen's, where I was sure she would literally walk in. 'You can do art online simultaneously,' I perhaps rather ambitiously suggested, as Dipti gave me 'the look'. Anyhow, Vallika applied somewhat half-heartedly, and after making the cut, as I had expected, she literally breezed through the interview. Dipti in the meantime, still wanted Vallika to apply to art schools in Bombay and Baroda. I had no problems with that but could not understand why Vallika should not go for the interviews on her own. With Veeha and Dipti tagging along, airfares would triple, I argued, and I simply did not have the funds to waste at that point of time.

The Government of India, with a lot of fanfare, had decided to change the college education system in the country and had introduced the FYUP or Four-Year Undergraduate Programme. I had gone with Vallika to St Stephen's to do her initial paperwork, and the staff in the office were nudging each other and saying Vallika was from the 'general category'. It was indeed sad, even after six decades of Independence, in India we continued to have so many reservation categories. I remember having gone to Miranda House, and the teachers there conducting interviews were in splits for a candidate who had the requisite marks to make the cut but had 'alternate English' as a subject. Just what we are doing to our education system would get further highlighted when a few months down the line, an increasingly frustrated Vallika vented her anger, 'They're teaching Shakespeare line by line,' since most of the students had come through the CBSE Board.

To make matters worse, I ran into the principal of St Stephen's College at the Bishop of Delhi's residence near St James's Church a few months later. Valson Thampu and I got talking about MCC, which according to him was very keen to have him as the principal, but then 'Stephen's is Stephen's' he added condescendingly. I had not planned to, but then I told him my daughter was studying there and he asked what were her other interests. I said she was an artist but commuting from Gurgaon to Delhi University and back every day, it took up three hours. He asked me if he could see any of her work, so I showed him a couple of paintings that I had photographed and had on my phone.

'I'll make an exception and give her hostel accommodation. She can then paint to her heart's content!' Thampu exclaimed, making sure the Bishop too heard him. 'Just drop by at my office tomorrow or day after and meet my PS and fill the application. Consider it done!

Like an idiot, that evening over dinner I told Vallika what her principal had promised. Naturally, she got all excited. Next two to three days, I went to the college, and each time I drew a complete blank.

A couple of months passed, and again by chance, I was invited by Joginder Mann to attend a Spelling Bee contest at the Mann Public School. Lo and behold, the chief guest was none other than Valson Thampu, who recognized me instantly and during the three-hour event, squirmed uncomfortably. Since we were seated side by side, every time there would be a break in the spelling rounds, Thampu would hold forth on how he was inspired by Gandhiji's teachings and how he started each day in St Stephen's by talking about one or two issues that the Mahatma had dwelt on. I was not planning to raise the art topic with him at all, but somewhere along the way, he leaned towards me and whispered in my ear, 'About your daughter. I was extremely tied up then. Please come and see me tomorrow. I have not forgotten my promise before the Bishop.'

So, the man has a conscience, after all, I thought to myself. It was such a non-issue to start with, but as we parted at the end of the event,

Thampu again in front of Joginder held forth about expanding educational horizons and with a flourish he asked me to drop by at the college and 'do the necessary formalities.'

Once bitten twice shy is the usual norm, but again, like an even bigger jackass, I told Vallika about what Thampu had said. Once again, a similar run-around started, and again one drew a complete blank. My credibility with my daughter was not only shot, she was convinced I had solicited her principal in the first place. Dipti too joined in, saying the least I could do was tell the truth. By then, the theme song that was beginning to emerge at home was that I had 'forced Vallika to go to St Stephen's!' At first, I thought it was just one of those things, said more in jest than with any seriousness.

David Davidar's growth in the publishing world had been phenomenal, and after his tenure with Penguin India, he had moved for a while to Penguin Canada. Our college-day tennis friendship had withstood the test of time, and to this day he falsely claims he got a set off me when we sometimes played in Delhi in the mid-1980s. Back in India, he had set up the Aleph Book Company which was a partnership with Rupa & Co. that was being run by Kapish Mehra after his father retired. I was none too happy with the marketing of *The Long Road to Siachen* and was complaining to David when he said wanted me to write a three-part series on the major wars that had been fought by India since Independence. 'However, before that, do an autobiography of General V. K. Singh.'

'You mean a biography? No way am I ghostwriting anything for anyone.'

'No, I mean an autobiography. You be the co-author, with a regular byline and sharing of royalties. It's the accepted thing.' The next few days he sent me two autobiographies—*It Doesn't Take a Hero* by General Norman Schwarzkopf and *My American Dream* by General Collin Powell. After I had dutifully read the books, there was a meeting with General VK and we started work on *Courage & Conviction*. Being from the same battalion as my father, 2 Rajput, and since I knew almost all the people he talked off, it was relatively easy to write. We would meet every alternate morning around 6 a.m. at his residence at 20 Mandir Marg, where he had shifted post-retirement, and talk for a couple of hours.

Courage & Conviction was published by the end of 2013, but by then I was working on the 1962 book at a fairly frenetic pace. All the years of research on the subject and the innumerable discussions were beginning to pay dividends. Yet, there were still many gaps, and at the time, one had very scanty information about the Chinese perspective of what had transpired. I got on the phone and dialled the listed number of the People's Republic of China. Frankly, I hadn't given it much thought, so was taken aback when the operator asked me in chaste Hindi who I wanted to speak to. Ten seconds were to elapse before the Military Attaché, presumably, a colonel with the PLA, was on the line, and once again, in perfect Hindi asked me what he could do for me.

Three hours later, I found myself sitting across the table in the colonel's office. I said I was writing a book on the 1962 War and was looking for any material I could get from their side of the hill. '*Aap log kyun usko war kehete hai? Yeh toh ek mamuli border skirmish tha*' (Why do you call it a war? It was but a minor border disagreement ...). If you did the math, what the Chinese were saying was true. In the two clashes that took place in October and November, there was a total of one brigade deployed in Ladakh and two at best in NEFA. I came away from the meeting with a translated version of a document titled 'Sino-India Border Self-Defence Counter-Attack Battle 1962' and a few other papers. As I was leaving, the colonel said he would send someone over with a film clip that I might find interesting.

Amazingly, the Chinese had filmed some of the fighting, albeit later in the day when the firing had died down. I was watching the footage, not sure if I wanted to expose the wounds in my father's heart after all these years when he walked in anyway and started to watch. '*Arre ... yeh to Balbir hai*' (Hey ... this is Balbir!), he said, recognition instantaneous even after half a century had passed. In the film, they had even re-enacted the capture of Brigadier John Dalvi, who was commanding the ill-fated 7 Brigade. The brigadier smiled wryly at the camera after which the Chinese narration switched gears and the film went on to show some of the other areas as well.

I had Lieutenant General Thorat's file on Exercise Lal Qila on my table for years. In March 1961 the general had, in a sand model exercise, told all the assembled commanders at Lucknow that the Chinese would attack in the third week of September 1962. Thorat had talked of a defensive line that ran about 25 miles from the foothills, which would force the PLA to stretch their lines of communication which would be harassed by the retreating Assam Rifles units. Though the Chinese film was in essence a propaganda film, it still had certain elements that answered some questions that were lingering in my mind. For example, after the unilateral ceasefire in November and the Chinese withdrawal, the PLA had lined up all the captured Indian equipment at Dirang Dzong and returned it to us. Footage of rows upon rows of vehicles and weapons belied what we ourselves had been conditioned to believe. Except for 2 Rajput and 1/9 GR that had de-inducted from NEFA and had been hurriedly brought back to Namka Chu, all other Indian units were reasonably well equipped. I began to realize, if you start asking the right questions, only then will you get meaningful answers.

The 1962 book was taking up all of my time, and I would sit with Blaise at my feet in the study and work till well past midnight. It was, to put it mildly, an extremely difficult book to write and I would often find myself in tears. 'This damn book is changing you as a person,' said Dipti accusingly on more than one occasion, 'it's taking over your entire life!'

It was a story of a defeat, a horrible one at that, and it involved people who were an extended part of our family. 'I know no one likes to read about a defeat. Even if it sinks without a trace, I feel I have to write it.' I was also acutely aware that my father was beginning to deteriorate physically, and I suppose subconsciously I wanted him to read it. Though we continued to discuss various aspects of realpolitik and its impact on the geopolitical scenario, we never discussed the 1962 book, though I did refer to his *Rivers of Silence* every now and then.

Dipti was getting more and more belligerent and accusatory, and I suspected, frustrated. Most of the time I wasn't sure if she was joking or not, for with mounting expenses, I simply did not have the luxury of taking my foot off the accelerator. I, on the other hand, started to feel she and the girls were completely removed from the issues that govern one's day-to-day struggle for survival, and I felt I could do with some help, but none was forthcoming. Unlike films, books, be they illustrated galactic tomes like the *Northeast Trilogy* or hardcore non-fiction as was the case with *1962: The War That Wasn't*, are by their very nature individualistic. Though we worked together when it came to writing captions for the trilogy, Dipti was barely involved in the photography and not at all in the endless slog of processing the images and doing the design.

The way out, in my opinion, was to go back to filmmaking. When I was shooting for the Assam Rifles, sometime in 2009 I had visited 2 AR that was deployed in the area between Churachandpur and the Mizoram border. The CO had been tasked by Shillong to try and get seven SUVs for a rally that would be flagged off in Delhi and terminate at Moreh. With pathetic connectivity, the CO had been dashing off letters to just about anyone he could think of, and so far had got a few indifferent bureaucratic replies. Though I had never met Anand Mahindra in person, we were in communication every now and then via e-mail, and I was always impressed by his down-to-earth attitude towards life. Driving twenty-odd kilometres to a point where there was signal to make a call, I connected with Anand and in less than thirty seconds he had said, 'Assam Rifles? No problem. We will give them all seven vehicles!'

I had sent a set of the *Northeast Trilogy* to Anand, and as usual, he was quick to respond. He suggested I explore the possibility of converting the books into a television series, and his office would fix a meeting with Mahesh Samat, who was heading the newly established Epic Channel in Mumbai. I had already written out a detailed 20-part synopsis for a series of 50-minute documentaries on the entire Northeast and I flew to Mumbai in August 2013 to meet with Mahesh, with whom I immediately struck a comfortable equation. In the meeting, there were a host of others, including Ravina Kohli who was in charge of development, and Aparna Pandey who was looking after content development. I was also introduced to Ekadish Bal who I was told would be coordinating things with me. In the meeting, I elaborated on the already very detailed summaries that we had written on all the twenty episodes and was surprised that there were actually no meaningful questions.

The pilot episode was to be shot on Sikkim. In my discussions with Mahesh I had told him I planned to use General VK as the narrator, for not only was his Hindi extremely good, he had an earnestness and simple approach that hopefully would see him emerge as the ideal *sutradhar*. 'Ah, the controversial guy ...' Mahesh nodded eagerly. I would eventually have to see if the general was comfortable and do a screen test, but I was quite confident it would work out. I also did not want to shoot the film myself, for unlike our earlier forays into the Northeast where we had the backing of the IAF, the army or Assam Rifles, we would be out on a limb and I would have a lot of coordination work to do. Given the nature of the terrain and the remoteness of some of the areas, I needed someone who was capable of enduring the slog. Sanjay Aggarwal, yet another classmate of Dipti's from FTII, had filmed with the Army Expedition on Everest and had also done some work with wildlife.

'You never get along with anyone from FTII,' said Dipti sullenly. 'I have no friends left, all thanks to you.'

I met Sanjay while Dipti abstained, and he was extremely excited with the project. We shook hands and then got down to the business of sorting out the required equipment. We would be shooting the first leg in December, and I told Mahesh the pilot would be based on what would eventually be less than thirty or forty per cent of the final film. Last I had shot a film was in 2009, and there had been a quantum leap in video camera technology. Sanjay, who I presumed was fully cued up, insisted we use Canon SLR cameras with all the requisite paraphernalia. 'It gives us a tremendous range when it comes to lenses,' he said earnestly, 'and believe me the results are right up there.' We did a couple of test shots and the footage seemed top draw, but I was still not too convinced about it.

'First you hire the guy,' said Dipti, 'now you want to impose your ideas! I still think you are the best person to shoot the entire series.'

I should have followed my instincts, for it would later transpire that Sanjay had, in fact, never used the equipment in that configuration before. The producer whom he worked with regularly had been toying with the idea of switching to this technology, so Sanjay wanted to shoot accordingly. By the time I found this out, we were halfway through our shoot in West Sikkim. I was getting extremely frustrated because with the adapters, etc., the still cameras were extremely difficult to pan, and zooming in or out was a major technical exercise that required focus adjustments by hand. These were theoretically possible, but practically impossible to do. By the end of the shoot, Sanjay himself was rather shamefacedly admitting he had bungled big time.

Nevertheless, after filming in West Sikkim and then the eastern part, we had got some extremely good footage and though we struggled with the edit for technical reasons, we had a fairly good pilot episode ready. General VK had, both in the on- and off-screen parts, done an extremely good job, though Dipti felt we needed to go for a younger person. I flew to Mumbai and once again an entire brigade of people trooped in to watch the pilot episode. I again reiterated that a major part of the film was yet to be shot in summer and that the pilot was a semi-trailer of things to come, and along with the others settled down to watch the film.

The screening was a complete disaster. Ravina Kohli said she could not relate to any of the names of the Chogyals, or any other people talked about in the film for she 'had never heard of them before'. She also said she had no clue who the narrator was, and audiences needed a 'known face'. Mahesh lamely said General VK was the former army chief and the 'controversial guy' but it cut no ice with the lady, who I figured was having one of her 'bad hair days!' Four or five days later, I got a call from Ekadish, who told me though the film was extremely well shot, it had been decided to bring in some younger 'script writers' who would help Dipti and me give it an acceptable shape!

Not sure how to react, I asked her what on earth did she mean. 'Well ... we feel you and Dipti are too close to the footage,' she said diplomatically. 'We need more action ... we need to bring in the Yeti and flying lamas, for example.'

'What?'

'Yes ... people associate Sikkim with that!' She paused, 'Look, I know how you feel, but let some of our script writers do their bit. Where is the harm?'

After receiving all sorts of inane queries from these otherwise faceless 'detached script writers', we received their revised script after a month or so, and frankly, even as a spoof, it couldn't have been worse. Dipti and I met Mahesh one last time when he visited Delhi, in a bid to salvage the project. Mahesh being from an advertising background, was by then talking a language which I for one just could not relate to. 'Surely you guys read the synopsis on the basis of which the series was commissioned. In the treatment of the Sikkim film, we have gone entirely by what we said we would do. How can we now deviate in this manner which is completely at odds with what we want to project about the region?'

'Kunal,' said Mahesh with a deadpan expression. 'We never read the script. There were too many pages! No one goes beyond page one or two!' At that point, we just gave up and that was the end of that!

I was much too preoccupied with *1962: The War That Wasn't* to waste any more time chasing the films with anyone else.

By the middle of 2014, even though Vallika was doing fine academically, the cacophony against me had turned into a tirade. I was being constantly accused of having nipped her art career in the bud. Around that time I got in touch with Martine Vaugel, an American sculptress who was settled in France. A former girlfriend of Bob Dylan, she had famously sculpted Mahatma Gandhi's bust, and the United States had even put her on a postage stamp. She conducted classes at her home in the south of France and I asked her if she would take Vallika under her wing for a few weeks during the winter break. Martine said she could, but then she would not take on other students and she quoted quite a large sum of money.

With some trepidation, I broached the subject and fortunately did not have my head blown off. Both the girls checked out Martine's website and got reasonably excited about it. Then, Dipti walked into the study and somewhat expectedly said Vallika obviously could not travel alone as she simply did not have the exposure. I said I was thinking of sending both the girls, but Dipti said that was a ridiculous thought and if anyone would go along, it would have to be her. 'Besides, have you thought about it? It'll be the height of winter. How do you expect the girls to manage?'

By October the arrangements had been made. I was as usual working on the 1962 book late in the evening when a call from my mother sent a chill down my spine. 'Come quickly by tomorrow's flight. Ashok has had a nasty fall in the evening.' I landed at Kullu the next morning and was taken aback at the pace at which my father seemed to have deteriorated in the couple of months since I had seen him last. He had gone for a walk with Pasha and in our own drive had collapsed. Luckily, Shamsher Thakur who lived next door saw him lying there with Pasha standing next to him and helped him home.

Velu Nair, by now a lieutenant general, was monitoring my father's condition from the R&R Hospital at Delhi. 'Try to arrange a blood transfusion,' he told me. Within hours, men of the ITBP's 2nd Battalion had lined up and the recovery was remarkable. Velu said, 'let him remain in Kullu till he's fit enough to drive down', but he also said the writing was now on the wall. At the end of October, my father bid adieu to Windsong, knowing in his heart he would never see the place again and drove down to Delhi. Two days later, he was admitted in R&R and the situation started to worsen by the hour. On 14 November, he had been shifted to the ICU, and the doctors said he would almost certainly not make it through the night. I had to sign a form which stated that under no circumstances was he to be put on a ventilator.

There was at the time a lot of trouble along the LOC in the region between Naushera and Poonch. Konsam Himalay Singh, by then a Lieutenant General, the first from the Northeast, was commanding XVI Corps. KH had his own equation with my father, and in the evening when I spoke to him, I told him according to the doctors it was all but over.

Having spent a restless night, I had finally fallen asleep in the morning when the phone rang around 7 a.m. It was KH, who had flown down to pay his final respects. Driving to the ICU straight from the airport, he was taken aback to find my father sitting bolt upright. Seeing KH, who was accompanied by a couple of doctors, my father took the mask off his face and asked him, 'What the hell are you doing here? There is firing all along your sector. Go back and give them (Pakistanis) hell!' He then griped about the fact that the ICU was full 'of old people', three of whom had died that night.

'Tiger ...' said KH, 'he's bloody upset with you, he wants you to get him out of the ICU immediately!'

The day my father was discharged and we brought him home to Beverly Park, Dipti and Vallika were to fly to France. Dipti had said we could cancel the trip, but it was almost a perfunctory sort of offer. The month of December was easily the worst time, for 1201-A got very little sunlight and there was almost constant fog outside. Veeha, however, was quite the little champion, doing everything that she could to make everyone comfortable.

My father, however, had a different agenda. After dropping Dipti and Vallika at the airport, I had barely got home when Veeha came and said Dadu is calling you. He got straight to the point. 'How much time before you finish your 1962 book?'

'I don't know ... maybe two months ...'

'There is no time. Finish it by the end of this month. Just do it. And give me a properly printed manuscript. I cannot read it off the computer.'

I started to say I'll try, but there was something about the way he was asking for the book, I knew it was, for all practical purposes, his last command. It seemed to me almost as if he had willed himself to last that little bit longer so that he could read what had been written.

After finishing three weeks under Martine's tutelage, Vallika and Dipti spent a couple of nights in Paris over Christmas, then flew back. As my parents prepared to move back to the flat in Noida earlier that day, I handed over the 400-hundred-plus pages. Since he loved to make notes in the margins, I also handed over properly sharpened red and blue pencils.

It would take him a full month to go through each page meticulously. 'He's just glued to your silly book,' my mother would complain, 'and sometimes he cries, for the words that you have written are impacting him deeply. Why can't you both just let the blasted war go?'

Dipti would nod in agreement. 'The book has completely changed you,' she would repeat every now and then.

Maybe it had, for it is not easy to live the horror of what had actually transpired, day in and day out. The only one who never said anything was

Blaise, for he just sat at my feet and would look very cross when I needed to wake him and go to bed every day well past midnight.

By mid-February, my father came home and gave me the manuscript back. Ours had never been a demonstrative relationship, and I did not expect him to say anything, for I was sure his comments would all be there, some in red, some in blue, a hangover from his days as a DS at the Staff College in Wellington. 'You know,' he seemed to be searching for the right words, 'after reading this, I know one thing for sure. It couldn't have happened any other way! The whole story finally rings true.'

He almost immediately was readmitted in hospital as his blood cells were packing up at an alarming rate. Velu said each day was a bonus, and then finally, in the early hours of 24 March 2015, the lights went out! Draped in his beloved Rajput regimental flag, surrounded by a few of his closest friends, many of whom had fought in Bangladesh with him, he was cremated to the sound of peacocks calling at Brar Square. The next day his ashes were immersed in the Ganga at Rajaji Sanctuary on the other side of Haridwar, and I could see some wild ducks take to wing as we entered the river's waters. The sun was setting, and we could also see the mahseer rising. One Circle of Life was complete.

25

The Summer of '62

My mother had always been by my father's side like a rock, and I wondered how she would cope with his passing. Six months shy of 80, he had left a void that would become even more acute when she moved to Kullu for the summer months. I was completely bogged down with the 1962 book's endless edits, and at times I felt the book would never actually see the light of day. With Pujitha Krishnan, this was the second edit we were doing, and she was relentless, making sure everything that was said in the book had the necessary supporting backup material available, which translated into making detailed end notes. The maps were also backbreaking, for I had decided to do them myself. I tried to get Vallika to help, but it just became another acrimonious argument with Dipti, who just didn't seem to understand the quantum of work involved. She would breeze in every now and then, offer some off-the-cuff suggestions and then lose complete interest. Her constant gripe was that I was losing interest in the family and was no longer interested in their lives. The accusations about ruining Dipti's film and Vallika's art career were gaining ground daily, to a point where I started looking for reasons to get out of town.

My mother had to return to Kullu around June and it was going to be an extremely traumatic experience. I felt it would be appropriate for all of us to move up to Kullu during the summer break, but the suggestion resulted in such a hostile response, for the first time the seriousness of the situation at home hit home. Until now I had believed all the ranting and raving about St Stephens and me having sabotaged Vallika's art career was a passing phase, but what Dipti now said had me staring at her incredulously. 'You've ruined your elder daughter's life ... now you want to do the same for Veeha. How can you not know it's her final board year?'

'You realize what you are doing? You're destroying our marriage. By going along with Vallika's ridiculous need to blame someone all the time, you're getting into an appeasement policy. Don't do that for God's sake!'

Even as I said that I realized Vallika was only echoing Dipti's behaviour pattern, for she too always blamed me for not having made a feature film. 'So, write the script,' I would say again and again. Even today there are dozens of incomplete scripts on my laptop, where she would not progress beyond page two or three.

I was in Kullu when Shri Ram held its end-of-term event. Like Vallika, Veeha too had become the chief editor of the school magazine. Dipti rang up shortly after the event, and she was ecstatic, and with good reason. 'Out of the five academic awards, your daughter has won five!' Frankly, I wasn't surprised though I had not quite expected anything like this. From the very beginning, I had seen an extraordinary streak in her. When she was in her ninth grade, her class teacher during the annual PTM had said how she was perplexed, for though she was one of the brightest kids she had ever seen, she was not scoring in exams. Until the previous year, the school had done away with exams as their new policy, and though the other children had quickly understood how to score, Veeha was in her own words, following my advice of 'getting at least seventy per cent but understanding what was happening rather than get a hundred or a ninety and not understand what was happening.'

'Let her be,' I had told Dipti as we drove back, 'you just watch and see, she'll outstrip all the other girls in the end ...' My wife did not respond, she just pursed her lips and looked out of the window. In case things went south in Veeha's case, another remark of mine had just been added to a fast-growing 'famous quotes' to be used against me. The problem with me was, I just wasn't looking at the writing on the wall!

The winter break came and went. I had taken Vallika to meet with Major Brijender 'Gucchan' Singh and over lunch he had suggested he knew a very good South African sculptor who specialized in sculpting wildlife. If Vallika was interested, he could talk to him, and she could apprentice with him for a month. She seemed interested, but then after a couple of days said she wanted to work on marble in Italy. I spent a few nights once again researching various options on the net. Dipti, however, was adamant that Vallika could not go on her own and this time she and Veeha would also go with her. This effectively doubled the cost factor and killed whatever possibilities that existed. I wanted to ask Dipti how come Veeha could go since now the Board Exams were on her head, but then there was no point putting one's hand further in the fire! I was also coldly told that now that Veeha's turn to go to college was coming up, and since I had ruined her life, I should keep my 'stupid opinions to myself'.

February 2016, *1962: The War That Wasn't* was formally launched at the India International Centre. I had asked Barkha Dutt to conduct the event and though she had missed her flight from Lahore where she was that morning, she had walked across the Wagah Border, caught the flight from Amritsar and joined General VK, Subramanian Swamy and myself on the dais straight from the airport. My mother did the honours and released the book. I so wished my father had lived long enough to be there. 1962 had not just been a conflict with the Chinese for him, it had obsessed him till the very end, as had the Battle of Ashuganj in 1971 where his battalion was not given the Battle Honour.[43]

I was surprised at the amount of press coverage the book was getting, with all the major news magazines giving it four or five pages, something which was quite unheard of. However, even then I was not quite prepared for what was to follow. Once again, it was Dereck Mountford, now a Director at the Goenka Group of Schools. 'Come and speak to the kids,' he said on the phone, 'I'll get all the history students here.'

Most of the time, we make up our minds based on preconceived ideas. I too had believed that the present-day generation was least interested in reading books or listening to details about wars that they

---

[43] His last words were to the Colonel of the Rajput Regiment, who had been allowed to see him in the ICU. Though 18 Rajput no longer existed and was now 13 Mechanised, he wanted the case reopened.

were not even aware of. However, Dereck was insistent, so with some trepidation, I drove across to the school which was on the outskirts of Gurgaon. I had at best expected some hundred odd students to be present, but Dereck had got other schools in the NCR to also participate and I was gaping at a sea of faces, wondering even more if I could hold their interest. It was to be a 45-minute talk, followed by a 15-minute Q&A session, but the session overshot mainly because of the quantum of questions that flowed from the audience. It was an eye-opener, for it began to dawn on me that if we treated school children as adults and put information across, they were hungry for knowledge. 'I told you,' Dereck laughed as he saw me to my car, 'not one kid was willing to go.'

Thanks to the extremely positive press coverage, there were a few invites for literary festivals, including one from the Doon School that had me pretty chuffed. The cherry on the cake was they wanted me to be the chief guest at the opening, which doubled the 'chuffness' factor manifold. Again, I was watching the boys like a hawk, and I was veering around to believe that they were indeed a far cry from what seemed to be universally accepted. On the contrary, they seemed to be hungry for knowledge. Peter McLaughlin, who spoke first, also seemed to be making the same mistake, for he kept insisting students were not really interested, and they had the briefest of attention spans, and hence he had jumped to back the idea of a literary festival. I couldn't help but think that even those students who wanted to expand their horizons were already being given a backdoor exit.

Two other events followed in quick succession, the Khushwant Singh and the Hindu Literature Festivals in Kasauli and Chennai. At Kasauli, I had long conversations with both Maroof Raza and Anil Dharker, and it was felt that given the interest levels around the 1962 book, it was certainly worth trying to pitch it at the school level.

'I'm frankly sceptical,' said Anil. 'But if we can get the younger generation to start looking at military history, especially in the post-Independence period, I feel it will not only have an impact but it's necessary. But so are other subjects, especially environment-related issues.'

Regardless of who I was talking to on stage and what I was saying on stage, I was watching the audience, trying to gauge the reactions. In Chennai the newspapers had played up the fact that I was from MCC, as a result of which I was in conversation with a dozen students who were presently studying there. They seemed extremely keen, almost insistent, that I come and speak to the college as well, but then I was due to fly back the next day.

In March 2016, *The War That Wasn't* was formally launched in Mumbai, once again to a packed audience. We followed this up with a second launch at the IIT in Powai. I was particularly delighted to have Wing Commander J. M. Nath, who was the holder of two MVCs for his role in both the 1962 and 1965 wars. Ashli Varma, Lieutenant General Prem Bhagat's daughter, who at the time of the conflict as the commandant's daughter, lived less than 200 metres from where we did, accompanied us from Delhi while Ayaz Memon conducted the two events. I reminded Ayaz of our meeting at the Srinagar airport where he had bought an artillery captain and me, coffee. The interest levels, especially among the IIT students, virtually helped me make up my mind, and I was now determined to find a way to make Alternate Education a reality. It would be a step-by-step process, and the first thing was to get at least one institution of repute to back me.

Like a moth drawn to the proverbial flame, I was once again tempted to broach the idea with the Doon School. 'You'll never learn,' sighed Dipti as I headed off to Dehradun. The time had come, I believed, to do at least once a month illustrated talks where one would restrict oneself to the larger picture of what had caused and led to the various conflicts, against the backdrop of geopolitics.

'I think it's a brilliant idea,' said Peter McLaughlin. 'I'll put it to the Board of Governors and revert to you in three-four days.' Anupama Joshi rolled her eyes when I told her what the HM had said, and true to form, that was that, for he never reverted.

My classmate and golf-playing partner, Ankur Bahl, and his wife Sangeeta had taken to mountaineering in a big way. In May 2015 Ankur had been left stranded at Camp II on Everest after a terrible earthquake had struck Nepal. Their team doctor had been killed at Base Camp and eventually Ankur along with hundreds of other climbers had to be evacuated by helicopter. Exactly a year later, on 19 May, which was also Veeha's birthday, Ankur became the first Doon School alumnus to summit the great Sagarmatha. It was a stupendous achievement, and we were all over the moon. On 12 July, to felicitate Ankur's feat, a bunch of us met at Magnolia in Gurgaon, where Darshan Singh had hosted the small get-together.

Darshan Singh had been a past president of the DSOBS and had done some climbing himself, having been to Bandarpunch while he was still in school. He was the Chairman of the Welham Boys' School, and as I got to know him, I was impressed by his ability to look beyond the horizon especially when it came to ideas related to education. He asked me if Peter had responded, for he was aware of our discussion. When I shook my head, he said, 'Unlike the Doon School, I do not necessarily have to take every idea to the Board. I inform them of course, but I am not necessarily handicapped by that one factor when it comes to decision-making. Go, meet the principal, Gunmeet Bindra, in Dehradun and let us take on military history at Welham Boys.'

Not particularly given to procrastination, I was sitting with Gunmeet soon enough. She had obviously been briefed by Darshan Singh, for she was listening to me, but I couldn't help but feel she was not really interested. I would later find out that her initial reaction was '*Hai, Chairman ne mere gale me ghanti band di*' (Oh hell, the Chairman has tied a bell around my neck!); so, I had read her right. 'How do you care,' said Darshan Singh when I reported back to him, 'you have my complete support. Just go ahead and set it up. You wanted to do this, well, here is your canvas!'

The problem, I was to soon realize was not that Gunmeet Bindra did not want to do anything. Institutions like the Doon School and Welham Boys' School were much too set in their ways and anything that involved additional work met with a lot of resistance. Plus, there was always the politics, which seemed to be just waiting behind every wall to rear its head. I had never met Dev Lahiri but had heard a lot of positive things about him. In a scathing post on Facebook, he tore into the military history initiative and said we were trying to turn Welham Boys' into a Military School. To my chagrin, he seemed to get a lot of 'likes' that were in support of his views. 'I've told you to ignore all the nonsense,' said Darshan Singh. 'Do not bother to respond. Just do what we have to do.'

Veeha had, as expected, done wonderfully well in her ISC board exams as well. Her percentage virtually mirrored her elder sister's earlier performance and like Vallika, she too could virtually pick and choose any college she wanted in the country. Veeha's entry into Ashoka where she opted to study psychology coincided with Vallika's graduation from St Stephen's, where she had finished fairly high up in the order of merit. I was pointedly not invited to her graduation ceremony. I was hoping she would apply to an art college and told Dipti under no circumstances encourage her to take a gap year. However, Vallika was adamant that she had missed the bus, and if she had to now take up art, she would have to do various art-related classes that were on offer in Gurgaon itself. Mainly at my insistence, she applied to a reputed art college in Bengaluru (formerly Bangalore) and promptly made the cut for the interview. Once again, Dipti insisted on accompanying Vallika, and they returned full of disdain, for even the people conducting the interview 'knew nothing'. By having asked her to apply, Vallika claimed I had further set her back in life! At some point, one just gives up, and I think by the third quarter of 2016, I had reached that point.

With just the *Northeast Trilogy* in our inventory, we had a very limited basket, and I was thinking of ways and means of expanding that. For lack of a better term, I started calling the new project I had in mind Alternate Education. If in the next three to four years, we could raise the resources and shoot in other parts of India, we could then look at making available extremely high-class material to our children. The most obvious, and the most important cog in this, would be a four-part wildlife series, a quartet of books that would not only cover the entire subcontinent, but also the continental shelves in the Bay of Bengal and the Arabian Sea, plus of course the islands on either flank. However, unlike the other subjects where I had literally done all the slog work myself, I would definitely need to put a team of photographers together. As was my wont, I started making a rough grid of the entire project and then discussed it with Dipti. Though she was not dismissive of the idea, she made it quite clear she was not going to get involved. Her focus, she announced, was on writing the script for a feature film, which in this case was based on the first general election that was held in independent India in 1951.

The 1976 batch had completed its fortieth year and we had decided to get together for a couple of days at Atali Ganga. We had an excellent turn out as some of the classmates flew in from various corners of the globe. Dipti, who was always otherwise game for the get-togethers, again flat refused to go. I was driving down to Rishikesh with Anoop Seth, and at that point of time we had known each other for forty-six years. 'Wife not coming? Man, your marriage is on the rocks!' We laughed as classmates do, but somewhere I felt Anoop was a lot closer to the truth than what I wanted to believe.

I knew of Latika Nath because she used to take music lessons from Leslie George, and though I had met her father, Dr L. M. Nath, who had been the director of AIIMS and a senior member of the Indian Board for Wildlife, I had never met her in person. We discussed the wildlife quartet, and I asked her if she was interested in helping me put it together. We also discussed doing a book on Ladakh together, for between us we had fairly extensive and unique coverage of the region. What I wasn't prepared for was Dipti's reaction, who threw a fit saying how could I so easily work with someone else when all our lives we had done everything together.

We had just had this conversation when a distraught Latika called up fairly late at night. An elephant, a tusker who was known by the sobriquet 'Sidda' was most probably dying and could I help? The situation was grim and though the locals had got a JCB and lifted the animal up, he was going to die unless someone did something. 'Hold on, calm down, will you? Tell me what has happened, and just where is all this happening?'

Sidda was a 35-year-old tusker that had strayed out of the Savandurga forest about a month ago and entered a village in Ramanagara District, some 40 kilometres from Bengaluru (formerly Bangalore). Blind in one eye, probably by a rocket fired at him during an earlier foray into the fields, he had been chased by villagers onto the nearby Manchanabele Dam. Unable to see what was happening on his blind side, the tusker had plunged into the water below, and by the look of it, had broken his leg. For weeks the elephant had been stranded in the backwaters of the Arkavathy

River, and in a complete turn of events, villagers from far and wide now started coming in droves to feed the wild animal. This had kept him alive, but obviously he couldn't stay in the water for the rest of his life. An NGO, Wildlife SOS, which ran the Bannerghatta Bear Rescue Centre, and was doing incredible work with rescued elephants and sloth bears in Mathura as well, had moved in along with a team of Forest Department veterinary doctors, and with the help of *kumkis* (trained domestic elephants), they had got him out of the water. After tranquilizing the tusker and treating his broken leg, they had then revived the animal and shooed him into the forest.

Earlier, three mornings previously, the tusker had re-emerged and started to show his leg to anyone who came within visual range. His condition worsening by the minute, he then collapsed in a field. 'He is dying Kunal ... we have to do something.' It was midnight and sitting in Gurgaon and Delhi respectively, there was little we could do. I told Latika to go to sleep, and if the animal survived the night, we would see how he could be propped up and treated. As I tucked Blaise near my feet for the night where he always slept, Dipti, who had been listening in, said to me coldly, 'Just look at you! Bleeding hearts about an elephant! You've ruined your own children's lives with your uncaring attitude and bullying manner, and here you are crying about a blasted elephant!'

I could hardly sleep that night, and towards the morning I had a wild plan in my head. It was barely dawn when I called up Lieutenant General Ray Narhona, the chief of staff, Southern Command. Ray was from the Rajput Regiment and I asked him if the Madras Engineering Group, which had its Centre in Bengaluru could move quickly and build a karaal where the elephant could be hoisted up. General VK had also been activated and he spoke to the army commander, and amazingly, by that afternoon, a convoy of army vehicles was on its way with bridging equipment with which they hoped to improvise a structure and get the elephant up. By then, the media had also picked up the story and it was breaking news all over. The army was on its way! Sidda, hold on, implored TV anchors![44]

---

[44] 'Injured Wild Elephant "Sidda" Treated By Expert Veterinarians In India', 27 October 2016, https://wildlifesos.org/chronological-news/injured-wild-elephant-sidda-treated-by-expert-veterinarians-in-india/

By then Dr Arun A. Sha, the SOS veterinary doctor, and others who had been brought in from across the country were talking to me almost by the hour. It would take two days for the army to set up a makeshift coral and hoist Sidda up, and once the animal was standing, he started to respond to treatment. The elephant had developed sores for he had been lying for almost a week on his side, and though it was a herculean task, it seemed he would pull through. The team of doctors then somehow managed to improvise a portable X-ray and Arun was ecstatic. 'The bone seems to be intact,' he said. He also said he thought the blind eye was not completely gone, and perhaps it could be treated. Latika started to explore how a veterinary doctor in Jersey who had treated a similar eye injury could be brought in from the UK. By the end of November, the elephant was eating close to 200 kilograms of fodder and seemed to be well on his way to recovery.

Anil Dharker was running the Times Literature Festival in Mumbai, and while we were in Kasauli, he had asked me if the year's edition could be launched with a debate on whether India and Pakistan could ever be friends. He had further developed the idea, and he called to say it would be Maroof Raza and myself pitted against Pavan Verma and Shashi Tharoor, with the journalist Vir Sanghvi moderating the event. The debate was to be held at the NCPA auditorium and with Shashi Tharoor's crowd-pulling ability, Anil felt the event would set the tone for the rest of the festival. The dates were finalized for the third week of November. 'Problem is,' I grumbled to Maroof, 'you'll cover the realpolitik angle and I'll handle the geopolitical aspect, but will these two gents let it be a serious discussion?'

'It's too good an opportunity to let pass,' said Maroof. Over the next few days, we divided up the various points between us and felt we had just about every base covered.

I had just flown into Mumbai when there was a call from Rakesh Loomba who was at the time in West Africa. The general was there in connection with his son Rahul's company, and while at Accra in Ghana, he had developed a good relationship with President John Mahama and his chief of staff, Michael 'Mike' Oboubi. At some point, my 1962 book had been presented either to the president or to Mike, which had resulted in an invitation for me to come immediately to Ghana as an observer for the presidential election that was scheduled for 7 December. 'Come immediately. Your tickets and visas are being done from here.' I told him there was no way I could get back to Delhi for another three days.

The opening session at the NCPA was a sell-out. Neither Maroof nor I had any illusions about the fact that the crowd puller was Shashi Tharoor. The audience was asked to respond to the question, 'Can India and Pakistan ever be friends?' by flashing their cards and the sentiment at the start was 'Yes' which was reflected in a sea of blue with a splattering of orange. Maroof and I were on the other side of the fence, and then the debate got underway. Vir Sanghvi, the host of the show, was at his gushing best, and even as he introduced the four panellists, he had already awarded the debate to Shashi, 'one of the greatest debaters on the planet!' Maroof was frowning, 'He's even forgotten Pavan Verma ...' he leaned across and whispered.

The debate, as we had expected, was a total farce, and was soon reduced to some Pakistani actress who some Indian producer had given or not given a role. Frankly, I was disappointed, for the topic deserved serious discussion and an insult to all those who had laid down their lives defending the western borders. At the end of the debate the audience was polled again, and this time we were happy to see a major shift in our favour. Vir Sanghvi was either suffering from myopia or had the biggest pair of blinkers on, for he obstinately insisted on mopping the floor in front of Shashi, who also seemed embarrassed by this rather partisan fan-struck demonstration. 'You see why,' Maroof said as we drove back to the Taj, 'Bollywood always gets anything to do with wars or the army so wrong. It's all about preconceived formulas.'

I landed in Accra a few days later and all the talk was about the elections being rigged. 'BBC, CNN and the entire Western media is going on and on about how President Mahama's government will rig the election,' explained Mike. 'The government has gone blue in the face saying it is not possible to rig the EVMs. Now here is where it gets complicated. We think the election is going to be tampered with, but just how we have no clue. The irony then is we are in no position to say the elections are rigged.' Mike placed a sheet of paper on the table in front of us. The exact percentage of votes that would be cast in favour of the two presidential candidates was there, and now time would tell if Mike's intelligence sources were right.

'It's a global phenomenon. After Gaddafi was taken out by the Americans in Libya, President Mahama was emerging as the pan-African leader. His subsequent speech at the UN Security Council where he talked of looking after the country and Africa's interests rather than US-British interests, has sealed the outcome against him.' Sure enough, once the counting started, Rakesh Loomba and I watched in disbelief as the final percentages settled at the exact numbers that had been predicted.

On 9 December at two in the morning, I was woken up by the shrill ringing of my phone. Even as I reached for it, I somehow knew something terrible had happened. It was Dr Arun Sha and his voice was choking with emotion, 'Sidda is dead!' I could hardly believe my ears for just the previous evening the elephant had eaten and drunk to his heart's content and seemed to be in a playful mood. In fact, Arun had earlier called wondering how to get a couple of dedicated vehicles to keep the flow of food coming.

Sidda, whom I had never seen physically, had just collapsed and died. More than anything else, I had begun to feel that in a world where man–animal conflict was becoming so very acute, the story of Sidda could be told in schools and colleges to help underline the desperate need for people to strike a balance. The reaction of the local population to the plight of the elephant had been, at one level, exhilarating. I just sat on the floor that night next to my bed and cried. It wasn't just an elephant that had died but with him all the work done by so many volunteers and the army. It was indeed a huge loss.

I flew back to Delhi, and it was decided that Rakesh Loomba and I would explore the possibility of setting up a think-tank, preferably in Mauritius. Once we had the blueprint in place, Mike would fly down to India. The think-tank would not only be looking at security-related matters but would also focus its attention on environmental and economic issues, with special emphasis on the East Coast of Africa and the Indian Ocean region. A series of meetings were held in Delhi with an assortment of people, while we sought an appointment with the prime minister of Mauritius.

In the meantime, Dipti and I were invited by the Bhutan government to come and speak on the 1962 War and the *Northeast Trilogy* at RIGSS —the Royal Institute of Governance and Strategic Studies. We were welcomed at Phuentsholing by the director, Dasho Chewang Rinzin, who most graciously had informed us earlier that we would be the guests of His Majesty's government and that we would be taken to Thimpu for a couple of days.

RIGSS could be compared to India's NDC, where those attending the course are a mix of the armed forces and various civil services, though in Bhutan they seemed to be much younger in age and service. Interestingly, army officers from the Royal Bhutan Army sat in half the room, while the civil officers occupied the other half. Both the sessions went off well, after which we proceeded to the Bhutanese capital from where I struggled up to the Tiger Nest Monastery. Bhutan with its policy of limiting itself to high-end tourism has, as a country, understood that the fragile mountain ecosystem of the Himalayas has to be protected, something that we in India seem unable to grasp despite repeated warnings dished out regularly by nature.

Rakesh Loomba and I flew to Mauritius and stayed with my cousin, Vijit Yadav, who was with the Afrasia Bank. The political scenario in Mauritius was going through a transition, with Sir Anerood Jugnauth having handed over to his son, Pravind Jugnauth. That the think-tank was also looking at the environmental aspect seemed to please the prime minister, who suggested we go and meet the director of the Mauritius Oceanography Institute at Albion. Her name, he said, with a twinkle in his eye, was Ruby Moothien Pillay. Obviously, his staff had briefed him, for Ruby had been in MCC with me, and we had travelled together on the train to Tambaram. By the time my ragging got over and I went looking for her, she was sitting across one of the drains that was the meeting place of most romantic couples and looking into the eyes of David Davidar.

Accordingly, we drove to Albion and met Ruby. The work being done by the Institute, combined with organizations in India like the Tata Institute of Fundamental Research (TIFR), was what we were wanting to do. I was in touch with Bheesette Satyanarayana who was then a senior scientist at TIFR and along with Dipti, was due to address their ASET colloquium in May. Simultaneously, along with a few former service chiefs, Rakesh Loomba and I were developing the security vertical, while others including some security experts based in Japan were to help with the economic aspect. While in Mauritius we also met with my former schoolmate, Major Rakesh Wahi, who owned CNBC Africa and had set up universities in Dubai and Johannesburg. A sapper, he had been a member of the Indian Army expedition to Antarctica. Both of us being from Hyderabad House, even though he was a year senior to me, I had stayed with him in 1985 in Pune and been in touch ever since. Wahi felt that with the growing, almost unchecked footprint of the Chinese in the region, the think-tank would have a major role to play in the future.

Dipti by then had developed her film script and she had drawn up an initial budget just to do the research and finalize the script. The figure projected was so low, I told her she was living in Cuckooland, and sat down and revised them with her. The talk at TIFR was a good opportunity to introduce Dipti to Pashupati Advani, who was from the 1972 Doon School batch and a good friend of mine. 'Putty' was a leading stock analyst and he could help with Dipti's feature film, but then I expected her to do all the follow-up work. The TIFR talk went off extremely well, and I couldn't help thinking we were addressing a room full of people whose minimum IQ level would be double ours! Two of my roommates, Hemant Kumar Jain and Nakul Bubna, also were in attendance. Every time the 'IQ' factor came to my mind, I just looked at the two of them and felt reassured!

Things were moving extremely fast, and I was using all my time to also develop the grid for the wildlife quartet of books. In April 2017, the prime minister of Bangladesh visited New Delhi and in what was a major break from the past where Indian involvement in the liberation of Bangladesh had been downplayed, she honoured the Indian dead who had laid down their lives to liberate Bangladesh. At the time of my father's passing, the military attaché from the Bangladesh High Commission had come and paid tribute to him, adding that His Excellency Syed Muazzem Ali would be happy to meet me. A year or so was to pass before I dropped in at the high commission, and the high commissioner was waiting at the door of his office. With me was General Rakesh Loomba and after making us comfortable, Syed Ali said he wanted to meet because he wanted to discuss the Battle of Ashuganj. I was a little taken aback, because on the Indian side, for various reasons, the battle had been glossed over and never given its real due. 'We in Bangladesh believe it was the turning point in the War of Liberation. I was not there physically but there were many officers from the EBR who were eyewitnesses to what happened with 18 Rajput.'

He went on to compare the Battle of Ashuganj with some of the greatest battles that had ever been fought, but then that was Bengali eloquence coming into play. My father had twice, along with Lieutenant General J. F. R Jacob visited Dacca and I was aware of the Bangladesh government's interest in the matter. 'The trouble is,' said Syed Ali, 'In India, no one wants to do anything about it.' I didn't want to get drawn into the reasons behind that, for it was perhaps one of the most shameful incidents of the war. Seeing me hesitate, the high commissioner said, 'We are aware of what happened and the subsequent court martial of Brigadier R. N Misra, but now we are wanting the men who died for our cause to be honoured.'

'That was one heck of a meeting,' said Rakesh Loomba when we came out of his office. 'I myself only vaguely had heard of the Battle of Ashuganj.'

A month before Sheikh Hasina's visit, Rakesh Loomba and I had met Syed Ali again at his office. Some officers had been working at compiling lists of Indian casualties, but the high commissioner lamented that those being honoured were those who had been awarded gallantry awards by the Indians. 'we were hoping to go beyond that,' he lamented. 'But it's a start at least.'

I attended the function at the Manekshaw Centre with my mother. Sheikh Hasina's address was followed by Prime Minister Narendra Modi. I had never interacted with the then army chief, General Bipin Rawat, but he and his wife Madhulika were frequent visitors at my parent's place in

Noida. Seeing me with my mother, the general walked up and said he had been speaking to the Bangladesh high commissioner who wanted Rakesh Loomba and me to pay a visit to Dhaka. He said his office would contact me the next day, but then nothing happened on that front.

General VK was the minister of state in the MEA, and he was equally keen the entire story of Pakistan's genocide be told. 'The ISI is overactive,' he had said, showing us a compilation of articles that had been published in book form. On the cover was the iconic photograph of dead cycle rickshaw pullers who had been murdered by the Pakistan Army and Razakars, while on the inside the caption said they had been shot and bayoneted by the Indian Army. 'Fly to Dhaka. I have spoken to His Excellency Abul Hassan Mahmood Ali, the foreign minister who had accompanied Sheikh Hasina. He will get you to meet their prime minister. We have to counter this rubbish.'

VK had been a twenty-one-year-old second lieutenant during the war and was serving as the intelligence officer of 2 Rajput. After the battalion had occupied Chittagong and the Pakistanis had surrendered, he had been sent to the Chittagong Medical College where there were rumours of a 'Race Improvement Camp' that was being run by the Pakistan Army. When he reached there with a couple of men, they were met with a horrifying sight, as hundreds of naked women, all in various stages of pregnancy, mobbed him and tried to get to his pistol so that they could shoot themselves. Kept naked so that they could not hang themselves because of their humiliation, the camp underlined the entire mental make-up of the Punjabi-dominated Pakistan Army towards the Bengali population. Among the many other horrors of the war where 3 million people had been killed, this incident had permanently scarred the mind of the general.

The foreign minister met us in his office, and after I had presented him with a set of the *Northeast Trilogy*, he spoke sadly of how, even after fifty years, the international community refused to recognize what happened in Bangladesh as a genocide. There already existed a genocide museum in Dhaka, but ironically, there was just the barest mention of the Indian Army there. 'We hope you can help us with that,' the minister said. He said we would have to make a second trip shortly to meet the prime minister, but we could start working on a blueprint of a plan that could be put up to her.

By the middle of 2017, with the beginning of the second academic term, I had started delivering monthly lectures at the Welham Boys' School. Confining myself to the immediate post-Independence era, I was extremely pleased at the response I was getting from the students, many of whom on subsequent visits kept telling me how they were reading books related to Partition and other related subjects. Darshan Singh, pleased at having finally gotten things underway, called me one evening. 'Look Kunal, Welham Boys' is fine as a single one-off platform. But I feel we need to take this further, involve other institutions.'

'What do you have in mind?' I asked.

'Hold a two-day military history seminar in October. Invite who you want as resource persons but work out the details. I don't care what it takes in terms of finances, we will do this for it simply has to be done.' He wrapped it up with his usual, 'Go meet Mrs Bindra. I'll talk to her just now.'

General VK was our first chief guest and we had quite a galaxy of generals, air marshals and admirals along with Captain Bana Singh, who was a living PVC. The buzz around the event was fantastic and the media promptly gave it the sobriquet, 'The Welham Initiative!' There were a total of six sessions and each one was extremely well received. In his opening speech, Darshan Singh, in the presence of General VK, warned that the Chinese were up to something, and it was a matter of time before something happened on our northern border. 'Get him onto your Mauritius think-tank,' said General VK to me as an aside tongue-in-cheek. We didn't know it then but the remarks were to be extremely prophetic three years later! Gunmeet Bindra was full of enthusiasm, and she came up with the idea of having RIMC cadets and Welham Boys' march in for the closing ceremony together while the IMA brass band playing *kadam kadam badaye ja*!

But what stood out was the participation of the girls. 'Why can't we ...' would be the beginning of all their questions, and it was pretty obvious to me that the days of the male-dominated armed forces were numbered.

Shortly after returning from Dhaka, there had been a call from M. G. Devasahayam. 'Come to the India International Centre I say,' he had said conversationally, 'there is someone here I want you to meet.' I set off from Beverly Park with Dipti immediately but unfortunately the moment we crossed the border, we ran into a horrendous traffic jam. To make matters worse, the cell phones were also not responding, and we just could not get through to MGD. After two hours, I managed to get a U-turn on the Jaipur Highway and we returned home.

A livid MGD said the gentleman who had wanted to meet had most kindly postponed his departure and could we please be there first thing in the morning. Thomas Franco at the time was the general secretary of the State Bank of India Officers' Association (SBIOA) based in Chennai. Extremely soft-spoken, for a few minutes I couldn't quite understand what he was saying. In effect, he had seen the *Northeast Trilogy* and MGD had also briefed him on my desire to expand the project as a part of the ambitious Alternate Education plan. Franco wanted to know what would it cost to do a similar trilogy on South India. SBIOA ran three or four schools, and he said they would be very happy to get involved with a programme as noble as this.

Never had I seen a more efficient and decisive organization, for by July 2017 I was on my way to Kanyakumari to do the first shoot and also spend some time with MGD at his residence in Nagercoil where we sat and planned what all the first volume on Tamil Nadu (and Puducherry) should contain. The first port of call was to be Chennai, where I was to sign the required agreement with Franco.

Chennai was home for me, the three years at MCC had been an eye-opener and I simply loved everything about Tamil Nadu. My classmate, M. Ct. P. Chidambaram was one of my closest friends, as was Alok 'Granny' Bhargava who was not only two years senior to me in Doon School but also in MCC. Strangely enough, I was in touch with more ex-DOSCOs in Chennai than with my former college mates. Granny had booked me into the majestic Madras Club which was on the Adyar River, and a few meetings had been arranged by another school senior, Ravi Katari, with some stalwarts including the 'chronicler of Madras,' S. Muthiah. The meeting we had over dinner started on a terrible note:'

Why are you, a North Indian, doing a book on Tamil Nadu? When there are people like me who have dedicated their lives to writing about Madras and its history?' A cranky Tamilian can get even crankier if you try to beat about the bush. That much knowledge I had acquired during my college days.

'Well sir,' I replied evenly, 'the fact that I and my wife are from outside the state perhaps is an advantage. I think, with all due respect to all of you, the caste divisions in society that you live with, they put blinkers on you. I am willing to bet you see yourself as a Chettiar first and then a Tamilian and then as an Indian.'

I don't think he expected that, for he busied himself with the menu. After a while, he said, 'I wish I was younger. I would accompany you on your shoots. Come and meet me when you have finished shooting. I wish you well.'

Compared to the Northeast, the shoots were obviously a lot easier, but at another level, they were also very difficult. Franko's banking community would help to some extent, but it was always a daunting task because wherever we went, especially the main temples, we were greeted by a sign saying 'No Photography'. I would trudge across to their office, find the relevant person, and then show him what we were doing. I was obviously quite persuasive because at times the person would drop the frowning demeanour, lead the way to the main complex, kick off his shoes or slippers, and even carry my tripod for me. In the final analysis, I do not think we were refused by anyone. But it took up a lot of time. No temple would, however, allow you to shoot the main central deity. That was something I never even asked to do. This level of cooperation was across the board, including government-run museums and even archaeological sites where red tape is a major impediment even with prior permissions.

Dipti came on the first shoot where we shot in Mahabalipuram and Kanchipuram. The sheer volume of what was all around us sometimes can be quite overwhelming. I also did not need Anoop Seth to tell me that our relationship was meandering towards its end, for by now the situation at home, especially when I was in Gurgaon, was becoming quite untenable. The shoots only underlined the fact that in reality, there was no real problem between us, we just did not know how to handle the explosive 'blame game' that had started soon after Vallika left school. At first, Dipti would admonish Vallika, saying you cannot talk to your father like that, but then she would sooner or later come under attack herself. Gradually, the shift began and I told Dipti more than once that the 'appeasement policy' of hers would only result in the family imploding. If counselling was suggested by me, the immediate retort would be that I was mentally unstable, a pathological bully and someone only interested in having a good time.

Sometimes I just wished Dipti could see for herself just how fortunate all of us were, who had grown up in secure homes and not been shackled by any social and cultural chains. In Madurai, on a subsequent shoot, we were in contact with Valli Annamalai who had played a major role over the years in battling the heinous practice of female infanticide. A common occurrence at one time in Uslimapatti, it was also widespread in Salem District. While driving back to Madurai, we listened to Valli as she described her battle against a mindset that was a part of the culture as recently as two decades ago. Valli also emphasized how the former chief minister, Jayalalitha, had supported her in battling the social practice.

On some of the shoots, I was accompanied by a couple of my classmates. Chiddu and his wife Chandrika opened up their residence at Kanadukathan, a village that is the virtual hub within Chettinad of the Chettiar community. Having them with me not only opened up doors, Chiddu's own depth of knowledge about his people and their culture kept opening up new vistas for me. In Chennai, Chiddu runs the M. Ct. M. Chidambaram School in Mylapore started by his mother, Sivagami Pethachi, who was the founder correspondent. It is among the best schools in the city today. I also got to photograph Chiddu's cousin's *Sashtiapthapoorthi* ceremony. This tongue twister celebrates the completion of a husband's sixty years of life, and a ceremony called the *santhi kalyanam* sees the couple once again reaffirm their wedding vows, complete with the tying of the *mangalasutra* and exchange of garlands while priests keep up their constant chanting. Since both Chiddu and I were also approaching the magical number,, we couldn't help but grin at each other.

Throughout my life, I was always in trouble for telling the wrong jokes at the wrong time. But it was much too delicious to miss, so in the car, I held forth about this Sardaji and his wife who fought and fought from dawn to dusk and through the night too. Fed up with their constant bickering, the rest of the village comes to them and tells them for thirty-five years they have been listening to their nonsense. Seeing a parakeet on a nearby branch nuzzling its mate, they tell the shamefaced Sardarji to go learn something from the parakeets. He goes across and asks the male bird what is the secret of his unending love. The parakeet looks left and right, then flies down and whispers in the Sardarji's ear, '*Roz ek nai totti liyanda hu* (I get a new female parakeet every day!)' While Chiddu howled with laughter, both he and I got the cold stare from Chandri!

For the Nilgiri leg of the shooting, I was joined by Hari Krishan Dhar, who was my batchmate from Hyderabad House and one of my closest friends. Based in Pune, he flew down to Coimbatore and then drove up to Wellington. I took Hari to see our old house, Mansarovar, in Wellington and both of us could not quite believe how as a 13-year-old, I had not only travelled entirely on my own all the way from Dehradun but had gone up and down regularly. In today's world where a school requires an indemnity bond from the parents to allow them to cross the street on their own, the world certainly had changed beyond recognition. From the Nilgiris we had dropped down to Kerala and then proceeded up the coast to Calicut. Not only was having Hari around great fun, he was the most helpful person under the sun, always quick to lend a hand.

While shooting in Vellore, Dipti and I spent the night at the Christian Medical College where another classmate, Sunil Aggarwal was a vascular surgeon. One of the most highly respected doctors, he was killed a year later in a tragic accident when the car he was travelling in burst a tyre, throwing him out of the vehicle. One of India's brightest doctors, the crowds that assembled for his funeral were a testimony to just how much he had done for the local community as well.

All this while, General Rakesh Loomba and some others who had been incorporated into the project were giving finishing touches to the setting up of the think-tank. Mike Oboubi then arrived in India in the second week of December 2017, and as the general was fond of saying, 'we were good to go!' We were preparing to host a dinner in Mike's honour in Beverly Park when all of a sudden he was taken unwell and rushed to Apollo Hospital. There he was diagnosed to have severe blockages in his arteries, and he was rushed in for an angioplasty. The next day I visited him in the hospital, and twenty-four hours later he had been discharged, only to be rushed back with some internal haemorrhaging. Then, just like that, Mike died. It was tragic and unbelievable, for no one had any inkling that he was ill at all.

I had now been working with Rakesh Loomba for quite some time, and I always marvelled at his ability to stay calm under even the gravest provocation. Not once had I seen him lose his cool, nor get flustered. Mike's abrupt death left him with a major problem, for the body along with his wife had to be sent back to Accra, which Rahul Loomba and his partner, Anant Ghanshyam did subsequently. In Ghana, they met the former President John Mahama, but with Mike out of the equation, though there was some talk of meeting in London, it was evident the Ghanaians were no longer interested. It also meant all the work we had put in to set up the think-tank, now went up in smoke.

I had my hands full with the *South India Trilogy*, for apart from just photographing Tamil Nadu, we were also shooting parts of Kerala and Karnataka, depending on when and what opportunities came up. Sometime in March 2018, MGD flew down to Delhi and gravely announced that we had a problem. Franco, he said, was due to retire in June and it had been presumed his deputy correspondent would take over. 'You'll have to just wrap up the Tamil Nadu book and raise funds for Kerala and Karnataka from elsewhere.'

Accordingly, with the *South India Trilogy* truncated, we worked overtime to finish the Tamil Nadu book. I had previously met K. Pandiarajan, who was the minister for Tamil language, Tamil culture and archaeology in his office with Chiddu in tow and presented him with a copy of the *Northeast Trilogy*. The minister had promptly called in his PA and said he was not to be disturbed and had gone through the books in great detail. It was due to him that I had been given free access to not only the Madras Museum, but also various smaller establishments spread across the various districts of Tamil Nadu. Franco had invited him in July to launch the book with all the accompanying fanfare. Unfortunately, the politics of the state at the time was going through an extremely turbulent stage, as a result of which, despite promising to get the book across to all schools in Tamil Nadu after translating the text into Tamil, Pandiarajan could not take the project forward either.

Another classmate from Doon, Dr Atul Bahadur Singh, along with a couple of my MCC batchmates too attended the launch. After the event, we had retired to the hotel where we were staying and everyone was talking of the minister's speech, but at the same time were extremely sceptical if anything at all would happen. MGD was also present, and

However, there was still an outside chance for alternate funding for the think-tank, since others from certain Pacific countries were involved. The Government of India, in its wisdom, had only allowed the Taiwan government to run the Taipei Economic and Cultural Centre, which also served as the de facto High Commission. Chung-Kwang 'James' Tien, suggested Rakesh Loomba and I attend a NATO conference in Taipei which focused not only on the immediate threat from the PRC across the Taiwan Sea but also looked at the global emerging scenario. Of the thirty-two delegates selected to speak, both General Loomba and I got a chance to put across India's perspective, while we also met various heads of agencies who were extremely keen on developing a 'listening post' off East Africa. The visit culminated with a meeting with President Tsai Ing-wen to whom I presented a copy of the newly released Tamil Nadu book. The next day we flew in a ROCAF C-130 to Kinmen Island, from where the city of Xiamen in Fujian is clearly visible. Having been extensively bombarded by the PLA in the early 1950s, the island is a maze of tunnels and fortified defences.

Veeha had opted to do her fifth semester at the University of Pennsylvania and she flew out of Delhi on 16 August. With her departure, the situation at home escalated almost immediately and the levels of hostility from not only Vallika, but even Dipti, made life almost impossible, both constantly accusing me of 'deliberately sabotaging' their careers. I was at the time watching the 10-part documentary series on the

Vietnam War by Ken Burns and Lynn Novick, so on an impulse, I applied for the visa, booked myself on a flight to Ho Chi Minh as the erstwhile Saigon was now called, and quietly slipped off a week after Veeha's departure. Other than my mother, no one knew where I was.

I boarded a train from Ho Chi Minh and headed north, chugging along in an Indian-built railway to Da Nang, which was where the Americans had landed after they intervened in what was a full-bloodied scrap between the colonial French and the Viet Cong. Almost half a century after the war, there were obviously no visible signs, but the countryside was extremely interesting, and I just sat and watched various places flash by. Near Da Nang I had booked myself into a comfortable resort called the Karma Cāy Tre that was at Hội An. As soon as I had checked in, I met Kass Tran, a Vietnamese by origin who was settled in Australia. Her boyfriend who was an Indian and was to join her in Vietnam had got stopped at Mumbai airport because he had earlier reported his passport to be stolen. Then there was Ishana and Vijay Maharaj, who were from Johannesburg and Priya and Vishwanath Janardhan from Bengaluru. The six of us then formed our own little group and did almost everything together over the next few days which suddenly changed the entire complexion of the trip. It was with a degree of sadness that I bid adieu to my newfound friends and flew to Hanoi on the next leg of my journey.

Vietnam impressed me as a country, as it does others who also visit the country. The people were incredible and had bounced back to the extent that there was very little evidence of the war. In the 1970s, it had also resolutely stood up to an invasion by the Chinese. Most of its army at the time was deployed in the south, but the border guards had taken on the PLA, fighting so efficiently that the Chinese had been effectively stopped. Given the fact that the entire 4,000-kilometre-long land border with China that runs from the Karakorams Range in Ladakh to Myanmar in the east is manned by the ITBP, I was most interested in the details of that operation. I could not help but feel that the Indian border management, especially when it came to China, could do with a lot of improvement. However, on the flip side, the terrain that we were deployed across was perhaps many times more harsh than what the Vietnamese were dealing with.

Back in India and Gurgaon, I was left with no choice but to move out of the house and shift to 1704-A. I was working on the 1965 book and the constant accusations and unbridled hostility was just too much for me to take. Blaise was beginning to show signs of age and he was loath to even come across the compound to the other flat, so I would keep him with me during the day and send him back to his familiar surroundings during the night. I also got busy with the second edition of the military history seminar for which I invited Air Marshal Philip Rajkumar as the chief guest. The LCA had by now been rechristened the Tejas and was entering frontline service with the IAF. It was around that time when Darshan Singh also asked me to go ahead with an illustrated book on Welham Boys' School. I decided to follow the blueprint I had drawn up for the Doon School a few years earlier and started photographing the events as they unfolded in the school. I was assigned Monica Chandel as the liaison teacher and together we worked out the various shoots. Some other teachers in Welham Boys', Srikanth Rajagopalachari and Om Prakash who was also from the Doon School, became good friends and we would often discuss what could be done to improve the existing system especially when it came to pastoral care and adjusting to the changing times.

The most interesting sessions, whenever I was in Welham Boys', would be with the senior boys. Abhay Singh Dhillon was the school captain and sharp at 4 p.m. he would be standing outside my door. We would then often walk around the campus and I would tell him the various names of trees and birds on the campus. The boys by and large were no different from what we had been, but I felt the education system was letting them down by not raising the bar adequately. The quantum of information available to children today at their fingertips is incredible, so there is a desperate need to constantly expand their horizons and mentally push them harder. Dhillon would move to a university in London subsequently and he continued to interact with me, as did some of the boys from the next batch, which included Chirag Bansal and Devraj Singhania, two outstanding young men who were in a class apart and would have stood out in any generation. Dhillon would often comment on how even our casual walkabouts and literal talks of 'birds and bees', prepared him more for the next level of education which was all about critical thinking. I think schools should, be they public schools or otherwise, boarding schools or day schools, take the feedback from the immediate batches that graduate and see how to improve the system from their perspective. I feel it would make a quantum difference.

I was waiting for Veeha to return from her stint at UPenn, literally counting down the days for I felt she would bring back a semblance of sanity to what by the end was looking like an irretrievable and hopeless situation. Repeatedly, doctor after doctor said the same thing to me, that these issues could only be tackled with counselling, but even the slightest attempt to suggest it would result in counter accusations. At Veeha's arrival after her four-month stint, I had gone to the airport to receive her and as she came out of the gate, she didn't even look in my direction. The realization that I had lost my family hit me then, and subsequently, it would get confirmed when in the list of accusations, I was told my physical attacks on Dipti and Vallika had led to Veeha being treated for PTSD in the US.

Dipti's mother too by then had packed up from Mumbai and moved to Beverly Park, so I had no choice but to move back to our own flat. The 1962 book had not only been well received, it had according to critics, set the bar for military history writing in India, and the challenge for me was to keep my foot on the pedal. More importantly, I was quite enjoying putting it all together though the red tape which the armed forces had wrapped themselves in, was quite unbelievable. Even if I asked a formation for a photograph of a brigade commander who had been in the hot seat half a century ago, the stock reply was please come through the 'proper channels'.

During this period, the Bangladesh project seemed to be moving on the right track. We made a second and a third trip to Dhaka, first to meet the finance minister, and then the Mukti Joddha (Ministry of Liberation War Affairs) minister, A. K. M Mozammel Haque, who were both extremely welcoming and positive. 'Unless we meet Sheikh Hasina herself, we'll keep shuttling up and down,' I said to our Bangladeshi hosts,

Muhammad Musa and his son, Mahmud Habib E. Akbar. Muhammad Musa had been bayoneted by a Pakistani soldier during Operation Searchlight and left for dead outside the Dacca University. Also present was Sherafat Ali, who told stories of bodies, women raped and their breasts cleaved off, stacked all along the waterfront. There were some other Mukti Joddhas also sitting with us, and one of them happened to be Dr S. A. Samad, a former principal secretary of Sheikh Hasina who had also served with Sheikh Mujibur Rahman. He promptly dashed off an impassioned plea to the Bangladesh prime minister but got no response.

Till now, we had kept the Indian High Commission out of the discussion, but now Muhammad Musa felt the time had come to push for a meeting with Sheikh Hasina through the high commissioner. Accordingly, I spoke to and then sent a letter to Riva Ganguly Das. The high commissioner wrote back saying we needed to contact the XP division in the MEA and if we wanted, she could connect us to Professor Muntassir Mamun, the chairman of the 1971 Genocide-Torture, Archive and Museum Trust. A rather dejected Muhammad Musa then called saying that his feedback was that there had been a meeting in Dhaka where the proposal was discussed, and the verdict was that it was a great proposal, but no Indians could be involved in it. Sometimes, one can only hold one's head in despair.

The military history seminars used to invariably straddle 5 October, and 2019 was no exception. The chief guest for the third edition was Air Marshal Nanda Cariappa, who was not only the son of the first Indian C-in-C but had also himself been shot down and taken prisoner by the Pakistanis in 1965. Field Marshal Ayub Khan, the president of Pakistan had written to General Cariappa saying he need not worry as his son would be well looked after, to which Kipper, as the Indian chief was known, had replied 'all Indian POWs with Pakistan were his sons'. Among the various invitees was Bittu Sahgal, and the session with him was about the 'enemy within'. Having parted acrimoniously over the Indravati film in 1987, three decades later it was good to bury the past and move on.

Earlier in July, I had been invited to Bhopal to be the chief guest for the Kargil Divas ceremonies in Bhopal and had stayed with Milan and

Epilogue

Flying from Kullu to Shimla and then on to Chandigarh, I was taking photographs of the Beas and Sutlej river valleys from the Dauphin helicopter in the second week of September 2021 with little or no idea of how life would change shortly thereafter. The edit of *1965: A Western Sunrise* was done and dusted, and the book was due to hit the stands in another three weeks. That evening I was looking forward to meeting the chief minister of Punjab, Captain Amarinder Singh and Lieutenant General 'Maun' Shergill at the former's farmhouse at Siswan. Both were Gentlemen Cadets at the IMA when my father was a platoon commander and together, they had authored *The Monsoon War* on the 1965 conflict, having also participated in it.

I was met at the Chandigarh airport by Pankaj Singh of the Browser who was also heading BluOne Ink, a relatively new publishing company with whom I had signed the contract to publish my autobiography. Pankaj had been one of the participants in the fourth edition of the Welham Boys' Military History Seminar in 2020, and since it was held online, I had never physically met him until then. Accompanying him was Anirudh Chakravartty, who Pankaj had said was 'one of the bosses' in his publishing set-up and whom he introduced as an extremely well-read 'military history buff'. We had a pleasant lunch together where we discussed the general flow of the autobiography, and then I asked Pankaj if he would like to come along with me to Siswan in the suburbs of the city. Having 'bumped' Anirudh off, even though I was told he had come all the way from Noida to meet me, we proceeded to demolish some excellent whisky with His Highness and Maun.

I was to catch the morning flight from Chandigarh to Delhi and then take a connection to Raipur where I was speaking to the Young Indians chapter on the 1962 and 1965 conflicts with China and Pakistan. Pankaj had offered to drop me at the airfield, and he arrived half an hour early with Anirudh in tow at the Punjab Bhawan where I was staying. During the unscheduled half an hour, I switched on my laptop and showed both the work I was doing on the Alternate Education programme. Apart from the three books on the Northeast and the single volume on Tamil Nadu and Puducherry, I was looking at completing an additional eight volumes, which included Karnataka, Kerala, a complete quartet on Indian wildlife, and two single volumes that would document the trans-Himalayan region and the military history of the subcontinent.

The illustrated volume on the military history of India, the last in the series, almost knocked Anirudh off his chair. I had sped-run through the first eleven volumes and even though only part of the book had been laid out, it was the grand finale, the final fly on the water that was about to be taken by the rising trout. 'This sir,' said Anirudh, 'is a national treasure!' Pankaj was nodding in agreement.

Sometimes, you don't have to strike with the rod for the fish hooks itself! As we drove to the airport, Anirudh asked me if I could be in Dehradun on the 30th of September to release a book on the history of 4 Kumaon by Brigadier Jasbir Singh. I would have to fly in from Coimbatore, and it was decided the next day Anirudh would get 'all his people' together in Mussoorie and I would run the idea of Alternate Education by them.

'We have to do this,' he repeated for the umpteenth time.

My mother's passing four months previously and the collapse on the home front had left me facing a future which felt like a free-fall through a night sky. Work on the various books had somehow allowed me to compartmentalize my existence and once the 1965 manuscript had been completed, I was back at work putting together and designing the wildlife books. Covid had created havoc and most of the projects I had been working on, especially in Bangladesh had come a cropper.

Sitting in the room with Anirudh, I looked around. Partho Sanyal (he was exactly twelve hours older than me, and it would subsequently turn out he was Teesta's classmate in Stephens, hence three years my junior!) was the mentor/director who decided which project the group would get involved with. Apart from him and Anirudh, there were Geetanjali Ahooja and Mugdha Misri, the other two directors of BluOne.

'Bringing India to Indians' was the term coined by Krishna Kumar Candeth (KK) when he commented on the *Northeast Trilogy* in the *Rosebowl*, the magazine that caters exclusively to ex DOSCOs. Somehow 'Alternate Education' for what we were attempting to put together was not sounding right, and for a couple of years I struggled to find a more apt nomenclature. While digging into a plate of delicious *idlis* in Chennai, I mentioned this to Dilip Krishna, the newly appointed All-India head for Young Indians, with whom I had been closely interacting ever since I addressed them at LBSNAA, Mussoorie a couple of years ago. 'Why don't you call it "Value Education"', suggested Dilip. The name stuck, and now only time will tell if we are able to contribute towards making education in the country more meaningful.

Living in the heart of the Himalayas, I have the Beas River below me and from my bedroom I can see the Rohtang area beyond which lies Lahaul and Spiti. Around me, in the name of 'development', one can see the phenomenal damage being done to the environment and today cloud bursts and landslides are a common occurrence in the region. The devastating floods in the lower reaches of Pakistan that have submerged close to a fifth of the country, are perhaps a sign of things to come. Human memory is short, for already in India we have forgotten the similar devastation that happened in Kerala in August 2018. Way back in the 1980s, when I returned from Kashmir and Ladakh, one had started writing about the need to preserve what we had. I've always believed we need to look beyond the horizon, for seeds that we sow will only bear fruit years later, perhaps well after we are gone.

This book is not so much 'my story', but also a documentation of some major events that impacted India's history. Many of the ensemble cast have passed on, and I have tried to be as accurate as possible. The fact that I kept diaries and even a logbook that recorded all my sorties first with the IAF and then with the navy and the army, helped tremendously. Events I could have otherwise sworn happened in 1994 had unfolded in 1995, which then meant charting the timelines accordingly. The other thing that kept a lot of the details of what had transpired alive in my head was the fact that a lot of what has been said in the book, was there on film/or tape as well, and one got to see the footage again and again on editing tables multiple times. There could be a few errors that may have crept in for human memory is flawed, but I have tried to check and double check events with quite a few of my fellow protagonists who sometimes amazed me by coming up with incidents that I had all but forgotten.

The world we grew up in has changed almost to a point where it is hard to even relate to the conditions then. Ours was perhaps the last of the 'non-AC' generation, for until I was in my early-20s, except for the brief stay in the United States, most of us had no idea what an air conditioner was. An 'AC car', more often than not, would 'conk it' if there was a gradient that had to be traversed for more than a few kilometres. Today, in a world where we grapple with artificial intelligence and have enough computing power on our individual cellphones to send a man to the moon many times over, we seem to be at a loss for basic answers that might help steady the planet, the only spaceship that we have on which to traverse through the cosmos.

I, for one, cannot but feel that in life after a certain stage the dynamics of time change completely. In ones' growing years, a day was a day, with minutes and hours ticking along slowly. Now it feels that one could easily do with another six or seven hours in each day, for days, weeks, months just flash by, and happily, the work keeps constantly piling up. Also, it's also not necessarily that only the big events stand out in life, for frankly every flower, every little creature, bird, animal or invertebrate that comes my way has had their own story to tell. Thanks to some incredible teachers in both the Doon School, Madras Christian College and Tiger Tops, I learnt to pause long enough and listen to those little tales, sometimes just the waving of an antenna underlining the marvels of creation. Having had the good fortune of being born in an incredible land on an incredible planet, all that I wish for now is to leave behind my own modest footprints that can in some way or the other, help future generations cherish what they inherit and then hopefully pass on to their children. I dedicate this book to my parents, Ashok and Usha ... and to all those who along the line had put their trust in me, giving me opportunity after opportunity to live life on my own terms. To my friends and those who continue to hold my hand, I could not have managed without them.

List of Abbreviations

ACAS	Assistant Ahief of Air Staff
ADA	Aeronautical Development Agency
ADC	Aide-de-camp
AFP	Agence France-Presse
AIIMS	All India Institute of Medical Sciences
ALC	Army Liaison Cell
AOC	Air Officer Commanding
AOR	Area of Responsibility
AP	Associated Press
ASET	Advances in Science, Engineering and Technology
ASTE	Armament & Systems Testing Establishment
ATC	Air-traffic Control
AVS	Assam Valley School
AWHO	Army Welfare Housing Organisation
BGS	Brigadier General Staff
BMP	Soviet amphibious tracked infantry fighting vehicle, BMP stands for Boyevaya Mashina Pyekhoty
BOAC	British Overseas Airways Corporation
BSF	Border Security Force
BVM	Birla Vidya Mandir
BVR	Beyond Visual Range
CAS	Chief of Air Staff
CB	Counter Bombardment
CBI	Central Bureau of Investigation
CBSE	Central Board of Secondary Education

CIA	Central Intelligence Agency
C-in-C	Commander-in-Chief
CISM	Conseil International du Sport Militaire (International Military Sports Council)
CITES	Convention on International Trade in Endangered Species of Wild Flora and Fauna
CNS	Chief of Naval Staff
CO	Commanding Officer
COAS	Chief of the Army Staff
COO	Chief Operations Officer
COP	Chief of Personnel
CSD	Canteen Stores Department
DBO	Daulat Beg Oldi
DDG	Deputy Director General
DFO	Divisional Forest Officer
DG	Director General
DGMI	Director General Military Intelligence
DGMO	Director General Military Operations
DLF	Delhi Land & Finance (real estate developer)
DNP	Desert National Park
DO	Demi Official
DOP	Director of Photography
DS	Directing Staff
DSC	Defence Security Corps
DSOBS	Doon School Old Boys' Society
DTC	Delhi Transport Corporation
EBR	East Bengal Rifles
ECB	Extremely Cold Beers
EME	Corps of Electrical & Mechanical Engineers

EVM	Electronic Voting Machine
FIR	First Information Report
FLG	Forward Landing Ground
FTII	Film and Television Institute of India
FYUP	Four-Year Undergraduate Programme
GC	Gentleman Cadets
GOC	General Officer Commanding
GS	General Staff
HAL	Hindustan Aeronautics Limited
HAPE	High-altitude Pulmonary Edema
HDFC	Housing Development Finance Corporation
HM	Headmaster
HOD	Head of Department
HQ	Headquarters
HRE	Himalayan River Exploration
HTA	Hindustan Thomson Associates
IAF	Indian Air Force
IAS	Indian Administrative Service
IB	Intelligence Bureau
ICU	Intensive Care Unit
IED	Improvised Explosive Device
IG	Inspector General
IIT	Indian Institute of Technology
IMA	Indian Military Academy
INA	Indian National Army
INS	Indian Naval Ship
IPKF	Indian Peace Keeping Force
IPS	Indian Police Service
IQ	Intelligence Quotient

ISC	Indian School Certificate
ISI	Inter-Services Intelligence, Pakistan
ITBP	Indo-Tibetan Border Police
ITC	formerly, the Imperial Tobacco Company, now a major Indian conglomerate, known as ITC Ltd
ITDC	India Tourism Development Corporation
IUCN	International Union for Conservation of Nature
J&K	Jammu and Kashmir
JCB	mechanical diggers and excavators
JCO	Junior Commissioned Officer
JIPMER	Jawaharlal Institute of Postgraduate Medical Education and Research, Puducherry
JS	Joint Secretary
JSW	Joint Services Wing, Clement Town, later the NDA, Khadakwasla
KMV	Kanya Maha Vidyalaya
LBG	Laser Guided Bombs
LBSNAA	Lal Bahadur Shastri National Academy of Administration, Mussoorie
LCA	Light Combat Aircraft
LG	Large Goose (cartridges)
LI	Light Infantry
LMG	Light Machine Gun
LOC	Line of Control
LST	Landing Ship, Tank
MCC	Madras Christian College
MEA	Ministry of External Affairs
MHA	Ministry of Home Affairs
MiG	Mikoyan-Gurevich Soviet-era fighter aircraft

MLA	Member of Legislative Assembly
MMG	Medium Machine Gun
MOD	Ministry of Defence
MV	Motor Vessel
MVC	Maha Vir Chakra
MWG	Military World Games
NA	Naval Assistant
NAL	National Aerospace Laboratories
NCC	National Cadet Corps
NCPA	National Centre for the Performing Arts, Mumbai
NCR	National Capital Region
NDA	National Defence Academy
NDC	National Defence College
NDTV	New Delhi Television
NEFA	North-East Frontier Agency
NID	National Institute of Design
NRI	Non-resident Indian
NSA	National Security Adviser
NTR	N. T. Rama Rao
NTSC	television broadcasting system used in North America and Japan
OIC	Organisation of Islamic Cooperation
OLQ	Officer Like Qualities
ORP	Operational Readiness Platform
PA	Personal Assistant
PAF	Pakistan Air Force
PAL	phase alternating line, one of the three major analog colour television standards, the others being NTSC and SECAM

PCCF	Principal Chief Conservator of Forests
PLA	People's Liberation Army
PM	Prime Minister
PMO	Prime Minister's Office
POK	Pakistan Occupied Kashmir
POW	Prisoner of War
PRC	People's Republic of China
PS	Private Secretary
PTM	Parent–teacher Meeting
PTS	Para Training School
PTSD	Post-traumatic Stress Disorder
PVC	Param Vir Chakra
Q&A	Question and Answer
QRT	Quick Reaction Team
R&R	Research and Referral hospital for the Indian armed forces, New Delhi
RAF	Royal Air Force
RAW	Research and Analysis Wing
RCL	Recoil-less
RD	R. D. Singh
RIAF	Royal Indian Air Force
RIGSS	Royal Institute of Governance and Strategic Studies
RIMC	Rashtriya Indian Military College
RIN	Royal Indian Navy
RNAC	Royal Nepal Airlines Corporation
RO	Range Officer
ROP	Road Opening Part
RP	Rajendra Pal Devgan
RPG	Rocket Propelled Grenade

RSO	Range Safety Officer
RT	Radio Transmitter
SAARC	South Asian Association for Regional Cooperation
SAIL	Steel Authority of India Limited
SAR	Search and Rescue
SASO	Senior Air Staff Officer
SBI	State Bank of India
SBIOA	State Bank of India Officers' Association
SDM	Sub-divisional Magistrate
SLR	Self-loading Rifle
SM	Subedar Major
SNF	Standing Naval Forces
SO	Staff Officer
SOP	Standard Operating Procedure
SSB	Services Selection Board
STD	Standard Trunk Dialling
SWAC	South Western Air Command
TA	Territorial Army
TACDE	Tactics and Air Combat Development Establishment
TC	Ticket Collector
TIFR	Tata Institute of Fundamental Research
TNT	Trinitrotoluene, an explosives material
TOT	Time Over Target
UAV	Unmanned Aerial Vehicle
ULFA	United Liberation Front of Asom
UNESCO	United Nations Educational, Scientific and Cultural Organization
UNI	United News of India
US	United States

USAF	US Air Force
VCD	Video Compact Disc
VrC	Vir Chakra
WWF	World Wildlife Fund
XP	External Publications
YC	Yellow Card